A HYMN OF CHRIST

Philippians 2:5-11
in Recent Interpretation
& in the Setting of Early
Christian Worship

RALPH P. MARTIN

InterVarsity Press
Downers Grove, Illinois

InterVarsity Press
P.O. Box 1400, Downers Grove, IL 60515
World Wide Web: www.ivpress.com
E-mail: mail@ivpress.com

InterVarsity Press®is the book-publishing division of InterVarsity Christian Fellowship/USA®, a student movement active on campus at hundreds of universities, colleges and schools of nursing in the United States of America, and a member movement of the International Fellowship of Evangelical Students. For information about local and regional activities, write Public Relations Dept., InterVarsity Christian Fellowship/USA, 6400 Schroeder Rd., P.O. Box 7895, Madison, WI 53707-7895.

ISBN 0-8308-1894-4

Printed in the United States of America

Library of Congress Cataloging-in-Publication Data

Martin, Ralph P.
   [Carmen Christi]
   A hymn of Christ: Philippians 2:5-11 in recent interpretation &
   in the setting of early Christian worship/Ralph P. Martin.
      p.   cm
   Originally published under title: Carmen Christi. London:
   Cambridge University Press, 1967, in series: Monograph series
   (Society for New Testament Studies); 4.
   Includes bibliographical references and index.
   ISBN 0-8308-1894-4 (alk. paper)
   1. Bible. N.T. Philippians II, 5-11—Criticism, interpretation,
etc.   I. Title.
BS2705.2.M3   1997
227'.606—dc21
                                                97-35894
                                                  CIP

21	20	19	18	17	16	15	14	13	12	11	10	9	8	7	6	5	4	3	2	1
14	13	12	11	10	09	08	07	06	05	04	03	02	01	00	99	98	97			

PREFACE

There are certain passages of scripture which both provoke and baffle study. Philippians ii. 5–11 is one such section, as all who have tried their hand at its interpretation know full well.

During the past half-century, this Pauline passage has been exposed to a searching scrutiny by a number of interpreters. Its apparent endorsement of the so-called Kenotic theory of the Incarnation has given it a special place in the field of systematic theology; its literary structure and style have made it suitable as a test-case for the tracing of early Christian liturgical fragments in the New Testament documents; and, more recently, it has taken on particular significance as a species of pre-Pauline confessional material, thus opening a window on what was believed and taught about the person and place of Jesus Christ in the Jewish-Christian and Gentile churches prior to the formative influence which Paul exerted on early Christian thought.

The tap-root of the present study, which seeks to investigate critically the form, setting and content of Philippians ii. 5–11 as these features are understood by recent scholarship, was put down by the author a decade ago. And so, by a coincidence, the appearance of the book in 1967 happens to agree with the advice given by Dr Vincent Taylor in *The Person of Christ in New Testament Teaching* (1958, p. 73) when he recommended that 'it seems to me the only way to enter into the meaning of a sublime, but difficult, passage (like Phil. ii. 5 ff.) is to summarize the views of many commentators and then to leave the summaries in storage for ten years'. As a result of this procedure, he anticipates, 'out of the welter of opinions we can form conclusions of our own'.

An attempt to expound the meaning of Philippians ii. 5–11 in the light of recent interpretation was made by the writer in 1960 and published under the title *An Early Christian Confession*. That brochure may be regarded as a tentative, and perhaps too hastily conceived, *Entwurf* of this larger work, which was originally composed as a Ph.D. exercise at King's College, the University of London and presented in 1963. A reassessment

vii

of the material has led to some modifications of the author's first views, chiefly in matters of the passage's form, dating and authorship; and these revisions are set out in the final chapter. But the important issue is the meaning of the hymn in the epistolary context of Paul's Letter, and this aspect calls for a comment.

That the hymn sets forth the Incarnation of Christ in His humiliation and subsequent enthronement is universally agreed. But that it depicts His example of humility and made an appeal to its first readers to follow in His steps, and that it is concerned with the mutual relationships of the Christian Godhead, are two assumptions which modern exegesis has seriously questioned.

The newer approach to the text, which is adopted in the following pages, sees the hymn as setting forth the story of salvation. The centre of gravity of this *carmen Christi* is the proclamation of Christ's lordship over all cosmic forces. The relevance of this understanding is a twofold one. In the context of early Christian worship the Christ-hymn proclaimed the drama of His descent to this world, His submission to death and His victory over spiritual powers. The hymn, which had an existence independent of the use which St Paul made of it, is cited by him in reference to the pastoral situation at Philippi in order to show how the Church came to be in the sphere of Christ's lordship; and this fact is made the basis of the ethical appeal.

It is a pleasant duty to record some expressions of the author's appreciation. Professor D. E. Nineham, now of Cambridge, supervised the study and made himself available for many hours of stimulating conversation on the themes of this passage. Professor C. F. D. Moule has added to his many kindnesses by offering the benefit of his criticisms and advice. Professor F. F. Bruce has taken the time and trouble to cast a vigilant eye over the proofs. Nor would the author wish to omit mentioning his sense of obligation to Professor A. M. Hunter whose interest in pre-Pauline Christianity first stimulated this study; and the late Professor T. W. Manson gave encouragement when the writer turned to post-graduate research in the complex area of Pauline studies.

These expressions of gratitude in no way hold the benefactors responsible either for the author's conclusions or for such errors in the text as remain. On the level of book production much valued assistance has been given by the staff and craftsmen of the Cambridge University Press who have had to cope with a difficult manuscript.

Finally and on a personal note, a word of thanks is due to Miss Marilyn Wagnell who typed the original MS; to Murray J. Harris who, in the midst of post-graduate studies in the Faculty of Theology, carefully compiled the indexes; to R. F. Broadfoot of Dunstable who has discussed with the author over many years some of the intricacies of Philippians ii; and to the writer's wife and family who have shown considerable forbearance during the period of this research, which must often have seemed to them to be almost interminable.

R.P.M.

Faculty of Theology
University of Manchester

PREFACE TO THE 1983 EDITION

The proposal to reissue this book, substantially in the format it had in 1967, has presented the author with an enviable set of choices. Aside from correcting a small number of misprints and improving an occasional infelicitous or ambiguous expression, one choice was to recast the work in its entirety in the light of recent studies, many of them critical of the original publication and its thesis; and in so doing to offer a response to these contributions to our understanding of a provocative passage in the Pauline corpus. Another possibility was to add extended footnote or endnote references to show the trends in contemporary research over the past decade and a half.

As it turns out, a different course has been chosen. This has been to offer a revised introduction to the existing volume and to state and evaluate selected studies which, in the author's opinion, have opened fresh avenues of interpretation. Thus this preface does not claim to have mentioned, let alone to have discussed, every item of periodical literature that has appeared since 1967. In defence of this decision two observations may be made. One is that the author's edition of the New Century Bible Commentary on *Philippians*,[1] prepared first in 1976 and reprinted with supplementary bibliography covering the years 1975–1979 in the year 1980, sought to take up the issues raised in current publications. Reference may be made to this commentary for titles and publication data; and an attempt has been made in what follows not to duplicate that commentary.

The other reason is more personal and needs to be stated with some delicacy. The author gratefully acknowledges all that has been written—as far as he has been able to see and appreciate it—on the several sides of the debate over the setting, meaning and significance of this *carmen Christi*. All critical reviews have been duly weighed, and contrary views noted. Yet it remains— and I hope this fact will not be put down to one person's incorrigible ignorance or resistance to change—that the author's gen-

---

[1] R. P. Martin, *Philippians* (New Century Bible) (London, 1976; Grand Rapid⁃ 1980).

eral understanding of Philippians ii. 5–11 is virtually the same as it was when the dissertation on which the book was based in 1963 was presented and defended. To be sure, I would wish to define more circumspectly what is implied in the so-called 'soteriological interpretation' as over against the equally ambiguous 'ethical interpretation'. And the discussion of the passage's authorship, hesitantly stated in a way that gave prominence to the two sides of the question, needs to be read in the light of the author's later view in the commentary and reopened in what follows.

In addition, the placing of this hymnic passage within the worshipping and cultic life of early communities of the Pauline mission needs to be developed by including a further dimension. From all the evidence we have, early hymns, especially those belonging to the *Gattung* of 'hymns to Christ', played a role in shaping christology and giving a response to pressing pastoral needs in Paul's communities. To set these verses in the context of Paul's answer to selfishness and envy in the Philippian church is the traditional way of exegeting the text. We must, however, press behind the symptoms of congregational strife to see what was the root malady plaguing the church in the Macedonian province. This is a feature of the more recent phase of Philippian studies; and in a closing section the issues are considered.

In setting out the areas of discussion, as described above, we have followed what seems to be a logical order as we try to assess what are the important matters under contemporary consideration.

I. THE PURPOSE OF PHILIPPIANS II. 5–11

There is universal agreement that these verses interrupt the flow of Paul's hortatory and pastoral writing. Addressing a series of distressing features evident in the Philippian church (ii. 1–4), Paul begins a personal admonition at verse 5 which has continued to vex commentators: τοῦτο φρονεῖτε ἐν ὑμῖν ὃ καὶ ἐν Χριστῷ Ἰησοῦ. The Greek text lacks a verb in the second part of the sentence and one has to be supplied. The addition of the verb ἦν, 'which *was* in Christ Jesus', makes it natural that Paul's subsequent citation of the noble passage will be seen as calling to some kind of 'imitation of Christ' (cf. the NIV heading 'Imitating Christ's Humility').

xii

R. B. Strimple[2] has championed this view, which 'allow[s] us once again to see the passage as setting Christ before us as the example that is to guide the Christian in his conduct toward others'. The grounds for this position are stated in opposition to the attempt to interpret the verse as: 'let this way of thinking be among you, as it is indeed needful-to-think [adding φϱονεῖν δεῖ] as those-in-Christ'. He proposes the following counter-arguments: (i) The two halves of the verse lose their tension, and the second part is tautological, with καί lacking exegetical sense.[3] (ii) ἐν Χϱιστῷ does not mean our incorporation in Christ but is 'a reference to Christ's own thought or attitude'. (iii) The exaltation motif in verses 9–11 is best understood as part of the same ethical interpretation and read in the light of II Corinthians viii. 9 (cf. II Tim. ii. 11). Romans viii. 17 might have been chosen as a better illustration of Paul's thought, 'we suffer now/we are exalted later'. (iv) Paul, it is said, does appeal to Christ's ethical example, e.g. Romans xv. 1–8; I Corinthians xi. 1; Ephesians v. 2; I Thessalonians i. 6. A denial of this, as in the sentence 'Paul never uses the earthly life of Jesus as an *exemplum ad imitandum*', is taken by L. W. Hurtado[4] as 'a rather astonishing statement', and he goes on to remark that though these references 'have to do mainly with the death of Jesus, they are nonetheless evidence that the earthly Jesus in his self-sacrifice could be cited by Paul as pattern for behaviour'.

This formidable array of objections, however, is not as convincing as may appear. All are agreed that the elliptical part-verse ὃ καὶ ἐν Χϱιστῷ 'Ιησοῦ poses problems. Nor is the matter really

---

[2] R. B. Strimple, 'Philippians 2:5-11 in Recent Studies: Some Exegetical Conclusions', *Westminster Theological Journal*, 41 (1979), 247–68. It should be observed that this essay, despite its title, considers only verses 5–8, and has little to say about verses 9–11. In my judgment, this is a fatal deficiency.

[3] R. Deichgräber, *Gotteshymnus und Christushymnus in der frühen Christenheit* (Studien zur Umwelt des NT 5) (Göttingen, 1967), p. 192, comments that καί is either regarded as meaningless or pushed aside in many interpretations of the text. But this is not so, if καί is given an ascensive force ('even') or an explicative meaning. See Blass-Debrunner-Funk, *A Greek Grammar*, sec. 442. This usage of καί would fit neatly into L. A. Losie's reconstruction of τοῦτο as the object of φϱονεῖτε, and it is this interpretation which gives due weight to ὃ καί and makes the verb look forward to the quoted hymn with its paraenetic appeal. See his 'A Note on the Interpretation of Phil. 2, 5', *ExT*, xc (1978), 52–54.

[4] L. W. Hurtado, 'Jesus as Lordly Example in Phil. 2:5-11', *From Jesus to Paul. Studies in Honour of Francis Wright Beare*, ed. J. C. Hurd and G. P. Richardson (Waterloo, 1983), ch. 9.

cleared up by opting, with G. F. Hawthorne,[5] to read the Byzantine text in verse 5*a*, τοῦτο φρονείσθω ἐν ὑμῖν: 'This way of thinking must be adopted by you', in order to gain a symmetry with verse 5*b*: 'which also was the way of thinking adopted by Christ Jesus' (ὃ καὶ ἐφρονεῖτο ἐν Χριστῷ 'Ιησοῦ). Hawthorne's readings do secure a parallelism ἐν ὑμῖν/ἐν Χριστῷ, but at heavy cost, namely accepting an inferior text. His statement, however, is correct: it is impossible to treat the two prepositional phrases as saying the same thing—which is precisely the point of Paul's admonition, linked as it is by καί, which may have an ascensive or elative force. The call is for his readers to 'adopt a way of life' (φρονεῖν is more than 'to think'; it signifies a combination of intellectual and affective activity which touches both head and heart, and leads to a positive course of action) in their mutual relations (ἐν ὑμῖν), which is indeed (καί) how they should live 'in Christ Jesus'.

To argue that 'in Christ Jesus' reflects Christ's own attitude, which is then spelled out in verses 6–8 as one of condescension, humility and obedience, runs into difficulty[6] once the question is put: Is it in fact 'the earthly Jesus in his self-sacrifice' that Paul is here making 'a pattern for behaviour'? Rather, Paul is appealing to the incarnation of a heavenly being in the verses under review. Hurtado grants as much on his next page, and proceeds to take the consequences in his stride. He writes: 'it is not impossible that such an action [of incarnation] might be so described as to make it exemplary for earthly behaviour'. Whether it may be described like this or not is irrelevant. What counts is that the becoming human of a divine being is by definition—as Hurtado explicitly says in his note 48—'unique', and if this is the case, Christians cannot imitate it except in an attenuated way. Then, what becomes of the summons in verse 5: 'Act thus . . . as Christ acted'?

The theological and logical impasse is worsened if we are inclined to see verses 9–11 as proclaiming a heavenly accolade

[5] G. F. Hawthorne, *Philippians* (Word Biblical Commentary) (Waco, TX, 1983, forthcoming). There is a full bibliography attached to the section on ii. 5–11 in this commentary.
[6] Noted by E. Käsemann, 'Kritische Analyse' (E.T. 'A Critical Analysis of Philippians 2:5–11', in *God and Christ. Existence and Province* (*Journal for Theology and Church* 5) (New York/Tübingen, 1968), p. 57 (E.T., p. 51).

granted to the Kyrios which is *also* applicable to Christians and so made part of Paul's admonition to the Philippians. Christ became man and was obedient by taking the role of a 'slave' (*doulos*); now He is exalted with the title of 'Lord' (*kyrios*). Granted there is a formal similarity here with the sequence, 'we suffer now/we shall be exalted then', it is striking that Paul does not invoke that principle in verse 12, which is his paraenetic appeal (ὥστε, ἀγαπητοί μου . . .) on the basis of the hymn. Rather he reverts to Christ's authority as Kyrios as requiring human obedience. He does not hold out the prospect of a reward for following Jesus in an exemplary way, which would be singularly inappropriate in the light of the self-interest he has rebuked in ii. 3, 4. Nor does he consider believers as receiving the status that God has graciously bestowed on Christ. There is only one Kyrios, a title as unique as the self-abnegation of verses 7–8, which in turn goes back to the decision taken uniquely by the heavenly one (verse 6).

The above statement has reviewed the grounds for what Käsemann called 'the ethical interpretation'. Perhaps that designation was ill-named, for it has evidently led to a polarization of that view with his antithetical position. But he has surely asked the right question of our text, How does the hymn function as a paraenesis? Why has Paul inserted a passage like this, with all its sacral-cultic terms and other-worldly scenario especially in verses 9–11, into a pastoral letter to deal with a fractious community?[7] His response, as is now well known, is in terms of a recital of soteriology, a dramatic story of the odyssey of Christ whose 'way' led from one eternity to His ultimate glory by acts of obedience, exaltation and acclamation. In verses 9–11, as the conclusion resumes the thought found at the beginning in a 'ring-composition', the picture is of the world ruler to whom all parts of creation are submissive; and the church is summoned to live in that realm where Christ's authority is paramount.

If the lordship of Christ is the hymn's 'center', it needs to be said clearly that (*i*) the lordly Christ still carries the human name Jesus and still retains an authority based on the cross; and (*ii*)

---

[7] Käsemann. Referred to on pp. 84–88, 90–93 below. Hurtado perceptively notes some possible reasons for Käsemann's opposition to the 'ethical idealism' of Old Liberalism in the light of his kerygmatic theology. For other reasons see H.-T. Wrege's discussion, referred to on p. xxx, n. 60 (*loc. cit.*, pp. 286 f.).

there are distinct ethical implications in that lordship that make the best designation of the hymn's purpose that of *paraenesis*.

Both these reminders depend partly for their cogency on some prior conclusions regarding a form-analysis of the text. Understandably some critics (e.g. M. D. Hooker[8]) have charged that the variety of proposals offered to account for the literary texture of the verses militates against the very idea of tracing a precomposed hymn in the section. But, as we shall see later, the poetic or hymnic character of the verses remains a virtual consensus in recent debate, with no serious attempt to overturn it. Less universally approved is the allied proposal that Paul has taken over a preformed hymn and edited it to suit his own purpose. Yet, even if more audacious suggestions are dismissed—for example, J. Jeremias' deletion of several lines of text—little support is given to O. Hofius' argument[9] that the line θανάτου δὲ σταυροῦ, 'even the death of the cross', is an integral part of the hymn in its original format. We may treat, with some confidence, these words as Paul's corrective addition to an already existing tribute—an idea that goes back to E. Lohmeyer,[10] who nevertheless failed to exploit its significance.

The presence of the earthly name 'Jesus' at the heavenly enthronement scene (verse 10), rightly discerned by C. F. D. Moule[11] and J.-F. Collange,[12] as well as the Pauline coda, 'even the death of the cross' (verse 8), have together been invoked by Takeshi Nagata[13] in his dissertation as laying the basis for Paul's exhortation (*paraenesis*). We propose to pursue this line in order to contend for the following interpretative positions: to show how the 'qualities' in verses 7 and 8 can still be taken up into a soter-

[8] M. D. Hooker, 'Philippians 2, 6–11', in *Jesus und Paulus. Festschrift* for W. G. Kümmel, ed. E. E. Ellis and E. Grässer (Göttingen, 1975), pp. 151–64.

[9] O. Hofius, *Der Christushymnus Philipper 2, 6–11* (Wissenschaftliche Untersuchungen zum NT 17) (Tübingen, 1976), pp. 3–12.

[10] E. Lohmeyer, *Kyrios Jesus*, pp. 8, 44 ff.; idem, *Philipper* (*MeyerKomm*), p. 96.

[11] C. F. D. Moule, 'Further Reflexions on Philippians 2:5–11', in *Apostolic History and the Gospel, Biblical and Historical Essays presented to F. F. Bruce on his 60th Birthday*, ed. W. W. Gasque and R. P. Martin (Exeter/Grand Rapids, 1970), pp. 264–76.

[12] J.-F. Collange, *L'épître de Saint Paul aux Philippiens* (*CNT*; Paris/Neuchâtel, 1973) (E.T. *The Epistle of Saint Paul to the Philippians* [London, 1979]), p. 95 (E.T., p. 106).

[13] T. Nagata, 'Philippians 2:5–11. A Case Study in the Contextual Shaping of Early Christology.' A dissertation submitted to Princeton Theological Seminary, unpublished (Princeton, N.J., 1981).

iological presentation of the hymn; to allow the 'center' of the hymn clearly to be Christ's present lordship set under the cross; and so to provide a reason for Paul's use of this passage in his dealings with pastoral problems at Philippi.

At the heart of this reconstruction is the axiom stated on p. 287 (see below) and still defended, although Strimple and Hurtado have challenged it. The hermeneutical assumption runs like this: we should isolate the meaning of the terms in the hymn from the use which is made of them by Paul in the verses which precede and follow them. To this statement needs to be added that the hymn may well have had one meaning in its original form and yet an altered meaning in the context of Paul's letter. Certainly this tearing asunder of the 'original' hymn (an *Urschrift*) and Paul's redactional use of it can be overdone. T. Nagata seems to be guilty of excess here when he concludes that 'the incarnational Christology of the hymn in Phil. 2:6–11 ... remains fundamentally alien to Pauline theology, and should not be utilized in discussing his theology'.[14] He has confused, we believe, ideas which are alien (e.g. Gal. i. 6–9; II Cor. xi. 4) and ideas which are regarded by Paul as inadequate. If the hymn is so inimical to Paul's thought, why did he choose to use it in the first place?

Let us assume that the 'original' composition celebrated the victory of Christ in a triumphalist manner, proclaimed a reign of Christ already begun—thereby ignoring the 'provisional' character of the present in anticipation of Christ's future rule at the parousia (the so-called *eschatologische Vorbehalt*)—and regarded the death as merely the extremity of His humiliation soon to be reversed and swallowed up in the glory of His exaltation. Then, it is not difficult to see how the phrase θανάτου δὲ σταυροῦ would function as a corrective insertion into the text, added by Paul to retain the centrality of the cross as the hymn's celebration of the victory of *the crucified*. The character traits in verses 7 and 8 serve the same function, namely to stress the lowliness and obedience of the one who 'came down' and who, though now enthroned in heavenly splendor as Lord of all creation, yet retains His character, which is not omnipotent might or despotic rule, but as the one who trod a path of obedience to the death of the cross, and is known by His earthly name, Jesus.

---

[14] Nagata, p. 359.

The lordship of Christ is indeed the hymn's *Mitte*; for that reason Paul quotes and uses it. This position, we believe, is still defensible—it is the only interpretation which can give a satisfactory reason for the inclusion of verses 9–11. These verses are not to be reckoned as an excursus (Dibelius[15]) nor can they rightly be regarded as 'exemplary', given their unique character in proclaiming the lordship of the world ruler, a status of κυριότης that can never be shared. The hymn, celebrating the 'way of Christ' (a *Weglied*, as K. Wengst[16] has rightly called it), moves to its climax in these latter verses, showing how the heavenly one (verse 6a) has returned to His *Heimat* where He has, after humiliation, abasement, obedience, death and vindication, received lordly power. The theological *Sache* of the entire passage is not, then, the atonement wrought by the Servant (Hofius[17]) nor strictly the incarnation, whether as an exercise in early dogmatics or as centered on the condescension of the pre-existent Christ and His selfless obedience to God. It is the exaltation of the once-humiliated one—who remains nameless throughout verses 6–8, a fact not always appreciated—who has received divine honors at the end of His itinerary that took Him from the presence of God *via* the becoming man and the obedience-unto-death back to that presence, *where He now enjoys the right to rule.*

The exaltation and authority of the Kyrios is, in our view, the basis of the paraenetic appeal. The summons to Paul's Philippian readers is that they should submit to Christ's divinely invested authority as Kyrios (clearly in verse 12: the obedient one must be obeyed). Yet in the crucible of Paul's soteriological thought the cross can never be separated from the resurrection, which is only vaguely hinted at in the *Urschrift* (but which is basic to Paul's pastoral theology, as we see from II Cor. iv. 7–15, xiii. 3–4); nor can the human Jesus be divorced from the exalted Christ (a criterion he applies in I Cor. xii. 1–3). His addition of the line in verse 8c and his appropriation of a hymn that did include elements of Christ's earthly humiliation and obedience served his purpose in recalling to his people that the *crucified Jesus* is the one they acknowledge as Lord. Their life 'in Christ Jesus' is to be

[15] M. Dibelius, *An die Thessalonicher, i, ii; die Philipper* (HzNT), p. 81.
[16] K. Wengst, *Christologische Formeln und Lieder des Urchristentums* (Studien zum NT 7) (Gütersloh, 1972), p. 144.
[17] O. Hofius, *Der Christushymnus*, pp. 56–64.

governed by that control, and thus such a 'reminder' (whether it is a baptismal or eucharistic *anamnesis* is difficult to decide[18]) should powerfully affect their conduct in their churchly relations. This, we submit, is the essence of the paraenetic appeal of the passage: it consists in giving a kerygmatic dimension to their life-in-Christ by anchoring what they understood as life under His lordly control in a 'theology of the cross'. The boundaries of Paul's understanding of Christ's achievement are set by His cross, which is not a station on the way to glory but of the *esse* of Christian existence, and by His humanity which is now elevated to share the throne of God.

II. DESCRIPTIONS OF JESUS IN THE HYMN

Recent interpretation has taken up with new submissions several exegetical matters that have preoccupied scholars over the past century. We may isolate these significant terms in the verses by way of continuing our 'history of interpretation' and trying to bring it up to date.

(*i*) ἐν μορφῇ θεοῦ ὑπάρχων (verse 6*a*). The debate here centers on the precise referent of the term μορφή and in particular whether it speaks of Christ's pre-temporal existence in this context. There is now a continuing consensus that μορφή cannot be used in a philosophical sense, as meaning 'form' or 'being'. G. F. Hawthorne is an exception as he reverts to μορφὴ θεοῦ as 'the essential nature and character of God'. The text, however, does not say that the heavenly being existed *as* the form of God (μορφὴ [τοῦ] θεοῦ) but that he was 'in' (ἐν) that μορφή, as Käsemann had noted, and he went on to submit that the only possible sense was *Daseinsweise* ('mode of being'). The immediate background, in this view, is the Gnostic world of a 'heavenly man' who shared a rank equal with God. But this setting has lost some of its appeal under attack from D. Georgi,[19] J. T. Sanders[20] and W. Pannenberg.[21]

---

[18] K. Gamber, 'Der Christus-Hymnus im Philipperbrief in liturgiegeschichtlicher Sicht', *Biblica*, 51 (1970), 369–76.

[19] D. Georgi, 'Der vorpaulinische Hymnus Phil. 2, 6–11', in *Zeit und Geschichte*, p. 264, n. 6.

[20] J. T. Sanders, *New Testament Christological Hymns: their Historical and Religious Background* (SNTS Monographs, 15) (Cambridge, 1971), pp. 66–69.

[21] W. Pannenberg, *Jesus. God and Man* (E.T. London, 1968), pp. 151–54.

'Phil. 2:6–11 lacks almost all the Gnostic anthropological motifs of *Corp. Herm. I*', writes Nagata,[22] who regards J. Behm's conclusion in Kittel's *Dictionary* as substantially sound: 'The most common meaning of the term μορφή is, as Behm correctly asserts, the visible outward form by which one can identify the concrete entity as such'.

Whether μορφή finds its semantic equivalent in εἰκών or δόξα continues to be discussed, while E. Schweizer's proposal[23] of μορφή as 'condition' or 'status' referring to Christ's original position vis-a-vis God has the added attraction that it allows a parallelism between verse 6*a* and 7*b* (the incarnate one's human condition as 'in the form of a *doulos*'). The chorus of objection, noted by Hawthorne, that there is an absence of such an understanding of μορφή in Greek literature is offset by an appeal to Tobit i. 13: 'Since I was whole-heartedly mindful of my God, the Most High endowed me with a presence (μορφή) which won me . . . favour' (NEB).

The chief issue, however, concerns what is involved if ἐν μορφῇ θεοῦ ὑπάρχων refers to Christ's pre-existent state, thereby giving to ὑπάρχων its full lexical significance. Or if the phrase ὑπάρχειν ἐν is idiomatic, as in Luke vii. 25, and may be rendered 'in the sense that Christ was clothed with the divine form' (Nagata), and if there is a conscious play on the theme of the first and last Adam, then it becomes arguable that 'the language was used *not* because it is first and foremost appropriate to *Christ*, but because it is appropriate to *Adam*, drawn from the account of Adam's creation and fall. *It was used of Christ therefore to bring out the Adamic character of Christ's life, death and resurrection . . . so Phil. 2. 6–11 is simply a way of describing the character of Christ's ministry and sacrifice*' without reference to His prior existence as a heavenly being (J. D. G. Dunn; his italics[24]). Already hinted at or explicitly stated by C. H. Talbert,[25] J. Murphy-O'Connor[26] and

[22] Nagata, p. 204.
[23] E. Schweizer (see p. 105, n. 2 below). Cf. Martin, *Philippians*, pp. 95 f. This meaning of μορφή as *'Stellung'* is accepted by Hofius, pp. 57 f.
[24] J. D. G. Dunn, *Christology in the Making. A New Testament Inquiry into the Origins of the Doctrine of the Incarnation* (London/Philadelphia, 1980), p. 120.
[25] C. H. Talbert, 'The Problem of Pre-existence in Phil. 2:6–11', *JBL*, 86 (1967), 141–53.
[26] J. Murphy-O'Connor, 'Christological Anthropology in Phil. II. 6–11', *RB*, 83 (1976), 25–50.

G. Howard,[27] this thesis has received considerable expansion in Dunn's christological enterprise. With some variation these writers agree on a central point: the hymn's initial strophe portrays Christ as the righteous one, the perfect image of God in the sense that 'he was totally what God intended man to be' (Murphy-O'Connor[28]), or that the sequence of the hymn's thought is 'first Adam/last Adam', as in I Corinthians xv. 45 ff., without reference 'to any particular time scale—pre-existence, pre-history or whatever' (Dunn[29]).

Dunn's exegetical position sets up a simple equation: what the Adam of Genesis i–iii lost, namely his possession of divine 'glory', has been restored to the last Adam whose 'glory' is described in ii. 9–11. The frontispiece of ii. 6a plays no role, Dunn insists, in portraying the 'glory' from which Christ came, nor does it allude to his pre-temporal, heavenly state. In this argument recourse is made to a single model of a two Adams teaching, which may well be the case. But in order to achieve the required result, i.e. the final glory of the last Adam, the hymn's sequence needs to begin with how it was with Christ's state *ab initio*. The hymn's thought cannot start from the Adam of Genesis but must go behind that Adam to Him who was the archetype (ἐν μορφῇ θεοῦ ὑπάρχων) of Adam. Only on this basis can the symmetry be established, and any real meaning given to the choice of Christ (in verse 6) which brought Him into the stream of humanity. Only as He existed 'in the beginning' can He properly be said to have regarded His state as a prize not to be exploited. Dunn has failed to press the hymn's 'logic' to inquire what is behind the first Adam's characterization as made in the divine 'likeness' (Gen. i. 26 f.). Pauline theology points to humankind's recovery of the *imago Dei* (Rom. viii. 29; II Cor. iii. 18; Col. iii. 10; cf. Eph. iv. 13, 24), which is not what Adam had but lost but what the heavenly Christ had.

(ii) οὐχ ἁρπαγμὸν ἡγήσατο τὸ εἶναι ἴσα θεῷ (verse 6). The precise meaning of these stately words remains as enigmatic as ever, though some notable advances have been made in our

---

[27] G. Howard, 'Phil. 2:6–11 and the Human Christ', *CBQ*, 40 (1978), 368–87.
[28] J. Murphy-O'Connor, p. 49.
[29] J. D. G. Dunn, p. 119.

understanding of them. R. W. Hoover's linguistic researches[30] into ἁρπαγμός as 'something to use for (one's) own advantage' have been applauded as throwing light on the meaning of the word per se. The remaining question is how we are to exegete the entire verse in this light.

If Hoover's interpretation is sound—as I believe it is—it confirms the meaning of μορφή as 'position', 'state', since Christ's being in the rank of God constituted the occasion for exploiting what He did have and reaching out after what could have been His prize. C. F. D. Moule has offered an alternative viewpoint with some anticipation in a previous discussion.[31] L. L. Hammerich[32] in 1966, and independently P. Florensky in 1915, sought a solution to the riddle of the rare word ἁρπαγμός in the translation 'rapture'. The contrast drawn is between what men strive to be, 'ecstatically caught up'—as in II Corinthians xii. 2–4—to be equal with God, and what the Son of God cannot do: His being equal with God is no snatching (*raptus*) since He is divine by nature. He chose to do the opposite, to empty Himself (ἑαυτὸν ἐκένωσεν). The keyword refers to a mystical experience of being 'caught up'. Moule fastened on this background to offer the following explanation: 'Jesus did not reckon that equality with God meant snatching; on the contrary, he emptied himself' ... 'precisely *because* he was in the form of God he reckoned equality with God as not a matter of getting but of giving.'[33] This fine statement, though inherently true as an incarnational sentiment, runs into problems. What I had said briefly in the *Philippians* commentary is elaborated by Nagata:[34]

> [that] v. 6*b c* cannot be reduced to a part of the static theological
> comment regarding how Christ thought of his equality with God
> ... which Christ possessed inalienably, followed by an interpre-
> tation that the self-emptying in v. 7 is to be understood as a positive
> exhibition of the essential characteristic of that equality, as Moule

[30] R. W. Hoover, 'The Harpagmos Enigma: A Philological Solution', *HTR*, 64 (1971), 95–119.

[31] C. F. D. Moule, 'Further Reflexions', pp. 271–74.

[32] L. L. Hammerich, *An Ancient Misunderstanding*. In addition to this work see his 'Phil. 2, 6 and P. A. Florenskij' (sic) Det Kongelige Danske Videskabernes Selskab Historisk-filosofiske Meddelelser 47, 5 (Copenhagen, 1976), pp. 4–16.

[33] C. F. D. Moule, 'The Manhood of Jesus in the NT', in *Christ Faith and History*, ed. S. W. Sykes and J. P. Clayton (Cambridge, 1972), p. 97 (his italics).

[34] Nagata, pp. 236 f.

argues. The explicit sequential progress from the pre-existent Christ (v. 6) to the incarnation of Christ (v. 7) cannot be replaced by the static paradox that the κένωσις is πλήρωσις.

The structure of the hymn's syntax οὐχ . . . ἀλλὰ militates against seeing two sides to Christ's being equal with God as if they were complementary. Instead [Nagata continues],

the negative sentence structure of v. 6, followed by ἀλλά, indicates that the movement of the story is already directed, from the beginning, toward the incarnation, without giving an independent status to the description of the pre-existent Christ.

This telling critique adds weight to the older interpretation that the soteriological drama moves forward from the station the pre-existent one held as ἐν μορφῇ θεοῦ ὑπάρχων to His decision not to use such a platform as a means of snatching a prize (τὸ εἶναι ἴσα θεῷ), but chose rather to divest Himself of that advantage and take the μορφὴ δούλου as an act of voluntary humiliation (ἐταπείνωσεν ἑαυτόν).

(*iii*) Terms such as μορφὴ δούλου, ἑαυτὸν ἐκένωσεν and ἐταπείνωσεν ἑαυτὸν have been given a specificity, namely the suffering servant in Second Isaiah's poems, that is still championed by Hofius, following J. Jeremias' earlier studies.[35] But it is still doubtful whether this clear identification can be sustained, not least on the general point that the hymn (minus the anadiplosis of verse 8c θανάτου δὲ σταυροῦ) attaches any salvific value to the obedience to death. Granted that this line marks out the death as saving event,[36] whereas without it the death could be taken simply as 'an unavoidable consequence' of humiliation, such a concession serves only to underscore the point. The original hymn sets out two sharply contrasting pictures: the pre-existent one who faced a choice whether to exploit His advantage, and the incarnate Christ who was obedient even if that entailed His becoming humiliated. We notice yet again that it is not said *how* He was humbled aside from the general term, 'he took a slave's rank'; nor is it explicitly remarked *to whom* He was obedient. We

---

[35] Jeremias (see below, pp. 182–90).
[36] J. Schneider, *TWNT*, VII (E.T. 1971), 575 f. on σταυρός; M. Hengel, *Crucifixion* (London, E.T. 1977), pp. 86–90.

assume it was to the Father's will, as Hofius implies by a 'cross-reference' to Hebrews x. 5 ff. or as G. B. Caird[37] openly states. But that idea has to be added to the text. Nor can we be sure that the verb ταπεινοῦσθαι is being used ethically. E. Käsemann[38] is more cautious when he comments that verse 8 is an eschatological affirmation, not an ethical portraiture. Still less are we persuaded that 'even unto death' necessarily means a vicarious death, as Hawthorne in agreement with Caird contends, or that this act of obedience presupposes an earthly ministry of Jesus that the hymn of Paul makes prototypical in a paraenetic way for Christians, as Hurtado argues.[39] Lohmeyer's original insight that the phrase 'obedient to death' can only refer to the act of a *divine* being runs exactly counter to this idea.[40]

In all this application which we are disposed to question, the text is being read in the light of other Pauline sections or else augmented by being related to a wider horizon of interest. Thus Hawthorne writes of being able to extract 'that the death of Christ was also vicarious . . . [it] can be correctly inferred, nonetheless, from the context', even if such teaching 'is not expressly stated'. And Hurtado consistently speaks of Christ's 'actions' as presenting 'a pattern to which the readers are to conform their behaviour'. In neither case, as we said, are these matters directly supported by the original text itself, which (*a*) in verses 6–8 never mentions Jesus by name; (*b*) regards the death as the ultimate limit of a freely willed obedience; and (*c*) refers only to a connected series of events which flow from one central, all-determinative 'act', namely 'he emptied himself'. The dramatic scene of John xiii. 3–17 may well have conceptual parallels with these verses, but such a mundane scenario is more coincidental than integral when set alongside the staccato statements of verses 7 and 8 and the other-worldly setting of verses 9–11, a point Hawthorne overlooks in an attempt to suggest a correlation.

We conclude therefore that the limpid verbs, 'He emptied Himself. . . . took the slave's form . . . humbled Himself and became obedient to death', are there to move the story of salvation to its

---

[37] Hofius, p. 15; G. B. Caird, *Paul's Letters from Prison* (New Clarendon Bible) (Oxford, 1976), p. 122.

[38] E. Käsemann, pp. 76 ff. (E.T., pp. 70 ff.).

[39] L. W. Hurtado, sec. iv.

[40] E. Lohmeyer, *Kyrios Jesus*, p. 72; idem, *Philipper*, p. 96.

appointed goal by showing how the initial 'decision' in the eternal realm was worked out in Christ's incarnate existence. He 'came down'—the kinetic imagery is still viable, notwithstanding E. Schweizer's recent but misplaced protest,[41] since it is not a matter of 'literal' descent and ascent—to the lowest levels of obedience, and endured the shame of 'death', whether seen as a power that enslaved Him or not, which represented for ancient society the final disaster and irretrievable loss. All this is necessary to show the extent of obedience and to pave the way for the turning point at verse 9. What the additional line of verse 8c, θανάτου δὲ σταυροῦ, does has already been mentioned, and we shall revert to it later.

(*iv*) The exaltation (implied in the elative verb αὐτὸν ὑπερύψωσεν) with the bestowal of a new name and the submission of all the powers—celestial, earthly and demonic—finds its powerful climax in the *terminus ad quem* of the entire passage: 'every tongue should acknowledge that "Jesus Christ is Lord" ', an ascription that is offered to 'the glory of God the Father'.

We may begin with O. Hofius' treatment since for him verses 9–11 are the clearest evidence that the hymn moves and stays within the orbit of Old Testament confessional material. He states his position clearly at the beginning of his study:[42]

> Phil. 2, 6–11 is a traditional early Christian hymn that celebrates the saving action of God in Jesus Christ, in which the pathway and story of God's Son are described. The extant form of the historical-hymnic report has its prototype (*Vorbild*) in those Old Testament Psalms which relate in confessional praise the historical saving acts of Yahweh. It can be seen from explicit reference to the divine oath in Is. 45, 23 [made in verses 10 and 11] that the Christ-hymn has literary connection with the *Gattung* of the historical Psalms of the Old Testament, to which it is related in terms of its content. The following study is based on the Old Testament background by which the hymn is to be understood, and it seeks to comprehend its message particularly in that setting.

It is an especially valuable feature of Hofius' exegesis that he explores thoroughly the Old Testament–early Jewish setting of

---

[41] E. Schweizer, 'Paul's Christology and Gnosticism', in *Paul and Paulinism. Essays in Honour of C. K. Barrett*, ed. M. D. Hooker and S. G. Wilson (London, 1982), pp. 119, 122.
[42] Hofius, Vorwort.

the enthronement language of the closing verses. In particular he has demonstrated the Old Testament rootage of the hymn's images, notably in regard to the use of Isaiah xlv. 23 and the Jewish synagogue prayers based on this text. Whether he has drawn the most convincing conclusions from these parallels will occupy our attention later. Here we simply look at his proposal as it has been refined by Nagata's study.

All students agree that the central point of this heavenly courtroom scene is the proclamation of Christ's lordly authority: it is 'the lordship of the acclaimed over the acclaimers', as Wengst remarks.[43] Hofius' bid[44] to apportion the triadic phrase in verse 10 to the three areas of angels in heaven, inhabitants of the earth and the dead in Sheol may be regarded as eccentric. Proof that verse 10 has the underworld dead in view is sought in Psalm xxii. 30, but this is unlikely, and the confession of faith in Christ's lordship that Hofius[45] regards as 'macabre' when attributed to demonic agencies is even more problematic in view of Psalms vi. 5 [6], xxx. 10, lxxxviii. 4 ff., cxv. 17 and Isaiah xxxviii. 18, all of which say nothing about proclaiming Yahweh's lordship whether now or in the future.

The moot question is what is meant by this universal confession, 'Jesus Christ is Lord', in which we recognize the overtone of the early Christian credal formulary (Rom. x. 9, 10; I Cor. xii. 3; Col. ii. 6). A clue is given in the use of Isaiah xlv. 23 as that text was used by the Tannaitic rabbis who appealed to Isaiah xliv–xlvii in their defence of the unity of God in the light of tendencies that put Jewish monotheism in jeopardy, a subject investigated by A. F. Segal.[46] The same Deutero-Isaianic passages, as Nagata re-

---

[43] K. Wengst, *Christologische Formeln*, p. 133: 'dass Jesus Herr über die ihm Akklamierenden ist.'

[44] Hofius, p. 53.

[45] Hofius, p. 40.

[46] A. F. Segal, *Two Powers in Heaven: Early Rabbinic Reports about Christianity and Gnosticism* (Leiden, 1977). This significant book's thesis relates to analyzing 'a whole constellation of traditions ... which speculated about the identity and character of the heavenly human [or angelic] figure' (p. 201) who acted as a divine hypostasis. Christians were but one of a number of apocalyptic or mystical groups who posited a primary angelic helper for God. 'The rabbinic attack against these groups had two thrusts. It damned the sectarian groups for having violated Jewish monotheism, using Dt. 32 and Is. 44–47, and Ex. 20 while suggesting that the dangerous scripture used by the sectarians really concerned God's aspects of justice and mercy or His *shekhina*' (p. 262). The 'two powers'

marks,[47] were taken up by Gnosticism in order to ridicule the ignorance of the Jewish God the creator, who did not know that there was a higher God.

Two possibilities deriving from this premise have been currently ventilated. First, Hofius[48] appeals to the Jewish prayers *Nishmaṭ Kol-ḥay* and *'Alenu* which seek to bring together the paradoxical relation between two biblical assertions: (*a*) God is eternally king (Ex. xv. 18), and (*b*) one day God will become king over all the earth (Zech. xiv. 9). He sees the use of Isaiah xlv. 23 in our passage as serving the same purpose. 'Basic to Phil. 2, 9–11 is the Old Testament and old Jewish theologoumenon that at the consummation of the age all creatures will fall down and worship Yahweh, the king of the world ... [It is to] Jesus Christ that universal, eschatological homage will be rendered',[49] and so the acclamation as a 'cry of allegiance' (*Huldigungsruf*), κύριος 'Ιησοῦς Χριστός in a context of the 'name' and the δόξα of Yahweh is the poet's way of claiming that the future hope has been partially realized in the present. He represents his Greek-speaking Jewish community that invokes Isaiah xlv. 23 as its proof-text as it lives 'in the confident expectation that this [eschatological] salvation will soon be universally visible'.[50]

---

seems to have been a basic issue over which Judaism and Christianity separated. But we should note that Segal also concludes (p. 264) that 'the earliest reports about "two powers" in the rabbinic texts were associated with gentiles', suggesting an origin of the teaching in 'a thoroughly Hellenized kind of Judaism or among gentiles attracted to synagogue services.'

[47] Nagata, p. 288; cf. Segal, pp. 234–59 (on Gnosticism whose origin is traced to the polarization of the Jewish community over the issue of the status of God's primary agent. The evidence from Nag Hammadi is illuminating: *Hypostasis of the Archons* 86. 28–87. 3; 94. 20–28; 94. 36–95. 7; *Origin of the World* 103. 6–21; *Apocryphon of John* 11. 18–21; *Gospel of the Egyptians* 58. 23–59. 4. These texts are mostly variations on the theme, 'I am God, and there is no other').

[48] Hofius, pp. 48–51, though the 'Alenu prayer is known only in a late, 3rd century A.D. form (G. F. Moore, *Judaism*, I, 434). Cf. L. Ligier, referred to in my *Philippians*, pp. 113, 116. The text is in S. Singer, *Authorized Daily Prayer Book*, pp. 76 f., 125 f. (*nishmaṭ*).

[49] Hofius, p. 51.

[50] Hofius, p. 67, n. 39; and even more emphatically F. Manns, 'Philippians 2, 6–11: A Judeo-Christian Hymn', *Theology Digest*, 26/1 (1978), 4–10, argues for a Jewish-Christian setting. Manns's arguments are based on literary forms of the text (*inclusio*, hook-words, chiasmus) and a familiarity with messianic themes, especially an 'Adamology'; but these items seem tenuous for tracing Philippians ii back to a Palestinian source. See Deichgräber, *Gotteshymnus*, p. 129, for eight *non*-semitic features.

There is thus, according to Hofius, a blend of enthronement teaching and a future hope of the *parousia* in a way comparable with the emphases of the epistle to the Hebrews. But this creates some problems. The futuristic elements of the eschatology of Hebrews are well attested (Heb. ix. 28, x. 13, 25, 37, 38) alongside an equally evident stress on the exaltation and session of the messianic high priest (Heb. i. 2*b*–14, viii. 1), and a possible way to account for this tension is to describe, in J. Jeremias' term,[51] the present office of the messiah as a 'provisional enthronement',[52] after the manner of a *regnum Christi* in I Corinthians xv. 24 ff. which one day will give way to a perfected *regnum Dei*. The problem is that Philippians ii says nothing of such a *Zwischenreich* or an interim lordship yet to be replaced in the future. Such a hope is already brought into the present in our text, and eschatology is collapsed into the present 'experience' of the acclaimers who offer their tribute to the already glorified Lord.

How then are we to bring these two divergent eschatological strains together? One device, to which Hofius refers,[53] is to suggest the contrast between what is invisible (Christ's present reign) and what is seen, namely the rule of Christ which is presently contested and awaits its perfection when 'all his enemies will have been set under his feet'. Here again we cannot see any place for this schema in Philippians ii, but the suggestion may help us in another way. The one hermeneutical key that could account for *both* the present enthronement of the Lord *and* His future universal acclamation—which our hymn runs together—is *the liturgical origin of the teaching.* As we recall that it is the church that sings the hymn, although the church is not directly included in a scenario (verses 9–11) which is transcendental and other-worldly, as Lohmeyer perceived, we can see how the singers would align themselves (by an act of *conformitas*) with the present victory of the crucified. In worship they reach out and grasp and express the future acknowledgement of all creatures as though it were a present reality. This idea has been well stated by C. F. D. Moule:[54]

[51] J. Jeremias, *New Testament Theology,* I (Philadelphia, E.T. 1971), p. 310 (=*Neutestamentliche Theologie*: erster Teil [Gütersloh, 1971], p. 294). Jeremias rejects this solution as 'forced'.

[52] Hofius, p. 98.

[53] Hofius, p. 98, n. 95.

[54] C. F. D. Moule, *The Birth of the New Testament* (London, 3rd ed. 1982), p. 149.

Always at moments of Christian worship, time and space are obliterated and the worshipping Church on earth is one in eternity
with the Church in the heavenly places.

Granted that such a picture needs to be complemented by the
thought of the church's existence *in via* and as not yet having
reached its goal *in patria*, it may well explain the confidence of
our hymn with its 'realized eschatology' and its telescoping the
future triumph into a present reality.[55] At all events, Paul's interest
is to secure a firm credal-confessional base for the lordship of the
exalted one, which he will use paraenetically since the Kyrios is
none other than the head of the church, to whom men and women
are accountable for their every decision and action (so in Phil. ii.
12).[56]

Secondly, it is a *sententia recepta* that the acclamation 'Jesus Christ
is Lord' is borrowed from an early Christian creed, usually thought
to be the initiatory confession required in baptism.[57] The hymn,
however, sets the cry in a cosmic, not a cultic, context, and thereby
it has reinterpreted it. Paul 'rescues' it from that setting to apply
it as part of his exhortation. But the question presses, What did
the formula connote in the context of the heavenly scene of verses
9–11?

Nagata's study has innovatively drawn our notice to Jewish traditions in the wisdom literature and sectarian Judaism in which
other divine beings or angelic vice-regents of God acted as inter-
mediaries between heaven and earth. We are familiar with wis-
dom-logos speculation that has been utilized as a background to
Philippians ii. 5–8, and the more recent studies of J. D. G. Dunn[58]
and E. Schweizer[59] have pressed these ideas into service. Partic-

[55] It will not do for Hawthorne then to write: 'How these purposes will be
fulfilled, or when they will be fulfilled, or whether they will be fulfilled are not
questions that can be answered from the statements of the hymn itself. Suffice
it to say in general that not always are purposes realized or goals attained. Not
even divine purposes and goals . . .'. This statement underestimates what the
text *does* say.

[56] W. Kramer, *Christ, Lord, Son of God* (London, E.T. 1966), pp. 169 ff.,
sec. 47.

[57] C. C. Marcheselli, 'La celebrazione di Gesù Cristo Signore in Fil 2,
6–11. Riflessioni letterario-storico-esegetiche sull' inno cristologico', *Ephemerides Carmeliticae*, 29 (1978), 2–42. I owe this reference to G. F. Hawthorne.

[58] Dunn, *Christology*, ch. vi. The role of various 'powers' (Aher, Metatron,
Merkabah, and the Angel of Yahweh) is discussed by A. F. Segal, *Two Powers in
Heaven*, pp. 60–73.

[59] E. Schweizer (see below, p. 319, and Schweizer's essay referred to on p. xxv).

ularly the picture of the suffering righteous man (in Wisdom ii–v) has been appealed to as affording a parallel to the career of Jesus in the first main section of the hymn. This follows the initial contribution of D. Georgi, to which we made brief allusion (see below, pp. 313, 318 f.) and which has been supported by Hans-Theo Wrege,[60] who indicated how Isaiah xl–lv has been reinterpreted, in post-biblical Judaism, to describe the destiny of the righteous one in the framework of the wisdom literature. Our criticisms have been developed by K. Wengst,[61] who notes how wisdom as a mediator—a common feature in this tradition—is lacking in Philippians ii, and asks how it came about that wisdom was identified with the righteous man and then transferred to Jesus.

What Nagata has done is to set this wisdom speculation on a broader, firmer base as part of a wider interest, especially in mystical Judaism, in angelology. He fastens on the 'name' of God, which was sometimes taken to refer to the highest angelic vice-regents of God on the basis of Exodus xxiii. 21, 'My name is in him', and accorded the honor of the title Yahweh (Kyrios).[62] In the hymn where the heavenly enthronement drama is played out and the ineffable name of Yahweh (Kyrios) is pronounced we are intended to see a rebuttal of an implied Jewish attack that such an arrogation of the divine title is blasphemous. The ground of such a resistance to the Christian claim (Jesus Christ is Lord) is that it imperils the unity of God in the same way that all talk of angelic beings and rivals to Yahweh was treated with disdain by the orthodox and repelled on the basis of an appeal to Isaiah xlv. 5: 'I am Yahweh, and there is no other' (cf. Isa. xlv. 14, 21, 22).

What this hymn, in its Jewish-Christian setting, contends for is a recognition, cast in polemical form by its use of a scriptural

[60] H.-T. Wrege, 'Jesusgeschichte und Jüngergeschick nach Joh 12, 20–33 und Heb 5, 7–10', in *Der Ruf Jesu und die Antwort der Gemeinde. Festschrift* J. Jeremias, ed. E. Lohse (Göttingen, 1970), pp. 275 f., n. 48.

[61] K. Wengst, *Christologische Formeln*, pp. 152 ff.

[62] Especially the principal angel, who is accorded the title *Yhwh hqtwn* (Yahweh the lesser), attributed to Metatron in the Merkabah tradition in III Enoch (H. Odeberg, *III Enoch* [Cambridge, 1928], p. 33; cf. M. Hengel, *The Son of God* [London, E.T. 1976], p. 46).

For some discussion of these ideas in 'esoteric' Judaism see C. C. Rowland, *The Open Heaven. A Study of Apocalyptic in Judaism and Early Christianity* (London, 1982), pp. 100–13; S. Kim, *The Origin of Paul's Gospel* (Wissenschaftliche Untersuchungen zum NT 2. 4) (Tübingen, 1981) (Grand Rapids, 1982), pp. 239–52.

prooftext already known in Judaism, that Jesus is now enthroned as the new eschatological *cosmocrator*. The counter-claim is registered by an appeal to God's own decisive interposition (verse 9) and to the universal homage of all sentient beings (verse 10) that the sovereignty Judaism expected at the end-time is already a reality. Such a divine prerogative as Jesus now has is seen to be approved by God Almighty Himself (verse 11). The drama of these verses, therefore, powerfully attests to a theological legitimization that (*a*) does not violate the divine unity; (*b*) is grounded in God's eschatological act which enshrines the principle of *Umwertung*, i.e. eschatological reversal, specifically 'the humble will be exalted';[63] and (*c*) has scriptural support. We are looking, according to Nagata, at 'a major theological reflection on the Jewish question about the unity of God, which is endangered by the incarnational divine christology, according to which Jesus is both the pre-existent divine figure and eschatological divine cosmic Lord beside God the Father.'

This illuminating treatment, which a later page (p. 148) will illustrate from the rabbinic definition of rebellion (cf. John v. 18), needs to be enriched by a reference to Philippians ii. 6 where the contrast is drawn between Christ's ἁρπαγμός and the 'advantage' it gave Him of reaching out after a prize of 'equality with God'. The way of combining the two ideas of *res rapta* and *res rapienda* we submitted (see pp. 143–53) allows us to complete the picture. The prize which the heavenly one chose not to seek after by a rebellious arrogating of Godlikeness, Moule's 'snatching' or 'getting', is now presented to Him, and He takes His place alongside Yahweh as Kyrios by divine appointment. The cosmic acclamation and *proskynesis* is the token in this setting that God's seal of approval is on the award. So the antithesis of 'snatching' or 'getting' by personal acquisitiveness or *hybris* is not so much 'giving' as 'receiving' (ὁ θεὸς ... ἐχαρίσατο αὐτῷ) with the emphasis not on what He *did* but on what *was done* to and for Him. God has bestowed on Him His own name and title, and installed Him in the seat of authority as the erstwhile incarnate, humiliated and obedient one. He is the exact opposite of the rebel son who 'makes himself strong as his father.' 'To the glory of God the Father' Jesus holds new office and receives the worship of all

---

[63] A. Contri, 'Il "Magnificat" alla luce dell'inno christologico di Filippesi 2, 6–11', *Marianum*, 40 (1978), 164–68.

creation. Nagata's proposal that in the polemical background is the Jewish claim to divine monarchy and exclusive honor to be paid to 'the one God' may well be the case. But if so, it is not a polemic against the incarnational christology the hymn depicts; rather it is directed against the hymn's insistence that Jesus who suffered ignominy and disgrace in His servant role is now exalted to such honor as only God can bestow. The hymn is another example of the axiom 'the humble shall be exalted' that seems to have informed Jewish-Christian apologetics according to the early speeches and prayers in Acts i–vii (e.g. ii. 23, 24; iv. 10, 11) and forms a link with Stephen's apology of the righteous one who was rejected (Acts vii. 52) and is now clothed with the glory of God (Acts vii. 55, 56).

It is time to review these two proposals and assess their contributions to the study of Philippians ii. 6–11. Both are linked by a common concern to see the hymn against its Old Testament-Judaic background and as directed to some kind of theological problem; for Hofius it was an eschatological issue, for Nagata the debate was christological. While not denying to these motifs a part of the total setting, the present writer is still convinced that the confessional acclaim, 'Jesus Christ is Lord' (which Hofius and Nagata agree is the 'center' of the hymn), has to be heard as the Christian's response to the Hellenistic feeling of helplessness and despair in the face of life's mysteries and the cosmos's apparent meaningless existence. There is no need to rehearse the reasons for this statement and the evidence on which it is claimed to be based. See a later section, pp. 306–11. I would simply add one factor which will serve as a bridge to the next section.

Philippians ii. 6–11 retains its interest as one example of several *carmina Christi* found in the New Testament, e.g. Colossians i. 15–20; I Timothy iii. 16; I Peter i. 20, iii. 18–22; Hebrews i. 3a–4; Apocalypse v. 1–14; John i. 1–14. The common element in most of—if not all—these tributes is the way the odyssey of Christ is depicted, climaxing in His exaltation to heaven where he received the accolade of a title and a new dignity as *cosmocrator*. I have elsewhere argued[64] that this 'model' is one of descent/ascent which replaced the earlier Judaic contrast of rejection/vindication, seen in the Acts kerygma. The real point of distinction that gave

[64] R. P. Martin, 'Some Reflections on New Testament Hymns', in *Christ the Lord. Studies Presented to Donald Guthrie*, ed. H. H. Rowdon (Leicester, 1982), pp. 37–49; cf. a summary in *ExT*, 94.5 (1983), pp 132–36.

these 'hymns to Christ' a new dimension is the *cosmological role* attributed to the person and work of Christ. In a double sense the use of this adjective is noteworthy. First, His pre-temporal activity in creation is made the frontispiece of the hymns. In our text this idea is muted save to describe His being as actively sharing in the 'form' (μοϱφή) or glory of God; and as we observed, only on that basis can the claim be meaningfully made that He came 'from God' in an act of self-abnegation or chose to accept the humility of incarnation and obedience (II Cor. viii. 9 as well as Phil. ii. 6–8).

Second, at the close of His earthly journey He took His place in God's presence by receiving universal homage and the acclamation of cosmic spirit-powers that, in confessing His lordship, were forced to abandon their title of rule over human destiny. The splendor that encompasses the exalted Christ in ii. 9–11 is indeed an eschatological inauguration of the new age already begun and a christological affirmation that He is one with the Father. But coming as the sequel to ii. 6–8, which shows how the incarnate one embraced His fate willingly (as seen in the reflexives ἑαυτόν [*bis*] and the word ὑπήϰοος), the final scene can only yield its deepest sense if it portrays vividly and performatively the conviction that henceforth Christ is the Lord of all life and holds the reins of cosmic and human destiny in His hands. This was the assurance the early believers in the Graeco-Roman world of Paul's day needed to hear; and as they gave voice to it in their worship of the heavenly Lord the message became real to them on earth.[64a]

III. THE USE OF THE HYMN IN CONTEXT: TRADITION AND REDACTION

This section may now turn to consider what is after all the nub of the exegetical task. Given that the passage had an independent existence as a pre-formed hymnic tribute, complete in itself and tracing the itinerary of a heavenly being from one phase of His existence to His final glory, the question is the use Paul has made of it by including it in his pastoral admonition. The traditional form of the verses is well attested by the criteria that are stated on pp. 24–41, and more recently developed by M. Barth[65] who

[64a] See now Karl Erich Grözinger, *Musik und Gesang in der Theologie der frühen jüdischen Literatur* (Tübingen, 1982), pp. 27–39, 56–75, 83–99, 335 f.

[65] M. Barth, 'Traditions in Ephesians'. Unpublished Paper for the seminar Traditionen in Corpus Paulinum, given at the SNTS meeting in Louvain, August 23–27, 1982.

adds features such as: the words at the end of the passage marking the resumption of the author's own speech (here in ii. 12); the absence of the name of Him who is praised; frequent use of the third person singular aorist verbs, and participles, with relative, final and/or consecutive clauses to express purpose or result (ii. 6–8, 9, 10); brevity achieved by the employment of anarthrous abstract nouns, set in parallelism and which are pleonastic or repetitive (ii. 7, 8); syllabic correspondences[66] especially to produce couplets (*parallelismus membrorum*) that are synonymous or antithetical or climactic, with a special device such as chiasmus (clearly in ii. 6 and 11); and one special example of chiasmus in *inclusio* or 'ring-composition' by which the conclusion resumes the topic found at the beginning. The application of such criteria leads, with a fair degree of confidence, to the conclusion that this pericope was composed earlier than the time when Paul wrote his pastoral letter to the Philippians and by a hand other than Paul's. Recent attempts, notably the one by S. Kim,[67] to support a Pauline authorship of this passage have not seemed impressive and have not faced the cumulative arguments referred to in *Philippians*, p. 113. We are on firm ground in stating that Philippians ii. 6–11 represents a hymnic specimen, taken over by Paul as a *paradosis* from some early Christian source with a Jewish background but slanted to address questions that faced the church as it moved out to confront the larger Hellenistic world of Graeco-Roman society.

Paul took over and redacted this lyrical composition, evidently because it was agreeable, with some emendation (in verse 8c notably), to his theology, and it suited his purpose in enforcing his apostolic call in Philippians ii. 1–4, 12. But it also is cited be-

---

[66] B. Eckman, 'A Quantitative Metrical Analysis of the Philippians Hymn', *NTS*, 26 (1980), 258–66, considers Philippians ii. 5–11 in the light of Greek poetic and metrical forms. Her scansion of the passage exposes many rhetorical traits (supplementing p. 37 below), but her method involves some unwarranted deletions in order to secure perfect symmetry. Moreover, she concedes that this attempt to see metrical regularity may be asking too much of the author.

[67] S. Kim, *The Origin of Paul's Gospel*, pp. 147–49. A. J. Bandstra's judgment that the question whether Paul used an earlier hymn or wrote Philippians ii himself is 'of remote concern to the minister' ('"Adam" and "the Servant" in Phil. 2:5 ff.', *Calvin Theological Journal*, 1 [1966], 213) may be accurate, but it is certainly an issue of some consequence for the New Testament interpreter, especially where the development of early christology is concerned.

PREFACE TO THE 1983 EDITION

cause it represented a shared possession with his readers, and
Paul could confidently assume that by quoting it he would command their assent to its chief thrust, namely that Christian existence is most tellingly understood and lived under the lordship
of Christ whose mandate—παράκλησις ἐν Χριστῷ (verse 1)—is
brought to bear on the troubles afflicting the Philippian
community.

Usually the problems arising within the church at Philippi are
dismissed as bad feeling (ii. 14), a quarrelsome disposition on
the part of some members (iv. 2, 3), a selfish rivalry driving
believers into unworthy ambitions and toward disunity (ii. 3,
4), and a confusion over ethical ideals (iv. 8, 9). But there was
certainly a more serious set of problems; or rather the most serious irritant within the Philippian congregation was a threatening false teaching that produced all these disfiguring symptoms.
Recent studies have tried to identify Paul's opponents confronted
in this letter and their influence on the Philippian Christians; and
only as we can achieve some success in isolating and appreciating
the nature of this influential teaching with its practical repercus-
sions may we hope to know why Paul chose to utilize the Philippian hymn. In this enterprise two matters are linked together:
(a) the precise nature of the situation at Philippi which required
the apostle's intervention, and (b) the function of cited material—
in this case, a *carmen Christi*—drawn from a liturgical setting but
used in a hortatory way.

(a) A recent study has noted how the meaning of the situational
context of the entire Philippian letter is bound up in two issues:
the literary questions of whether the letter is a unity or a pastiche
of epistolary fragments, written at different times and in response
to various needs and put together in loose fashion to form what
we know as Paul's letter to the Philippians; and, secondly, the
question of the opponents in the letter(s) (notably referred to at
i. 28 and iii. 2 ff., 18 ff.) and their influence on the Philippian
congregation. The bewildering variety of proposals in these areas,
chronicled by B. Mengel,[68] makes a decisive statement of how the
Philippian problems are to be analyzed problematical, and the
present writer can only plead that, as he has discussed some of

[68] B. Mengel, *Studien zum Philipperbrief* (Wissenschaftliche Untersuchungen
zum NT 2. 8) (Tübingen, 1982), pp. 191–221.

XXXV

these matters in another place,[69] some tentative conclusions may here be drawn, as a basis for further research.

We assume that at iii. 2 ff. the presence of Jewish Christian enemies is to be understood. They have all the marks of the emissaries who resisted the Pauline mission at Corinth (II Cor. x–xiii), and proclaimed a triumphalist understanding of the Christian life removed from suffering and loss. Hence Paul's impassioned justification of his life as a suffering apostle (Phil. i 15–18, 28 f.) and of the vicissitudes that befell his colleague Epaphroditus (ii. 25–30). The charge that the intruders led the Corinthians into a freewheeling morality (II Cor. xii. 20 f.) reappears in their attitudes depicted in Philippians iii. 18 ff. Their proud boast in circumcision reflects their claim to represent the true Israel, and is linked to a perfectionist teaching that imagined that since they had attained a present enjoyment of a heavenly life on earth their 'exalted . . . self-consciousness . . . released [them] from the imperfections of time and morality'[70] (iii. 12–16), and gave them a lopsided view of the resurrection—which for Paul is still a future hope (iii. 11, 20, 21)—and caused them to deny the *parousia* which Paul affirms repeatedly throughout the letter (i. 10; ii. 16; iii. 20 f.; iv. 5 [?]). A plus factor in this identification is that it pinpoints a single common issue on which Paul offers his response, and relates the encroachment of false teachers on the Philippian scene to other situations in the mission churches where similar ideas were being introduced, notably at Galatia and Corinth. At the heart of Paul's retort is the exposure of what he regarded as the chief distressing feature of this alien influence. There was a misguided eschatology and a lack of humility because the cross was pushed into the background and its significance as both the foundation of Christian existence and a pattern for Christian living denigrated.

At a practical level the Philippians were enticed into thinking that a Christian community could know a life exempt from hardship, strife and loss since it was a pneumatic fellowship raised with Christ to a heavenly life already begun. The other side of this proud claim was that the Christian vocation as a commitment to

---

[69] *Philippians*, pp. 22–36. What follows will, I hope, repel the charge brought by Strimple, 'Philippians 2:5–11', pp. 267 f.: 'Martin can object . . . only because he refuses to interpret the passage in the context of Paul's exhortation to the Philippians.'

[70] R. Jewett, 'Conflicting Movements in the Early Church as Reflected in Philippians', *Novum Testamentum*, 12 (1970), 387.

lowliness and suffering was forgotten; hence the ugly symptoms of selfish egotism and a disdain of Paul's suffering (i. 26) as of Christian vulnerability in general (i. 28 f.).

This interpretation of the Christian life is countered by Paul. Suffering is shown to be God's will (i. 28–30), just as Paul's prison experience is a sign, not of his spurious apostleship but of its God-given authenticity (i. 12–18). 'Perfection' belongs only to the future, and meanwhile the believer like Paul is required to exert all his powers to press onward (iii. 12–15) to a future resurrection; and the hope of the *parousia* (iii. 20 f.) makes ethical demands on him now. Above all, it is life under the sign of the cross that characterizes the Christian attitude since the path the church treads in the world is one of weakness (iii. 10, 11) as it follows its Lord who came to His final glory only by accepting a servant role and becoming obedient to death.

It should now be apparent that the paraenetic section i. 27–ii. 18 is a close-knit unit, and forms Paul's total response to the Philippian malaise. More importantly it is his controversy with sectarian teaching that informs his writing here. As the frontispiece is Paul's theodicy of suffering (i. 29), which leads him to consider Christ's suffering. His pastoral appeal puts its finger on the outward signs of disunity and selfish attitudes (ii. 1–4) where each Philippian is looking to his or her own interests and not the well-being of the community whose 'health' (ii. 12) Paul's teaching (I Cor. xii) set at the center of congregational life as κοινωνία πνεύματος (ii. 1). The last thing Paul needed to do, then, was to appeal to some hedonistic ethic that promised a future glory if only the Philippians would take the road of humility. Christ's own 'exhortation' is seen in what is expected of those who share His life in community (ii. 5) and who praise Him in a hymn that celebrates His lordship as the obedient one who is now exalted. The paraenetic call comes at ii. 12: the obedient one is to be obeyed. And the practical outworking is applied in verses 14–16, with Paul's own life of self-giving service as an apostle appealed to (ii. 17, 18).

The two lines of the quoted hymn drive home Paul's paraenesis: 'the death of the cross' (verse 8c) and 'Jesus Christ is Lord' (verse 11). If the original version of the hymn is best understood as a triumphant assertion of the cosmic authority of the *Pantocrator,* it is not difficult to see how Paul would take it over (perhaps because it represented the sectarian theology at Philippi and may have been a hymn the teachers had introduced to epitomize their message that Christ the Lord calls His people to share His present triumph)—but only with modification. The *Vorlage* needed corrective reworking, and Paul does it by the simplest of devices. He uses the terminology of the hymn in his 'build-up' (in ii. 1–4) as he describes the Philippian scene as marked by κενοδοξία in place of a needed ταπεινοφροσύνη and calls on his readers to 'consider' (ἡγούμενοι) others' interests; and he inserts the line θανάτου δὲ σταυροῦ to make it clear how Christ's present lordship is exerted under the sign of the cross. True Christian living is at furthest remove from a *theologia gloriae,* the sectarians' watchword. Rather Paul's theology, involving both his exposition of Christ's work, past and present, and his statement of the church's life, is essentially a *theologia crucis.* This setting of 'the cross' as the decisive criterion of Christian existence means that Jesus' death is more than a fact of past history and greater than a station on the way to His ultimate glory. It is the hallmark of all that characterized Jesus' person and saving significance, so that to proclaim Him is to proclaim the cross (I Cor. i. 18), to be called to suffering is for the sake of the cross (Gal. vi. 12–14), and to die to self is to be crucified with Him by sharing His death (Gal. ii. 20; Phil. iii. 10; Rom. vi. 4). To deny this is to subvert Paul's gospel by removing its *skandalon* (I Cor. i. 23; Gal. v. 11). So his editing of the Philippian hymn is directed at those who are sadly called 'enemies of Christ's cross' (iii. 18).

(*b*) M. Hengel's study[71] 'Hymn and Christology' remarks how the genre 'Christ hymn', offered to the enthroned Lord, is an 'extremely old christological formula ... it appears in different periods of time, at different places, and in different contexts in tradition history'. He notes the three features that distinguish this class of hymnic praise: (*i*) Christ's sacrificial death is the reason for his exaltation; (*ii*) the receiving of a name is part of His being glorified; and (*iii*) all creation is subject to Him as κύριος. There are Old Testament anticipations of these claims, chiefly in Psalm cx. 1, but their appearance on the scene is not the result of considered reflection or scripture study. We should trace these hymns to the activity of 'anonymous, spirit-filled poets' who led the congregation in worship and gave expression to eschatological joy

[71] M. Hengel, 'Hymn and Christology', in *Studia Biblica* 1978, *III. Papers on Paul and Other New Testament Authors,* ed. E. A. Livingstone (*JSNT* Suppl. Series 3) (Sheffield, 1980), pp. 173–97. German version 'Hymnus und Christologie', in *Wort in der Zeit. Festgabe für Karl Heinrich Rengstorf zum 75. Geburtstag,* ed. W. Haubeck and M. Bachmann (Leiden, 1980), pp. 1–23.

(ἀγαλλίασις) which was linked to the joy of the heavenly world perhaps by the use of a glossolalic utterance (I Cor. xiii. 1, 'tongues of angels'); when they rendered such tributes into intelligible speech they became 'teachers'. 'A unity ... was established between the praising ἀγαλλίασις community and the spirit-filled διδασκαλία community'.[72]

The 'service of worship' in I Corinthians xiv inevitably springs to mind as we read these suggestions. We recall also the 'spirit-filled enthusiasm of the primitive church',[73] and note how Paul was compelled to sound certain warnings and set up controls to regulate such unbridled outbursts at Corinth.[74] One of the criteria he appeals to (I Cor. xii. 1–3) is that the confession κύριος 'Ιησοῦς stands in opposition to and in correction of the cry ἀνάθεμα 'Ιησοῦς.[75] The preceding study of Philippians ii. 6–11, whose text and theme (now most adequately shown to be 'The Way of Christ') also closes with that note, has, we trust, drawn out one further reminder. In the formula κύριος 'Ιησοῦς Χριστός it is for Paul not enough to claim enthusiastically that the heavenly κύριος is world ruler and is present in the congregation which now shares His reign. His name 'Ιησοῦς casts its shadow back on His earthly life of self-abnegation and humiliation; and His present lordship was achieved—and is exercised—only because He became 'obedient unto death', with the cross erected[76] as Paul's warning notice that no version of Christ's triumph or the church's vocation and destiny can claim to be authentic unless it is seen *sub specie crucis*.

R. P. M.

Advent 1982

---

[72] Hengel, p. 195 (German p. 23).

[73] Hengel, p. 185 (German p. 13); cf. R. P. Martin, *The Worship of God. Some Theological, Pastoral, and Practical Reflections* (Grand Rapids, 1982), ch. 10.

[74] A forthcoming title, 'The Spirit and the Congregation: Studies in I Corinthians 12–15', will seek to investigate how Paul did this.

[75] To my list of possible meanings, given in *The Worship of God*, pp. 175–78, should be added: J. M. Bassler, 'I Cor. 12:3—Curse and Confession in Context', *JBL*, 101 (1982), 415–18.

[76] Cf. H. Weder, *Das Kreuz Jesu bei Paulus* (FRLANT 125) (Göttingen, 1981), pp. 212 f., who notes this fact: 'The insertion of the "death on the cross" has then far-reaching consequences for the interpretation of the entire hymn. It becomes its center, from which the other statements (of the hymn) appear in a new light.'

The centrality of the *theologia crucis* in Paul has been well described by E. Dinkler, who writes of 'the character of the cross as a divisive and decisive sign (*als scheidend-entscheidendes Zeichen*)' of Christian existence; 'Das Kreuz als Siegeszeichen', *ZfTK*, 62 (1965), pp. 1–20 (p. 19) = *Signum Crucis* (Göttingen, 1967), pp. 55–67 (p. 74).

PREFACE TO THE 1997 EDITION

I. INTRODUCTION

It is a rare privilege (and accompanying responsibility) to see one's earlier literary work reintroduced to the reading public. The volume, now published under the title *A Hymn of Christ,* thus translating the original Latin title *Carmen Christi* and hopefully making its appeal more accessible, first appeared in 1967. The sub-title *Philippians ii. 5-11 in Recent Interpretation and in the Setting of Early Christian Worship* was intended to explicate the Latin. It also served to demarcate the limits of the biblical text and indicate the author's intention to investigate the way scholars in modern times have understood the verses. The purpose was then to suggest a life-setting of the Pauline period in a liturgical frame. A reprint, with an extended preface to take account of the ongoing debate from 1963 to 1983—a twenty-year span in which the output of secondary literature devoted to Philippians 2:5-11 showed no sign of abatement—followed in 1983. The tide of scholarly productions continues to flow up to the present day, with no hint of receding.

This continued exegetical activity is a healthy index of the state of Scripture study. It reminds us that the quest for understanding Scripture's meaning in its contextual setting is never-ending, and each generation of scholars brings its own interest, acumen and agenda concerns to the text. Yet there are other reasons that Philippians 2:5-11 continues to be a focus of study: we acknowledge that this text has not yet yielded its full secrets or rich treasures. Reasons for this enduring quality are not far to seek.

It taxes the skill of the translator, since many of the key words used in relation to Christ, in what traditionally are regarded as his threefold states of pre-existence, incarnate life and exalted office, baffle the lexicographer's expertise and present a wide variety of choice and interpretation. Since many of these terms are rare in biblical Greek and even rarer in the Pauline vocabulary, the translator's difficulty is compounded. For this reason Philippians 2:5-11 is frequently prescribed in Greek and English exegesis courses in the university and seminary curriculum—or even at the college level.

The literary form of the passage gives a window of access into the worshipping life of early Christians. Depending on the outcome of investigation into the pre-history of a text like Philippians 2, it becomes feasible to gain entree to the earliest Pauline (or pre-Pauline, if Paul took over an earlier version of the passage, generally classified under the genre "hymnic" or "poetic") congregations, where the exalted Lord was being hailed as worthy of liturgical praise on a par with Israel's covenant God. Interest in early Christian worship is stimulated by this text. Modern liturgy makers and hymnists are encouraged to know how the first hymns in the New Testament period reflected an experience and practice of veneration offered to the enthroned (but once crucified) head of the church and Lord of creation. Any study of "a symphony of New Testament hymns," to cite a recent (1996) title,[1] is bound to give pride of place to Philippians 2:5-11.

In our day Christology is a perennial topic of interest in the allied fields of biblical study, early Christian doctrine and church history, and systematic theology. The tribute paid to the church's Lord in our passage is often regarded as the starting point (or a likely starting point) for all future development, picking up the evaluations that in this Pauline passage we have the oldest evidence of what was later to become the ground plan of all christological thinking (so Jeremias),[2] "perhaps the most rich in christological content in the New Testament" (Cullmann)[3] and "the earliest witness to an explicit formulation of pre-existence and kenosis" (Hengel).[4] Inasmuch as the section 2:6-11, often regarded as epitomizing the "the story of salvation" or "the way of the redeemer," is set in a wider context of ethical and pastoral exhortation and admonition (2:1-4, 12-16), Paul's grounding of his ethical instruction in salvation teaching sets a pattern for a modern discussion of the proper basis for Christian ethical endeavour and interpersonal relations within the church.[5]

A tacit reason that a biblical text continues to engage scholarly interest is, of course, that its meaning is complex. It can be approached from various angles, and it can be understood in several ways. This is

---

[1]Robert J. Karris, *A Symphony of New Testament Hymns* (Collegeville, Minn.: Liturgical, 1996).

[2]J. Jeremias, "Zur Gedankenführung in den paulinischen Briefen," in *Studia Paulina in Honorem J. de Zwaan*, ed. J. N. Sevenster and W. C. van Unnik (Haarlem: Bohn, 1953), pp. 146-54 (154).

[3]O. Cullmann, cited in "Ernst Lohmeyer† (1890-1946)," in *Theologische Zeitschrift* 7.2 (1951), pp. 158-60: "Die christologisch vielleicht gehaltsvollste Stelle des NTs" (p. 159).

[4]M. Hengel, "The Song About Christ in Earliest Worship," in *Studies in Early Christology* (Edinburgh: T & T Clark, 1995), p. 289.

[5]For one such consideration, see Richard B. Hays, *The Moral Vision of the New Testament* (New York: HarperCollins, 1996), pp. 28-32.

why no two interpreters are likely to come up with identical answers to the exegetical conundrums posed by the text. All of this makes a book purporting to chronicle the history of interpretation a worthwhile project. Two disclaimers, however, must be entered at this point.

First, an inquiring reader, anxious to know what the most recent bevy of scholarship concludes regarding the passage, is likely to be bewildered by a cataloguing of names, opinions and theories, when all that is essentially needed is a broad-stroke sketch of proposals that are (in the reviewer's estimate, to be sure) most plausible and thus the most worthy of attention. This new preface, therefore, has eschewed the simple recital of names and bibliographical references, which in any event can easily be called up by electronic means in our day—a service that was not technologically possible or at least as widespread in 1983, when the older preface was prepared. Admittedly, some selectivity of judgment is involved in making decisions as to what should and should not be included; but on balance the method chosen in the following pages will, I believe, be found less confusing and more serviceable to students and the general reader, even at the loss of comprehensiveness and providing a full bibliographical thesaurus. The prospect of "information overload" is such that the purpose behind this re-issue could be defeated were I to attempt comprehensive cataloguing.

Second, currently in preparation is a symposium dedicated to a study of Philippians 2:5-11 from different perspectives, including exegetical, ethical, liturgical and pastoral points of view. Several of the essays, from ten or so contributors, contain ample bibliographies to point the would-be inquirer in the direction of the latest trends. The symposium will also feature a critical interaction with current literature alongside a statement and an evaluation of some groundbreaking proposals. It seemed a needless expenditure of effort to duplicate this major addition to the growing library of resources, and as editor of this volume, *Where Christology Began,* I have been greatly impressed and assisted by the fine contributions of several colleagues, all experts in their fields. To add further distinction to this symposium—and to place all students in their debt—two of our team of essayists have produced essays that are part translation, part exposition, part evaluation of the two landmark publications in the history of interpretation. I refer to the seminal works of Ernst Lohmeyer and Ernst Käsemann (the former was hitherto untranslated). Both writers' works and their significance are now made available and expressed in a nuanced fashion.[6] The latter point is worth emphasizing, since both Lohmeyer and Käsemann wrote on Philippians 2 in a style and against a background such that the simple translation from German to English required a great deal of glossing to bring out the full sense. Both essayists have offered selections and provide running commentaries that all students will find valuable.

It is time now to state what objectives this new edition of *A Hymn of Christ* seeks to achieve.[7] There are two chief concerns, with the second subdivided so as to isolate the aspects of the passage that are central in more recent discussion.

1. The first preoccupation has been to provide a re-statement and, to an extent, a more nuanced set of conclusions on this passage as it affects New Testament exegesis with its christological emphasis and in particular the role of "hymns to Christ"[8] as a genre within the multifaceted diversity of New Testament literature. At this stage, and before becoming bogged down with too much exegetical detail, it is desirable to express this re-assessment in easily accessible language without loss of integrity.

[6]Lohmeyer's *Kyrios Jesus: Eine Untersuchung zu Phil. 2, 5-11*, SHAW Jahrgang 1927/1928 (Heidelberg: Carl Winter, Universitätsverlag, zweite Auflage, 1961) has never been translated into English until now. Käsemann's "Kritische Analyse von Phil. 2, 5-11," *ZfTK* 47 (1950), 313-60, reprinted in *Exegetische Versuche und Besinnungen* 1 (Göttingen: Vandenhoeck & Ruprecht, 1960), pp. 51-95, was translated by A. F. Carse as "A Critical Analysis of Philippians 2:5-11," in *God and Christ: Existence and Province*, ed. R. W. Funk, *Journal for Theology and the Church* 5 (New York: Harper & Row, 1968), pp. 45-88.

Colin Brown and Robert Morgan have written chapters on these titles in the forthcoming *Where Christology Began: Essays on Philippians 2* (Louisville, Ky.: Westminster John Knox, 1998).

[7]All recent substantial commentaries on Philippians devote considerable space to 2:5-11. Among these may be listed G. F. Hawthorne, *Philippians*, Word Biblical Commentary 43 (Waco, Tex.: Word, 1983); W. Schenk, *Die Philipperbrief des Paulus* (Stuttgart: Kohlhammer, 1984); M. Silva, *Philippians*, Wycliffe Exegetical Commentary (Chicago: Moody Press, 1988); M. D. Hooker, *Philippians*, New Interpreter's Bible 11 (Nashville: Abingdon, forthcoming); P. T. O'Brien, *The Epistle to the Philippians*, New International Greek Testament Commentary (Grand Rapids: Eerdmans, 1991); R. R. Melick, *Philippians, Colossians, Philemon* (Nashville: Broadman, 1991); G. D. Fee, *Paul's Letter to the Philippians*, New International Commentary on the New Testament (Grand Rapids: Eerdmans, 1995). See too E. A. C. Pretorius, "A Key to the Literature on Philippians," *Neotestamentica* 23 (1989), 125-53.

[8]It is well to state here what this term entails. R. Deichgräber, *Gotteshymnus und Christushymnus in der frühen Christenheit*, Studien zur Umwelt des Neuen Testaments (Göttingen: Vandenhoeck & Ruprecht, 1967), 5-106, has defined it thus, in answer to his question "What is a Christ-hymn?": "We understand by this such passages whose contents speak of Christ and his work (especially his humiliation and exaltation) and because of whose vocabulary, style and construction can truly be described as poetic."

2. The other main consideration, which arises from the obvious fact that this new edition is appearing in 1997, some fifteen or so years after the preface to the 1983 edition was written, is to enter into dialogue with some significant recent interpretations. These interpretations address questions suggested by the two principal parts of this book's new English title: (1) hymn (2) of Christ. The two questions that need to be discussed are as follows.

(*a*) How much, if at all, is Philippians 2:6-11 to be seen as a *hymn/song* (for evidence that such existed in Pauline assemblies, see Col 3:16-17 = Eph 5:19-20; cf. 1 Tim 3:16),[9] originally composed to be used in worship and only later finding its way into Paul's hortatory purpose in writing to the Philippians? Is it still appropriate to place the passage in the genre of "New Testament hymn," or is it to be regarded as a set of narrative sentences dictated by Paul in a poetic and exalted style?[10]

While this may seem to be a pedantic question, arising from the difficulty of classifying literary forms of an ancient text, there is a deeper issue at stake. The issue is whether Paul is here utilizing a pre-formed composition that on stylistic and theological grounds may not inevitably reflect his own theology. Yet he uses it as a shared possession with his readers, to establish a common ground for his ethical-soteriological call (heard in 2:1-4, 12). Paul may have altered the pre-Pauline version by inserting lines to emphasize theological motifs that were not explicit, thereby giving to the "hymn," now set in a pastoral context, an added dimension, with its hinge at verse 5 and its enforcement in verse 12. This may be expressed in a way familiar to all students of form- and redaction-criticism as the distinction between a text's "setting in life" *(Sitz im Leben)* and the subsequent "setting in literature" *(Sitz in der Literatur)*. The pristine version of the hymn in six couplets (see later for this analysis) arose in a liturgical context as an ode to Christ; Paul's adaptation and use in a pastoral context suggests a secondary function in his epistolary (literary) setting.

The alternative view is that Paul took his cue from the ethical injunctions in 2:1-4 as an occasion to compose a lyrical rhapsody

---

[9]Reasons for isolating such passages may be seen in the author's contribution "Hymns, Hymn Fragments, Songs, Spiritual Songs," in *Dictionary of Paul and His Letters,* ed. G. F. Hawthorne, R. P. Martin and D. G. Reid (Downers Grove, Ill.: InterVarsity Press, 1993), pp. 419-23, with bibliography.

[10]This way of viewing Philippians 2:6-11 has been expressed by Fee, *Philippians,* pp. 193-94, and his article "Philippians 2:5-11: Hymn or Exalted Pauline Prose?" *Bulletin for Biblical Research* 2 (1992), 29-46. The above comments are directed to these pages, which seek to challenge the assumption of 2:6-11 as hymnic.

celebrating Christ's humility (and enthronement as a natural complement; verses 9-11), then returned to the Philippians' scene at 2:12 with a summons to act as Christ acted (implied in verse 5).

(*b*) How far, if at all, is Philippians 2:6-11 to be regarded as a tribute to the person and accomplishment, crowned with attendant honours, of the church's Lord, that is, as a christological statement, even if it indirectly and by extension, throws light on the character of "God the Father" (as verse 11 describes the chief actor in the drama of verses 9-11)? Is it still appropriate to designate the passage a hymn *of Christ*?

Bound up with this question are a number of ancillary matters, all of some moment. Assuming that we are right in detecting the literary form and genre of "New Testament hymns," is there a subset entitled "christological hymns"?[11] And if so, are we justified in seeing here a liturgical veneration of Christ, as hymns were sung in his honour as well as tributes paid to him in the narrative form that was earlier suggested? The relation of the cosmic Christ, both in his pre-temporal existence (if verse 6 is so regarded) and in his post-enthronement status, to the one God of Judaism and Hebraic Christianity thus becomes a burning issue. Some have settled this by recourse to Paul's redefined "christological monotheism"—that is, his belief in one God which is flexible enough to pay honour to the cosmic-exalted Christ.

One bid to ease the tension and so avoid the charge of binitarianism (or better, di-theism) as that problem raised its head in subsequent centuries is to see Philippians 2:6-11 as strictly *theo*logical rather than christological. It then takes on its distinctive character as a story about God (albeit revealed in Christ)[12] rather than a strict "confession of faith"—paving the way for the second article of the later creeds—that traces the road travelled from the state of being "in the form of God" by way of self-renunciation and obedience unto death onward to sharing the divine throne. In the latter reconstruction much is made of the progression from one level (on a par with God) to another (humanity-death) and then to an even higher plane (elevation to assume the title Lord and the allegiance of the cosmic powers), with the decisive choice held to be implied in verse 6 ("*although* he was . . . yet he did not exploit his advantage but chose to attain equality with

[11]In the terms set out by R. Deichgräber; see note 8.

[12]Fee, "Philippians 2:5-11," p. 40, note 38. N. T. Wright, "ἁρπαγμός and the Meaning of Philippians 2:5-11," *JTS* 37 n.s. (1986), 321-52 (esp. 350-52), with a later version in his *The Climax of the Covenant: Christ and the Law in Pauline Theology* (Edinburgh: T & T Clark, 1992), pp. 56-98 (esp. 84). Subsequent references will be to the later work.

God by obedience") and the subsequent vindication (verses 9-11) which bestowed on him the honours he might have seized (albeit in disobedience).

The strictly theological connotation of the drama tends to see less movement and shift in Christ's odyssey. Key is the rendering of verse 6 (*"since* he was . . . he did not exploit his advantage,"[13] for this is the way God acts). The entire passage is a noble tribute to the Godlikeness of God, whose character is seen on display in Christ's self-giving. It is a character of giving sacrificially, not grasping or clutching to one's possession.

II. PHILIPPIANS 2:5-11: ITS POINT AND PURPOSE

The interpretive key that in the following pages will be used to get to the heart of this Pauline passage may be expressed in the following way.

All students concur that these stately lines almost baffle analysis, as we might expect once we recognize them to be poetic, imaginative and quite probably liturgical. The passage is an early Christian hymn, composed originally in praise of the church's Lord. It traces the "way" he took from the Father's eternal presence to his ultimate glory alongside God's throne through becoming human (verse 7), choosing obedience-to-death (verse 8) and being exalted (verses 9-11). Evocative metaphors are drawn from the Old Testament, with three most prominent: Adam, who aspired to be "like God" (Gen 3:5); the suffering servant of Isaiah 53:12, who "poured out" his life in death, later to be "highly exalted" (Is 52:13); and the vindicated King-Messiah of Psalm 110:1, who shares the divine throne. Less likely is the

---

[13]Proposed by C. F. D. Moule (see Wright, *Climax,* p. 83, note 110). See his earlier discussion, "Further Reflexions on Philippians 2:5-11," in *Apostolic History and the Gospel: Biblical and Historical Essays presented to F. F. Bruce on His Sixtieth Birthday,* ed. W. W. Gasque and R. P. Martin (Exeter, U.K.: Paternoster; Grand Rapids: Eerdmans, 1970), pp. 264-76. Later commentators (Hawthorne, Fee) have followed suit. But it is held to be undermined on stylistic grounds by Robert H. Gundry's analysis ("Style and Substance in 'the Myth of God Incarnate' According to Philippians 2:6-11," in *Crossing the Boundaries: Essays in Biblical Interpretation in Honour of Michael D. Goulder,* Biblical Interpretation Series 8 (Leiden: Brill, 1994), pp. 271-93 (283).

T. Yai-Chow Wong, "The Problem of Pre-existence in Philippians 2, 6-11," *Ephemerides Theologicae Lovanienses* 62 (1986), 267-82, calls attention to the weakness in Moule's interpretation (noted earlier, pp. xxii-xxiii), namely that "the antithesis between v 6 and v 7 is completely destroyed" (p. 276), though she takes the first part of verse 6 to be not concessive ("though he was . . .") but causative ("since he was . . ."—p. 275). This latter view is hard to maintain in the light of her stress on ἀλλά, "but," as setting up a "real contrast" beginning with verse 7a. The full value of the adversative ἀλλά is given by M. Thekkekara, "A Neglected Idiom in an Overstudied Passage (Phil 2:6-8)," *Louvain Studies* 17 (1992), 306-14 (312).

background of a Gnostic redeemer figure who comes from the heavenly sphere to lead earthlings back to the divine world. Less clearly obvious too is the figure of Wisdom in both Old Testament and intertestamental literature—a personification of God (some say a hypostasis) who lives with God, comes to dwell with humankind, especially the prophets, and is praised for her virtues in a genre called "aretalogy."[14]

In our approach to the passage's meaning, we should begin by asking two questions: (*a*) What does the hymn mean on its own? (*b*) How does Paul use it by working it into the fabric of his letter-writing prose?

(*a*) The hymn is a carefully constructed tribute to Jesus Christ, who is now elevated to share the Father's throne and is the universal Lord (verses 9-11). The church, like the one at Philippi (which must certainly have known this hymn already, at least in its original form), that sang this hymn did so to express its confidence in Christ's victory over all his foes—and theirs. In particular they celebrated the reign of Christ, now begun (1 Cor 15:25), and in worship exulted in their union with a victorious Lord and sought to bring that reign to bear on their situation as a persecuted and harassed community (Phil 1:28-30; 2:14-15). This is the rationale for Christ-hymns in the New Testament church and even to the present: to praise God for his mighty deeds in creation and redemption, and in so doing to make his once-for-all acts in salvation history our story today.

So Philippians 2:6-11 traces the saga of salvation: He who enjoyed the Father's glory did not use his privilege as a means of self-aggrandizement (like Adam) but chose to stoop to the utter limits of obedience. His death shows the extent of that obedience. Yet that death is but a prelude to his ultimate reward. He is now enthroned by God's appointment and accorded the very name of Yahweh himself, with all hostile powers brought into subjection. The noble hymn closes with the ringing credal confession that Jesus Christ is Lord. Thus the circle of movement that began with the pre-mundane choice (verse 6) concludes with the co-equality of the obedient one with God (verse 11).

(*b*) The more puzzling question is why Paul chose to quote the hymn at this point in his epistolary correspondence. At first glance the hymn looks entirely appropriate and in place. Clearly Paul was facing a proud

---

[14]See, for example, B. W. Witherington III, *Jesus the Sage: The Pilgrimage of Wisdom* (Philadelphia: Fortress, 1994), pp. 257-66; idem, *Paul's Narrative Thought World* (Louisville, Ky.: Westminster John Knox, 1994), pp. 97-105.

and wayward congregation (2:1-4, 14; 4:2). So his call to humility is reinforced by his recital of the path of humility taken by the Lord (2:8). Verse 5, which introduces the hymn, is often taken to mean "Act as he acted, and resemble the one who revealed God as self-giving, humble love." The hymn, then, reminds us of how gracious God is and elevates Christ's example, spurring hearers and readers to follow his steps.

The pages that follow will seek to challenge this (still) popular view of Philippians 2:5-11. The grounds for that challenge, which I still believe to be valid though some expressions should probably be more circumspectly put, are several.

(*i*) All translations of 2:5 have to make sense of the elliptical Greek that Paul writes. In leaving us with a verbless second part of the verse, literally "which also . . . in Christ Jesus," he has set the translator a conundrum, since some complementary expression has to be added to fill the gap. Probably the best (neutral) rendering is that of the RSV: "which is yours in Christ Jesus." It has the merit of leaving the key word *yours* (not in the Greek but supplied to complete the sense) to be interpreted variously, whether as "your example" as the "mind of Christ Jesus" or "your way of life" that is determined by your being "in Christ Jesus" (as I have proposed). One writer even submits that there is no difference in these choices,[15] but that tends to blur distinctions that are inevitable.

(*ii*) An issue that haunts the discussion and presents a continuing problem to those who find Paul's purpose to set forth Christ's humility as an example to be followed lies in verses 9-11. Why did Paul see fit to cite the passage in its entirety, assuming he is quoting a pre-formed hymn? The question is more urgent if he is composing for the occasion, since presumably he has control over what he writes. One is left to suppose that Paul's prose took on a lyrical cast in an unexampled way; not even 1 Corinthians 13 comes close to such an extended encomium linking Christ's heavenly and earthly states. The call to follow Christ's humility is complete at verse 8; why go on to demonstrate God's vindication and elevation of the obedient one to a rank that, by definition, is without peer and unique? To occupy the divine throne is, again by its scenario, an honour that belongs to one who is the unrivaled Lord of the universe, to whom all agencies, human, angelic and demonic, are subject. How can *that* proclamation be the ground

---

[15]J.-F. Collange, *De Jésus à Paul: L'éthique du Nouveau Testament* (Geneva: Labor et Fides, 1980), p. 201: "'Imiter Christ' n'est donc pas autre chose être 'en Christ' . . ." He does go on to describe "being in Christ" as living in the community of those who put themselves under Christ's lordship.

for the ethical call to exemplary human conduct?

Clearly, however, the entire quotation of the hymn is meant to enforce an ethical appeal. If the rationale is only shakily to be treated as "act as he acted," should we not find it rather in what verses 9-11 do most obviously proclaim—the lordship of Christ—and see *that* as the ruling motif to guide Christian conduct? Rather than subsuming the hymn under the title "The Example of Christ," we should give it the title "Living Under Christ's Lordship" and find in verse 12 a confirmation as a continuance of what began at verse 5 ("let this way of life be among you which befits those who are 'in Christ Jesus' "). "Being in Christ"—a capsule expression for being a Christian in the Pauline sense—entails living in obedience to the obedient one in a pattern of social behaviour that, to be sure, entails selfless regard for others and lowly demeanour. Such conformation to the pattern arising out of "life in Christ" receives the approbation of God.

(*iii*) What "conformity to Christ" means is further spelled out as we recognize the significance of Paul's makeover of the earlier hymn. In a later section we will consider the proposal that four lines look to be the apostle's way of correctively emphasizing what the first draft of the hymn may have passed over. These are

taking the servant's form (verse 7),

even death on a cross (verse 8),

the heavenly, earthly and demonic (verse 10), and

to the glory of God the Father (verse 11).

All these emphases are designed to enforce the momentous proposition that life lived "in Christ" is set under the lordly control over all powers of the one whose title to lordship came through an acceptance of the servant role, whose obedient death reached the very nadir of submission (on a Roman cross, with all the suggestiveness of ignominy, shame and curse-bearing [1 Cor 1:18, 23; 2 Cor 13:4; Gal 3:13; 5:11; 6:12, 14]) to God's salvific plan, and whose present authority has the endorsement of the Father's will, since it sets up no rival dichotomy or challenge to God's sole rule (a theme to be expanded in 1 Cor 15:20-28).

If this proposal—a two-step development in which a pristine version of the christological hymn, celebrating cosmic authority and (maybe) a proud, triumphalist notion of selfish disregard of others, was pressed into service by Paul and suitably adapted to meet the urgent pastoral needs at Philippi—is taken into account, a way of joining the soteriological and exemplary functions of the hymn may be offered.

The reason Paul chose this method of answering the Philippians' problems as he saw them may well lie in *his pastoral strategy:* that is, he called on a hymn the Philippians knew already (and sang?) but edited it to remove false impressions. This device is attested elsewhere in the Pauline corpus (see p. lvi).

Paul has brought out the elements of lowly condescension to death (since Christ's death was on a cross, verse 8). He has shown the character of Christ's incarnate life as essentially the servant form. He has moved to the second part of the hymn as its centre of gravity and highlighted the lordly rank of the world-ruler, κύριος, who, however, came to his throne only along the road of humble obedience to God and self-sacrifice. This blend of lordship and the theology of the cross exactly met the pastoral needs we may discern from the rest of the Philippian letter, and in advance has paved the way for Paul's plea, based on his life, to be "conformed" to Christ's way (2:5) and Christ's death (3:10).

It is time now to see the wider implication of this approach.

III. PHILIPPIANS 2:5-11 IN ITS CONTEXTUAL SETTING

One of the firmest conclusions in more recent studies of the letter is the way 2:5-11 fits into the wider context of the thematic unit of 1:27—2:30.[16] Paul's admonitions take their starting point in the

---

[16]On the general question, see D. Peterlin, *Paul's Letter to the Philippians in the Light of Disunity in the Church,* Novum Testamentum Supplements 79 (Leiden: Brill, 1995).

L. G. Bloomquist, *The Function of Suffering in Philippians,* JSNT Supplements 78 (Sheffield, U.K.: Academic, 1993), has approached the letter from the vantage point of rhetorical criticism and shown how (*i*) the humbling and obedience of the servant (based on Isaiah's עבד יהוה figure) is central to the hymn and (*ii*) this same figure governs the presentations elsewhere in the letter. "Close observation of the recurrence of the language and imagery in 2.6-11 throughout the letter reveals the way the experience of Christ, the experience of Paul, and the experiences of Paul's co-workers are interwoven" (p. 164). That Philippians 2:6-11 is a key unit within the letter, classified on rhetorical grounds as an encomium in praise of Christ and functioning in context as a hortatory "profession of faith," is suggested by C. Basevi and J. Chapa, "Philippians 2.6-11: The Rhetorical Function of the Pauline 'Hymn,'" in *Rhetoric and the New Testament,* ed. S. E. Porter and T. H. Olbricht, JSNT Supplements 90 (Sheffield, U.K.: Academic, 1993), pp. 338-56.

The thematic centre of the letter at 2:6-11 is argued for, in an elaborate chiastic structure, by Peter Wick, *Der Philipperbrief,* Beiträge zur Wissenschaft vom Alten und Neuen Testament 135 (Stuttgart: Kohlhammer, 1994), pp. 58-63, 78-81. In more general terms, P. Perkins, "Philippians: Theology for the Heavenly Politeuma," in *Pauline Theology,* ed. J. M. Bassler (Minneapolis: Fortress, 1991), 1:89-104, argues for the Christ-hymn as governing metaphor in the letter and stresses the link between 1:27 and 3:20-21 on the basis of the root πολιτευ- ("citizen-life"). And that 2:6-11 in its setting of 2:1-12 looks on to the problems surrounding Euodia and Syntyche in view of the

reminders of his own absence from the beloved community he had founded and the Philippians' perceived need to face threats that loomed large, at least before his eyes (1:27). The Philippian church, like any religious community in a hostile society, was (in his pastoral vision) clearly in danger, both physically (1:28-30) and in-house, for it was fractured and racked by in-fighting (2:14) and moral confusion (4:8-9). Using a word of special relevance to those who lived in a Roman colony (Acts 16:12, 21), he recalled their citizen life in an outpost of the Empire and applies it to their current life together with a higher allegiance to God's (Christ's) kingly rule as his citizens and servants. This is the heavy theological, ecclesiological and ethical freight contained in his quasi-political term πολιτεύεσθε: "let your life in the polis of God's realm be worthy of your adherence to the good news" (1:27)—that is, the work of Paul and his colleagues as preacher and church leader under God (1:5, 12; 1:27, twice; 4:3, 15). The "worthy life" is seen in two commendable and necessary virtues: courage and unity. The twin call is therefore to be brave (1:28) and to be united (2:1-4).

First, Paul's readers are to conduct themselves in a hostile world with confidence that God is with them to drive out their fear (1:28). The church's salvation, meaning their welfare and integrity, as in 2:12 at the conclusion and enforcement of the christological section, is in higher hands than those that would destroy them. Paul turns the tables on the persecutors with a well-known moral maxim: "Destruction to the destroyer" (see 1:28; see 1 Cor 3:17 for a clear example applied to failing professed Christians). In the light of this confidence, let the Philippians take courage and close ranks (1:27).

The call, however, is not simply on grounds of prudence and common sense, reminding them that they would be easy prey if they fell apart in disarray—and so incidentally Paul's own work as church founder would go for nothing (2:16). Significantly, Paul provides a theological reason for his assurance that all will be well. He is not in the business of handing out simple bromides to boost faltering faith. Rather, he offers a theodicy (1:29) as a tonic to lift drooping and nervous spirits and sets the suffering of the Philippians within the

link-phrase of "a common mind" is suggested by N. A. Dahl, "Euodia and Syntyche and Paul's Letter to the Philippians," in *The Social World of the First Christians: Essays in Honor of Wayne A. Meeks*, ed. L. M. White and O. L. Yarborough (Minneapolis: Fortress, 1995), pp. 3-15. See too P. S. Minear, "Singing and Suffering in Philippi," in *The Conversation Continues: Studies in Paul and John in Honor of J. Louis Martyn*, ed. R. T. Fortna and B. R. Gaventa (Nashville: Abingdon, 1990), pp. 202-19.

framework of God's overarching providence, as he viewed his own—and Christ's—fate in terms of God's gracious provision (1:29, "it has been granted in grace" (ἐχαρίσθη); cf. "bestowed in grace" (ἐχαρίσατο), repeated in 2:9).

Then the Philippian Christians are reminded of their responsibility to keep together in unity, born out of their shared possessions, listed in 2:1. Their life together should be marked by what they have in common and by what they think of themselves and others (2:3-4). The key to this moral incentive is their selfless regard for others and an active desire to promote their neighbours' well-being and interest in preference to their own.

Above all (in 2:1-4) there is to be humility, a moral quality that in this section is to be seen in Paul's telling the story of the Lord of glory who became the servant of all (verses 6-11) by an act of self-humbling, which in turn is expressed in obedience to the point of death (verse 8). Interestingly, when Paul drives home the application, the moral incentive the Philippians are to find in the incarnational motif, it is Christ's obedience that is the centerpiece (verse 12), not his humility.

The admonition that flows directly from a recital of Christ's path from highest honour to even higher exaltation (verse 9) is tersely expressed in the maxim "The obedient one is to be obeyed!"[17] This is the apostle's method of driving home his pastoral point; and given this assumption and relating it to his concern for the congregation's wholeness (called "salvation" in verse 12), much of what follows falls into place. The Philippian assembly, as we have observed, was racked by a divisiveness and prideful preference for individual rights (verses 1-4). On a wider front, their confusion arose from a "questioning" (verse 14 has the exact term) over the hardness of their lot as a suffering community (1:28-30) and, beyond that, over the reason that Paul, their beloved leader (4:1), should be in jail and absent from them at a time when they needed him on hand (implied in 1:12, 24-26) [18] Hence the reassurance is given that the God who brought the church into existence in the first place (1:6) may be relied on to pledge his continuing protection (the "salvation" referred to in 1:28) and goodwill that is actively at work on their behalf (2:13).

[17]This way of linking 2:6-11 to 2:12 goes back to P. Bonnard, *L'épître de S. Paul aux Philippiens*, CNT 10 (Paris, 1950), p. 49.
[18]We may refer to the still-important contribution of R. Jewett, "Conflicting Movements in the Early Church as Reflected in Philippians," *Novum Testamentum* 12 (1970), 362-90 (see earlier, p. xxxvi).

Moreover, in spite of enforced separation because Paul is a prisoner on their behalf (1:13), the lines of communication between apostle and congregation need to be kept open. That is part of the reason for Paul's letter-writing in the first place (1:12) and his desire to send messengers who will report to the Philippians the circumstances of his imprisonment and unpreventable absence (2:19, 25). The two persons[19] who are brought on to the scene will act as Paul's representatives and make up for his being at a distance. The other main justification for Paul's supplying an antidote to his readers' "grumbling" or "questioning" lies in the way both men are characterized, along with Paul's own self-designation. The trio all have lives marked by the commonality of suffering that to some degree is what "life in Christ" is all about.

Paul's own life experience serves as a reinforcing of his moral exhortations to courage, unity and selflessness. Links between the hymn's language and ideology and Paul's autobiographical writing in this letter have often been noted. His imprisonment, which posed the problem of enforced absence from Philippi at a time when he was needed, and his suffering set the scene for what he describes. His life is being "poured out" (2:17) just like that of the suffering servant (2:7; cf. Is 53:12). His reflection on his life's ambition to reach out to grasp the prize (3:12-13) runs parallel, though in human terms, to the idiom used in 2:6-8. The heavenly Christ always had a place in the life of the Father as his "form" (2:6). Yet he was presented with a choice to snatch "equality with God" by seizure or exploitation, just as an athlete or swimmer might leap off a springboard[20] and use it to his or her advantage. Christ, we are told, did not aspire to gain his lordship *in this way;* yet Paul wants to respond to the call to go forward (3:14). So the parallel is not exact.

Nor is the parallelism often adduced between 2:6-11 and 3:20-21 exactly appropriate. The hymnic conclusion, as was observed, brought the obedient Christ to a dignity that is conferred on him as a gracious act (2:9) and that installed him as sovereign Lord. The hope of resurrection and final conformity to his likeness (3:21) at the end time of the parousia are indeed part of God's saving design bestowed in

[19]On the role played in this letter by Paul's colleagues, see P. T. O'Brien, "The Gospel and Godly Models in Philippians," in *Worship, Theology and Ministry in the Early Church,* FS R. P. Martin, ed. M. J. Wilkins and T. Paige, JSNT Supplements 87 (Sheffield, U.K.: Academic, 1992), pp. 273-84.
[20]For this imagery, see later p. 145.

grace, but there is no confusion between the Savior (3:20) and the saved (3:21). Nor is there a hint of Christians' being finally rewarded for their meekness and selfless regard for others, called for in 2:1-4. Indeed, such a prudential motive, called "eschatological reward" or "vindication"[21] (be humble now . . . so that you may share in Christ's otherworldly glory and office), is explicitly denied in 2:4 (don't look to your own interests).[22]

More to the point is Paul's eagerness to be obedient at any cost, because only in such an understanding of being "in Christ" lies the secret of true "partnership" (a key term—κοινωνία—in the letter)[23] with Christ's sufferings and a conformity to his pattern of dying-to-live (3:10), with the promise of resurrection a future goal, still unrealized (3:11).

Timothy's worth (2:22) and Epaphroditus's courage in a near-death trauma (2:27) are brought forward to illustrate the "story of Christ," epitomized in 2:6-11. These men and their "story" make up the trio, along with Paul's autobiographical detail. Timothy has earlier been referred to in the letter's opening (1:1) as a "servant [δοῦλος] of Christ Jesus," just as Jesus himself took the rank of a servant (2:7). Timothy is also said to have "served" (ἐδούλευσεν, 2:22) the interests of the gospel as one bound to Paul in filial relationship. Timothy's sterling character is further praised as unrivalled among Paul's co-workers (2:20; the term used is ἰσόψυχος, RSV "I have no one like him," lit. of "like soul," a phrase recalling ἴσα θεῷ in 2:6 of the heavenly Christ who disdained the opportunity to be "like God"). Clearly Paul's language in this section (2:19-24) is designed to portray his colleague as one who lived out the Christ model.

In similar fashion Epaphroditus (2:25-30) is commended as Paul's kinsman in the faith, fellow worker along with other unnamed persons (4:3), fellow soldier in the struggle Paul is enduring (1:30), as well as a messenger who had been sent by the Philippians to bring gifts by which Paul's needs were relieved (4:14-18). On every count Epaphroditus was a choice person in Paul's eyes.

[21]Fee, "Philippians 2:5-11," p. 44, uses both words. See too Stephen E. Fowl, *The Story of Christ in the Ethics of Paul: An Analysis of the Function of the Hymnic Material in the Pauline Corpus,* JSNT Supplements (Sheffield, U.K.: Academic, 1990), pp. 94-95.

[22]This reading of 2:4 is challenged by O'Brien, *Epistle to the Philippians,* pp. 183-85. But he is so wedded to the so-called ethical example interpretation of verses 5-11 (see p. 185: "it does not harmonize with the example of Christ set forth in the following hymn") that Paul's altruism is blunted.

[23]See B. W. Witherington III, *Friendship and Finances in Philippi* (Valley Forge, Penn.: Trinity Press International, 1994).

Yet there is more. At some point in his travels Epaphroditus had fallen sick and was grieved when this intelligence got back to Philippi. Indeed, he was at death's door (verses 27, 30), a real experience that Paul draws attention to evidently in order to deflect criticism from his colleague, who seems to be under fire for having overstayed his time away. Epaphroditus is suggested as a role model when Paul notes that his illness brought him "close to death" (verse 30 NRSV), rendering μέχρι θανάτου, a phrase that is the same as "to the point of death" (NRSV) in the hymn in 2:8. Once more, as with Paul's own life story (3:13), the parallel is not precise: Epaphroditus did not actually die, whereas Christ's obedience led to his death on the cross. The point, however, is that Epaphroditus exhibited the same spirit of sacrifice in his loyalty to the Pauline mission, as one whose life "in Christ Jesus" (2:5) arises from the greater sacrifice of a unique obedience to death.

That point would not be lost on the factious, self-seeking Philippian readers, who, in the frontispiece of the hymn, are admonished to act without regard to "their individual interests" (2:4, τὰ ἑαυτῶν, in contradistinction to the sad complaint of 2:21, where those around Paul are "seeking their own interests," τὰ ἑαυτῶν ζητοῦσιν). The "interests of Jesus Christ" are held up as a motivating force to check self-centeredness and to spur the readers to pursue the interests of others (2:4). The essence of Christ's paradigmatic actions stands out in the lineaments of the hymn, and they are exemplified in his servants like Paul, Timothy and Epaphroditus, whose lives are made conformable to his pattern of service, sacrifice and above all obedience (3:17; spelled out in 4:9 as a call to *do* as Paul *did*).

IV. SALIENT ISSUES IN PHILIPPIANS 2: A REVIEW

1. *Philippians 2:6-11 as Hymn*

The classification of the Philippians 2 passage as "hymnic" invites us to consider the background to New Testament hymns in general and the techniques that modern scholarship has used to detect such specimens. Some account of these particulars may be read in another place,[24] and the author's approach need not be repeated here. Yet

---

[24]Again, I refer to Martin, "Hymns, Hymn Fragments," pp. 419-23; cf., also in *Dictionary of Paul and His Letters*, J. L. Wu, "Liturgical Elements," pp. 557-60; W. H. Gloer, "Homologies and Hymns in the New Testament: Form, Content and Criteria for Identification," *Perspectives in Religious Studies* 11 (1984), 115-32; and now M. Lattke, *Hymnus: Materialen zu einer Geschichte der antiken Hymnologie* (Freiburg: Universitätsverlag; Göttingen: Vandenhoeck & Ruprecht, 1991); W. Kennel, *Frühchristliche Hymnen? Gattungskritische Studien zur Frage nach den Liedern der frühen*

some recent challenges (notably by G. D. Fee) to the idea that Philippians 2:6-11 encloses a christological hymn do require a comment, with special attention directed to the following issues.

(*a*) What are the features that make this passage much more than an example of "exalted prose"?[25]

(*b*) How may the form analysis of 2:6-11—that is, the arrangement of the verses into strophes and lines—contribute to our understanding of the contents and then point in the direction of worship offered to the exalted Lord?

(*c*) If Paul took over and set this pre-formed passage into his epistolary prose, while he may be presumed to have agreed with its main thrust, does it seem likely that he edited the hymn to bring it more closely in line with his purpose in citing it in the first place? New Testament hymns, in particular the christological examples both here and in Colossians 1:15-20 and Ephesians 2:14-16, as well as credal sections like Romans 3:24-6, bid us examine the principle of tradition and redaction.[26] The author's use of traditional forms does not preclude the redacting (editing) of such deposits in such a way as to correct potentially misleading ideas, emphasizing "truths" that were passed over in the original version and supplying additions that represent more adequately the author's theological viewpoint. This conclusion rests on such firm exegetical bases that it simply will not do to dismiss it pejoratively as "exegetical nihilism" or "anarchy," or "exegetical tour de force."[27]

Christenheit, Wissenschaftliche Monographien zum Alten und Neuen Testament 71 (Göttingen: Vandenhoeck & Ruprecht, 1995); R. Brucker, *"Christushymnen" oder "epideiktische Passagen"?* FRLANT 176 (Göttingen: Vandenhoeck & Ruprecht, 1997).

The notion of a hymn is opposed by R. H. Gundry ("Style and Substance"), who argues for an elaborate arrangement of concentric chiasms that allegedly smooth out the numerous asyndeta in the text and result in a set of paired couplets, composed after the manner of Paul's "own exalted prose . . . rather than an early Christian hymn" (p. 288). Of his five sets of couplets in the schema (A-B-C-B^1-A^1), the final one (comprising verses 9-11) is so gigantic that it throws the preceding chiasms out of balance and makes the total picture look decidedly odd. Yet I am supportive of his seeing verses 9-11 as the "center of gravity" (p. 280).

By my hypothesis of Pauline lines added to a *Vorlage*, many of the asyndeta producing breaks in the flow of the hymn are removed.

On the various examples of Christ-hymn see C. M. Mountain, "The New Testament Christ-Hymn," *The Hymn* 44, no. 1 (1993), 20-28.

[25]Fee's terms ("Philippians 2:5-11").

[26]I have attempted a discussion and demonstration of how apostolic writers took over and adapted pre-composed texts in *Reconciliation: A Study of Paul's Theology* (rev. ed.; Grand Rapids: Zondervan, 1989; reprint Eugene, Ore.: Wipf & Stock, 1997).

[27]Terms variously used by Fee (*Philippians*, p. 43; "Philippians 2:5-11," pp. 34-35) as a putdown.

(*d*) If within the overall category of New Testament hymns we may detect a subset of "Christ hymns," what chief emphases in this group may be isolated that contribute to the growth of Christology? Moreover, if the person of Christ is seen in the frame of his saving work, how do these christological-soteriological examples function as teaching vehicles, to impress on the nascent congregation not only Christian theology but also incentives to live the Christian life in this world? In other terms, what is the nexus between soteriology and ethics, and what transition points move us from statements about transcendental and cosmic issues (he came from God; he rules over the powers and receives the accolade of their subjection to his authority) to the writer's admonition that readers/hearers/singers should base their lives and shape their social conduct accordingly?

This listing of agenda items looks formidable, and the preceding discussion has touched on several of these matters. It will, however, be helpful if we address them in turn.

(*a*) Clearly 2:6-11 interrupts the flow of Pauline prose writing that opens at 1:27 with an imperative-ethical exhortation to the Philippian readers. They are kept steadily in view, especially in 2:1-4, until we reach verse 6, with verse 5 serving as a pivot on which turns the illustration or rationale of what Paul expected of his readers in response. The exegetical issue of verse 5 has already been alluded to. The choice is to see Paul's enigmatic language as introducing Christ's humility as a virtue to be imitated, since (it is said) the key words of verses 1-4 are repeated in verses 6-8. The influence, of course, could go the other way, and Paul's choice of terms in verses 1-4 may well be dictated by what he knows will follow in his citing of the hymn. This alternative is the one I have argued for, since (*i*) the grammatical forms in verses 6-11 are all third person and do not have the readers directly in their sights; (*ii*) the vocabulary, idioms and style of verses 6-11 are rare, ceremonial, hieratic and full of *hapax legomena*, words not found elsewhere in Paul or in some instances elsewhere in the Greek Bible or exiguous in Greek literature. If Paul is believed to continue his dictating in the manner of epistolary prose, however "exalted," one is left to wonder why and how he produces this extended series of words, terms, ideas and rhythmic style at this point in his concerns for pressing problems in a local congregation. (*iii*) Tellingly, the language at verse 12 reverts to such pastoral issues at Philippi, and the call is *not* to cultivate the virtues of verses 6-8 but to yield obedience to the obedient one who is now hailed as cosmic Lord (verses 9-11).[28]

(*b*) Amid the welter of suggestions as to how the lines should be arranged, granted that Paul has utilized a pre-formed hymn—and the multiplicity of suggestions is no real barrier to the value or validity of the general proposal—the simplest is still, in our view, the best.[29] The verses divide naturally into two main strophes: verses 6-8 and 9-11, with a break clearly indicated at verse 9. The connection between the two strophes is one of contrast (hence the suggestion that verses 9-11 are antistrophe in contrast to the strophe of verses 6-8),[30] with the opening of verse 9, διὸ καί, "therefore . . . also," functioning as a *peripeteia* in Greek drama, which reverses the hero-victim's fate and sets out the road to recovery and reinstatement in honour.

The interrelatedness of the lines within the two strophes is best (in my judgment) regarded as a set of *couplets*, based on the parallelism of Hebrew poetry. The original insight of Lohmeyer was that in Philippians 2:6-11 the second line is matched with the first of each stanza, with the third line producing a conclusion and a starting point for the next stanza. This device, called sorites, is suggestive, but there is some problem with this reconstruction, since it is difficult to see a strict pattern other than the sequential flow of action, with the stanzas building one on another, as Colin Brown points out (see note 30). It is better to stay with the concept of *parallelismus membrorum*, with added support now from Old Testament literary studies that suggest that in Hebrew poetic couplets the second line completes and enriches the thought of the first. Indeed, one can go further and argue for a "dramatization" in the complementary line that adds a new dimension to the initial statement.[31]

The most recent submission of a form analysis of the hymn takes seriously this arrangement in couplets. It regards the hymn as joining

---

[28]The NRSV translation, "Just as you have always obeyed *me*," is unwarranted. It reflects A. Plummer's similar understanding (see p. 216, note 1 in this book).

[29]See later, pp. 36-41. M. D. Hooker is sometimes quoted for the view that "the fact that different scholars produce different poetic structures makes one slightly hesitant about the value of this exercise" ("Philippians 2.6-11," in her *From Adam to Christ* [Cambridge: Cambridge University Press, 1990], pp. 88-100 [93-94]). Yet that verdict does not preclude her from attempting an arrangement (not very symmetrical, to be sure), nor does it cast doubt on the worthwhileness of the enterprise. In the field of technical New Testament scholarship scholars very rarely agree!

[30]Colin Brown's discussion of Lohmeyer's *Formanalyse* is valuable and innovative. See note 6 above.

[31]See James L. Bailey and Lyle D. Vander Broek, *Literary Forms in the New Testament* (Louisville, Ky.: Westminster John Knox, 1992), sec. "Poetry and Hymn," pp. 76-82, with reference to Robert Alter and James L. Kugel on biblical and especially Hebrew poetry.

verses 6-8—Christ's pre-temporal life and incarnate existence, climaxing in his death—to verses 9-11, with its new sequence marked by a change of subject (God's action replaces Christ's own decisions, as in the reflexive ἑαυτόν, "himself," twice). The second stanza (verses 9-11) emphasizes God's action in two parallel clauses with (we may note) increased intensity, followed by two results, again with the second line of verse 10 augmenting the significance of the first. In verse 7, it is submitted, we should drop the line "taking the form of a servant" as Paul's later enrichment. If in conjunction with this proposal of Werner Stenger[32] we utilize and extend the earlier arguments of Joachim Jeremias[33] about the detecting of Paul's own hand in the four lines, then we are looking at a *symmetrical whole* thus:

I. v. 6   ὃς ἐν μορφῇ θεοῦ ὑπάρχων
          οὐχ ἁρπαγμὸν ἡγήσατο τὸ εἶναι ἴσα θεῷ,

II. v. 7   ἀλλὰ ἑαυτὸν ἐκένωσεν
          [μορφὴν δούλου λαβών,]
          ἐν ὁμοιώματι ἀνθρώπων γενόμενος·

III.   καὶ σχήματι εὑρεθεὶς ὡς ἄνθρωπος

v. 8   ἐταπείνωσεν ἑαυτὸν γενόμενος ὑπήκοος μέχρι θανάτου,
          [θανάτου δὲ σταυροῦ.]

IV. v. 9   διὸ καὶ ὁ θεὸς αὐτὸν ὑπερύψωσεν
          και ἐχαρίσατο αὐτῷ τὸ ὄνομα τὸ ὑπὲρ πᾶν ὄνομα,

V. v. 10   ἵνα ἐν τῷ ὀνόματι Ἰησοῦ
          πᾶν γόνυ κάμψῃ
          [ἐπουρανίων καὶ ἐπιγείων καὶ καταχθονίων]

VI. v. 11   καὶ πᾶσα γλῶσσα ἐξομολογήσηται
          ὅτι κύριος Ἰησοῦς Χριστὸς
          [εἰς δόξαν θεοῦ πατρός.]

I. v. 6   [It is he][34] who was in the form of God,
          Yet he did not regard it as a prize to be equal with God,

---

[32]See W. Stenger, "Two Christological Hymns (Phil. 2:6-11; 1 Tim. 3:16)," chap. 12 in his *Introduction to New Testament Exegesis* (Grand Rapids: Eerdmans, 1993), pp. 118-32, for a clearly expressed statement of how redactional analysis assists exegesis.
[33]See later in this book, pp. 32-35.
[34]J. C. O'Neill takes ὅς, "who," to mean "he it was who" by analogy with parallels in Sirach (46:1; 48:1-2; 48:12; 49:8; 50:1). See "The Source of the Christology in Colossians," *NTS* 26 (1980), 87-100 (90). The relative pronoun is one of the telltale marks of quoted

II. v. 7	But he emptied himself,
	[taking the form of a servant,]
	being born in human likeness.
III.	And disclosing himself in human appearance,
v. 8	He humbled himself, becoming obedient to death
	[even death upon a cross].
IV. v. 9	So therefore God highly exalted him,
	And engraced him with the name high above all names,
V. v. 10	That in the name of Jesus,
	Every knee should bow
	[of heavenly and earthly and subterranean powers]
VI. v. 11	And every tongue acknowledge
	That "Jesus Christ is Lord"
	[to the glory of God the Father].

(*c*) However drastic the bracketed deletions from the given text may seem at first glance, some reasoning lies behind this way of seeing an original version which Paul has subsequently redacted. The line "taking the form of a servant," while it seems to belong integrally to the hymn as matching "form of God" (verse 6), fits in exactly with what I have said earlier about the servant motif in the letter as a whole and gives in verse 7 a soteriological character to the self-humbling and the death of the incarnate one. The links in terminology with Isaiah 53 (noted by Robinson and Jeremias) [35] are thus maintained if we see Paul's concern to stress and clarify the point that the kenosis of verse 7a was a genuine enfleshment (ὁμοίωμα, "likeness," may well have suggested otherwise; it does not necessarily imply identity with the human race, as Rom 8:3 makes clear) and points forward to a vicarious death (important for

material in the New Testament epistolary corpus, and the fact that sometimes it is introduced with a preparatory phrase (e.g., 1 Tim 3:16, "confessedly") and sometimes with no hint (e.g., Col 1:15) suggests the authors were expecting the audience-readers to recognize well-known confessional-hymnic material. This is a priori more likely than Fowl's view that "the pictures of Christ presented in these hymns were new to the specific groups Paul was addressing" (*Story of Christ*, p. 43).

[35] See later in this book, pp. 182-90, for these references and in particular pp. 199-211 for a discussion, in reliance on O. Michel, who is one of the few writers on 2:7 to have wrestled with the paraphrastic style of the text. I am more disposed now than in the earlier edition to see intertextually some echoes of Isaiah's יהוה עבד. (See too Gundry, "Style and Substance," in robust defense of Isaiah 53's servant idea in the text.) The multiple occurrences of δοῦλος to translate עבד in the LXX should be recognized: Isaiah 42:19; 48:20; 49:3, 5 (Wright, *Climax*, p. 60).

Paul with his concentrated emphasis on the *pro nobis* factor in soteriology), which the first draft of the hymn lacked.

It is this lifting up of the saving significance of Christ's obedience-to-death that required the line "even death on a cross." All the overtones (although not spelled out) could be implied by this line, as a hint of Paul's *theologia crucis*. This stands as a corrective measure in a hymn that conceivably carried triumphalist teaching by regarding that death as an interlude on the road to the incarnate one's worldwide victory. Paul could not so regard it and thus inserts the powerful, pungent reminder of the "cross-death" as a shorthand nota bene of his kerygma of Christ *crucified*.

The expansion in verse 10 of the scope of the Victor's reign is made by adding to "every knee shall bow" the threefold demarcation of the entire universe, expressed in plerophoric language, typical of liturgical terminology. Thus Paul makes plain that no part of sentient creation is outside its control, and in particular there is no hostile power that can work ultimately to defeat Christ's purpose or destroy his people. At this juncture Paul's pastoral interest surfaces. He is concerned to answer the implied necessity to offer a theodicy for the church's suffering and to stimulate faith in the final outcome of God's saving design (1:6) and the church's ultimate triumph in Christ (3:20-21). More to the point, however, his editing of the hymn is to supply a midrashic expansion and explication of the Isaianic phrase "every knee" (Is 45:23) to include all the malevolent forces that were ranged against the Philippian conventicle.

He adopts a similar expedient in the line "to the glory of God the Father" by returning the hymn to its beginning in the glory of God (verse 6—as Lohmeyer's insight perceived). Also by promoting a christological monotheism that both places the exalted Lord on God's throne as co-regent and also safeguards the monarchy of the Father, he accomplishes a paraenetic purpose. This is to round off the hymn on the note of "reconciliation"[36] (the last word in the line is *Father*, which may well evoke ideas of the church as family in which all brothers

---

[36]This point picks up Lohmeyer's comment based on the connection he infers between the "father"-"son" (*Sohn*) relationship and the verb "to reconcile" (*versöhnen*) which his German language can make. See Lohmeyer's *Philipper*, p. 98, referred to in Martin, *Reconciliation*, p. 222. His words are: "In order to snatch back the world from the power of Satan, and to reinstate God, he who was in the form of God took the road from heaven to earth. That he has become Lord is the sign that the victory is won, and therefore the word 'Father' betokens that now God and the world are 'reconciled' [*versöhnt*] and are one."

and sisters are to live in harmony and altruistic concern for one another, as in 2:1-4 but also a theme to reappear in 2:15).

(*d*) The most important element in this discussion regarding the hymnic genre of Philippians 2 has to be its value in contributing to Christology. Along with some other examples in the Pauline corpus—Colossians 1:15-20; 1 Timothy 3:16—the obvious feature, judged by the content of these passages, is that here we are in touch with the main deposits of belief about the person of Christ and the raw materials of later christological development. We are led to inquire what are (to change the metaphor) the chief contours of this Christology and, interestingly, to face the question of how such christological statements function in pastoral contexts where the apostolic writers were addressing ethical issues. The interrelation of Christology and ethics is brought to the fore as a pressing concern, since Christology is not speculative or systematic at this period of the church's history, and (as we observed in relation to Phil 2:1-11 in the framework of 1:27—2:30) moral incentives are girded with a strong doctrinal buttress, which cannot be characterized as "Follow Jesus and do your best." Indeed, discipleship ethics is strangely missing from Paul's role as apostolic counselor and guide.[37]

In these sections that I have classified (along with a virtual consensus opinion) as Christ hymns, the Christian's Lord is set forth in a cosmological role in the double meaning of that adjective. First, his pre-existence, as having a life in God before his becoming human, and his pre-temporal activity in creation are made the frontispiece of the hymns (especially Col 1:15-20, with later parallels in Heb 1:1-4; Jn 1:1-18). In that divine order in which he exists as one with God, as his image/form/reflection/glory,[38] he enters the human lifestream as the

---

[37]G. F. Hawthorne writes on "The Imitation of Christ: Discipleship in Philippians," in *Patterns of Discipleship in the New Testament,* ed. R. N. Longenecker (Grand Rapids: Eerdmans, 1996), pp. 163-79, but runs into all sorts of difficulties. For example, *discipleship* is not Paul's word; rather, Paul pleads with his converts "to become Christ's followers by imitating his thoughts and actions" (p. 166). What this model-to-be-imitated is Hawthorne spells out: "they should strive to emulate the attitude and actions of servanthood that marked the character and conduct of the preexistent Christ" (p. 169). But Christ's pattern of servant (2:7) is that of his earthly life (the Jesus of history, in Hawthorne's concession), not of his pre-existent state (2:6). Whatever else verse 6 refers to, it describes a unique act, involving the choice of incarnation ("the divine who became human," as Hawthorne calls it), which leads on only subsequently in the flow of the hymn to the topic of his "taking the status of a servant." Conceivably Paul's call is to pattern human lives on Christ's servant role; it is inconceivable that the once-for-all decision, reflected in verse 6, could be the *ground* of such model.

[38]Fowl (*Story of Christ,* p. 54) epitomizes in a sentence the results of recent discussion on

incarnate one in an epiphany,[39] a subgenre that has been suggestively offered to include 2 Timothy 1:9-10 (verse 10a: "has now been manifested"), Titus 2:11-14 (verse 11a: "has been manifested") and Titus 3:4-7 (verse 4b: "were manifested") as well as 1 Timothy 3:16. Second, at the conclusion of his earthly life, marked by obedience and suffering, he is taken up into the presence of God and honoured as a sharer not only of the glory he once enjoyed but also of the divine throne that rules over all. The token of this dignity and stature is that he receives the universal homage of all creation (notably expressed in the hymns of Rev 4-5) and the submission of the cosmic spirit-powers, which confess his lordship (see 1 Pet 3:22 as the finale to the putative hymnic 3:18ff.) and so are forced to abandon their title of control over human and cosmic destiny.[40] This last-named feature expresses vividly

μορφή (and its semantic near-equivalents, especially εἰκών, "image"). See later in this book, pp. 102-18. He writes: "By locating Christ in this glory [by which God's majesty is made visible], it conveys the majesty and splendor of his pre-incarnate state." Less happy is his remark that it is God's "glory . . . by which the majesty of God is made manifest *to humanity*" (my italics), since it is difficult to relate verse 6 (on my reading) to such an appearance to humans. Rather, the setting is that of John 17:5, 24 (though John 8:56; 12:41 could be appealed to as implying how the pre-incarnate glory could be perceived by mortals, *pace* Brown in the forthcoming *Where Christology Began*).

A challenge to this linguistic argument is mounted by D. Steenburg, "The Case Against the Synonymity of *Morphê* and *Eikôn*," *JSNT* 34 (1988), 77-86. Yet all this study shows is that while precise equivalence may not be proved, the terms μορφή, εἰκών, and δόξα overlap, with the first word carrying the "more visual element" to convey the thought of the representation of God in contrast to the less specific εἰκὼν θεοῦ (p. 85). Yet the use of צלם in Daniel 3:19 (rendered μορφή in LXX) is one occurrence; otherwise it is translated by εἰκών; and this evidence (admittedly not very great) is a pointer to the merging of concepts. And how is it that δόξα (glory) hides Yahweh yet "manifests his nature and/or presence" (p. 80)? Again we are faced with overlapping, if not strictly equivalent, terms to express the ineffable.

[39]See C. M. Mountain, "The New Testament Epiphany-Hymn," *The Hymn* 45, no. 2 (1994), 9-17. There is clearly, on his showing, an overlap with the category of "Christ-hymn" (see note 8).

[40]M. Hengel, " 'Sit at My Right Hand!' The Enthronement of Christ at the Right Hand of God and Psalm 110:1," in *Studies in Early Christology* (Edinburgh: T & T Clark, 1995), pp. 119-225, argues that "session at God's right hand" (akin to sharing the throne of glory, based on Jer 17:12 [p. 156]) antedates the Pauline doctrine of the granting by God of the title κύριος (Rom 14:9), by which Christ is given the "unspeakable name" of יהוה. But our passage brings the two ideas together. Christ's exaltation is to exercise the role of κύριος, as "equality with God" is now assumed. So C. A. Wanamaker, "Philippians 2.6-11: Son of God or Adamic Christology?" *NTS* 33 (1987), 179-93 (187). A suggestive attempt to conflate ideas drawn from Isaiah 45, stories of the righteous sufferers and Greco-Roman ruler worship—all under the rubric of "right to rule"—is made by David Seeley, "The Background of the Philippians Hymn (2:6-11)," *Journal of Higher Criticism* 1 (1994), 49-72. On the use of יהוה texts to relate to the exalted Christ, I am pleased to refer to the work of my research student C. J. Davis, *The Name and Way of the Lord: Old Testament Themes, New Testament Christology*, JSNT Supplements 129

the anxiety that pervaded first-century society with demonic dread and uncertainty over life's meaning and purpose, arising from a pessimistic addiction to astrology and the "elemental spirits of the universe" (Col 2:8, 20).

To meet this felt need the New Testament hymns enunciated, in bold strokes and utilizing the cosmological scenario suited to the occasion, the saving work of the redeemer whose mission is to bring together the two disparate parts of the universe (celestial and terrestrial) and to reconcile the opposing forces by a deed of pacification and harmony. The cross is set in this light (Col 2:15)—and maybe Ephesians 2:14-17 in its earlier form—which gives the notable imagery of conflict[41] and victory; and the triumph of the redeemer brings his subjugated foes in his train (Eph 4:8) en route in his ascent to his high station. So the hymns are essentially *soteriological* in their purpose, setting forth and relating the person of Christ (in his obedience to God, in light of the mission on which he came, his victory and the cosmos over which he now rules as viceregent) to his achievement as reconciler and world-ruler.

Two consequences follow from this declaration: one ethical, the other christological. Both derive from the acknowledgment by God and his rival spirit-powers that Jesus Christ is Lord since, as Philippians 2:9-11 puts it, God has "super-exalted" him over all competing intelligences (the stress on the double ὑπέρ, "above," in the verb, verse 9, and the preposition cannot be fortuitous). Since Paul's congregations may well have shared the contemporary "fear of the unknown world" (clear in Colossians)[42] and faced hostility from human sources (Phil 1:27-30; 2:15; 4:6), the assurance of the lordship of Christ would have profound ethical implications. As we saw as a background to Philippians, the readers' confusion over moral questions and their falling apart on account of strife and selfishness would require the same direct reminder that Christ's lordly power was to be exercised in their submission in obedience to his presence in their midst (2:12; 4:4). And

(Sheffield, U.K.: Academic, 1996).

[41]On Ephesians 2:12-19, see Martin, *Reconciliation*, pp. 167-76, and my *Ephesians, Colossians and Philemon*, Interpretation (Louisville, Ky.: Westminster John Knox, 1991), pp. 23-28. The conflict motif in these Pauline texts is considered by Daniel G. Reid in Tremper Longman III and D. G. Reid, *God Is a Warrior* (Grand Rapids: Zondervan, 1995), pp. 146-64.

[42]The setting of Colossians in the world of Asian magic and cultic taboos is well demonstrated by Clinton E. Arnold, *The Colossian Syncretism: The Interface Between Christianity and Folk Belief at Colossae*, Wissenschaftliche Untersuchungen zum Neuen Testament 2.77 (Tübingen: J. C. B. Mohr/Paul Siebeck, 1995; Grand Rapids: Baker, 1996).

in the issues of life and death, that same power would finally at his parousia bring them to his glory (3:20-21).

The christological component emerges from the equating of what Christ has done and what God was expected to perform in Jewish eschatology. God would assert his royal claims on the world and bring all cosmic, refractory forces into alignment with his sovereignty by receiving a universal submission. The line of connection between Christ and God seems to run thus: inasmuch as he has accomplished what God alone could do, in the neutralizing of hostile powers of the universe and the enthroning of a true lordship in defeat of the usurping claimants (the devil, in his various names and titles and symbols),[43] and has received from God's hands the right to true human life and to be the judge of history, it was but a short step—yet full of moment—to set him on a level with God as worthy of worship.

At this nerve centre in the growth of early Christianity, hymnology and Christology merge in the praise of the one Lord who is no rival to the one God but the most adequate and (for Christians) final realization of God's rule over the world (and all worlds) he has created. The New Testament churches responded to the acclamation "Jesus Christ is Lord!" with worship, joining all sentient creation in hailing the "one God, one Lord" (1 Cor 8:6)[44] in creation and reconciliation. Later Christians would address a hymn "to Christ as to God" (so Pliny reports, c. A.D. 112),[45] and the Te Deum would express liturgically:

Thou art the King of Glory, O Christ,
Thou art the everlasting Son of the Father.

2. *Philippians 2:6-11 as Christology*

In this section we respond to a reading of the hymn by N. T. Wright which sees its theological emphasis "not simply [as] a new view of Jesus. It is a new understanding of God." In this reading God's nature is best described by the word ἀγάπη, "love," which though it is "not used in the hymn itself (as it is in vv. 1-2), vv. 6-8 might almost serve as a

---

[43]See Lohmeyer's bid to find in the hymn the story of cosmic rivalry (*Philipper,* p. 98, cited in note 36 above).

[44]See L. W. Hurtado, *One God, One Lord* (Philadelphia: Fortress, 1988).

[45]On Pliny's text and the key sentence *carmenque Christo quasi deo dicere secum invicem*—the Bithynian Christians met "to chant a hymn to one another alternately [offered] to Christ as to God"—see now the study "Liturgy at the Beginning of the Second Century," in Allen Cabaniss, *Pattern in Early Christian Worship* (Macon, Ga.: Mercer University, 1989), pp. 11-21.

definition of what it means in practice—and vv. 9-11 would then affirm that this love is none other than the love of God himself."[46] The step from this interpretation to an implied use of the hymn as a call to imitation is natural. The link idea is the thrust of verses 9-11, by which Wright maintains that "God endorsed Jesus' interpretation of what equality with God meant in practice" and will "recognize self-giving love in his people as the true mark of the life of the Spirit." So "Christ's own example is held up for the church to imitate; not that his incarnation, death and exaltation are *merely* exemplary, but they are *at least* that."[47]

Yet that divine approval of Jesus' loving example does not await his exaltation (on this reading); it is expressed truly in verses 6-8, in which ironically "the humiliation *was* itself exaltation."[48] Wright's view is open to the criticism that this "static" nature of the recital of events is less the case than the "sequential" progress of the hymn (for which I have argued) and that the tension required by the contrast at verse 6 ("but [ἀλλά] he emptied himself") is not to be slackened. So Wright's view must now concede that there is a "real change of state" for the pre-existent one, which conveys to faith "the full revelation of what it meant, in practice, to be equal with God. The one who was eternally 'equal with God' expressed that equality precisely in the sequence of events referred to in vv. 6-8."[49]

Wright draws some corollaries from this interpretation: (*i*) Verses 6-7 are translated as "who, being [precisely because he was] in the form of God, did not regard this divine equality [supplying the demonstrative] as something to be used for his own advantage, but rather emptied himself . . ." with the implication that the governing motif of the incarnation was Christ's "recognition"[50] that equality with God was to be understood in this way, namely, as giving not getting.

(*ii*) Therefore the choice presented to the pre-existent Christ stemmed from his possession of equality and consisted in understanding it in a specific way, in regarding it as the way of self-giving and then in acting on it. Its essence is expressed in the *attitude* he took

---

[46]Wright, *Climax*, pp. 84, 87; cf. Hawthorne, who writes more recently: "[The passage is] not so much a 'hymn' about Christ or to Christ . . . as a marvelous anthem of praise that in effect describes the true nature of God" *(Where Christology Began)*.

[47]Wright, *Climax*, p. 87 (his italics).

[48]Moule, "Further Reflexions," p. 274.

[49]Wright, *Climax*, p. 90.

[50]This is Moule's word ("Further Reflexions").

toward what he already had—and continued to have and hold;[51] the issue turns on whether he would or would not take advantage of this possessed object.

(*iii*) Instead of exploiting his status as "equal with God" by taking advantage of it, he (re-)interpreted it as a "vocation" to obedient humiliation and death. This "understanding" God the Father acknowledged as the true one by exalting Christ to share his own glory.[52] But this exaltation implies and states that Jesus was "receiving no more than that which was always, from before the beginning of time, his by right."[53]

(*iv*) Finally, verses 6-11 are not to be seen "in any way as detached, or even detachable" from their context as a "hymn to/about Christ."[54] This designation is firmly rejected, presumably because the passage is less christological (certainly not soteriological) than theological, with its main topic (its *Sache*, or theological point, judging what is meant by what is [allegedly] said[55]) being the characterization of God in which

[51]Wright (*Climax*, p. 78) is in support of R. W. Hoover, "The *Harpagmos* Enigma: A Philological Solution," *HTR* 56 (1971), 95-119. Cf. J. C. O'Neill, "Hoover on *Harpagmos* Reviewed, with a Modest Proposal Concerning Philippians 2:6," *HTR* 81 (1988), 445-49, who ends up with the desperate expedient of submitting that a scribe, puzzled over the presence of τό, which suggested that Christ's pre-existent state was not one of equality with God, changed τό to μή (the negative). When the μή is read, the translation runs: "who being in the form of God thought it not robbery [O'Neill's preferred word to Hoover's] *not* to be [μὴ εἶναι] equal with God" (p. 449). In point of fact, while he regards the translation "robbery" as "near nonsense," O'Neill's alternative rendering of the Pauline phrase as "to think of something as an occasion for acting as robber, snatcher back or reaper of advantage" (p. 447) does fit the context well and nicely chimes in with my understanding, once the identity of "form of God" and "equality with God" is discounted (which O'Neill does not do [p. 448], though he attributes such a break to a puzzled scribe who made a textual emendation, noted above).
Hoover, whose suggestion of a proverbial sense of ἁρπαγμὸν ἡγεῖσθαι τι as "something to use for his own advantage" ("*Harpagmos* Enigma," p. 118) seems well grounded (though O'Neill makes some telling criticisms), takes exception to what he regards as my bid to combine what Christ had *de jure* and what he rejected as temptation, namely, the de facto exercise of power. He remarks that no text "carries both active and passive senses at the same time" (p. 101), yet later (p. 107) he concedes that very point regarding ἅρπαγμα (used synonymously with ἁρπαγμός [108]); and his final translation (118) looks as if it does unite both active and passive meanings.
See later in this book, p. 149, for C. K. Barrett's interpretation, evidently now abandoned in his latest treatment, *Paul* (London: Chapman, 1994), pp. 105-9, where it is unclear whether his line 6 ("obedient to death") is pre-Pauline or added by Paul.
[52]Wright, *Climax*, p. 97.
[53]Ibid., p. 94; cf. p. 86: not "exaltation to a divine rank or nature, not already possessed"; but cf. p. 87, note 123. Cited later.
[54]Ibid., p. 98.
[55]This definition of *Sachkritik*, distinguishing between what is said and what is meant

"incarnation and even crucifixion are to be seen as *appropriate* vehicles for the dynamic self-revelation of God."[56]

I have reproduced the substance of Wright's view of Philippians 2:6-11 for several reasons. At face value it is attractive and undoubtedly conveys a meaning that most readers of the text would initially assent to. Who would wish to challenge the thesis that God's love—even though the word ἀγάπη is missing—is seen pre-eminently in the gift and sacrifice of his Son, who has defined God's character for all time? Yet there are several problematic underpinnings of this presentation which raise the question whether it has adequately come to terms with the main thrust of the hymn—or, as we may rephrase it, whether its correct *Sache* has been located. Wright's interpretation runs counter to the one I have espoused, defended against earlier critics and set forth in the following pages; this new preface gives a platform to make some response, without rehearsing all the reasons contained in the subsequent book. Some page references, however, may assist those who wish to read a fuller defense.

The systematic history of more recent interpretation from which I have just drawn really turns on the exegesis of 2:6 and two troublesome technical terms: (*a*) ἁρπαγμός, literally "a thing to be seized" and then retained or exploited, either way used with advantage to the subject, and (*b*) "to be equal with God." On any showing these are the critical terms whose meaning determines how the hymn's message is viewed in toto.

Over against Wright's notion that "being equal with God" is the virtual equivalent of "being in the form of God" and that ἁρπαγμός relates to an understanding of equality with God which Christ refused because he would not and did not exploit it as something to be used for his own advantage, my correlation of the terms runs as follows. While accepting the proverbial sense for ἁρπαγμὸν ἡγεῖσθαι τι ("to treat something as a piece of good fortune," "to regard it as a treasure trove"), my view sees the choice differently. It is that Christ refused to use his being in the form/image of God, which he had in his life in God, as an advantage (like a springboard) from which he might have

(zwischen Gesagtem und Gemeintem unterscheidet) and measuring the one by the other, derives from R. Bultmann, "Das Problem einer theologischen Exegese des Neuen Testaments," in *Das Problem der Theologie des Neuen Testaments,* ed. G. Strecker (Darmstadt: Wissenschaftliche Buchgesellschaft, 1975), p. 253.
[56]Wright, *Climax,* p. 84 (italics in the original).

seized equality with God. Rather, he let the advantage go (verse 7a) and chose to condescend to be born in human form and to die in obedience. God set his seal on this action, and Christ attained by God's gift (verse 9) his rank as Lord, which accorded him equality with God, which he now enjoys.[57]

However the taxonomy of this understanding of ἁρπαγμὸν ἡγεῖσθαι τι might be defined (with reference to the debate over *res rapta*, *res retinenda* and *res rapienda*—for these terms see pp. 134-52), it is time to address Wright's six more substantive criticisms[58] against this position.

1. It is said that, on my showing, the proverbial idiom cannot be appealed to, chiefly because "one cannot decide to take advantage of something one does not already have."[59] But when this criticism is more clearly phrased as "that which one might seize, one does not already possess: that which one does not possess, one cannot relinquish,"[60] it is overlooked that (logically) one can forgo the opportunity to use a prize that is held out in prospect. There is a middle term between Christ's status (μορφή, verse 6, or more correctly "being *in* the μορφή of God") in the divine form (which he had eternally) and his being equal with God. It is the opportunity for advancement that lay in his power. His "decision" viewed as temptation[61] was to refuse such a prize—to disprize it, to use the old Elizabethan verb, which seems apropos to the sense of ἁρπαγμός—and choose to attain the title to lordship by a life of obedient submission.

This view of ἁρπαγμός, I continue to believe, makes sense of the basic idea behind the noun, seen in the corresponding verb ἁρπάζειν, "to seize" (cf. Jn 10:12, 28; Acts 8:39), and the fact that one can conceivably "seize" opportunities that one already has, as in the epigram *carpe diem*, "seize the day." It also accounts for the flow of the drama in its movement both downward (in con*descension* and obedience to death) and upward (elevation in verse 9 and exalted station before which the powers "bow down"). Furthermore, it gives point to a real choice. On the alternate view, one is left to wonder whether that viable decision (implied in the verb ἡγεῖσθαι) has been weakened. If the pre-existent one had divine equality as his possession, and that surely is the ultimate

---

[57]See later in this book, pp. 151-53; R. P. Martin, *Philippians*, New Century Bible (Grand Rapids: Eerdmans, 1989), pp. 96-97.

[58]Wright, *Climax*, pp. 72-73, summarized in O'Brien, *Epistle to the Philippians*, pp. 212-13.

[59]Wright, *Climax*, p. 82.

[60]Ibid., p. 72, note 69.

[61]This is Lohmeyer's insight into the *nature* of the ἁρπαγμός (*Kyrios Jesus*, p. 25: "What is the religious significance of the picture? It is, in brief, the thought of temptation").

PREFACE TO THE 1997 EDITION

good (in Anselm's language) "than which nothing greater can be conceived," wherein is the choice except to see it in a particular way? If one already has and holds "equality with God" as the greatest good, we may ask the question *"Cui bono? To what profit?"* when he is said not to have exploited it to his (further) advantage. If it is objected that being in the divine form and holding on to equality with God are *precisely* the starting point from which God's character as giving, not gaining, is seen, then it needs to be asked why a word like ἁρπαγμός with its inbuilt idea of "advantage" came to be used.

2. The supposed wedge driven between Christ's being in God's form and his refusal to act in what would be tantamount to disobedience (here the Adam-Christ contrast is pertinent) turns on the way the Greek phrases are syntactically related. Wright and others bring out examples of the way the articular infinitive is used in a bid to prove the point that τὸ εἶναι ἴσα θεῷ, "to be equal with God," must grammatically hark back to ἐν μορφῇ θεοῦ, "being in the form of God," in the preceding line. It is even suggested that, to make the connection one of identity, we should insert *this*, to read "who, being in the form of God, did not regard *this* divine equality as something to be used for his own advantage. . . ."[62] This is quite arbitrary, since there is another way of understanding this grammatical connection.[63]

3. At the conclusion of his "career" as the hymn unfolds it in ever-greater dramatic intensity, the exalted one is accorded a dignity as world-ruler (cosmocrat)[64] or, in biblical terms, Lord with sovereign rights over all created orders (verses 9-11). This is granted him (note the verb, verse 9) as a tribute to his obedience, not simply his suffering and death. Lordship attained any other way would be arrogance. This answers the query, Why should world lordship be a thing to which Christ should not aspire? It is illustrated (though, in my view, only illustratively) in the temptations of the historical Jesus (Mt 4:1-11 par. Lk 4:1-13). That is the force of "more-than-highly exalted" (in verse 9)

---

[62]Wright, *Climax*, p. 83 (emphasis added).

[63]We grant that BDF §399 (1) lists the articular infinitive of Philippians 2:6 as anaphoric, which supports Hawthorne and Wright. Alternatively, however, the article could function to identify εἶναι ἴσα θεῷ as the direct object ἡγήσατο rather than ἁρπαγμόν, which precedes it, since εἶναι with an accusative following ἡγεῖσθαι would normally indicate a predicate accusative. Cf. Philippians 3:8, ἡγοῦμαι πάντα ζημίαν εἶναι, where ζημίαν εἶναι is predicate accusative; Job 30:1 LXX, οὓς οὐχ ἡγησάμην εἶναι ἀξίους, where εἶναι ἀξίους is predicate accusative (cf. BDF §157 [3]).

[64]On the propriety of this term in the history of the exegesis of Philippians 2, see D. V. Way's note in *The Lordship of Christ: Ernst Käsemann's Interpretation of Paul's Theology* (Oxford: Clarendon, 1991), pp. 94-100.

and the possession of a divine equality that *in the nature of the case* could not be his as pre-existent, that is, in the pre-temporal and so pre-cosmic state represented by "being in the form of God." This is so clear (to me!) that no surprise is registered that Wright admits this and reports, "In his exaltation Christ does not merely return to the state of glory corresponding to that of his pre-existence, but is now exalted as *man*, God's intended ruler of the world."[65] Incidentally, this stands in plain contradiction to the remark (cited earlier, p. xvii) that he received "no more than that which was always, from before the beginning of time, his by right."

4. The propriety of the term *soteriological* should now be evident, since the hymn does not spell out ontological or trinitarian relationships. Nor is it concerned with moral traits, save that of obedience, which in Paul's hands becomes the linchpin of the human response to the kerygma in the *ordo salutis*. If Christ's obedience in the double (not single, as is mistakenly alleged) sense of *first* refusing to accept the prize by aggrandizement (implied in οὐ[κ] . . . ἁρπάζειν, which is the verb form underlying ἁρπαγμός) and *then*—in consequence, but with distinct contrast, ἀλλά, "but"—emptying himself (the reflexive underscores the volitional element) holds the key to the hymn, the nexus between soteriology and paraenesis (in verses 1-4, 12) is clear. In the "obedience of faith" (Rom 1:5; 16:26; cf. Rom 6:12, 16-17; 10:16; 15:18; 16:19) believers identify with Christ and his obedience to death (exactly as at Phil 2:12).

Adopting the "same mind" (τοῦτο φρονεῖτε) may refer to the response of the "obedience of faith,"[66] after the pattern established by Christ, by which believers come to be "in Christ." As elsewhere (Gal 5:6) for Paul, the fundamental response of "obedience of faith" provides the basis for ethical endeavour and styles of behaviour, namely, "faith [basis] working through love [ethical behaviour]." We may compare Romans 12:1-3, "present yourselves as a living sacrifice . . . be transformed by the renewing of your minds [basis] . . . do not think more highly [ὑπερφρονεῖν] than you ought to think [δεῖ φρονεῖν] [ethical response]."[67] Later Paul will apply this as a call to

[65]Wright, *Climax*, p. 87, note 123 (his italics).
[66]Lynn A. Losie tells me that he tends now to make this connection (at 2:5) rather than the link he suggested earlier (in "A Note on the Interpretation of Phil 2:5," *ExT* 90 [1978], 52-54). I am glad to incorporate some other suggestions from him in this section.
[67]There is some justification for the inclusion of δεῖ in Philippians 2:5; see later in this

show love to one's fellow Christians (Rom 13:8-10).

The hymn, on this showing, is soteriological in both its primary (as the story of salvation centred on the *via crucis*) and its secondary (as the pattern for believers: see earlier, pp. xlviii-xlix) meanings. The salvation teaching is borne out by how Paul writes in 2:12: "work out your own *salvation* . . . for it is God who is at work among you."

5. The accusation that "the parallel between Adam and Christ is obscured" sits ill with my appeal to the Adam-Christ typology,[68] even though the parallel is not exact; and several images, resonances, "symbolic fields," intertextual echoes and textual subplots also lie in the background of the hymn. The contrast between what Adam did (in defiance and disobedience) and what Christ refused to do (in humble submission and obedience) is as telling as it can be.

6. The final critique returns to the paraenetic function of the hymn. I have argued that the incorporation of the hymn in its Pauline version needed both the frontispiece of 2:1-4 and the admonition of 2:12 to make its moral force felt (let us recall that the readers are not brought into the picture in 2:6-11; there is no stress on "for us and for our salvation" made explicit, precisely as in the quoted Col 1:15-20 and inserted in the framework of Col 1:12-14, 21-22).

The assertion that the hymn (at least verses 6-8) centres on the verb "he emptied himself"[69] rather than on the obedience-unto-death motif lacks probative appeal, since I have called attention to obedience as the master thought governing both Christ's way and the hortatory application. In fact, the tables are turned at this point, for we are left to wonder what is the theological import of the self-emptying if the real decisive moment of the choice lies in Christ's taking up of an "attitude" (a key term in the reconstruction I am opposing) and a way of "interpreting" what equality with God means and implies.

A final observation reverts to the importing of divine ἀγάπη as the defining motif (see earlier, p. lxv) and the revisionist interpretation

---

book, pp. 68-74.

The seeking of an adequate *grounding* for Pauline ethics in God's "merciful acts" (Rom 12:1) is offered by H. D. Betz, "The Foundations of Christian Ethics According to Romans 12:1-2," in *Witness and Existence*, FS S. M. Ogden, ed. P. E. Devenish and G. L. Goodwin (Chicago: University of Chicago Press, 1989), pp. 55-72. The tie-in connecting the indicative (God's "history of salvation" acts [Rom 1:17]) and ethical "obligation" (Greek ὀφειλή) as a moral imperative calling for a response has several parallels in Philippians 2:1-12.

[68]See later in this book, pp. 150-51, 161-64.

[69]Wright, *Climax*, p. 73.

that places all emphasis on our reading off the divine character as love from the text's story. We are in the realm of a hypothetical meta-story that floats above the text and is not (in spite of all the exegetical acumen and industry that has gone into this revision) as closely linked to the text as it professes to be. The text speaks of Christ's self-humbling and obedience-unto-death, *not explicitly* of God's love and sacrifice for others (as the neutral reader might well have anticipated from the introit in 2:1-4). There is no *explicit* mention of Christ's death as atonement (or even on a cross, in the putative *Vorlage* or original text of the hymn: that Pauline phrase of course may well be exegeted as implying ὑπὲρ ἡμῶν, "for our sakes," as in Gal 3:13; 2 Cor 5:21; Rom 5:8, where, however, the application is added *expressis verbis*). The nub of the problem for all proposals that try to find in the hymn an ethical example to provide the basis for the paraenesis in 2:1-4, 12-13 is, in fact, that *the hymn in all six Pauline verses does not speak of any action of Christ on behalf of others.*

Additionally, any reconstruction is bound to be inadequate that fails to account for the clear storylike movement that gives the hymn a dynamic quality. Talk of Christ's attitude and the way he supposedly "(re)interpreted"[70] his status as "vocation"[71] lends an air of detachment and flatness, even matter-of-factness, to what is essentially a drama with a plot unfolding whose contours and tensions should not be smoothed out. It disregards the momentous shift in that progress (from downward[72] to upward), pivoting on verse 9: διὸ καί, which marks the turning point and brings the direct action of God, in contrast to Christ's own volitional acts in verses 6-8, to the front of the "plot." It throws into high relief the enthronement of the obedient/crucified one as the total hymn's centre of gravity.

"Jesus Christ is Lord" is indeed the banner under which the hymn, as both a christological tribute and the basis for ethical endeavour, has to be seen. It is such a credal tag that epitomizes the "way of Christ" and permits us to see "Christ hymns"[73] as a distinct New Testament

[70]Ibid., p. 83.
[71]Ibid., pp. 84 (twice), 97.
[72]When Wright (ibid., p. 90) sums up, "The one who was eternally 'equal with God' expressed that equality precisely in the sequence of events referred to in vv. 6-8," one reader is left to ask what then has become of the kenosis? I call attention once more to the spatial and kinetic language used (see p. 277).
[73]Whether Philippians 2:6-11 is regarded as a *carmen Christi* (a hymn sung to Christ) or *carmen Christo* (a hymn about Christ, as in Pliny) is really immaterial. The point is that it is *christological*, a point tacitly accepted by Wright in his chapter heading in *Climax,*

category and the birthplace where Christology began.

V. FINALE

Given that this new preface marks a milestone in a series of publications that go back to 1959,[74] some may view devoting some forty years to a study of a six-verse biblical passage as a tedious and exacting chore. Yet it has been a task lightened by many assistances: post-graduate advisors' counsels, students' inquiries, faculty debates (a notable one in particular),[75] reactions of colleagues in the academic enterprise—and above all, the chance to penetrate the mind of whoever wrote the hymn, the experience of those who first sang,[76] heard or were challenged by it, and the wisdom of the apostle who recorded it.

This 1997 preface is the outcome of my latest lucubrations; and I mean it to be final.

R. P. M.

Lent 1997

"Jesus Christ Is Lord." On his showing he ought really to have titled it "The Story of God" (as in his chapter in *Bringing the Church to the World* [Minneapolis: Bethany House, 1992], pp. 100-108).

[74]The Tyndale lecture in that year appeared as *An Early Christian Confession: Philippians 2:5-11 in Recent Interpretation* (London: Tyndale Press, 1960), with a short note on μορφή in *ExT* 70 in 1959.

[75]Or rather a series of debates, held with Daniel P. Fuller in his class on hermeneutics and extending over a fifteen-year period, once and even twice a year.

[76]See the jocular remark in Fee, *Philippians*, p. 226, note 42, that "the passage obviously sings, even if it was not originally a hymn!" (sic!).

LIST OF ABBREVIATIONS OF REFERENCE WORKS, COMMENTARIES, AND JOURNALS (including series of publications)

Abh. T. ANT	*Abhandlungen zur Theologie und Geschichte des Alten und Neuen Testaments* (Zürich)
AJT	*The American Journal of Theology* (Chicago, 1897–1920)
ASNU	*Acta Seminarii Neotestamentici Upsaliensis:* curavit A. Fridrichsen (Copenhagen/Lund)
Bh. ZNTW	*Beihefte zur Zeitschrift für die neutestamentliche Wissenschaft* (Giessen/Berlin)
BJRL	*Bulletin of the John Rylands Library* (Manchester)
CB	*Cambridge Bible for Schools and Colleges* (Cambridge)
CBQ	*Catholic Biblical Quarterly* (Washington)
CNT	*Commentaire du Nouveau Testament* (Neuchâtel/Paris)
CQR	*Church Quarterly Review* (London)
DB	*Dictionnaire de la Bible* (Paris)
EvT	*Evangelische Theologie* (Munich)
Expos.	*The Expositor* (London, 1875–1925)
ExT	*The Expository Times* (Edinburgh)
FRLANT	*Forschungen zur Religion und Literatur des Alten und Neuen Testaments* (Göttingen)
HTR	*Harvard Theological Review* (Cambridge, Mass.)
HzNT	*Handbuch zum Neuen Testament* (ed. Lietzmann, H.–Bornkamm, G., Tübingen)
IB	*The Interpreter's Bible* (New York/Nashville)
ICC	*The International Critical Commentary* (Edinburgh)
JBL	*Journal of Biblical Literature* (Philadelphia)
JCP	*Journal of Classical Philology* (London)
JSNT	*Journal for the Study of the New Testament* (Sheffield)
JTS	*Journal of Theological Studies* (1900– ; 1950 new series, Oxford)
MeyerKomm.	*Kritischer-exegetischer Kommentar über das Neue*

	Testament (ed. Meyer, H. A. W., Göttingen)
MNTC	*Moffatt New Testament Commentary* (London)
NTD	*Das Neue Testament Deutsch* (Göttingen)
NTS	*New Testament Studies* (Cambridge)
RAC	*Reallexicon für Antike und Christentum* (Stuttgart)
RB	*Revue Biblique* (Jerusalem/Paris)
RGG	*Die Religion in Geschichte und Gegenwart*[3] (ed. Galling, K., Tübingen)
RHPR	*Revue d'Histoire et de Philosophie religieuses* (Strasbourg/Paris)
RHR	*Revue de l'histoire des Religions* (Paris)
RSR	*Revue des Sciences religieuses* (Strasbourg)
SBT	*Studies in Biblical Theology* (London)
SJT	*Scottish Journal of Theology* (Edinburgh)
ST	*Studia Theologica* (Lund)
ThBl	*Theologische Blätter* (Leipzig, 1922–42)
Theol. Revue	*Theologische Revue* (Münster i. W.)
ThQ	*Theologische Quartalschrift* (Tübingen)
TLZ	*Theologische Literaturzeitung* (Leipzig)
TSK	*Theologische Studien und Kritiken* (Hamburg/Gotha, 1828–1942)
TWNT	*Theologisches Wörterbuch zum Neuen Testament* (ed. Kittel, G. and Friedrich, G.). Band. i–vii (1933–60), Stuttgart
WC	*Westminster Commentary* (London)
ZfTK	*Zeitschrift für Theologie und Kirche* (Tübingen, 1891–1917; new series 1920–)
ZNTW	*Zeitschrift für die neutestamentliche Wissenschaft* (Giessen/Berlin)

INTRODUCTION

I. THE MEANING OF CARMEN CHRISTI IN EARLY
CHRISTIAN WORSHIP

The Roman official Pliny held office as governor of the province
of Pontus and Bithynia in Asia Minor for a period of fifteen
months or so in A.D. 111–12. During that time he corresponded
with the emperor Trajan. One piece of extant correspondence is
of great interest to the student of Christian history.[1]

Pliny had sought to enforce an edict which proscribed the
profession of Christianity. But he was uncertain as to the correctness of the procedure he had adopted. He wrote, therefore, to
Trajan seeking guidance. He explained the method of procedure
he had hitherto followed; and in the course of his letter he related
some information about Christian practices which he had
received from certain Christian apostates.

> They asserted that this was the sum and substance of their fault or
> their error; namely, that they were in the habit of meeting before
> dawn on a stated day and singing alternately a hymn to Christ as to
> a god, and that they bound themselves by an oath, not to the com-
> mission of any wicked deed, but that they would abstain from theft
> and robbery and adultery, that they would not break their word,
> and that they would not withhold a deposit when reclaimed. This
> done, it was their practice, so they said, to separate, and then to
> meet together again for a meal, which however was of the ordinary
> kind and quite harmless. (*Epp.* x, 96–7: Lightfoot's translation.)

Our special attention is directed to the words rendered by
Lightfoot 'before dawn on a stated day and singing alternately a
hymn to Christ as to a god' (*stato die ante lucem. . .carmenque Christo
quasi deo dicere secum inuicem*). These words give an insight into
the practice of Christian worship in the second century, which is
known otherwise only from occasional references. The earliest
documents apart from the canonical literature are I Clement (*c.*
A.D. 96); Ignatius' epistles, written *en route* to his martyrdom (*c.*
A.D. 108); and the enigmatic Church Order known as the

---

[1] The historical background is given in E. C. Kennedy, *Martial and Pliny*
(1952), *ad* x, 96; B. J. Kidd, *A History of the Church to A.D. 461*, I (1922), 234 ff.

Didache which possibly belongs to the decades A.D. 80–100. In chronological sequence the next liturgical text is that contained in Justin's *Apology* (*c.* A.D. 150–3).[1] If this attempt at dating the second-century literature is anywhere near correct, what is virtually the sole extant witness to Christian worship in the half century or so which separates Ignatius and Justin is contained in Pliny's letter. A special significance, therefore, attaches to this text.

The record which has been cited above presents certain problems of identification. The 'fixed day' may be taken as referring to the Christian 'Sunday', the Lord's day. For the observance of this day there is attestation in the canonical Acts of the Apostles, the Apocalypse, the *Didache*, Ignatius and Barnabas;[2] but the data are capable of various interpretations.[3] The oath which is mentioned has been understood to refer to the reciting of the Decalogue. It is suggested[4] that, as the reciting of the Law takes place in the Sabbath worship of the Jewish synagogue, the allusion to a similar form of oath-taking confirms that the Christian service in Bithynia still retained its Jewish-Christian character. An alternative suggestion is made by J. H. Srawley[5] that the oath relates to the baptismal vow when the neophytes renounced those practices which were out of character with their Christian profession. *Ante lucem* seems clearly to point to an early morning gathering, held before the day's work began. Tertullian

---

[1] I Clem. LIX–LXI; Ignatius, *Eph.* IV; VII, 2; XIX; *Trall.* IX; *Smyr.* I. The belief that Ignatius introduced antiphonal singing to the Church at Antioch is mentioned by Socrates, *H.E.* VI, 8. But this claim was evidently not undisputed in view of Paul of Samosata's criticism, in Eusebius, *H.E.* VII, XXX, 10. *Did.* ix–x; and Justin, *Apol.* I, lxvii, 3; lxv; lxvi. These are the chief texts which contain *liturgica*.

[2] Acts xx. 7; Apoc. i. 10; Ignatius, *Magn.* IX, 1; Barn. xv, 9; *Did.* xiv. 1; and later in the second century Justin, *Apol.* I, lxvii.

[3] Cf. A. A. McArthur, *The Evolution of the Christian Year* (1953), pp. 13–29; H. B. Porter, *The Day of Light* (1960); H. Dumaine, 'Dimanche', *Dict. d'archéol. chrét. et de lit.* IV, 1 (1920), 858 ff. More recent discussions are those by H. Riesenfeld, 'Sabbat et Jour du Seigneur', *New Testament Essays in memory of T. W. Manson* (1959), pp. 210–17; and C. W. Dugmore, 'Lord's Day and Easter', *Neotestamentica et Patristica in honorem Oscar Cullmann* (1962), pp. 272–81.

[4] So C. J. Kraemer, 'Pliny and the Early Christian Church Service', *JCP*, XXIX (1934), 293–300; and E. C. Ratcliff, 'Christian Worship and Liturgy', *The Study of Theology*, ed. K. E. Kirk (1939), p. 419.

[5] *The Early History of the Liturgy*[2] (1947), p. 30.

uses a similar term for Christian assemblies held before dawn. 'We take also, in meetings before daybreak (*antelucanis coetibus*), ... the sacrament of the Eucharist' (*de Coron.* III); and in *Apol.* II, 6 there is a phrase which Tertullian uses in reference to the allusion in the Pliny text: *coetus antelucanos ad canendum Christo ut deo.* This latter description is of importance when we come to ascertain the meaning of the *carmen* which the Bithynian Christians offered to Christ.

From the foregoing data it seems that what was intended in the description which was supplied to the Roman governor was an eye-witness account of the Sunday morning worship of the Church in Asia Minor in the early part of the second century. And the picture the data give is tolerably clear.

More controversial, however, are the terms which Pliny employs to describe the precise actions of the Christians at their Sunday *synaxis*. At least four different meanings have been assigned to the key-term *carmen* in the phrase *carmen...dicere.*

(*a*) Some writers hold that *carmen* means an Old Testament psalm. This view is taken mainly on the ground that the Bithynian Christians had apparently incorporated into their worship the chief elements of the Jewish Sabbath service. C. J. Kraemer notices that *sacramentum* ('they bound themselves by an oath') is parallel with the Decalogue confession; and he wishes to refer the *carmen* to a psalm borrowed from the Jewish psalter.[1] The phrase *secum inuicem* is apparently in keeping with this idea, for it is claimed that the antiphonal singing of psalms—assuming that the phrase does mean 'antiphonally'—is part of the *pietas Judaica* of the synagogue worship.[2] But this suggestion, although offered by W. O. E. Oesterley as a feature of the *Jewish Background of the Christian Liturgy*,[3] is debatable. Although antiphonal responses were used by the congregation in the Hebrew syna-

[1] C. J. Kraemer, *loc. cit.*

[2] It is not disputed that antiphonal psalm-singing is known in the worship of the Old Testament. Some references are only incidental in character: e.g. when the people responded at the dedication of Solomon's Temple, or at the reformation under Hezekiah; or at the foundation-laying of the second Temple. Congregational responses in these cases were in terms of the traditional Amen or longer benedictions and thanksgivings. See further R. P. Martin, *Worship in the Early Church* (1964), pp. 40 ff.

[3] *The Jewish Background of the Christian Liturgy* (1925), p. 75. Cf. O. Cullmann, *Early Christian Worship* (E.T. 1953), pp. 21, 22.

3

gogues of the first century, congregational psalm-singing is unattested.[1]

But the possibility that a Jewish psalm, interpreted Messianically, may have been sung to Christ cannot be ruled out. Justin witnesses to the adaptation of Psalm xlv to Christian purposes, and declares that the Psalm is an evidence that Jesus is to be worshipped as 'God and Christ'.[2] But *secum inuicem* is left unexplained on this supposition.

S. L. Mohler has proposed that *carmen* refers to a Christianized version of the Jewish confession of faith, the *Shema'*.[3] The evidence that the *Shema'* was recited antiphonally in the synagogue is better attested than the practice of psalm-singing.[4] Both liturgical prayer and the confession of faith were led by the representative of the synagogue assembly, the *šeliaḥ ṣibbûr* (שליח צבור), as part of his liturgical function.[5] The congregation responded with *Amen* and certain short *bʰerākôt*, in an antiphonal manner. But there seems little support for this suggested meaning of *carmen* in the context of Christian worship apart from the evidence of a series of antiphonal responses in the synagogue liturgy.

(*b*) J. B. Lightfoot accepts that the sense of *secum inuicem* implies antiphonal responses, and calls in witness many pagan and Jewish literary parallels. But he remarks that *carmen* can be used of 'any set form of words', and does not necessarily presuppose a metrical composition.[6] J. Stevenson takes over this alternative in his adaptation of H. M. Gwatkin's translation of Pliny's words. He renders them, 'recite by turns a form of words'.[7] H. Lietzmann endeavoured to place this text in a baptismal setting by submitting that the phrase *carmen. . .dicere*

[1] So I. Elbogen, *Der jüdische Gottesdienst in seiner geschichtlichen Entwicklung*[4] (1931 = 1962 reprint), pp. 249, 494 ff.

[2] Justin, *Dialogue with Trypho* LXIII (Migne, *PG* VI (1857), 622): cf. A. L. Williams, *Justin Martyr: The Dialogue with Trypho* (1930), 132.

[3] 'The Bithynian Christians Again', *JCP*, xxx (1935), 167–9.

[4] On the use of the *Shema'* cf. E. Schürer, *History of the Jewish People*, E.T. II, ii (1893), 77 ff.

[5] For the office of שליח צבור see Strack–Billerbeck, *Kommentar z. N.T.* (1922–28), IV, 149–52; Elbogen, *Der jüdische Gottesdienst*, pp. 487 ff.

[6] Ignatius, *The Apostolic Fathers*, II, i (1889), 51.

[7] *The New Eusebius* (1957), pp. 14 f., adapting H. M. Gwatkin, *Selections from Early Christian Writers* (1902), p. 29.

signifies the 'question and answer of a formulated baptismal confession'.[1] The grounds for this novel interpretation which has been accepted by some recent Continental scholars (notably W. Nauck[2]) are three. First, Lietzmann quotes two pieces of evidence in which *carmen* is used to signify a baptismal symbol.[3] Then, the phrase *secum inuicem* may be understood as the *interrogatio de fide* and the baptizand's *responsum*, as in the early baptismal formularies.[4] Thirdly, Lietzmann is able to account for the ambiguity of *carmen* by observing that it also carries the sense of a magical incantation or invocation. What to the Bithynian Christians was a cherished symbol and badge of their faith seemed to the pagan official a mere charm or incantation.

(c) This view of Lietzmann's is opposed by F. J. Dölger in his full study of the term.[5] The merit of Dölger's conclusion is that it explains both the implicit interrogation of Pliny and the Christians' response thereto. Pliny asks if the Christians worship idolatrously and offer *preces infelices* which are subversive of the state in their tendency. The Christians strenuously rebut these implied charges: 'Our *carmen* is directed to no unlawful gods, or magical spirits, or dead deities: we call upon the living Christ.' The true meaning of *carmen*, Dölger avers, is therefore *supplicatio*. He concludes: 'What Pliny ascertained from the cross-examination was an invocation of Jesus' (*eine Anrufung Jesu*). This 'invocation' may have been either a hymn or a solemn prose formula—Dölger leaves it an open issue, yet inclines to the former alternative—but it must have been accompanied by a response because *secum inuicem*, which he translates as 'reciprocally' (*wechselseits*), implies a response to the ejaculation.

Other commentators on the Pliny letter have sought to sug-

---

[1] 'Die liturgischen Angaben des Plinius', *Geschichtliche Studien Albert Hauck zum 70. Geburtstag* (1916), pp. 34–8 (37). Cf. F. Kattenbusch, *TLZ*, XLV (1920), 224.

[2] *Die Tradition und der Charakter des ersten Johannesbriefes* (1947), p. 161, n. 4.

[3] 'Die liturgischen Angaben des Plinius', citing *Rhein. Mus.* 71 (1916), 281 f. and Faustus of Reji I, 1 and *Acta S. Arcelli Papae*, § 4.

[4] For specimens of this 'question and answer' formulation see Hahn's reference work (A. and G. L. Hahn, *Bibliothek der Symbole und Glaubensregeln der alten Kirche* (1897 = 1962 reprint), § 31 a).

[5] Section 6, 'Das an Christus gerichtete *Carmen* der Christen Bithyniens' in *Sol Salutis: Gebet und Gesang im christlichen Altertum*[2] (1925), pp. 103–36.

5

gest what this response may have been. Some think that the Christians repeated the invocation as they were being instructed by their Christian teacher. Newman and Dom Connolly take this view. The latter renders:[1] they repeated 'among themselves an invocation of Christ'. W. Lockton[2] thought more of a liturgical response, and submitted that, in answer to the *carmen* offered by the leader, the assembled company replied: 'Lord, have mercy' (*Kyrie eleison*). Dölger[3] took the same line of interpretation, and imagined that the carmen was 'a hymn to Christ as God' (*ein Gesang an Christus als Gott*), recited by bishop, priest or deacon, and evoking some such catena of response as:

> Come, Lord Jesus!
> *Mārānâ thâ* (i.e. our Lord, come!)
> σῶσον ἡμᾶς
> ἐλέησον ἡμᾶς
> Κύριε ἐλέησον

These suggestions can only be considered as very tentative. There is no way of testing their accuracy; and it seems better to admit that we do not know the nature of the *carmen* and the response which it called forth. Attempts have been made to find some antecedents for antiphonal responses in the New Testament (in I Corinthians xvi. 22–4 and Apocalypse xxii. 17–21) and in *Didache* x. 6.[4] These texts have been regarded as arranged in the liturgical shape of a dialogue between the presiding minister (or celebrant at the Eucharist) and the congregation.

[1] Cited, without reference, by Srawley, *Early History of the Liturgy*, p. 30.

[2] 'Liturgical Notes', *JTS*, xvi (1915), 548–50.

[3] *Sol Salutis*, pp. 135–6.

[4] Both G. Bornkamm, 'Das Anathema in der urchristlichen Abendmahlsliturgie', reprinted in *Das Ende des Gesetzes, Paulusstudien* (1961), pp. 123–32 and J. A. T. Robinson, 'The Earliest Christian Liturgical Sequence?', reprinted in *Twelve New Testament Studies* (1962), pp. 154–7, have noted the similarity between I Cor. xvi. 22 and *Didache* x. 6. 'Beide Texte sind hinsichtlich ihrer sakral-rechtlichen Stilisierung und ihrem Inhalt nach eng verwandt', comments Bornkamm (123). Both scholars, moreover, accept the conclusion of H. Lietzmann, *Messe und Herrenmahl* (1926), p. 229 (*Mass and Lord's Supper* (E.T. Fasc. IV, 1953), pp. 192 f.), that *Didache* x. 6 is set in the shape of a dialogue between the Celebrant and the Congregation at the Eucharist.

A dialogue pattern in Apoc. xxii. 17–22 is detected by J. A. T. Robinson, *loc. cit.* 156 f. Cf. E. Lohmeyer, *Die Offenbarung des Johannes*[2] (*HzNT*, 1953), pp. 182 f.

But there is no certainty that this arrangement of the verses is correct.[1]

(d) If *carmen* carries the sense of a composition, whether as a metrical hymn to be sung or as a form of words in prose, can we be sure that it was only a single invocatory sentence or baptismal question? O. Casel refuses so to regard it,[2] and wishes to understand the word not according to its Latin usage but as a translation of the Greek ὕμνος. In support of this we may observe that Eusebius uses the cognate verb ὑμνεῖν in the account he gives of the Pliny letter.[3] Dölger has objected to this equivalence, however, on the ground that Pliny would scarcely have rendered ὕμνος by *carmen* in preference to *hymnus*.[4] The attestation of *hymnus* in the lexica, however, is very slight, and it may be that Pliny chose to use the commonest word in his vocabulary. But the matter may again be left an open question; and we have no means of knowing whether the *carmen* was short or lengthy. On balance, the conclusion that *carmen* means a hymn addressed to Christ seems more likely.[5]

This conclusion has been challenged by those who prefer to translate *carmen* as 'a form of words', and to regard the corresponding verb as meaning that this form of words was recited, not sung. This translation is doubtless based on the plain meaning of *dicere* (= 'to say', 'to declare'); and accepts the alternative sense of *carmen* as 'formula' or 'declaration'. But there are two points which tell against this way of interpreting the text.

First, whatever the phrase *carmen. . .dicere* may have meant to Pliny, it is indisputable that the earliest 'commentator' on the text, Tertullian in his reference to it in *Apol.* II, 6, believed that a hymnic composition was intended,[6] as his use of the verb *canere*

---

[1] It is criticized by C. F. D. Moule, 'A reconsideration of the context of Maranatha', *NTS*, VI (1960), 307–10 and in the same author's *Worship in the New Testament* (1961), pp. 43 f.

[2] Review of Dölger's *Sol Salutis*[1] in *Theol. Revue*, XX (1921), 183.

[3] Eusebius,[2] *H.E.* III, xxxiii, 1–3.

[4] *Sol Salutis*[2], p. 117.

[5] This conclusion is accepted by most translators and by J. Quasten, 'Carmen', *RAC* II, 907; *carmen* is no magical formula, but a composition directed to Christ as God; D. M. Stanley, 'Carmenque Christo quasi Deo dicere', *CBQ*, XX (1958), 173–91, writes, 'The. . .phrase *carmen* etc., which might seem to suggest choral recitation of the psalter, undoubtedly is an attempt to express the liturgical practice of community hymn-singing' (176).

[6] As Dölger observes, *Sol Salutis*, p. 124, n. 4.

7

shows in his transcription *ad canendum Christo ut deo*.[1] And the meaning of *canere* is shown by the use he makes of the same verb in *Apol.* xxxix. Moreover, the same writer uses *carmen* of a hymn in *de Orat.* xxvii, and gives further references to Christian psalmody in *ad Uxor.* ii, 8 and *Exhort. ad Cast.* x.

The witness of Eusebius is unequivocal also in the account he gives, in dependence upon Tertullian, of the descriptions of Christian worship in Pliny's letter, although it appears that the historian is simply relating what he has learnt from Tertullian and does not know the Pliny text at first hand.[2]

The second method of finding out the precise connotation of the words *carmen...dicere* is one which has been strangely overlooked. This is the enquiry into the usage in Latin authors. The chief authority here is Horace who uses the noun and the verb on two occasions. In *Carmen saeculare*, line 8: *Dicere carmen*; and *Odes*, iv, xii, lines 9, 10:

> Dicunt in tenero gramine pinguium
> Custodes ovium carmina fistula

the phrase is employed; and in both instances the meaning is 'to sing a song to the gods'.

The usage of the phrase in Latin and the later Christian comment upon the text endorse the conviction of those writers who wish to see in the description of early Christian worship an allusion to a hymn to Christ. But what is perhaps of greater moment is the evidence which this text affords of the cultic practices of Christians in the second century. They evidently had it as their custom to hail their Lord Christ as cultic God;[3]

[1] See the commentary by T. H. Bindley in his edition of the *Apologeticus* (1889), p. 9. The reading *Christo et deo* is to be rejected.

[2] 'That Eusebius knew nothing of the correspondence between Trajan and Pliny except what he learnt from the Greek version of Tertullian's Apology' is the opinion of Lawlor and Oulton, *Eusebius*, ii (1928), 105.

[3] On the subject of worship offered to Jesus, cf. J. M. Nielen, *Gebet und Gottesdienst im Neuen Testament* (1937), pp. 163 ff. who concludes his discussion of the New Testament references to the worship of God and Christ with the remark: 'Therefore there is no doubt that the primitive Christian worship knew of solemn prayer to Jesus' (169). The New Testament texts (Acts vii. 59, 60; Eph. v. 19, 20; Col. iii. 16; Phil. ii. 6–11; II Cor. xii. 8; Rom. x. 12) show, he avers, that 'not only did Paul and the early Christians pray in His Name to God, but also, in the strict sense, prayed to him in person as to God'

to set Him at the centre of their worship as they brought homage to Him; and to do so in a way—by the offering of a *carmen* to Him—which became a regular feature of later Christian worship, as Tertullian, Eusebius and Clement of Alexandria confirm.[1] In addition to the references to Christological hymns which are given by these authors, there are sections of sub-Apostolic literature which read as though they were hymnic in form. The most notable instances are in the writings of Ignatius and in the *Didache*.

II. REFERENCES TO HYMNIC FORMS IN SUB-APOSTOLIC LITERATURE

(i) As far as the *Didache* is concerned, there is no record of Christian hymnody attested. The one place where hymnic forms have been traced is the Eucharistic prayers of chapters ix–x.[2] The language of these prayers is exalted and hieratic, with doxological ascriptions of praise (in ix. 2, 3 and 4; x. 2, 4 and 5). There is also the possibility that x. 6 may contain a dialogue which stands as a frontispiece to a Eucharistic service. The motif of these chapters is thanksgiving to God on the occasion of some special Church gathering; and the ministry of 'prophets' (x. 7) is spoken of in this connection.

(167). This is 'New Testament evidence for Pliny's Christo quasi Deo' (168). But an invocation of God *through* or *in the name of* Christ is also found, thus safeguarding the worship of the Church from degenerating into the worship of a Hellenistic cult-deity (I Cor. viii. 5, 6). There is no suspicion that Christ is a δεύτερος θεός or a rival of the one God. Cf. C. F. D. Moule, *Worship in the New Testament* (1961), 70–3; G. Delling, *Worship in the New Testament* (E.T. 1962), pp. 117 ff.

[1] Tertullian, *ad Uxor.* II, 8: 'chant to their Lord'; Eusebius, *H.E.* v, xxviii, 5: 'all the psalms or songs (ψαλμοί...ᾠδαί) written from the beginning by faithful brethren, which celebrate (ὑμνοῦσι) the Logos of God, even Christ, and speak of him as God (θεολογοῦντες)'; Clement Alex. *Strom.* VII, vii, 49. Cf. Origen, *contra Celsum* VII, 67 and Socrates, *H.E.* VI, 8.

[2] The case for regarding chapters ix and x as containing both *Agape* and Eucharistic prayers, the opening liturgy of the Eucharist being marked at x. 6, is stated with cogency by M. Dibelius, 'Die Mahl-Gebete der Didache', *ZNTW*, XXXVII (1938), 32–41; and is accepted by J. Jeremias, *The Eucharistic Words of Jesus* (E.T. 1955), pp. 84 f. But the most recent commentator on the *Didache*, J.-P. Audet, *La Didachè: instructions des Apôtres* (1958), pp. 410 ff. thinks that the prayers relate to a special service, preliminary to the 'eucharistie majeure' in ch. xiv.

These facts led E. Peterson[1] to suggest that the Thanksgiving prayers in the chapters are part of a Christ-hymn used by Christians of Jewish extraction in Palestine, which was later incorporated into the Eucharistic liturgy. But whether these verses contain the lines of a Christological hymn as distinct from the utterances of a rhythmical prayer in elevated and ceremonial language may be doubted.

(ii) In his letter to the *Ephesians* IV, Ignatius has a highly rhetorical passage in which he appeals for the unity of the Church on the basis of obedience to the bishop, on the part of both presbytery and people. The desiderated unity and concord are likened to the principle of harmony in music. The presbyters are in tune with the bishop as the strings to a harp. The people are encouraged to follow this example and to form a united choir which, 'being harmoniously in concord', will receive the 'key of God in unison, and sing with one voice through Jesus Christ to the Father'. Indeed, when the Church attains to concord and harmonious love, 'Jesus Christ is being sung'.

The use of technical musical expressions[2] and the mention of Jesus Christ as both the object and the medium of Divine worship seem to show clearly that Ignatius is drawing upon some well-known features of Christian public worship in his day.[3]

But these allusions to practices of Christian worship remain obscure; and there is no passage in which Ignatius says explicitly that he is quoting a Christian hymn. Nevertheless, there are

[1] 'Didache cap. 9 e 10', *Ephem. litur.* 58 (1944), 3–13 (not accessible, but referred to by J. A. Kleist, in volume VI of *Ancient Christian Writers* (1957 ed.), p. 153).

[2] The words ὁμόνοια, σύμφωνος and χρῶμα are examples of a technical vocabulary in *Eph.* IV, 1–2. Cf. Dölger, *Sol Salutis*, p. 127.

[3] The words διὰ τοῦτο ἐν τῇ ὁμονοίᾳ ὑμῶν καὶ συμφώνῳ ἀγάπῃ 'Ιησοῦς Χριστὸς ᾄδεται seem to point to the practice of offering a religious song to Christ. This is the inference drawn by J. Kroll, *Die christliche Hymnodik bis zu Klemens von Alexandreia* (1921), p. 19: 'Ignatius has undoubtedly in mind in his exhortation the worship of Christians. Praise to Christ and to the Father constitutes the essence of divine worship.' Similarly, W. Bauer, *Die apostolischen Väter* II (*HzNT*, 1920), 204: 'The phrase 'Ιησοῦς Χριστὸς ᾄδεται proves, by its unusual form, the Church's custom of hymnic praise to Jesus Christ.' Casel, *Theol. Revue*, XX (1921), 184 disputes this interpretation, arguing that ᾄδεται is purely metaphorical, called forth by the words συμφώνῳ ἀγάπῃ. More recently, H. Schlier, *Die Verkündigung im Gottesdienst der Kirche* (1953), pp. 48, 49 has suggested that Ignatius' references show that he was acquainted with the Pauline *Gemeindeversammlung* in the canonical Ephesians v. 15–21.

parts of his letters where the literary style is elevated and poetic, and where the words may be arranged into regular lines and couplets, and, in one notable instance, the lines may be set into strophes. This is the 'Song of the Star' (*Ephesians* xix, 2, 3).[1] The theme is that 'the Incarnation marked the overthrow of the reign of those malign powers which ruled men from the stars, holding the superstitious in the iron chains of Fate. The coming of Christ released mankind from the debasing fears of astrology and magic.'[2] The most plausible 'Form-analysis' is that suggested by E. Lohmeyer who divided the lines into six strophes as a 'Christ-hymn',[3] improving upon C. F. Burney's earlier attempt to arrange them into four strophes on the basis of the Syriac.[4] The resultant analysis produces the following:

A star shone in heaven
Beyond all the stars,
And its light was unspeakable,
And its newness caused astonishment;

And all the other stars,
With the sun and the moon,
Gathered in chorus round the star.

It far exceeded them all in its light;
And there was perplexity:
Whence came this new thing, so unlike them?

By this all magic was dissolved,
And every bond of wickedness vanished away;
Ignorance was removed.

The old kingdom was destroyed,
For God was manifest as man
For the newness of eternal life.

And a beginning was received
Of that which had been prepared by God.
Hence all things were disturbed,
Because the abolition of death was planned.

[1] Cf. Virginia Corwen, *St Ignatius and Christianity in Antioch* (1960), pp. 176 ff. and H.-W. Bartsch's full exposition of chapter xix in his *Gnostisches Gut und Gemeindetradition bei Ignatius von Antiochien* (1940), pp. 133–59 in which he seeks to distinguish between the Church tradition and a Redeemer-myth which Ignatius has fused together (156–8).

[2] J. Lawson, *A Theological and Historical Introduction to the Apostolic Fathers* (1961), p. 118.

[3] *Kyrios Jesus: Eine Untersuchung zu Phil. 2, 5–11*, 1928 (reprint 1961), p. 64.

[4] *The Aramaic Origin of the Fourth Gospel* (1926), pp. 161 ff.

The meaning of this strange composition—as far as we can understand it—will concern us at a later stage; its immediate interest lies in its existence as a specimen of early Christian hymnody. Admittedly we cannot say whether this composition was set to music and sung. There are no metrical standards available at this point in the development of Christian worship.[1] Metrical verses came later;[2] and it is only in the third century that we have examples of anapaestic metre and musical notation.[3] The criteria which are available are stylistic tests, of which the most obvious traits are: a certain rhythmical lilt ascertainable when the passage is read aloud, a correspondence between words and phrases which are placed in the sentences in an obviously carefully selected position, not always *ad sensum*; the use of *parallelismus membrorum* (i.e. an arrangement into couplets); and traces of a rudimentary metre and the employ-

---

[1] On the development of music in Christian worship cf. E. Jammers, 'Christliche Liturgie', *RGG³*, IV, cols. 407, 408. J. Quasten, *Musik und Gesang in den Kulten der heidnischen Antike und christlichen Frühzeit* (1930), p. 103 writes: 'For the first two centuries the evidence for the lyrical and musical formation of divine worship is slender.'

[2] Cf. *Oxyrh. Pap.* xv, 1786:

ὁμοῦ πᾶσαί τε θεοῦ λόγιμοι
α...αρ...π(ρ)υτανήω σιγάτω
μηδ' ἄστρα φαεσφόρα λ(ειπ)έ-
[σ]θων...ποταμῶν ῥοθίων
πᾶσαι ὑμνούντων δι' ἡμῶν πα-
τέρα χ' υἱὸν χ' ἅγιον πνεῦμα
πᾶσαι δυνάμεις ἐπιφωνούντων
ἀμὴν ἀμὴν ἀμὴν κράτος αἶνος
δωτῆρι μόνῳ πάντων ἀγαθῶν
ἀμὴν ἀμήν

This papyrus is dated by B. P. Grenfell and A. S. Hunt in the late third century (*The Oxyrhynchus Papyri*, Part xv, 1922, 21–5). The metre is purely quantitative and uninfluenced by accent, while the rhythm is anapaestic in a series of dimeters. It has special importance as being 'by far the most ancient piece of Church music extant' (Grenfell and Hunt, *op. cit.*)—a verdict in which Quasten concurs: 'das älteste datierbare Stück christlicher Kirchenmusik, das wir besitzen' (*op. cit.* 100).

[3] A. B. Macdonald, *Christian Worship in the Primitive Church* (1934), p. 118 traces this to Ambrose's introduction of what we understand by congregational hymns. The references to Ambrose are supplied by Kroll, *Die christliche Hymnodik*, p. 8 and discussed by C. W. Dugmore, *The Influence of the Synagogue upon the Divine Office* (1944), pp. 98 ff.

ment of rhetorical devices such as *homoeoteleuton,* alliteration, antithesis and *chiasmus.*

The detection of this passage in Ignatius as poetic and lyrical in form, and its isolation from the epistolary context in which it stands as a Christ-hymn, raise the issue which is the *raison d'être* of our present study. So far our concern has been with the Christian literature of the second century; and we have noticed certain allusions—sometimes veiled, sometimes explicit—to the practice of hymnody in Christian worship. May we not press back into the first century and examine the literature of the New Testament in the hope of detecting both allusions to, and examples of, early Christian *carmina?*[1] This is the spirit and the aim of our enquiry.

The word 'detect' was used earlier; and this is an appropriate term to use, for we are to be taken up with the task of literary detection. But detection of this nature must have not only the evidence before it, but also some clues to assist and to encourage. Before we address ourselves to the major undertaking of New Testament research in this field, one excellent clue is to be noticed. In his *Apology,* Tertullian gives in chapter XXXIX a full description of the Christian assembly *(curia).* In the course of this account he writes: 'After washing of hands and bringing in of lights, each is asked to stand forth and sing *(canere),* as he can, a hymn to God, either one from the holy scriptures or one of his own composing.'

Our study will be concerned to sift the data of the New Testament and to examine the cultic setting of such references as there are to Christian *carmina*—especially Christological hymns —in the Apostolic Church. Pressing backwards from the age of the sub-Apostolic period and of the literature of the early Church fathers we shall attempt to investigate those hymnic forms in a period when hymns and canticles 'from the holy scriptures' came into existence as the compositions of the men and women of the New Testament Church.

[1] An older collection of those New Testament texts which may conceivably be regarded as liturgical is to be found in F. Cabrol and H. Leclerq, *Monumenta ecclesiae liturgica: Reliquiae liturgicae vetustissimae,* Part I (1900), 1–51. But this list would need some drastic revision if cognizance were taken of New Testament studies in the last sixty years.

CHAPTER I

TRACES OF CARMINA IN THE
NEW TESTAMENT

A. BACKGROUND TO NEW TESTAMENT HYMNOLOGY

That the Christian mesage should appear on the scene of history attended by an upsurge of spiritual fervour and power is what we might expect in view of the claim which the New Testament makes that in such a message God is visiting His people. And that this spiritual energy, newly released by the Pentecostal Spirit, should find expression in songs of praise is again a natural consequence.

But Christian song did not break forth upon a world which had hitherto been dumb and in which hymns were unknown. The Church was cradled in Judaism, and borrowed many of its forms and patterns of worship from the worship of the Temple and synagogue. There is some doubt as to the extent to which the singing of divine praises had developed in the Palestinian synagogues in the first century A.D. It is probable that the synagogues of the Dispersion were more advanced in the use of psalmody than their more conservative brethren. But there can be no doubt that the early believers in Jesus inherited the desire to express their gratitude to God in the offering of vocal praise, as their use of the Psalter in the early prayers in Acts and the references in Colossians iii. 16, Ephesians v. 19 and James v. 13b show. The canticles of the Nativity in Luke i–ii have a distinct Old Testament colouring as they look back to the best hopes and fervent aspirations of the Old Testament saints; and forward to the proximate fulfilment of God's redeeming purpose in the coming of the Messianic herald, John the Baptist, and the dawn of the new age of emancipation.

Another preparation of a different order was going on in the pre-Christian centuries. The world into which Christ came was a world of intense religious questings (Acts xvii. 22) which had known for centuries how to sing hymns to the Greek deities. Many of these hymnic compositions contain elevated thoughts and worthy aspirations (e.g. Cleanthes' *Hymn to Zeus*) and their style set a pattern which was to become familiar in Greek-speaking Christianity. But there is a gulf set between the religious ideas of pagan and Christian hymnology.

Christian hymns stand in relation to both Jewish antecedents and Greek examples as the fulfilment stands to the longing which precedes it. That which explains the transition is the Gospel of God. This brings with it to the Church the awareness of living in the decisive hour of human history wherein God has visited and redeemed humanity. It is this feature which is the key to the newness of the songs which the New Testament Church sings (Apoc. v. 9; xxi. 1–5). Because the New Testament claims to be the record of the divine interposition into history of Christ and of the human response thereto, it would be singular indeed if no voices of praise and acknowledgment proclaimed that event.

B. ENCOURAGEMENTS FOR THE STUDY OF NEW TESTAMENT HYMNS

When we turn to enquire whether there are any definite examples of Christian hymns in the New Testament, we are encouraged in this quest by certain verses which tell us of the existence of such hymns. These clues are given in I Corinthians xiv. 26; Colossians iii. 16 and Ephesians v. 19, 20. But the evidence is more broadly-based than these few verses would imply. It is a conclusion of modern Biblical study that the documents of the New Testament have their setting in the worshipping life of the Churches. Much of what forms the New Testament was written to be read at the assembling of Christians for worship and instruction (Col. iv. 16; I Thess. v. 27; Apoc. xxii. 16). This understanding of the genesis and form of the literature should prompt us to ask whether hymnic pieces are embedded in the Epistles in particular; and if so, whether they may be detected and classified.

Certain criteria are proposed for this task. These include the presence of introductory formulas (as in Eph. v. 14; I Tim. iii. 16); the use of a rhythmical style and an unusual vocabulary which are different from the style and language of the surrounding context of the letter in which the verses appear; the presence of theological concepts (especially Christological doctrines) which are expressed in language which is exalted and liturgical; and the setting of certain passages in a cultic *milieu* (for example, the baptismal motifs are clear in Eph. v. 14).

C. CLASSIFICATION OF NEW TESTAMENT HYMNS

A number of putative hymns have been located, but no attempt has been made to place them in families. The following classification may, therefore, be suggested:

(i)   the Lukan canticles;
(ii) hymns in the Apocalypse;
(iii) Jewish-Christian fragments and ejaculations ('Amēn, Hallelû-jah, Hôša'nā, Mārānâ thâ, 'Abbâ);
(iv) distinctively Christian forms.

The fourth section may be subdivided. But this classification is not rigid; and examples tend to overspill from one category into another. Any one hymn may be classified in more than one way:

(*a*) sacramental (Eph. v. 14; Tit. iii. 4–7); (with hesitation Rom. vi. 1–11; Eph. ii. 19–22);
(*b*) meditative (Eph. i. 3–14; Rom. viii. 31–9; I Cor. xiii);
(*c*) confessional (I Tim. vi. 11–16; II Tim. ii. 11–13);
(*d*) Christological (Heb. i. 3; Col. i. 15–20; I Tim. iii. 16; John i. 1–14; I Pet. i. 18–21, ii. 21–5; iii. 18–21; Phil. ii. 6–11).

D. THE MEANING OF THE CHRIST-HYMNS

(i) *Form*

All these texts may be set out (with varying degrees of plausibility and success) in verse-form and in stanzas, showing evidence of a rudimentary rhythm and—in some cases—even rhyme. This feature is natural, for when Christians write and speak about their Lord, their thoughts will tend to be expressed in lyrical terms. Religious speech tends to be poetic in form; and meditation upon the person and place of Jesus Christ in the Church's cultic life is not expressed in a cold, calculating way, but becomes rhapsodic and ornate. This fact should prepare for the correct elucidation of some of the key-terms which the hymns contain.

(ii) *Content*

Certain Christological themes run through these verses. The main examples are the pre-existence of Christ and His pretemporal activity; the concept of the Servant; and His rôle as cosmological Lord who receives the homage of all the orders of creation in heaven, earth and the underworld. The redemption which Christ achieves according to these hymns is set in a cosmic context; and His person is viewed in relation to that work.

Both these features are clearly to be seen in Philippians ii. 6–11, a passage in the Pauline corpus to which the remainder of our study will be devoted.

E. PHILIPPIANS II. 6–11 IN RECENT STUDY

'This section belongs to the most difficult passages of the Pauline letters', comments E. Lohmeyer in the introductory sentence of his commentary on these verses.[1] In this estimate Lohmeyer is but re-echoing the sentiments of many scholars who have addressed themselves to the task of elucidating this passage.[2] And there appears to be no interruption in the flow of scholarly literature which this section of six verses has called forth. If A. B. Bruce in 1876 could write of the diversity of opinion as 'enough to fill the student with despair, and to afflict him with intellectual paralysis',[3] that sombre appraisal of the situation is even more confirmed in 1967. For a task which begins with an attempt at the exegesis of some few verses quickly takes on the proportion of the exploration of an entire library of research. Karl Bornhäuser's observation is a sober assessment of the situation: 'When one has gathered what has been written and issued (on these verses), one has a library';[4] while T. Arvedson,

---

[1] E. Lohmeyer, *Der Brief an die Philipper*[10] (*MeyerKomm.*) (1930 = 1953, ed. W. Schmauch), p. 90.

[2] Thus, for example, H. Schumacher opens his massive exposition of *Christus in seiner Präexistenz und Kenose nach Phil. 2, 5–8*, Part I (1914), 1 by remarking that 'the Christological reference in Phil. 2, 5–11 is not only the most interesting, but also the most difficult, in the entire New Testament'; and quotes earlier scholars who have concurred that 'it is the mystery *par excellence* of New Testament interpretation'.

[3] *The Humiliation of Christ* (1876, = 1955 reprint), p. 8.

[4] *Jesus Imperator Mundi* (1938), p. 15.

commenting on the same feature, states that 'a whole literature has grown up around these verses'.[1]

Yet the Pauline text induces a fascination which invites the attempt to study it closely. The passage is important for its own sake, as expressing the quintessence of Pauline thought on the Person of Christ.[2] Nonetheless, it is true to say that the importance of Philippians ii. 6–11 is appreciated, in more recent study, not simply for its own sake, but because it represents a type of Christian literature which has been detected and classified as 'cultic' or 'confessional'.[3] The verses are best described as a piece of early Christian kerygmatic confession which found a place in the cultus of the primitive Church[4]—although this conclusion anticipates the results of the pages which follow. The Christological significance of Philippians ii. 6–11 has always been recognized and stressed by exegetes. Within the last sixty years or so—and it is this period of time which delimits the phrase 'in recent interpretation'—a new understanding has been sought as scholars have endeavoured to place the section in the cultic life of the early Church.[5] It has been treated—for reasons which are to be investigated shortly—as a *carmen Christi*, a Christological ode, devoted to the praise of the Church's Lord and hailing Him in confession and worship as *Maran-Jesus*. If *carmen Christi* is a true description, it presupposes a cultus,[6] i.e. a clearly defined religious devotion on the part of the

[1] 'Phil. 2, 6 und Mt. 10, 39', *ST*, v, i–ii (1951), 49–51.

[2] 'The amplest and most deliberate of all St Paul's declarations on the theme' declares H. R. Mackintosh, *The Doctrine of the Person of Jesus Christ* (1913), p. 66.

[3] On this section as a confession, cf. A. Seeberg, *Der Katechismus der Urchristenheit* (1903), pp. 181, 182.

[4] Nothing has 'been more characteristic of recent research than the gradual detection of early kerygmatic fragments in the New Testament, in which the original eschatological meaning of the christological titles used in the *kerygma* is still apparent, and is clearly distinct from their later metaphysical use' (J. M. Robinson, *A New Quest of the Historical Jesus* (1959), pp. 111, 112, quoting Philippians ii. 5–11 as illustration).

[5] A. M. Hunter, *Paul and his Predecessors*[2] (1961), p. 82.

[6] See W. Morgan, *The Nature and Right of Religion* (1926), pp. 181 f. on the meaning of this: 'That Jesus is the Kyrios means much more than the possession of moral authority and leadership. It means on the one hand that He is Divine being, a god; and on the other that He is subordinate to the supreme God...He exercises, in fact, all the functions of Deity. And believers claim

early believers which centred upon Him as Lord and which drew its inspiration from His living presence in their midst. Modern studies have shown that hymn and creed are not rigidly separated in the New Testament.[1] It is also of some importance for us to notice that the endeavour to place the passage in the worshipping life of the Christian community has led to an understanding of Philippians ii. 6–11 as a Christological confession.[2] The Church which sings this hymn thereby proclaims her faith in her Lord as pre-existent, incarnate and exalted; and it is this expression of the 'states of Christ' (in Jeremias' phrase[3]) which gives an added importance to the passage. For the first time, in extant Christian literature, we meet a clear formulation of these three 'epochs' in the existence of the Church's Lord. He is hailed and confessed as pre-existent (in the form of God), incarnate and humiliated (as taking the form of a servant) and

for Him and render to Him the religious homage proper to Deity. Prayers are directed to Him and baptism administered in His name. That a few years after the Crucifixion there was in operation a fully developed cult in which Christ was worshipped as a God no one now disputes.'

[1] Some of the evidence is given by the present writer in *Worship in the Early Church*, chs. 4 and 5.

[2] Lohmeyer, *Kyrios Jesus*, describes it as 'the so-called *locus classicus* of Pauline and early Christian Christology' (pp. 4, 89).

[3] J. Jeremias, 'Zur Gedankenführung in den paulinischen Briefen: Der Christushymnus', *Studia Paulina in honorem J. de Zwaan*, ed. J. N. Sevenster and W. C. van Unnik (1953), p. 154: 'drei Seinsweisen Christi'. This description of the 'three states' covered by the passage depends for its aptness on Jeremias' attempted Form-analysis. In this he strikes a new line inasmuch as previous writers were content simply to see in the section of *vv*. 5–11 a twofold status of Christ. As H. Lietzmann put it, Phil. ii. 5–11 is 'the classical mould' (*die klassische Ausprägung*) for the later scheme (which he finds in Hippolytus and the *Apostolic Constitutions*) of 'Humiliation–Exaltation: Suffering–Resurrection' ('Symbolstudien', *ZNTW*, xxii (1923), 265), with canonical examples in Romans i. 3; II Timothy ii. 8; I Corinthians xv. 3 ff.; I Peter iii. 18–22; and later in Ignatius, *Eph.* xvii, 2; *Trall.* ix; *Smyr.* i, 1–2. R. Bultmann, *Theology of the New Testament*, ii (E.T. 1955), 155 f. has also detected the threefold pattern—of 'the incarnation of the pre-existent one, the cross, and the exaltation' (156)—in Philippians ii. 6–11. Furthermore, he discovers a similar linking together of the three themes of pre-existence, incarnation and exaltation in I Peter by adding i. 20 to the hymnic creed of iii. 18, 22. E. Lohmeyer, *Die Offenbarung des Johannes*[2] (*HzNT*, 1953), comments on Apoc. i. 18 that this verse pictures the 'drei Stadien des Daseins Christi: sein Leben in Gott, seinen Tod auf der Erde, seine Erhöhung zum ewigen Leben und Weltenrichter'.

triumphant (as exalted by the Father and receiving the homage of all orders of creation). Philippians ii. 6–11, Jeremias declares, 'is the oldest evidence for the teaching concerning the three states of Christ's existence which underlies and delimits the whole Christology of later times'.[1]

With these prolegomena our study proceeds to consider the Philippians passage in the light of modern interpretation. Some preliminary chapters will deal with its literary character (i.e. whether and to what extent it is hymnic in form); its authorship (i.e. whether it is Apostolic or pre-Pauline); and its setting in the pastoral context of the letter to the Philippian Church (i.e. whether it sets forth Christ as an ethical example for the believers to imitate, as the traditional view maintains) and its treatment by modern scholarship. In this last-mentioned part we shall consider some of the main interpretations which have been offered in the present century.

This preparatory investigation will set the stage for an exegetical enquiry into the meaning of the text; and the words and sentences of the passage will be discussed *seriatim* in the light of modern research.

---

[1] *Studia Paulina*, p. 154.

CHAPTER II

PHILIPPIANS II. 5–11: ITS LITERARY FORM[1]

A. SOME INDICATIONS BY OLDER WRITERS

It is a singular fact that it was not until the beginning of the twentieth century that the unusual literary character of Philippians ii. 5–11 was detected and classified. Johannes Weiss first recognized the poetic, stately and rhythmical genre, and arranged the verses into two main strophes, of four lines each. He drew attention to 'der vorhandene Rhythmus', noting that the four clauses of verses 6–8 are balanced by the four clauses of verses 9–11.[2]

(1) ὃς ἐν μορφῇ θεοῦ...	(1) διὸ καὶ...
(2) ἀλλὰ...	(2) καὶ ἐχαρίσατο...
(3) ἐν ὁμοιώματι...	(3) ἵνα ἐν τῷ ὀνόματι...
(4) ἐταπείνωσεν...	(4) καὶ πᾶσα γλῶσσα...

This arrangement was followed by that of Adolf Deissmann who divided the section into two main stanzas of seven lines, in full recognition of its poetic character.[3]

Later writers have accepted one or other of these proposals. For example, A. T. Robertson in America accepted the versified scheme of Weiss, conceding that 'the words are balanced with rhetorical rhythm', with two strophes of four lines each;[4] and J. Moffatt in Britain also accepted the same conclusion about the

---

[1] This chapter reproduces, with some modification, the author's contribution in *Studia Evangelica*, II (ed. F. L. Cross), *TU* 87 (1964), 611–20.

[2] J. Weiss in *TLZ*, IX (1899), 263; and similarly in the collected works *Studien J. B. Weiss* (Göttingen, 1897), pp. 190 f. (*Beiträge zur paulinischen Rhetorik* (1897), pp. 28, 29).

[3] *Paulus*[2] (1925), pp. 149 f. (E.T. *St Paul* (1912), pp. 169 f.). C. Guignebert, 'Quelques Remarques d'exégèse sur Phil. 2. 6–11', *RHPR*, III (1923), 533, commented on the psalm-like appearance of the passage and its place in Christian worship.

[4] *Paul's Joy in Christ* (1917), p. 123 (later edition, n.d., p. 69).

literary structure of the passage.[1] In recent times, K. Grayston[2] has reproduced the pattern which was first described by Deissmann.

A hint that the hymnic character of the verses was being recognized was given in a discussion of the passage by H. Lietzmann. He has a chapter, in his monumental study of the Eucharist,[3] on the antecedents of the Eucharistic prayer in Hippolytus, and refers to the evidence of the Pauline literature to supply him with a canonical model. He writes: 'The characteristic feature of this Hippolytan preface is the thanksgiving—a term derived from the preface which reads—εὐχαριστοῦμέν σοι, ὁ Θεός—in the form of a "Christological Hymn", for what God has given the Church through Christ. Such confessions of Christ in the form of hymns are frequent in Pauline writings. In Philippians ii. 5–11 there rings out with striking force the hymn of him who was equal with God and became obedient unto the death of the cross, whom God highly exalted to be Lord, before whom all things bow, in heaven, in earth, and under the earth.' Lietzmann then proceeds to set down the lines of verses 5–11 in seventeen lines, but with no attempt to analyse further the poetic structure or to versify the whole.

B. ERNST LOHMEYER'S ANALYSIS

E. Lohmeyer made his important contribution, in an epoch-making study of the passage in 1928,[4] on the assumption that what we have in these verses is a Christological hymn set in rhythmical form and composed of six strophes, each with three lines. It is 'ein carmen Christi in strengem Sinne'.[5] He thus improved on Lietzmann's earlier arrangement in two ways.[6]

---

[1] An Introduction to the Literature of the New Testament[3] (1918), pp. 167 f. and earlier, p. 57.

[2] The Epistles of Paul to the Galatians and Philippians (1957), pp. 91, 92.

[3] Messe und Herrenmahl, p. 178 (E.T. Mass and Lord's Supper, Fasc. IV, p. 145). Another arrangement, manifestly based on Lietzmann's work, divides the hymn into eleven uneven lines. This appears in Andreas Duhm's Gottesdienst im ältesten Christentum (1928), pp. 23, 24.

[4] Kyrios Jesus. [5] Lohmeyer, op. cit. p. 7.

[6] Most of these points are taken from Lohmeyer's opening section, op. cit. 4–13; but his commentary, Der Brief an die Philipper[10] (MeyerKomm.) (1930) ad loc. has also been consulted.

First, he separated, in verse 6, the phrase τὸ εἶναι ἴσα Θεῷ from the preceding verb and made it a separate line; and also detached τὸ ὄνομα τὸ ὑπὲρ πᾶν ὄνομα from the foregoing words of the line, in verse 9, and so turned the phrase into a new line.

Secondly, this led to the possibility of setting down the lines in versified form with a strophic symmetry and regularity which Lietzmann's version lacked. But this harmony which Lohmeyer sought and of which he spoke in the sentence, 'each strophe has lines of approximately the same length', was not secured without some cost; for he goes on to say that there is an apparent exception in the last stichos of the third stanza. This line—θανάτου δὲ σταυροῦ—must be deleted from the original version of the hymn as a Pauline gloss, added by the Apostle as an interpretative comment for the sake of the Philippian Church.

With Lohmeyer's study other features in the literary analysis of the passage came into prominence. These may be tabulated:

(*a*) He acutely detected that the verses formed a self-contained unity. There are two reasons why this may be affirmed. First, the hymn possesses an introductory formula (ὁ καὶ ἐν Χριστῷ Ἰησοῦ) which Lohmeyer takes to mean 'a sort of formula of citation',[1] as though the writer were preparing his readers for a quotation. It would be the near equivalent of our literary device of using a phrase like 'As such-and-such an authority says. . .' to preface a statement. In the second place, he notes that the theme of the hymn begins with God in eternity, and concludes with the same thought. It is no snatch of liturgical writing, incomplete in itself or quoted in part.[2]

(*b*) It has every appearance of being a studied composition

---

[1] In *v.* 5 the preposition, according to Lohmeyer, carries a paradigmatic meaning, corresponding to the Hebrew בְּ which is used (e.g. in the Mishnah, tractate *'Aboth* iii. 7: 'it is written in David': cf. Rom. xi. 2; Heb. iv. 7) to introduce an authoritative quotation. So in Phil. ii. 5 it paves the way for the hymn in which the example of Christ is made authoritative for the Philippian community. E. Käsemann, 'Kritische Analyse von Phil. 2, 5–11', in his *Exegetische Versuche und Besinnung*, vol. 1 (1960), 91, has characterized this interpretation as Lohmeyer's taking a wrong turning. The reasons for this criticism will appear later, p. 85.

[2] So Lohmeyer, *Kyrios Jesus*, p. 7; cf. P. Henry, 'Kénose', *Supplément au Dictionnaire de la Bible*, 1950, Fasc. xxiv, 7–161, who comments: 'L'hymne se clôt comme il a commencé, en Dieu' (37); and Dibelius, *An die Philipper*[3] (1937), p. 82 who notices that verses 11, 12 picture the goal to which the purposes of God are tending.

with a definite progression and climax of theme. This fact is established by a series of proofs.[1] The way in which the sentences are constructed, with such features as *anaphora* and parallelism; the positioning of the participles; the way in which it is common for the third line of the strophe to take up again the content of the first line or the first line to take up the third line of the preceding strophe; the unusual vocabulary with *hapax legomena* in full measure and the presence of terms which have a stately, liturgical and ceremonial character; the way in which the 'plan' of the hymn hinges on verse 9, as the words διὸ καί exactly divide the piece into two equal parts—all these points cannot be incidental or accidental. Rather they betray the work of an author of a carefully composed portion of ancient liturgy.[2]

(*c*) The linguistic and stylistic evidence goes to show that the hymn was both pre-Pauline and a product of a Jewish-Christian community. There are features which make it likely that it was composed first in a Semitic tongue and later translated into Greek.[3] Traits of style which are 'impossible' in Greek; phrases which appear to be simply 'translation equivalents' from a Semitic language into Greek; and the use of words and expressions which are drawn directly from the Old Testament[4]—all these facts indicate the Semitic provenance of the hymn in its putative original form; and the best description of the section, Lohmeyer declares, is that it is a Judaeo-Christian psalm.

(*d*) Then follows a surprising conclusion in Lohmeyer's patient analysis. The early Jewish-Christian community which is credited with the composing of the hymn is located in Jerusalem; and Lohmeyer further submits, with an apparent *tour de force* which has not met with much favour from succeeding scholars,

---

[1] Appendix to this chapter (pp. 38 ff.).

[2] Lohmeyer concludes: 'daß hier nicht ein Stück gewöhnlicher brieflicher Rede, auch nicht eine rhetorisch gesteigerte Prosa, sondern ein sorgsam komponiertes und bis in alle Einzelheiten hinein abgewogenes strophisches Gebilde, ein carmen Christi in strengem Sinne vorliegt' (*Kyrios Jesus*, p. 7). Similarly, Henry concludes: 'L'ensemble de ces traits révèle une composition soignée, d'une rhétorique presque recherchée' ('Kénose', 10).

[3] See appendix to this chapter (pp. 39 ff.).

[4] The instance which Lohmeyer quotes and uses as proof of this is the phrase εὑρεθεὶς ὡς ἄνθρωπος (verse 8 *a*). Not only is the construction with the participle non-Greek, but the words ὡς ἄνθρωπος thinly disguise the underlying original כברראנש, which is drawn directly from Dan. vii. 13 (*Kyrios Jesus*, pp. 39, 40).

that the ode to Christ belongs to the Eucharistic liturgy of the Jerusalem Church and was sung at the celebration of the Lord's Supper in that early community.[1]

If we except the final conclusion, we may say that Lohmeyer erected landmarks which subsequent study has largely confirmed. To him belongs the credit of the first detailed analysis of the verses and of general observations on the stylistic features which have orientated later study in a new direction altogether. As Ernst Käsemann puts it, somewhat drily, 'Lohmeyer's works do mark a turning-point insofar as they lift us out of the old ruts, and therefore have forced "the exegetical fraternity" and their usual readers to face new and suggestive questions'.[2] As far as Form-analysis is concerned, Lohmeyer's treatment has shown the poetic and hymnic form of the passage, and has produced the linguistic evidence to support his main contentions.

Since 1928 there has been no attempt to reverse the description of the verses as a liturgical composition. It has become a *sententia recepta* of literary criticism that Philippians ii. 6–11 is clearly to be distinguished from the neighbouring verses of the Epistle; and its language and style must be treated as totally unlike the language and style of epistolary prose.[3] The latest

---

[1] This hypothesis of the Eucharistic setting of the hymn was anticipated by Lietzmann, 'Symbolstudien', *ZNTW*, xxii (1923), 265. Cf. his assessment of 'the liturgical character' of Phil. ii in *The Founding of the Church Universal* (E.T.[2] 1950), p. 107; it 'was employed especially in working out the form of prayer used at the eucharistic Lord's Supper, when the assembled Church expressed its thanks, through the lips of the priest, for Christ's incarnation and act of redemption'.   [2] 'Kritische Analyse', 53.

[3] Of the twelve criteria of credal formulas in the New Testament suggested by E. Stauffer, *New Testament Theology* (E.T. 1955), Appendix III, the following are to be noted as applicable to Philippians ii. 5–11: (a) A different linguistic usage, terminology and stylistic form from its context are apparent. The ceremonial character of the section with its artistic structure, rhythmical style and well-formed phrases (e.g. τὸ εἶναι ἴσα Θεῷ) stands out in vivid contrast to the narrative style of the surrounding verses. (b) What Stauffer calls the 'monumental stylistic construction' of the confessional formulas is evident in the passage. The antithetic construction of the whole hymn dividing into two contrasting halves is the most obvious point. This feature is strengthened by such rhetorical devices as *chiasmus* in, e.g., vv. 7, 8:

ἀλλὰ ἑαυτὸν ἐκένωσεν
ἐταπείνωσεν ἑαυτόν

This example of chiasmus (ἐπάνοδος) is noticed by O. Michel, 'Zur Exegese von Phil. 2, 5–11', *Theologie als Glaubenswagnis*, Festschrift K. Heim (1954),

writers who have turned their attention to this Pauline text can, therefore, say without further argument, after remarking on Lohmeyer's demonstration of the hymnic character of the verses: 'This is generally acknowledged.'[1] Lohmeyer's arrangement of the text into lines and stanzas may now be set down:

I   (a) (ὅς) ἐν μορφῇ Θεοῦ ὑπάρχων
    (b) οὐχ ἁρπαγμὸν ἡγήσατο
    (c) τὸ εἶναι ἴσα Θεῷ

II (a) ἀλλὰ ἑαυτὸν ἐκένωσεν
    (b) μορφὴν δούλου λαβών
    (c) ἐν ὁμοιώματι ἀνθρώπων γενόμενος

III (a) καὶ σχήματι εὑρεθεὶς ὡς ἄνθρωπος
    (b) ἐταπείνωσεν ἑαυτόν
    (c) γενόμενος ὑπήκοος μέχρι θανάτου (θανάτου δὲ σταυροῦ)

IV (a) διὸ καὶ ὁ Θεὸς ὑπερύψωσεν αὐτόν
    (b) καὶ ἐχαρίσατο αὐτῷ
    (c) τὸ ὄνομα τὸ ὑπὲρ πᾶν ὄνομα

pp. 79–95 (82). (c) The employment of participles and relative clauses is a sign of the presence of *liturgica* in ancient religious literature, as E. Norden has demonstrated. There are five participles in a relatively small literary piece: ὑπάρχων, λαβών, γενόμενος (*bis*), εὑρεθείς, and the hymn opens with a relative pronoun (ὅς, like I Timothy iii. 16). (d) The truths of salvation-history are the theme of a credal formulation. Philippians ii. 5 ff. may be described as a record of Christ's salvation-history (*Heilsgeschichte*). Käsemann, 'Kritische Analyse', 76, has called attention to this in his words: 'All these statements are not intended to give a definition of (Christ's) nature in the sense of early Church Christology; rather they speak of events in a connected series...Christology is here being presented in the framework of soteriology' (71).

[1] J. Jervell, *Imago Dei: Gen. i. 26 f. im Spätjudentum, in der Gnosis und in den paulinischen Briefen* (1960), p. 105; and a similar assumption of the hymnic form of Phil. ii, composed of traditional material, is made by H. Conzelmann *ad* Col. i. 15 and G. Friedrich *ad* Phil. ii. 5 ff. in the latest revision of their commentary in the series *NTD*, 1962. Cf. too D. M. Stanley, 'The Theme of the Servant of Yahweh in Primitive Christian Soteriology and its transposition by St Paul', *CBQ*, xvi (1954), 420 f. and the same author's *Christ's Resurrection in Pauline Soteriology* (1961), p. 100. No effort has been made to upturn the judgment of Lohmeyer as to the form of the passage; and nothing that has been written since Lohmeyer's book appeared affects Lohmeyer's conclusions. We have in mind J. J. Müller, *The Epistles of Paul to the Philippians and to Philemon* (1955), p. 78 and W. Hendriksen, *New Testament Commentary: Exposition of Philippians* (1962), pp. 102–18.

V (a) ἵνα ἐν τῷ ὀνόματι 'Ιησοῦ
  (b) πᾶν γόνυ κάμψῃ
  (c) ἐπουρανίων καὶ ἐπιγείων καὶ καταχθονίων
VI (a) καὶ πᾶσα γλῶσσα ἐξομολογήσηται
  (b) ὅτι Κύριος 'Ιησοῦς Χριστός
  (c) εἰς δόξαν Θεοῦ πατρός

In the years from 1928 until the present day the main interest of *Formanalyse* in reference to Philippians ii has been in modification of Lohmeyer's original enterprise. At the same time there have been many who hâve been content to endorse his thesis as to the literary form of the passage,[1] while most scholars are unpersuaded by his theory of the Eucharistic *milieu*, and some unconvinced by his arguments for a pre-Pauline authorship. The chief suggestions by way of amendment of Lohmeyer's versification may be reviewed.

C. M. DIBELIUS

Dibelius registered the influence of Lohmeyer's monograph and commentary, not only in the new descriptive heading which he placed over the verses in the third edition of his commentary in the Lietzmann series,[2] but also in his criticism of the way in

[1] Among those who have accepted Lohmeyer's six-strophe arrangement we may give the following: W. K. L. Clarke, *New Testament Problems* (1929), pp. 143 f.; Hunter, *Paul and his Predecessors*², pp. 40 f., 123; and the same author's Layman's Commentary, *Galatians to Colossians* (1960), pp. 93 ff.; J. Héring, *Le Royaume de Dieu et sa venue* (1937), pp. 159 ff.; Macdonald, *Christian Worship in the Primitive Church*, p. 119; P. Benoit, *Les épîtres de S. Paul*³ (1959), pp. 26 ff.; O. Cullmann, *The Earliest Christian Confessions* (E.T. 1949), p. 22; and the same author's *The Christology of the New Testament* (E.T. 1959), pp. 174, 175; F. W. Dillistone, *Jesus Christ and his Cross* (1953), p. 103; P. Henry, 'Kénose' (1950), 9; E. Andrews, *The Meaning of Christ for Paul* (1949), p. 156. F. W. Beare, *A Commentary on the Epistle to the Philippians* (1959), pp. 73, 74, and the same author's *St Paul and his Letters* (1962), p. 130; D. M. Stanley, *Christ's Resurrection in Pauline Soteriology*, p. 96; M.-E. Boismard, *Quatre Hymnes baptismales* (1961), pp. 12, 13; A. W. Wainwright, *The Trinity in the New Testament* (1962), p. 87, who accepts Lohmeyer's suggestion of an Aramaic original, but questions whether this is necessarily pre-Pauline.

[2] *An die Thessalonicher; an die Philipper*³ (*HzNT*) (1937), *ad loc.* His second edition (1923, pp. 61 f.) reads 'Die Demut Christi...und Erniedrigung und Erhöhung'. This was replaced in the third edition by 'Der Christushymnus' (72 ff.).

which Lohmeyer arranged verses 7 and 8. Dibelius maintains that it is wrong to separate the close of verse 7 and the opening of verse 8. There should be no break between the two sentences, as Nestle's edition wrongly suggests by its punctuation with a full stop after γενόμενος. The reasons for Dibelius' observation are two. First, he notes that ὁμοιώματι (in verse 7) and σχήματι (in verse 8) are linked by similarity of sound in the final syllables (i.e. the use of the rhetorical device of *homoeoptoton*),[1] and in meaning the two phrases connote one another. This leads to the second point, that the two sentences of verses 7 and 8 are joined exegetically: 'Both lines describe solemnly the Incarnation of Christ.'[2] It is erroneous for Lohmeyer to force a distinction of meaning between them.

In his analysis, Dibelius sets down verses 6, 7 and 8*a* in seven three-accented lines. This enables him to construct the remainder of the hymn in four stanzas of three lines each. Verse 8*b* (ἐταπείνωσεν ἑαυτόν) begins a new stanza; and it marks, he says, a change both of rhythm and action in the drama. But this point is not apparent at all. Furthermore, the grouping of verses 6–8*a* into one opening strophe is cumbersome and disproportionate. His criticism of Lohmeyer's tearing asunder of verses 7 and 8 is valid; but it may be asked whether his attempt to put these verses into one unwieldy stanza is correct.

In a second way he parts company with Lohmeyer. This is in his acceptance of the line θανάτου δὲ σταυροῦ, which Lohmeyer had deleted as a Pauline gloss. Dibelius places the phrase as the third line of a strophe; and on exegetical grounds he defends its necessary place in the hymn as signifying the last step in the Lord's humiliation.[3] In his retention of θανάτου δὲ σταυροῦ Dibelius is not alone. L. Cerfaux, W. Michaelis and E. Stauffer all remain unconvinced by Lohmeyer's argument;[4] but a considerable body of opinion has sided with Lohmeyer.

---

[1] For ὁμοιόπτωτον, see Quintilian, *Institutio Oratoria*, Bk. IX, iii, 78.
[2] Dibelius, *op. cit.*[3] 77.
[3] *Ibid.* 78.
[4] L. Cerfaux, *Le Christ dans la théologie de S. Paul* (1954), p. 294 (E.T. 1959, p. 392); W. Michaelis, *Der Brief des Paulus an die Philipper* (1935), p. 39; Stauffer, *New Testament Theology*, p. 284.

D. L. CERFAUX

In his contribution to the *Festschrift* for A. de Meyer in 1946, L. Cerfaux writes on 'L'hymne au Christ — Serviteur de Dieu'.[1] In his Form-analysis of Philippians ii he offers an arrangement of the lines into three stanzas comprising verses 6–7*a*; 7*b*–8; 9–11. He objects to the analysis which begins the second main sentence with καὶ σχήματι; and also to Dibelius' suggestion that the first stanza should include the three lines which begin with μορφὴν δούλου λαβών...ἐν ὁμοιώματι...γενόμενος and σχήματι εὑρεθείς. He follows instead the idea of Deissmann who proposed to link together the two clauses which are connected with καί; and, so as to keep the parallelism between the first and the second clause, to begin both of them with a similar phrase: ἐν μορφῇ and ἐν ὁμοιώματι. This division, he remarks in another place,[2] is favoured by the sense of the passage. The first strophe ends with the idea that Christ took human nature, while the second stresses that this state will later become the occasion for an even deeper humiliation.[3]

E. J. JEREMIAS

A further revision of Lohmeyer's thesis has been suggested by the latest writer on the theme of our discussion. J. Jeremias,[4] while paying tribute to Lohmeyer's 'brilliant analysis', calls in question a singular feature of Lohmeyer's work, namely, that only strophes III and VI end with the completion of a sentence. This is perhaps not unusual once we recall that the hymn divides at the end of strophe III and concludes at the end of strophe VI. But it does raise the question whether a better arrangement is possible.

The correct scheme, Jeremias proposes, would be found if we observed that 'the entire hymn is built up in couplets', in a

---

[1] In *Miscellanea historica Alberti de Meyer*, I (1946), 117–30, reprinted in *Recueil Lucien Cerfaux*, II (1954), 425–37.

[2] L. Cerfaux, *Le Christ*, p. 289.

[3] Cerfaux's analysis is followed, with slight alteration, by J. Dupont, 'Jésus-Christ dans son abaissement et son exaltation d'après Phil. II. 6–11', *RSR*, XXXVII (1950), 500; and A. Hamman, *La Prière: Le Nouveau Testament* (1959), p. 253.

[4] *Studia Paulina*, pp. 152–4.

device known as *parallelismus membrorum*.[1] This feature is most clearly seen in the three strophes covering verses 9–11 in which there are four lines in pairs, viz.

(i) διὸ καὶ ὁ Θεὸς αὐτὸν <u>ὑπερύψωσεν</u>
(ii) καὶ <u>ἐχαρίσατο</u> αὐτῷ τὸ ὄνομα τὸ ὑπὲρ πᾶν ὄνομα
(iii) ἵνα ἐν τῷ ὀνόματι Ἰησοῦ πᾶν γόνυ <u>κάμψῃ</u> κ.τ.λ.
(iv) καὶ πᾶσα γλῶσσα <u>ἐξομολογήσηται</u> κ.τ.λ.

The verbs which are underlined show the pattern of the *parallelismus membrorum*.

Jeremias finds fault with Lohmeyer's separation of verses 7 and 8*a* (here following Dibelius' criticism); and prefers Cerfaux's reconstruction which keeps them together in the same strophe. He largely concurs in Cerfaux's results[2] which give three strophes with four lines, five lines and six lines progressively. The novelty of the hypothesis of Jeremias comes out, however, in the way in which he is prepared to excise more phrases than Lohmeyer's θανάτου δὲ σταυροῦ as Pauline glosses. Accepting, as he does, the pre-Pauline character of the hymn he goes farther than Lohmeyer in his omissions, and hence he achieves what Cerfaux's analysis did not produce, a perfectly balanced symmetry of three stanzas each with four lines.[3] The offending phrases are: (i) ἐπουρανίων καὶ ἐπιγείων καὶ καταχθονίων in verse 10; and (ii) εἰς δόξαν Θεοῦ πατρός in verse 11. In both cases the arguments for the later addition of these phrases are: (*a*) their position at the end of their sentences is unusual. In verse 10 the verb κάμψῃ comes between the noun γόνυ and the phrase; and in verse 11 there is an entire line ὅτι Κύριος Ἰησοῦς Χριστός between ἐξομολογήσηται and the connecting phrase; (*b*) and, Jeremias continues, these phrases are

---

[1] This feature had been observed by R. Bultmann in a footnote to his discussion on 'Bekenntnis- und Liedfragmente im ersten Petrusbrief', *Coniectanea Neotestamentica*, XI (1947), p. 6, n. 10.

[2] The indebtedness may conceivably be reversed in the light of Cerfaux's footnote in *Le Christ* (p. 283, n. 9) in which he says that Jeremias communicated his views on Phil. ii to him in a letter under the date 16 Aug. 1950.

[3] In his *Jesus' Promise to the Nations* (E.T. 1958), pp. 38 f. and his commentary *Die Briefe an Timotheus und Titus* (*NTD*, 1953), pp. 22–4, Jeremias finds the same triple-action of early coronation hymns in the New Testament.

in the typically Pauline style in contrast to the rest of the hymn which is linguistically un-Pauline.[1] Thus Jeremias reaches a conclusion which is the *ultima Thule* of literary criticism, viz. a perfectly arranged hymn, set in three strophes, with four lines to each strophe and built up by *parallelismus membrorum*; and conforming to Aristotle's judgment that a perfect literary composition requires 'a beginning, a middle and an end'.[2] Granted his presuppositions and the legiti-

[1] The first member of the triadic expression in *v.* 10 is a favourite Pauline term, especially if the occurrence of ἐπουράνιος in Ephesians is included (e.g. I Cor. xv. 40, 48, 49; Eph. i. 3, 20, ii. 6, iii. 10, vi. 12; cf. II Tim. iv. 18). For ἐπίγειος the following instances may be noted: I Cor. xv. 40; II Cor. v. 1 and Phil. iii. 19. Καταχθόνια is a New Testament *hapax*.
On εἰς (τὴν) δόξαν, Jeremias comments: it is 'an expression which Paul loves. The Apostle's thought does not rest until it comes to rest in the glory of God' (*loc. cit.* 154, n. 2). This phrase is, to be sure, often found in Paul (Rom. iii. 7, xv. 7; I Cor. x. 31; II Cor. iv. 15; Phil. i. 11; I Thess. ii. 12), and stands out from the rest of the hymn which (so Jeremias maintains) employs 'an un-Pauline idiom' (p. 153). But a similar (if not identical) expression occurs in I Peter (i. 7, v. 10). Jeremias' conclusion, therefore, is not as un-assailable as he gives us to think; and we prefer to leave it an open question as far as the lexical evidence is concerned. E. Schweizer, *Erniedrigung und Erhöhung bei Jesus und seinen Nachfolgern* (1955), p. 32 n. 224, accepts Jeremias' decision to treat the phrases as Pauline additions, but on the grounds of the metrical arrangement of the whole which is spoilt by these two extra phrases (he does not include the triadic formula of verse 10); and likewise G. Friedrich, *Die kleineren Briefe des Apostels Paulus; Der Brief an die Philipper* (1962), p. 111. On the other hand, A. M. Hunter, *Paul and his Predecessors,*[2] p. 123 dismisses Jeremias' procedure as 'Procrustean'; while R. H. Mounce, *The Essential Nature of New Testament Preaching* (1960), p. 107, endorses Jeremias' right to excise the words (but without any independent discussion).
At an earlier date, J. Schmitt, *Jésus ressuscité dans la prédication apostolique* (1949), p. 97 had noticed how the words εἰς δόξαν 'semble bien trahir la main de l'Apôtre terminant son exposé, selon sa manière habituelle, par une doxologie à "Dieu le Père"', quoting additional references in Rom. xi. 36, xvi. 27; Phil. iv. 20; I Tim. i. 17; II Tim. iv. 18; Rom. i. 25, ix. 5; II Cor. i. 3, xi. 31.
It is also of interest to note that R. Bultmann, *loc. cit.* p. 6, n. 10, had commented, independently of Jeremias, in reference to εἰς δόξαν Θεοῦ πατρός: 'It is an extra third line of the Christ-hymn whose construction I regard differently from Lohmeyer. Whereas he claims throughout that there are verses of three lines, I believe that there are two-line verses all the way through, up to the final verse.'
[2] Aristotle, *Poetics* 1450b 26: ὅλον δέ ἐστιν τὸ ἔχον ἀρχὴν καὶ μέσον καὶ τελευτήν. Cf. L. Cooper, *Aristotle on the Art of Poetry* (1913), p. 28. Arising from this description, the question may be asked whether Jeremias' *schema*

macy of his excisions, it is hard to see how literary analysis can go beyond, and improve upon, this latest modification offered by Jeremias. It is accepted by the latest commentator, G. Friedrich in the series *Das Neue Testament Deutsch*,[1] who bases the reasons for his acceptance partly on the presuppositions which lie at the heart of Jeremias' work. Thus, the words ἐπουρανίων καὶ ἐπιγείων καὶ καταχθονίων do not belong to the original hymn, are probably an addition—because they do not fit in with the *parallelismus membrorum*—and emphasize the universality of the adoration which is already contained in the expressions 'every knee...every tongue'. The final line εἰς δόξαν Θεοῦ πατρός is 'possibly a Pauline observation which likewise mars the texture of the hymn'.[2]

There is one outstanding difficulty in the scheme of Jeremias. He describes the way in which each of the three stanzas depicts a distinct aspect of 'the three levels of Christ's existence'. The first stanza deals with His pre-existence; the second with His earthly life; and the third with His exaltation. But Jeremias has also declared his conviction that the cryptic phrase in verse 7, ἑαυτὸν ἐκένωσεν, refers to the 'surrender of life, not the *kenosis* of the incarnation'.[3] The issue now is to explain how the first strophe which is said to deal with His pre-temporal existence can jump in thought straight to the Cross. A possible solution of this difficulty was offered some years ago by H. Wheeler Robinson,[4] and this will be examined in due course.[5] It will suffice here to comment that this solution is somewhat involved and is by no means universally approved. Yet, as far as Jeremias' Form-analysis is concerned, it is dependent for the cogency of its arrangement into three strophes covering the three states of Christ's existence upon some such explanation. In fine, Jeremias has failed to account for the fact that in the first stanza, which deals (on his analysis) with 'the pre-existence', one of the stichoi 'refers to the sacrifice of His life' upon the Cross.

fails to do justice to the place of the 'turning point' in verse 9 which came, in Lohmeyer's arrangement, exactly at the middle and formed the περιπέτεια.

[1] *Der Brief an die Philipper*⁹ (1962), p. 111.
[2] Friedrich, *loc. cit.*
[3] *The Servant of God* (E.T. 1958), p. 97; from *TWNT*, v, 708.
[4] H. W. Robinson, *The Cross in the Old Testament* (1955 ed.), p. 106.
[5] This matter is discussed in Chapter VII.

F. A SUGGESTED ANALYSIS

Of all the attempts at literary analysis which have been surveyed there is none which meets with general agreement. The pioneering work of Lohmeyer probably has the least difficulty, and possibly for that reason is the most favoured. Lohmeyer considered the line θανάτου δὲ σταυροῦ to be a later addition;[1] and this has raised the question in the minds of later scholars whether other phrases may also be regarded as Pauline comments on an existing text. If the additional phrases which Jeremias has mentioned be treated as the Apostle's comments, the remaining text lends itself to the following arrangement.

It is submitted that we should discard the notion of a hymn in three nicely balanced strophes covering the three periods of Christ's existence; and, instead, think of the verses as forming a series of couplets,[2] in six pairs; and arranged in such a way that they could have been chanted[3] in an antiphonal manner. The pattern is thus:

A   (a) (ὃς) ἐν μορφῇ Θεοῦ ὑπάρχων
     (b) οὐχ ἁρπαγμὸν ἡγήσατο τὸ εἶναι ἴσα Θεῷ

B   (a) ἀλλ' ἑαυτὸν ἐκένωσεν
     (b) μορφὴν δούλου λαβών

C   (a) ἐν ὁμοιώματι ἀνθρώπων γενόμενος
     (b) καὶ σχήματι εὑρεθεὶς ὡς ἄνθρωπος

---

[1] It is only part of Lohmeyer's argument that the words θανάτου δὲ σταυροῦ are to be deleted from the original hymn *metri causa*. His other arguments—on the grounds of content—will be discussed in Chapter VIII: cf. the present writer's *An Early Christian Confession: Philippians ii. 5-11 in Recent Interpretation* (1960), pp. 31 f., 63 f.

[2] This submission takes up the hint dropped by R. Bultmann, 'Bekenntnis', p. 6, n. 10.

[3] The Jewish practice of reading a sacred text with a rhythmical melody (נעימה נגון) is an interesting background to this suggestion. The art of cantillation is highly developed in the synagogue worship. E. Norden, *Die antike Kunstprosa*, I³ (1915), 55 ff. has described the practice in the ancient world; and the cultivation of the art in modern Judaism has evoked such books as S. Rossowsky, *The Cantillation of the Bible* (1957) (for the American scene) and A. W. Binder, *Biblical Chant* (1959). Cf. B. Gerhardsson, *Memory and Manuscript* (1961), p. 166. The need to read *aloud* Phil. ii. 6-11 in order to appreciate its rhythmical quality is stressed by Deissmann, *Paulus*, p. 170 and P. Bonnard, *L'épître aux Philippiens* (*CNT*, 1950), p. 47.

D (a) ἐταπείνωσεν ἑαυτόν
   (b) γενόμενος ὑπήκοος μέχρι θανάτου
E (a) διὸ καὶ ὁ Θεὸς αὐτὸν ὑπερύψωσεν
   (b) καὶ ἐχαρίσατο αὐτῷ τὸ ὄνομα τὸ ὑπὲρ πᾶν ὄνομα
F (a) ἵνα ἐν τῷ ὀνόματι Ἰησοῦ πᾶν γόνυ κάμψῃ
   (b) καὶ πᾶσα γλῶσσα ἐξομολογήσηται ὅτι Κύριος Ἰησοῦς Χριστός

There are certain marks of rhetorical form. A (a, b)–B (a, b) may suggest a chiastic arrangement of the pattern a–b: b–a; and there is a clear instance of homoeoteleuton, and possibly anaphora (in A (a) and B (b)). C (a) and (b) are linked, as Cerfaux noticed; and traces of homoeoptoton and homoeoteleuton are to be seen. In the case of each couplet the thought of the first member is completed (whether by a complement, an expansion or a contrast) by the second member; and the movement of the hymn proceeds by these regular stages. For example, the meaning of the compound verb ὑπερύψωσεν (in E (a)) is clarified by the cognate phrase τὸ ὑπὲρ πᾶν ὄνομα (a trace of polyptoton?) in E (b). And the πᾶν γόνυ of F (a) is picked up in the parallelism of πᾶσα γλῶσσα in F (b).

It is submitted that, on this arrangement, the pattern of the lines exhibits the three necessary qualities which Quintilian[1] regards as important in any artistic structure: order; connection; and rhythm. It is easy to imagine, furthermore, how a hymnic structure like this could lend itself to antiphonal chanting or recitation; and it may be that the carmen Christi of these verses is indeed a forerunner of the carmen quasi Deo which Pliny reports as a part of early Christian worship, in which a carmen was offered to Christ responsively.[2] A translation of this putative

[1] Quintilian, Institutio Oratoria, Bk. IX, iv, 22: 'In omni porro compositione tria sunt genera necessaria: ordo — iunctura — numerus' (cf. IX, iv, 147). The desideratum, he lays down, is 'a spontaneous flow' (sponte fluxisse).
[2] There have been analyses of the literary form of Phil. ii which have been offered, but with no reason given and no discussion of the merit of the proposed construction. The following have been noted: F. C. Grant, An Introduction to New Testament Thought (1950), pp. 234 f.; M. Meinertz, Theologie des Neuen Testamentes, II (1950), 63; F. F. Bruce, An Expanded Paraphrase of the Epistles of Paul (1965), p. 167; a novel reconstruction of the hymn (five stichoi, each of 4 lines with a discernible pattern of syllabic rhythm) has been offered by G. Gander, 'L'hymne de la Passion: Exégèse de Philippiens i. 27–ii. 18' (unpublished diss. Geneva, 1939). Among more recent scholars (especially in Europe and U.S.A.) the

original hymn may be set down:[1] The hymn concerns Christ Jesus:

A (a) Who, though He bore the stamp of the divine Image,
    (b) Did not use equality with God as a gain to be exploited;
B (a) But surrendered His rank,
    (b) And took the rôle of a servant;
C (a) Accepting a human-like guise,
    (b) And appearing on earth as the Man;
D (a) He humbled Himself,
    (b) In an obedience which went so far as to die.
E (a) For this, God raised Him to the highest honour,
    (b) And conferred upon Him the highest rank of all;
F (a) That, at Jesus' name, every knee should bow,
    (b) And every tongue should own that 'Jesus Christ is Lord'.

LOHMEYER'S VIEWS OF THE LITERARY FEATURES OF PHILIPPIANS II

In the history of the literary criticism of Phil. ii. 5–11, J. Weiss[2] had noted certain correspondences in the placing of words in the passage, e.g. μορφῇ in v. 6: μορφήν in v. 7, and γενόμενος in v. 7: γενόμενος in v. 8. But it was E. Lohmeyer who carried this investigation into great detail. From his studies we may observe the following features:

(a) The words διὸ καί divide the whole into almost equal halves.

tendency has been to accept the analysis of Jeremias as definitive. Thus, the following have pronounced favourably upon his version of the structure of the passage: Michel, 'Zur Exegese von Phil. 2. 5–11', 81; J. M. Robinson, 'A Formal Analysis of Col. i. 15–20', *JBL*, LXXVI (1957), 284; and *A New Quest of the Historical Jesus*, p. 50; G. Bornkamm, 'Zum Verständnis des Christus-Hymnus', *Studien zu Antike und Urchristentum. Gesammelte Aufsätze*, II (1959), 178 n. 2, observes that Lohmeyer's analysis has not gone unchallenged, and refers to Jeremias as illustration.

[1] This translation presupposes many of the results of our exegetical study in the body of the text, and should, strictly speaking, come at the end. It is placed here, however, for convenience' sake—although it was composed at the end of the study. Acknowledgment is made to the late T. W. Manson for guidance in the early days of the author's interest in Philippian studies, and ii. 5–11 in particular, and to his book *The Beginning of the Gospel* (1950), p. 111.

[2] *Beiträge zur paulinischen Rhetorik*, pp. 28 f.

The stress in the first part falls on ἀλλά.. .καί; and on ἵνα.. .καί in the second.

(b) Within each strophe there is an emphatic line (in four out of the six strophes it is the second line).

(c) In strophes I–III it is a characteristic that in each the verb is in the framework of two participles.

(d) In strophe V the genitives of line 3 are dominated by the cry 'Jesus Christ is Lord', which joins lines 1 and 3 of strophe VI.

(e) There are examples of synonymous parallelism, e.g. in v. 6 Θεοῦ – Θεῷ; in vv. 7, 8 ἄνθρωπος – ἀνθρώπων; in vv. 10, 11 πᾶν – πᾶσα. There are examples of antithetic parallelism, e.g. vv. 6, 7 μορφὴ Θεοῦ – μορφὴν δούλου; vv. 6, 8 ὑπάρχων – γενόμενος; vv. 8, 9 ἐταπείνωσεν – ὑπερύψωσεν, and examples of assonance in vv. 7, 11 δοῦλος – Κύριος; vv. 6, 7 μορφὴ Θεοῦ – μορφὴν δούλου; vv. 7, 8 ὁμοιώματι – σχήματι.

(f) In regard to the content of the passage, Lohmeyer was able by arranging the verses into stanzas to show that the first three strophes are concerned with Christ's katabasis, and the second three with His anabasis. At the head of both parts (in strophes I and IV) is the record of a heavenly 'resolution' (Ratschluss); and each part relates a miraculous happening (i.e. Incarnation in part one, Exaltation in part two). The διὸ καί of v. 9 marks the turning-point in the story of salvation, as the hymn tells it. Such a περιπέτεια is a common literary and theatrical device in Greek tragedy.[1]

(g) The linguistic peculiarities will be considered in the chapter on the hymn's authorship, but we may note here the following stately and liturgical expressions which give evidence of a studied literary composition, as Lohmeyer was the first to perceive: τὸ εἶναι ἴσα Θεῷ: τὸ ὄνομα τὸ ὑπὲρ πᾶν ὄνομα: εἰς δόξαν Θεοῦ πατρός.

Another feature of this passage's unusual literary form, according to Lohmeyer, was the evidence for a Semitic background:

(a) The use of participles. The participial style which is found in the first part of the hymn is a well-known feature of Semitic hymnic prayer-speech, with the participle doing the job of the finite verb and preserving the continuity of thought and action. This produces what Lohmeyer called 'a ballad-like tone'.[2]

Furthermore this is a linguistic trait which is possible only in Semitic writing. 'Only in Semitic language can a finite verb be continued by a participle' (9). Illustrations of this unusual feature of the use of the participle are found in the Old Testament (e.g. Ps. lxxxix) and in the Odes of Solomon (Od. xix, xxxi, xxxiii). See further for this trait, E. Norden, Agnostos Theos, pp. 201 f.

---

[1] Cf. Aristotle, Poetics, 1452a 22.   [2] Kyrios Jesus, p. 10.

(*b*) Constructions are found which are out of place in a Greek composition. The phrase εὑρεθεὶς ὡς calls forth Lohmeyer's brusque verdict that it is not only un-Pauline but un-Greek too (8).

(*c*) Another distinguishing feature which indicates to Lohmeyer that the hymn had a Semitic origin is the arrangement of the section in threes. There are three stresses to a line (actually this is true only in his strophes I–IV), three lines to a strophe, three strophes to each part of the entire composition. The first half contains three steps downwards from the Lord's heavenly state to His humanity and Servanthood and ultimately the humiliation of death itself. And there is the threefold division of the cosmos in *v.* 10.

This list of references to the use of 'three' looks impressive until it is closely inspected. It makes certain assumptions, however, which require proof. For example, it assumes a descent to Hades in the third stage of His incarnate life; and in some of the corroborating material which he cites (e.g. Apoc. xviii. 21–4) there are two-stress lines as well as three-stress. Moreover, the '*Dreizeiligkeit*' in Ignatius' hymn (*Eph.* xix) does not suggest a Semitic *Urschrift* for it. Lohmeyer's predilection for analysing Biblical texts into groups of three comes out clearly in his commentary on Mark (*MeyerKomm.*) and his comments on, e.g., Apoc. i. 18 (*HzNT*).

(*d*) Perhaps the most impressive argument for an Aramaic *Urschrift* of Phil. ii. 6–11 is the simple fact that the Greek can be turned back into a putative Aramaic hymn. When this is done—and it is attempted below, with the help of P. P. Levertoff's contribution to W. K. L. Clarke's *New Testament Problems*, p. 148—the text has a rhythm and evenness of flow that may well be the mark of an authentic composition, as Lohmeyer claimed.

But the theory of an Aramaic original has not universally commanded assent. W. Michaelis[1] recognizes that the use of threefold expressions in the hymn is common, but remarks that Lohmeyer's scheme is too precise. E. Käsemann[2] rejects Lohmeyer's theory by denying his fundamental assumption that the hymn emanates from a Jewish-Christian source; and the same verdict is passed by F. W. Beare.[3] Yet most of the scholars (listed above, p. 30, n. 1) are impressed by the evidence for an Aramaic *Grundtext*.

A possible Aramaic original, based on Lohmeyer's analysis, would read:

I 1   בדמותו דאלהא איתהי

2   וחשבא לא הוא לשללא

3   איתהי לפחמא דאלהא

---

[1] *Der Brief an die Philipper* (1935), pp. 39, 40.

[2] '*Kritische Analyse von Phil. 2, 5–11.*'

[3] *A Commentary on the Epistle to the Philippians* (1956), p. 76.

II 1   אלא סריך והפשט את נפשה
      2   ודמותא דעבדא נסבא
      3   בצלמא דאנשא איתהי

III 1   איך ברנשא אשתכח
      2   ונפשה שפל ומכח
      3   עדמא למותא אשתמע

IV 1   [מותא דצליבא]
          על־כן אגבהי אלהא
      2   ויהב לו שמא סגיהא
      3   דגביהא מכל שמהין

V 1   דבשמא דישוע
      2   תכרע כל־בירכא
      3   דבשמיא ובארעא ודלתחת דארעא

VI 1   וכל־לישן נודי
      2   ישוע משיחא הוא מרא
      3   לשובחא דאלהא אבוהי

PHILIPPIANS II. 5–11: ITS AUTHORSHIP

A. THE PLACE OF THE VERSES IN ST PAUL'S LETTER

In the previous section of our study an attempt was made to demonstrate that Philippians ii. 5–11 represents a Christological hymn set in rhythmical form and composed as a confession of faith in the Church's Lord in the three 'states' of His pre-existence, incarnation, and exaltatioh. The main lines of evidence for this conclusion, which is largely accepted now as proven, were given as (i) stylistic, which shows that we are dealing with the language of liturgy rather than epistolary prose; and (ii) linguistic, which reveals many exceptional terms, phrases and words in the section; and confirms the impression that we have before us a piece of literature which is quite distinct from that of pastoral letter-writing. There is a third clinching argument which may be adduced in support of the view that Philippians ii. 5–11 is detachable from the epistolary context of the Pauline letter of which it forms a part. This is the contextual evidence.

Philippians i. 27–ii. 18 forms one closely-knit section of the Epistle.[1] Its continuity should not be broken at the chapter division in the English Bible. The dominant theme is exhortation.[2] G. Heinzelmann sums up the contents of the verses as 'What Paul expects from the Church'.[3] Now it is obvious, irrespective of the reason which may be given for the fact, that the verses 5–11 clearly interrupt the flow of the hortatory theme, and this points to the conclusion that the section has been inserted at this juncture as a citation by the Apostle of what

[1] So Ewald, *Der Brief...an die Phil.*[4] (*ZahnKommentar*), revised by G. Wohlenberg (1923), p. 131, who describes Phil. i. 27 ff. as 'der Anfang der Ermahnungsreihe'.

[2] The technical expression is παραινετικόν (= exhortation), as defined by Quintilian, *Inst. Orat.* Bk. IX, ii, 103. For the significance of Pauline *paraenesis* see Hunter, *Paul and his Predecessors*[2], pp. 52 ff. and Dibelius, *An die Thessalonicher I–II*[3], pp. 19, 20.

[3] *Der Brief an die Philipper* (*NTD*, 1955), p. 93.

would seem to him to be the appropriate quotation to support his admonition to the Philippian Christians.[1] The only alternative possibility is that Paul composed the lyrical piece *currente calamo*, which indeed is not impossible; but the use of the introductory formula in verse 5 and the way in which the key-terms which are found so appositely in the neighbouring verses are placed in carefully selected positions in the hymn, sometimes contrary to normal usage and in such a way as to produce a rhythmical cadence—both these facts tell against the suggestion of a spontaneously composed canticle.[2] The verdict which sees the hymn as a separate composition, inserted into the epistolary prose of Paul's writing, commands an almost universal assent in these days.[3] The conclusion, then, is that Philippians ii. 5–11 is a

[1] The distinctiveness of the *Abschnitt* in contrast to the surrounding verses of the chapter was recognized, first of all, by J. Weiss in his review of M. R. Vincent's commentary in *ICC* (1897) in *TLZ*, 9 (1899), 263. He based his argument on (i) the rhythmical and symmetrical features; and (ii) the fulness of detail and 'prolixity' (*Umfänglichkeit*) of the passage. Weiss concluded that it was a prepared and 'lovingly thought out *Einlage*' which certainly had an existence independent of the rest of the Epistle. It is interesting that Weiss did *not* say 'prior' existence; nor did he say that the section was non-Pauline.

[2] A further argument of the view that Paul is quoting a separate hymnic composition is given by J. Jervell, *Imago Dei*, p. 209. Granting that verses 6–8 illustrate the exhortation of verses 1–4, he observes that only these particular verses of the hymn do, in fact, illustrate the exhortation. Verses 9–11 serve no purpose, in this context, but Paul goes on to add them because he is quoting, in its entirety, a hymn which he had before him.

We may question the premise of this argument that verses 9–11 do in fact 'serve no function' (as Jervell declares). Are they not necessary to show the lordship of Christ and thereby to give point and purpose to the exhortation to the Philippians as those who are 'in Christ' and therefore under His lordship? And is it incredible that Paul, having once begun to quote, should go on to complete the citation, even if the latter half had no *strict* relevance to the *paraenesis* he had just placed before his readers? Jervell is influenced by his further theory that the two parts of the hymn (verses 6–8: verses 9–11) contain two distinct Christologies (*op. cit.* p. 213). This theory will be scrutinized later (see appendix to ch. IX, p. 247).

[3] Since Weiss's day, the verdict on the separate character of Philippians ii. 5 ff. has been endorsed. W. K. L. Clarke comments: 'The more we press the actuality of Philippians as a genuine letter, the more probable it is that St Paul did not pause in his dictation to compose an exquisitely balanced and rhythmical piece of prose' (*New Testament Problems*, p. 146). This judgment was evoked by E. Lohmeyer's commentary which, in 1929, had

pendant, attached by verse 5 to a Pauline section of *Mahnrede* and utilized by the Apostle to buttress his appeal to his converts at Philippi. It is marked out as a fragment of liturgy by its unusual style and the employment of rare expressions which are more in keeping with the style of poetry and worship than the result of the dictation, presumably *ad hoc*, of a letter to a factious, local community of Christ's people at Philippi.[1] Added to this evidence is the way in which it breaks into the continuity of

labelled the verses 'a self-contained *carmen Christi*'. Hunter, *Paul and his Predecessors*, p. 42, writes of the hymn as resembling 'a "purple patch" stitched into the fabric of the exhortation'.

[1] The evidence of the unusual language may here be assembled. The first writer thoroughly to examine the vocabulary and draw attention to the *hapax legomena* and rare expressions was Lohmeyer, on the Continent, while A. M. Hunter and W. K. L. Clarke did the same thing for English readers. Supplementary studies have followed by L. Cerfaux, P. Henry, J. Jeremias and E. Schweizer.

(a) Many of the key-terms are *hapax legomena* in the entire New Testament: ἁρπαγμός is absent from the LXX and quite rare in secular Greek. ὑπερυψοῦν appears in an Old Testament citation in I Clement xiv. 5, which is the only other reference supplied in Bauer–Arndt–Gingrich, *Lexicon*, p. 849. The threefold enumeration of the universe in verse 10: ἐπουρανίων καὶ ἐπιγείων καὶ καταχθονίων, is unique in the New Testament, while καταχθόνιος is a New Testament *hapax* and is unknown in the LXX.

(b) Some words and expressions are used in an unusual way. Μορφή is found only once elsewhere in the New Testament. This is in the Markan appendix at Mk. xvi. 12. The verb 'he emptied himself', translating ἑαυτὸν ἐκένωσεν, presents an interesting problem. The verb κενοῦν is used in four other places in Paul (Rom. iv. 14; I Cor. i. 17; ix. 15; II Cor. ix. 3), but never with the precise meaning it has in Phil. ii. 7. There it is used absolutely in contrast to the other Pauline usages which are in the passive voice, except I Cor. ix. 15 which has the verb in the active voice. But as Lohmeyer acutely observed the other references construe the meaning of the verb *sensu malo*, in contrast to Phil. ii. 7. The phrase ἐν τῷ ὀνόματι Ἰησοῦ is something of a unique specimen in the Pauline writings. His customary term is 'in the name of the Lord Jesus' (I Cor. i. 2, 10, v. 4, vi. 11; Col. iii. 17; II Thess. i. 12, iii. 6). Σχῆμα occurs again in Paul only in I Corinthians vii. 31 in reference to 'the appearance' of the world; while ὑπήκοος, 'obedient' has a special meaning in the context of Phil. ii. 8, which is not found elsewhere. In classical Greek it usually connotes political obedience (cf. Liddell–Scott–Jones, *Greek–English Lexicon* (1940), *s.v.*). In the two other New Testament examples, it is obedience to men (to Moses, Acts vii. 39; to Paul himself, II Cor. ii. 9) which is in view. In the sense of religious obedience to God its usage in Phil. ii. 8 is unique in canonical literature, while the masculine singular form is only rarely attested (no examples in Liddell–Scott–Jones *ut supra*).

44

the surrounding verses by interposing an elaborate Christological digression, which (although it is germane to Paul's admonition) seems to be too fulsome and ornate for an illustration coined on the spur of the moment.[1] II Corinthians viii. 9 stands in contrast to the Philippians passage. One can readily imagine that Paul momentarily turned his thought to the noblest of examples to reinforce his appeal for generosity at Corinth. One can hardly concede the same in respect of the studied and finely balanced hymn of the Philippians ii psalm.

B. THE ARGUMENT AGAINST PAULINE AUTHORSHIP

The designation of the section as a Christological tribute has a distinct bearing on the matter of authorship. E. Lohmeyer first put forward the argument that the verses must be pre-Pauline, and, therefore, incorporated by Paul into his letter.[2]

We shall now proceed to set down the grounds on which he and later writers up to the present have denied the Apostolic authorship of this *carmen Christi*. This statement of the case will then be followed by a summary of the counter-arguments which have been brought forward in defence of the Pauline authorship. If the last part of this section may be anticipated, it will be seen that the arguments on both sides are finely balanced, and there is a reluctance to make a final decision. The matter will be left open until we have considered the results of the exegetical chapters; and our final section (p. 287) will try to indicate which alternative in the debate concerning the hymn's authorship may be accepted.

---

[1] The section stands out in vivid contrast to the tenor of the Epistle as a whole. Benoit, *L'épître aux Philippiens*, describes Philippians as a letter which is 'plus affective que dogmatique' (p. 11). In this letter which Benoit calls (17 f.) 'un entretien cœur à cœur', Phil. ii. 6 ff. stands out as 'le magnifique cantique sur la "Kénose" du Christ, qui en est comme la perle'. Similarly D. M. Stanley writes: 'It seems clear that in a letter, whose tenor, for the most part, is that of a friendly "thank you" note, the presence of such a deeply theological passage as Phil. 2, 6–11 is best explained as a citation already familiar to the Philippians' (*Christ's Resurrection in Pauline Soteriology*, p. 102).

[2] *Kyrios Jesus*, pp. 8 ff.

45

(a) The form of the verses

Lohmeyer contrived to show that the Greek text must be based on an underlying Semitic original. 'The poet's mother-tongue was Semitic'; and this is evidenced by the traces of Semitic style in the surviving Greek text. We have already called attention[1] to the participial style which is found in verses 5–7 (Lohmeyer's stanzas I–II–III) as a well-known feature of Semitic hymnic prayer-speech, with the participle doing the job of the finite verb and preserving the continuity of thought and action, thus producing what Lohmeyer called a 'ballad-like tone'. This is a linguistic trait which is possible only in a Semitic writing. Furthermore, he mentions constructions which are unlikely in a Greek composition. The phrases ἑαυτὸν ἐκένωσεν[2] and εὑρεθεὶς ὡς call forth his brusque verdict that they are not only un-Pauline but also un-Greek, while the expression ἐπουρανίων καὶ ἐπιγείων καὶ καταχθονίων is, he says, possible only as a Greek expression. The hymn has, therefore, a double background. His conclusion is that although the author composed in Greek, his native speech was Semitic. In other words, the passage is a Jewish-Christian psalm.[3]

Now, up to this point, all that Lohmeyer's thesis leads to is the strong possibility that the Greek text of Philippians ii. 5–11 had an *Urschrift* in a Hebrew or Aramaic original.[4] Even when

---

[1] Chapter II above, p. 39.

[2] J. Jeremias has more recently argued that ἑαυτὸν ἐκένωσεν goes back to a Semitic original. On the phrase he remarks, 'it is attested nowhere else in the Greek, and is grammatically harsh in the extreme' (*Studia Paulina*, p. 154, n. 3). Comment on this proposal is deferred until ch. VII.

[3] In addition to the data provided by the isolated phrases, Lohmeyer also perceptively noted that, in the second half of the hymn—his stanzas IV–VI —the presence of Semitic overtones may be detected in the style used. On verse 10 he comments (*Philipper*, p. 96) that 'the language which up to now has been terse and economical becomes ornate and full of Old Testament expressions'. This feature is seen in a direct allusion to the Old Testament (i.e. Isa. xlv. 23); moreover, the main verbs (ὑπερύψωσε and ἐχαρίσατο) are followed by subordinate clauses with the copula καί (*bis*) rather than participles.

[4] On the question of a putative Aramaic original underlying the Greek text, interpreters since Lohmeyer have noted the possibility of the theory, but have either rejected or accepted it without much discussion. It has been rejected because some have denied the early dating of the hymn, taking with

this is granted it does not immediately preclude Pauline author-ship, for we have in the Apostle himself a writer whose mother-tongue was Aramaic (see Acts xxi. 37–xxii. 3; cf. Acts xxvi. 14) and who enjoyed equal facility in the use of Greek.[1] But Loh-meyer, following a hint in Lietzmann,[2] put forward another point of evidence which took the authorship away from Paul and located it in the early Jewish-Christian community at Jerusalem.[3]

the theory of an Aramaic *Urschrift* the allied suggestion by Lohmeyer that the hymn goes back to the Jerusalem Church. It has been accepted on the ground that some harsh Greek expressions are difficult to account for otherwise. Examples of the former tendency are in Käsemann, *loc. cit.* and E. Schweizer, *Erniedrigung und Erhöhung.* Those who have followed Lohmeyer include: L. Cerfaux, *Le Christ,* p. 283: 'un hymne chrétien primitif...composé pro-bablement en araméen'; J. Héring, *Le Royaume de Dieu et sa venue,* pp. 159 ff.; and O. Cullmann, *The Earliest Christian Confessions,* p. 22; and the same author's *The Christology of the New Testament* (E.T. 1959), pp. 174 f.

A submission of Michel, 'Zur Exegese von Phil. 2, 6–11', 80, breaks new ground; and defends the Aramaic theory on a different basis. He contrasts 'the traditional material' which forms the basis of early Christian παραδόσεις and on which (he holds) Paul drew extensively in the formulation of his Christology (see *infra,* p. 54, n. 1) with early hymns of the Church. He con-cludes: 'It is my considered opinion that the various elements of the παρα-δόσεις found in the epistles display clearly their Aramaic or Semitic origin, whereas the hymns appear very much more strongly hellenized.' The unusual combination in Phil. ii. 5–11 of a Semitic 'style' and the clear influence of Hellenistic doxological language and concepts leads him to propose that the reason for this combination is that the Greek of the present text is 'transla-tion-Greek' (*Übersetzungsgriechisch*). In this way he explains the expressions which 'either are not in accordance with the liturgical style of a hymn or which in Greek sound extraordinarily harsh' (83). He postulates an under-lying Aramaic παράδοσις which is rendered somewhat woodenly into Greek with the result that the Semitic origin—the *Grundcharakter* of the hymn—shows through (80).

[1] The possibility that Paul himself composed the hymn in Aramaic, and subsequently turned it into Greek, has been recognized also by a recent writer. Cf. Wainwright, *The Trinity in the New Testament,* p. 87. And for the wider perspective of Paul's background see W. C. van Unnik's conclusion, *Tarsus or Jerusalem* (E.T. 1962), pp. 55 f.

[2] 'Symbolstudien', 265.

[3] Later discussion by those who are sympathetic to Lohmeyer's theory of the literary origins of Phil. ii tends not to follow him in this idea. First, J. Héring, *Le Royaume de Dieu et sa venue,* pp. 160 ff. (and earlier in his art. 'Kyrios Anthropos', *RHPR,* xvi (1936), 196–209), and then Hunter, *Paul and his Predecessors* in 1940 made proposals which take the place of the

(b) The language test

There is the linguistic argument which builds on the impartial evidence of the use of rare, non-Pauline words and expressions. This test of vocabulary has been accepted by most subsequent writers who have taken cognizance of Lohmeyer's brochure and commentary, and some further points in the treatment of the linguistic data have emerged. The case falls into three parts:

(i) There is the presence of terms which are *hapax legomena* in Paul's extant writing. Some of the words are indeed used only here in the entire New Testament corpus.

(ii) Then, theological ideas are expressed which are foreign to Paul as we know him from the rest of his Epistles. E. Schweizer[1] places in this category the following: the concept of Jesus as 'equal with God' (contrasting the subordination of I Cor. xv. 28);[2] the designation of Him as δοῦλος; the use of the verb (ὑπερ-)ὑψοῦν which is Johannine rather than Pauline[3] (Paul's customary verb is ἐγείρειν); the thought that Christ

hymn's origin away from Jerusalem. Héring, while still adhering to the notion of an Aramaic original and a pre-Pauline provenance, denied a connection with Jerusalem (*op. cit.* 160) on the ground that the relations between Paul and the Palestinian churches were infrequent and that Paul was often at pains to maintain an independency of them (cf. Gal. i. 13–24). On the other hand, we know that he had close connections with Damascus, at the time of his conversion and later. He kept in touch with the Churches of Syria where, at Damascus and Antioch, there were Aramaic-speaking Christians. Of the two cities, Antioch has stronger claim as the home of the Philippians psalm, for it was noted for its population of Greek-speaking Jews. It was 'indeed a home-from-home for Hellenistic Jews' (Hunter, *op. cit.* 42); and we know that Paul spent a good deal of his life there when not busy with his missionary labours. Héring, *Le Royaume de Dieu*, p. 160, calls it 'sa seconde patrie'.

D. M. Stanley, in two recent contributions, has championed the view that Antioch is the place to which we may look for the origin of the hymn. It formed part of the baptismal liturgy (so 'The theme of the Servant of Yahweh etc.', *CBQ*, xvi (1954), 424 f.) or the Eucharistic liturgy (so his *Christ's Resurrection*, p. 102) in that city.

[1] *Erniedrigung*, p. 52, n. 224 (not in E.T. *Lordship and Discipleship*, 1960), [2]p. 93, n. 373.

[2] Cf. the Johannine use of the phrase in John v. 18. The Jews plan to kill Jesus because He called God His Father, thus claiming to be equal with God (ἴσον ἑαυτὸν ποιῶν τῷ Θεῷ).

[3] The verb ὑψοῦν is found in John iii. 14, viii. 28, xii. 32, 34, with only one attestation in Paul (II Cor. xi. 7).

received (χαρίζεσθαι)[1] a gift from God, whereas Paul normally uses the verb of men as being the recipients;[2] and the threefold division of the cosmos in verse 11, which is subjugated to a new Lord rather than redeemed from sin.

(iii) The noticeable absence of those themes which we associate with Paul's Christology and soteriology,[3] e.g. the doctrine of redemption through the Cross, the Resurrection of Christ and the place of the Church, is another strong piece of objective evidence. Although it is on the Cross that the Lord of glory brings His life of obedience to a climax, no redemptive significance is attached to that death. Indeed, as was noted earlier, the Cross may not be mentioned in the original version of the hymn. The downward path of the Incarnate One ends in His obedience 'unto death' *simpliciter*. In any case, there is no thought of the sinner's personal interest in the work of the Crucified (contrast Gal. ii. 20); and no hint of ὑπὲρ or περὶ ἡμῶν (Gal. i. 4; Eph. v. 2; II Cor. v. 14 ff.; I Thess. v. 10).[4] There is no mention of the

[1] On the place of χαρίζεσθαι in the hymn D. M. Stanley comments: 'That the exaltation of Christ should be regarded as a grace to the Sacred Humanity is an idea that is unparalleled in the Pauline writings' (*CBQ*, xvi, 423). The meaning he attaches to the verb is clarified in his subsequent discussion (*Christ's Resurrection*, p. 101): 'The most convincing proof of the pre-Pauline origin of this Christian hymn is...(that) Paul never conceives Christ's glorification as a reward for his sufferings.' That this is the most satisfactory exegesis of the text remains to be seen.

[2] The meaning of χαρίζεσθαι in the Pauline corpus is: (i) to show favour: Gal. iii. 18; (ii) to bestow: Rom. viii. 32; I Cor. ii. 12; Phil. i. 29; Phm. 22; (iii) to grant favour: II Cor. ii. 7, 10, xii. 13; Eph. iv. 32; Col. ii. 13; iii. 13.

[3] D. M. Stanley, *CBQ*, xvi, 423; Schmitt, *Jésus ressuscité*, p. 98 and Hunter, *Paul and his Predecessors*, p. 42 make these points.
J. R. Geiselmann, *Jesus der Christus* (1951), p. 132 goes a little deeper in his observation. He sets the soteriological structure of St Paul's thinking (in terms of Christ's death and resurrection) over against that of the hymn (which he regards as 'the humiliation of the pre-existent One in His becoming man, followed by His exaltation as *Kyrios*').

[4] There is no *propter nos et propter nostram salutem*, remarks Stanley, *CBQ*, xvi, 423.
The noticeable omission of any significance and personal application of the death of the Kyrios calls for some comment. The issue is not so acute, however, if the line θανάτου δὲ σταυροῦ is allowed to stand in the original of the hymn, for there is the witness of I Cor. i. 18 ff. that Paul used the term ὁ σταυρός as a metonymy for the redemption of Christ in all its aspects. H. Schlier writes that ὁ σταυρός is an 'Ideogramm für das Erlösungsgeschehen' (*ad* Gal. vi. 14, *Der Galaterbrief*[11] (*MeyerKomm.* 1951)). The doctrine of

Resurrection which, as I Corinthians xv shows, was a central theme of the Pauline *kerygma*.[1] In Philippians ii. 9 the thought proceeds directly from the Cross to the exaltation of the Lord.[2] And, finally, there is no explicit reference to the Church as the company of those for whom Christ died (contrast Eph. v. 25). Instead the reconciliation is in terms of the cosmic submission rather than the religious worship which the Lord of the world receives at His enthronement and acclamation; and the whole order of created life is embraced in the scope of His authority.[3]

reconciliation may, therefore, be *implicit* in the reference to the Cross. On the other hand, most literary critics have excised, following Lohmeyer's lead, the phrase θανάτου δὲ σταυροῦ as 'a Pauline interpretative gloss' (*Philipper*, p. 96). If there is solid ground for this deletion—and we take up the discussion in a later chapter—then it remains that the hymn makes no reference to the manner of His death. The fact of the death as the nadir of obedience is recorded, but the text 'ne donne aucune indication sur la signification rédemptrice de cette mort' (Bonnard, *L'épître aux Philippiens*, p. 45). This omission leads E. Schweizer, *Erniedrigung*, pp. 111–17, to infer that an understanding of the mission of Christ which is *toto caelo* different from the Pauline soteriology is taught in the hymn. Our final chapter takes up this question.

[1] The centrality of the Resurrection in the Pauline *kerygma* is one of the most universally accepted conclusions of modern New Testament scholarship. Thus, F. V. Filson's title *Jesus Christ the Risen Lord* (1956) is rightly named as an exposition of Pauline thought (cf. *op. cit.* 31). E. Peterson, 'La libération d'Adam de l'ἀνάγκη', *RB*, LV (1948), 209 regards the omission of the Resurrection as 'decisive' for attributing the hymn to Jewish Christians; similarly in his later *Frühkirche, Judentum und Gnosis* (1959), p. 121, which repeats the earlier conclusion.

[2] That the verb ὑπερυψοῦν in verse 9 refers to the Exaltation of Jesus rather than His Resurrection is shown by J. G. Davies, *He Ascended into Heaven* (1958), p. 29. His conclusion is that ὑψοῦν and its intensive form ὑπερυψοῦν may be considered as the equivalents of ἀναβαίνειν and may, therefore, be understood to refer to the Ascension. This concentration on the *Himmelfahrt* and the entrance upon the kingly and priestly office is characteristic of the Epistle to the Hebrews where the Resurrection of Christ is mentioned explicitly only once (in xiii. 20), as M. Dibelius, art. 'Der himmlische Kultus nach dem Hebräerbrief', *ThBl*, XXI (1942), 1–11 has noted. He finds the central saving event, not in the Cross and Resurrection, but in the 'entrance into the heavenly sanctuary', according to the Epistle. Jeremias, 'Zwischen Karfreitag und Ostern', *ZNTW*, XLII (1949), 194–201, observes how, in Heb. ix. 11 ff., the entrance into heaven follows on directly from the sacrifice of Good Friday (198).

[3] Lohmeyer, *Philipper*, p. 97, saw this and stated it in forceful terms: 'Es herrscht kosmische, nicht ekklesiastische Betrachtung, und Herr sein bedeutet darum zunächst Herr der Welt sein, nicht aber Herr der Gemeinde.'

One piece of evidence which militates against the Apostolic authorship has recently been offered by E. Schweizer. He writes:[1] 'It cannot be shown in any other of Paul's writings that he would assemble together such a long series of Christological expressions unless led to do so by the context.' To sum up the argument so far. The apparent force of these linguistic and Christological *characteristica* provides the ground for a denial of the Apostle's hand in the composing of the hymn, with the exception of the interpretative Pauline gloss θανάτου δὲ σταυροῦ in verse 8. Could he have written a noble tribute to the Lord, it is asked, and expressed himself in language and style otherwise unattested, and, at the same time, omitted those very ideas and emphases which we know to have been so vital to his theology?

(c) The Servant of Yahweh teaching

Still continuing the history of the arguments brought against the Pauline authorship we pass on to consider a factor which Lohmeyer hinted at but which has been developed since his day. Lohmeyer traced one of the main categories of interpretation to the Old Testament teaching of the Servant of Yahweh, whose obedience, submission and glorification are the prototype of the presentation of Christ in the Philippians canticle. Now it is a fact that Paul's use of this category is only very weakly attested elsewhere. The argument here is dangerously near to becoming circular; but many commentators (as we shall see) hold that the verbal similarities and ideological connections between Isaiah liii and Philippians ii. 5–11 are too numerous to be ignored, or regarded as fortuitous. This provides them with a fixed starting-point. The Christology which employs the categories of the Servant of the Lord is found mainly in the Acts of the Apostles and I Peter, but is strangely absent from Paul. May it be that Philippians ii. 5–11 derives from that area of Christological development in which Pauline influence was largely not felt?[2]

This use of the 'Servant doctrine' is considered by Vincent Taylor to be the strongest argument in favour of a non-Pauline

---

[1] *Erniedrigung und Erhöhung*, p. 52; [2]p. 94.

[2] This sentence epitomizes the argument of D. M. Stanley, in his various contributions, and J. R. Geiselmann, *Jesus der Christus* (1951), p. 133.

authorship;[1] and others share this conviction. P. Bonnard puts the case very clearly:[2] 'One can understand the Christologies of Paul and of the fourth Gospel as developments of these verses, but certainly not as formulations leading up to those of the hymn. After the Pauline Epistles and the Johannine writings our verses would have had difficulty in finding their place in the development of primitive Christology.'

There are various reasons which may be conceivably given in explanation of the apparent neglect of the 'Servant teaching' in Paul's doctrine of Christ.[3] But the fact remains; and has led to a judgment that has become virtually a piece of critical orthodoxy, viz., 'Paul never makes use of any of the Servant language, except where he is quoting tradition which he has received from pre-Pauline Christianity'.[4]

(d) Paul's debt to his predecessors

The dependence of Paul upon his predecessors, those who were 'in Christ' before him (Rom. xvi. 7), is often used as a factor to explain the literary origin of the Philippians ii Christology. Indeed it may be said that research into pre-Pauline Christianity has stimulated the interest concerning the literary *milieu* which has been suggested for the hymn in Philippians ii as for other credal and liturgical fragments in the New Testament. We may sketch the present conclusions of scholars who have endeavoured to investigate the development of Paul's thought in the formative years which followed directly on his conversion.

It must be confessed that a curtain of silence covers 'those baffling years of which nothing is known beyond the bare facts that S. Paul visited Arabia, returned to Damascus, went up to Jerusalem "after three years", and then "came into the regions

---

[1] *The Person of Christ in New Testament Teaching* (1958), p. 63.

[2] *L'épître aux Philippiens*, p. 48.

[3] E.g. the explanations offered by Taylor, *The Atonement in New Testament Teaching*[3], pp. 65 ff. and the same author's 'The origin of the Markan Passion Sayings', *NTS*, I, 4 (1954), 159–67; L. L. Carpenter, *The Doctrine of the Servant* (1929), pp. 85 ff.; Stanley, *Christ's Resurrection*, p. 99, n. 21; O. Cullmann, *The Christology of the New Testament* (E.T. 1959), pp. 79 ff.; M. D. Hooker, *Jesus and the Servant* (1959), pp. 154 ff.

[4] R. H. Fuller, *The Mission and Achievement of Jesus* (1954), p. 57; cf. Cullmann, *The Christology of the New Testament*, p. 79.

of Syria and Cilicia" (Gal. i. 17 ff.), to be sought out eventually by Barnabas who found him at Tarsus and brought him back to Antioch' (Acts xi. 25 ff.).[1]

Johannes Weiss,[2] who calls attention to the important fact that the theology of the Epistles is that of an already mature thinker, draws the conclusion which later research has seriously questioned. This is that, on the basis of Galatians i. 16, 'I conferred not with flesh and blood', Paul must be regarded as a 'spiritual man' or mystic who thought of his beliefs and experiences as proceeding *directly* from God through the Spirit. The effect of this thesis is to picture Paul as receiving his distinctive beliefs in isolation from and independently of his Christian contemporaries. This exegesis of Galatians i. 16 is open to criticism. What Paul *is* asserting, in a highly polemical passage, is that he did not owe his Christian conversion or instruction to the Twelve in Jerusalem. On the contrary, he was converted by a special and direct 'revelation' (ἀποκάλυψις), and in that very experience he received his Apostolic authority from the risen Lord. But the working-out of this conversion-experience was not in isolation from other believers nor in an ecclesiastical vacuum. His baptism was at the hands of a fellow-Christian, probably Ananias, at Damascus; and it is certain that the rite of initiation would be followed by a welcome into the society of believers who received him as 'a brother in the Lord'. It is historically most probable, therefore, that the early days of Paul's Christian life were spent in contact with—and therefore under the influence of—the worshipping life and practice of the early Christian communities in Syria and Palestine.[3]

This discussion raises the question of the origin of Paul's Christology. Various explanations have been given of the most dominant influence which fashioned his picture of Christ. Amid the variety of theories the thesis of Wilhelm Bousset has had an important place.[4] He ascribed the formation of Paul's thought to the Hellenistic-Christian Churches with which Paul

[1] A. E. J. Rawlinson, *The New Testament Doctrine of the Christ* (1926), p. 115.

[2] *Earliest Christianity*, 1 (1959 edit. of E.T.), pp. 196 ff.

[3] So Fuller, *The Mission and Achievement of Jesus*, pp. 66 f. in connection with Paul's receiving the tradition of the Lord's Supper narrative (I Cor. xi. 23 ff.).

[4] *Kyrios Christos*[3] (1926), ch. III (pp. 75–104).

was brought into contact. The Christology of these Greek-speaking Christians in Syria was characterized chiefly by a cultus of Jesus as Lord (κύριος). The picture Bousset paints is that of a worshipping community which invoked Jesus as their cult-deity in the same way as contemporary religious groups worshipped Isis or Serapis. He thus explains the Kyrios-religion, with such cultic rites as baptism and the Eucharist; and above all, he is able on this basis to draw a picture of the throbbing devotional life of such early Christian meetings as are described in I Corinthians xii–xiv. In such an atmosphere there would be formulated a 'doctrine of Christ' which matched the cultic needs of the community. We read of men prophesying, speaking in strange 'tongues' (*glossolalia*) and evincing abnormal gifts from the Spirit's direct inspiration. They saw visions, were rapt in ecstasy and found an outlet for such pent-up, highly-charged emotions in psalms, hymns and odes inspired by the Spirit, as they made melody in their hearts to the heavenly Kyrios.

This account has been given because of the part it has played in the proposal that it was in such pre-Pauline Christian circles that the Philippians psalm originated. It is an illustration of the larger theory which is current coin in these days that Paul's theology is παράδοσις-theology[1] which he received from those who were believers before him and which he saw it as his responsible duty to hand on to his converts in the Gentile churches (cf. I Cor. xi. 23 ff., xv. 3 ff.). On this view it is natural that Philippians ii. 5–11 may be thought of as a liturgical fragment which he first heard in some Hellenistic-Jewish community,[2] and passed on to the Philippians as a species of Christian praise in honour of the Lord.

[1] Hints of the importance of 'the tradition' in Paul are given by Norden, *Agnostos Theos*, pp. 288 ff. and most fully worked out and applied by O. Cullmann, 'Paradosis et Kyrios', *RHPR*, xxx, 12–30; and the same author's study in *The Early Church* (E.T. 1956), 'The Tradition' (55–9); W. G. Kümmel, 'Jesus und der jüdische Traditionsgedanke', *ZNTW*, xxxiii (1934), 105–30; and especially B. Gerhardsson, *Memory and Manuscript* (1961), pp. 288 ff.

[2] The importance of the rôle of 'prophets' whose utterances at public worship are thought to be at the basis of much New Testament literature (in confessions of faith, hymns and baptismal catechesis and exhortation) is alluded to by R. Schnackenburg in his recent survey of current trends of New Testament study, *La Théologie du Nouveau Testament* (1961), p. 46.

C. THE ARGUMENT FOR PAULINE AUTHORSHIP

On the matter of authorship the evidence, however, is not all on the one side. The historical survey reveals that, in the main, the ground-breaking arguments of Lohmeyer, popularized to English readers by A. M. Hunter and supported by some new and telling points of Eduard Schweizer, have carried the majority of those scholars who have turned attention to the issue. But, as is often the case in the field of New Testament criticism, a challenge to a traditional position provokes a response from that side; and the debate about the authorship of Philippians ii. 5–11 is no exception. The chief proponent of Pauline authorship has been L. Cerfaux, although, it must be confessed, his treatment is slender.[1]

(a) The hymnic style and content

To champion the cause of Apostolic authorship in the instance of this *pericope*, it has to be conceded, is not an easy business, especially when the arguments ranged against it are so strong and

[1] *Le Christ*, pp. 283 ff. Henry, 'Kénose', 11 f. and Schmitt, *Jésus ressuscité*, pp. 98 f. notice that the hymn contains liturgical elements, but the presence of Pauline traits also convinces them of the hymn's authenticity. Among others who have seen no solid reason to cast doubt on the Pauline authorship are: F. Tillmann, *Die Gefangenschaftsbriefe des heiligen Paulus*[4] (1931), p. 139, who grants the rhythmical character of the passage which he explains by the elevated theme which is handled; but remarks that the hypothesis of a pre-Pauline *carmen Christi* is an 'unproved surmise'; M. Meinertz, *Theologie des Neuen Testamentes*, II (1950), 63 f. assumes rather than defends the Apostolic authorship; F. Büchsel, *Theologie des Neuen Testaments*[2] (1937), p. 200, n. 6, states the Pauline authorship in criticism of Lohmeyer's thesis, and A. A. T. Ehrhardt, 'Jesus Christ and Alexander the Great', *EvTh.* I–II (1948/9) has accused Lohmeyer of 'a lack of critical caution' (pp. 101 ff.); S. Lösch, *Deitas Jesu und antike Apotheose* (1933), p. 74 regards the hymn as an 'excerpt of Paul's preaching of the Cross and the Easter theme', drawn from his contacts with the Philippian Church at the season of Passover (Acts xx. 1 ff.); W. D. Davies, *Paul and Rabbinic Judaism*[2] (1955), pp. 41 f., 355 bases his support of the Pauline authorship on the use which is made of the Second Adam doctrine in the hymn; and 'there is nothing in the text to indicate that Paul is quoting the work of any other person; he employs the hymn as if it were part and parcel of his customary exhortation' (p. 42); G. V. Jones, *Christology and Myth in the New Testament* (1956), says that there is 'no inherent improbability' in Pauline authorship (p. 66, n. 2). More recent writers who have championed the cause of Apostolic authorship of the hymn are noted below.

clear. Cerfaux begins where all discussion must do, in the acknowledgment that the style is unusual in its solemn and 'hiératique' tone. Also the arrangement of the sentences is more studied than in a piece of epistolary prose. He grants that the passage may rightly be called a hymn or a poem. The rhythmical and liturgical style of the piece, betraying an early Christian confession, may be taken as proved. But this one concession may in itself explain some of the features which Lohmeyer, Hunter and Schweizer have so acutely detected, viz., the unusual vocabulary and the absence of certain ideas which the Apostle elsewhere elaborates in great detail. If the section was originally composed as a hymn, or confession of faith, in tribute to the Church's Lord, the employment of exceptional words and constructions might well be expected. Presumably the author had a certain picture in mind of the Subject in whose praise and honour the hymn would be written. It would be unnatural to ask that every truth about Him and His work should be included in one short tribute. The author would have to be selective of his ideas, and this one fact may go far to explain the omission of those features which we find in the undoubtedly Pauline works. As Henry reminds us simply, 'Un silence n'est pas une négation'.[1]

There are two points which must be taken up at this stage of the discussion. First, it has already been mentioned that this is a short tribute, compressed into six verses and with a total of seventy-six words. The exiguousness of the hymn material as a whole raises the question (as G. B. Caird has perceptively observed[2]) whether we have sufficient data on which to base a judgment concerning authorship. One of the most prominent features of recent Pauline studies has been the growing distrust of word-statistics in the determining of authorship, and an admis-

[1] Henry, 'Kénose', 33.
[2] *The Apostolic Age* (1955), p. 114: 'It is true that the passage contains three *hapax legomena* and one word (κενοῦν) used in an unusual sense. But one of the *hapax legomena* is a compound word of the kind that Paul delighted to create...Moreover, Philippians has a higher proportion of *hapax legomena* than any other Pauline Epistle. The linguistic evidence, therefore, is by no means incompatible with Pauline authorship.' He cites P. N. Harrison, *The Problem of the Pastoral Epistles* (1921), pp. 21, 23 for evidence that the ratio of unusual expressions in Philippians is above the average per page of the *Corpus Paulinum*.

sion that we cannot say with dogmatism just what he could and could not have written.[1]

This leads on to the observation that Paul is capable of an exalted and poetic style when the occasion serves. The evidence is set out in detail by Johannes Weiss who draws on the pioneering work of E. Norden.[2] There are many places in his authentic corpus where he scales the heights of sublime poetry and composes in a literary genre which is as far removed from that of epistolary prose as is Philippians ii.[3] There are other examples which may have been his guide and incentive in, for instance, the liturgical Psalms and Servant poems of Isaiah. The conclusion is that we should hesitate before saying confidently that Paul was not capable of producing such a composition as Philippians ii.

(b) The argument from the hymn's omissions considered

The second observation will lead us directly to the next section. It concerns the omission of certain theological concepts in the Philippians lyric, e.g. the reference to the Cross. But Lohmeyer himself agrees that the phrase θανάτου δὲ σταυροῦ must be the Apostle's own addition because the offending words break the metrical symmetry. The interesting thing is that when Paul adds his own phrase even that phrase contains no distinctively Pauline

---

[1] See B. M. Metzger, 'A Reconsideration of certain arguments against the Pauline authorship of the Pastoral Epistles', *ExT*, LXX, 3 (1958), 91-4. For some observations on the use and misuse of the principle of literary statistics, cf. C. F. D. Moule, *The Epistles to the Colossians and Philemon* (1957), pp. 61 f. and E. E. Ellis, *Paul's Use of the Old Testament* (1957), pp. 7 f.

[2] J. Weiss, *Earliest Christianity*, II, 406 ff., drawing upon E. Norden, *Die antike Kunstprosa*, I³ (1913).

[3] The Apostle 'loves that rhythm of style for which his taste had been sharpened by the language of the Prophets. Whole sections of his epistles can be divided into short complete lines like poetry in prose' (H. von Soden, *Early Christian Literature*, E.T. 1906, p. 25). This assessment covers passages such as Romans viii. 31 ff. and I Corinthians xiii which Michaelis, *Der Brief an die Philipper*, p. 43 quotes as a parallel to Philippians ii. 5-11. But there are other passages in which 'le style se rapproche de la prose rythmée', as Héring comments on II Corinthians xi. 21b-33 (*La seconde épître de saint Paul aux Corinthiens* (*CNT*, 1958), p. 83). Paul's poetic gift, known 'from a number of splendid outbursts in his epistles', is a pointer to Apostolic authorship, according to E. F. Scott, *The Epistle to the Philippians* (*IB*, 1955), p. 47.

doctrine; and all that Schweizer has said about the absence of a personal interest in the redeeming work of Christ is not altered even when the Apostle does add his own contribution. Does not this expose the weakness of the whole approach which makes the absence of certain ideas a determining criterion in matters of authorship?

W. D. Davies[1] has offered a positive suggestion when he maintains that the teaching about our Lord as the last Adam is characteristically Pauline. In his discussion of the Second Adam doctrine he reaches the conclusion that 'the conception of Christ as the Second Adam was probably introduced into the Church by Paul himself'. If this is so, and we shall hope to show that this concept is one of the ruling ideas in the interpretation of the passage, our hymn is the most conspicuous example, along with Romans v and I Corinthians xv, of the way his renewed mind was working in the formulating of the contrast between the first Adam and the last Man from heaven.

Turning to the matter of language, L. Cerfaux has pointed out that there are many verbal similarities between the hymn and the adjacent verses: 'The Hymn fits the exhortation (to the Church)...and the ideas and even the wording echo it.'[2]

---

[1] *Paul and Rabbinic Judaism*[2], pp. 41 ff., against C. F. Burney, *The Aramaic Origin of the Fourth Gospel* (1926), p. 47.

[2] *Le Christ*, p. 284 (E.T. *Christ in the Theology of St Paul*, p. 376).

The linguistic affinities between the verses of the hymn and the surrounding verses may be tabulated:

ἡγούμενοι (ii. 3):	οὐχ ἁρπαγμὸν ἡγήσατο (ii. 6)

(The verb ἡγεῖσθαι is frequent in chapter iii)

κενοδοξίαν (ii. 3):	ἑαυτὸν ἐκένωσεν (ii. 7)
ταπεινοφροσύνη (ii. 3):	ἐταπείνωσεν ἑαυτόν (ii. 8)

See also iii. 21, iv. 12.

εὑρεθῶ (iii. 9):	εὑρεθεὶς ὡς (ii. 7)
μετασχηματίσει (iii. 21):	σχήματι (ii. 7)
ἐχαρίσθη (i. 29):	ἐχαρίσατο (ii. 9)
εἰς δόξαν...Θεοῦ (i. 11):	εἰς δόξαν Θεοῦ πατρός (ii. 11)

N. Flanagan, 'A Note on Philippians iii. 20–21', *CBQ*, XVIII (1956), 8–9, has remarked on the close linguistic parallel between Phil. ii. 6–11 and Phil. iii. 20 f. No fewer than six words in the latter text are reminiscent of the language of the hymn (ὑπάρχει, Κύριον, μετασχηματίσει, ταπεινώσεως, σύμμορφον, δόξης) and the final words (ὑποτάξει αὐτῷ τὰ πάντα) are expressive of the meaning of the close of the hymn, as Michaelis, *Der Brief an die Philipper*, ad loc., has observed. The cosmic confession, Jesus Christ is

Admittedly this is a double-edged argument, for one cannot say that, because there are numerous parallels between the verses 5–11 and the neighbouring verses, Paul's appeal to the Philippians *must* have influenced his choice of words in the hymn. It might equally have been the other way round. Cerfaux leaves his position exposed at this point. It is safer to maintain with E. Stauffer that Paul here is incorporating his own hymn which he composed at an earlier time.[1] It is the text of the hymn which explains the remarkable correspondence between the words in the hymn and the surrounding verses.

Some justification was given above for the exceptional vocabulary. It remains to say, with G. Delling,[2] that some of the words and terms are typically Pauline, whether we think of certain words like σχῆμα or his use of the Old Testament citation from Isaiah xlv. 23, or the common Christological appellation Κύριος 'Ιησοῦς which occurs in Romans x. 9 and I Corinthians xii. 3.[3] It is this which leads E. Stauffer to oppose Lohmeyer's hypothesis and to identify the section as a Pauline incarnation formula.

(c) Pauline doctrine in the hymn

However much the language and ideas of the hymn may be regarded as foreign to the thought-world of the Apostle there can be no denying the compatibility of at least two ideas with

Lord, is (he says) a sign of the subjugation of all things to the victorious Christ. Apart from the similarities of language, it may be affirmed (as by W. Maurer, *Bekenntnis und Sakrament* (1939), p. 10, n. 4) that the setting of the hymn in a framework of the Apostle's sufferings and the Philippians' vocation to share like sufferings is an interesting point.

[1] Stauffer, *New Testament Theology*, p. 284, n. 372. This conclusion is shared by Michaelis, *op. cit.* pp. 43, 44, and Schmitt, *Jésus ressuscité*, pp. 98, 99; G. Delling, *Der Gottesdienst im Neuen Testament* (1952), p. 86.

[2] *Worship in the New Testament* (E.T. 1962), p. 88, n. 3 (corrected by the original, *Der Gottesdienst*, p. 86, n. 59), notes the following in proof of his statement: 'The terminology of Phil. 2. 6 ff. contains important Pauline elements': ὁμοίωμα, cf. Rom. viii. 3; σχῆμα, cf. Phil. iii. 21; εὑρεθεὶς ὡς, cf. I Cor. iv. 1 and II Thess. iii. 15 (but these are not precise parallels). This list (it must be confessed) is not very impressive; and hardly bears out Delling's categorical remark quoted above; rather it justifies the stricture passed by Schweizer, *Erniedrigung*, p. 52, n. 225.

[3] But there is some evidence that the use of this Christological title in these texts is part of traditional teaching which Paul has taken over.

the teaching of his undisputed letters. These are his concept of
Jesus as the Lord of glory which we trace back to his conversion-
experience before the gates of Damascus[1] and regard with H. W.
Beyer as the controlling source of his theology,[2] whilst granting
the place of his early contacts with pre-Pauline Christianity in
the explication of the initial revelation that came peculiarly to
him; and the second major theme of his Christology was the
schema of obedience in Christ which reversed the primal disobedience of the first Adam, a theme which is worked out in
considerable detail in Romans v, and lies at the heart of the
Pauline Christology, as J. Héring has shown.[3] W. Michaelis has
noted this central feature[4] of the hymn, and says categorically
that in all important particulars the hymn chimes in with the
Pauline Christology. Ancillary to these emphases the place
given to the exaltation of Christ and the bestowal of a Name
upon Him (cf. Eph. i. 20–3) may be noticed.[5]

If an underlying Semitic *Grundtext* may be taken as demonstrated by Lohmeyer, then this raises an obvious question. May
not the Apostle himself be the author? We require, as candidate
for authorship, a writer whose mother-tongue is Aramaic and
who writes with equal facility in Greek. The Apostle has just
that qualification.[6]

[1] So A. E. J. Rawlinson, *N.T. Doctrine of the Christ*, pp. 118 ff., who speaks
of Paul's conception of Jesus as the Lord of glory as 'the element in the
Christology which, so far as our evidence goes, appears to be new' (p. 120).

[2] *Der Brief an die Galater* (*NTD*, 1955), p. 12; cf. H. A. A. Kennedy,
St Paul and the Mystery Religions (1913), pp. 192 ff.

[3] *La seconde épître de Paul aux Corinthiens*, pp. 184 ff. treats of Paul's
'Adamologie'.

[4] *Der Brief des Paulus*, p. 39: 'One thought runs (through the hymn) with
powerful emphasis: Christ's obedience to the will of the Father.'

[5] The link with Ephesians i. 20 ff. is regarded as important by Hamman,
La Prière: Le Nouveau Testament, pp. 253–4. He calls attention (as Caird
does, see n. 41 above) to Paul's fondness for verbs and adverbial expressions
with ὑπέρ; this construction 'signale la main paulinienne' (253, n. 3).

[6] In addition, the opportunity for Paul to give utterance to the hymn
whilst he was conducting Christian worship may be noticed. It was a
synagogue custom for the one who led in prayer to be very often himself the
hymnographer. Cf. E. Stauffer, *New Testament Theology*, p. 310, n. 653; and I.
Elbogen, *Der jüdische Gottendienst*, pp. 484 f. with reference to the leader of the
worship (חזן הכנסת).

J. Jeremias, *ad* II Timothy ii. 11–13 (*NTD*, 47), raises the question whether Paul may have been responsible for turning the original form of these

(d) *The status quaestionis*

A final sentence of summing-up endorses the verdict of the most recent contributor to this debate:[1] 'Arguments against the authenticity of Philippians 2, 6–11 based upon considerations of vocabulary, context and poetic form, cannot be said to be conclusive or even really convincing. The theological argument may fairly be said to be still *sub judice*'; while we should add that this appears to be the present state of affairs in this country, it is far different on the Continent. British scholars are inclined to dismiss the issue (or at least to grant the possibility) and then pass on as though the verses were authentically Paul's. German and French commentators, since Lohmeyer's time, are mainly persuaded by him, with certain exceptions.

We have tried to set down, in as objective a way as possible, the arguments for and against the Pauline authorship of Philippians ii. 5–11, concentrating on the positive contributions of various scholars and not always stopping to notice how their views may be open to criticism. When the arguments are thus set side by side, it may be felt that no clear decision one way or the other is possible. The issue is finely balanced. Both positions are arguable and neither is absolutely certain. And in this state of indecision we prefer to leave the matter until the exegetical section has been dealt with. Only after an examination of the words of the hymn in their context, and of the meaning of the various Christological ideas which the hymn contains, shall we be in a position to make any clear judgment. This latter task is attempted in the final chapter when we seek to place the hymn in its first-century setting.

D. OTHER POSSIBILITIES

Two final positions regarding authorship remain briefly to be noticed, although they must be considered somewhat as aberrations. The view of E. Barnikol appeared in 1932 under a title which explains it: *Der marcionistische Ursprung des Mythos-Satzes*

verses (which Jeremias says is quite un-Greek and obviously Semitic) into Greek; and it may be that he is the author of the original too.

[1] J. M. Furness, 'The authorship of Philippians 2. 6–11', *ExT*, LXX, 8 (1959), 240–3.

Phil. 2. 6–7.[1] He regarded the verses as a Marcionite composition and artificially inserted into the letter in the second century. There is not a shred of evidence to support this, textually or otherwise. In fact, the use of the quotation from Philippians ii in Eusebius, *H.E.* is a decisive point against.[2]

In recent years F. W. Beare[3] has taken up the position that Philippians ii. 5–11 is not Pauline or pre-Pauline, but was composed by a contemporary of the Apostle and utilized by him in the letter with the Apostle's *imprimatur*. It is hard to evaluate this view. Presumably there must have been a compelling reason why the commentator refuses to credit Paul himself with the authorship; but none is given. He objects to using the hymn as an evidence of pre-Pauline Christianity, but prefers to seek the author in 'a gifted writer of his (Paul's) own circle' who came under his influence. This seems too elaborate. If the hymn expresses so forcefully the Pauline thought, why is Paul not allowed to expound his own doctrine?

[1] This is part of his *Apostolische und Neutestamentliche Dogmengeschichte als Vor-Dogmengeschichte* (1938), pp. 53 ff. Cf. E. Esking, *Glaube und Geschichte in der theologischen Exegese Ernst Lohmeyers* (1951), pp. 160 f.

R. M. Hawkins, *The Recovery of the Historical Paul* (1943), pp. 251 ff. has espoused (but without reference to Barnikol) the view that the verses 5–11 are a later insertion, 'written by one who could not accept the reality of a genuine incarnation' (252). The verses, moreover, are marked by an 'utter inapplicability' to the situation at Philippi (251). Hawkins does not tell us how late he proposes to date this 'insertion', and it would therefore be unfair to class his view with that of Barnikol who places the hymn in the middle of the second century. But the allusion to 'one who denied the real incarnation' seems to point to a Docetic source. Marcion's Docetism was founded on Phil. ii. 7: cf. E. C. Blackman, *Marcion and his Influence* (1948), p. 107.

[2] Eusebius, *H.E.* v, ii, 2. Dibelius, *op. cit.* 73 exposes the weakness of this *Interpolationshypothese*, referring to Harnack, *Marcion*[2] (1924), p. 123.

[3] *The Epistle to the Philippians*, pp. 30, 78.

CHAPTER IV

PHILIPPIANS II. 5–11: MAIN LINES OF TWENTIETH CENTURY INTERPRETATION

This part of our study attempts what German New Testament scholarship calls *Auslegungsgeschichte* in respect of Philippians ii. 5–11. This entails passing under review the main lines of interpretation of the passage which have been offered in the last sixty years or so.

As our investigation is not concerned with studies which appeared before the turn of the century we are permitted to pass over the task of disentangling the tortuous complexities with which the nineteenth-century Lutherans discussed the problems of the passage as they saw them. But three questions placed in the foreground of that discussion were carried over into the present century.

A. THE NINETEENTH CENTURY LEGACY

(i) The 'Dogmatic' View

The Lutheran contribution identified the Subject of the 'Hymn' with the historical Christ.[1] The *time* of the action of the verbs, 'He emptied Himself' because 'He thought it not robbery to be equal with God' (A.V.), is located, not in some pre-temporal existence or in the presence of God from which the Lord of glory came forth on His redemptive mission, but in the course of His earthly life when He was faced (as in the Temptations of Matt. iv = Luke iv) with a choice to be equal with His Father but in which He declined to oppose the Father's will.[2] The effect

---

[1] For example, M. Jones, *The Epistle to the Philippians* (WC, 1918), p. lxxiii, comments on the prevalence of this identification in the Lutheran tradition.

[2] J. Ross, 'ἁρπαγμός Phil. II. 6', *JTS*, x (1909), 573 f. sought to understand Philippians ii. 6 in this way. His view will be considered later (ch. VI). Sometimes the Temptation story is used as illustrative of the Philippians

of this interpretation is to place the phrase, 'Being in the form of God' as a description of Jesus in His incarnate state, so that He is held to be both 'in the form of God' and 'in the form of a servant' at one and the same time. Since 1900 there has been some support for this view. A. Sabatier championed it in 1906,[1] as did F. Loofs in a celebrated study in 1927–28,[2] and occasionally (e.g. J. H. Michael) it is

text or *vice versa*, as by Fuller, *The Mission and Achievement of Jesus*, p. 39: 'Had Jesus performed signs as a proof of his Messiahship, he would have been treating the Messiahship as an ἁρπαγμός, a thing to be grasped at.'

[1] *The Apostle Paul* (E.T. 1906), p. 257: 'The apostle is thinking, not of some celestial being, but of the historical Christ; and it is His earthly life that he so admirably sums up in the idea of renunciation and obedience'; (259): 'The subject of the whole paragraph is the historical Christ, rising to glory through humiliation.' The chief point in favour of this view is that, if St Paul were setting forth the example of the pre-existent Christ, there could hardly have been any ethical value for the Philippian readers, who were never faced with the choice which was His. Against this, however, we may note that His humiliation is seen in His obedient and submissive life on earth as well as in the Incarnation; and, decisively, the above interpretation does not accord with the structure of the hymn in which there are three, not two, stages in the process. His choice goes back to His eternal rank. See further M. Jones, *op. cit.* lxxiii–lxxv. This view also begs the question concerning the purpose of the passage, i.e. it decides in advance that Paul is inculcating some ethical admonition by setting forth the picture of Christ as an example to be followed.

[2] 'Das altkirchliche Zeugnis gegen die herrschende Auffassung der Kenosisstelle (Phil. 2, 5 bis 11)', *TSK*, c (1927–28), 1–102. After stating the evidence for the view that the subject of Phil. ii. 6–7a is the λόγος ἄσαρκος in certain Church Fathers (Clem. Alex. onwards) (3 f., 10–16, 66 ff.), Loofs shows that there is a parallel line of interpretation, found in Novatian, 'Ambrosiaster', and Pelagius, which treats the person of the historical Jesus Christ as the subject of these texts (27 ff., 63 ff.). It is this latter tradition which he seeks to maintain.

There is criticism of his historical assessment by J. Gewiess, 'Zum altkirchl. Verständnis der Kenosisstelle (Phil. II. 5–11)', *ThQ*, cxx (1948), 463–87.

On the basis of his assumption that the Subject of the *kenosis* is Christ-made-man, Loofs goes on (*loc. cit.* 94) to explain ἑαυτὸν ἐκένωσεν which he paraphrases: 'Christ, the historical Lord, emptied Himself of the fulness of the Spirit, of the πλήρωμα of the Godhead which dwelt bodily in Him (Col. i. 19, ii. 9). But this, as Bornkamm, 'Zum Verständnis des Christus-Hymnus'; 179, n. 4 remarks, falsifies the sense of the text. For where are we told, in this or in any passage, that Christ emptied himself of the fulness of the Spirit? 'Loofs himself has to water down (*abschwächen*) the word ἐκένωσεν to an "as though"', says Bornkamm, who cogently maintains that it must be the

alluded to only to be passed over.[1] This rejection is mainly on the ground that the participle of verse 6 is ὑπάρχων;[2] and that pre-existent One whose self-emptying is first referred to in connection with the Incarnation in verses 7 ff. Cf. also for criticism of Loofs, A. Oepke, *TWNT*, III, 661: 'Subjekt zu ἐκένωσεν ist nicht der Fleischgewordene, sondern der Präexistente.' Loofs's view has recently been revived by F. X. Durrwell, *The Resurrection* (E.T. 1960), p. 44; but with no real persuasiveness.

[1] J. H. Michael, *The Epistle of Paul to the Philippians* (*MNTC*) (1928), pp. 83 f.

[2] A. Plummer, *Commentary on St Paul's Epistle to the Philippians* (1928), p. 42, cites the witness of the participle of verse 6: ὑπάρχων which he says 'points clearly to the pre-existence of Christ, to the period before the Incarnation'. A comment on this participle is called for.

Ὑπάρχειν can mean simply 'to exist', 'to be'; and we may compare the very frequent usage of the participle with a predicate noun to mean 'who is', 'since he is'. There is also the connotation of 'what belongs to someone', 'his possession'; or in the phrase ὑπάρχει μοί τι, 'something is at my disposal' which expresses a thought which may equally be conveyed by the simple verb, 'I have'. Thus in Ecclus. xx. 16: 'A fool will say, I have no friend' (οὐχ ὑπάρχει μοι φίλος) and Acts iii. 6: ἀργύριον καὶ χρυσίον οὐχ ὑπάρχει μοι. Perhaps this nuance is needed when the exegesis of Philippians ii. 6 is examined. The Lord in His pre-incarnate state had the possession of 'the form of God'. The usage of ὑπάρχειν to denote an original or fundamental possession is attested by I Corinthians xi. 7. Man is the εἰκών and δόξα of God, but not by acquirement. Rather he is that by nature, i.e. in virtue of his original creation at the hands of God (Gen. i. 27: κατ' εἰκόνα LXX: cf. Col. iii. 10 and for an early interpretation of Gen. i. 27, Ecclus. xvii. 3). The Pauline text seems to mean: 'Although He possessed the divine form....'

The 'time' of this possession has been debated. J. B. Lightfoot, *Philippians* (1896), *ad loc.* regards ὑπάρχων as implying the contrast between the original and the subsequent state of Christ. Cf. his note on Galatians ii. 14. On Phil. ii. 6 he writes that the word there denotes 'prior existence' but not necessarily 'eternal existence'. The latter idea, however, he goes on, proceeds from the conception of the divinity of Christ which the context presupposes. But see B. W. Horan, 'The Apostolic Kerygma in Philippians ii. 6–9', *ExT*, LXII, 2 (1950), 60 for the meaning of ὑπάρχων as 'being essentially', i.e. with no time-reference at all. This seems the safest conclusion to draw; and certainly has more warrant than E. H. Gifford's elaborate argument in which he endeavours to show that the participle means not only pre-temporal existence in the form of God, but Christ's continuing existence in that form during His incarnate life. That conclusion *may* be valid, but it is a *tour de force* to base it on the meaning of an introductory participle (E. H. Gifford, *The Incarnation* (1911 ed.), pp. 8–12).

An even more detailed discussion of the force of ὑπάρχων is given by H. Schumacher, *Christus in seiner Präexistenz und Kenose nach Phil. II 5–8*, II (1921), 229–40. His conclusion may be quoted: Christ's 'ἐν μορφῇ Θεοῦ ὑπάρχων

the words μορφὴν δούλου λαβών go closely with the main verb ἑαυτὸν ἐκένωσεν and form part of the description of the way in which He emptied Himself, e.g. He emptied Himself by taking the servant's form. This can refer only to the Incarnation, although it is an open question (shortly to be considered) whether in His self-emptying He exchanged His μορφή in the Godhead for His human μορφή, or in accepting the form of a servant He continued to be in the form of God. A spirited defence of the latter view was made by E. H. Gifford in 1897;[1] while the increasing tendency in modern commentaries is to favour the former interpretation, largely in view of the different connotation given to μορφή from that of Gifford and Lightfoot. A swing back to the older view, however, is found in certain writers on dogmatic grounds, e.g. in Karl Barth.[2]

(ii) The Kenotic Theory

In the early part of our period the spell of the Kenosis controversy rested over this Scriptural passage, and tended to haunt the commentators as they approached the exegetical task. The essence of 'Kenosis' (derived from the Greek of verse 7) is stated clearly by J. M. Creed.[3] 'The Divine Logos by His Incarnation divested Himself of His divine attributes of omniscience and omnipotence, so that in His incarnate life the Divine Person is

speaks of Christ's pre-existence in the divine essence which remains unaltered during the subsequent stages of His taking the form of a servant and His exaltation' (p. 240). He thus interprets the participle as meaning 'an indefinite continuance of being'; but that in Hellenistic usage ὑπάρχειν had a weakened sense (as equivalent to εἶναι) is observed by the grammarians (Liddell–Scott–Jones, Lexicon, ad loc.; Moulton–Milligan, The Vocabulary of the Greek New Testament (1914–30), p. 650; Bauer–Arndt–Gingrich, Lexicon, p. 845; A. T. Robertson, Grammar (1914), 1121; Blass–Debrunner–Funk, A Greek Grammar of the New Testament (1961), § 414, 1; J. H. Moulton, Grammar of New Testament Greek, 1 (1908), 127 sounds a warning on the New Testament use of a timeless present participle: 'Grammar speaks to exegesis here with no decisive voice').

[1] Op. cit. (in 1911 ed. 8–12, 48); similarly Müller, The Epistle to the Philippians, p. 78 and note.

[2] K. Barth, Erklärung des Philipperbriefes (1928 (= 1947)), ad loc. (E.T. 1962); and the same author's Church Dogmatics, IV. The doctrine of Reconciliation, 1 (E.T. 1956), 180.

[3] 'Recent Tendencies in English Christology', Mysterium Christi, ed. Bell and Deissmann (1930), p. 133.

revealed and solely revealed through a human consciousness.' There are antecedents of this Christology which go back to the early centuries of the Church's history,[1] but in its classical formulation it belongs to the middle of the last century, to the writing of G. Thomasius whose *Christi Person und Werk* (Part II, 1857) is described by F. Loofs as 'the masterpiece of the modern theory of Kenosis'.[2] The same historian of dogma also shows that there is nothing in ancient Christian thought which provides a substantial precedent for the theory of Christology which goes by the name of Kenosis.

Since Thomasius then, and parallel with the rise of grammatico-historical exegesis, the main interest in Philippians ii became devoted to the question whether verse 7 could be used to support, or rebut, a Kenotic theory of the Person of Christ. In more recent times this concern has been displaced by the virtual consensus of opinion that the truth or error of Kenoticism, whether in a strict or modified form,[3] cannot be decided by a single verse which is not a pronouncement of dogmatic theology.[4] The restoring of Philippians ii. 7 to its context and the need to view the Philippians section as a whole, together with (it must

---

[1] The history of the Kenosis-doctrine is comprehensively sketched by Henry, 'Kénose', 136 ff. and E. R. Fairweather, 'The Kenotic Christology' in F. W. Beare's *Commentary on Philippians*, pp. 159 ff. Certain antecedents are traced in Apollinarius of Laodicea by C. E. Raven, *Apollinarianism* (1923), pp. 202–8; but cf., for a criticism, Henry, *loc. cit.* 78.

[2] 'Kenosis', *Realencycl. für prot. Theol.* x (1901), 248; and the same author's contribution *s.v.*, Hastings's *ERE* vii (1914), 680–7. Of Thomasius he says, in the latter place, that he 'gave the doctrine its scientific formulation' (686).

[3] For an example of modified Kenoticism, cf. the study of V. Taylor, *The Person of Christ in New Testament Teaching* (1958), esp. ch. xix, pp. 260–76.

[4] Käsemann, 'Kritische Analyse', 70 speaks for many modern commentators when he remarks that the passage does not answer the question put by dogmatic theology of 'the simultaneity of the supra-temporal and temporal being' of Christ. All it records is a succession of phases in the drama of redemption. It is therefore wrong to seek any *Kenosislehre* in our hymn.
J. S. Lawton, *Conflict in Christology* (1947), p. 132 repeats this verdict: 'It is impossible to assign to the passage that decisive place which it obviously holds in the construction of kenotic Christology'. Likewise E. R. Fairweather concludes: 'It is clear enough as it is that the supposed *locus classicus* for Kenoticism, literally interpreted, has in fact no direct bearing on the question' (*loc. cit.* 162), while M. Jones says plainly: 'St Paul's statement is only utilised to buttress an idea (*sc.* Kenoticism) derived from other sources' (*The Epistle to the Philippians*, p. lxxix).

be confessed) a partial eclipse of the Kenotic doctrine on theological grounds,[1] have largely accounted for the disappearance of this aspect of discussion from the scene.

(iii) The 'Ethical Example' Interpretation

Of more permanent influence has been the approach to the Pauline *pericope* in the interest of finding here the ethical example of Christ. On this interpretation[2] the Apostle is concerned with a Christian community where pride had raised its ugly head (Phil. ii. 3, 4, iv. 2, 5), and where the unity of the Church was being destroyed by division and quarrelling (Phil. i. 27, ii. 2–4, iv. 2). So he writes with the pastoral needs of the Philippians uppermost in his mind. To recall them to humility and unity he gives them a picture for their imitation; and what finer enforcement of his appeal could there be than the reminder of their Lord who was both humble and obedient? So Paul will urge upon his readers an obedient submission to his own Apostolic authority for their corporate good.

This interpretation which is widely held today (although it has suffered considerably at the hands of German criticism since Lohmeyer's day)[3] rests upon certain presuppositions:

[1] E.g. in D. M. Baillie, *God was in Christ* (1948), pp. 94–8.

[2] It is usually referred to in German books as 'the ethical interpretation' (*die ethische Interpretation*); cf. J. R. Geiselmann, *Jesus der Christus*, pp. 134 ff. which devotes a section to 'The different ways of understanding Phil. 2, 5–11'; and Käsemann, 'Kritische Analyse', 77 who calls it 'der ethische Deutungsversuch'. The ethical view is clearly stated by A. Schlatter, *Der Brief an die Philipper* (1928), p. 76: 'The Church must go the way of Jesus in that pure, selfless love which can deny its own greatness and honour.'

[3] Lohmeyer, *Kyrios Jesus*, and the same author's *Philipper*. The decisive significance of these works has been recognized generally: W. K. L. Clarke, *New Testament Problems* (1929), pp. 141–50 was the first writer in this country to call attention to 'the extraordinary importance' of Lohmeyer's treatment of the passage.

In the same year, J. Moffatt in a review in *ExT*, XL, 11 (1929), 519 f. praised the monograph (*Kyrios Jesus*) as 'one of the most brilliant and stimulating contributions to the discussions (of the lordship of Christ)...that have been made for long'. R. Bultmann's review in *Deutsche Literaturzeit.* LI (1930), 774 ff. showed great sympathy for Lohmeyer's 'sachliche Interpretation' (774). J. Héring praised Lohmeyer's treatment as 'die fundamentale Abhandlung' on the passage (*Die biblischen Grundlagen des christlichen Humanismus* (1946), p. 29). A. B. Macdonald, *Christian Worship in the Primitive Church*

(*a*) It assumes that Philippians ii. 5–11 is 'a piece of popular theology'[1] rather than a formal discussion of Christology; and side by side with this appraisal goes the cognate assumption that Paul is not using the language of philosophical speculation or metaphysics.[2] These two points were clearly stated by H. A. A. Kennedy in a commentary which has exerted a wide influence.[3] If we grant the legitimacy of both assumptions, it is an easy step to the conclusion that Paul is making use of the Incarnation of Christ simply to enforce the great lesson of humility as essential to unity and concord within the Philippian Church. In effect he says, Christ was humble. Therefore we should be.[4] The passage is 'an ethical sermon' (as O. C. Quick put it).[5]

(*b*) This view looks directly for its support to verse 5 which is something of a *crux interpretum*. The difficulty in translating the

(1934), pp. 119 ff. utilized the results of Lohmeyer's 'distinguished monograph' (as he calls it); and A. M. Hunter's *Paul and his Predecessors*[1] (1940), pp. 45 ff. registered a direct influence of Lohmeyer's works. Jeremias, *Studia Paulina*, p. 153, described Lohmeyer's 'brilliant analysis' of Phil. ii. 6 ff. as the most important of all his numerous and basic works. O. Cullmann, *The Christology of the New Testament* (E.T.) pays a similar tribute: 'All later exegetical investigation of this text builds upon this fundamental work' (174 f.). F. W. Beare, *Commentary on Philippians*, p. 74 expresses an indebtedness to Lohmeyer's commentary.

[1] A. T. Robertson, *Paul's Joy in Christ*, pp. 68 f. (1917 ed. 123 f.).
[2] As Sabatier thought, *The Apostle Paul*, p. 259. He calls the words ἐν μορφῇ Θεοῦ ὑπάρχων 'the most exalted metaphysical definition ever given by Paul to the Person of Christ'.
[3] H. A. A. Kennedy, *The Epistle to the Philippians* (*ExGreekT*, 1903), p. 435.
[4] The ethical ideal is usually regarded as that of self-effacing humility. For instance, F. Prat writes: 'Paul urges the faithful to brotherly unity, to humility, and to that generous self-denial which makes us prefer the interests of others to our own, in imitation of him who is our perfect model' (*The Theology of Saint Paul*, 1 (E.T. 1933), 312).
An application of this humility-motif appeared early in Christian literature, viz. in I Clem.xvi: 'For Christ is of those who are humble-minded, not of those who exalt themselves over the flock...humble-minded (ταπεινο-φρονῶν), as the Holy Spirit spake concerning Him (quoting Isa. liii and Ps. xxii). You see, beloved, what is the example (ὑπογραμμός: cf. I Pet. ii. 21) which is given to us; for if the Lord was thus humble-minded (ἐταπεινο-φρόνησεν), what shall we do who, through him, have come under the yoke of His grace?' (Kirsopp Lake's translation).
[5] O. C. Quick, *Doctrines of the Creed* (1938), p. 82; and in similar vein, O. Holtzmann, *Das neue Testament nach dem Stuttgarter griechischen Text*, II (1926), 684: 'Paul sets the example of the Christ before the eyes of the Church.'

verse arises partly from a textual uncertainty. We may accept the reading φρονεῖτε in the first part of the sentence as the better attested reading: 'Have this mind in you (or, among you)'. The second half of the sentence reads only ὃ καὶ ἐν Χριστῷ Ἰησοῦ, where it is clearly necessary to supply a verb *ad sensum*. The A.V. adds a form such as ἐφρονήθη or ἦν to produce the translation: 'which was (the mind which was) in Christ Jesus';[1] but this reads harshly, and is partly due to the A.V.'s acceptance of the inferior reading of φρονείσθω in the first part of the sentence.[2]

The majority of modern editors, following Deissmann and Kennedy,[3] supply φρονεῖτε (or φρονεῖν δεῖ) to give a parallelism with the first part of the sentence. The sense is then: 'Have this mind among yourselves (i.e. in your church-life)[4] which you have as those who are in Christ Jesus.' But we have still to determine what 'in Christ Jesus' represents. Two possibilities are open to us.

First, we have the suggestion of a mystical sense given to the preposition ἐν, as though Paul were writing, 'Have this mind among you as you have in communion with Christ Jesus'.[5] In this way Deissmann (in a view akin to his theory of a 'mystical genitive'), Michaelis and C. H. Dodd interpret.[6] For the last-

---

[1] Luther translates the exhortation as 'dieselbe Gesinnung zu haben, die Jesus Christ gehabt hat'. A similar understanding of the text is given by Plummer, *op. cit.* 41: 'The meaning almost certainly is "Think in yourselves that which He also thought in Himself", understanding ἐφρονήθη: "Model your thoughts on His."' If this were the correct translation, it would (as G. Friedrich has recently said, *Der Brief an die Philipper*, p. 109) make the passage as a *Christuslied* impossible and unintelligible, for 'if Christ is an example of selfless disposition, then verses 6–8 are sufficient', and the remaining verses cannot be explained.

[2] This reading is accepted by Ewald–Wohlenberg (*ZahnKomm.*), pp. 112–13 but without justification, as Käsemann has shown, 'Kritische Analyse', 91.

[3] Kennedy, *The Epistle to the Philippians*, p. 434. The provision of φρονεῖτε or φρονεῖν δεῖ was first suggested by Hofmann; and the submission was given its final form and expression by J. Kögel, *Christus der Herr*, Beiträge z. Förd. christl. Theol. (1908), II, pp. 10 ff.—a reference taken from Käsemann, *loc. cit.* 57. See below, pp. 84 ff. O. Holtzmann, *op. cit.* 684: 'zu ergänzen ist ὃ καὶ ἐν Χριστῷ Ἰησοῦ φρονεῖν δεῖ'.

[4] Cf. Mark x. 43: ὃς ἂν θέλῃ μέγας γενέσθαι ἐν ὑμῖν.

[5] Or 'in union with Christ Jesus', as J. Bonsirven suggests (*L'évangile de Paul* (1948), p. 64).

[6] Deissmann, *Paulus*, pp. 149 f. (E.T. p. 170); Michaelis, *Der Brief an die Philipper*, p. 33; C. H. Dodd (quoting Haupt), *The Apostolic Preaching and its*

named the Philippians passage is an example of 'ethics developing directly out of "Christ-mysticism"'.[1]

Secondly, a more recent (and more likely) explanation gives to the preposition ἐν an attested Pauline connotation of 'in the company of Christ's people'.[2] The whole passage reads then: 'Think this way among yourselves which you think in Christ Jesus, i.e. as members of His Church.'[3] The call, therefore, is to the Philippians to live together in personal relationship in such a way that their social conduct (in the light of the situation in the Church described in ii. 2–4) will befit those who are in the body of Christ as His members.

It would be idle to deny that, on the surface, this type of interpretation which sees the passage in Philippians ii. 5–11 as setting forth Christ as an *exemplum ad imitandum* looks natural and appropriate. Yet there are some facts which cast doubt upon it.

(i) We have noted the impossibility of the A.V. and R.V. translation except with the addition to the text of the verb 'to be'. This addition is unlikely because, first, ἐν Χριστῷ 'Ιησοῦ is rather to be taken in a technical sense, as Barth and Käsemann[4]

Developments (1944 ed.), pp. 64 f. Similar opinion is expressed by J. H. Michael, *The Epistle of Paul to the Philippians*, p. 85; Bauer–Arndt–Gingrich, *Lexicon*, p. 874; J. S. Stewart, *A Man in Christ* (1935), p. 159; A. M. Hunter, *Interpreting Paul's Gospel* (1954), p. 37.

[1] C. H. Dodd, *op. cit.* 65.

[2] Cf. Bultmann, *Theology of the New Testament*, I, 311: '"In Christ", far from being a formula for mystic union, is primarily an *ecclesiological* formula.' We should perhaps note the word translated 'primarily'; Bultmann does not deny outright that ἐν Χριστῷ carries a mystical sense, as A. M. Hunter, *Interpreting Paul's Gospel*, 99 suggests that he does. See, too, R. N. Flew, *Jesus and His Church*[2] (1943), p. 153: 'The phrase "in Christ" is used as defining the community', instancing Gal. i. 22; I Cor. i. 30, iv. 15; Rom. xii. 5; Col. i. 2, i. 28. He concludes: 'These passages do not contradict any other passages where a reference may be to the communion of the individual believer with Christ. But they do prove that, for Paul, communion with Christ was not a mere individual possession or private privilege. It was inseparable from the thought of membership in the Ecclesia. Indeed it was the characteristic and constitutive mark of the Ecclesia.'

[3] So Grayston, *Commentary*, p. 91; with similar translations by Barth, *Philippians*, p. 59; P. Bonnard, *L'épître aux Philippiens*, p. 42; Dibelius, *Philipper*, p. 72; A. D. Nock, 'Early Gentile Christianity', *Essays on the Trinity and the Incarnation*, ed. A. E. J. Rawlinson (1928), p. 102.

[4] Barth, *The Epistle to the Philippians*, p. 59: '*En Christō Iēsou* designates in point of fact the reality, the place, the area in which the people addressed

show; and secondly, if the second suggestion given above is accepted, so that the complementary second verb is 'which *you think* in Christ Jesus', then special force is given to καί and to ἐν ὑμῖν which are evidently placed in the sentence for a purpose and not as otiose words which they are in the A.V., R.V. rendering.[1]

(ii) But the most cogent objection to the ethical-imitation theory is on a broader canvas than a number of grammatical and syntactical peculiarities. It is that Paul only rarely uses the idea of the ethical example of Jesus to enforce an exhortation. The conclusion is (although this has been disputed)[2] that Paul makes little use of the *imitatio Christi* pattern as a ground for his ethical appeal;[3] and that when he does make an allusion to the example of Jesus it is His earthly life rather than the theological or Christological significance that is drawn upon (e.g. Rom. xv. 3).[4] For the Apostle the Christian life was not simply a matter of

exist. They exist in the *fellowship* of Christ Jesus, they are members of his *body*.' E. Käsemann, 'Kritische Analyse', 57: 'ἐν Χριστῷ is to be understood not as a paradigm but as the technical formula so common in the writings of Paul in the sense of "under the domination of Christ"; and therefore verse 5 can no longer be thought of as offering an example-motive.' Cf. *loc. cit.* 91, which is discussed on pp. 84 ff.

[1] See appendix A at the end of this chapter (p. 84).

[2] The extremes of interpretation are found in W. Michaelis, *TWNT*, IV, 671–6: 'Die Forderung einer imitatio Christi hat in den paulinischen Aussagen keine Stütze' (676); E. Lohse, 'Nachfolge', *RGG*[3], 1286–8; E. Käsemann, 'Kritische Analyse', who discount the use of the 'imitation of Christ' idea in Paul; E. J. Tinsley, *The Imitation of God in Christ* (1960), pp. 134–65; and W. P. de Boer, *The Imitation of Paul* (1962), who has a full-scale discussion of the New Testament material. The latter is somewhat insensitive to the eschatological elements of the Gospel and the dynamic significance of baptism as a dying and rising with Christ rather than a following in His steps. And his exegesis at times founders on this very rock. For example, it is inadequate to say, on Mark x. 42 ff., 'He (Christ) holds himself before them as a model of self-giving and service, (and)...finds in himself a true model of greatness' (*sic!*) (*op. cit.* 54).

[3] Cf. D. E. Nineham, 'Eye-witness testimony and Gospel tradition', *JTS*, XI, 2 (1960), 256, who points out further that when Paul wants a practical example to set before his readers he normally quotes himself and his fellow missionaries, e.g. I Cor. iv. 16, xi. 1; Phil. iii. 17, iv. 9. So also C. A. Anderson Scott, *The Fellowship of the Spirit* (1921), pp. 93 f., but cf. Davies, *Paul and Rabbinic Judaism*[2], pp. 147 ff.

[4] A possible exception is II Corinthians viii. 9, but see appendix A (p. 87), and recently, A. Feuillet's discussion, *RB*, LXXII, 4 (1965), 497 f.

following in the footsteps of the historical Jesus, but sharing His risen life by the Holy Spirit.[1] Since the publication of Lohmeyer's lecture in 1928 (one of its novel conclusions is stated in the author's commentary published in 1928—the Christological psalm 'has to do with the portrayal of a divine-human event, not the representation of an ethical concept')[2] the trend of German criticism has been turned in a new direction.[3] While British and American commentators are still content to follow the ethical example view,[4] with only an occasional reversion to the older dogmatic approach,[5] Con-

[1] A. Nygren, *Commentary on Romans* (E.T. 1952), *ad* Rom. x. 9: 'To be a Christian is to have a risen Lord, and through Him to share in His resurrection life.' Cf. A. D. Nock, *St Paul* (1938), p. 240. Ignatius' plea 'allow me to imitate the passion of my God' (*Rom.* VI, 3) is quite unthinkable for Paul, as R. Bultmann, 'Ignatius und Paulus', *Studia Paulina*, p. 50 (E.T. in *Existence and Faith* (1961), p. 277) and W. A. Beardslee, *Human Achievement and Divine Vocation in the Message of Paul* (1961), pp. 128–30, have shown.

[2] E. Lohmeyer, *Philipper*, p. 98.

[3] This is Käsemann's expression, 'Kritische Analyse', 53: 'markieren Lohmeyers Arbeiten...einen Wendepunkt'.

[4] As typical of many writers, E. Andrews, *The Meaning of Christ for Paul* (1949), p. 155 says: 'Paul's thought is here controlled by the profound ethical significance of the humiliation of Christ; and his main concern is to use the fact of the Incarnation as the supreme motive or incentive to humble Christian love.' Cf. J. Moffatt, *Love in the New Testament* (1929), pp. 192–4. Not all Continental scholarship shows the influence of Lohmeyer, e.g. G. Heinzelmann's commentary (*NTD*, 1955) sees the motive of the passage as Christ's humility in love: 'seid eins in demütiger Liebe wie Christus sie lebte' (94), the hymn is 'Hinweis auf die Gesinnung Christi' (95). But the difference between this standpoint and that adopted by Friedrich in his revision (1962), under Lohmeyer's and Käsemann's influence, is strikingly marked.

[5] E.g. in R. C. H. Lenski's commentary (1946), pp. 769 ff. and W. Hendriksen's *Philippians*, pp. 102 f. Perhaps Barth's *Philipperbrief* (1928), should be included here. He registers no sign of Lohmeyer's influence, although the latter's lecture had been given in 1927. Barth makes the 'Incarnation-motif' the ruling factor in his interpretation. He views the Incarnate Lord as concealing His glory in His humanity. For this reason he refuses to accept the prevailing view that verse 9 marks a new phase of Christ's glory; and he objects to the thought of the exaltation as a prize offered to the obedient Christ. This piece of exegesis falls to be considered later, but it is noteworthy that the emphasis Barth places on the incarnate glory hidden in the obscurity of Him who took the servant's form makes all thought of ethical example impossible. 'It is not by reference to the *example* (*Beispiel*) that Paul would strengthen what was said in verses 1–4' (*op. cit.* 57;

tinental scholars have looked to *religionsgeschichtlich* and historical—as well as the Biblical—sources for suggested parallels and the key to the understanding of the passage. It is possible to tabulate a series of hypotheses from Lohmeyer to the present day.

B. TWENTIETH CENTURY HYPOTHESES

(a) The background in heterodox Judaism

Ernst Lohmeyer traced two main sources for the hymn.[1] He utilized the Old Testament background of the Servant of Yahweh (a source which earlier writers had noted); but he broke new ground in treating the phrase, 'as a man' in verse 8 as the equivalent of כבר אנש in Daniel vii. 13. From this identification he worked out the theory that Paul (or the pre-Pauline *auctor*, he would say) employed an Iranian myth of the Primal Man (*Urmenschmythos*) who, as a heavenly redeemer, descends from heaven to accomplish a saving mission for mankind, then reascends into heaven, taking back with him the trophies of his victory and becoming the forerunner of those who will follow him.[2] The point of contact between the Danielic 'Son of Man' and this Oriental-syncretistic figure of Gayōmart is the book of Enoch which, it is held, merges the two traditions. And it is this

E.T. 59). Thus Barth has no place for ethical Idealism. For him the drama of salvation and its different stages are set out as the unfolding of a paradox which is to be understood dialectically. Christ is at the same time God and man; and is so even in His humiliation. The hinge of the drama is the Resurrection, when the veil which enveloped His hidden glory is thrown off, and He is revealed as One who was all the time God's equal. The pity is, for this exegesis (as Käsemann somewhat caustically remarks, 'Kritische Analyse', 58), that there is no reference to the Resurrection in the hymn!

[1] *Kyrios Jesus*, pp. 13 ff., 68 ff. His conclusion is succinctly stated in the words: 'daß die Tradition vom Menschensohn mit der anderen vom "Knechte Gottes" schon in vorchristlicher Zeit zusammengewachsen ist' (69).

[2] The connection of the Philippians text with a possible Gnostic background and the use of the *Anthropos* myth goes back to F. C. Baur, *Paulus, der Apostel J.-C.* (1845), pp. 458 ff. And C. Clemen, *Primitive Christianity and its non-Jewish Sources* (E.T. 1912), drew attention to some parallels of expression (pp. 158 f., 368: 'The idea of the Son of Man comes ultimately from Parsism, and the speculation in this system regarding the Primal Man probably lurks behind such passages as 1 Co 15. 45 ff. and Ph 2. 6 f.'). But Lohmeyer was the first to work out the full implications of this theory.

fusion of the Jewish and Oriental-Hellenistic thought which lies in the background of the presentation of the pre-existent, incarnate and finally glorious Redeemer in the hymn of Philippians ii. The plausibility of this account will be discussed later. What is of interest at this juncture is to note the introduction of a new feature into the question of the background of the Philippians psalm. With this myth in mind the main purpose of the hymn is not the presentation of a moral ideal or even a Christological message answering the question, Who is Jesus Christ? Rather it is a story of salvation, set in the framework of the cosmogonic 'myth' of a heavenly being who descended from his high estate, became enslaved by death but at length was victorious. Out of this victory—which in Christian terms means the lordship of Christ—a new world-order is created in which God and the world are reconciled and brought into unity. The agent of the cosmic unity is Jesus Christ whose lordship is solemnly acclaimed by all the orders of created existence (Phil. ii. 10, 11). And Lohmeyer believed that this faith in the cosmic Christ was part of the Church's Jewish heritage, for the Christ-hymn was first sung in the Jerusalem Church.

The application of the hymn is seen in its illustration of the principle that exaltation follows humiliation. Lohmeyer recognized the transcendental setting of the events which the hymn portrays—it speaks of 'a happening between heaven and earth'[1] —but he is loth to deny any ethical application in terms of our becoming obedient to that law or principle of which Christ is the representative norm. But it is Lohmeyer's clear analysis of the hymn as setting forth a cosmic drama against a mythological background which remains his chief contribution. This is the novel turn which followed directly upon Lohmeyer's epoch-making treatment, although it was left to a later generation of his students to draw out the implications.

[1] *Kyrios Jesus*, p. 85: 'ein Geschehen zwischen Himmel und Erde'. See Käsemann's acute comment on this ('Kritische Analyse', 56 f.); and Lohmeyer's questionable use of an analogy borrowed from Idealism is criticized by E. Esking, *Glaube und Geschichte in der theologischen Exegese Ernst Lohmeyers*, pp. 165 ff., 208, 209.

(b) The Hellenistic background

The impact of this new setting for the interpreting of the hymn is seen in M. Dibelius[1] who, while not denying the ethical application of the piece, labelled it a *Christushymnus*; and cited the parallels from contemporary pagan sources. The full working-out of this influence is found in E. Käsemann[2] who rejects all ethical application and sees the hymn in the context of the cosmic drama of redemption and in the form of the *Urmensch* gnostic myth, with no direct Old Testament background. For him here is no ethical example (*Vorbild*) because, although the Incarnate One shows obedience, He does not show how it is to be translated into imitation. On the contrary, there are no traits of personality attributed to the human Jesus—a point which is characteristic of R. Bultmann's school[3] of which Käsemann is a member—only theological saving acts (*Heilsgeschehen*) of the Redeemer (*Urmenscherlöser*), set in a suprahistorical and mythical framework. The dominant motif is not a Christological statement defining either the Person of Christ or His 'natures'; but a tracing of the stages through which He passed from pre-existence to exaltation as a series of events in a drama of salvation. The effect of this recital is not to set an ethical pattern but to elicit a response of confession, acclamation and adoration, that by Him the new Age has arrived, in which the Church now lives.

Many items in this treatment have appealed in different ways to different scholars. O. Cullmann takes issue with Käsemann for his 'anchoring the hymn thus in the thought world of Hellenism',[4] and is disposed to interpret it exclusively against an Old Testament backcloth. Indeed, Cullmann works out a thorough hermeneutic on this line. But he shares Käsemann's view that the hymn teaches nothing about Christ's 'natures'; the Christology is 'functional', not speculative.[5] He thus parts company with the older orthodoxy.

---

[1] See appendix B at the end of this chapter (p. 89).   [2] *Ibid.*
[3] See, for example, R. Bultmann, 'Die Bedeutung des geschichtlichen Jesu für die Theologie des Paulus', *Glauben und Verstehen*, I[2] (1933 (= 1945)), 188–213, esp. 206 f., and later in *Existence and Faith* (E.T. 1961), pp. 123 f., 138.   [4] *The Christology of the New Treatment* (E.T. 1959), pp. 175 f.
[5] This is very clearly stated in Cullmann's *Christus und die Zeit* (1946), pp. 94 f. (E.T. 1949, p. 109).

P. Bonnard[1] accepts many of the suggestions put out by Lohmeyer, but traces the origin of the hymn to a possible 'Judaeo-Gnostic' circle which may have exposed itself to syncretistic and Hellenistic influences in the first centuries B.C. and A.D.

The tendency represented by Käsemann to cut the hymn free from all connections with Judaism, whether orthodox or Hellenistic, is found in the latest commentators on the Epistle, F. W. Beare[2] and G. Friedrich.[3] The former places the *Sitz im Leben* of the hymn in a wholly Hellenistic, non-Jewish environment. He finds parallels in the literature of the Gnostics and the *Hermetica*, which were current in the early days of the Church. They were put together or borrowed structurally by a Gentile Christian, and utilized to set forth the cosmic drama of saving history in Christ by the suitable application of Christian terms and phrases.

G. Friedrich re-echoes much of the teaching of Käsemann. Accepting the view that the hymn is a non-Pauline composition, set in a mythical framework, and portraying the three stages of Christ's existence in dramatic form, he concludes: 'Christ is not presented as an ideal which can never be attained. The hymn speaks primarily of the transformation of the world which is entered through Christ.' The hymn tells the story of Christ in its different phases, not as the record of an individual life—one life among many—but as a decisive happening which determines the life and behaviour of all men. It is directly from this

[1] *L'épître de saint Paul aux Philippiens (CNT)*, p. 49: 'Une adaptation parénétique, par Paul, d'un hymne qui, primitivement, chantait l'apparition sur la terre de l'Homme céleste, en termes judéo-gnostiques' is his description of the passage.

[2] *The Epistle to the Philippians*, p. 77: 'There is nothing specifically Jewish about this language [of *v.* 8]. The "form of God", and the thought of "equality with God" are hardly compatible with any late form of Judaism. The whole tone is peculiarly and distinctively *Christian*, and Christian against a Hellenistic, non-Jewish background.' Yet this judgment is modified in the following piece of exegesis which looks to the Old Testament for a possible background to *vv.* 10 f.: 'The enthronement of Jesus and the conferring of the title of Lord mark his installation as God's vicegerent in the government of the universe. This is entirely in keeping with the Old Testament patterns of Messianic kingship' (Beare, *op. cit.* p. 87).

[3] 'Der Brief an die Philipper', in *Die kleineren Briefe des Apostels Paulus*[9] (*NTD*, 1962).

Christology (i.e. what Christ has *done* for the world) that the exhortation springs.[1]

Yet Bonnard, Beare and Friedrich do not completely ignore the Old Testament background, and have recourse to it in further explanation of many of the leading ideas of the hymn. In this they are drawing upon a source which has always been regarded as of the first import, especially by British scholars. To this we may now turn and sketch the leading motifs.

(c) The Old Testament background

The two chief parts of the Old Testament[2] which have been laid under tribute have been (i) the Servant poems of Isaiah xl–lv, with their characterization of the Servant of Yahweh in his humiliation, obedience unto death and glorification; and (ii) the portrayal of Adam or Lucifer, both of whom are depicted as snatching at a prize before them and suffering a penalty in consequence of a vain rivalry of God and a transgression of a God-imposed limit of their respective authority. Of the two possibilities in this latter source the Adam-story is much more likely, especially as that story was treated in Rabbinic and Hellenistic Judaism. We shall have occasion to investigate these avenues of interpretation in some detail later.

In addition to the above sources the following, more esoteric lines of interpretation may be mentioned.

(d) Specific Hellenistic examples

A. A. T. Ehrhardt[3] and W. L. Knox,[4] apparently independently of each other, proposed a type of interpretation which

---

[1] Friedrich, *op. cit.* 109.

[2] The most comprehensive and distinguished treatment of New Testament Christology on its Old Testament background is that by Geiselmann, *Jesus der Christus*, which well deserves the encomium of Schnackenburg, *La Théologie du Nouveau Testament*, pp. 43 f. Geiselmann interprets Philippians ii. 6 ff. as 'the synthesis of the theology of the Servant of God and that of the Kyrios', *op. cit.* 130 ff.

[3] *EvT*, I–II (1948–49), 101–10; and 'Jesus Christ and Alexander the Great', *JTS*, XLVI (1945), 45–51.

[4] 'The "Divine-Hero" Christology in the New Testament', *HTR*, XLI, 4 (1948), 229–49. Knox's *point d'appui* is that Paul had come to think of and describe Jesus 'in very much the same light as some of the most popular cult-

may be called the 'Divine Hero' Christology. This anchors the Philippians passage in the world of Greek history and mythology. The former scholar seeks, from a common use of the key-term ἁρπαγμός in verse 6, to draw out the parallel between Jesus and Alexander the Great. He finds in Philippians ii. 5–11 a number of terms which suggest the antithesis of the emperor-worship formulas and motifs. W. L. Knox also refers to Plutarch's *de Alex. fortuna aut virtute*, and comments that it is hardly likely that Paul would have heard of such a view of Alexander, but he may have known such ideas applied to Herakles whom Alexander imitated. The point which he makes is that Paul in this section is comparing Jesus and the popular cult-figures of the ancient world. The objections to this interesting speculation are strong and compelling, as Günther Bornkamm and P. Henry have indicated.[1]

E. Schweizer[2] has sought to understand the hymn in the light of its setting in early Christianity. Philippians ii, he says, presupposes a Church for which the meaninglessness of life and the impossibility of eluding fate (εἱμαρμένη) were the great distress;

figures of the hellenistic world', and that the language used in Phil. ii shows 'a close affinity with the descriptions and panegyrics of these figures of the pagan world, of whom Heracles was the most prominent'. While granting there is no evidence of direct dependence, Knox relates both types of writing to 'a common stock of ideas... carried over into the liturgical and homiletic language of the hellenistic world, including that of the Church'. Beare, *The Epistle to the Philippians*, p. 81 shares this view. Earlier Holtzmann, *Das neue Testament*, p. 685 had noted that the mention of the obedience of Christ, followed by his glorification, was reminiscent of the saga of Herakles.

[1] G. Bornkamm, 'Christus und die Welt in der urchristlichen Botschaft', *Das Ende des Gesetzes: Paulusstudien*[3] (1961), pp. 160 ff.; Henry, 'Kénose', 39, 40. The arguments against this theory are:

(i) In the Philippians text the pre-existent Christ is already divine because He is 'in the form of God'; and His humiliation is voluntarily accepted. These elements are missing from the Greek story.

(ii) Jesus' death was not like Herakles' death, a mere *epiphenomenon* of His career; rather it was the necessary consequence of His humiliation.

(iii) The real difference lies in the exaltation of the figures. For Herakles exaltation means deification, but this is relatively unimportant; whereas Christ is exalted as Lord of the world and possesses cosmic dominion.

A consideration of these points, and a reference to M. Simon's *Hercule et le christianisme* (1955), follow in chapter VI.

[2] *Erniedrigung* (E.T. with modifications *Lordship and Discipleship*, 1960). The relevant pages are 51 ff. and 112 ff. of the original book.

and the believer needed, above all, to be assured that the Lord had conquered all the spiritual forces which were hostile to the Church. In this way Schweizer explains such features as the omission of the Church, for she is present in the passage as the singer of the hymn; the stress on the Exaltation rather than the Resurrection, for it is the enthronement that is important as signifying the dominion of the exalted One to whom all cosmic powers are subjugated; and the Hellenistic framework of two spheres, heavenly and earthly, rather than the Hebraic setting of two ages, 'this age' (העולם הזה) and the Messianic era (העולם הבא) with the fulfilment of prophecy joining them: κατὰ τὰς γραφάς (I Cor. xv. 3 f.).

This scheme of interpretation marks a real step forward in the exegesis, although whether it is a step in the right direction we shall have to consider when the passage has been examined in detail.

(e) Historical allusions

Closely associated with Ehrhardt's and Knox's view is that of K. Bornhäuser[1] who takes the reference historically. Paul here has in mind the emperor Caligula, who, although a common man, snatched at divine honours, whereas Jesus who was divine became one of us (ἑαυτὸν ἐκένωσεν; so Bornhäuser interprets). For this reason God gave Jesus the status of Caligula who claimed the title of Kyrios for himself. The background thus depicted was occasioned by the historical circumstance of the letter of the Philippians, for the readers lived in a military town[2] and a centre of Caesar-worship.[3]

This interpretation must be pronounced more ingenious than convincing, especially when Bornhäuser proceeds to draw a further parallel between Nero who took the form of a slave—corresponding to the Pauline μορφὴν δούλου λαβών—in order to move around in Rome incognito. The force then of Paul's

---

[1] Jesus Imperator Mundi (1938), pp. 21–4.
[2] Bornhäuser, op. cit. 8 ff. The view that the Church at Philippi was composed for the most part of Roman veteran soldiers is stated by Feine-Behm, Einleitung in das neue Testament[11] (1956), p. 179. Bornhäuser places the origin of Philippians in Rome; the Apostle was surrounded by the praetorian guard who were the Emperor's personal bodyguard.
[3] Bornhäuser, Jesus Imperator Mundi, pp. 14 f.

exhortation is: Imitate your Emperor, the Christ (cf. Acts xvii. 7). Do not imitate Caligula who sought divine honours by violence. Rather be like Nero who took a slave's form. But the parallel is surely a superficial coincidence; and Henry[1] gives a just appraisal when he remarks of Bornhäuser's view that imagination can hardly go to more extreme limits than in his theory.

(f) A baptismal setting

Before we attempt a summing-up, there is one further modern theory to be ventilated. This has to do with the setting of the hymn in the worshipping life of the early Church. Lohmeyer tried to place the hymn in this way as an example of an early Eucharistic liturgy.[2] Later attempts have been made to put the hymn in a baptismal setting.[3] The grounds for this notion are given in a recent study by J. Jervell, *Imago Dei: Gen. 1. 26 f. im Spätjudentum, in der Gnosis und in den paulinischen Briefen*.[4] He offers three points:

[1] Henry, 'Kénose', 41. There has been, not surprisingly, little enthusiasm for this hypothesis of Bornhäuser. We refer to it again in chapter VI.

[2] See appendix C at the end of this chapter (p. 94).

[3] The first of these attempts is apparently that of A. Seeberg, *Die Didache des Judentums und der Urchristenheit* (1908), pp. 74 f. He based his case on the meaning of the confession of the name (in Phil. ii. 10, 11) which he thought was comparable with the confession of the *Shema*' required in Jewish proselyte-baptism. E. Käsemann, 'Kritische Analyse', 95 is inclined to favour a baptismal *milieu* for the hymn in view of its content. It speaks of a new world which Christ has brought; and baptism is the token that the Church lives in that order of life. But he does not work out this idea.

[4] Jervell, *op. cit.* 205 ff. has subjected Lohmeyer's theory to penetrating examination. It is quite false, he begins, to regard the worship of the Church at Corinth described in I Corinthians xiv as the prototype of early Christian worship in general. Furthermore, it is wrong to understand Paul as having a tradition of 'holy words'. He does not say, in I Corinthians xiv. 26, 'let each one bring what he has', but 'what each one has let him bring *to edify the Church*'. Lohmeyer has misquoted, and therefore misrepresented, the Pauline text.

All that Lohmeyer states of the eschatological perspective as confirming (in his view) the Eucharistic setting of the hymn, is equally applicable to baptism; and there is more positive evidence to support this latter view as the correct *Sitz im Leben* of the hymn in baptism, where the eschatological standpoint is especially in view (Rom. vi. 4; Col. ii. 12; and Phil. iii. 10—*sic*!). And 'we find in Phil. 2, 6-11 a series of indications leading to the conclusion that the

(i)   The confession of the lordship of Christ in verse 11 is held to correspond to similar confessions in a baptismal context. The lordship of Christ, Jervell further argues, is to be understood against a background of the defeat of the evil spirit-forces and the acclamation of Christ as the World-Ruler. He finds also a reference to the Lord's victory over the powers in other baptismal contexts (e.g. Col. i. 15–20).

(ii)   The part played by the Name is well-known as a feature of early Christian initiation-rites; and similarly, he maintains, in Philippians ii. 9, 10.

(iii)   A third argument turns upon the use of μορφή and its meaning in verse 6. This he equates with εἰκών; and then he proceeds to maintain that these concepts make sense only in the context of Christian experience in which the believer is united to his Lord's likeness and conformed to His image (esp. Phil. iii. 10, 21; cf. II Cor. iii. 18; Rom. viii. 29; Gal. iv. 19). Now, he concludes, the sacramental means by which such a union is made possible is baptism (Rom. vi. 3–5; Gal. v. 24; Col. ii. 12). This endeavour to relate the texts in sequence is interesting and will need closer inspection at the conclusion of our study. Of immediate interest is the way in which Jervell's argument has brought together the soteriological and the ethical strains of teaching, by relating them to that place in early Christian experience and worship where they blend together, namely, in baptism.

C. SUMMARY

The undermentioned characteristics may be picked out as summing up the history of interpretation of our passage during the last half-century.

(i)   The placing of the hymn in the cultic life of the early Church has made it impossible to regard Philippians ii. 5–11 as a pronouncement of dogmatic theology. Sometimes this has been taken to extremes as in Dibelius' third edition of his commentary which denies any doctrinal significance at all; but it is clear that the fresh understanding of the section as a liturgical fragment has guarded against the dogmatic interpretation.

hymn was closely connected with baptism' (*Imago Dei*, p. 206). These 'indications' are tabulated in the text of the thesis, and discussed in chapter XII.

(ii) The 'ethical example' view which sees the hymn as a call to follow Christ in His traits of humility has been challenged from the side of German scholarship which construes the hymn in terms of soteriology, not Christology. As Käsemann puts it, Philippians ii tells us what Christ *did*, not what He *was*.[1] With this description of the passage as a piece of *Heilsgeschichte*, relating the drama by which men are redeemed, it becomes more and more impossible to think of the believer as treading in His footsteps.

(iii) The conflict is still over the question of background. The choice is sometimes unduly narrowed to two stark alternatives and modern interpreters are classed as those who look to the Old Testament as the quarry for the Christological material, and those who would anchor the hymn in the world of Hellenism as part of the wider concern to detect 'Gnostic motifs' (Bultmann) in the New Testament. For the former the background of the hymn in the picture of the suffering Servant links on to an exegesis of Philippians ii in terms of the redemptive mission of Christ, with His obedience unto death related to His atoning work on the Cross. The second view places the mission in the world of Hellenism, and sees the hymn as illustrating the cosmic triumph over the spirit-forces of the world and bringing a deliverance from these powers rather than from guilt.

This conclusion about the message of the hymn is in line with views concerning the provenance of the hymn. A Judaic *milieu* is likely to go with the first interpretation; a setting in some Hellenistic community (with Beare) matches the other. But it may be that we are not, in fact, faced with an 'either–or'. Recent studies[2] have shown that there was, in Hellenistic (and even in

---

[1] 'Kritische Analyse', 72.

[2] Cf. the important statement in D. Daube, *The New Testament and Rabbinic Judaism* (1956), p. ix: 'It is becoming ever clearer that Palestinian Judaism of the first century was far more varied and flexible than preoccupation with the particular line which ultimately prevailed would lead one to assume...the sharp distinction between a Hellenistic and a Rabbinic Judaism in the New Testament period is being abandoned as it is found that many Hellenistic ideas have crept into, or been consciously taken over by, Rabbinism long before, and that the process, though slowed down, was not halted.' Cf. similarly S. Lieberman, *Hellenism in Jewish Palestine* (1950); and F. W. Beare, 'New Testament Christianity and the Hellenistic World', *The Communication of the Gospel in New Testament Times* (1961), 57 ff. Two

Palestinian) Judaism, a tendency to be influenced by outside forces. The frontiers between Rabbinic Judaism and Hellenism were constantly being crossed by an interchange of thought. We may, therefore, keep before us the third possibility that, in view of both Jewish and Hellenistic elements in the hymn, the origin of Philippians ii. 5–11 may be sought in some Greek-speaking Christian community whose Biblical traditions had been modified by Hellenistic Judaism.

APPENDIX A

THE 'ETHICAL INTERPRETATION' OF PHILIPPIANS II. 5

The purpose of this detached note is to draw attention to the criticisms which have been brought against the view which sees in Phil. ii. 5 an indication that the following passage in verses 6–11 sets forth Christ as an example to be imitated. This interpretation is often summarized in the phrase, the 'ethical view'.

(a) W. P. de Boer[1] considers the objections which have been made to this view of ethical imitation which has a *prima facie* attractiveness about it. But the only reply of substance he has to give is that 'the ἐν ὑμῖν and ἐν Χριστῷ 'Ιησοῦ each at the end of their respective clauses match each other perfectly. So do the τοῦτο and ὃ καί, each at the beginning of their respective clauses. Hence one would expect that the ἐν in both instances would express the same thought, and that the τοῦτο could not only refer backward, but must in some way have ὃ καί in mind.' But this argument is doubtful. The ἐν in ἐν Χριστῷ seems definitely to have a technical sense[2] and is quite unlike the use of the preposition in ἐν ὑμῖν or in Phil. i. 30: ἐν ἐμοί. Moreover, that verse 5 is a recapitulation of verses 1–4 is unlikely as Käsemann[3]

important statements may be mentioned in addition: W. D. Davies, 'A Quest to be resumed in New Testament Studies', reprinted in his *Christian Origins and Judaism* (1962), p. 16; and M. Bouttier, *En Christ. Étude d'exégèse et de théologie pauliniennes* (1962), pp. 106 f., who has observed how these two backgrounds (which he calls 'les deux pistes') are often set in antithesis, whereas 'il est souvent impossible de les démêler l'une de l'autre' and 'ces deux sources. . .se trouvent concomitantes souvent, car c'est par le biais du bas-judaïsme que les spéculations orientales, vulgarisées dans le monde hellénistique, se sont introduites dans le christianisme'.

[1] *The Imitation of Paul*, pp. 60 f.
[2] So E. Percy, *Die Probleme der Kolosser- und Epheserbriefe* (1946), p. 120, n. 92.　　　　　　　　　　[3] 'Kritische Analyse', 91.

(following Haupt and Barth) remarks. On de Boer's view, only half the passage is accounted for and, had he considered it, he would have been driven to regard verses 9–11 as an 'appendix', with no relevance to the exhortation. Only on Käsemann's interpretation is this embarrassment overcome. To this view we turn.

(b) E. Käsemann[1] has addressed himself to the task of meeting the exegetical demands of verse 5 in the light of the entire hymn. He refuses to treat the second strophe (verses 9–11) as an 'Exkurs' or 'Überhang' (p. 91). The only way through the difficulty, he avers, is to dismiss the idea that Christ is set forth as an example (Vorbild). The key to the passage is found in the phrase ἐν Χριστῷ 'Ιησοῦ which is a technical expression for 'in the domain of Christ'; and it introduces, not the example of His conduct (as Lohmeyer thought, and thereby took a false step), but the story of the events of salvation. Verse 5 therefore introduces a hymn with the Apostolic preface that the Philippians are to act one to another as is fitting to those who are in the sphere of Christ's rule ('im Bereich des Christus',[2] loc. cit. p. 57) as His people. He is appealing to his readers to recognize that they are those who are in the state of salvation through the One who was in the divine form and emptied Himself and took on Himself in obedience the slave's form. There are two elements in Käsemann's interpretation which are important:

(i) He understands the hymn as setting forth a soteriological drama. The Christology is not concerned with the relationships of the Father and the Son in the Christian Godhead, and therefore the latter's obedience is recorded simply as a fact. No moral is drawn from it, for it is not said to whom the Son was obedient. This omission, he remarks, destroys the bulwark of the ethical interpretation.[3] It is the fact of obedience that is noted, not the relationships of the Godhead from which some paradigm of virtue could be deduced for the Christians' example.

(ii) Käsemann builds, as we have seen, on the technical meaning of 'in Christ'. The Philippians had been guilty of quarrelsomeness and arrogance (ii. 1–4). They have set before them in this passage of ii. 6–11 not a lesson to imitate or an ethical ideal to follow, but a solemn reminder that they are 'in Christ' and as such brought into the sphere of redemptive history, i.e. into the Church by the One who was obedient and wrought salvation by placing them in a new world.[4] Let them confess with all creation the lordship of Christ and take upon themselves the true obedience in submission to His authority. They belong to that new world where He is Lord of all,

---

[1] *Op. cit.* 90 ff.   [2] *Op. cit.* 57.
[3] 'Kritische Analyse', 77.   [4] *Op. cit.* 94.

and that means that they are called to obedience (see verse 12). Käsemann interprets, in a play on words which we note also in E. Brunner's *Das Gebot und die Ordnungen*,[1] the Pauline call as follows: 'We become obedient, therefore, not through an example, but through the word which bears witness that we belong to Him' ('Gehorsam werden wir..., das uns als ihm gehörig bezeugt').

Thus the hymn states the indicative of divine action—what God has done to bring His people, through a decisive event, the Incarnation, which means nothing less than 'the turning-point of the ages',[2] into the realm of Christ's rule. There goes out now the call (in the sacrament of baptism, at the beginning of the Christian life, but also sounding through all life) to live out the meaning of that membership of Christ's Church. This is the application of the hymn to the Philippians' situation. The story of 'the event of salvation which is inseparable from and forms the foundation of the status of a Christian'[3] is also the imperative of *paraenesis*. The hymn tells how they came to be 'in Christ'; now they must let their lives be controlled as those who are truly His.

(c) It is perhaps inevitable that such a novel interpretation as Käsemann's should invite criticism and bring forth a defence of the ethical view. Edvin Larsson in his *Christus als Vorbild. Eine Untersuchung zu den paulinischen Tauf- und Eikontexten* (1962) has recently appealed to the Philippians passage as an important Pauline text in the presentation of Christ as an example for Christians to follow. The following paragraphs will notice the chief lines of his argument:

(i) He begins with a 'necessary presupposition' (p. 231), viz. that the Church at Philippi was a persecuted community. The unity of the Church was important, therefore; and Paul issued a timely call to unity and humility. In the course of his letter he has reached a point when he can introduce 'the great example for such a way of life (*Lebensführung*) in his exhortation'. This example is 'Christ Himself and His freely willed renunciation of the heavenly power and glory which He possessed before His Incarnation' (p. 232). Larsson thus claims that the passage has directly to do with Christ as *Vorbild*, and this assertion leads him to a denial of Käsemann's position (pp. 232 f.).

(ii) He has four main points to bring against Käsemann's understanding.

First, if φρονεῖτε is added to the text, then the Philippians are made the subjects of the second half of the verse. This produces a 'strictly tautological' aspect to the verse, for the phrase ἐν ὑμῖν has then

---

[1] 1932 (E.T., *The Divine Imperative* (1937), p. 116).
[2] *Op. cit.* 94.   [3] *Op. cit.* 91.

become the equivalent of ἐν Χριστῷ 'Ιησοῦ. This is wrong, he states; and the alternative proposal must stand. The Philippians must have among themselves the same disposition (*Gesinnung*) and so the same manner of life (*Lebenshaltung*) which was (ἦν) in Christ Jesus. This interpretation opposes the idea that ἐν Χριστῷ 'Ιησοῦ is to be taken ecclesiologically. Paul is not referring to the Philippians' member-ship of the Body of Christ, but to Christ as an individual person in whose character the Philippians are meant to see a model, though in a later part of his treatment Larsson brings back the notion of a corporate application by stressing that the exalted Christ is not alone but includes the Head and the members as 'a collective concept' (p. 260).

Secondly, according to Käsemann the *paraenesis* is excluded at verse 4, and with verse 5 we have the presentation of the redeeming event from which the *paraenesis* of the introductory verses is drawn. The hymn on this view has no hortatory function (p. 233). Larsson objects that this would mean 'an unexpected sharpness of division between the fact of redemption and the derivative *paraenesis*', which is contrary to the characteristic texture of other Pauline texts. But this criticism overlooks the fact that Phil. ii. 6–11 is inserted as a piece of independent material and one may very well expect an exception to the rule that in other Pauline texts there is 'a characteristic inter-weaving of soteriological and ethical elements' (p. 234) if Paul is consciously introducing some quoted material.

In the third place, Larsson argues that in several other verses in the Pauline literature an example is presented for the behaviour pattern of Christians, in particular, II Cor. viii. 9 and Rom. xv. 1–7. In the former text, 'the unexpressed but unavoidable conclusion is that the Corinthians should part with their earthly goods for the benefit of others. They should take the behaviour of Christ as an example. . . It is difficult to show why the self-emptying of Christ in Phil. 2, 5 ff. cannot have a similar paradigmatic function', although in reply it must be said that the pre-existent 'choice' of the heavenly Christ and the dramatic nature of His self-impoverishment are not spelled out in the Corinthians passage of a single verse, and (decisively) Paul there does directly relate the action of Christ to his readers' immediate situation by placing the δι' ὑμᾶς at the centre. He does the same in Rom. xv. 7 and in that text there is no hint of an incarnational formula which may be thought to set the paradigm. If the thought of imitation is present, it is based on Jesus' earthly life and self-denying regard for the interests of others. But there is nothing comparable with the majestic sweep of the Incarnation-Exaltation drama in Phil. ii. Larsson's conclusion: 'It seems probable then that the

"Christ-hymn" in Phil. 2 has a paraenetic lesson and that it does not have in view simply a description of the redemption-event' (p. 235) can hardly be sustained by a comparison with other Pauline materials for the simple reason that the presence in our passage of a long, Christological hymn drawn from independent sources and not anticipated in the context of the Epistle—as E. Schweizer[1] has remarked—stamps Paul's address to the Philippians as a unique case.

Finally, Larsson faces the problem raised by Käsemann of the relevance of the second part of the hymn. He writes (p. 253): 'With this—the conclusion of verse 8—the *paraenesis* appears to be ended. Verses 9–11 at first sight appear to be put in simply because they belong to the hymn, but this raises the question whether perhaps this final section was not regarded by the Apostle as having some exemplary meaning for the Christians. Perhaps the paraenetic consequences of Christ's exaltation were so obvious as not to need explicit statement.'

Larsson, granting that Paul does not make explicit the meaning and purpose of verses 9–11, nevertheless goes on to fill the lacuna by the following argument. 'The Exaltation of Christ is understood as prototypical for Christians' (p. 261)...'As Christ was exalted and glorified as a "reward" for His humble obedience, so also His followers will be exalted and glorified. That this thought is not expressly stated is perhaps due to the fact that it cannot have the same paraenetic function as the teaching about the humility and obedience in the first part of the "hymn". Besides this, the Exaltation of Christ is portrayed in such superlative terms that these could not be directly applied without danger to the eventual glorification of the Christians, although certainly this is seen as a counterpart of the Enthronement of Christ' (p. 262).

This paragraph has been reproduced *in extenso* because it indicates the amount of inference from the text which has to be made in order to account for the place of verses 9–11 in the whole scheme of Paul's citation. There is nothing in the text which hints at the Church's glorification with her Lord, however well attested elsewhere this idea may be. Käsemann's verdict stands, therefore: if the hymn depicts an ethical example for the believers' *imitatio*, the final three verses must be treated as an appendix and so irrelevant. In fact the teaching of 'reward' is a positive hindrance to disinterested ethical endeavour, and this in turn reflects upon the correctness of this starting-point of exegesis.

[1] *Erniedrigung*[2], p. 94.

APPENDIX B

THE VIEWS OF M. DIBELIUS AND
E. KÄSEMANN ON PHILIPPIANS II. 5-11

(a) M. Dibelius' commentary *An die Philipper* appeared in a third edition in 1937. His main contribution was, in fact, a novel one, for he denied that the key-terms of the hymn should be interpreted as technical theological expressions. 'The solemn style proves that this section does not have a dogmatic, but rather a poetic-hymnic character.'[1] Käsemann (noted below) found fault with this line of interpretation.

Other points from Dibelius' commentary may be noticed. In his second edition (1925) he cited many parallels from the Hellenistic cults and was disposed to see the dominant motif of the passage as 'ein Höllenfahrtsmythos', used Christologically and set in a mythical framework.[2] For the application of the teaching of this passage Dibelius has recourse to the picture of the humiliated Christ who sets the ethical pattern for the Church. The picture of humiliation in verse 8 is the 'clothing' (*Einkleidung*) of the principle. 'Insofar as the humiliation of Christ is here presented as an act of free obedience, the myth is moralized', comments Käsemann,[3] by way of interpreting Dibelius.

Once this picture is drawn in verse 8, the rest of the passage has little meaning. Verses 9 ff. are therefore treated as an 'excursus'; and regarded as really immaterial to the teaching of the passage—a view shared by W. Lueken:[4] 'The whole is really only a subordinate clause which has the purpose of setting forth the exemplary humility of Christ'; and Ewald-Wohlenberg who took the view that verses 9-11 are 'an obvious digression' which the Apostle slipped in as a matter of course to complete the picture of Christ.[5]

The influence of Lohmeyer on Dibelius is seen clearly and in many ways in the third edition of his Commentary. We have observed earlier in our chapter II the new structure of the passage as 'a Christ-hymn' which Dibelius found. He still maintained in the revised edition the value of the 'Urmenschmythos' as an interpreting idea in the hymn, but is convinced by Lohmeyer that an ethical Idealism is

---

[1] *Op. cit.* 80.
[2] *Op. cit.* 63. Cf. his *Geisterwelt im Glauben des Paulus* (1909), pp. 203 ff., for this myth.   [3] 'Kritische Analyse', 59.
[4] 'Der Brief an die Philipper', *Die Schriften des Neuen Testaments*[2] (1917), p. 390.
[5] *Der Brief des Paulus an die Philipper*, Zahn's *Kommentar*, revised Wohlenberg (1923), p. 112.

to be found in the passage's use of the law of humiliation and exaltation. He makes use of what Käsemann calls the 'speculative dialectic'[1] which Lohmeyer had employed. Käsemann goes on to challenge this, stating that the best service perhaps that Dibelius renders is to expose the embarrassment which his acceptance of Lohmeyer's interpretation has created for him!

(b) Ernst Käsemann's 'Kritische Analyse', reprinted in his *Exegetische Versuche und Besinnungen*, is the most weighty and important contribution made to the study of Philippians ii. 5–11 in the post-Lohmeyer period. It is concerned with two things. He states and criticizes the main lines of (Continental) interpretation which have been adopted in recent study; and in the course of the historical and exegetical survey which he conducts, he drops hints and gives suggestions as to his own position, which is then briefly stated in some closing sections. It is not easy to compress his salient contribution into a short note, but the attempt must be made.

His starting-point is that the hymn does not purport to set out an *imitatio Christi* pattern. Nor is it concerned to depict the mutual relations of the Godhead. 'Not a relationship, but an event, a drama, is here portrayed, in the various phases which follow one another. Against Lohmeyer and his followers we may say that Christology is here set forth in the framework of soteriology.'[2] This sentence may be taken as the Ariadne's thread guiding to the heart of Käsemann's often tortuous discussion.

The verbs which the earlier commentators had seized upon as clear indications of the moral acts of the human Jesus, 'He emptied Himself' and 'He humbled Himself', Käsemann says, do not reveal the historical life of the earthly Jesus at all. Rather they describe the theological saving acts of the Redeemer in a supra-historical and mythical framework. The 'mythical framework' is that of the Gnostic Redeemer myth which has been christianized to produce the following result.

The hymn falls into two parts, corresponding to Lohmeyer's two main strophes (verses 6–8; 9–11). 'The One who was equal with God became a slave and became obedient...To the question of the why of His abasement, the first strophe merely answers: of His own free will. To the similar question of His exaltation the second strophe answers explicitly: because He became abased and obedient. What else can this mean except this: that the manifestation of the lowly One and the obedient One was actually an eschatological event?'[3] This means that it is no ordinary happening such as a history-book

---

[1] 'Kritische Analyse', 61.   [2] *Op. cit.* 71.
[3] *Op. cit.* 79.

may record. The event of Christ's coming into the world has a decisive significance for all time. It begins a new era; it opens the door on a new world.

Because this is so, there is no room for the ethical view, for who could possibly tread in the footsteps of the heavenly Redeemer who descended and is exalted to the throne of the universe? The picture of Christ in the hymn is painted in terms of His status as the heavenly Man of Hellenistic speculation. But this does not mean that His relations with the Father are described; no Kenosis-doctrine may legitimately be derived from the hymn; and no teaching as to the person of Christ can be deduced from the various terms which are used of Him. If His pre-existence and glory are mentioned, it is only 'to bring to light clearly the miracle of the saving event. But in the lines (of the hymn) which follow, we always find primary mention of what Christ did, not what He was'[1] (*loc. cit.* p. 72). This is another seminal thought in the exposition which Käsemann offers.

No definition of His nature is given. The hymn is concerned with events in a connected series; and events which show contrasts.[2] The hymn tells the story of a heavenly Being (*nicht irgendein Mensch*— literally 'not just any man')[3] who comes down and is obedient. Finally He is exalted and enthroned as World-Ruler over all the spiritual forces which the ancient world thought of as peopling the inter-space between the planets and stars, and exercising a malign influence upon the dwellers upon earth. But as He is and remains a heavenly *Anthropos*, the obedience He shows (and not to His Father, an assumption which the commentators read into the text) cannot be displayed for our imitation. Thus, 'He reveals obedience but not for our imitation. He is *Urbild*—the original pattern, the prototype, not *Vorbild*, the example, to put it in a nutshell' ('er ist Urbild, nicht Vorbild, um es zugespitzt zu sagen').[4]

In the final section of his essay Käsemann tackles the question: What is the significance of the 'story of salvation' represented in the hymn for the readers of Phil. ii and for the Church today? He begins by defining once more the place of the believers as those who are under the régime of Christ the Lord. He became obedient and is now exalted in His present status as Lord over the world, having subdued all cosmic forces which molest man. This is the present lordship, and the deliverance He offers is a present and final reality. This, Käsemann remarks, is the distinctiveness of the Christian message over against that of Jewish apocalypticism which was ever forward-looking, and the Greek myths which attached no decisive significance

---

[1] *Op. cit.* 72.   [2] 'Kritische Analyse', 76; cf. 80.
[3] *Op. cit.* 80 f.   [4] *Op. cit.* 81.

to the stories of the gods and 'divine men' who appeared on earth. Though, therefore, the hymn uses the framework of a Hellenistic myth, it breaks free at one important point. For what is unique about the Christian myth is the eschatological motif. It speaks of nothing less than the end of the old age where man is under the dominion of evil forces and the beginning of a new Aeon wherein all the hostile powers are defeated. The early Church knew this as a present experience, and so 'in this hymn the Christian Church on earth makes her simultaneous response with those who adore before the throne of God'.[1] She is caught up into the eschatological event, and is a witness on earth of the enthronement of Him who was obedient.

This leads finally to the standpoint of the hymn. It is meant to be sung by those who are in the new era. They are thus because they are 'in Christ', the new man. The hymn explicates what it means to be 'in Christ'. And, to return to Käsemann's almost concluding words to his main theme, there is no ethical pattern set up, but a basis is provided in the hymn for the call to live as those who are in the Church 'upon whom the end of the ages has come' (I Cor. x. 11).[2]

A notable contribution to the modern discussion of Phil. ii has brought certain objections against Käsemann's understanding of the passage, particularly his use of the Gnostic redemption myth as an interpretative key. This is the article by Dieter Georgi, 'Der vor-paulinische Hymnus Phil 2, 6–11'.[3] Georgi argues that Käsemann's use of the *Erlösermythos* as a soteriological concept in terms of a descent into the world of matter, a freeing of enslaved elements in this world and a return to the heavenly realm is ill-founded. He adduces seven reasons why 'our text is not directly attributable to this form of the myth'; and these may be summarized, as we draw attention to the most important items in his list.

Käsemann admits that in Phil. ii the presentation of the 'primal destiny' of the *Urmensch* plays no part, and at certain decisive points the Gnostic 'Saviour' and the Christian Redeemer figure are different. For example, the former becomes incarnate only as a masquerade (contrast verse 8) and ascends by his own initiative to a place which he had before his descent with no 'increase' of power. The Christian figure in the passage is exalted by the sovereign and wonderful act of God (ii. 9) and receives an Enthronement-proclamation which places the entire world at His feet. Käsemann has described this ' new worthiness' which the exalted Christ was given, and

---

[1] 'Kritische Analyse', 94 f.   [2] *Op. cit.* 95.
[3] Contributed to *Zeit und Geschichte, Dankesgabe an Rudolf Bultmann zum 80. Geburtstag*, ed. E. Dinkler (Tübingen, 1964).

no doubt would regard this novel feature in the Pauline passage as part of the christianizing of the myth, to which attention was drawn above.

Georgi finds an important difference in the worship which is offered to the 'redeemed Redeemer'. No explicit mention is made in Phil. ii to Christ's active confrontation with God-denying spirit-forces—except of course that they prostrate themselves and render submission as they cry, Jesus Christ is Lord (v. 11); and the type of *proskynesis* which they offer, derived from the language of Isaiah xlv. 23, suggests to Georgi[1] that the background is that of later Judaism, not the Gnostic mythology. He concludes (p. 266): the use of Isa. xlv. 23 is 'a compelling reason for believing that the "conceptual world" (of the hymn) is to be sought not in religious Hellenism in general, and not in an extension of non-Christian gnosis, but in Hellenistic Judaism in which the LXX was a sacred text'. And in particular, the homage of the closing verses of the Philippians psalm derives not from the spirit-powers, but from the Godless men whose attitudes to the righteous appear in *Wisdom*, chapters v and xviii.[2]

As a comment on this viewpoint, we may confess that the similarity between Phil. ii and the righteous man's enemies in *Wisdom* is by no means clear, and there is nothing in the latter text to suggest the cosmic grandeur and finality of Phil. ii. 10, 11. Further, Georgi's tentative notion that the acclamation may originally have read ὁ δίκαιος υἱὸς Θεοῦ εἰς δόξαν Θεοῦ πατρός (on the basis of *Wis.* xviii. 13; cf. ii. 16) with Κύριος Ἰησοῦς Χριστός being substituted as a later Christian addition[3] does not inspire confidence in his proposal to deny a transcendental framework to Phil. ii. 6–11.

Georgi has, however, performed a most important service in (a) calling attention to some vital *differentiae* which mark out the Phil. ii Christology from the mythical framework of Hellenistic speculation; and (b) pointing to Hellenistic Judaism as a source of the humiliation–exaltation motif, as E. Schweizer had earlier done. The great weakness in his argumentation is that it builds too much on the portrayal of the righteous man in the *Wisdom of Solomon* whose vindication lacks those transcendental descriptions which make the picture in Phil. ii. 10, 11 so stately.

---

[1] 'Der vorpaulinische Hymnus', 265.
[2] *Op. cit.* 290.   [3] *Op. cit.* 275, 293 n. 90.

93

APPENDIX C

THE EUCHARISTIC SETTING OF
PHILIPPIANS II. 5-11

There are three arguments which Lohmeyer adduces in favour of the hypothesis that the setting of the Christ-hymn is in a Eucharistic context.[1] First, he argues that this is the appropriate setting because of the witness of I Cor. xiv. 26. Each member of the Corinthian Church is to bring respectively 'a psalm, a teaching, a revelation, a "tongue", an interpretation'. The fact that hymns are not explicitly alluded to leads Lohmeyer to conclude that they had no place in the *ordinary* worship of the Church at Corinth.

Secondly, hymns embodied Christian traditional teaching, and Lohmeyer states that, in the service described in I Cor. xiv, there could not have been any tradition of 'holy words'. We may interpret this remark to mean that, for Lohmeyer, hymns contained teaching too sacred for public proclamation. The teaching of the hymns belonged to the *disciplina arcani* of the Church.

In the third place, he avers that the hymn of Phil. ii demands an occasion 'in which the faith of the Church is directed to a purely eschatological goal'.

Now this close link between the tradition of 'holy words' and the eschatological outlook of the community, Lohmeyer believes, is found only in the Lord's Supper. The conclusion is then stated with clarity: Phil. ii. 6 ff. is a fragment of Eucharistic liturgy, and its Palestinian background is confirmed.[2] The place of the hymn in a letter whose *Leitmotiv* is martyrdom—both Paul's and the Church's—is a further proof that 'dieser Christuspsalmus ursprünglich zur Liturgie des Abendmahles gehörte'.[3]

The reception accorded to this theory has been decidedly cool and critical. Most scholars have passed an unfavourable verdict upon it. The fact that there are no specific and characteristic Eucharistic terms such as redemption, the new covenant, fellowship (κοινωνία) and the *parousia* in the Psalm was quickly pointed out by H. Windisch.[4]

J. Marty,[5] in criticism of a similar view of the Eucharistic setting of Phil. ii propounded by Lietzmann,[6] comments that this view is

[1] *Kyrios Jesus*, pp. 65 ff.   [2] *Ibid.* 66.
[3] *Ibid.* 66, 62.   [4] In his review, *TLZ*, LIV, xi (1929), 246-8.
[5] 'Étude des textes cultuels de prière contenus dans le N.T.', *RHPR*, III, 4/5 (1929), 369.   [6] 'Symbolstudien', *ZNTW*, XXII (1923), 265.

'difficult to maintain in the absence of other passages which are comparable and which are certainly Eucharistic'.

Some critics are content to quote Lohmeyer's suggestion with the briefest of comments. For instance, W. D. Davies[1] says simply that the proposal is 'mere conjecture'; and J. N. D. Kelly[2] repeats this verdict in almost identical language.

More recently, N. A. Dahl has sought to refurbish the theory by submitting that all the hymnic passages in the New Testament are concerned to 'evoke the remembrance of Christ' by the believers as they gathered for public worship. He builds upon the Pauline statement in I Cor. xi. 23 ff. that at the table the Lord's death is proclaimed (καταγγέλλειν) until the *parousia*. This 'proclaiming' is the verbal declaration of the person and saving mission of Christ (so J. Schniewind, *TWNT*, i, 70) as the verb καταγγέλλειν corresponds to the usage of הגיד in the Paschal *Haggadah*. Furthermore, this καταγγέλλειν is connected with thanksgiving over the bread and wine; and 'we are able to identify the form this commemoration of Christ took at the Supper in the Pauline Churches; for a text like Philippians ii. 6–11 corresponds to the Eucharistic thanksgiving in the later liturgy of Hippolytus. As Lietzmann detected, there is every reason to suppose that it is a similar formula which was used to "recall" Christ at the Supper in Paul's day.'[3]

A Eucharistic background to Phil. ii is mentioned as likely by L. Cerfaux,[4] mainly on the ground that the use of the divine names betrays a liturgical usage; the style is exalted and appropriate to a solemn occasion like the Eucharist; and the title of Jesus as 'Servant' is indicative of a liturgical setting (as in *Didache* x. 2, etc. and *I Clem.*):
'Les cantiques du Serviteur...ont été des hymnes d'action de grâces, et leur lieu littéraire naturel fut d'abord la liturgie de la Cène' (p. 130).

[1] *Paul and Rabbinic Judaism*[2], p. 355.
[2] *Early Christian Creeds* (1950), p. 18.
[3] 'Anamnesis: Mémoire et Commémoration dans le christianisme primitif', *ST*, i, i (1947), 86.
[4] 'L'hymne au Christ', 129.

PART II

AN EXEGETICAL STUDY OF THE HYMN IN PHILIPPIANS II. 6–11 IN THE LIGHT OF RECENT INTERPRETATION

CHAPTER V

THE PRE-EXISTENT BEING

ἐν μορφῇ Θεοῦ ὑπάρχων (verse 6a)

Our interest in this phrase is immediately focused upon the word μορφή, translated in the A.V. and R.V. as 'form'. That this is the most adequate rendering of the Greek word is doubted, even by those commentators (such as M. R. Vincent[1]) who cannot propose a better alternative. L. Cerfaux[2] comments that 'le substantif μορφή...est intraduisible en français'; and the same admission must be made in respect of all attempts to render the word into any modern language (as D. M. Stanley remarks[3]).

The discovering of the exact meaning is handicapped by the fact that the term is found only here in St Paul's writing, although it is true that cognate forms of the root μορφ- are elsewhere used by him. In recent discussion three main explanations of the word in the context of Philippians ii. 6 have been offered; and to a survey of these explanations we turn.

But a word of explanation about this method of treatment itself is required before we embark upon the classification of the various views which have been propounded. Ostensibly we are concerned with the task of discovering the meaning of a single Greek word in the context of a phrase. But this one Greek term stands at the head of the Christ-hymn; and in a way it sets the stage for all that follows in the next six verses. It would therefore be no exaggeration to say that μορφὴ Θεοῦ is the key-term of the entire hymn; and thus its significance calls for extended comment. The exegesis of the one phrase has bearing upon the interpretation of the whole passage.

This feature will be apparent as we address our enquiry to a consideration of recent discussion in sections B and C. It will be needful to set the interpretation of μορφή within the larger frame

---

[1] *The Epistles to the Philippians and to Philemon* (*ICC*, 1897), p. 57.

[2] *Le Christ...*, p. 290.

[3] *Christ's Resurrection in Pauline Soteriology*, p. 97.

of the current understanding of New Testament Christology. In section B we shall attempt this as we see how the modern 'Biblical theology' movement treats a text like Philippians ii. 6, seeking to find linguistic parallels and similarities and building up an imposing structure on the basis of etymological equations and reminiscences—a procedure which has evoked the criticism of J. Barr in his recent studies of Biblical semantics.[1]

In section C the background of μορφή Θεοῦ will be sought in the first century world of speculative thought. Some commentators on the Pauline text—notably those on the Continent—have proposed that Philippians ii. 6 is but one instance of the debt of New Testament Christology to the redemption-myths which were supposedly current. A discussion of this setting will therefore be included.

Our first section, however, looks at the exegesis of Philippians ii. 6 in the older writers at the turn of the past century.

A. THE PHILOSOPHICAL BACKGROUND OF 'MORPHE THEOU'

The standard commentary of J. B. Lightfoot, published first in 1868 and subsequently revised but without material alteration, provides a convenient starting-point in the history of modern interpretation.[2]

Lightfoot made the following points in his search for the true linguistic background to Philippians ii. 6.[3]

(a) The entire phrase ἐν μορφῇ Θεοῦ ὑπάρχων points back to the time prior to the Incarnation. Thus, the μορφή in which Christ was refers to His pre-temporal existence.

(b) Μορφή and σχῆμα are compared in detail. The relevance of this discussion is seen when it is observed that σχῆμα occurs in Philippians ii. 8. Lightfoot concludes that μορφή stands in contrast with σχῆμα as that which is intrinsic and essential stands in contrast with that which is accidental and outward. The nuance of σχῆμα suggests that which is changeable and variable, while

---

[1] *The Semantics of Biblical Language* (1961); and the same author's article, 'The Position of Hebrew Language in Theological Education', *The International Review of Missions*, L, 200 (1961), pp. 433–44.

[2] *Saint Paul's Epistle to the Philippians* (1868). References are to the 1896 ed.

[3] *Op. cit.*, 'The synonymes μορφή and σχῆμα', 127 ff.

μορφή denotes that specific character of an object or person, a quality of abiding and permanent worth. It is eminently suitable, therefore, to be used in the Pauline context where 'it must apply to the attributes of the Godhead'.

(*c*) After citing some parallels from Plato and Aristotle, he concludes that, in the scriptural context of Philippians ii. 6, 'it (*sc.* the term μορφή) is used in a sense substantially the same which it bears in Greek philosophy'. With Plato, the μορφή is the impress of the 'idea' on the individual. Its meaning is not necessarily that of something which is perceptible; but equally its philosophical or metaphysical aspect is undeveloped. For Aristotle, however, the philosophical sense is pronounced and μορφή comes to take on the meaning of the essence (οὐσία) of a thing. It is this connotation which Lightfoot gives to the Pauline phrase. He admits that Paul need not be thought of as consciously deriving his use of the term from any philosophical nomenclature. He may rather be influenced by the speculations of Alexandrian and Gnostic Judaism which brought the philosophical terms of ancient Greece within his reach, just as λόγος may have entered the vocabulary of the author of the Prologue of John i. 1–14 along the same channel. Nonetheless, Lightfoot's conclusion is clearly stated: 'Though μορφή is not the same as φύσις or οὐσία, yet the possession of the μορφή involves participation in the οὐσία also.' This last phrase of Lightfoot's summing-up distinguishes his position from that of the Roman Catholic scholar H. Schumacher who took μορφή as the exact equivalent of οὐσία; and saw in the Pauline term a clear proof of the deity of Christ. The last-named writer[1] relied on certain indications in Aristotle where the term has this precise metaphysical sense.[2] He therefore interpreted the phrase as 'Being in (or, as being) the substance or essence of the Godhead'. Virtually the same understanding of μορφή is found in E. H. Gifford for whom μορφὴ Θεοῦ 'is the Divine nature actually and inseparably subsisting in the Person of Christ'.[3] The term 'includes the whole nature and essence of Deity'.[4] The

---

[1] Schumacher, *Christus in seiner Präexistenz und Kenose*, vol. II, esp. pp. 141–217 with his conclusion, p. 221. [2] *Op. cit.* pp. 188–91.
[3] *The Incarnation* (1911 ed. (first published 1897)), p. 16.
[4] *Op. cit.* p. 19.

ancestry of this view can be traced back to the Fathers of the Church.[1]

Lightfoot does not go to the extent of identifying μορφὴ Θεοῦ with the actual being of God; but says that, possessing the μορφή, the pre-incarnate One shared in the divine essence without actually being identified with it. This may seem to be a hair-splitting refinement; and hardly alters our conclusion that Lightfoot depends upon classical Greek authorities,[2] as does Gifford, for the parallels he adduces.

The influence of Lightfoot's discussion has been widely marked. Since his day his treatment of the word is accepted by H. R. Mackintosh[3] and H. C. G. Moule,[4] to name only some influential British writers of this older period. Both scholars are content to refer to Lightfoot and accept his conclusions. M. R. Vincent[5] challenged the latter's dependence upon classical parallels, but his discussion reaches a conclusion which is virtually the same as that of Lightfoot: 'to say that he was ἐν μορφῇ Θεοῦ is to say that he existed before his incarnation as essentially one with God'.

B. SEPTUAGINTAL BACKGROUND

One of the turning-points of New Testament study has been the investigation of the Old Testament background of many of the key-terms of the Christian gospel. This may be illustrated from the term now under discussion. The appearance of H. A. A. Kennedy's commentary in 1903 showed the influence of this

---

[1] Cf. 'Ambrosiaster''s dictum: '*forma Dei nihil differt a Deo*' quoted by Ewald–Wohlenberg, *Philipper*, p. 115. The reference is in Migne (*P.Lat.* XVII, 408).

[2] The chief references in Plato and Aristotle are: Plato, *Rep.* II, 381 C and *Phaed.* 271 A; and for a clear equation of μορφή and φύσις in the latter, φυσικὴ ἀκρόασις, II, 1 (cited by Schumacher, *Christus*, p. 187).

[3] *The Doctrine of the Person of Jesus Christ*, pp. 66 f.

[4] The Epistle to the Philippians (*CB*, 1899), pp. 64 f.; and the same author's *Philippian Studies* (1902), p. 92.

[5] 'Excursus on Vs. 6–11', *The Epistles to the Philippians, etc.*, p. 84; and similarly, Müller, *The Epistles of Paul to the Philippians and to Philemon*, p. 78; Jones, *The Epistle to the Philippians* (*WC*), p. 30: 'the phrase declares the essential Divinity of Christ, that which is inseparable from the essence and nature of God'; and E. F. Scott, *Philippians* (*IB*), p. 48: Christ 'was of the same nature as God...the principle of his being was essentially divine'.

new trend.[1] He indicated that from the usage of μορφή in the LXX 'the word had come, in later Greek, to receive a vague, general meaning far removed from the accurate, metaphysical content which belonged to it in writers like Plato and Aristotle'. An examination of the word in the LXX reveals that εἶδος and ὁμοίωμα are synonymous with it;[2] and this would give the sense of the outward form or appearance of the thing so described. Hence Bauer's *Wörterbuch* gives the meaning as 'äußere Erscheinungsform',[3] along with other possibilities; and similarly J. Behm in his contribution to Kittel's *Theologisches Wörterbuch*.[4] Kennedy went on, however, to state that the word 'always signifies a form which truly and fully expresses the being which underlies it'.[5] Confirmation of this is offered in the parallels from the papyri in Moulton–Milligan's *Vocabulary*.[6]

The upshot of this discussion is seen in the tendency to move away from the philosophical usage according to which μορφή carries the meaning of 'substance, essence'; and to relate it to the visible form which is characteristic of the object under consideration. Vincent Taylor[7] accepts this by quoting the later phrase μορφὴ δούλου which he takes to imply that the slave is recognized and known by the form he assumes. So the pre-existent Lord possessed a visible form which was characteristic of His being. Of this 'form of God' the best thing we can say is that it is His 'glory', the shining light in which, according to the Old Testament and inter-Testamental literature, God was pictured.[8] On this view, the term μορφή is not to be rendered by

---

[1] *The Epistle to the Philippians* (*ExGT*, 1903), pp. 435 f.

[2] For the synonymous meanings of εἶδος, ὁμοίωμα and μορφή in LXX, cf. Jud. viii. 18; Tobit i. 13; Job iv. 16; Wisd. xviii. 1; Isa. xliv. 13; Dan. iii. 19; IV Macc. xv. 4.

[3] W. Bauer, *Griechisch-Deutsches Wörterbuch* (1952), *ad loc.* (E.T. 1957, 530).

[4] J. Behm, *TWNT*, IV, 753–5.

[5] Kennedy, *The Epistle to the Philippians*, p. 436.

[6] Moulton–Milligan, *Vocabulary of the Greek New Testament*, p. 417.

[7] Taylor, *The Person of Christ in New Testament Teaching*, p. 75.

[8] That God was thought of as enveloped by an effulgent light, which also radiated from His person and was seen as a light-stream—and that His angels and other heavenly beings shared in this effulgence—seems clear from many strata of Old Testament and post-Old Testament sources: Ex. xvi. 10; xxiv. 16; xxxiii. 17–23; xl. 34 f.; I Kings viii. 11; Isa. vi. 3; lx. 1, 2; Ezek. i. 28; xliii. 2; xliv. 4; II Macc. ii. 8; III Macc. vi. 18; I Enoch xiv. 21, l. 4, cii. 3, civ. 1; Test. Levi iii. 4; II Esd. viii. 21; *Asc. Isa.* x. 16; Philo, *De*

'essence' or 'nature' in the ontological sense; but rather by some such expression as 'condition' or 'state' or even 'stamp',[1] 'character';[2] for as P. Bonnard[3] acutely points out the first translation cannot be fitted into the required meaning of Philippians ii. 7. It is, he says, the situation, the historical condition, the humble obedience of the slave that is there described. Bonnard offers the rendering 'condition' or 'position' or 'glory'. The last-mentioned word had been used by earlier writers.

H. A. W. Meyer, in the commentary[4] which is part of the series which bears his name, had defined μορφή as the divine 'glory'; it denotes 'the form of being corresponding to the essence and *exhibiting* the condition'. This idea of the interrelation of inner being and outward expression has been appealed to recently by E. Schweizer[5] who comments that Old Testament thinking 'does not separate form and substance as the Greek does, but regards the existence of a thing as bound up with its appearance'.

J. Weiss[6] similarly maintained that '"the divine form" which he possessed before becoming man (Phil. ii. 6) was nothing less than the divine *Doxa*, and may we not understand this statement to mean, in the Pauline sense, Christ was from the beginning no other than the *Kabōd*, the *Doxa*, of God himself, the glory and radiation of his being, which appears almost as an

Monarch. i, 6; and for Philo, cf. E. R. Goodenough, *By Light, Light: The Mystic Gospel of Hellenistic Judaism* (1935), pp. 11 ff., esp. p. 27, for his idea of God under the symbol of a light-stream. On the picture of God in II Enoch, Goodenough says: 'it is interesting to see that the view of God as Light had become so proverbial in Hellenistic Judaism as to be axiomatic even in an apocalypse' (267). Angels and other celestial beings are described in *Asc. Isa.* ix. 9; II Enoch xix. 1; xxii. 7; Test. Levi xviii. 5; I Enoch lxii. 15, xxii. 8; II Bar. li. 10; II Esd. ii. 39.

[1] This translation is suggested by G. R. Beasley-Murray in *Peake's Commentary on the Bible*[2] (1962), *ad loc.* It assumes that μορφή is synonymous with χαρακτήρ (cf. Heb. i. 3; and Ignatius, *ad Magn.* v, 2).

[2] This is Stanley's rendering: *Christ's Resurrection*, p. 96.

[3] *L'épître aux Philippiens*, pp. 42 f. D. G. Dawe, 'A Fresh Look at the Kenotic Christologies', *SJT*, xv, 4 (1962), 337–45 translates the text as 'of the divine realm', 'in the divine condition' (340).

[4] *Commentary on the New Testament, The Epistle to the Philippians* (E.T. 1876), pp. 77 ff. (quoted by Taylor, *The Person of Christ*, p. 68).

[5] *Erniedrigung und Erhöhung*, p. 54, n. 234 (not in E.T.).

[6] *Earliest Christianity*, ii, p. 478.

independent hypostasis of God and yet is connected intimately with God?' And in a later decade J. Behm[1] in the article contributed to *Kittel* arrives at the same conclusion: '"The form of God", in which the pre-existent Christ was, is nothing else than the divine "glory"; the Pauline "being in the form of God" corresponds completely with John xvii. 5: "the glory which I had with thee before the world was".'

The interpretation which we have just outlined wears all the suggestiveness of something novel and unheard-of; and it has called forth a measure of criticism.[2] We have now to trace the

[1] *TWNT*, IV, 759 drawing upon Calvin's commentary *ad* Phil. ii. 6: 'Christ, then, before the creation of the world, was in the form of God, because from the beginning He had His glory with the Father, as He says in John xvii. 5.'

[2] The most direct challenge to this interpretation has come from Käsemann, 'Kritische Analyse', 65–9 who argues that the translation of ἐν μορφῇ as 'Erscheinungsweise' is inadequate; and prefers a translation such as 'Daseinsweise' (following Dibelius, *An die Philipper*[3], p. 75). The ground for this proposal is that, in Hellenistic usage, μορφή has the meaning of 'existence in the divine substance and power'. Celestial beings and 'divine men' who appeared on earth with preternatural powers are spoken of as wearing the divine *morphe* by which is meant that they exercised a miraculous power as though they were 'equal with God'. 'Divine power' and 'divine nature', Käsemann maintains, go together (*loc. cit.* 68); and the terms μορφή Θεοῦ and ἰσόθεος φύσις are parallel and synonymous.

Further, Behm's view cannot do justice to the force of the preposition ἐν in the phrase. It is used in the technical sense to signify the sphere in which a person stands. Used of the pre-existent One it means that He was established in a place of divine power. But this implies a corresponding nature. Only in this way can the preposition be interpreted meaningfully. We may speak of a man 'having an appearance', but not his being 'in that appearance' (*loc. cit.* 68; and Geiselmann, *Jesus der Christus*, p. 138 similarly).

Another point is taken up by Schweizer, *Erniedrigung und Erhöhung*, p. 54, n. 234. Is there any proof of the meaning of μορφή as 'position', or 'condition'? The same allegation is brought by Jervell, *Imago Dei*, p. 230, n. 220, which regards the proposed translation of μορφή as 'position' as a 'makeshift' (*Notbehelf*), and lacking in demonstrable proof. Jervell criticizes the attempt which Schweizer makes to suggest a possible parallel. According to this attempt, 'if the Genesis creation story of man as made in the "image" of God really means his establishment in the "position" of a ruler over all creation, then this would be some kind of parallel. For the unity of being and appearance, this passage (writes Schweizer) is enlightening.' He goes on to cite a Jewish prayer in which Adam calls for salvation from ἀνάγκη; and calls upon his original 'form' (μορφή) in Paradise and the πνεῦμα which gave life to it. It is possible, Schweizer declares, 'that by this his glory is

way in which it developed and to ask whether there is any real justification for it. Clearly the correctness of such a view will have distinct bearing upon some wider issues. The traditional interpretation of Philippians ii. 6 has been regarded as giving metaphysical basis for the Person of Christ in New Testament teaching, and as providing some justification for the later Church doctrine of the Two Natures definition of the Councils. While our concern at the moment is with the history of linguistic interpretation of a Biblical text, it is clear that within the same area of Christian thought there is a growing consensus of opinion, represented by such scholars as R. Bultmann,[1] O. Cullmann,[2] E. Brunner,[3] and John Knox,[4] that the New Testament contains no evidence for a metaphysical statement of Christology. The modern emphasis rather is upon a functional Christology which is set within the framework of the Redeemer's saving acts. As Cullmann has expressed it: 'All speculation concerning his natures is therefore un-Biblical as soon as it ceases to take place in the light of the great historical deeds of redemption.'[5]

The first thorough investigation of μορφή in the light of the Old Testament terms צֶלֶם and דְּמוּת goes to the credit of J.

referred to, which according to Jewish thought betokened above all things his position in the sight of God and with reference to angels and other created things' (loc. cit. 54, n. 234).

But this view raises the same difficulty as Käsemann had earlier noted. Can there be true 'position' without a corresponding 'nature' or 'essence'? As Jervell phrases it, 'So kann man von Position nicht sprechen, ohne zugleich Substanz zu erwähnen' (loc. cit. note 220).

Käsemann's positive contribution to the debate on the significance of μορφή will be considered later in section C.

[1] *Theology of the New Testament*, I, p. 191.

[2] *The Christology of the New Testament*, pp. 3 f.; but a clearer statement of his attitude is in his *Christ and Time* (E.T. 1951), pp. 126–8. Cf., however, his clarification in his article translated as 'The Reply of Professor Cullmann to Roman Catholic critics', *SJT*, xv, 1 (1962), 36–43.

[3] *The Christian Doctrine of Creation and Redemption, Dogmatics*, II (E.T. 1952), pp. 357 ff.

[4] J. Knox, *Jesus, Lord and Christ* (1958), esp. pp. 225 ff.

[5] O. Cullmann, *Christ and Time*, p. 128 (*Christus und die Zeit* (1946), 114); *Christology*, p. 326: 'All mere speculation about his natures is an absurdity. Functional Christology is the only kind which exists.' For a criticism of these statements and their implications, see J. Frisque, *Oscar Cullmann, Une théologie de l'histoire du salut* (1960), pp. 241 ff.

THE PRE-EXISTENT BEING (VERSE 6a)

Héring. In a series of articles and in his book *Le Royaume de Dieu et sa venue*[1] he took up a hint dropped by Lohmeyer that the LXX often uses μορφή to translate the word צלם in its meaning of 'image, likeness'. A good example of this usage is in Daniel iii. 19 where the Aramaic equivalent צְלֵם is rendered into the Greek as ἡ μορφή (*sc.* τοῦ προσώπου αὐτοῦ): 'the form of his (*sc.* the king's) countenance' was changed. An even more interesting comparison of the Hebrew and the LXX is in the Creation story of Genesis i. 26 ff. where the divine pronouncement runs: 'Let us make man in our image, after our likeness.' It seems clear that the two concepts, 'image', 'likeness' must be taken as synonyms.[2] The Hebrew צלם is rendered by εἰκών in the LXX. Thus by a simple equation of terms Héring came to the solution of the curious expression in Philippians ii. 6: 'Si l'on traduit μορφή par "image", tout s'éclaircit.'[3] This simple expedient, which cuts through a veritable jungle of complexity by opening up a straight path, was welcomed enthusiastically by those who examined it. A. M. Hunter[4] thus comments: 'If μορφή here has the sense of "image", at once we get a clue to what follows. Now there is evidence that μορφή can translate the Aramaic word for "image". That meaning fits our passage like a glove—

> Who being in God's image
> Did not consider equality with God
> Something to be seized.'

O. Cullmann,[5] the latest writer to turn his attention in a detailed way to Philippians ii. 6, arrives at the same conclusion:

[1] 'Kyrios Anthropos', *RHPR*, xvi (1936), 196–209; 'Les bases bibliques de l'humanisme chrétien', *RHPR*, xxv (1945), 18 ff.; *Le Royaume de Dieu et sa venue*, 159 ff. A. M. Hunter mentions Héring's art. in *Recherches théologiques* (1) (1936), 12–25, which is now unobtainable.

[2] Or interpreted to mean that דמות limits צלם; so P. Humbert, 'Trois notes sur Genèse 1': note 2: 'L'image de Dieu' (88–90), *Interpretationes ad vetus Testamentum pertinentes: Mowinckel Festschrift* (1955), pp. 85–96. But this is opposed by I. Engnell who comments on Gen. i. 26: it is 'an expression, the second half of which I confess I am absolutely unable to consider as a limitation of the former, but as an equivalent and strengthening of it' ('"Knowledge" and "life" in the Creation story', *Wisdom of Israel*, etc., Rowley *Festschrift* (1960), p. 112).

[3] Héring, 'Kyrios Anthropos', 161, n. 2. He wishes therefore to render the text: 'Il existait en tant qu'*image de Dieu*' (162). Some corroboration for this is found in the Peshitta version which reads: *baḏmûṯâ da'lâhâ.*

[4] *Paul and his Predecessors*[2], p. 43.   [5] *Christology*, p. 176.

107

'Thus μορφή in Philippians ii. 6 is immediately related to the concept εἰκών, since the Semitic root word דְּמוּת or its synonym צֶלֶם can correspond to either of the two Greek words.' This quotation brings the word εἰκών into the arena of discussion; and we must now look closely at the data. The issue may be stated at the outset. The argument for the equation of μορφή Θεοῦ with εἰκών or δόξα rests upon a number of different grounds; and the total impact, its proponents say, is cumulative.[1] If it were to be established that μορφή and εἰκών/δόξα were equivalent terms and could be used interchangeably, then the suggested interpretation of the Christological text would be: 'As the image and glory of God in His pre-existent state, our Lord uniquely shared in the divine splendour.' He possessed that image perfectly because only He is God's Son in the unique sense.[2] The lines of evidence for this thesis are:

(a) It may be shown that εἰκών and μορφή are used as interchangeable terms in the Greek Bible, and are regarded as synonyms in other places. It is not necessary to conduct an independent enquiry into the literary connections of these two terms because the ground has been comprehensively covered in the recent work of F.-W. Eltester, *EIKON im Neuen Testament*, which surveys the *Sprachgebrauch* of εἰκών in various authors. The most important text is Genesis i. 26 where 'image' and 'likeness' appear in a parallelism. The corresponding Semitic terms צלם and דמות may thus be judged as equivalents, if there is corroborating evidence. This is forthcoming.[3]

---

[1] But we should, strictly speaking, keep separate the equations μορφή = εἰκών and μορφή = δόξα, although many writers do not do so. It is possible to hold that while μορφή is a variant of δόξα, the term εἰκών 'must not be confused with it' (so Behm, *TWNT*, IV, 760).

[2] See L. S. Thornton, *The Common Life in the Body of Christ*[3] (1950), p. 292.

[3] Eltester, *op. cit.* 13 ff. Cf. G. S. Duncan, *Jesus, Son of Man* (1948), p. 193. In short compass, the data are: the LXX uses εἰκών to render דמות in Gen. i. 26, 27, v. 3, ix. 6; the same Greek term is used to translate צלמא in Dan. ii (4 times) and iii (9 times), and μορφή is used to translate צלמא in Dan. iii. 19. We have already noticed that the Syriac has *baḏmûṯâ* to translate ἐν μορφῇ in Phil. ii. 6; and it is worth a mention that Delitzsch translates both Col. i. 15 and II Cor. iv. 4 by using צלם. Further discussion of the linguistic data is in K. L. Schmidt, art.'"Homo Imago Dei" im alten und neuen Testament', *Eranos-Jahrbuch*, XV: *Der Mensch* (1948), 149–95; and C. Ryder Smith, *The Bible Doctrine of Man*

One extra piece of supporting witness for the equation εἰκών = μορφή may be found in the *Corpus Hermeticum*.[1] The importance of this text lies in its attestation of many of the key-words of Philippians ii. 6 ff. Eltester[2] draws attention to the presence of μορφὴ θεοῦ, εἰκὼν τοῦ πατρός and ἴσος θεῷ side by side in the same context; while another recent word-study, *Imago Dei* by J. Jervell,[3] has pointed out the presence of terms like κενόω, μορφὴ δούλου, δοῦλος, all of which are found in the Philippians passage. The conclusions of Eltester on *C.H.* I, 12: 'εἰκών und μορφή sind hier offenbar synonym und bedeuten beide "Gestalt": die "Gestalt" ist dann als Ausdruck des "Wesens" zu fassen', and those of Jervell on the same passage: 'εἰκών hat dieselbe Bedeutung wie μορφή. "Morphe" heißt dann nicht mehr "Form" oder "Gestalt", sondern "Wesen"', differ slightly in their interpretation, but they are one in the matter of the essential synonymity of εἰκών and μορφή. The Semitic צלמא/צלם or דמותא/דמות is the translation-equivalent for both.

(*b*) That εἰκών and δόξα are parallel and equivalent terms is shown in the LXX's translation of תְּמוּנָה by both these words. Here again the detailed researches of Eltester have comprehensively examined the data.[4] Attention has also been drawn to the use of δόξα in the LXX by L. H. Brockington in an article under that caption.[5] Noting that Genesis i. 27 is directly quoted

(1951), pp. 94 f. He examines the usages of the Hebrew words תמונה, דמות and צלם with their LXX equivalents, and concludes that 'for the LXX translators the three *Hebrew* terms were synonyms' (95).

[1] *Corpus Hermeticum*, I, 12–15 (in the edition of A. D. Nock and A.-J. Festugière (1945), 10–12). The most important phrases are: ὁ Νοῦς, ὢν ζωὴ καὶ φῶς, ἀπεκύησεν Ἄνθρωπον αὐτῷ ἴσον οὗ ἠράσθη ὡς ἰδίου τόκου· περικαλλὴς γάρ, τὴν τοῦ πατρὸς εἰκόνα ἔχων, ὄντως γὰρ καὶ θεὸς ἠράσθη τῆς ἰδίας μορφῆς. The importance of this text, in the elucidation of Philippians ii. 6 ff., will be discussed later. We may note now the linguistic similarity, about which Henry comments ('Kénose', *Supp. DB*, 21): 'In this text μορφή is much nearer to εἰκών than to οὐσία and signifies the external appearance rather than the specific character; it is sometimes almost a synonym of "reflection".'

[2] This text is discussed by Eltester, *EIKON*, pp. 80–8, 133 n. 14 (*op. cit.* p. 10 for the equivalence of εἰκών and μορφή in the light of this documentary evidence).

[3] *Imago Dei*, pp. 228 f.

[4] Eltester, *EIKON*, pp. 23, 24; Behm, *TWNT*, IV, 759, n. 53.

[5] 'The Septuagintal Background to the New Testament use of δόξα', *Studies in the Gospels* (ed. D. E. Nineham) (1955), p. 2.

in I Corinthians xi. 7 (man is 'the image and glory') he comments that 'it may well be that δόξα is here virtually a synonym of εἰκών seeing that δόξα translates *t^emunah* "form" in Numbers xii. 8 and Psalm xvii (xvi). 15'. To this fact may be added the relevant detail that תמונה is also found in Job iv. 16 where the LXX translates by μορφή. This linguistic study endorses the verdict of J. Schneider in his treatise on the word: ' δόξα erscheint damit zugleich als verstärktes Synonym von εἰκών.'[1]

(c) This close association in the writings of the LXX of the concepts of 'image' and 'glory' leads us on to consider those places in the New Testament where Jesus is described as 'the image and glory of God'. There are two passages where the teaching is clear; and remaining verses where it is probable or possible.

In the first category we place II Corinthians iv. 4[2] which is undoubtedly Pauline; and Colossians i. 15 where the Apostolic authorship has been disputed since the time of Holtzmann's essay.[3] In the former reference the text reads: 'in whom (*sc.* οἱ ἀπολλύμενοι) the god of this age has blinded the minds of the unbelieving that the light of the gospel of the glory of Christ, ὅς ἐστιν εἰκών τοῦ Θεοῦ, should not dawn upon them'. The close juxtaposition of the terms δόξα and εἰκών is striking. The main drift of the teaching is clear. Εἰκών is used to set forth the relationship between God and Christ, as Schlatter and Jervell[4] have shown. The former writes: 'Vielleicht besaß er (*sc.* Paul) im Begriff, "Bild Gottes" eine Denkform, mit der er sich das ewige Verhältnis des Vaters zum Sohn verdeutlicht hat (2 Kor. 4, 4: Kol. 1. 15).'[5]

The gospel according to Paul is one of the revelation of God's glory (cf. I Tim. i. 11; Tit. ii. 13). This divine δόξα is the otherworldly splendour in which the Old Testament envisages the immediate presence of Yahweh. It is used in the Old Testament under the Hebrew term כָּבוֹד as 'a kind of totality of qualities

---

[1] *Doxa. Eine bedeutungsgeschichtliche Studie* (1932), p. 54.

[2] On this passage and Col. i. 15 cf. Eltester, *EIKON*, pp. 130 ff.

[3] H. J. Holtzmann, *Kritik der Epheser- und Kolosserbriefe* (1872).

[4] Jervell, *Imago Dei*, pp. 214 f. Indeed, he comments that 'in the presentation of Christ as the image of God we find the central affirmation of the Pauline theology'.

[5] A. Schlatter, *Die Theologie des Neuen Testaments*, II (1910), p. 299 (cited by Jervell, *op. cit.* p. 214).

which make up his divine power; it has close affinities with the holiness which is of the nature of deity and it is a visible extension for the purpose of manifesting holiness to men'.[1] Yet no finite being can see the uncovered glory of God in its full blaze of light and majesty. Normally, therefore, it is veiled behind a cloud (Ex. xvi. 10; Num. xvii. 7); and Moses is permitted to see only the reflection of the *k^{e}bod Yahweh* (Ex. xxxiii. 18 ff.).

There is an important development of teaching in the writing of Ezekiel. According to this prophet, the 'glory' is not merely a manifestation of God in concrete form (as it had been earlier, in such phenomena as fire, earthquake and cloud); but is identical with Him. Thus God and His *kabod* are interchangeable. But no man can see Him in Himself; yet He reveals Himself in His glory. Thus we arrive at an important conclusion, endorsed by Ezekiel i. 26–8, that God cannot be seen in His essence—the unfailing witness of the scripture in both Testaments—but only in His image.

We may suppose that Paul inherited this line of theological reasoning in II Corinthians iv where verses 4 and 6 explain each other. The gospel promises the dispelling of human darkness and the lifting of the veil of unbelief (cf. II Cor. iii. 12–18) by an exhibiting of the divine glory. But this outward shining of the inner being of God may not be known directly. The rubric of John i. 18: 'No man has seen God at any time' is true for Paul as for all the scripture-writers (cf. Col. i. 15; I Tim. vi. 16). His manifest presence is shown forth in the person (πρόσωπον, verse 6) of His Son in whom the glory of God appears to men (e.g. John i. 14). Jervell's estimate of the New Testament teaching is important for this line of interpretation: 'Doxa Christi ist nichts anderes als die Doxa Gottes, die in Christus anwesend ist.'[2] Christ, in the Corinthians passage, is portrayed as the risen and exalted heavenly being who appeared to Saul on the Damascus road (Acts ix. 3, xxii. 6, 11, xxvi. 13) as to Stephen at an earlier point in the record (vii. 55).[3]

[1] E. Jacob, *Theology of the Old Testament* (E.T. 1958), p. 79.

[2] *Imago Dei*, p. 214 (cf. 216).

[3] May the καί be epexegetical in this reference? If so, we should read: Stephen 'saw the glory of God, that is, Jesus standing at the right hand of God'. For the New Testament picture of the exalted Lord as one of irradiated brightness, 'the visible radiance of the divine light' (Kittel, *TWNT*, II, 240,

The Colossians text (i. 15) speaks of Christ as ὅς ἐστιν εἰκὼν τοῦ Θεοῦ τοῦ ἀοράτου. The clue to the meaning of εἰκών here is found in the complementary description of the same verse. Christ is also 'the firstborn of all creation'. The term πρωτό-τοκος is comparative and is used with the sense of 'the firstborn *before* all creation', as L. S. Thornton has argued.[1] This sense is required by the context, for the writer goes on immediately to say that in Him all creation sprang to birth; and that He is before all things (verse 17: πρὸ πάντων). The purpose of these descriptions of Christ is clearly polemic. Against an incipient Gnosticism which would reduce the status of Christ and inter-pose angelic and spiritual powers as mediators between the high God and the world of men, the author insists that Christ is the sole intermediary because His office is unique. He alone is the sphere in which creation began; He alone is its sustainer (verse 17*b*); and He alone is its ultimate goal (verse 16 end). And these unique functions ascribed to Him are proper because He is *sui generis* in His relationship to God. He is the image of the invisible God.

The distinction between the teaching of these two passages may be stated. In the earlier text Paul declared that his gospel is the true demonstration of the glory of God. The controversial background is clearly that of the Judaizers' claim that the glory of the Mosaic dispensation did not require any 'new order' (chapter iii). At Colossae the author is concerned to prove that the divine 'fulness', 'the totality of the essence of God', resides in Christ and may therefore be seen in Him and not in the spiritual powers.

From these two sections of the New Testament, each with its different background, it is possible to draw one firm conclusion as to the Biblical meaning of εἰκών. The term 'image of God' is not fully understood by the meaning of 'representative of God', however perfect that representation may be thought to be. The phrase must include the thought that God Himself is personally

251), cf. G. H. Boobyer, *St Mark and the Transfiguration Story* (1942), pp. 66 ff.: 'When Christ's radiant appearance is mentioned by the New Testament, it is predominantly around the thought of his shining form in heaven...' (68); and for the special relation between Paul's idea of the glorified Lord and the Damascus road experience, cf. H. A. A. Kennedy, *St Paul's Conceptions of the Last Things* (1904), pp. 90–3.

[1] *The Common Life in the Body of Christ*, p. 293.

present, *Deus manifestus*, in His Son.[1] The detailed consideration which Lightfoot gives to the word in his Colossians commentary[2] under the headings of Representation and Manifestation may be supplemented by the important observations of Vincent Taylor,[3] C. F. D. Moule,[4] H. Kleinknecht,[5] C. Masson[6] and E. Lohse.[7] Kleinknecht, in his article, shows that in ancient thought an εἰκών was not held to be a mere representation of an object but was believed in some way to participate in the being of the object it symbolized. In some sense, it *was* the object it represented. As he puts it, it is the reality itself coming to expression.[8] It is the 'objectivization' of the essence of the object so described.

As a Christological term it refers to the coming into full expression, in the experience of men, of the divine glory.[9] 'In His face we see the *shekinah* present in visible form.'[10]

This last allusion to the *shekinah*, a rabbinical term for the manifested glorious presence of Yahweh,[11] may help to explain some other verses where the thought of Jesus as the glory of God is in view. The following places have been interpreted in this way:[12]

Ephesians i. 17: 'The God of our Lord Jesus Christ, the Father of the glory.' The genitive may be substantival in which case it is

---

[1] This is very clearly expressed by E. Lohse, 'Imago Dei bei Paulus', *Libertas Christiana, Festschrift Friedrich Delekat* (1957), pp. 122–35: 'In Christus offenbart sich Gott selbst'(126); 'In Christus ist der unsichtbare Gott offenbar geworden—nur in ihm' (129).

[2] *St Paul's Epistles to the Colossians and to Philemon* (1904), *ad loc.*

[3] *The Names of Jesus* (1954), pp. 124 ff.

[4] *The Epistles to Colossians and to Philemon*, pp. 62 ff.

[5] *S.v.* εἰκών, *TWNT*, II, 391 ff.

[6] *L'épître de S. Paul aux Colossiens* (*CNT*, 1950), pp. 98 f.

[7] 'Imago Dei bei Paulus', pp. 122–35.

[8] Kleinknecht, *TWNT*, II, 386 (cf. *loc. cit.* 393 f.).

[9] This thought is expressed very clearly by Lohse, 'Imago Dei', 127. Commenting on the apparent contradiction of the phrase εἰκὼν τοῦ Θεοῦ τοῦ ἀοράτου, he remarks that the contradiction is resolved when 'we observe that by the term "image" is meant the "becoming-evident" (*das Sichtbarwerden*) of that which up to now has been hidden'. This manifestation of God in Christ is related to the Christian conviction that in Christ the new age has dawned, and in Him the invisible God has revealed Himself (*loc. cit.* 129). [10] Taylor, *The Names of Jesus*, p. 127.

[11] See G. F. Moore, *Judaism*, I (1927), pp. 419 ff. for the *shekinah* (שְׁכִינָה; Aram. שְׁכִנְתָּא).

[12] These verses are considered by A. M. Ramsey, *The Glory of God and the Transfiguration of Christ* (1949); and H. Kittel, *Die Herrlichkeit Gottes* (1934), pp. 183 ff.

a title for Christ, or descriptive (as most writers take it) in which case it refers back to the Father as 'glorious'.

Colossians i. 27: 'Christ in you, the hope of glory.' It is submitted that the glory, no less than the mystery, may be equivalent to 'Christ in you'; but this seems unnatural.

James ii. 1 is a well-known *crux*. The Greek reads: τοῦ Κυρίου ἡμῶν 'Ιησοῦ Χριστοῦ τῆς δόξης. Among the possible interpretations J. B. Mayor takes the sense to be 'our Lord Jesus Christ, the glory'; meaning that Christ is Himself the *shekinah* in the midst of the congregation and this will have a sobering effect upon those guilty of social snobbery. 'This interpretation makes good sense, and it fits the Greek better than the others' (A. M. Ramsey).[1] John i. 14 is one of the clearest indications of the point under review. Both verb (ἐσκήνωσεν, with Old Testament associations of Tabernacle and Temple, the holy σκηνή) and noun seem to have the thought that the incarnate Word expresses what God is *in se*. The commentary of C. F. Burney has produced cogent evidence of the Old Testament and Rabbinic setting of this part of the Prologue.[2]

All in all, then, the summing up of A. M. Ramsey will appear not unreasonable:[3] 'There seems to be good evidence that the early Church thought of Jesus as Himself the manifestation of the glory of God.'

There are other places in which the equation or equivalence of εἰκών and δόξα has been traced, although (it must be confessed) some of the correspondences seem more fortuitous than by design, and therefore some of the conclusions are questionable.

(i) If we draw together the strands of teaching in I Corinthians xv. 49 and Philippians iii. 21, the result will be a 'demonstration' of the equation εἰκών = δόξα as applied to the resurrection bodies of the faithful. Paul announces, in the first text, 'As we have borne the image of the earthy, we shall also bear the image (εἰκών) of the heavenly'. In the latter text he goes on to set forth the same contrast in terms of 'the body of our lowly estate' which we know under terrestrial conditions and the body which will be ours when the present 'frame' (II Cor. v. 1 ff.) is

[1] *Op. cit.* p. 149.
[2] *The Aramaic Origin of the Fourth Gospel*, pp. 35 ff.
[3] Ramsey, *The Glory of God*, p. 150.

made to conform (σύμμορφον) to the body of His glory (σῶμα τῆς δόξης αὐτοῦ). One further interesting point is the use of the adjective here: σύμμορφον, of which the English 'con*form*ed' is the exact equivalent. The form (μορφή) of the new body (σῶμα πνευματικόν) will be that which belongs to the body of glory which is His in His Exaltation.

(ii) II Corinthians iii. 18 uses closely corresponding language for the believer's present spiritual conformity to the image of his Lord. 'We all, with unveiled faces, reflecting as a mirror the δόξα of the Lord are transformed (μεταμορφούμεθα) into the same image (τὴν αὐτὴν εἰκόνα), from glory to glory, as by the Spirit of the Lord.' The difficult phrase, ἀπὸ δόξης εἰς δόξαν, we may interpret, with Héring, to mean: 'from His glory to our being like Him in the final state'.[1] This process of inward renewal and increasing approximation to the pattern of Christ is elsewhere spoken of as a 'taking shape' of Christ in the believer (Gal. iv. 19: the verb is μορφωθῇ). It seems clear in these references that the final 'image' into which the Christian is being transformed is nothing else than the 'glory' of the heavenly Man; and the verb which denotes this change is that which comes from the root μορφ-.

(iii) Romans viii. 29 speaks of the purpose of God to bring every Christian to this conformity to the likeness of Christ His Son, so that the family likeness may be apparent throughout the whole company of Christ and His people, thought of as a unity, the *totus Christus*. In the next verse, moreover, this plan is described as a 'glorifying' of those who are thus united to Christ in election, calling and salvation. The equivalence of the terms image and glory (it is implied) could hardly be more clearly proved.[2]

From these allusions in the Pauline writing with their illustration of the way in which μορφή, εἰκών, and δόξα are used in

---

[1] This phrase perhaps illustrates the unwarranted length to which this type of exegesis can go. It may be that all that Héring (*La seconde épître aux Corinthiens* (*CNT*, p. 40)) draws out of this phrase is implicit; but on the other hand it is clearly possible that the expression is but a rhetorical one and with no precise significance (like Rom. i. 17: ἐκ πίστεως εἰς πίστιν: thus E. Lohse, *loc. cit.* 134, n. 51).

[2] Thus Jervell, *Imago Dei*, pp. 271–81; cf. Lohse, 'Imago Dei', 133; Michel, *Der Brief an die Römer* (1955), p. 182; Thornton, *The Common Life in the Body of Christ*, pp. 181 f.; J. A. T. Robinson, *The Body* (1952), pp. 80 f.

interchangeable ways, we have sought to demonstrate that the interpretation of ἐν μορφῇ Θεοῦ can legitimately be taken as κατ' εἰκόνα... or ἐν δόξῃ Θεοῦ. There is one special application of this picture Paul gives of Jesus as 'the image and glory of God', viz., his doctrine of the last Adam. To this teaching we now turn.

Recent studies in the background of Pauline Christology have fastened upon his so-called 'Second Adam' teaching as an important factor in the shaping of his thought. The relevance of this concept is seen clearly in two places especially, viz., I Corinthians xv. 20–2, 45–50, and Romans v. 12–21. In the second reference the parallel is drawn between the first man Adam who is regarded as the head of the race, because of whose sin the whole of humanity is implicated in sin and death (in line with Rabbinical teaching); and the One whom the first Adam 'typified' (v. 14: τύπος τοῦ μέλλοντος). The advent of the 'second Adam' is by contrast one of hope and salvation. By His obedience He has reversed the stream of humanity as far as those who are justified by the grace of God in Him are concerned.

The contrast is more succinctly put in the Corinthians passage. Here the expression, ὁ ἔσχατος Αδαμ, is actually in the text; and the issues of life and death are clearly depicted. Death entered through the first man who is 'the man of dust' (cf. Gen. ii. 7, iii. 19), whereas life reigns through the 'second Man' who came from heaven and has become πνεῦμα ζωοποιοῦν, conferring His life upon those who are His. They will ultimately share His heavenly image even as they here and now, as members of the human race, share the image of 'the man of dust' (v. 49). It seems that there are two main strands of teaching in the Apostle's discussion here. There is the estimate he gives of Jesus as the embodiment of the perfect image of God. For that reason He provides the prototype of the heavenly image into which Christians will finally be changed. They will bear His likeness by becoming immortal or heavenly beings (I Cor. xv. 49).

There is equally a statement of the present activity of the second Man in the lives of His people. The purpose of God in the creation of the first Adam was frustrated for a time by the entry of sin. The effect of the advent of Christ is to reverse this calamity; and this He does by becoming, by virtue of His Resurrection and Exaltation, a 'life-imparting spirit', conferring on those who are joined to Him His own pneumatic life and uniting them in a spiritual union so that they are formed into 'one spirit' in Him (I Cor. vi. 17).

This process of incorporation into Christ is further described in terms which are reminiscent of the creation of the first man. The relevant texts are: Colossians iii. 10; Ephesians ii. 15 and iv. 22 ff. The putting on of the new man, in the first text, is elsewhere the equivalent of the putting on of Christ in Galatians iii. 27, Rom. xiii. 14, with the same verbs used in all instances. At Colossians iii. 10 there is some doubt as to whose image it is which forms the ground-plan of renewal. A first reading would suggest that it is the image of God the Creator which provides the pattern. But Lohmeyer has brought forward strong reasons for taking Christ as the Creator of 'the new man'.[1] And this is confirmed, Matthew Black[2] urges, by a comparison with Ephesians ii. 15 and iv. 22–4. Ignatius, *ad Ephes.* xx, 1 and *Barnabas* vi, 11, 12 show how this teaching was understood in the later Church.

In this discussion of the Pauline 'Second Adam' teaching two other sections of the *Corpus Paulinum* have been utilized. They are I Corinthians xi. 7 and those verses which set forth Paul's doctrine of the Church as the 'body of Christ'. The latter theme has been investigated by W. D. Davies[3] who concludes that the

---

[1] *Die Briefe an die Kolosser und an Philemon⁹* (*MeyerK.*), p. 142. The argument is based on the way in which the Apostle can speak of the Christian as putting on Christ (Gal. iii. 27; Rom. xiii. 14); and the declaration of Colossians iii. 11 that Christ is both everything (πάντα) and 'in all' (ἐν πᾶσιν), i.e. indwelling all the members of His Church. Lohmeyer concludes: 'So kann das für unsere Stelle kaum anderes bedeuten, als daß Christus der neue Mensch ist' (142). See the full discussion in Eltester, *EIKON*, pp. 158 ff. and Lohse, 'Imago Dei', 134; cf. Cullmann, *Christology*, p. 174.

[2] 'The Pauline Doctrine of the Second Adam', *SJT*, vii, 2 (1954), 170–9 (175). Cf. E. F. Scott, *The Epistles to the Colossians, to Philemon and to the Ephesians* (*MNTC*, 1930), p. 172: 'Thus Paul speaks of Christ as performing in himself a new act of creation... Christ was the Adam of a new type of human beings.' The full discussion of S. Hanson, *The Unity of the Church in the New Testament. Colossians and Ephesians* (1946), pp. 144 f. concludes that the expression ἕνα καινὸν ἄνθρωπον refers to the New Race incarnated in Christ as the Second Adam (parallel references in Eph. iv. 22 ff.), i.e. 'Christ incorporating saved humanity' (145).

[3] *Paul and Rabbinic Judaism²*, pp. 36 ff.

origin of Paul's ecclesiological teaching is Rabbinic speculation on the place of Adam as the protoplast of humanity. Men were thought of as 'in Adam', the common eponymous ancestor of the race. Paul boldly takes over this concept and applies it to the unity of the Church 'in Christ'; and thus, says W. D. Davies, evidence is forthcoming that this conception (of Christ as Second Adam) 'played a far more important part in his thought than the scanty references to the Second Adam in I Corinthians and Romans would lead us to suppose'.[1] This argument is important in suggesting that Paul came into touch with a circle of ideas, even in Rabbinic Judaism, which made it possible for him to use the figure of Adam as ground-plan for his Christology.

The passage in I Corinthians xi has been drawn into this discussion, notably by A. E. J. Rawlinson.[2] He regards the statements, in a context that deals with women's dress, that man is 'the image and glory' of God and that woman is the 'glory of man' as looking back to Genesis ii. 21 f. and as teaching that the first woman was derived from the first man. The Corinthians passage suggests, on its surface, that 'image' and 'glory' are equivalent expressions. Further, the idea of 'glory' suggests a source whence it derives. The Christ, therefore, who as the heavenly man was from the beginning of the creation as the image and glory of God and at the same time the Son of His love (Col. i. 13) must be regarded both as deriving His being from God, and also as reflecting, like an image seen in a mirror, the divine glory, as Christians in turn are to reflect with unveiled faces the 'glory' of the Lord Jesus. So Rawlinson argues, and proceeds to link up this train of thought with the 'wisdom' Christology of Colossians i. 15 ff.

We have surveyed the linguistic usages of the Pauline terms of μορφή, εἰκών, and δόξα in their Christological contexts. The conclusion which many Biblical scholars draw is that because the terms appear to be used interchangeably in various contexts their meanings are to be regarded as equivalent;[3] and when this

---

[1] Op. cit. p. 53. See R. Scroggs, The Last Adam (1966).

[2] The New Testament Doctrine of the Christ, pp. 132 f. Cf. Lohse, 'Imago Dei', 124-6.

[3] It would be an interesting enquiry to investigate this approach as the Christian parallel to the Rabbinic hermeneutical device known as gᵉzērâh šāwâ (גזירה שוה). This means that where two identical (or parallel) words occur in different contexts, one is justified in putting them together and

fact is applied to Paul's Christology it throws light on the second Adam teaching which provides Paul with 'the scaffolding, if not the basic structure, for his redemption and resurrection Christology'.[1] All this paves the way for the conclusion that the enigmatic phrase ἐν μορφῇ Θεοῦ in the Philippians περιοχή *may* be taken in the following sense:

'The form of God' is to be read against an Old Testament background. The μορφὴ Θεοῦ may be the equivalent of εἰκών = δόξα of God; and thus describes the first man, Adam at his creation (Gen. i. 26, 27). Adam reflected the glory of the eternal Son of God who, from eternity, is Himself the 'image' of the invisible and ineffable God. Both Adams are thought of as the possessors of celestial light. What Paul had learned at the feet of Gamaliel about the 'glory' of the first Adam—the idealized picture of the Rabbinic schools[2]—he transferred to the last Adam as He had revealed Himself to him in a blaze of glory. This contrast is the key to the phrase ἐν μορφῇ Θεοῦ; and points us back to the pre-temporal existence of the heavenly Lord in His unique relationship to God. It also prepares for the soteriological mission on which He came in 'the fulness of time'.[3] For His coming and redeeming enterprise is nothing other than the recovery of the 'image' in His people. In taking our nature upon Him (Rom. viii. 3) and fulfilling the rôle of the obedient last Adam as the perfect Man in whom the image of true manhood is seen, He reversed the baneful effect of what the first Adam did. So He is described as the 'last Adam' (I Cor. xv. 45); 'the second Man' (I Cor. xv. 47) and the 'new man' whose image— the image of humanity as God intended it (so Kittel)[4]—is renewed in His Church (Col. iii. 10; cf. II Cor. iii. 18; I Cor. xv. 49; Rom. viii. 29; Ignatius, *ad Ephes.* xx, 1).

This argument assumes that μορφὴ Θεοῦ may be accounted for simply on the basis of the LXX equivalents. We move on to interpreting their meaning reciprocally. Cf. J. Jeremias, 'Zur Gedanken-führung in den paulinischen Briefen', *Studia Paulina*, p. 149, for the Jewish authorities on this principle.

[1] Black, 'The Pauline Doctrine of the Second Adam', 173.

[2] The Rabbinic material is cited by Kittel, *TWNT*, II, 249 ff.

[3] The soteriological emphasis on εἰκών in Paul's thought is brought out by Lohse, 'Imago Dei', 133, 135.

[4] *TWNT*, II, 394 f.; cf. S. V. McCasland, '"The Image of God" according to Paul', *JBL*, LXIX (1950), 85–100.

consider another line of discussion which, while it rejects the philosophical backgrounds of μορφή, and partly accepts the Genesis story as controlling the Apostle's thought in Philippians ii. 6 ff., declares that the underlying motif is the *Erlösungsmythos* of the Heavenly Man. The types of theory which are called in to explicate Philippians ii may be classified in the following way:

(*a*) The concept of the Redeemer in Iranian religion (Lohmeyer);

(*b*) a Judaic version of this myth (Héring, Bonnard);

(*c*) an incipient 'Gnostic' redemption saga, which later blossomed in such documents as the Hermetic *Poimandres* and the Gnostic apocryphal literature (Reitzenstein, Bousset and R. Bultmann. Our attention will be particularly devoted to those scholars who have come under Bultmann's influence and have written on Phil. ii. 6 ff., especially E. Käsemann and G. Bornkamm). What is common to all these writers is the conviction that a doctrine of the Primal Man (*Urmensch*), whether in Oriental or Hellenistic forms or a mixture of both, lies at the heart of the Pauline *pericope*. The next section may therefore be conveniently labelled

C. THE 'RELIGIONSGESCHICHTLICH' APPROACH

The common feature which joins together the interpretations which may be described under this heading may be stated in one sentence. It is the recognition that the hymn uses the framework of a *myth*[1] in order to set forth its Christological message. The descriptions of the pre-existent Christ as 'in the form of God' and 'equal with God' are thus quite characteristic, for the same appellations are found in Hellenistic religious documents

---

[1] This term requires some definition. Its meaning has tended to become blurred in the current 'de-mythologizing' debate. See the wise comments by Virginia Corwen, *St Ignatius and Christianity in Antioch*, pp. 127 ff. She offered the following definition which also covers the different meanings which the commentators on Philippians ii give to the term: 'Myth, as we are using it, is a statement of truth cast in dramatic form to suggest the dynamic inter-relations of the divine, the world, and man.' This would be acceptable—as a lowest common denominator—to all the writers mentioned in the text, but some (e.g. Bultmann and his early followers) would wish to go beyond it.

For myth in the New Testament, cf. Bultmann's 'Mythos und Mythologie im NT', *RGG*[3], IV, 1278–82; and the same author's *Theology of the New Testament*, I, pp. 164–83.

and in the Gnostic literature. In these sources the terms are used to portray the heavenly state of the *Urmensch* or Primal Man, and when the myth is found in a Jewish *milieu* this character is designated 'Adam'.

Discussion may be kept in these two categories. First, the myth of the Heavenly Redeemer in its pagan and Gnostic setting will be treated. Then, the Judaized version of the Anthrōpos speculation in Hellenistic Judaism will be mentioned.

(a) The Heavenly Man myth

E. Lohmeyer's treatment, as we have seen, is notable in many ways. It is important in this connection because it was his brochure[1] which introduced prominently the figure of Gayō-mart, the principal character of the Iranian myth, into the explanation he gave of Philippians ii. 6 ff. In this he was not innovating. Ever since the rise of the *religionsgeschichtliche Schule*, traces of this teaching in Paul's Christology had been detected. The contributions of Reitzenstein,[2] Clemen and Weiss sought to do just this. C. Clemen, for example, writes:[3] 'It is chiefly in the Christological statement of Ph 2. 6 f. that Paul seems to me to be indebted to the doctrine of the Primal Man, in the form in which we find it in the Poimandres.' He had earlier[4] adduced evidence to support his opinion that 'the Persian origin of the doctrine in question (*sc.* that of the Primal Man) has been sufficiently plausible'.

This myth of Gayōmart in its pristine Zoroastrian form may be set down in outline, under the direction of C. H. Kraeling who describes in this way the chief *persona* of the drama:[5] 'The Anthropos, it appears, represents in all probability the Hel-

[1] *Kyrios Jesus*, pp. 23, 68 f.
[2] The importance of R. Reitzenstein's work is noted by Carsten Colpe, *Die religionsgeschichtliche Schule* (1961), pp. 34 ff. A clear statement of Reitzenstein's conviction that Paul's Christology was shaped by a conception of 'a divine Man (*Anthropos*) as a bearer of the true religion, a conception which is already found in Hellenistic and Palestinian Judaism and is derived originally from Iranian sources' is found in his *Die hellenistischen Mysterienreligionen*[3] (1927 = 1956), p. 423.
[3] *Primitive Christianity and its non-Jewish Sources* (E.T. 1912), p. 158.
[4] Clemen, *op. cit.* p. 157.
[5] *Anthropos and Son of Man* (1927), p. 187.

lenistic and syncretistic form of the ancient Iranian *gaya-maretan*, "mortal life",[1] a mythical person originally devoid of a proper name and not removed from the ideas of bisexuality, and one of whom story told that he had formed a part of the preexistent spiritual creation of Ahura Mazdā in the capacity of prototype of humanity, had been embodied in the ensuing material creation, had occupied a role of great importance in the fatal primordial battle with the evil forces of Ahriman, had at the moment of death become the progenitor of humanity, had contributed elements to the formation of material cosmos and would in the future life occupy a prominent place among the blessed.'

The statement is important mainly for the place it holds in the realm of comparative religion; but also it gains interest for the New Testament interpreter because it is the starting-point from which developed the myth of the Heavenly Redeemer.[2] It is in Manichaeanism, Mandaism and the documents known as the Hermetic literature that, in the later centuries, the myth finds its full form.[3] These documents and movements are known to us in their post-Christian form, but it is the contention of the scholars of this Comparative Religion school that the gnosis which forms the basic idea of all the movements is a pre-Christian phenomenon. The religious groups in question are concerned chiefly with an anthropology. In their estimate of man, he is thought of as a soul with a divine nature which is imprisoned in a world of darkness and evil and from which he has to be liberated and restored to the world of light. Man's essence is derived from the Primal Man who is humanity's protoplast. This Original Man was in the divine likeness and was sent forth from God in the beginning of time. He fell prey to the powers of darkness and was victimized by them to such an extent that, although he was 'rescued' by the Father of all and restored to the realm of light,

[1] The various meanings of this term are considered by Sven S. Hartman's full study, *Gayōmart, Étude sur le syncrétisme dans l'ancien Iran* (1953), pp. 13–44.

[2] The close nexus between the figure of Gayōmart and that of the *Urmensch* in Gnostic speculation is, however, denied by Colpe, *Die religionsgeschichtliche Schule*, p. 153; against Kraeling, *Anthropos and Son of Man*, pp. 85 ff.

[3] The literature which has grown up around this problem is vast. Of fundamental importance is Reitzenstein's description of the myth in *Das iranische Erlösungsmysterium* (1921), pp. 117 ff.

he left behind him in the world a part of the heavenly elements from which the soul of man in the world is derived. Man's origin, his destiny in the world, and his ultimate hope, therefore, rest upon this Primal Man who, now exalted, carries with him the pledge of man's final deliverance. The *Poimandres* tract of the Hermetic Corpus[1] puts all this drama in terms which have suggested a distinct reminiscence of the *Christuslied* of Philippians ii. The first Man is spoken of as one who 'bore the image of his father' (τὴν τοῦ πατρὸς εἰκόνα ἔχων). For God loved him as ἑαυτῷ ἴσον, and he is described as 'his own form' (τῆς ἰδίας μορφῆς). The myth continues: 'Now he has entrusted to him all his works... and since he possessed, in himself, all power over the world, he broke through the "circle of the spheres" (τὴν περιφέρειαν τῶν κύκλων) and bowed himself down hither, and revealed to nature below the beautiful form of God... Immortal he was, and had the power over all things—now he suffers the fate of the mortal because he is subject to destiny (τῇ εἱμαρμένῃ): he was exalted above the circle of the spheres (ἐπάνω τῆς ἁρμονίας)—now he is exiled in the circle, a slave he has become' (ἐναρμόνιος γέγονε δοῦλος). The greatest interest attaches to this passage for the reason to which F.-W. Eltester[2] draws attention, namely, that in one context we find the significant expressions of Philippians ii. 6 f.: τὴν τοῦ Θεοῦ μορφήν: τὴν τοῦ πατρὸς εἰκόνα: ἴσος in close association. J. Jervell[3] adds to this list the expressions κενοῦν and δοῦλος/δούλου μορφήν.

It is the belief of those who regard this myth as the framework of the Christian message that Paul's doctrine has been fitted into such a pattern. For him, J. Weiss says,[4] the coming and death of Christ is by no means only a 'historical', human, earthly occurrence. The gnosis of Paul places the event of Christ in the centre of cosmic happenings and indeed considers it as in itself a cosmic

<hr />

[1] Cf. Reitzenstein, *Poimandres* (1904), pp. 81 ff. The most up-to-date translation is that by F. C. Grant in R. M. Grant, *Gnosticism: An Anthology* (1961), pp. 213 f. And for commentary, cf. W. Scott, *Hermetica*, I (1924), pp. 121 ff., II, 36 ff.: H. Jonas, *Gnosis und spätantiker Geist*, I (1934), pp. 326–48; and the same author's *The Gnostic Religion* (1958), pp. 147–73: C. H. Dodd, *The Bible and the Greeks* (1935), pp. 145–69; and the same author's *The Interpretation of the Fourth Gospel* (1953), pp. 41 f.

[2] See above, p. 109, n. 2.

[3] See above, p. 109, n. 3.   [4] *Earliest Christianity*, II, pp. 491 ff.

event. The actors are not chiefly Pilate, Caiaphas and the people; the agents are the evil powers, 'the rulers of this Age' who conspired to bring about the death of Jesus, but who in that act were overcome and vanquished. The divine Christ, the Lord of glory, had laid aside the body of His glory, descended into the lower spheres of the earth and placed himself under the yoke of servitude to these powers, both in life and death; but they were not able to hold their victim and were forced to release Him. He is now returned to His heavenly glory as the beginning of a new humanity which looks to Him as the pledge of its final victory over the dark powers of evil; and has taken again His glorious body. The demonic powers acknowledge Him as Lord.

This account of the meaning of Christ for Paul has been restated in recent times in forceful terms by R. Bultmann[1] and W. Schmithals.[2] The use by Paul of the Gnostic framework is the starting-point in their discussions. With them, however, the myth is more than a piece of ancient folk-lore; it has profound significance for modern man. In effect, like the ancients, they are concerned with anthropology. Bultmann, in particular, sees behind the Pauline Christology and the Gnostic 'redeemer myth' the same human *Seinsverständnis*, namely, the feeling that human life is threatened by cosmic powers which imprison man

[1] *Theology of the N.T.* 1, p. 175. Hewrites: 'But most of all the Gnostic stock of concepts served to clarify *the history of salvation*. According to these concepts the Redeemer appears as a cosmic figure, the pre-existent divine being, Son of the Father (with a reference to his earlier description of the Redeemer-figure, *op. cit.* 129 ff.), who came down from heaven and assumed human form and who, after his activity on earth, was exalted to heavenly glory and wrested sovereignty over the spirit-powers to himself. It is in this conception of him that he is praised in the pre-Pauline Christ-hymn which is quoted in Phil. 2: 6–11'; and in even clearer terms in *RGG*[3], IV, 1281.

[2] *Die Gnosis in Korinth* (1956): Excursus II: 'Der erlöste Erlöser' (pp. 82–134). In regard to Philippians ii. 5–11 Schmithals finds in that text a clear proof of the pre-Pauline character of the Redeemer-myth. 'We can say with certainty that it was not Paul himself who linked the gnostic conceptions and thought-world with the message of Jesus as the earthly appearance of the Redeemer. On the contrary, he found them already united and received before he began his so-called missionary journeys' (124 f.). In a footnote to this statement he remarks: 'This is shown in the gnosticizing Christ-hymn (Ph 2, 6–11) which Paul received. It originated in hardly any other circle of Christian gnosis than that in which the gnostic character of the Redeemer-myth was clearly set forth. This also had become connected with Jesus of Nazareth previously to Paul.'

and bind him in a world in which he realizes himself to be an alien in his deepest being or existence. Thus, in relation to Philippians ii. 6 f., he transposes the Incarnation into an existentialist key: 'The coming of the redeemer out of the world of light is a self-humiliation...and everything which souls now experience, was previously experienced by the redeemer in a primeval period.'[1] The Pauline Christology is in this way geared to man's present-day *Daseinsverständnis*, his understanding of human existence in this world.[2]

The immediate issue to be settled is whether a pre-Christian redemption myth has set the framework for the picture of the heavenly Christ in Philippians ii. 6. This assumption is accepted by E. Käsemann and G. Bornkamm.[3] The latter is most emphatic in rejecting Cullmann's interpretation that the hymn makes use of the Creation-story and pictures Christ as 'the antitype' (*als Gegentypos*) of Adam. The term μορφή is not to be treated as the equivalent of εἰκών. It refers rather to the heavenly nature of Christ which He gave up when He became man. 'The term μορφή (which is found in verses 6 and 7) indicates not merely the outward form and shape in contrast to the being (*Wesen*), but signifies actually His being (*Wesen*), showing that "the form of a servant" is not a part that He plays but the being He becomes.' He quits His heavenly existence (*Dasein*) and takes instead a human existence—an existence of unredeemed man

[1] R. Bultmann, *Orient. LZ* (1940), no. 5/6, 169 (cited by H. N. Ridderbos, *Paul and Jesus* (E.T. 1958), p. 112).

[2] See Conzelmann's exposition *ad* Col. i. 15–20 (*NTD* 1962), p. 139.

[3] Käsemann, 'Kritische Analyse', 65–9, seeks to justify the meaning of ἐν μορφῇ Θεοῦ as 'Daseinsweise' (see p. 105, n. 2) on the grounds that the closest parallel of the Pauline text is in the *Sibylline Oracles*, VIII, 458: βροτέην ἐνεδύσατο μορφήν; and the description of the *Urmensch-Erlöser* in *C.H.* I, 13 f.: ἔδειξε...τὴν καλὴν τοῦ θεοῦ μορφήν (the latter providing 'a striking analogy to our text' in Philippians ii. 6); and that in Hellenistic usage μορφὴ θεοῦ was used of the power and the nature of certain gods and god-like men who were worshipped. The μορφή of these figures is often synonymous with their person or essence. Käsemann might have drawn upon the researches of Reitzenstein (*Die hellenistischen Mysterienreligionen³*, pp. 357 f.) who showed from the evidence that μορφή as a current designation of a divine figure could often be used absolutely and directly invoked (e.g. in the papyrus cited by him: πρόσεχε, μορφὴ καὶ πνεῦμα, 358).

Bornkamm's discussion is taken from his essay 'Zum Verständnis des Christus-Hymnus', 179–81. In similar vein G. Friedrich comments on the text (*Philipper* (*NTD*)), pp. 108–9.

which is seen as that of slavery under the tyranny of the cosmic powers.

With this view the wheel has turned a full cycle; and we are back with the earlier interpretation of μορφή as 'nature', 'being'—not in the sense of a proof of Christ's divinity within the Godhead, but rather of His place as the heavenly Redeemer who was thought of (in Hellenistic religion) as a divine being, with a nature which made Him worshipful (ἰσόθεος φύσις). This nature He abandoned when He came down on His errand of redemption. And Philippians ii. 6 f. is one illustration of the use which the New Testament makes of this myth of a descending and finally 'redeemed' Redeemer.

It is Bultmann's advocacy of this background of New Testament Christology which has made this a burning question again. Some present-day writers[1] are content to refer to the arguments which earlier scholars (such as J. M. Creed,[2] A. E. J. Rawlinson[3] and W. Manson[4]) used against the *religionsgeschichtlich* school of the first two decades of this century. The position of Bultmann has been assailed in a detailed study by the Scandinavian scholar, E. Percy.[5] His conclusions may be stated.

The matter of dating is a chief consideration. Percy argues that, except for the Mandaean and the Hermetic literature, the figure of the Gnostic Redeemer rests upon a syncretism with the Christian conception of the Saviour. And where the Mandaean writings speak of a Redeemer who descends from the heavens and appears in human history, Christian influence is unmistakable. Where, in the other parts of the literature, the descent of the divine Son is spoken of in a non-Christian context, there is no doctrine of redemption mentioned. The 'Redeemer' is here a

---

[1] A. Richardson, *An Introduction to the Theology of the New Testament* (1958), pp. 141–4 gives a good summary of objections to the Gnostic redeemer-myth theory; and for an up-to-date *Forschungsbericht* see J. Munck, 'The New Testament and Gnosticism', *Current Issues in New Testament Interpretation. Essays in honor of O. Piper* (1962), pp. 224–38 (= *ST*, xv, 11 (1961), 181–95).

[2] 'The Heavenly Man', *JTS*, xxvi (1925), 113–35; cf. Edwyn Bevan, 'The Gnostic Redeemer', *Hellenism and Christianity* (1921), pp. 89–108.

[3] *The New Testament Doctrine of the Christ*, pp. 125 ff.

[4] *Jesus the Messiah* (1943), Appendix D.

[5] *Untersuchungen über den Ursprung der johanneischen Theologie* (1939): 'Der Ursprung des Gnostizismus' (pp. 287–99).

pre-historical, mythological, hero-figure, who carries on a struggle with all sorts of primaeval powers, but who is not set forth as redeemer.[1] This means that where the notion of redemption is found in the texts it is a Christian importation. Percy explicitly denies that there is any link between the Iranian figure of Gayōmart and the Christian Redeemer on this ground.[2] He lays it down that outside of Christianity and those religious conceptions which have fallen under its influence (such as Manichaeanism) the entire notion of redemption does not appear in the religions of the Near East.[3] In the Mandaean books where the notion is to be found that a redeemer shares the fate of those whom he comes to redeem the idea is only infrequently mentioned,[4] and even then those few references stand under a Christian influence.[5] This study has persuaded such as J. Jeremias[6] that the doctrine of a 'redeemed Redeemer', according to which a divine Primal Man redeems fallen humanity by himself becoming identified with it and delivered from engulfing matter, has no bearing upon the New Testament teaching. Whatever the figures of the redeemer may have been in Persian and pre-Christian thought this teaching cannot have been the origin of the humiliated and exalted Redeemer of the New Testament. Bultmann himself[7] has accepted the force of much of Percy's contention, although he still holds to his original position. The main point of comparison between the myth and the New Testament picture is the common idea of descent and re-ascent such as we find in Philippians ii. The historicity of Jesus, His ethical significance for His Church, His personal presence in the experience of Paul arising from His Resurrection and the Damascus road encounter—these are all Christian *differentiae* which stamp the Christian redemption mystery as quite unlike its mythical counterparts, however much the framework may

---

[1] Percy, *op. cit.* 296.

[2] Percy, *op. cit.* 278–87 with conclusion: 'Es fehlt...vor allem...jede Spur dafür, daß man Gayōmart als einen Erlöser betrachtet habe' (281).

[3] Percy, *op. cit.* 290; cf. R. McL. Wilson, *The Gnostic Problem* (1959), p. 225.

[4] Percy, *op. cit.* 240–56.   [5] Percy, *op. cit.* 271–3.

[6] *ThB* (1940), 277.

[7] *Orient. LZ* (1940), no. 5/6, 173: Percy 'has adduced a great deal of what is correct in opposition to a number of hasty hypotheses, and I (i.e. Bultmann) am not in a position to say anything decisive about it' (quoted by Ridderbos, *Paul and Jesus*, p. 152).

seem to have a common origin. The mythical account of Gayōmart may safely therefore be left in the background when we come to ask about the immediate influences upon the Pauline text.[1] C. H. Dodd, however, in passing his verdict upon this matter puts us on the track of another allied suggestion: 'Adam is probably more directly the ancestor of the Hellenistic Ἄνθρωπος than Gayomard.'[2]

(b) Adam speculation in Judaism

The background to Philippians ii. 6 in the Genesis story has already been touched upon; and the various suggestions of the semantic equivalence of μορφή, εἰκών, and δόξα noted, in the light of their corresponding Hebrew terms in the Creation narrative. Some scholars have taken this discussion a stage farther than the proposal of a simple linguistic correspondence by maintaining that Philippians ii reflects dependence upon a Judaeo-Gnostic account of the first Man of Hebrew anthropology. The chief differences between this proposal and the suggestion referred to above may be given in the words of C. H. Dodd again:[3] 'Even if Iranian mythology gave an impetus to such speculations, the Ἄνθρωπος doctrine in its familiar Hellenistic forms owes much to direct reflection by Jewish thinkers and others influenced by them, upon the mysterious

---

[1] But the discoveries at Nag-Hammadi seem to have re-opened the issue; and the results of the later study of the documents tend to be more open-minded than the pronouncements of the first translators were on the possible existence of a pre-Christian redemption myth. Thus, what G. Quispel, 'The Jung Codex and its significance', *The Jung Codex* (E.T. 1955), p. 78, says: 'There would appear to be good grounds for supposing that it was from Christianity that the conception of redemption and the figure of the Redeemer were taken over into Gnosticism. A pre-Christian redeemer and an Iranian mystery of redemption perhaps never existed', and R. McL. Wilson, *The Gnostic Problem*, pp. 75, 250 has endorsed: 'The "Gnostic Redeemer-myth" is...largely a scholars' reconstruction, and it has not been satisfactorily shown that such a myth existed in pre-Christian times' (98)—these categorical statements are to be tempered lest 'too sweeping a conclusion' be drawn (so W. R. Baird, Jr., 'Current Trends in New Testament Study', *JR*, xxxix, 3 (1959), 144 f.); cf. W. R. Schoedel, 'The Rediscovery of Gnosis', *Interpretation*, xvi, 4 (1962), 387–401.

[2] *The Bible and the Greeks*, p. 147 n.

[3] *Ibid.*

story of man's origin told in *Genesis*, and possibly to more fantastic forms of that story handed down in Jewish tradition.'

As far as the Pauline text is concerned, Lohmeyer[1] had noted the relevance of the Adam literature as a background to the passage. He detected a cosmic motif which entered Judaic thought through the Adam speculation of the apocalyptic writers. In these writers (e.g. the Enoch literature, Sirach, the Sibylline Oracles, and indeed the earlier graphic descriptions in Job xv. 7 ff., Ezekiel and the Daniel apocalypses) there is the highly ennobled picture of the first Man.[2] His glory when created was above that of every living thing. From his abode in Paradise which was the third heaven he could see the angels before God's throne. Indeed, he was himself an angel, a ruler of the earth.[3] He is the symbol of the cosmos, a perfect microcosm of the universe. All this status would be implied in the Pauline phrase when applied to the first Man: he was 'in the form of God'.

The Rabbinic literature[4] carries this process of the 'idealization' of Adam to an inordinate length. In the hands of the Rabbis the resultant picture borders on the grotesque and the fantastic. Our concern, however, is to pay attention to the way in which his glory is set down in fulsome detail. Adam is thought of as immortal, with a splendour derived from God Himself. The brightness of his feet (not to speak of his face!) darkened the sun in the heavens. He is worthy of the angels' worship and even Satan is commanded to offer obeisance to him. He is praised for his wisdom as the vicegerent of the universe.

As Judaism came into contact with the Hellenistic world its 'Adamology' (to use the expressive phrase of Héring) was affected. We may see the influence at work in Philo's contribution to this subject. In true Platonic manner Philo detects in the Creation accounts a distinction between the heavenly Man of Genesis i and his earthly counterpart in Genesis ii. The beauties

---

[1] *Kyrios Jesus*, pp. 28 ff.

[2] See N. A. Dahl, 'Christ, Creation and the Church', *The Background of the New Testament and its Eschatology: Essays in honour of C. H. Dodd*, ed. Davies and Daube (1956), pp. 422–43.

[3] A. Dupont-Sommer, 'Adam, Père du monde', *RHR*, (1939), 182–96.

[4] W. D. Davies, *Paul and Rabbinic Judaism*[2], pp. 42, 46; Jervell, *Imago Dei*, pp. 99 ff. who gives the full references to the glory of Adam in Rabbinic sources. Cf. R. A. Stewart, *Rabbinic Theology* (1961), pp. 68, 74.

and glory of the earthly Adam are transferred to the Original who now becomes the prototype for the race of men. It is at this point that the doctrine of the Two Adams has entered Christian thought, according to those who are concerned to investigate the background of the Philippians passage. J. Héring has worked out this theory in fullest detail.[1] He locates the psalm in an environment where this Hellenistic-Jewish speculation would be familiar teaching, namely, in Antioch in Syria; and relates the phrase ἐν μορφῇ Θεοῦ ὑπάρχων to the pre-existent Christ who is pictured in these terms as the Celestial Man who provides the 'image' in which the protoplast of the race was made.[2] Bonnard[3] follows this with the clearly expressed hypothesis that the hymn belongs to a Judaeo-Gnostic *milieu*; it was originally a hymn sung in honour of the heavenly Man who is invested with divine honours. Paul the Christian has taken it over and adapted it by applying it to Christ and by using it in a paraenetic context in his letter to the Philippians.

Paul's use of the Second Adam teaching is shown by W. D. Davies[4] who argues that this doctrine was 'probably introduced into the Church by Paul himself'. Whether this is a valid assumption or not, it cannot be doubted that Paul was familiar with the comparisons which were current (notably at Corinth) between Adam and Christ. It would then appear to be somewhat gratuitous to go to an unknown Jewish-Gnostic myth for the scaffolding when it is clear that the parallels between the first Man and the 'second Man from heaven' were current coin in the early Church. The suggested linguistic correspondences are impressive enough on their own; it seems unnecessary to add complications by introducing the evidence of a postulated myth as lying in the background.

The latest interpreter of our passage, J. Jervell,[5] looks to this Judaeo-Gnostic source for the key to the entire hymn, or at least verses 6–8 which he says 'contain ideas which originate in Gnostic theology' as it developed in a Hellenistic Jewish environment. 'Here we see the pre-existent "Heavenly Man".

[1] *Le Royaume de Dieu et sa venue*, pp. 147 ff. For Philo's teaching, we may compare C. K. Barrett, *From First Adam to Last* (1962), pp. 7 f., 75.
[2] Héring, *op. cit.* 160.
[3] Bonnard, *L'épître aux Philippiens*, pp. 48 f.
[4] W. D. Davies, *Paul and Rabbinic Judaism*[2], pp. 41 ff.
[5] *Imago Dei*, p. 213.

In Phil. ii. 6–8 we have exact and detailed parallels to the Gnostic presentation of the *Uranthropos*.' The first part of the text 'deals with a Gnostic original version (*Vorlage*) which is handled non-controversially, but in an epistolary and cultic context. It is altered only in so far as the statements now refer to Christ and not to the Primal Man.'[1] This thesis of Jervell expands therefore the theory put out by Bonnard. He does break new ground, however, in seeking a Christological explanation of the Pauline passage in the light of the place of the Primal Man in Gnostic speculation.

He builds his reconstruction of the hymn's Christology upon the fact that in Gnostic thought the Man in the form of God is said to be 'in the Father'. This is the starting-point of his discussion on the meaning of the phrase ἐν μορφῇ Θεοῦ. 'All Gnostic thought starts from the point that the Father, the most high God, "thinks" himself, projects his image, as a result of which the Image takes on the appearance of a person. In order to describe this, reference is made (in the Gnostic literature) to Genesis i. 26, 27. *Morphe*, then, is partly the Father as prototype (*Urbild*), and partly the Son of God as the copy (*Abbild*) of the most high God.'[2] The Greek word μορφή (which in oriental Gnosis is rendered as the Aramaic צלמא) stands for the Form of the most high God, his pneumatic Substance. At the same time, by this close association between the high God and his Son, the same word may be used of the Son as the copy of the Father. And the justification for this close unity between Father and Son (in Gnostic thought) is found in Genesis i. 26 f. in the Greek translation of which μορφή and εἰκών are both employed.[3]

On this view μορφή comes to stand for all that God is in Himself and all that Christ is *vis-à-vis* the Father. Jervell later explains how the Father–Son relationship was seen in Gnosticism. 'The Anthropos is ἐν μορφῇ Θεοῦ just because God is in him or he is in God; and yet they are always thought of as two separate persons. For that reason, we understand that the Primal Man is equal with God (ἴσος Θεῷ) just because he is the Image, because God is in him. To be equal with God, therefore,

---

[1] Jervell, *op. cit.* p. 229. [2] *Ibid.* pp. 204 f.
[3] In the *Sibylline Oracles*, Gen. i. 26 f. is quoted as: ποιήσωμεν ἰδοὺ πανομοίϊον ἀνέρα μορφῇ ἡμετέρῃ in VIII, 440; but εἰκών is used in the citation of Gen. i. 26 in VIII, 264 ff. Cf. VIII, 257, 270 ff.

does not mean to be exactly the same as God, to have the same outward appearance of likeness to God etc., but to be in God without, therefore, simply being the most high God himself.'[1] The pattern of the myth is brought into connection with the Christian message of God and Christ by relating Christ to Father as One who is 'in Him'. Both share a common substance or nature; and the pre-existent One stands on an equality with God. Yet he is distinguished from God as the Father's Image, an exact replica (an *Abbild*, in Jervell's word) of the high God Himself. He makes this point clear when he comes to deal with the nature of the *kenoma*, i.e. the Incarnation, in Christian terminology. 'Just because Christ is the second Person *in* the Godhead, for His divinity is something which He possesses as being in the Father, His self-emptying is therefore to be understood as 'a stepping out of the Father' (*ein Aus-dem-Vater-Treten*) in order to take human form; and this is where the ἑαυτὸν ἐκένωσεν of verse 7 comes in...Christ had His true self, according to the best Gnostic teaching, only in the Father, just as the Gnostic had his inner being or true self in heaven, without therefore being distinguished as a person'.[2]

On this view μορφή means 'nature' or 'substance' of the Deity.[3] It is applicable strictly to God, but insofar as Christ has a community of interest with the Father it may be used of Him. Christ shares in this heavenly 'Pneumasubstanz' as the Christian counterpart of the Anthropos who was made 'in the image of God'. On this assumption Jervell is able to account for the preposition ἐν; for it is the slavish translation-equivalent of the Hebrew בּ in Genesis i. 26 f.

A critique of this stimulating theory which is a refinement of the Judaeo-Gnostic theory raises again the double issue of dependence and dating. The detailed sources on which Jervell draws are taken from the post-Christian era, and the question of which source came first is raised in an acute form. If the Gnostics are utilizing a treatment of Genesis i–ii which derives from a Jewish or early Christian period, it will be unnecessary to look any further for a background to Philippians ii. If, on the other hand, the construction in the later Gnostic documents is

---

[1] Jervell, *Imago Dei*, p. 230.
[2] *Ibid.*
[3] *Ibid.* p. 228.

original, can the author have been influenced by a late production?[1]

On balance, the truth seems to lie in a mediating position. There seems to have been much speculation in the world of the first century about a Heavenly Original Man in Hellenized Judaism—and indeed Rabbinic orthodoxy may well have been brought within the ambit of these tendencies, as the studies of S. Lieberman and H. J. Schoeps have shown[2]—so that it is not inconceivable that Saul of Tarsus—or the author of the original Christology—came into touch with this line of speculative interest. The *auctor* of our hymn is indebted to this interest in the state of the first Man for the framework of his Christology. Important new factors appear in the Christian version (e.g. the historical Jesus, the eschatological element of the drama and a freely willed identification of Jesus with men)[3] which suggest that it cannot be interpreted *solely* within the bounds of a borrowed scaffolding; but that some use is made of a current 'myth' seems evident.

[1] And as a minor point Jervell skates all too lightly over the difficulty raised by Schweizer in his criticism of Käsemann's parallel theory. If ἐν μορφῇ Θεοῦ means that the pre-existent Christ was 'in the substance of the high God', what possible meaning can be attached to His 'Substanzwechsel', so that He comes to take 'the substance of a slave'? What is 'the substance of a slave?' asks Schweizer, pointedly (*Erniedrigung und Erhöhung*, p. 54, n. 233). The only solution to the difficulty is to deny (with Lohmeyer, *An die Philipper*, pp. 93f.; Jervell, *op. cit.* p. 230) that μορφή has the same meaning in the two verses (6 and 7).

[2] S. Lieberman, *Hellenism in Jewish Palestine*; H. J. Schoeps, *Paul* (E.T. 1961), ch. 1: 'Problems of Pauline research'; cf. C. K. Barrett, *From First Adam to Last*, p. 7.

[3] Cf. W. Manson, *op. cit.* p. 2; R. McL. Wilson, *The Gnostic Problem*, p. 225; and especially T. Preiss, 'The Mystery of the Son of Man', in *Life in Christ* (E.T. 1954), p. 53. G. Bornkamm, 'Zum Verständnis des Christus-Hymnus', p. 182 comments, 'There is no place (in the Gnostic myth) for obedience in humiliation and bodily suffering'.

CHAPTER VI

HIS CHOICE

οὐχ ἁρπαγμὸν ἡγήσατο τὸ εἶναι ἴσα Θεῷ (verse 6*b*, *c*)

The term ἁρπαγμός poses one of the most thorny questions in the whole field of New Testament exegesis. There is, on the one hand, the need to ascertain the precise connotation of the word; and, on the other hand, the task of interpreting in the most satisfactory way the peculiar significance of the Pauline phrase οὐχ ἁρπαγμὸν ἡγήσατο in relation to the Christological thought of the passage.

The assignment of discovering the true meaning of ἁρπαγμός is no new enterprise. Commentators and exegetes in the early centuries of the Church's life were busy in this matter. Nor is the confession of perplexity a recent one. Oecumenius admits to uncertainty when he writes of the term: ἐν αἰνίγματι γέγραπται.[1] A modern commentator shares the same difficulty in his confession, 'There is hardly a more famous word in the whole of the New Testament'.[2]

There is no help available from contemporary usage of the word. It is *hapax legomenon* in the New Testament; and is not found at all in LXX. It is very rarely used in Greek literature generally, and such occurrences as there are shed very little light on the Biblical use.[3] Its attestation is strongest in Plutarch who employs it in the sense of 'robbery'.[4] We shall see shortly that this meaning in the Philippians ii. 6 context is next to impossible.

[1] Oecumenius, *PG* (ed. Migne), cxviii, 1281 (cited by Henry, 'Kénose', *Supp. DB*, 22).

[2] J. Rickaby, *The Epistles of the Captivity* (1911), p. 78.

[3] Liddell–Scott–Jones, *Lexicon*, p. 245 quote the Plutarch reference (n. 4) and Vett. Val. 122. 1: ἁρπαγμὸς ὁ γάμος ἔσται. For reference in Christian authors, cf. *A Patristic Greek Lexicon*, Fasc. 1, ed. G. W. H. Lampe (1961), p. 228; and Arndt–Gingrich–Bauer, *Lexicon*, p. 108.

[4] Plut. *De lib. educ.* 12A: καὶ τοὺς μὲν Θήβησι καὶ τοὺς [ἐν] Ἤλιδι φευκτέον ἔρωτας καὶ ἐν Κρήτῃ καλούμενον ἁρπαγμόν, τοὺς δ' Ἀθήνησι καὶ τοὺς ἐν Λακεδαίμονι ζηλωτέον.

A. THE ACTIVE SENSE OF HARPAGMOS

The only conceivable way in which this active meaning could be applied is in the explanation offered by J. Ross.[1] Taking the word to carry the sense of 'an act of robbery or usurpation' (with ἁρπαγή as a cognate form), Ross concedes that the active force of 'an act of plundering' would not be understood by Paul's readers as though he meant that our Lord were robbing God, but rather (he proceeds) that he was telling them that the Messiah, Christ Jesus, did not think that to be on an equality with God spelt rapacity, plundering, self-aggrandizement. On the contrary, He voluntarily and gladly rejected the earthly idea of Messiahship for the spiritual. Ross finds this choice illustrated in the Temptation presented to Jesus in the wilderness (Matt. iv. 1–11 = Luke iv. 1–13) when He was tempted by the devil to seize the Kingdom in opposition to the will and purpose of God.

But this interpretation (which is offered also by Ewald[2] in the Zahn *Kommentar* and P. W. Schmidt[3]) faces the decisive question: What exactly was it that our Lord refused to plunder? There is no satisfactory answer to this question which presses for a reply if an active signification is given to the key-term. There is no object to the phrase οὐχ ἁρπαγμὸν ἡγήσατο if ἁρπαγμός is taken as an implicit subject; and this omission of an object leads W. Foerster[4] to regard this view as 'unerträglich'. The Latin Vulgate (which is followed by the A.V.) in translating *rapina* has misled many of the older writers, as A. Plummer rightly points out.[5] Nevertheless there has been a revival of this view by S. H.

---

[1] 'ἁρπαγμός, Phil. II. 6', *JTS*, x (1909), 573 f. Cf. the comments on this article by J. M. Furness in *ExT*, LXIX, 3 (1957), 93. B. Reicke, 'Unité chrétienne et Diaconie', *Neotestamentica et Patristica* (1964), 209 has also defended the active sense, suggesting a synonym in ἁρπαγή (= 'occasion de rapine'). F. E. Vokes in his study of the word in *Studia Evangelica*, II (1964), 667–72 argues similarly.

[2] P. Ewald–G. Wohlenberg, *Komm. zu den Gefangenschaftsbriefen (Zahn-Komm.* 1910), *ad loc.*

[3] *Neutestl. Hyperkrit.* (1880), p. 59: Christ had 'das Wesen seiner Gottgleichheit nicht in einem Rauben gesehen…'.

[4] *TWNT*, I, 473: 'aber das Fehlen des Objektes ist unerträglich, man würde dann statt ἁρπαγμός ein Verbum erwarten, das kein Objekt fordert, etwa κυριεύειν'.

[5] *Philippians*, p. 43.

Hooke[1] who wishes to translate ἁρπαγμός by 'grasping for oneself'; and earlier by A. Feuillet.[2] It is difficult, however, to avoid the impression that these interpretations are more in the nature of paraphrases than strict renderings of the Greek; and P. Henry[3] assesses the trend when he says: 'De plus en plus les exégètes, d'accord avec tous les philologues s'intéressant au texte, abandonnent le sens actif.' Lightfoot and Gifford led this movement away from the active sense which seemed generally to be given to ἁρπαγμός because, in addition to the point raised earlier about the absence of an object, it appeared to them[4] incompatible with the validity of the Lord's claim to be on an equality with God and also because, in its context, one would expect the clause immediately following to begin with a concessive phrase such as 'nevertheless' or 'yet, however'.

There seems to be a general agreement that the passive sense must be attributed to the word in this context. On this reading ἁρπαγμός has a synonym in ἅρπαγμα, together with a list of related terms (εὕρημα, ἕρμαιον, εὐτύχημα). The sense of these expressions is 'that which is seized', whether in the bad sense of 'what is stolen', 'prey' or 'booty'—Foerster[5] uses 'das Geraubte', 'die Beute'; or, if the phrase is construed *sensu bono*, 'prize', 'gain' ('ein Gewinn').

This equivalence of ἁρπαγμός and ἅρπαγμα has been widely accepted since Lightfoot's day. The effect of this identification is to introduce a term which is held to be truly synonymous, i.e.

---

[1] *Alpha and Omega* (1961), pp. 257 ff. W. Barclay, 'Great Themes of the New Testament, I. Philippians 2. 1–11', *ExT*, LXX, 2 (1958), 40–4 (42) accepts an active meaning for the term: 'Jesus Christ did not consider His own equality with God an act of seizure and of plundering. There was no necessity that He should do so, for that equality was His...by right.' But on this view, it becomes very difficult to make sense of the next words, ἀλλὰ ἑαυτὸν ἐκένωσεν.

[2] A. Feuillet, 'L'homme-Dieu considéré dans sa condition terrestre (Phil., 2, 5 seq. et parall.)', *RB*, LI (1932), 58–79 (= *Vivre et Penser*, second series) with conclusion on ἁρπαγμός (64).

[3] Henry, 'Kénose', 24.

[4] Lightfoot, *Philippians*, 'Different Interpretations of οὐχ ἁρπαγμὸν ἡγήσατο', pp. 133–7; Gifford, *The Incarnation*, pp. 34–6. See further Michael, *The Epistle of Paul to the Philippians*, p. 88 for a decisive rejection of the active sense. Arndt–Gingrich–Bauer, *Lexicon*, dispose of it by treating it as 'next to impossible' (*s.v.*).

[5] W. Foerster, *TWNT*, I, 472.

ἅρπαγμα, into the arena of the discussion. This latter term is much commoner than its postulated equivalent, occurring seventeen times in the LXX.[1] It is sometimes objected that this equivalence of ἁρπαγμός and ἅρπαγμα cannot be shown. Thus recently S. H. Hooke[2] justifies his seeking an active signification for ἁρπαγμός on the ground that 'in New Testament usage the forms ending in μος and μα are not generally interchangeable'. Hence, on this view, ἁρπαγμός should not be treated as though it were the same as the passive object (ἅρπαγμα) in its connotation. The evidence however, which Hooke doubts, is forthcoming, as Schumacher[3] and Henry[4] have amply demonstrated by comparing the usage of such words as φραγμός/φράγμα; βδελυγμός/βδέλυγμα; σταλαγμός/στάλαγμα. Their conclusions are clearly stated: 'Eine kurze Umschau bestätigt die Tatsache, daß die Bedeutung der Wörter auf μος und μα ineinander übergeht' (Schumacher), and 'Il est constant d'ailleurs que le substantif en -μός signifie aussi bien que celui en -μα, le résultat de l'action, et que bien des doublets en -μός et en -μα sont employés dans le même sens, passif et concret' (Henry).

B. THE PASSIVE SENSE OF HARPAGMOS

We have still to determine the exact meaning even if the passive translation of ἁρπαγμός be accepted. The issue is to decide whether the 'prize' or 'booty' was something which the pre-incarnate Christ was tempted to hold fast to (in which case 'prize' would be the obvious translation), or something which He refused to snatch violently (taking ἁρπαγμός *sensu malo*, 'booty', 'prey'). It is a statement of the controversy which has centred upon the choice of the terms *res rapta* and *res rapienda*.

[1] Lev. vi. 4; Job xxix. 17; Ps. lxi. 10; Sir. xvi. 13; Mal. i. 13; Isa. xlii. 22; lxi. 8; Ezek. xviii. 7, 12, 16, 18, xix. 3, 6; xxii. 25, 27, 29; xxxiii. 15; Ps. Sol. ii. 28.

[2] *Alpha and Omega*, p. 258.

[3] *Christus in seiner Präexistenz*, II, p. 278.

[4] 'Kénose', 24. See, for example, the usage of φραγμός and φράγμα in Matt. xxi. 33; Mk. xii. 1; Lk. xiv. 23; Eph. ii. 14.

(i) *Res Rapta*

This is a shorthand expression for the sense of ἁρπαγμός as a prize which, already in the possession of the owner, is held on to. The Christological meaning is that the pre-existent Christ was faced with the temptation (which is inferred from the negative verb: He did not reckon it as an ἁρπαγμός) to hold tightly to the gain which He already had. This 'gain' is usually taken to be the equality He enjoyed with God the Father (τὸ εἶναι ἴσα Θεῷ of the next line). The chief point that Paul is making—on this understanding of the text—is the assertion that He already possessed this equality and, being tempted to hold on to it, He chose rather to let it go in His decision to become incarnate. This is the drift of Lightfoot's exposition of the crucial words. He translates:[1] 'He did not look upon His equality with God as a prize, a treasure to be greedily clutched', i.e. He already possessed divine equality and resolved not to cling to it. Again, he writes at a later point, 'He did not look upon equality with God as a prize which must not slip from His grasp'. This interpretation commands a following in current expositions of the passage, whether in the sense which Lightfoot gives it,[2] or in the idea which Karl Barth introduces,[3] or as in the current revival of the *res rapta* teaching in modern Continental scholarship.[4] Barth's

[1] Lightfoot, *Philippians*, p. 134; cf. *op. cit.* p. 111.

[2] Schumacher, *Christus in seiner Präexistenz*, I, pp. 108 f. conveniently lists those who follow Lightfoot's view. More recently it has been accepted by M. Jones, *The Epistle to the Philippians* (WC), 30 f.; Müller, *The Epistles of Paul to the Philippians*, pp. 79 f.; Stanley, *Christ's Resurrection*, p. 97.

There is a variant of the same idea. On this interpretation, the sense runs: He did not regard equality with God as a prize to be grasped because He had it already, and therefore there was no need for Him to snatch it because it was already His as the eternal Son of God.

[3] *Erklärung des Philipperbriefes*, esp. pp. 59 f. (E.T. *Philippians*, 61–2); and the same author's exposition in *Church Dogmatics*, IV, *The Doctrine of Reconciliation*, I (E.T. (1956)), p. 180.

[4] Käsemann, 'Kritische Analyse', 69 ff.; Bornkamm, 'Zum Verständnis des Christus-Hymnus', 180; Schweizer, *Erniedrigung und Erhöhung*, 54, n. 235 (55); Friedrich, *Philipper (NTD)*, p. 109; Jervell, *Imago Dei: Gen. i. 26 f. im Spätjudentum*, etc., pp. 229 f.; Larsson, *Christus als Vorbild* (1962), p. 242. The view which these writers have in common—that ἁρπαγμός is to be understood in the sense of *res rapta*—is founded upon the assumption that μορφὴ Θεοῦ (in verse 6) and τὸ εἶναι ἴσα Θεῷ (in the same verse) are to be equated. Jervell speaks for this group of scholars: 'In this context, therefore, τὸ εἶναι

138

teaching rehabilitates the ancient Alexandrian doctrine[1] associated with the names of Apollinarius and Cyril who both taught that the Incarnation implies a retaining of the divine 'form' and an 'adding' of the 'form of a servant'. The key phrase in the Cyrillan system was 'besides this' (πρός γε τούτῳ or προσέτι τούτῳ). Barth has given a full re-statement of this view. He takes the words ἁρπαγμὸν ἡγεῖσθαι to mean 'to hold something convulsively' (*krampfhaft an etwas festhalten*) as a robber would clutch his prize and hold it to himself. There is no thought, says Barth, of the abandoning of His Godhead which He retained throughout His incarnate existence. The kenosis 'consists in the renunciation of His being in the form of God alone...He did not treat His form in the likeness of God (τὸ εἶναι ἴσα Θεῷ) as a robber does his booty...In addition to His form in the likeness of God He could also—and this involves at once a making poor, a humiliation, a condescension, and to that extent a κένωσις—take the form of a servant.'[2] The result is that 'He is God equally in the obscurity of the form of a servant',[3] and His pre-incarnate choice is that of accepting the servant's form while at the same time retaining the divine form which was His. The views of modern Continental New Testament scholars may be treated later when we have seen the implications of the rival theory.

(ii) *Res Rapienda*

Criticism of the older interpretation outlined above has fastened upon a number of important points. As early as 1890 J. A. Beet stated the difficulty which was hotly debated in the

ἴσα Θεῷ and ἐν μορφῇ Θεοῦ ὑπάρχων and ἁρπαγμός are to be understood in the sense of *res rapta* (230). Christ's being 'in the Godhead' as the heavenly Man means that He has equality with God; and it is this equality which He surrenders when He leaves His divine μορφή and assumes an earthly one.

But for Käsemann and Bornkamm (as we shall see) *res rapta* shades off into *res rapienda* in the thought that Christ might have used His heavenly nature for His own ends. See pp. 145 f.

[1] For this type of ancient Christology, see R. V. Sellers, *Two Ancient Christologies* (1954), p. 85; and Bindley-Green, *The Oecumenical Documents of the Faith*[4] (1950), pp. 121 f.

[2] Barth, *Church Dogmatics*, p. 180.

[3] Barth, *Philipperbr.* p. 60: 'Er ist Gott...gleich in der Verborgenheit der Knechtgestalt.'

pages of the *Expository Times* in that decade.[1] Beet rejected Lightfoot's understanding of ἁρπαγμός, arguing that the verb behind the noun means 'always...taking hold of, or snatching, something not yet in our hands'.[2] He denied that the verb ever has the sense of refusing to let go something which is already in the possession of the subject. The emphasis is therefore upon attainment more than on renunciation. This line of attack was pursued by H. A. A. Kennedy[3] at the turn of the century. The verb, he declares, means 'to snatch violently', 'to seize',[4] with the overtone that what is taken in this way is not in the possession of the person concerned. It is not permissible to glide into the sense of 'to hold fast'.

A second critique of the *res rapta* hypothesis begins at the opposite end of the Christological drama in Philippians ii. In verse 9 the text reads that God αὐτὸν ὑπερύψωσεν at the close of the Redeemer's saving mission upon earth. The prefix ὑπερ- in the verb presents a difficulty, and is usually taken, as Cullmann[5] says, as a sort of rhetorical pleonasm which actually means no more than the simple verb ὑψοῦν. The study of J. Héring,[6] however, has shown that the compound verb carries a fuller meaning than the simple form; and must be taken to imply that,

---

[1] J. Agar Beet made his first contribution to the subject in *The Expositor*, 3rd series, v, 115–25 in 1887. This article was substantially repeated in *ExT*, III (1891–2), 307–8, with a further discussion (in response to an article by J. S. F. Chamberlain, IV (1892–3), 189–90) in VI (1894), 526–8. This called forth further items by F. G. Cholmondeley, VII (1895–6), 47–8; J. Massie, VII (1895–6), 141 and F. P. Badham, XIX (1907–8), 331–3. Meanwhile, Beet's commentary had appeared in the *Expositor's Bible* series, 1890. This latter is notable for Beet's arguments against Lightfoot (65 ff.).

[2] Beet, *Commentary, ut supra*, 64. He cited Chrysostom, *Hom.* VI, 2 (text in *Expositor*, v (1887), 117; and comment in Henry, *loc. cit.* 88) for the word as 'a forcible seizure of something not yet in our hand'.

[3] *The Epistle to the Philippians* (*ExGrTest*), pp. 436 f. He concluded: 'Are we not obliged, then, to think of the ἁρπαγμός (= ἅρπαγμα) as something still future, a *res rapienda*?' (437).

[4] Compare the use of the verb ἁρπάζειν in John vi. 15; Acts viii. 39, xxiii. 10; II Cor. xii. 2; I Thess. iv. 17; Jude 23; Apoc. xii. 5; and very clearly in Eusebius, *HE*, VIII, xii, 2 (τὸν θάνατον ἅρπαγμα θέμενοι τῆς τῶν δυσσεβῶν μοχθηρίας). But Henry, *loc. cit.* 25 objects that this is not the exclusive sense.

[5] *Christology*, p. 180; but he will have none of this explanation.

[6] *Le Royaume de Dieu et sa venue*, p. 163. This is (he comments) 'the only meaningful interpretation of the word ὑπερυψοῦν'.

at the Exaltation of Jesus, God gave Him 'une dignité supérieure à celle dont il avait joui dans sa préexistence'. This greater dignity is understood in the context to follow from the fact that, in His eternal status, Christ was in the image of God, but not then King of the universe. The choice which faced Him was whether He would aspire to the dignity in His own right by snatching at it, or receive it from the Father by treading the path of lowly submission and obedience. He chose the latter course; and is rewarded by being exalted above the rank which He enjoyed as the eternal image of God. This gives precise nuance to the full verb. God did more-than-highly exalt Him above His former position, His ἐν μορφῇ Θεοῦ ὑπάρχων; and the proof of this elevation is the according to Him of the title Kyrios. This title is the name of God *par excellence*; and it is this name which is the correct equivalent of equality with God. 'Christ thus receives the equality with God which in the obedience of the Heavenly Man he did not usurp as "a thing to be grasped". God has now given him this equality.'[1]

Now it is clear that if this is the tenor of the whole passage it can only be so interpreted if ἁρπαγμός means that equality with God was not, at the time represented by the participle ὑπάρχων in verse 6, within the grasp of the pre-existent One. Therefore the whole phrase οὐχ ἁρπαγμὸν ἡγήσατο cannot refer to an actual possession which He was tempted to hold on to. By definition it must relate to 'a possibility soon to materialize, *which must not be lost*' ('eine in Bälde sich realisierende Möglichkeit, die mann sich *nicht entgehen läßt*'), as Foerster defines it.[2]

This double criticism has cleared the ground for a statement of the *res rapienda* view. In the Pauline context, it expresses the truth that He was tempted to seize what He did not actually possess, namely, the equality with God. Only on this construction, it is maintained by the proponents, is full justice done to the basic idea of the verb ἁρπάζειν. C. A. A. Scott gives a very lucid exposition of this meaning in his translation, 'He did not regard it as a thing to be grasped at to rise to equality with God' and in another place, 'He could have grasped it by the assertion of

[1] Cullmann, *Christology*, p. 180.
[2] W. Foerster, *TWNT*, I, 473. This definition is contrasted with the other possible meaning: 'a thing already possessed, which is *utilized*' ('eine fertig vorliegende Tatsache sein, die *ausgenutzt* wird').

Himself by insistence on His own interests. But He refused.'[1]
The corollary of this rendering and argument is that the very
thing which the Lord of glory refused to aspire to became His
at the Exaltation. In the history of interpretation this view has
become the standard one, at least among English-speaking
commentators; and an impressive array of names may be cited as
adherents of this position.[2] We should not fail moreover to notice
that the view of *res rapienda* is bound up with the idea that the
background is that of the First–Second Adam contrast which is
believed to hold the key to the correct understanding of the
entire piece.[3] Thus Cullmann[4] lays it down that 'without the
background of Paul's doctrine of the two Adams...these words
can scarcely be understood'; and Héring[5] and A. M. Hunter[6]
are no less emphatic that this implied contrast is the Ariadne's
thread guiding us to the only satisfying solution to the problems
of the Philippians psalm. The latter comments: 'There is a clear
reference to the Genesis story of the First Adam's fall. τὸ εἶναι
ἴσα Θεῷ echoes "*eritis sicut dei*". The Second Adam might have
conceived the senseless project of seizing by force (ἁρπαγμός =
res rapienda) the equality with God he did not as yet possess, but
conquering this temptation to which the First Adam fell, he
chose the way of obedience unto death.' It is plain from the
Genesis narrative that Adam's being in the image of God did not
eo ipso mean that he possessed a status 'as God'; else the
serpent's promise, 'You shall be as God', would have been pointless. This was the specious promise at which Adam and his wife
clutched in their disobedience. The Second Adam 'recapitu-
lates' this choice in obedience to the divine will, resists the
'urge' to claim that which is still unattained and opts to
receive it, in the gracious pleasure of the Father (ἐχαρίσατο), at
the end of His mission and sacrifice. The coherence of the two

[1] *Footnotes to St Paul* (1935), p. 192; and the same author's *Christianity according to St Paul* (1927), pp. 271 f.

[2] Kennedy, *The Epistle to the Philippians*, pp. 436 f.; Michael, *The Epistle of Paul to the Philippians (MNTC)*, pp. 87–9; Andrews, *The Meaning of Christ for Paul*, p. 159; Beare, *The Epistle to the Philippians (Black's NTC)*, pp. 79 f.; (apparently so): Stauffer, *New Testament Theology*, pp. 118 and 284; R. Leivestad, *Christ the Conqueror* (1954), p. 112.

[3] See the Appended Note: 'Suggested Backgrounds to Philippians ii. 6b', pp. 161 ff.   [4] *Christology*, p. 177.

[5] *Le Royaume de Dieu*, p. 163.   [6] *Paul and his Predecessors*[2], p. 43.

sets of circumstances has often been noticed (perhaps most evidently in the chart of F. C. Synge[1]); and has proved a powerful incentive to the adoption of the view that goes under the cipher of *res rapienda*.

(iii) *A third possibility*

There is a modification of the second of these two rival theories as to the precise flavour of ἁρπαγμός which has the effect of drawing it nearer to the concept implied in the term *res rapta*. It would be too much to say that a third view is being propounded—*tertium datur*. Rather a mediating position is taken up if we follow this newer line of thought. This view begins with the assumption that ἁρπαγμὸν ἡγεῖσθαι is a proverbial expression. The origin of this assumption may be traced back to W. Jaeger's contribution to the journal *Hermes* in 1915;[2] and in 1921 H. Schumacher commented on the phrase ἁρπαγμὸν ἡγεῖσθαι as 'eine sprichwörtliche Formel'.[3] The whole phrase means 'to treat as a piece of good fortune', 'to regard as a lucky find', 'to regard as a treasure trove', as though the word were εὕρημα or ἕρμαιον. Since those dates various renderings have attempted to bring out the proverbial flavour in this way:

He did not regard equality with God as a piece of good luck (A. D. Nock);[4]

ἁρπαγμόν...is translated as if it were εὕρημα—'a lucky find', almost 'treasure trove' (W. K. L. Clarke);[5]

'...considérer ou traiter quelque chose comme une bonne aubaine' (L. Cerfaux).[6]

The evidence for this translation is particularly full and interesting.[7] Some data were noticed as early as the date of Gifford's book[8] which called attention to Heliodorus' equiva-

[1] F. C. Synge, *Philippians and Colossians* (*Torch BC*) (1951), p. 29.
[2] W. Jaeger, 'Eine stilgeschichtliche Studie zum Philipperbrief', *Hermes*, L (1915), 537–53, esp. 550–2.   [3] *Christus in seiner Präexistenz*, II, p. 285.
[4] 'Early Gentile Christianity' in *Essays on the Trinity and the Incarnation*, ed. A. E. J. Rawlinson (1928), p. 99; and the same author's *St Paul* (1938), p. 224.   [5] *New Testament Problems*, p. 144.
[6] *Le Christ dans la théologie de St Paul*, p. 289 (E.T. 384).
[7] Full documentation in *A Patristic Greek Lexicon*, Fasc. I, 228; and Arndt–Gingrich–Bauer, *Lexicon*, p. 108.
[8] Gifford, *The Incarnation* (in 1911 ed., p. 34).

lence of ἅρπαγμα and ἕρμαιον.[1] Isidore of Pelusium[2] states the same fact, while Cyril of Alexandria has an interesting sentence (*De Ador.* I, 25[3]): Lot does not regard the angels' demand as ἁρπαγμός: οὐχ ἁρπαγμὸν τὴν παραίτησιν ὡς ἐξ ἀδρανοῦς καὶ ὑδαρεστέρας ἐποιεῖτο φρενός. The best illustration of this popular meaning of ἁρπαγμός as 'windfall' or 'piece of good fortune' is drawn from Plutarch, *de Alex. fortuna aut virtute*, I, 8 (330 D)[4] which again Lightfoot and Gifford had noted and mentioned as illustrating the sense of ἁρπαγμός which is equivalent to ἕρμαιον and denotes 'a highly-prized gain, an unexpected possession'. The text refers to Alexander in his refusal to overrun Asia on a looting expedition, 'treating those territories as falling to him by the fortune of war, and so his to seize...'. These pieces of analogous material are germane to the Philippians text once we concede two things: first, that ἁρπαγμός is being used in a popular and proverbial sense rather than in its strict etymological usage; and, secondly, that ἁρπαγμός finds a proper equivalent in ἕρμαιον or εὕρημα. Not all commentators agree that these suppositions are well-founded. Dibelius,[5] for instance, criticizes this group of parallels as 'trivial' if the phrase means 'an unexpected piece of luck' (*ein gefundenes Fressen*); but he does admit that there is evidence for it. The present state of the question is the recognition that the more popular sense is more likely to be the right one; and

---

[1] Heliodorus VII, xx. 2: νέος...γυναῖκα ὁμοίαν καὶ προστετηκυῖαν ἀπωθεῖται καὶ οὐχ ἅρπαγμα οὔτε ἕρμαιον ποιεῖται τὸ πρᾶγμα. Further references to Heliodorus in Dibelius, *Philipper*[3], p. 75.

[2] Isidore, *Epist.* IV, 22: εἰ ἕρμαιον ἡγήσατο τὸ εἶναι ἴσον, οὐκ ἂν ἑαυτὸν ἐταπείνωσεν...δοῦλος μὲν γὰρ καὶ ἐλευθερωθεὶς καὶ υἱοθεσίᾳ τιμηθείς, ἅτε ἅρπαγμα ἢ εὕρημα τὴν ἀξίαν ἡγησάμενος, οὐκ ἂν ὑποσταίη οἰκετικὸν ἔργον ἀνῦσαι.

[3] Cyril, *de Ador.* I, 25 (Migne, *P. Gr.* LXVIII, 172C). In this context with reference to Gen. xix. 3 ἁρπαγμός has the sense of 'a godsend', a 'piece of luck' (so *Patristic Lexicon*): οὐχ ἁρπαγμὸν τὴν παραίτησιν ὡς ἐξ ἀδρανοῦς καὶ ὑδαρεστέρας ἐποιεῖτο φρενός.

[4] Plut. *de Alexandri fortuna*, I, 8 (330D): οὐ ληστρικῶς τὴν Ἀσίαν καταδραμὼν οὐδ' ὥσπερ ἅρπαγμα καὶ λάφυρον εὐτυχίας ἀνελπίστου σπαράξαι καὶ ἀνασύρασθαι διανοηθείς.

[5] *An die Philipper*, p. 75. A. Fridrichsen, 'Quatre conjectures sur le texte du NT', *RHPR*, III (1923), 441 deals critically with Jaeger's suggestion of 'le caractère populaire de la locution' of ἁρπαγμός. He asks: 'Would Paul make allusion to a sacred fact which reveals the mystery of divine love—by using terms which were popular and familiar?'

recent scholars champion this notion. Some representatives may be mentioned:

(a) P. Bonnard[1] takes the illustration of 'a spring-board' (*tremplin*), treating the phrase as conveying the meaning of that opportunity which the pre-existent Christ had before Him. He existed in the 'divine condition' as the unique image and glory of God but refused to exploit His privileges and assert Himself in opposition to His Father. It remains an open question whether the windfall had already been seized and is waiting to be used, or whether it is still to be appropriated; but it seems more in keeping with the tenor of the passage as a whole to interpret ἁρπαγμός as the actual holding of a privilege which opens up the future possibility of advantage, if only the possessor will exploit it to his own profit. This is the train of thought suggested by Bonnard's commentary, although we have supplied it in words other than his own.

(b) E. Käsemann[2] introduces, at the suggestion of R. Bultmann, a parallel text from Philippians iii. 7: 'But whatever gain I had, I counted it as loss' (ἥγημαι...ʒημίαν) and says that the verses are to be taken as parallel. Thus the meaning of the one will illumine the sense of the other. Paul had in his possession certain advantages as a Pharisee. They were his to be used for his further advantage. But when he became a Christian he set these on one side; indeed, as Barth says,[3] he rejected them with

---

[1] *L'épître aux Philippiens*, p. 43; cf. the 'fishing' metaphor suggested by B. Reicke, 'Unité chrétienne', 210.

[2] 'Kritische Analyse', 70. He opposes the view known as *res rapienda*, which suggests that Christ had the possibility to aspire to divine equality and 'decided' not to avail Himself of it. He comments: 'I can find from the text no justification for this meaning. As I read the expression, it describes not a decision, but a relationship, an objective fact; and also it appears to me to be a proverbial expression. A rendering in the sense of *res rapta* would therefore be possible, not merely on the basis of a comparison with *Corpus Herm.* I, 13 f. [see above, ch. v], but we must take note further of the very clear antithesis between verses 6 and 7 f. from which we may derive a very much closer rendering [of the text]. Christ gives up what He actually possessed. And finally we ought to throw into the scales [of the argument] the witness of Phil. iii. 7. The expression ʒημίαν ἡγεῖσθαι forms an antithetic parallelism with ἁρπαγμὸν ἡγεῖσθαι, and refers to a present possession (*ein vorhandenes Gut*).'

[3] *Philipperbrief*, pp. 96 f. In fact, Käsemann's use of Phil. iii. 5 ff. was anticipated by F. C. Porter, *The Mind of Christ in Paul* (1931), pp. 215 f.

horror ('...nicht: liberal werden, indifferent werden gegen das, was man vorher gewesen ist, verehrt und getrieben hat, sondern: sich entsetzen darüber'). It is this background which gives Käsemann his clue. The pre-existent Christ had His place as the Redeemer in glory, but refused to treat it as 'an existing possession' (*ein vorhandenes Gut*) and utilize it for His own advantage.[1] Käsemann's adoption of the *res rapta* formula is to be observed; for he comments, Christ gives up what He actually possesses. It is at this juncture that the re-entry of the *res rapta* idea may be understood. The difference between the older and the newer views may be underlined, however. On the older classical view, Christ refused to hold on to His divine glory or equality. With Käsemann, however, what He does not use for His own profit is the advantage which inheres in His heavenly office as the *Urmensch*.

(c) L. Cerfaux[2] takes a somewhat similar line, accepting the view which makes the prize neither *res rapta* nor *res rapienda*, but rather 'un objet possédé sans doute justement mais dont il ne faut pas user orgueilleusement et comme par bravade'. To the same effect P. Henry writes, as his conclusion,[3] 'nous préférons dire que "l'égalité avec Dieu" est le bien, possédé, que le Christ renonce à exploiter', and finds confirmation in Eusebius' citation of the passage in *H.E.* v, ii, 2.[4]

---

[1] Käsemann, 'Kritische Analyse', 69 f. is somewhat suspicious of the rendering of ἁρπαγμὸν ἡγεῖσθαι as 'to utilize to one's own advantage' (*etwas für sich ausnutzen*); but this thought seems implicit in his use of Philippians iii. 7. And Bornkamm quite clearly includes the notion that the pre-existent Christ refused to make use of what He had. He writes (*loc. cit.* 180): The expressions in verses 6 and 7 'show that the pre-existent Christ *was* equal with God, and that He gave up this divine nature. The Fathers [Bornkamm should perhaps have qualified this by adding "Greek"; the Latin Fathers took the opposing view] were right when they spoke of this as "res rapta". We must, however, point out that this extraordinary expression (*sc.* ἁρπαγμὸν ἡγεῖσθαι) should not be understood literally, but as having been originally a weakened expression from common speech ("to take possession of something for oneself")'. Similarly, Friedrich (*op. cit.* 109): 'He had this equality with God, but He did not exploit (*ausbeuten*) it in a selfish manner.'

[2] L. Cerfaux, *Le Christ*, pp. 289 f. (E.T. p. 385).

[3] Henry, 'Kénose', 27.

[4] Eusebius, *H.E.* v, ii. 2: The martyrs refuse to exploit their sufferings as an occasion for proud display. 'They neither proclaimed themselves martyrs nor indeed did they permit us to address them by this name...they refused

(*d*) We come back to the seminal writings of E. Lohmeyer.[1] He too pointed out the direction of this newer line of thought and enquiry. It is impossible, in his estimate, to decide between the two formulas *res rapta* and *res rapienda* if they are regarded as mutually exclusive. Lohmeyer recognizes that the motif of the hymn is the determination of the path Christ chose as the way to His lordship. In contrast to the aspiration of Satan,[2] He resolved to gain His lordship by the way of sacrifice and suffering. He exemplifies the maxim *Per aspera ad astra*: the path leads 'durch menschliche Niedrigkeit zur göttlichen Hoheit'.[3] The goal set before Him is no other than the lordship which is the same as equality with God.[4] But, unlike Satan, He can only achieve this end by the abasement of His humanity and death. There is thus a paradox at the heart of the Philippians story. It is 'through His becoming Man that His way leads to His being Lord' ('durch das Mensch-werden zum Kyrios-sein führt).[5] Lohmeyer relates this paradox to the theme of election which he traces back to Isaiah's doctrine in the picture of the Suffering Servant. 'To be chosen by God means to suffer upon earth.'[6] So the way of Christ to His lordship is necessarily one of suffering in

the title of martyrs.' And in this, says the historian, they were emulators and imitators of Christ who counted it not a ἁρπαγμός to be equal with God.

A somewhat similar interpretation is offered by T. Arvedson, 'Phil. 2, 6 und Mt. 10, 39', *ST*,v, 1–11 (1951), 49–51. He begins with the Lord's words in Matt. x. 39: 'He who finds (ὁ εὑρών) his life will lose it.' He wishes to equate the verb with the phrase in Phil. ii. 6 on the basis of the usage of εὑρίσκειν in the LXX (e.g. Ps. cxix. 162; II Sam. xx. 6; I Sam. xxv. 8 = 'to have in one's hand' in the sense of 'to have at one's disposal'; cf. Num. xxxi. 50, Jud. v. 30). The substantive εὕρημα is used as the translation of שָׁלָל ('booty of war'). Arvedson then brings over this meaning of the root into the New Testament. Jesus' word means: He who will snatch his life as a prize and use it for himself will lose it. And he finds confirmation of this meaning in the following verses (Matt. x. 37–9; cf. Mk. viii. 31 ff.; Lk. xvii. 33) where the opposite is 'to renounce oneself', 'to empty oneself' as Jesus did in Phil. ii. The true disciple will follow his Lord who refused to exploit the prize of His favoured state and renounced all that might have accrued to Him as His lawful possession.

[1] *Kyrios Jesus*, pp. 23 ff.; *Philipper*, pp. 92, 93.
[2] For this possible background, see Appendix, pp. 157 ff.
[3] *Kyrios Jesus*, p. 74. This maxim is discussed in ch. IX (below).
[4] *Philipper*, p. 92: 'So bedeutet "Gott gleich sein" nichts anderes als Kyrios sein.'   [5] *Philipper*, p. 93.
[6] *Philipper*, p. 93: 'Von Gott erwählt heißt auf Erden leiden müssen.'

pursuance of the vocation of the Servant of Yahweh. But as with the Servant His vindication follows and His installation as Kyrios betokens that 'equality with God' which He refused to aspire to in His own right. Yet it properly belonged to Him; hence *res rapta* is true equally with *res rapienda*. The whole movement is one of 'from lordship to lordship': from what was due to Him as a divine being to what is His after His own act ('Dies Gestalt ist Kyrios kraft ihrer göttlichen Art und wird Kyrios wieder durch die eigene Tat').[1]

(iv) *Conclusion*

It remains now to sum up the implicates of this position as they bear upon the Christology of Philippians ii. 6. We submit that the clue is found in the phrase τὸ εἶναι ἴσα Θεῷ. The best parallel is John v. 18: Jesus called God His Father, making Himself equal with God (ἴσον ἑαυτὸν ποιῶν τῷ Θεῷ). Both the immediate context and Rabbinical parallels support the exegesis that the phrase ἴσον ἑαυτὸν ποιῶν τῷ Θεῷ means 'He made Himself independent of God'.[2] The Greek phrase would represent the Rabbinic: משוה את עצמו לאלהים. The Rabbis spoke of a son who rejects paternal authority as one who משוה עצמו לאביו, i.e. makes himself equal with his father. The Johannine text is a rebuttal of the Jewish insinuation that Jesus is a rebel against the divine government, a blasphemer who lays claim to a status which usurps the place of God.

Now this text throws light on the enigmatic Pauline verse. The pre-incarnate Christ had as His personal possession the unique dignity of His place within the Godhead as the εἰκών or μορφή of God, a vantage-point from which He might have attained that equality with God which the later verses show to be the bestowal of the name of Lord and the function which that name implies. He possessed the divine equality, we may say, *de jure* because He existed eternally in the 'form of God'. He could have seized the glory and honour of the acknowledgment of that position *vis-à-*

---

[1] *Philipper*, p. 93: *Kyrios Jesus*, p. 29: '...sowohl eine res rapienda als auch eine res rapta'.

[2] W. F. Howard, *Christianity according to St John* (1943), p. 71; with the Rabbinic authorities cited and discussed by H. Odeberg, *The Fourth Gospel* (1929), pp. 203 f. Cf. C. H. Dodd, *The Interpretation of the Fourth Gospel* (1953), pp. 325 ff. A comparative text is Philo, *Leg. All.* I, xxxi, 49.

vis the world if He had grasped His sovereignty *de facto* by His self-assertion and desire for power in His own right. He considered the appropriation of divine honour and lordship *in this way*[1] an intolerable temptation. He rejected it and chose to be proclaimed equal with God and to exercise the office of Kyrios over the universe by accepting His destiny as the incarnate and humiliated One.

Not to re-state this summary, it is still needful to pick out some of the salient points of this discussion:

(1) The passive connotation of ἁρπαγμός meaning a 'prize' or 'gain' may be accepted as the most satisfactory. A subsidiary meaning (as though it were the equivalent of ἕρμαιον, εὕρημα, εὐτυχία, εὐτύχημα) is certainly a distinct possibility, and there is much to favour it.

(2) From this premise the old controversy between *res rapta* and *res rapienda* need not be settled by a choice of one term to the exclusion of the other. When E. Stauffer states:[2] 'So the old contention about ἁρπαγμός is over: equality with God is not a *res rapta*...a position which the pre-existent Christ had and gave up, but it is a *res rapienda*, a possibility of advancement which he declined', he overlooks a way of combining the two notions. There is the concept of *res retinenda*: He had the equality with God as His Image, but refused to exploit it to His personal gain.[3]

(3) The force of the verb ὑπερυψοῦν in verse 9 may be brought into the discussion; hence it is an over-simplifying to say with the latest commentator, J. Jervell,[4] that verse 6: ἐν μορφῇ Θεοῦ ὑπάρχων represents *ein Maximum*, as though nothing more could be added to the fulness of Christ consequent upon His Exaltation. If the exercise of lordship over the cosmos

[1] E. F. Scott, *The Epistle to the Philippians* (*IB*), p. 48: 'What Christ resisted was not merely the prize but the means of obtaining it.'

[2] *New Testament Theology*, p. 284.

[3] Or else the way of combining *res rapta* and *res rapienda* may be put slightly differently, as by C. K. Barrett in his exposition, *From First Adam to Last*, pp. 69 ff.: '[Paul] affirms that for Christ equality with God was both *res rapta* and *res rapienda*. As the eternal Son of God, he had it; yet emptied himself and became obedient (cf. II Cor. viii. 9). As Man, the new Adam, he had it not; yet did not snatch at it, but chose rather the life of obedient and dependent creatureliness for which God made him' (72).

[4] *Imago Dei*, p. 212; cf. Käsemann, 'Kritische Analyse', 83.

is taken as the 'extra' which the exalted One could only receive subsequent to His obedience and vindication, there is no need to postulate, as Jervell does, two conflicting Christologies in verses 6–8 (a doctrine of the pre-existent 'Heavenly Man' who came down, but with no word as to His ascension) and 9–11 (a typical Christology of the early Christian community, in which Jesus is promoted to the rank of Kyrios at the Resurrection). He envisages that verses 6–8 belong originally to a Gnostic source and were taken over by the Hellenistic wing of the Church which added the teaching (by applying it to Christ) to verses 9–11 (which originally came from a Jewish-Christian source), thus fusing the two parts 'in order to give greater prominence to the cosmic importance of Christ'.[1] There is no doubt as to the ingenuity and novelty of this reconstruction of Philippians ii. 6–11; but it is a desperate expedient to divide the verses unless it is imperatively required.

(4) The decisive issue in the interpretation of the phrase ἁρπαγμὸν ἡγεῖσθαι is its relation to the preceding ἐν μορφῇ Θεοῦ ὑπάρχων (in verse 6a). This issue is in turn influenced by the meaning of μορφὴ Θεοῦ. As we have already seen, we are confronted with two ways in which this may be viewed. On the one hand, the phrase may be linked with the concept of the pre-existent Christ as the Image of God (as in Gnostic thought) who is distinct from God but on a par with Him. He has, in His eternal existence, the equality of One who is 'in God'. On this view μορφὴ Θεοῦ describes 'a mode of existence' (*Daseinsweise*); and (when linked with the later phrase in verse 6b) speaks of the place of the heavenly Christ, the Primal Man, within the Godhead. He had divine equality as His own prerogative; but gave it up when He exchanged the mode of existence in heaven for the mode of existence as Man upon earth. At the conclusion of His earthly career, He is taken back and reinstated as World-Ruler, but in open display and commanding universal dominion. This is the sense of the verb ὑπερυψοῦν (in verse 9), and the meaning of the acclamation in verses 10, 11.

On the other hand, the relation of verse 6a to verse 6b may be seen in a far different way. The pre-existent One is likened to the first Adam. Both wore the likeness of the divine glory; and both had within their reach the attainment of a higher prize. To

[1] Jervell, *op. cit.* p. 213.

that extent, both figures lacked the achievement of a destiny which lay before them. The Adam of Genesis ii–iii aspired to an equality with God—a promise held out to him by the serpent—but found only disaster and misery in his self-assertion. The last Adam 'did not think that equality with God was a prize to be seized' by the exercise of His own choice; and chose rather to be given that equality at the close of His incarnate and self-surrendered life. The equality was future to Him in His heavenly existence, and could be His either by snatching it (which He refused to do) or by His receiving it from God (which is, in fact, what He chose).

On the intermediate view, which gives a proverbial meaning to ἁρπαγμὸν ἡγεῖσθαι, there is a further refusal to be forced into an 'either–or' choice: either *res rapta* or *res rapienda*. The phrase τὸ εἶναι ἴσα Θεῷ so far has been treated as a piece of metaphysical dogma, and made to refer to the 'inner-Trinitarian relations' of the Christian Godhead (if we may use Markus Barth's phrase[1]). The heavenly Christ either *has* or *does not have* equality with God. But there is another way of phrasing the issue, if we start from the assumption that 'equality with God' should be interpreted dynamically as the exercise of an office, the office of Lord. This is the direction in which the studies of Lohmeyer,[2] Käsemann[3] and Cullmann[4] have been pointing,

[1] M. Barth, 'The Old Testament in Hebrews', *Current Issues in New Testament Interpretation, Essays in honor of Otto A. Piper*, ed. W. Klassen and G. F. Snyder (1962), p. 62.

[2] *Kyrios Jesus*, p. 53, shows that the final stage of Christ's pathway leads to His cosmic dominion. This explains (as we have already observed) His lordship (cf. above, p. 147).

[3] 'Kritische Analyse', 83. For Käsemann the story of Christ in the hymn is not concerned with Trinitarian relations but with events in a soteriological drama (*loc. cit.* 71). The new thing which is Christ's at the end of His mission as Redeemer is the open proclamation of the name of Kyrios. Herein lies the secret of the prefix of the verb ὑπερ-ὑψοῦν: 'It would be pointless to speak of an increase in the power of the Kyrios which the One equal with God did not beforehand possess. The "more" is connected with the name. Christ is no longer the hidden Godhead. He is now revealed; and openly rules in the fullest sense' (83).

[4] *Christology*, p. 235: 'Although Christ was ἐν μορφῇ Θεοῦ from the very beginning, he became equal with God for the first time with his exaltation.' This 'becoming equal with God' is later defined more closely as the exercise of His office of Kyrios in the *Heilsgeschichte*-scheme, which Cullmann discovers throughout the New Testament (*op. cit.* pp. 306 ff., 315 ff.).

however opposed they may be in regard to the background of the passage. The descriptions of the hymn are set in the framework of soteriology[1] and are not intended to offer precise information about the mutual relations of the Godhead. It is Christ *vis-à-vis* the world (or, better, the cosmos of verse 11), not *vis-à-vis* the Father-God of the Trinity, who is depicted. In this way, it is possible to bring together the two notions, expressed in the two Latin tags. The μορφὴ Θεοῦ is *res rapta*, for the pre-existent Christ has His place within the Godhead. He is 'the Image' of the Father. Bound up with this existing possession is the exercise of cosmic dominion, which the hymn calls the name and office of Kyrios. This authority constitutes a *res rapienda*; and the issue before the pre-incarnate One is whether He will treat His possession of His μορφή as a vantage-point, *ein Vorsprung*, from which He will reach out to the exercise of lordship in His own right and independently of God the Father. This picture—and it is a picture, full of metaphorical and symbolic language, as the use of the illustrations ('a windfall', 'a piece of good luck', 'a jetty', 'a spring-board') makes clear—assumes a popular meaning of the *crux* ἁρπαγμὸν ἡγεῖσθαι and the possible undertone of a Jewish-Christian debate in which it was insinuated that our Lord was a blasphemer who set Himself up as a rebel Son of Israel by claiming to be 'equal with God'. On the contrary, the hymn declares, He did not raise Himself up in proud arrogance and independence—although He might have done so—but chose by the path of humiliation and obedience (*vv.* 7 ff.) to come to His lordship in the way that pleased God (*v.* 9).

In short, His heavenly station, His 'being in the form of God' as the Image of the heavenly Man, is *res rapta*; but is given up when He comes to accept the station of a Man and a servant. The lordship which is implicit in His pre-existent state and waits to be exercised *de facto* over the world is the *res rapienda*; and the meaning of the verse is that He did not reach out from His favoured place and grasp at that authority. He chose, on the contrary, to be installed as World-Ruler and *Cosmocrat* at the

---

[1] Ewald–Wohlenberg, *Philipper*, p. 127 had earlier spoken of 'the soteriological situation' envisaged by these verses: 'nicht daß J. Christus dem *Range* nach über das Gotte gleiche Sein hinaus gehoben ward, was in sich undenkbar ist, sondern nach *seiner soteriologischen Stellung*'.

completion of a mission of self-humbling and lowly obedience unto death.

It remains now, for the sake of completeness, to touch upon some final possibilities in the exegesis of the word under debate. W. Foerster[1] cuts the Gordian knot of difficulty by taking the phrase as a complete proverb which has no Christological value, except perhaps an incidental one. He looks to Plutarch's evidence for support in maintaining that the phrase means no more than something like: 'It is a great fortune to be on an equality with God, and everyone would take advantage of that.' He builds upon the common meaning of 'piece of good fortune', and thinks that Paul is deliberately adopting the standpoint of human reasoning. Plutarch uses the word in the sense that the behaviour of 'the man in the street' (*jedermann*) tends to throw into relief the opposite action of a man of high principle (*ein nach höheren Prinzipien Handelnder*). So, in Philippians ii. 6, Christ, being the supreme example of this high principle, will *not* do what everyone does. It is not surprising that this view has convinced very few.

Deserving of only the briefest comment is the admission of despair in the conjectural emendation of F. Kattenbusch[2] and A. Fridrichsen[3] who, apparently independently of each other, suggested a transposition of the letters of ἁρπαγμόν into ἄπραγμον. According to Goguel[4] there were earlier attempts at emendation; but all are equally unconvincing as he admits: 'I do not think the text can be corrected as there is no ambiguity in the manuscripts and the meaning is perfectly clear.' We may endorse the first of these observations, while, at the conclusion of this intricate discussion, reserving the right to doubt the second!

[1] W. Foerster, *TWNT*, I, 473 f.

[2] "Ἁρπαγμόν? Ἄπραγμον! Phil. 2, 6. Ein Beitrag zur paulinischen Christologie', *TSK*, CIV (1932), 373 ff. He suggested also the conjecture that the text should read: οὐχὶ πρᾶγμα ἡγήσατο.

[3] *RHPR*, III (1923) translates: 'Le Christ ne regarda pas l'égalité avec Dieu comme une *sinécure*' (ἄπραγμον), which he believes a second-century scribe altered to ἁρπαγμόν (442).

[4] M. Goguel, *The Birth of Christianity* (E.T. 1953), pp. 210, 211 n. 4.

APPENDIX

SUGGESTED BACKGROUNDS TO PHILIPPIANS II. 6B

The way in which the phrase οὐχ ἁρπαγμὸν ἡγήσατο is written has suggested to many commentators that there is a latent contrast in the mind of the writer. He has in view not only the spirit which animated the pre-incarnate Christ but, as though to form a backcloth to His exemplary action in not seizing or clinging to 'equality with God', the spirit of some person who *did* aspire to this equality as a desirable thing and who *did* from a favourable position reach out after his own glory.[1] The chief point in favour of this search for intended parallels is the negative form in which the sentence is cast. It seems strange that the author of Philippians ii should trouble to introduce this negative construction if his purpose would have been served just as well had he written: 'Being in the form of God and not counting equality with God a *harpagmos*, He emptied Himself. . . .'

Not all scholars are attracted to this notion of an implicit background, and some have branded it as bizarre and unnecessary. W. Foerster[2] and A. Plummer[3] may be mentioned in this category. As we have seen the former gives only a popular connotation to the word ἁρπαγμός with the underlying thought: 'It is a great fortune, a godsend, to be on an equality with God, and "everyone" would take advantage of that if he had the chance.' There is then no justification for seeking any extraneous background. A. Plummer similarly writes: 'There is no need to suppose that he is thinking of the First Adam who was tempted to become as God (Gen. iii. 5), or of the fall of Lucifer (Is. xiv. 12–17).'

The two possibilities mentioned above are the main ones. But there are others; and it is with these that we may begin this survey.

[1] This point is made forcefully by L. Bouyer, ''Αρπαγμός', *RSR*, xxxix (1951–2) in honour of J. Lebreton, 281–8. If we assume, he states, an implicit parallelism throughout the verses, we are relieved of difficulty over the philological problem of ἁρπαγμός. For the meaning of the word says 'que Jésus n'a pas fait ce qu'un autre avait fait. . .c'est de l'autre que cela devra s'entendre' (284).

[2] *TWNT*, i, 473: 'Man braucht also nicht zur Rechtfertigung der negativen Formulierung an Adams. . .oder des Teufels Fall zu denken.'

[3] *Commentary*, p. 44.

HIS CHOICE (VERSE 6*b*, *c*)

A. HISTORICAL PARALLELS

The older writers, Lightfoot and Wettstein, had drawn attention to the use of ἅρπαγμα in Plutarch; but it was left to Jaeger[1] and A. A. T. Ehrhardt[2] to indicate that, in their view, both Plutarch and Paul are going back to the same historical allusion in the life and destiny of Alexander the Great. Ehrhardt goes a step farther in his suggestion that in writing to the Philippians Paul actually set Christ opposite to Alexander. 'To Jesus Christ, according to St Paul, is granted success far surpassing that denied to Alexander.'[3]

The justification for this hypothesis lies obviously in the lexical correspondence and in the supposed similarity of situation which confronted the two characters. The occurrence of the rare ἅρπαγμ- in both instances has been noted. The historian says of Alexander: 'He did not overrun Asia like a brigand, nor did he form the design of rending it and ravaging it as a brigand's plunder and the spoils obtained by luck (ὥσπερ ἅρπαγμα καὶ λάφυρον εὐτυχίας ἀνελπίστου); but wishing to make all mankind a single people, he so fashioned himself (οὕτως ἑαυτὸν ἐσχημάτιζεν).' This last phrase seems to refer to Alexander's taking Asiatic dress in order to ingratiate himself with the people whom he sought to bring in obedience to one logos (ἑνὸς ὑπήκοα λόγου τὰ ἐπὶ γῆς).

There are many points of similarity in this citation. Jaeger mentioned: (*a*) The οὐ...ἀλλά correspondence; (*b*) the presence of the terms ἅρπαγμα/ἁρπαγμός which are cognate, if not exactly equivalent; (*c*) the correspondence between ἑαυτὸν ἐσχημάτιζεν and σχήματι εὑρεθεὶς ὡς ἄνθρωπος; and (as (*d*)) there may be added the use of the expression γενόμενος ὑπήκοος which is found in Plutarch as ὑπήκοα. Jaeger observed the main difference on his view of ἁρπαγμός as a *res rapta*. Christ possessed what He renounced, whereas Alexander gives up only the possibility of conquering what lies beyond his reach. Now it is clear that if ἁρπαγμός carries the nuance of *res rapienda*, the parallel is even closer. But Jaeger was content to notice the general similarity and to find a connection in the same inner attitude which bound together the two figures of history.

Ehrhardt goes considerably farther and proposes that Christ is set forth as the direct counterpart of the Greek general. He brings into his discussion the way in which Alexander and Herakles are associated as the former imitated the latter and was regarded as 'equal to

---

[1] *Hermes*, L (1915), who refers to Lightfoot and Wettstein (550–2). The Plutarch reference is in note 4 on p. 144.

[2] 'Jesus Christ and Alexander the Great', *JTS*, XLVI (1945), 45–51, now reprinted in *The Framework of the New Testament Stories* (1964), pp. 37–43.   [3] Ehrhardt, *loc. cit.* 48.

the gods'. Herakles 'was honoured on an equality with the gods' (ἴσα θεοῖς ἐτιμήθη); and Alexander's military prowess would be especially relevant in a letter addressed to the Roman colony and garrison town of Philippi. This reference to Herakles leads on to an allied suggestion that it is the Greek 'divine-hero' whose image lies in the background.[1]

W. L. Knox[2] has remarked on the importance of this myth as providing Paul with a point of contact with the ancient Hellenistic world as he sought to present the Gospel and to represent Jesus 'in very much the same light as some of the most popular cult-figures of the hellenistic world'. This suggestion is taken to its full length in A. Toynbee's section in *A Study of History*, vol. VI[3] where the Christian story of Jesus is regarded as simply the Herakles myth *réchauffé*. This account has been trenchantly dealt with by M. Simon in his detailed study, *Hercule et le Christianisme*.[4] His two main contentions are worth noting: First, the contrast between the legendary and the historical is plain, even if we qualify this stark antithesis by saying that the Herakles myth has certain elements believed to be historical, and the historical person of Jesus has gathered to itself certain mythical accretions. Secondly, the Herakles-theology developed in a polytheistic context, whereas there is no doubt of the absolute monotheism of Judaeo-Christianity and the Logos Christology. As far as our immediate concern with Philippians ii. 6 is affected—and this observation is germane to the case of Alexander also—the decisive difference which makes the comparison no more than interesting is the attitude of the cult devotees to their object of worship. Christ is pre-existent when faced with the choice and is already 'in the form of God' as divine. As to the cult-heroes, whether human (like Alexander) or semi-human, semi-divine (like Herakles), they aspire to divinization. Their 'progress' involves no incarnation, no humiliation, no *katabasis*, although it does hinge upon an exaltation, an *anabasis*. A. D. Nock[5] puts it in a sentence: 'It was easy enough for an ancient to think of this mortality putting on immortality, Heracles being the most famous instance...but the reverse process was not envisaged.'

---

[1] Cf. Beare, *The Epistle to the Philippians*, pp. 80 f. for a sympathetic discussion of these hypotheses.

[2] 'The "Divine Hero" Christology in the New Testament', *HTR*, XLI (1948), 229–49. A possible use of this myth was noted by O. Holtzmann in his commentary, p. 685; and W. Grundmann, *ZNTW*, XXXVIII (1939), 65–70 attempted to explain such phrases as ἀρχηγὸς τῆς ζωῆς and σωτήρ as Luke's hellenizing process which incorporated features from the Herakles-myths of exaltation. [3] (1939), vol. VI, 266 ff., 465 ff.

[4] (1955), esp. pp. 197 f. [5] *Conversion* (1933 (in 1961 ed. p. 237)).

HIS CHOICE (VERSE 6*b*, *c*)

Karl Bornhäuser[1] has sponsored a view which treats Philippians ii. 6 historically. Paul has in mind the emperor Caligula who, although a common man, snatched at divine honours, whereas Jesus who was divine became one of us (ἑαυτὸν ἐκένωσεν: as Bornhäuser interprets it—'Jesus ward uns armen Menschen gleich': Rom. vii. 22–4; viii. 3). The outline of this novel reconstruction has already been given, but comment may be made on the way Bornhäuser interprets οὐχ ἁρπαγμὸν ἡγήσατο.[2] He finds a clue in the use of the verb ἡγεῖσθαι in III Macc. iii. 15 ἡγησάμεθα μὴ βίᾳ δόρατος and this enables him to take the Pauline phrase as 'to snatch with violence, with a show of force (*mit Waffengewalt*). Christ, unlike the Roman emperor who sought to impose the cult of his divinity with a show of force and with a display of blasphemous madness (*im lästerlichen Wahnsinn*), refused this road to lordship and treated it as a violence to be resisted. He interprets the sense of ἁρπαγμός as that of 'violent seizure', quoting Matthew xi. 12. Whatever may be the meaning of this enigmatic Synoptic text, ἁρπάзειν does not have in every instance the notion of violence; and it would be unwarrantable to insist upon it here in Philippians ii. 6 as a prop to a very dubious theory which most scholars who allude to it dismiss as highly improbable.[3]

B. CHRIST AND SATAN

The dramatic account of the pride and ambition of Lucifer in Isaiah xiv. 12 f., where it originally refers to the *hybris* of the king of Babylon, has for centuries, in both the Hebrew and Christian traditions,[4] been taken as imaging the aspiration and fall of Satan.

In the apocalyptic literature Satan's fall from heaven was regarded as the result of his *pleonexia*, the desire to grasp more than his due

[1] *Jesus Imperator Mundi*. An adumbration of this view appeared in F. G. Cholmondeley's art. *ExT*, vii (1895–6), 47 f. Caligula used his position as a means of grasping...he laid violent hands on them (his subjects) at will, to gratify his own pleasure, without thought of pity. Christ took the opposite rôle. He did not value His equality with God for what it would enable Him to exact of His subjects, but for what it would enable Him to do for them.

[2] Bornhäuser, *op. cit.* pp. 15 ff.

[3] Thus J. Behm, *TWNT*, iv, 760, n. 58 sardonically refers to the theory as Künstelei'—the same word as M. Meinertz had employed (*Theologie*, ii (1950), p. 64, n. 1).

For some more sympathetic references, cf. A. Victor Murray, *Personal Experience and Historic Faith* (1939), pp. 294 f. and Davies, *Paul and Rabbinic Judaism*[2], p. 355; and earlier, Deissmann, *Light from the Ancient East* (E.T. 1927), pp. 349 ff., esp. 355 had detected an allusion to the Roman Emperor.

[4] Strack–Billerbeck, *Kommentar*, i, 137 ff.; ii, 167 (*ad* Luke x. 18).

which God has appointed him. E. Stauffer,[1] in particular, has drawn attention to the Enoch-literature where the devil is described as the most glorious of the angelic host, being in fact their leader.[2] But in a decisive hour he refused to obey God. In language directly borrowed from Isaiah xiv, he is made to say: 'If He be wroth with me, I will set my seat above the stars of heaven and will be like the Most High.' His fear of the divine wrath was justified and he was cast out of heaven and down into the depths. Reminiscence of this expulsion of the devil is found in the canonical scriptures in, for example, Luke x. 18; II Peter ii. 4 ff.; Jude 6; and Apocalypse ix. 1, xii. 9.

Stauffer is in no doubt that this tradition lies behind the Philippians ii. 6 reference to ἁρπαγμός. The Apostle is deliberately contrasting the picture of Satan and his *superbia* with the picture of Christ and His *humilitas*. The *tertium comparationis* is the desire to rival God. Satan aspired to this in his senseless ambition, but the preincarnate One rejected this temptation. The Enoch literature and the *Life of Adam and Eve* xii–xvii put this Satanic ambition in a very dramatic way. Satan had his heavenly nature and was honoured as the chiefest of God's creatures, but he strove after equality with God. The test came when he refused to worship Adam; and in his proud disobedience he was robbed of his glory.[3]

There are many points of contact in this myth, both in linguistic and conceptual correspondences. The allusions to the equality with God, the divine glory which invested Satan, his desire to exploit his position are the most obvious ones. Moreover, Satan is set forth as a celestial being, so that the contrast is made between beings on the same plane of ideas, as it were. Both Satan and Christ have a heavenly nature *ab initio*; the test is whether they will remain content with that which God has apportioned to them, or whether, in vain pride, they will seek to reach out after divine status in a rivalry with the Most High.

It is clear that this comparison, and therefore the plausibility of this contrast, is possible if ἁρπαγμός is taken in the sense of *res rapienda*; and Stauffer is convinced that this must be the case.

A further point in favour of this background is the use Paul makes elsewhere of the Satan–Adam story (in II Cor. xi. 1–15), even to the extent of drawing upon the legend of the seduction of Eve and the transforming of Satan into an angel of light, which is not in the

---

[1] *New Testament Theology*, pp. 64 f.

[2] *Slavonic Enoch* xxix, 4, 5 (in *The Book of the Secrets of Enoch*, ed. W. R. Morfill and R. H. Charles (1896), p. 36).

[3] J. Pedersen, 'The Fall of Man', *Interpretationes ad vetus Testamentum pertinentes in honorem S. Mowinckel* (1955), pp. 162 ff. calls attention to this legend in the *Life of Adam* (169 f.).

Biblical account but is derived from the non-canonical *Life of Adam and Eve*.[1] It seems from this evidence that Paul (Stauffer assumes the Pauline authorship of the hymn) was well acquainted with the extra-Biblical traditions and might easily have found in Satan's original status, testing and rebellion a parallel to the ἁρπαγμὸν ἡγεῖσθαι which confronted the pre-existent Christ.

If there were no detailed comparison with Adam elsewhere in the Pauline corpus, the above suggestion would seem the most likely. But the force of Stauffer's contention is lessened when we recall that in some important places Paul has no hesitation in linking Christ and the Adam of primal history as comparables. In fact Adam is no less than a type (τύπος) of the coming One (Rom. v. 14).

It remains, then, that this construction is possible; and has commanded a certain following. Among the adherents are Lohmeyer,[2] Lueken,[3] Goguel,[4] J. Knox,[5] and Dibelius in the earlier edition of his commentary and in his full study on 'The Spirit-World in Paul's faith'.[6]

C. Guignebert[7] quotes the even more dramatic account of Satanic rebellion in the *Ascension of Isaiah*, x. 20 ff.[8] This is a post-Christian

[1] *Life of Adam and Eve*, x (Charles' *Apocrypha and Pseudepigrapha*, II (1913), 136).

[2] *Philipper*, pp. 92 f.: 'His aim (*sc.* the devil's) and object are by all means to attempt to be equal with God. This being equal with God means literally to be Lord; and this hymn which tells how Christ became Lord through suffering and death is a song of triumph because the lordship of the devil who once attempted to be Lord by robbery is thereby for ever broken.'

[3] *Der Brief an die Philipper* (*SNT* 1917, II), p. 391: 'There appears to be an allusion to an old myth', contained in Isa. xiv, of the fall of Lucifer.

[4] *Introduction au nouveau Testament*, IV (1926), p. 396 n. 1: 'Le caractère négatif des déterminations fondamentales du morceau montre que Pl. a vu, dans l'œuvre du Christ, l'antithèse de celle de Satan.'

[5] *Jesus, Lord and Christ*, p. 159; 'It is hard to resist the conclusion that Paul is thinking of this divine person (in Phil. 2: 5 ff.) in contrast to the mythological Lucifer (see Isaiah 14: 12 ff.) who *did* seek to seize "by robbery" equality with God, and in consequence was thrown out of heaven.'

[6] *An die Philipper*[2], pp. 53 f.; *Die Geisterwelt im Glauben des Paulus* (1909), pp. 103–9.

[7] 'Quelques remarques sur Phil., II. 6–11', *RHPR*, III (1923), 522–32.

[8] The most germane section is *Asc. Isa.* x. 29: 'And again He descended into the firmament where dwelleth the ruler of this world and He gave the password to those on the left, and His form was like theirs, and they did not praise Him there; but they were envying one another and fighting; for here there is a power of evil and envying about trifles'; cf. x. 30: 'And I saw when He descended and made Himself like unto the angels of the air, and He was like one of them' (*The Ascension of Isaiah*, ed. R. H. Charles (1900), p. 74).

work which describes the descent of Christ through the lower spheres. His way is resisted by the denizens of the cosmic spheres, but He changes His appearance and passes through by setting the spirits against one another in envy. According to Dibelius' conjecture,[1] Paul 'set the prince of the future aeons over against the spirit-powers of this Age, fighting and robbing one another; what they could not gain by robbery He gains by humble obedience'. This type of 'antagonistic' Christology plays an important part in early Christian teaching, both in the canonical and later sources.[2] Its place in I Corinthians ii. 8 and Colossians ii. 15 should put us on our guard against a too hasty dismissal of it as grotesque, especially when we read Ignatius' 'Song of a Star' (*Ephes.* xix) which speaks of Christ's being manifested to the Aeons (cf. I Tim. iii. 16; I Pet. iii. 22). A final decision about this possible background may be postponed until we have considered Philippians ii. 10, 11. In its later form, however, as mentioned above—and this applies also to the Gnostic version of the same idea in the Hermetic literature[3] and the 'Hymn

[1] *Die Geisterwelt*, pp. 92 ff.

[2] See the full study of Leivestad, *Christ the Conqueror*, pp. 108 ff. for the relevance of this text in *Ascension of Isaiah* and the dramatic and antagonistic elements in the New Testament generally.

[3] We have noted the prominence which Käsemann gives to *C. Hermet.* I, 12 ff. (above, ch. v). He is particularly impressed by the presence of the phrase in *C.H.* I, 13: ἔδειξε τῇ κατωφερεῖ φύσει τὴν καλὴν τοῦ θεοῦ μορφήν. He comments: 'Both passages (i.e. Phil. ii and *C.H.* I) are so closely connected both in period and subject-matter and yet so undoubtedly independent of each other that only a common tradition could explain this relation' ('Kritische Analyse', 69). But his conclusion that there is a 'gemeinsame Tradition' underlying both needs careful inspection.

It is true that the correspondence of key-terms in both passages is noteworthy; but this fact immediately raises the issue of dating. A. D. Nock (in the edition of *C.H.* by Nock–Festugière (1945), Intro. p. vii) dates the *Poimandres* document in the centuries which separate the years 100 and 300 of the Christian era. Further, while there is a remarkable verbal agreement, the *Urmensch-Erlöser* is *not* said to be 'ἐν μορφῇ θεοῦ'; and there is a difference of motive in his descent. In the Christian version He comes down of His own free will (as Käsemann has fully realized, *loc. cit.* 79); but in the Gnostic account the Redeemer is under some constraint (ὑποκείμενος).

It is still a matter of debate then how far the dependence goes; and Käsemann's conclusion of a common pre-Christian Gnostic tradition would be disputed by most British scholars who treat this Gnostic Redeemer myth with characteristic *Vorsichtigkeit*. But that there was a widespread myth of the Primal Man in the pre-Christian Near East seems very possible, as S. Mowinckel (*He That Cometh* (E.T. 1956), pp. 420–37) has shown. The issue is how far Paul or the early Church may have been influenced by it in their Christological systems.

of the Pearl' in the *Acts of Thomas*, 108–13[1] which many Continental scholars quote as a rough parallel—we seem to have drifted a long way from the Pauline text into another world of thought—and into another century!

C. CHRIST AND ADAM

The possibility that Philippians ii contains a latent allusion to Adam was first suggested many years ago. One of the earliest British scholars to draw attention to the parallel between Genesis ii–iii and Philippians ii was F. P. Badham in 1908;[2] and a year afterwards the same reference was given by A. H. M'Neile in *HDB*.[3] The history of this suggestion, however, goes back to an earlier age. G. Estius, *Comm. in Ep. Pauli* (1631),[4] draws a parallel between the choice registered by the devil or the first man and Christ: 'Ubi latenter taxatur diaboli et hominis superbia qui divinitatem appetendo quodammodo eam rapuerunt', taking ἁρπαγμός in the sense of 'rem alienam et ex rapto usurpatam'.

Hugo Grotius[5] translated ὡς ἄνθρωπος in Philippians ii. 8 as *tanquam Adam* with which he compared ὁ πρῶτος ἄνθρωπος (I Cor. xv. 47), in a work dated 1732.

The immediate antecedents to Badham's article which was evidently the first serious proposal in English were H. F. Ernesti's contributions to *Studien und Kritiken*, xxi (1848) and xxiii (1851) which carried the significant title, 'Phil. II. 6–11 aus einer Anspielung auf Gen. II.–III. erläutert'.[6]

The way in which this line of thought developed in the minds of modern interpreters of Paul has been considered in a section in which we considered Adam speculation in Rabbinic and heterodox Judaism.[7] It was H. J. Holtzmann[8] who brought into the discussion the idea

---

[1] The 'Hymn of the Pearl' in *Acts of Thomas* is translated and discussed by H. Jonas, *The Gnostic Religion*, pp. 112–29; and the same author's *Gnosis und der spätantiker Geist*, I², pp. 320 ff. The pre-Christian elements are considered by A. Adam, *Die Psalmen des Thomas und das Perlenlied als Zeugnisse vorchristlicher Gnosis* (1959), pp. 48 ff.

The most important phrase in this drama is *Act. Thom.* 110: υἱὸς βασιλέων ὑπάρχων δουλικὸν ὑπεισῆλθες ζυγόν (cf. *Gnosticism*, ed. R. M. Grant, pp. 116 ff.). [2] 'Phil. II. 6, 'Ἁρπαγμός', *ExT*, xix (1908), 331.

[3] *S.v.* 'Adam', *Dictionary of the Bible*, ed. J. Hastings (1909), p. 12.

[4] Fol. 657 (cited by Henry, 'Kénose', 43).

[5] *Opera theol.* iii (1732), 912 (cited Henry *ut supra*).

[6] *TSK*, xxi (1848), 858–924; xxiv (1851), 596–630.

[7] See above, ch. v, section C.

[8] H. J. Holtzmann, *Lehrbuch der N.T. Theologie*, ii (1911), pp. 92–102. He suggested that in Paul's anthropology Adam was thought of as created in the

that Paul was drawing upon Jewish speculations about the celestial and earthly Adams.

The Pauline doctrine of the two Adams in the strict sense of that expression, i.e. the first Adam and Christ the last Adam, was impressed into the service of the exegesis of Philippians ii by a number of commentators and writers in the nineteenth and early twentieth centuries. Some writers, notably D. Somerville in 1897,[1] saw in this teaching the master-key to the entire Pauline Christology.

One firm conclusion seems to emerge from a historical survey of the literature of this period. As scholars came to interpret ἁρπαγμός as *res rapienda* with equality with God as a prize to be attained by the pre-incarnate Lord it became natural to turn to the Genesis account for a likely background, for this idea of a future prize to be gained by snatching is exactly the content which is given to the specious promise of the serpent: 'You shall be as God' (Gen. iii. 5).[2] It is not surprising therefore that the two interpretations should go hand in hand, for they are strictly complementary, as Schumacher has remarked.[3]

The lines along which the parallels are drawn have already been described;[4] and have convinced certain commentators that Paul is tacitly contrasting the two Adams in his Christology. O. Cullmann puts it categorically: 'Except for this background of the Pauline teaching of the two Adams' this verse (ii. 6) 'is scarcely intelligible'.[5]

From this premise the meaning of ἁρπαγμός is illuminated. The first ἁρπαγμός was attempted as Adam, 'the son of God' (Luke iii. 38) and made a little lower than God (Ps. viii. 5 R.V.), with the enjoyment of a glory which made him the most illustrious of God's creation and therefore a proper reflection of the eternal Son in whose

image of the pre-existent 'ideal' Man (an idea drawn from Philo, *Leg. alleg.* I, xxxi. 49; *de Opif. Mundi*, LXIX, cxxxiv. 32) which Palestinian Judaism took to be in the image of angels (cf. Weber, *Jüdische Theologie*² (1897), pp. 155, 209; Jervell, *Imago Dei*, pp. 52 ff.).

Jewish speculation on the celestial and earthly Man, the two Adams, was utilized by J. Héring, art. 'Kyrios Anthropos', *RHPR*, xvi (1936), 196–209.

[1] *St Paul's Conception of Christ or the Doctrine of the Second Adam* (1897).

[2] See E. Jacob's exposition, *Theology of the Old Testament* (E.T. 1958), pp. 170 f.

[3] H. Schumacher, *Christus in seiner Präexistenz*, etc., I, p. 126. Cf. R. S. Franks, *The Doctrine of the Trinity* (1953), p. 30.

[4] See above, ch. v, section B.

[5] Cullmann, *Christology*, p. 177, cf. 175; L. Bouyer, *RSR*, xxxix (1951), 281–8 made this the master-key of the hymn. Christ is set in contrast to another. The whole hymn, he averred, is constructed as a contrast between the first and second Adams. Only on that basis can it be interpreted.

image he was made, asserted himself to be 'as God'. This was in response to the serpent's promise in Genesis iii. 5. Adam was given a relative dominion (κατακυριεύειν, LXX: Gen. i. 28, ii. 19, 20), but he sought an absolute lordship in his own right and independently of God his Maker. But he failed in this senseless aspiration; and in consequence of his disobedience and rivalry he 'died' and was expelled from Eden with his 'innocence' destroyed (Gen. iii. 22: ἰδοὺ Αδαμ γέγονε ὡς εἷς ἐξ ἡμῶν, LXX).

The Son of God, however, faced with a parallel temptation, refused to exploit His unique position within the Godhead as the 'image and glory of God' and to assert Himself in opposition to His Father. In direct contrast to the first Adam, He refused the opportunity to snatch what lay before Him, i.e. an acknowledged 'equality with God', by disobeying God; and chose rather to be obedient to the Father in a pathway that led to lordship through Incarnation, humiliation and suffering. The main attractiveness of this scheme has always been its obvious *prima facie* plausibility. The linguistic agreements between the LXX and the Greek text of Philippians ii are impressive; and the conception of our Lord as the last Adam is attested Pauline teaching in Romans v. 12–17 and I Corinthians xv. 20–49. But some important criticisms have been registered.[1] The parallelism may be displayed in tabulated form:

ADAM	CHRIST
Made in the divine image	Being the image of God
thought it a prize to be grasped at	thought it not a prize to be grasped at
to be as God;	to be as God;
and aspired to a reputation	and made himself of no reputation
and spurned being God's servant	and took upon Him the form of a servant
seeking to be in the likeness of God;	and was made in the likeness of men;
and being found in fashion as a man (of dust, now doomed),	and being found in fashion as a man (Rom. viii. 3),
he exalted himself,	He humbled Himself,

[1] For instance, G. Friedrich, *Philipper* (*NTD*), p. 108 denies any allusion to Adam—and the same denial holds for the suggestion of a background in *The Life of Adam and Eve*—because, on his view, the pre-existent Christ already had His divine existence in equality with God and thus had no need to reach out after it, or to contend for it. For Friedrich the parallelism of the two Adams in Rom. v. 12 ff. is not apparent in the Philippians psalm.

ADAM	CHRIST
and became disobedient unto death.	and became obedient unto death.
He was condemned and disgraced.	God highly exalted Him and gave Him the name and rank of Lord.

CHAPTER VII

HIS INCARNATION

ἀλλὰ ἑαυτὸν ἐκένωσεν
μορφὴν δούλου λαβών (verse 7 *a*, *b*)

A. LINGUISTIC EVIDENCE

The meaning of the verb κενοῦν in secular Greek is straightforward. It carries the sense of 'to empty, to make empty' in the literal application of the word; and then, by inference, 'to make of no effect'. This literal meaning is found in the LXX (e.g. Gen. xxiv. 20 where ἐξεκένωσεν is used of Rebekah's emptying the water from her pitcher into the trough). The simple verb κενοῦν is found only twice in the LXX:

Jeremiah xiv. 2: αἱ πύλαι αὐτῆς (*sc.* τῆς 'Ιουδαίας) ἐκενώθησαν.
Jeremiah xv. 9: ἐκενώθη ἡ τίκτουσα ἑπτά.

In both instances the Greek translates the *puʻal* of the root אמל with the sense of 'to languish'. This is an important fact because it focuses attention upon the metaphorical, as distinct from the literal, use of the verb.

In the New Testament, κενοῦν is found only four times (apart from the Phil. ii. 7 reference); and in three cases it is in the passive voice. It is also of some importance, as A. Oepke in his article *s.v.* in *TWNT*[1] has pointed out, at least by inference, that with these verses the sense required by the passive is undoubtedly metaphorical. So in Romans iv. 14; I Corinthians i. 17; II Corinthians ix. 3. The same holds good for the one case of the active voice in Paul. In I Corinthians ix. 15 the translation will be 'to make ineffectual' (Oepke, *unwirksam machen*).

The New Testament evidence which is considered so far will prepare for Philippians ii. 7 and dispose the interpreter to consider not only a literal application, but also a figurative one, if this latter is required on other grounds.

The interpretation of the Christological text begins with the

[1] *TWNT*, III, 661 f.

question, Of what did Christ empty Himself in His resolve not to cling to, or clutch at, divine equality but to take the form of a servant? This is a legitimate question only if the literal meaning of κενοῦν is insisted upon. When this is done, there are three possible answers:

(a) It is the contention of those theologians who support some aspect of the 'Kenotic' theory of the Incarnation that it is the 'form of God' which was the pre-existent nature of Christ which was surrendered at the Incarnation, as He emptied Himself of this divine nature.[1]

(b) For those who interpret ἁρπαγμός as His possession, as His state or status which He voluntarily let go, and find the phrase 'equality with God' (τὸ εἶναι ἴσα Θεῷ) as a synonym for this possession, the consequence follows that He was willing to forgo, for the period and purpose of the Incarnation, the equality He had known from all eternity. Lightfoot so regards the meaning of the word:[2] '*Though* He pre-existed in the form of God, *yet* He did not look upon equality with God as a prize which must not slip from His grasp, *but* He emptied Himself, divested Himself (not of His divine nature, for this was impossible), but of the glories, the prerogatives, of Deity.' This He did by taking the form of a servant.

(c) The view that ἁρπαγμός is to be taken as referring to the prize which lay within the reach of the pre-existent Son but which was not His actual possession in His eternal state has been mentioned earlier. On this reading of ἁρπαγμός the equality with God was not His possession, but was what He received at His glorification. The ἁρπαγμός He refused to clutch at, or exploit, was a future possibility which He declined to possess by seizure. On this interpretation He cannot have

[1] For example, H. A. W. Meyer, *Commentary*, p. 88 writes: Christ 'emptied *Himself*, and that, as the context places beyond doubt, of the *divine* μορφή, which he possessed, but now exchanged for a μορφὴ δούλου'. C. Gore makes this piece of exegesis the pivot of his Christology: 'The question has been asked, Does St Paul imply that Jesus Christ abandoned the μορφὴ Θεοῦ? I think all we can certainly say is that He is conceived to have emptied Himself of the divine mode of existence (μορφή), so far as was involved in His really entering upon the human mode of existence (μορφή)' (cited without reference by F. J. Hall, *The Kenotic Theory* (1898), p. 64, n. 1).

[2] *Philippians*, pp. 111, 112. The quotation in the text is a conflated one, made up from what Lightfoot says on two consecutive pages.

emptied Himself of that which He did not then possess, and those commentators who adhere to this view of ἁρπαγμός as *res rapienda* have to look elsewhere for their explanation of the content of the verb κενοῦν. They find it in 'the conditions of glory and majesty that inevitably pertained to his divine nature' (J. H. Michael).[1] Or alternatively, they submit that the verb may be taken in the sense of the general antithesis to the temptation of snatching at the equality which He refused. In an article which is one of the few serious discussions of the phrase in the early part of the century, W. Warren chose to treat the verb ἑαυτὸν ἐκένωσεν in a general way as 'He poured out Himself', teaching that He did not 'consider the equality with God as an opportunity of self-aggrandizement', but effaced Himself and all thought of self and poured out His fulness to enrich others.[2]

This way of taking ἑαυτὸν ἐκένωσεν brings us directly to the possibility of treating the verb in a non-literal way. Ought we to expect a secondary object, and is it right to press the question, Of what did He empty Himself? Warren clearly does not think so. And this conclusion has been set on a firm exegetical ground in recent linguistic study.

The importance of the Hebrew idiom has been stressed by L. S. Thornton.[3] He draws upon Pedersen's description of the way in which the Hebrew mind associates 'emptiness' with 'distress'.[4] Jeremiah xv. 9 is a good example of this tendency:

'She who bore seven has languished (ἐκενώθη);
she has swooned away.'

The distressed mother 'languished' so that she is no longer able to bear children. Her strength has ebbed out, and she is reduced to weakness. The same imagery is employed in II Samuel xiv. 14: 'We must needs die, and are as water spilt upon the ground.'

The link with κενοῦν is also provided by Genesis xxiv. 20. Rebekah poured out the water, and so emptied her pitcher, thus making it bare. It is of some interest that the Hebrew verb here translated by the LXX καὶ ἐξεκένωσεν is ותער, i.e. the *pi'el* of ערה which means literally 'to make bare'.

---

[1] *Philippians*, p. 90; and M. Meinertz, *Theologie*, II, p. 65.
[2] 'On ἑαυτὸν ἐκένωσε', *JTS*, XII (1911), 461–3.
[3] *The Dominion of Christ* (1952), pp. 94 ff.
[4] J. Pedersen, *Israel, Its Life and Culture*, I–II (1926), pp. 149 ff.

A study of the usage of עֶרָה reveals that the verb has a wide range of meanings. It is variously translated as 'to lay bare', 'to pour out', 'to humiliate' by exposing to shame. A key link-verb is found in Isaiah liii. 12, and this text has played an important part in the exegesis of Philippians ii. 7 since Warren called attention to its significance as a translation of ἑαυτὸν ἐκένωσεν.[1] The M.T. runs:

הערה למות נפשו

i.e. the *hiph'il* of עֶרָה is used; with the LXX this sentence becomes παρεδόθη εἰς θάνατον ἡ ψυχὴ αὐτοῦ.

A difficulty is met once the submission is made that Philippians ii. 7 goes back to this reference to the Servant who 'poured out his soul unto death'. We shall be concerned with the deeper issues of suitability and context later; for the present there is the obvious point to be faced. The LXX reads παραδι-δόναι as a translation equivalent, but the author of the Philippians passage uses κενοῦν. L. S. Thornton[2] is one of the few writers who take up this matter, and he makes the following suggestions to account for the difference of translation verbs. The writer chose—and Thornton accepts the Apostolic authorship of the hymn—the verb κενοῦν because (i) παραδιδόναι had already acquired something of a special nuance in Paul's theology; and (ii) only κενοῦν carried the double meaning of 'pour out' in the combined Old Testament senses of עֶרָה, i.e. voluntary self-giving to the utmost limit *and* the idea of shameful humiliation, which is more clearly denoted in the next main verb ἐταπείνωσεν (*v.* 8).

The full argument for the lexical equivalence of ἑαυτὸν ἐκένωσεν and the M.T. הערה נפשו can only be presented within the wider context of the postulated identification of Jesus in the form of a servant with the Servant of Yahweh in the Isaiah songs; and this will be considered separately. On the purely linguistic issue the conclusion may be stated within more restricted limits that a figurative connotation of κενοῦν is clearly possible on the basis of the lexical data drawn from the Old Testament. Thus ἑαυτὸν ἐκένωσεν may be taken in a number of diverse ways:

(*a*) ἑαυτὸν ἐκένωσεν does not necessarily require a secondary

---

[1] *JTS* xii. Similarly Isaiah liii. 12 was regarded as the background by Michael, *Philippians*, p. 90.
[2] *The Dominion of Christ*, p. 95, n. 1.

object; but if one is to be found, it will be ἡ μορφὴ τοῦ Θεοῦ or τὸ εἶναι ἴσα Θεῷ.[1] The latter is the more usual, but both are due to the predilection of the interpreter according to the type of Christological doctrine he finds elsewhere in the hymn.

(*b*) The adoption of a more general sense which takes the phrase as 'He poured out Himself' without further enquiry into the content of the verb is certainly permissible; and this would link on naturally to the participial clause which follows: 'by taking the form of a servant'.

With these linguistic observations before us we turn to tabulate the different conclusions which have been drawn about the meaning of the key-words ἑαυτὸν ἐκένωσεν and μορφὴν δούλου.

B. VARIOUS INTERPRETATIONS OF VERSE 7 (*a*, *b*)

It will be most convenient to take the two lines of verse 7 together:

(*a*) ἀλλὰ ἑαυτὸν ἐκένωσεν
(*b*) μορφὴν δούλου λαβών

and pass under review the various types of explanation which have been offered in the past half-century.

(*a*) The 'Kenotic' view: 'He gave up the form of God'

The first line of the text has acquired some distinction in that it has given its name to the so-called 'Kenotic' theory of the Incarnation. The Greek phrase ἑαυτὸν ἐκένωσεν has thus become part of theological vocabulary in providing a name for that Christological construction which sets out 'to show how the Second Person of the Trinity could so enter into human life as that there resulted the genuinely human experience which is described by the evangelists' (H. R. Mackintosh).[2] The impor-

---

[1] W. Hendriksen, *Exposition of Philippians* (1962), p. 107 lists the older adherents of this view; and Henry, 'Kénose', 28 expresses himself in a sanguine manner in regard to this alternative: 'If we see in the τὸ εἶναι ἴσα Θεῷ the object of the Kenosis...a condition given up by Christ voluntarily at the moment of His Incarnation...the text presents no difficulty, whether exegetical or theological.' But this is countered by Hall, *The Kenotic Theory*, pp. 463 f. in a series of telling arguments.
[2] *The Doctrine of the Person of Jesus Christ*, p. 266.

tance of this doctrine in the history of Christian thought may be gauged by the fact that P. Henry, who writes as a severe critic of it, is led by the historical evidence to call it 'le quatrième grand essai d'explication théologique de l'être du Christ'.[1]

To assess the theological merits and demerits of this Christological scheme does not fall within the province of this discussion, but it is germane to notice that modern exponents of the theory in its modified form (e.g. P. T. Forsyth,[2] V. Taylor[3]) no longer base their case on the exegesis of the Pauline words *simpliciter*. When J. S. Lawton writes,[4] 'It is impossible to assign to the passage (Phil. ii. 7) that decisive place which it obviously holds in the construction of kenotic Christology', he is referring to the place which was assigned to Philippians ii. 7 in early Anglican 'Kenoticism' associated with the name of C. Gore.[5] Later scholars who espouse a 'Kenotic Christology' uses the verse more as illustrative of their teaching than as a main prop or proof.

The abandonment of the support which was formerly sought in the Philippians reference is due to the perception that the verb κενοῦν is used here in a metaphorical sense[6] and that the participle λαβών, in the second stichos, is related syntactically to the main verb in the first line. The meaning is clarified when we translate on this assumption: 'He emptied Himself in that He took the servant's form.' Henry draws attention to this point of syntax:[7] 'L'action marquée par l'indicatif aoriste paraît être concomitante avec celle du participe aoriste qui suit, comme en Eph. i. 9, et la kénose, au sens large, consisterait bien dans le fait même de "prendre la forme d'esclave".' V. Taylor who writes as a champion of a revised 'Kenoticism' shares the same view, as an exegete of the Biblical text: the reference in the words

[1] Henry, 'Kénose', 156.
[2] *The Person and Place of Jesus Christ* (1909), pp. 308 ff.
[3] *The Person of Christ in New Testament Teaching* (1958), pp. 77, 260 ff.
[4] *Conflict in Christology* (1947), p. 132.
[5] For a full discussion of this teaching, see Hall, *The Kenotic Theory*, pp. 20 ff.; L. B. Smedes, *The Incarnation: Trends in Modern Anglican Thought* (n.d., about 1953).
[6] This is the conclusion of F. J. Hall's study, *op. cit.* 65, 67, 155.
[7] Henry, 'Kénose', 28; cf. Hall, *op. cit.* 64: 'The clauses which follow are epexegetical and limit the meaning of ἐκένωσε according to the Greek idiom.'

ἑαυτὸν ἐκένωσεν is 'to a pre-incarnate renunciation coincident with the act of "taking the form of a servant"'.[1]

Whatever then may be the attraction (or, as its proponents say, the necessity) of the Kenosis principle in our understanding of the Incarnation, it seems clear on strictly linguistic grounds that the verses 6 and 7 cannot mean that the pre-existent Christ emptied Himself of the μορφὴ Θεοῦ and instead took the μορφὴ δούλου. That was blandly asserted in the hey-day of Kenoticism; and is occasionally met with in modern works.[2] Barth[3] is found to use this expression, but seeks forthwith to modify the force of this 'abandonment' of the divine form by interpreting this latter phrase as the outward appearance of God rather than His 'nature' as God. There are two further objections to this 'Kenotic' explanation:

(i) It is generally agreed by modern scholars that Philippians ii does not state any 'Two Nature' Christology.[4] This verdict is endorsed in a variety of ways. H. A. A. Kennedy[5] has shown that 'Paul does not speculate upon the great problems of the nature of Christ'. An American writer H. F. Rall[6] fastens upon an important point when he comments: 'The idea of loosely attached "attributes" or powers which can be laid off and taken on like a garment corresponds to nothing in our knowledge of the personal life, nor does it do justice to Paul.' And O. Cullmann in a full examination of New Testament Christology has indicated that while there is (in his conviction) no fundamental opposition between the New Testament and the dogma of Chalcedon the Biblical texts present a functional Christology.[7] The New Testament is concerned with the saving work of God in Christ, not with answering those questions about the Being of

---

[1] V. Taylor, *The Person of Christ*, p. 77. The classification of the participial form would be that of coincident action (J. H. Moulton, *Grammar*, I, 130 f.).

[2] Cf. the short, but incisive, discussion in E. L. Mascall, *Christ, the Christian and the Church* (1946), pp. 25 f.

[3] *Philipperbrief*, p. 60: '...kann er sich der "Gottesgestalt"...auch entäußern... kann auf das diesem Sein entsprechende Erscheinen und Gelten auch verzichten' (E.T. pp. 62 f.).

[4] See above, ch. v.

[5] *The Epistle to the Philippians*, p. 435.

[6] *According to Paul* (1944), pp. 130, 131 (cited by Andrews, *The Meaning of Christ for Paul*, p. 155).

[7] Cullmann, *Christology*, p. 326.

God and the natures of Christ which subsequent centuries were to throw up. The metaphysical aspects are not so much denied —Cullmann in his latest apologia now states they are implicit in the New Testament[1]—as treated with indifference.

(ii) W. Michaelis[2] contradicts any 'Kenotic' reading of verses 6 and 7 by observing that if Paul meant that the pre-existent One exchanged His divine form for His form as a δοῦλος by emptying Himself of the former he would have written: ἑαυτὸν κενώσας. . . ἔλαβεν. The construction as we have it in the text, he says, militates against the 'Kenotic' idea.

(b) 'Non-technical' sense: 'He became poor'

According to Dibelius no precise meaning may be drawn from the words of the verse in question. These words are to be understood according to the rubric which Dibelius states:[3] 'Alle diese Erwägungen (that Paul says nothing which enables the reader to decide whether *res rapta* or *res rapienda* is in his mind: that he does not show how 'being equal with God' is connected with the 'form of God' and the title Κύριος: that Paul does not say exactly what it was that Christ gave up) sprechen gegen eine streng terminologische und für eine poetisch-hymnische Interpretation.' This rubric then applies to all the key-terms of the hymn. Applied to verse 7 and to the words ἑαυτὸν ἐκένωσεν it means that it will not do for us to ask the precise nature of the renunciation. The phrase stands in parallelism with ἐταπείνωσεν ἑαυτόν later; and both are to be understood as saying, with the use of figurative language, that Christ became poor: 'Er machte sich arm.' Dibelius quotes in support Luke i. 53; Ruth i. 21; and II Corinthians viii. 9 is equally germane if we are disposed to give a weakened sense to ἐπτώχευσεν there.

This line of reasoning has commanded little support. P. Henry remarks[4] that our Lord's poverty is not referred to explicitly; and we would expect at the first line of verse 7 some

[1] Article cited as 'The Reply of Professor Cullmann to Roman Catholic critics', *SJT*, xv, 1 (1962), 36–43.
[2] *Der Brief des Paulus an die Philipper*, p. 37.
[3] *An die Philipper*[3], p. 77; cf. *op. cit.* 80 where Dibelius draws attention to the style of the passage. This style, he infers, 'shows that this fragment has a character which is not dogmatic, but poetic-hymnic'.
[4] 'Kénose', 29.

allusion to the fact of the Incarnation itself quite apart from the historic conditions of the life on earth upon which the Incarnate later entered. Dibelius' fellow-German colleagues have dealt more stringently with his approach. E. Käsemann raises two points by way of criticism:[1]

(i) In the context of the hymn some technical definitions in the language may well be expected; and in any case Dibelius' antithesis 'wissenschaftlich' and liturgical-poetic is false. It is a *petitio principii* to divorce them so widely, and to say that the technical terms of theology have no place in the language of devotion and the cultus.

(ii) This is also true because there is no criterion by which we can measure what is liturgical and distinguish it from the dogmatic element in the early Christian literature. 'Were not the early hymns dogmatic in character, and who can deny that early Christian confessions of faith were couched in hymnic style?' asks Käsemann rhetorically.[2] Dibelius' method, therefore (Käsemann concludes[3]), 'suffers shipwreck'; and on his assumptions that Philippians ii is dealing only in poetic forms and figurative language serious exegesis is at an end. He is left with only fragments of the whole in his hands!

The same points are made *contra* Dibelius by J. Jervell who accepts the validity of Käsemann's 'severe and correct criticism', as he labels it.[4] Dibelius has overlooked the fact that we are concerned in the Philippians psalm 'with the liturgical, Christological confession in which there are statements of a logical-terminological-theological character expressed strongly with clarity and precision'. This seems a fair estimate of the whole passage; and thereby puts the Dibelius type of approach out of court.

[1] 'Kritische Analyse', 60 ff. See above, ch. IV, pp. 89 f. for the criticisms of Käsemann.

[2] *Loc. cit.* 60, taking up the issue raised in Dibelius, *op. cit.* 80 (cited in n. 3, p. 172.

[3] *Loc. cit.* 60 f., 'Mit dieser Methode kann man doch nur Schiffbruch leiden...Er behält nur Bruchstücke [an ironical allusion to Dibelius's own term—dieses Stück—in the above quotation?] des Ganzen in seiner Hand.'

[4] Jervell, *Imago Dei*, p. 209, n. 142.

(c) Sociological theories: 'He became a member of the slave class'

The same general objections may be brought against the rather bizarre views of Bornhäuser[1] and Maurenbrecher.[2] The former writer was content to see in the phrase ἑαυτὸν ἐκένωσεν only an illustration of the self-abasement of Jesus modelled on the mock humility of Nero who dressed himself in a slave's garb and mingled with the Roman populace. Maurenbrecher endeavoured to place Jesus in the social context of His times, insisting that 'the significance of Jesus' earthly life is to be viewed according to economic, political and social factors' (Esking). The words μορφὴν δούλου λαβών are thus given a social twist, and mark out His life as a member of the proletarian class. His δουλεία is to be understood quite literally, and is a part of His credentials in His rôle as leader of proletarian opinion against the capitalist Temple authorities and the totalitarian power of Rome. If a reading back of nineteenth- and twentieth-century European political and economic struggles into the Gospels and Epistles is permitted, this exegesis may have a claim; but not otherwise.

(d) Incarnational ideas: 'He became Man'

We are now to consider the view which may fairly be called the traditional one, although it has a number of different emphases. The common feature which binds these together is the idea that His taking the form of a servant relates directly to the Incarnation and carries forward the sequence of thought in the hymn to that point of time when the pre-existent One becomes the Incarnate One.

The general and common background may be filled in after this fashion. The words ἑαυτὸν ἐκένωσεν relate to the consequences of His pre-temporal choice. He refused to lay hold upon equality with God. This act of decision (implied in ἡγήσατο) was followed by certain definable consequences. This is borne out by the structure of the sentence: 'He did not...but...', where the strong adversative ἀλλά prepares for the statement of what the Incarnation meant to Him on its positive side. On the

---

[1] *Jesus Imperator Mundi*, pp. 15 f.
[2] M. Maurenbrecher, *Von Nazareth nach Golgotha* (1909), p. 126 (cited by E. Esking, *Glaube und Geschichte*, p. 26).

one hand, He refused to succumb to the temptation represented by the term ἁρπαγμός; and, on the other hand, He followed the inevitable consequence of His choice not to cling to His heavenly μορφή or to exploit the dignity which His status conferred. We have observed earlier the ways in which this choice has been understood. What seems to be a common factor is the supposition that His choice to become man was costly, with the cost variously described.

If the meaning of ἁρπαγμός is in terms of *res rapienda* and He consented not to grasp at Divine equality which (in some way) was held out to Him, the self-emptying is simply explained as His acceptance of the consequences of this self-imposed discipline and denial. The train of thought runs smoothly from verse 6 to verse 7. The pre-existent Christ was faced with a choice. Would He grasp at equality which was before Him? He declined to do so, and thereby deprived Himself (ἑαυτὸν ἐκένωσεν) of what might have been His. This self-abnegation looks back to His pre-temporal decision; and looks onwards to the sequel in the remainder of the hymn. His refusal to seize equality and His acceptance of the consequences meant that He took the servant's form, i.e. became man at the opposite end of the scale to God. The polarity of the expressions δοῦλος – Κύριος fits in with this view, and is important for the following reasons.

(i) It helps to explain why δοῦλος is in fact the selected word. The hymn might have contained the sentence, 'He emptied Himself, taking the form of man'. Lightfoot[1] notices that this is not the case and comments that δοῦλος is used instead of ἄνθρωπος (which is the obvious parallel with Θεός in verse 6) because the former is the stronger word, and it contrasts with the Κύριος of verse 11: 'He, who is Master (Κύριος) of all, became the slave of all.'

(ii) The fact that δοῦλος is found in the text—and it is used only here in the New Testament of Christ—is *prima facie* evidence that there is an intended contrast with Κύριος, and this note of contrast would chime in with the entire stress of the hymn. The pre-incarnate Christ refused lordship in His own right by an act of seizure, but at the end of His career as the humiliated and obedient δοῦλος He is granted that κυριότης which *might* have been His in His pre-existence.

---

[1] *Philippians*, p. 112.

(iii) Δοῦλος emphasizes obedience to the will of another person, in this context κατ' ἐξοχήν God Himself; and the obedience of Christ, at length vindicated and rewarded, is a dominant motif in the entire passage.

This last observation brings us to the exposition of W. Michaelis[1] for whom the obedience of Christ is the central meaning of the phrase under discussion. He has the distinction of addressing himself in his treatment of this verse to a question which many commentators pass over lightly: Why is Christ's coming to earth spoken of as the taking of the form of a δοῦλος? Schlatter[2] dismisses this difficulty with the statement that 'weil wir es sind, wurde er es'; and Heinzelmann[3] similarly takes the expressions to imply that, as all men are slaves qua sinners, Christ did not hold Himself aloof from His brethren but 'subjected Himself to the accursed ordinances under which we groan as men'. Heinzelmann does not elaborate the meaning, but it is possible he has in mind such an event as the Baptism of our Lord when He identified Himself with those who came to John's baptism of repentance, and thereby declared Himself to 'fulfil all righteousness'. This may be the case, but Michaelis takes issue with this understanding of Philippians ii. 7 on the ground that the idea that men are slaves lacks Biblical proof, a criticism which Käsemann has approved.[4] Nor does Michaelis find Haupt's view any more acceptable that the δουλεία which Christ assumed was His life of dependence upon God: 'Mensch sein heißt ein abhängiges Wesen sein.'[5]

Michaelis therefore is forced, in default of any satisfactory alternative, to deny that the phrase μορφὴν δούλου λαβών has any reference to the Incarnation. The manhood of Christ, he says, is described clearly and sufficiently in the following sentence with the help of the words ἐν ὁμοιώματι ἀνθρώπων γενόμενος. It is these words which set forth the Incarnation as the tell-tale ἀνθρώπων makes clear. What, then, is the purpose

---

[1] *Philipper*, p. 39: 'one thought runs through the hymn with intentional insistence (*Einseitigkeit*): the obedience of Christ in relation to the Father's will'.

[2] *Der Brief an die Philipper* (*Erläut. z. NT*, 1928), ad loc.

[3] *Der Brief an die Philipper* (*NTD*), ad loc.

[4] Käsemann, 'Kritische Analyse', 73.

[5] E. Haupt, *Die Gefangenschaftsbriefe* (*MeyerKomm.*) (1902), p. 60.

of verse 7*b*? Its meaning can only be decided by our study of what constitutes the nature of a slave. The answer is simply, that he has a lord, whose will is influential for him. He has to subordinate his will to that of his master to whom his life is one of obedience. Thus ἑαυτὸν ἐκένωσεν (*er entleerte sich*) means that Christ 'abandoned His self, His own will, He made Himself empty (*leer*) in so far as He became an obedient Servant'.[1] This is where the accent falls in verse 7*b*. Michaelis is guarded in claiming only this limited application of the line. The Incarnation is not in view here; there is no hint of His 'human nature' in opposition to His divine nature—'speculation as to divine and human natures and their relation is far away'[2]—and it is not even said *why* He was obedient (a question which Paul discusses at length in Romans v) or that He was obedient 'for us'. It is simply His obedience and the execution of the Divine will that are stressed in this line.

(*e*) E. Käsemann's hypothesis: 'He placed Himself under demonic powers'

This 'minimal' interpretation of Michaelis is rejected by most commentators, but not for the same reasons. E. Käsemann,[3] however, puts his finger on the chief weakness when he points out that the lines of verse 7 are in parallelism, and the two participial clauses:

7*b* μορφὴν δούλου λαβών
7*c* ἐν ὁμοιώματι ἀνθρώπων γενόμενος

run together. The whole of verse 7 then must refer to the Incarnation, and cannot be split up as Michaelis had imagined. Käsemann, moreover, praises one feature of the earlier construction. This is the way in which the obedience of Christ as an act of free will is brought out. Käsemann's own view[4] may be divided into two parts, and both are important because they have commanded an influential following among writers in this field.

---

[1] Michaelis, *Philipper*, p. 37.   [2] Michaelis, *op. cit.* p. 38.
[3] 'Kritische Analyse', 62, 71.   [4] *Loc. cit.* 72 ff.

The first area is concerned with the general approach to this section of the hymn; and the second has to do with the meaning of 'the form of a servant'.

The emphasis of the hymn, indeed its preoccupation, is not in any way to do with the mutual relationships of the Godhead. All that verse 7 says is that the One who was equal with God became a slave and became obedient. To the question: Why did He abase Himself? the only answer of the hymn is: Of His own free will. The strophe portrays not a relationship between God and Christ, but an event, a drama in which the various phases follow one upon another in succession. The early verse has said that Christ was in the divine form which He gave up and 'came down' as man. Upon the modern query, How can this be? How can He be God and man at the same time? the only light which the hymn throws is to assure us that this is not the thing at stake. The central issue is that the Redeemer has passed through successive phases of existence and is at length exalted as Lord of the cosmos. We require to know not *who He is* but *what He did*; and the stress falls upon His acts. This is the significance of the reflexive ἑαυτόν in the phrase ἑαυτὸν ἐκένωσεν (*v.* 7). And this act is only of interest to us as we can perceive in it not so much the moral decision of Jesus as the way in which God is acting for our salvation.

Verse 7, then, on this reading of the text means that God became man, nothing more and nothing less. The *kenosis* of Christ is His incarnation. The text does not say of what He 'emptied Himself', or what the relation of the 'two natures' is. It refers to Christ who voluntarily gave up His heavenly existence and limited Himself by becoming man. It was His free act which inspired this; and no fate impelled Him. The Incarnation is in no way explained; the facts are simply stated. He who was God is now man; but this is only a preparation for His final enthronement as Kyrios. The important thing here is 'not the identity of the Person in the various phases of His existence, but the continuity of a miraculous occurrence' ('nicht die Identität einer Person in verschiedenen Phasen...sondern die Kontinuität eines wunderbaren Geschehens').[1]

Summarizing this novel interpretation, then, we may regard the following points as salient:

---

[1] Käsemann, *loc. cit.* 76.

(i) The framework of the hymn is a mythical drama.[1]

(ii) It is concerned with events in an other-worldly setting.

(iii) The intention and purpose of the hymn is not to describe who Christ is in His Person nor to relate that Person to the Father. The statements of the hymn concern His actions.[2]

(iv) When we read that 'He emptied Himself', 'He took the servant's form' these statements do not give a definition of His nature, but speak of events in a connected series.[3]

(v) All we are required to learn from them is that the Lord of the universe acted freely and was under no compulsive, external power when He entered upon that stage in His progress which is represented by the second strophe of verse 7.

(vi) He did voluntarily, however, place Himself under the yoke of submission in two ways. In His acceptance of humanity's bondage to the elemental spirits of the universe (this is Käsemann's way of taking μορφὴν δούλου λαβών), and in His enslavement by the demonic power of death, He entered upon His humiliation.

This last point brings us directly to the second aspect of Käsemann's understanding of verse 7, viz., his treating the δουλεία as bondage to the evil spiritual forces which were thought to rule over the destinies of men in the Graeco-Roman world of the first century. O. Holtzmann has called attention to Galatians iv. 3 in this connection.[4] The bondage of men under the στοιχεῖα becomes in this context the frontispiece for Paul's doctrine of the Incarnation in Galatians iv. 4 as he goes on to speak of Christ who came 'under the law'. We may take this description of the coming of Christ as a δοῦλος to be yet another piece of evidence that His gospel was understood and pro-

---

[1] 'The myth describes the metamorphosis of the Deity: the heavenly nature is laid aside, the earthly is put on', *loc. cit.* 72. For a similar conclusion, see J. Schneider, *TWNT*, v, 197. Only by the use of a mythical pattern can the miracle of the Incarnation be expressed.

[2] '...Fakta feststellten, nicht Verhältnisse beschrieben' ('Kritische Analyse', 77).

[3] Käsemann, *loc. cit.*: 'all diese Sätze eben nicht eine Wesensdefinition ...sondern von der Ereignisfolge eines in sich zusammenhängenden Geschehens sprechen' (76).

[4] 'die Vorstellungen...an den die Menschen gebunden sind (Gal. 4. 3). Jetzt aber wurde der Messias den Menschen gleich, also auch ὑπὸ τὰ στοιχεῖα τοῦ κόσμου δεδουλωμένος', comments O. Holtzmann, *Das NT*... *übersetzt u. erklärt* (1926), p. 684.

claimed in the first century against a background of human need. The belief that these 'rulers', 'authorities' and 'powers' held sway over human life and fortune produced an atmosphere which, in turn, struck fear into Hellenistic man. It led to a sense of futility and 'failure of nerve', of which E. Bevan[1] and Gilbert Murray[2] have written. Speaking of the στοιχεῖα H. A. A. Kennedy[3] remarks that this was perhaps 'the most crushing weight which oppressed human souls' in this period, and that the burden of them was felt like an 'iron yoke' throughout the Hellenistic world. Moreover, this dread of cosmic powers beyond man's control was associated with the fear of death (Heb. ii. 15) and a general pessimism and despair. The following couplet sums up the *Zeitgeist*:

'I, a stranger and afraid
In a world I never made.'[4]

The Christian gospel came as good news into such a situation, declaring the overthrow of these cosmic and alien forces by the victory of Christ who voluntarily placed Himself under these powers and overmastered them. To give a rationale of this victory in Pauline theology is not a simple matter. Paul seems more concerned to proclaim the fact of Christ's triumph than to explain how it was accomplished. What is clear, however, is the stress he lays upon the identification of Christ with men in their servitude because this fact provides the foundation and basis for his later appeal to his converts that they may share the benefits which their victorious Lord has won for them. He disarmed principalities and powers by engaging them at first hand, not holding Himself aloof; and has thereby secured the release from tyranny of those who are 'in Him'. And this liberation was made possible because He took upon Himself the form of a slave and though acting with freedom consented to submit to the yoke of Destiny (εἱμαρμένη).[5]

---

[1] *Hellenism and Christianity* (1921), esp. 81–8.
[2] *Five Stages of Greek Religion* (1935 ed.), ch. IV: 'The Failure of Nerve'. The texts are cited in Part III below.
[3] *St Paul and the Mystery Religions* (1913), pp. 24 f., citing Gal. iv. 8, 9.
[4] A. E. Housman, *Last Poems*, xii.
[5] The grip which the belief in εἱμαρμένη had on the men of the first century is described by H. Jonas, *Gnosis und spätantiker Geist*, I² (1954), 156–72.

This interpretation which is expounded by E. Käsemann[1] and others who follow him (e.g. G. Bornkamm,[2] J. Jervell;[3] and, by inference, R. Bultmann[4] in his treatment of a similar passage in I Peter) assumes that the hymn is correctly anchored in the thought-world of Hellenism, and represents a borrowing of the pattern of a current Gnostic myth.[5] At the opposite end of the spectrum stand other scholars who deny the legitimacy of such teaching; place the understanding of verse 7 in an exclusively Biblical tradition and, not unnaturally, come to quite a different interpretation of what the phrase 'the form of a servant' implies. It is interesting to note that both lines of explanation stem from a common source. It was E. Lohmeyer who fathered both suggestions which have subsequently dominated the exegesis of this verse. He pointed to the possibility of dependence upon myth—in the Iranian form of Gayōmart; and at the same time put out the idea that the terminology of the Philippians Christ-hymn may go back to the Old Testament. He comments on such a phase as εὑρεθεὶς ὡς that 'it is not only un-Pauline but un-Greek'; and is led to postulate an Aramaic *Grundlage* for the

---

[1] 'Kritische Analyse', 73, 79.

[2] 'Zum Verständnis des Christus-Hymnus', 181: 'The existence of un-redeemed man is seen as that of slavery (δουλεία), that is, of imprisonment and servitude under the rule of the cosmic powers, the "elements of the world".' The evidence for this is found in Gal. iv. 1–5, 8 f.; and equally in Rom. viii. 21: δουλεία τῆς φθορᾶς and Col. ii. 20 ff. and Heb. ii. 15. In these texts where the Incarnation of Christ is set forth (i.e., Gal. iv and Heb. ii. 14f.), this coming of the Son in the flesh and His being made under the law are 'for the freeing of those who are enslaved by the cosmic powers'. Hence, Bornkamm concludes, 'it is understandable, in the light of this, that Phil. 2. 7 equates His being a slave and His being a man'.

For Hebrews ii. 15, cf. Käsemann, *Das wandernde Gottesvolk* (1939), pp. 98 ff.

[3] *Imago Dei*, p. 229 who quotes as 'convincing' the parallel in *C.H.* 1, 15: ὑπεράνω οὖν ὢν τῆς ἁρμονίας ἐναρμόνιος γέγονε δοῦλος. The *Urmensch* is depicted as 'subject to Destiny. Though he is superior to the framework, he has become a slave in it.'

[4] 'Bekenntnis- und Liedfragmente im ersten Petrusbrief', *Coniect. Neotest.* XI (1947), pp. 6 f.

[5] A number of scholars, including some British writers, have drawn attention to this background: J. Weiss, *Earliest Christianity*, II, p. 493: 'Paul calls this "form of a servant" because he, though born Lord of all things, became like men, the slave of "the elements of the world"'; M. Werner, *The Formation of Christian Dogma* (E.T. 1957), p. 127: the 'form' of a slave (*sc.* of the angelic powers which ruled the world); J. A. T. Robinson, *The Body* (1952), pp. 38 f.; G. B. Caird, *Principalities and Powers* (1956), pp. 97 f.

entire passage. Later scholars have taken up this notion in relation to verse 7 and the words ἑαυτὸν ἐκένωσεν and found in them a reflection of Isaiah liii. 12, with the following words μορφὴν δούλου λαβών to confirm them in their hypothesis that here is an allusion to the suffering Servant of Yahweh.[1]

(*f*) *The 'Ebed Yahweh portrait: 'He took the rôle of Isaiah's Servant'*

We turn now to sketch this line of development. It is introduced by J. Jeremias,[2] although it is found earlier in W. Warren's article.[3] The latter simply called attention to Isaiah liii. 12 by saying that ἑαυτὸν ἐκένωσεν was 'perhaps an equivalent' for the Hebrew. In 1926, however, H. W. Robinson[4] took up this idea and elaborated it, arguing that the Greek of Paul's letter depends upon the Hebrew of Isaiah. This discussion is noteworthy in two ways. First, Robinson asserted a direct dependence upon Isaiah liii as distinct from a mere literary allusion. And then, he went on to translate the Hebrew, 'Because he emptied out his life to death'. Secondly, as far as the Pauline text is concerned, the emphasis falls upon the death of Christ: 'the Kenosis was properly that of the Crucifixion, though naturally involving the Incarnation'.[5] Both these insights have been taken up into recent exegesis, with some interesting results. C. H. Dodd in 1938,[6] apparently independently, expressed a similar readiness to find a parallel to Philippians ii. 7 in the words נפשו הערה of Isaiah liii. He suggests that Paul is using an already established form of expression—a possibility which too has been taken up and carried forward in recent discussions[7] by O. Michel and L.

---

[1] E. Lohmeyer noted this connection, *Kyrios Jesus*, p. 36; *Gottesknecht und Davidsohn* (1945), pp. 3 ff.

[2] 'Zur Gedankenführung in den paulin. Briefen', *Studia Paulina*, p. 154, n. 3; and the same author's art. *s.v.* παῖς, *TWNT*, v, 708.

[3] *JTS*, xii (1911), 461 ff. See the discussion of the early developments of this idea by D. R. Griffiths, "Ἁρπαγμός and ἑαυτὸν ἐκένωσεν in Philippians ii. 6, 7', *ExpT*, lxix (1958), 237–9. C. Taylor, *The Sayings of the Jewish Fathers*[2] (1897), pp. 165–7 may be added.

[4] *The Cross of the Servant* (1926), pp. 72–4. The pagination followed in the notes is that of the composite volume, *The Cross in the Old Testament* (1957), pp. 103–5.   [5] H. W. Robinson, *op. cit.* 105.

[6] In a review of a *Lieferung* of *TWNT*, *JTS*, xxxix (1938), 292; cf. his later discussion of the matter in *According to the Scriptures* (1952), p. 93.

[7] See below, footnotes 2, 3 on p. 188.

Cerfaux. Dodd seeks linguistic support on the evidence that the *pi'el* of ערה is translated three times[1] by ἐκκενοῦν in LXX, and that the *hiph'il* of the same verb is found in Isaiah liii. 12. He would therefore boldly translate this latter text into Greek as ἐξεκένωσεν τὴν ψυχὴν αὐτοῦ εἰς θάνατον. A. M. Hunter[2] enthusiastically received this submission in 1940 as part of a wider concern to relate the entire psalm in Philippians ii to the picture of the suffering Servant.

J. Jeremias has continued this tradition, noting that ἑαυτὸν ἐκένωσεν is found nowhere else in Greek[3] and is grammatically harsh. Therefore, 'it can only be regarded as a literal rendering of הערה נפשו (Is. liii. 12) and refers to the sacrifice of His life and not to the self-emptying of His Incarnation'.[4] Thus Jeremias accepts the two points made earlier by Wheeler Robinson. And it is upon exactly these two matters that criticism has fastened.

(i) *The linguistic validity of the theory.* Most commentators are content either categorically to dismiss what Käsemann[5] disdainfully labels the *Gottesknechttheorie*[6] or eagerly to welcome

---

[1] In Gen. xxiv. 20; II Chron. xxiv. 11; Ps. cxli. 8.

[2] A. M. Hunter, *Paul and his Predecessors* (1940), p. 50 ([2]1961, p. 43) and similarly W. K. L. Clarke, *New Testament Problems*, p. 144.

[3] The suggested parallel in Isaiah xlix. 4: κενῶς ἐκοπίασα καὶ εἰς μάταιον καὶ εἰς οὐδὲν ἔδωκα τὴν ἰσχύν μου is listed by P. Henry, *loc. cit.* 46; Cerfaux, *Le Christ*, p. 286 (E.T. 379) and D. M. Stanley, 'The Theme of the Servant of Yahweh, etc.', *CBQ*, xvi (1954), 422; but this suggestion is far-fetched.

[4] J. Jeremias, *Studia Paulina*, p. 154, n. 3: '...bezieht sich dann auf die Preisgabe des Lebens, nicht auf die Kenose bei der Inkarnation'.

[5] 'Kritische Analyse', 73.

[6] In this category may be placed: Dibelius, *An die Philipper*, pp. 74 f. who declares that δοῦλος signifies (any) man in contrast to God—a meaning which would be ruined if the Servant of Isaiah liii were meant, or any special or elect person, chosen from among men; Ewald–Wohlenberg, *Philipper*, pp. 115 f.: 'Gar nicht in Betracht kommt natürlich der jesajische Gottesknecht. Denn dafür pflegen LXX παῖς zu brauchen' (116, n. 1); Michaelis, *Der Brief an die Philipper*, p. 37 who says explicitly: 'Auch an den "Knecht" Jes 53 ist übrigens nicht zu denken'; Schweizer, *Erniedrigung und Erhöhung*, p. 135 (see below, p. 191); Jervell, *Imago Dei*, p. 229; G. Bornkamm, 'Zum Verständnis des Christus-Hymnus', 180 who fastens the following criticism on Jeremias' theory that the Greek of Phil. ii. 7: ἑαυτὸν ἐκένωσεν, is a translation of Isaiah liii. 12: 'Even linguistically we should have to admit that the Hebrew "lammaweth" (unto death), as well as the object "naphscho" (his soul) could not have remained untranslated', if the Pauline text were an attempted Greek version of a Hebrew original. 'There is no mention

it,[1] but very few seem anxious to investigate the linguistic question whether ἑαυτὸν ἐκένωσεν can mean the equivalent of Isaiah liii. 12. One writer who does essay this task is M. D. Hooker.[2] She writes, 'There is no linguistic evidence for regarding the words ἑαυτὸν ἐκένωσε...μέχρι θανάτου as a reference to Isaiah 53. 11 (sic). While κενόω is a possible translation of עָרָה, it is not used in this sense in the LXX.' Now ערה means 'to lay bare', and then with a developed sense, 'to lay bare by removing the contents, to empty': so Genesis xxiv. 20, II Chronicles xxiv. 11. It also carries the sense (noted by C. K. Barrett[3]) of 'to kill' in Psalm cxli. 8. It is this last usage which is most apposite for an understanding of Isaiah liii. 12: 'He poured out His life unto death.' But there is also another group of meanings of ערה which is notable. In Lamentations iv. 21 the hithpa'el of the verb is used of 'making naked', 'being humiliated'. It could therefore express

of the death in our text until the last line of the first strophe and not in verse 7a'; Friedrich, Philipper (NTD), p. 110 dismisses the possibility of an allusion to Isa. liii because the phrase means the situation of men who are enslaved by cosmic forces. He follows Käsemann's line: 'Die "Knechtsgestalt" meint das Dasein des Menschen, sofern es den Mächten ausgeliefert ist' ('Kritische Analyse', 74).

[1] Cullmann, Christology, pp. 76 f. simply reports: 'Phil. 2. 7 certainly includes the idea of the ebed Yahweh in the humiliation of Christ's incarnation: μορφὴν δούλου λαβών ("taking the form of a servant"). Ebed is translated here by δοῦλος.'

The following writers have supported, with varying degrees of conviction, the identification of Jesus' 'taking the form of a servant' with the picture of Isaiah's servant: Lohmeyer, Philipper, p. 94; Kyrios Jesus, p. 36; and Gottesknecht und Davidsohn (1945), pp. 7, 8; K. Euler, Die Verkündigung vom leidenden Gottesknecht aus Jes 53 in der griechischen Bibel (1934), pp. 45–8, 101, 103 ff.; G. Stählin, s.v. ἴσος κ.τ.λ., TWNT, III, 354; Bornhäuser, Jesus Imperator Mundi, pp. 19–21; P. Joüon, 'Notes philologiques sur quelques versets etc.', RSR, xxviii (1938), 228 f.; G. Kittel, s.v. εἰκών, TWNT, I, 225; A. Feuillet, 'L'Homme-Dieu etc.', RB, li (1942), 66; Davies, Paul and Rabbinic Judaism², pp. 274, 355; Geiselmann, Jesus der Christus (1951), pp. 140 f.; Michel, 'Zur Exegese von Phil. 2, 5–11', 83 ff.; Michael, The Epistle to the Philippians (MNTC), p. 90; Henry, 'Kénose', 45 f.; A. Richardson, An Introduction to the Theology of the New Testament (1958), p. 304, n. 1; B. Reicke, 'Unité chrétienne et Diaconie', Neotestamentica et Patristica (Novum Testamentum Suppl. vi) (1962), 210 f.

[2] Jesus and the Servant, p. 121.

[3] 'The Background of Mark 10: 45', New Testament Essays. Studies in memory of T. W. Manson (1959), p. 5. M.T. reads: אַל־תְּעַר נַפְשִׁי (i.e. do not kill me; do not pour out my life); LXX: μὴ ἀντανέλῃς τὴν ψυχήν μου.

quite easily the sense of 'to expose to disgrace and shame'; and would then link up with the meanings of κενοῦν in Jeremiah xv. 9 where the mother now reduced in strength (ἐκενώθη) is no longer capable of bearing children and enters under this 'humiliation'. Rightly, we feel, L. S. Thornton[1] concludes: 'Thus the double meanings of the two verbs employed in Isaiah and Philippians are not far apart.' If the question is pressed, If 'Paul' is *citing* Isaiah liii, why does he not quote verbatim from the LXX? the answer is:

(1) The LXX παρεδόθη has for him already acquired something of a technical meaning;

(2) moreover, he requires a new verb not because of necessity only, if (1) be true, but because he wishes to convey the nuance of humiliation. This is seen in his employment of an imagery which suggests the exact notion he is at pains to make clear. In Hebrew thought, as Pedersen has shown, the life of distress and misery is described as a life wherein the soul (נפש) is poured out: 'The anguished soul is empty': 'the miserable soul has poured out his *nephesh*, i.e. emptied it of its fulness and strength.'[2] This thought may well have motivated the choice of the rare verb κενοῦν with the voluntariness conveyed by the Hebraic use of the reflexive to replace the words τὴν ψυχὴν αὐτοῦ of the original.

(3) Later, in verse 8, the author will write: μέχρι θανάτου which is the equivalent of εἰς θάνατον in Isaiah liii. 12.

It would appear, then, that the linguistic challenge to the equivalence of the Isaiah liii. 12 and the Philippians reference cannot stand.

But this is only a preliminary skirmish as far as the challengers are concerned; and other points are raised which need now to be faced.

(ii) While there seems no lexical barrier to impede the semantic equation of the term נפשו הערה and ἑαυτὸν ἐκένωσεν, another difficulty emerges concerning the place of such a reference in the structure of the hymn. *This is the contextual impropriety* of relating the sacrifice of the Cross before the actual Incarnation has been mentioned. M. D. Hooker proceeds (in

[1] *The Dominion of Christ*, p. 95, n. 1.
[2] J. Pedersen, *Israel: Its Life and Culture*, i–ii, pp. 149 ff. Cf. Job vii. 11, xxx. 16; Ps. xlii. 5, cxli. 8.

the above quotation) to say of the use of κενόω: 'nor is its primary meaning in this passage (sc. Phil. ii) the actual death of Christ'.[1] Jeremias boldly says that ἑαυτὸν ἐκένωσεν refers not to the *kenosis* of the Incarnation but to the surrender of His life upon the Cross; and this raises an obvious difficulty if we expect the hymn to proceed in chronological fashion to cover the *curriculum vitae* of Christ. The structure of the hymn has been broken by mentioning the death of the Lord before the circumstances of the incarnate life have been given. How far we are to expect formal consistency here with logical, historical order is the issue. There are a number of factors to be borne in mind before this theory is held to be embarrassed by an insistence upon a strict order. First, H. Wheeler Robinson[2] faces the objection and grants that, on first reading, it would appear that the Incarnation is in view in ἑαυτὸν ἐκένωσεν, but the Apostle's parenthetic style may account for the peculiar form and order of the clauses. 'When he has begun to express this divine humiliation unto death, with the memorable words of Isaiah liii. 12 in his mind as its apt expression, he checks himself after saying, "He emptied himself"—before adding the completing words "to death", at the remembrance of the human life which was the necessary pathway to that death of the Cross, and describes the humiliation of this life on earth as a "servant" prior to the great humiliation of the Cross; hence the parenthetic clauses, which grammatically follow the word which envisages the goal of the Cross, though logically they precede this, as the preparation for it.' But this explanation of the mental processes of the hymn-writer seems very strained.

Secondly, we may remark upon the way in which the text of Isaiah lii–liii appears to be used in the hymn without any reference to logical or historical sequence. For example, the glorification of the Servant in Isaiah lii. 13 with the key-verb in the LXX ὑψωθήσεται is the frontispiece of the chapter of his humiliation, whereas in the Philippians text at ii. 9 it comes as the climax of the hymn and as the result of His obedience unto death.

Thirdly, the above observation has been differently explained

---

[1] *Jesus and the Servant*, p. 121.
[2] *The Cross of the Servant*, p. 104, n. 23.

by other writers (G. von Rad[1] and H. W. Wolff[2]) who regard the prophet as speaking of the suffering and dying of the 'Ebed only from the standpoint of exaltation. If this exegetical principle is applied to Philippians ii. 6 ff. it would mean that the ταπείνωσις of the Lord who takes the servant's form derives its true meaning from the ἐν μορφῇ Θεοῦ ὑπάρχων in verse 6. Thus His high estate, on this view, does in fact stand at the head of the hymn and gives point and purpose to all that follows.

(iii) The argument moves on to consider *the propriety of the use of* μορφὴ δούλου to designate the 'Ebed Yahweh of the Isaianic poems. This is a point mentioned by a variety of editors. K. Rengstorf[3] in *TWNT* notes that παῖς is the correct translation-equivalent for עבד, while some writers aver that the concepts underlying עבד '" = παῖς Θεοῦ which are those of dignity and honour are absent from δοῦλος which underscores the element of shame and humiliation.[4] To take the lexical point first:

(a) While it is true that the expected equivalent of the title 'Ebed Yahweh is παῖς Θεοῦ, C. F. Burney[5] has shown that 'both Greek terms (δοῦλος, παῖς) are indifferently used in the LXX to render the עֶבֶד of Deutero-Isaiah, but the preference[6] is for παῖς (δοῦλος in 49. 3, 5;[7] παῖς in 42. 1, 49. 6, 50. 10, 52. 13)'. The way in which the two titles are interchangeably used is brought out in the exhaustive examination conducted by K. Euler[8] which has convinced Lohmeyer[9] and Cerfaux.[10] Euler[11] distinguishes the words as follows: δοῦλος emphasizes the depen-

---

[1] G. von Rad, 'Zur prophetischen Verkündigung Deuterojesajas', *Verkündigung und Forschung* (1940), p. 62: 'Erst unter diesem eschatologischen Gesichtspunkt (also: vom Ende her!) kann es in seiner Bedeutung recht verstanden werden' (cited by Wolff, see note 2).

[2] *Jesaja 53 im Urchristentum*[3] (1953), pp. 31 f.

[3] *S.v.* δοῦλος, *TWNT*, ii, 282.

[4] Thus M. D. Hooker, *Jesus and the Servant*, p. 120.

[5] *The Aramaic Origin of the Fourth Gospel*, p. 108.

[6] The reason for this preference of δοῦλος instead of παῖς is hinted at by Cerfaux, *Le Christ*, p. 340 (E.T. p. 455) and Cullmann, *Christology*, p. 284. They point out that παῖς means both servant and son. Cf. A. Richardson, *An Introduction*, p. 304.

[7] Add Isaiah xlii. 19, xlviii. 20.

[8] *Die Verkündigung*, pp. 54 ff.

[9] *Gottesknecht und Davidsohn*, pp. 3 ff.

[10] *Le Christ*, pp. 284 ff., 293 ff. (E.T. pp. 377 ff., 385 ff.).

[11] *Op. cit.* p. 91.

dence of a man upon his lord or the Lord; παῖς is the more intimate term describing him as the member of a family and stressing his relationship to the *paterfamilias*. But within the context of the Servant songs there is no vital distinction and both are permissible translations of עבד.

(*b*) This conclusion is endorsed by the variation in textual tradition. In Isaiah lii. 13 Aquila reads ὁ δοῦλος in place of ὁ παῖς.[1] Moreover, the verb δουλεύειν is used in the LXX at Isaiah liii. 11 which suggests that there is no great distinction between the two terms.

(*c*) On the assumption that Isaiah liii is in the author's mind, not only δούλου but even the entire phrase μορφὴν δούλου may be traced to this corpus of prophecy. O. Michel[2] and L. Cerfaux[3] have drawn attention to the textual tradition underlying Isaiah lii. 14 where the LXX reads τὸ εἶδος and ἡ δόξα. These same Greek words corresponding to מראהו ותארו recur in Isaiah liii. 2. Aquila reads for this pair ὅρασις αὐτοῦ καὶ μορφὴ αὐτοῦ in Isaiah lii. 14; and there is a variant reading of μορφή at Isaiah liii. 2. The upshot of this textual peculiarity is that Aquila and Philippians ii in these places agree with each other against the LXX; and this fact leads Michel to suggest that both later authorities refer to an older Greek translation of the Isaiah text.[4] L. Cerfaux[5] remarks that this is not the only place where Paul's quotations agree with Aquila against the LXX. If there is substance in this claim then we can read back into Isaiah's portrait of the '*Ebed* not only Paul's designation of the Incarnate Christ

[1] Euler, *op. cit.* p. 29; cf. Cerfaux, *op. cit.* 285, n. 4 (E.T. p. 378, n. 30).
[2] 'Zur Exegese von Phil 2, 5–11', 92. [3] *Le Christ*, p. 285 (E.T. p. 378).
[4] This possibility had been mooted by Euler, *Die Verkündigung*, p. 48: 'Sollte...in Phil 2, Symm und Aquila eine ältere uns unbekannte Textgestalt vorliegen, die von dem heutigen LXX-Text abweicht?' The question is answered affirmatively (e.g. *op. cit.* 106: μορφή in Aquila's version is regarded as the 'ältere Lesart', a reading which Aquila has fallen back upon in his reproduction of the LXX text). Cf. Behm, *s.v.* μορφή, *TWNT*, IV, 759, n. 52.
[5] Cerfaux, *Le Christ*, p. 290 (E.T. 386). The most interesting examples are I Cor. i. 20 where Paul's word γραμματεύς agrees with Aquila against the LXX's γραμματικοί (Isa. xix. 12; xxxiii. 18); and I Cor. iii. 19 (Job v. 12, 13) on which Héring, *The First Epistle of Saint Paul to the Corinthians* (E.T. 1962), *ad loc.*, comments: 'Perhaps Paul had read Job in another translation than the LXX.' See further O. Michel, *Paulus und seine Bibel* (1929), pp. 64 f.

as the Servant, but also His appearing in the form (μορφή) of that character.

(d) A subsidiary argument introduced by Cerfaux[1] is that Paul who used the title of δοῦλος (Phil. i. 1, etc.) of himself *qua* Apostle viewed his apostolate in terms of the suffering Servant passages.[2] Cerfaux describes Paul's 'rôle' not as though he imagined himself to be a new Servant of Yahweh as Windisch thought,[3] but as perpetuating the Messianic ministry begun in Jesus, as T. W. Manson[4] has expounded it in another connection. The relevant texts are Galatians i. 15; II Corinthians vi. 2; Philippians ii. 16; II Corinthians iv. 6; Romans xv. 20 f., x. 1–21. On this idea the use of δοῦλος is in exact parallelism with the LXX's use of παῖς.

We address our enquiry now to the nub of the problem. We have seen that there is no linguistic objection to the equation of the New Testament phrases ἑαυτὸν ἐκένωσεν μορφὴν δούλου λαβών with the Servant of Isaiah. But do the two conceptions fit together? In Isaiah lii–liii the title παῖς/עבד is one of honour. The full examination of G. Sass,[5] 'Zur Bedeutung von δοῦλος bei Paulus', indicates that, in the semantic development of the word, *'Ebed* is a title of honour (*Ehrentitel*); and this is seen in the

---

[1] 'Saint Paul et le "Serviteur de Dieu" d'Isaïe', *Recueil Lucien Cerfaux*, II, 439–54. His conclusion in that Paul's ministry and apostleship were viewed 'en continuation du Christ, dans l'accomplissement de la prophétie du Serviteur'. But there is criticism of his view in Hooker, *Jesus and the Servant*, pp. 115 f.

[2] And Stanley, 'The Theme of the Servant of Yahweh', *CBQ*, XVI (1954), 415–18 finds answer to the question, What authority had St Paul for thus casting himself in the rôle of the Servant of Yahweh? in Acts xxvi. 12 ff. where the Apostle learns that he is 'destined to prolong in his own person the salvific work of Christ, the Ebed Yahweh' (418).
See further for Paul's conversion and prophetic call in the light of the Old Testament scriptures, J. Munck,'La vocation de l'apôtre Paul', *ST*, I, i–ii (1947), 131–45.

[3] *Paulus und Christus* (1934), p. 137.

[4] *The Church's Ministry* (1948); *Ministry and Priesthood; Christ's and Ours*, Lecture I (1953).

[5] 'Zur Bedeutung von δοῦλος bei Paulus', *ZNTW*, XL (1941), 24–32.
This conclusion as to the basic meaning of *'ebed* (in the light of δοῦλος in Phil. ii. 7) is shared by Lohmeyer, *Philipper*, p. 94: 'To be a servant in the religious language of Judaism meant to be one chosen by God; the greatest saints of the past have been proud and honoured to call themselves this.'

LXX in the translation-term δοῦλος as much as παῖς. Euler[1] has a similar analysis which shows how *'Ebed* is used of men as *Jahwe-Verehrer* who are called δοῦλοι. It cannot be asserted, then, as M. D. Hooker does, that δούλου carries in Philippians ii. 7 a connotation which παιδός would not have done.

A far more perceptive criticism is that given by G. Bornkamm[2] who asks how the two pictures of Isaiah lii–liii and Philippians ii can tally. 'For the Servant of God there is distinguished in nature and action from other men, even when he suffers vicariously their punishment.' Bornkamm has in mind Isaiah lii. 14 which tells 'how many were astonished at him—his appearance was so marred beyond human semblance, and his form beyond that of the sons of men'. What is emphasized here is the apartness and uniqueness of the Servant, not his identity with men as in the Christ-hymn. Therefore, Bornkamm concludes, 'We could not paraphrase "He took the form of the Servant of God"; it is rather that His servant-form (no definite article!) places him in identity with men, as the further expressions show most emphatically'. There is some force in this acute observation, but its importance is mitigated by the reasoning of Michel who also has noted the difficulty. He quotes Isaiah lii. 14 which means (he says) that the Servant lives a life 'which separates him from the rest of humanity, but which does not take him out of humanity' ('die ihn von den Menschen trennt, ihn aber nicht aus dem Menschsein herausnimmt').[3] Whereas Isaiah lii. 14 emphasizes that the Servant is separate from the rest of men, Philippians ii. 7 is expressing the thought that even the emptying and humiliation have not destroyed or relinquished the secret of the pre-existent One. He is truly Man, but He is not merely Man: for He calls forth the wonder and amazement of those who regard Him. This is the characteristic in the Christology of the hymn, according to Michel, that the Subject who is truly one with His creation—else no judgment could be passed on sin on the Cross—nevertheless hides His true destiny and keeps His secret. Verse 7 is thus 'an attempt to preserve the secret of the pre-existent One in His humanity'.[4]

[1] *Die Verkündigung*, pp. 85–8, esp. the table (87) of men who are called δοῦλοι and were the worshippers of Yahweh.
[2] G. Bornkamm, 'Zum Verständnis des Christus-Hymnus', 180.
[3] O. Michel, 'Zur Exegese von Phil. 2. 5–11', 92.
[4] O. Michel, *loc. cit.* 93.

(g) E. Schweizer's interpretation: 'He became the righteous sufferer'
One more line of interpretation of verse 7 falls to be considered.
This is the treatment supplied by E. Schweizer[1] who begins by
expressing, if tacitly, dissatisfaction with all current views. It is
not difficult to share his feelings. If Lohmeyer's hint which led to
the *Gottesknechttheorie* were as simple as is sometimes maintained
it would be a revelation of Jesus as the one foretold by the
prophet, and not necessarily as a man in the full empirical
sense. Schweizer here faces the full force of the way in which the
uniqueness of the Servant is underlined. Whatever else Philippians ii. 7 declares, His true identity with men is apparent.
Besides which, if the *'Ebed Yahweh* were in mind, the text would
have read μορφὴν δούλου Θεοῦ in full. By parity of reasoning, if
Käsemann's view were correct, we should have expected the text
to include something like: He became a servant to the powers of
nature, or a slave of 'the elements of the world'—an addition to
the text which J. Weiss actually makes![2] The parallels which
Käsemann and Jervell cite from *Corpus Hermeticum*, I, 15 which
relates the myth of how man fell from his high estate, became
subject to fate (εἱμαρμένη) and became a slave within the universal frame (ὑπεράνω...ὢν τῆς ἁρμονίας ἐναρμόνιος γέγονε
δοῦλος) are dismissed as out of place in the context of Philippians ii. 6 ff.[3]
If these possibilities are refused, is there another candidate for
the office of δοῦλος left? Schweizer affirms that there is, and
finds him in the obedient righteous man in Judaic thought. With
a wealth of data he shows that 'the concept that the righteous
individual man must pass through the suffering, humiliation,
and shame imposed by God in order, finally, to be exalted by
him, is widespread in the Judaism of the time'.[4] *'Ebed* was a key-

[1] *Erniedrigung und Erhöhung*, p. 135 (E.T. p. 63).
[2] *Earliest Christianity*, II, p. 493.
[3] Schweizer, *op. cit.* p. 136 (not in E.T.). In any case, he remarks, the use of
the term ἁρμονία in *C.H.* I, 15 is a strange way of describing an evil 'necessity' which enslaves man. He grants that the Hellenistic community may
have thought of man's slavery as that of a domination by 'the powers', but
prefers to see in the reference here in Phil. ii a picture of the way of Jesus in
obedient relationship to God. There is some inconsistency in this exposition,
for elsewhere Schweizer places the hymn in a Hellenistic setting.
[4] Schweizer, 'Discipleship and Belief in Jesus, etc.', *NTS*, II, 2 (1955), 88,
which is a summary of his *Erniedrigung*, pp. 35 ff.

term in Jewish martyrology since the time of the Maccabees. E. Lichtenstein[1] has maintained that two issues stood out prominently in later Judaism: 'the understanding and meaning of the suffering of the pious and the eschatological question of the resurrection of the dead'. Now these are the elements which Schweizer finds in Philippians ii. The drama is one which depicts the abasement and humiliation of Jesus as a servant and His ultimate vindication by God. He is called Servant not because He fulfils the rôle of the *'Ebed* in Isaiah liii but because every righteous one who took upon himself suffering and humiliation for God's sake was so called; and He is the righteous One *par excellence*. This study of the way in which Jewish piety saw life under the Torah as characteristically one of obedience and in which all the great men and heroes of the Jewish faith are known as 'the servants of God' provides the best background for the Pauline text. Thus he writes on 'Servanthood': 'es ist der Begriff, der in spezifischer Weise den eigentlichen, den frommen Menschen bezeichnet, der sich Gott gegenüber zum Gehorsam verpflichtet weiß'.[2] Schweizer breaks new ground with this idea of the servant who is called to live in a hostile world which will invariably prove his persecutor. His life will necessarily involve hardship, suffering and death, for this is his calling as one who chooses God as his *Gegenüber*,[3] but God will at length vindicate him as He did the *'Ebed* of Isaiah's prophecy. For such a pious individual the quintessence of religion is *obedience*. As Bousset–Gressmann[4] define it, 'To the mind of late Judaism religion is obedience (ὑπακοή)...Humble, servant-like (*knechtische*) submission of the human will to God's almighty, inscrutable will, acting according to His commandments, comprehensible or incomprehensible, at every moment of life—this is piety (*Frömmigkeit*).' In this context servanthood describes the behaviour of the righteous man, and has the title of 'Lord' as its correlative.

The Incarnation depicted in verse 7 means Jesus' acceptance of this life of humanity. Not only was He born of woman, He

---

[1] 'Die älteste christliche Glaubensformel', *ZfKirchengeschichte*, LXIII (1950), 4–74 (20).
[2] Schweizer, *Erniedrigung*, p. 55.   [3] Cf. s.v. δοῦλος, *TWNT*, II, 270f.
[4] W. Bousset–H. Gressmann, *Die Religion des Judentums*[3] (*HzNT*, 1926), p. 375 (quoted by Schweizer, *op. cit.* p. 36).

was born 'under the law'. He came to take His place among the heroes of the ancestral faith, and indeed to fulfil perfectly the office which they faintly adumbrated. The obedience He showed to the pre-mundane will of God in consenting not to hold fast His divine status is now complemented by His appearing upon earth as the One who is perfectly submissive to that will in all the circumstances of His earthly lot. He accepts 'tous les risques historiques' (as Bonnard puts it[1]) with unflinching surrender to the divine will and unquestioned obedience to His God. In the context of the Christian community which sang this hymn, this meant that He took on Him true humanity when He took the form of a servant.

Eduard Schweizer's proposals have been attacked by G. Bornkamm[2] mainly on the ground that 'the motive of obedience does not occur until several clauses later and is introduced with its own, quite new force. The expression "form of a servant" refers exclusively to the Incarnation of the pre-existent Christ, that is, to His assuming of human nature, and has no bearing upon His life as a man. It is only in this sense that the three stages in the Way of Christ can be seen in their dramatically paradoxical order—Equality with God: Servant: Lord.' This line of reasoning may be disputed. The obedience of Christ belongs to His pre-incarnate choice (cf. Heb. x. 5 ff.) and His earthly life may very well be summed up as that of a servant. Bornkamm objects to this because he holds that there are no Old Testament examples of the equation of terms 'Being a man = being a servant'; and it is the Incarnation which is exclusively depicted in verse 7*b*. He therefore reverts to Käsemann's position that the Hellenistic background most illuminates the phrase's meaning. Μορφὴ δούλου means that 'the existence of unredeemed man is seen as that of slavery, imprisoned and enslaved under the rule of the cosmic powers... The Incarnation is for the freeing of those who are enslaved by the cosmic powers. It is understandable, in the light of this, that there is the equating of being a slave and being a man (*die Gleichsetzung von Knecht- und Menschsein*).'[3]

The attractiveness of this approach is that it conserves strict

---

[1] *L'épître aux Philippiens* (*CNT*), p. 44.
[2] 'Zum Verständnis des Christus-Hymnus', 181 f.
[3] Bornkamm, *loc. cit.* 181.

progression of thought throughout the hymn. It insists that each line says one thing and one only; and that in logical order. If this is the criterion, it puts under suspicion the '*Ebed Yahweh* proposal and Schweizer's view. But it lays down too firm a standard by which exact logical order is to be expected. This canon, moreover, overlooks the fact that other confessional pieces in the New Testament have an unusual order. Jacques Marty[1] in his study of these quotes I Timothy iii. 16 where one would expect 'elevated in glory' (by the Ascension) to *precede* 'preached to the Gentiles'. 'Logical strictness', he comments, is not found.

C. TENTATIVE CONCLUSION

We are now to attempt the difficult task of reaching some conclusion. Amid the plethora of diverse interpretations of the Pauline words the following ruling ideas seem to stand out as important:

(*a*) The verb κενοῦν seems to carry in this context a metaphorical as distinct from a metaphysical meaning.[2] It would be wrong then to insist that the text teaches the surrender of divine attributes and the exchanging of Christ's deity for His human nature. To be sure, the verb does link verses 6 and 7; and joins the parallel terms ἐν μορφῇ Θεοῦ and μορφὴν δούλου. He who existed eternally in a heavenly station surrendered that high place and gave up the position of being the 'Image of God' and humbled Himself to accept the rôle of the servant. He emptied Himself in that He took the servant's form—this is the exegetical connection between verse 7*a* and *b*; and this necessarily involved an eclipsing of His glory as the divine Image (μορφή = εἰκών) in order that He might come, in human flesh, as the Image of God incarnate. He condescends to come 'in the flesh', thereby fulfilling the rôle of the last Adam as the Man in whom the image of true manhood is to be seen.

(*b*) This implies that His Servanthood is a synonym for His

---

[1] 'Étude des textes cultuels de prière contenus dans le NT', *RHPR*, III, 4/5 (1929), 369.

[2] This was recognized by Vincent, *ICC*, p. 59: The verb is 'not used or intended here in a metaphysical sense to define the limitations of Christ's incarnate state, but as a strong and graphic expression of the completeness of his self-renunciation'.

humanity, as Dibelius remarks,[1] and betokens His taking man's place *vis-à-vis* God. Verse 7*b* runs in parallelism with 7*c*; and both describe the Incarnation (against Michaelis). The verse sets forth the coming of the pre-existent One into the world and His taking of our humanity upon Him. It is not a special quality of humanity that is in view, whether His social state or His special office as *the* Servant of Isaiah's prophecy. The evidence for the former is negligible; and the wording of the text makes the *'Ebed Yahweh* theory less than certain. The data for this latter proposal are such that while a case may be sustained for this identification one or two points are left unexplained. A possible resolving of the difficulties may be the way in which the title *'Ebed Yahweh* is used of a variety of persons in Judaism. It is a much wider term than its use in Isaiah liii, where Christian thought and devotion has seen a single individual, might suggest. E. Schweizer's suggestion that it applies to the righteous man who suffers for his loyalty to God and that the early Church saw in Jesus the pre-eminent example of this type is a fruitful one. The *'Ebed* of Isaiah is a notable illustration of this pattern which reaches its peak example in the career of Jesus.

(*c*) If this concept of the Righteous one is the background there are additional features which are true of no prophet or martyr in Israel. Only the Church's Lord is pre-existent; and He comes into humanity from without by way of an unimaginable condescension and a flawless obedience. This is underlined in the wording of the verse. Of His own volition and unfettered choice He made Himself as nothing,[2] setting no store upon His possession of His dignity as the μορφή of God. His refusal to use what He had to His own advantage (ἁρπαγμός) meant His acceptance of the office of Man upon earth—and to this extent a *kenosis*. Jervell's contribution here is a significant one.[3] For, as he

---

[1] *An die Philipper*[3], p. 74: 'Sein Sklaventum ist seine Menschheit. Δοῦλος heißt der Mensch im äußersten Gegensatz zu Gott.' E. Larsson, *Christus als Vorbild*, pp. 244 f. takes this view, but combines it with the *'Ebed Yahweh* identification.

[2] Cf. *NEB ad loc.*: 'but made himself nothing'.

[3] *Imago Dei*, p. 230: 'Because Christ is "the second person *in* the Godhead", for His divinity is something which He possesses only by being in the Father, His *kenoma* is then to be understood as a stepping-out-of-the-Father in order to take human form like man; and this is where "He emptied Himself" (verse 7) comes in.'

sees, Christ's divinity is something which He possesses as being in the Father. His kenosis, then, is His willingness to step out of the Father and this He must do in order to take human form. It entails a suspension of His rôle as the divine Image by His taking on an image which is Man's—a rôle that will blend together the pictures of the obedient last Adam and the suffering servant. And, at the last, with His mission and self-giving completed, He is elevated to a rank to which no prophet could aspire and given a name beyond that of all mortal men.

CHAPTER VIII

HIS ABASEMENT

ἐν ὁμοιώματι ἀνθρώπων γενόμενος
καὶ σχήματι εὑρεθεὶς ὡς ἄνθρωπος
ἐταπείνωσεν ἑαυτόν,
γενόμενος ὑπήκοος μέχρι θανάτου,
θανάτου δὲ σταυροῦ. (verses 7 c–8)

A. THE FORM OF VERSES 7c–8

In the history of the Form-analysis of the hymn, the relations of verses 7c and 8a have been variously assessed. E. Lohmeyer placed 7c: ἐν ὁμοιώματι ἀνθρώπων γενόμενος at the conclusion of the second stanza, and began a new stanza with 8a: καὶ σχήματι εὑρεθεὶς ὡς ἄνθρωπος.[1] This arrangement, as we observed earlier, was criticized by M. Dibelius on two grounds.[2] He maintained, first, that it was wrong to separate the two lines by placing them in different stanzas because they belong together in rhetorical form. The first words of each line:

7c: ἐν ὁμοιώματι
8a: καὶ σχήματι

are linked by similarity of sound, which produces rhetorical devices known as *homoeoptoton* and the anaphoral style.

But there is a second reason why Lohmeyer wished to consider the two lines as separate. He considered the meaning of the two lines to be quite different. Verse 7c: 'being born in the likeness of men' refers to the Incarnation; but the next sentence should be translated 'And appearing on earth as the Son of man'. The words ὡς ἄνθρωπος, according to Lohmeyer, thinly disguise the underlying Aramaic כבר-אנש which is drawn directly from Daniel vii. 13.[3] And Dibelius, in common with

---

[1] *Der Brief an die Philipper*, p. 95; *Kyrios Jesus*, pp. 37 ff.
[2] *An die Philipper*[3], p. 77; and similarly, Jeremias, *Studia Paulina*, 'Zur Gedankenführung in den paulinischen Briefen', p. 153. See ch. 1.
[3] Lohmeyer, *Kyrios Jesus*, pp. 39 f.

most subsequent writers, has found fault with this proposal which Lohmeyer offered.[1]

Dibelius therefore declared that verses 7*c* and 8*a* must go together.[2] This means that the two participles γενόμενος and εὑρεθείς are dependent, not on the preceding main verb ἐκένωσεν, but on the verb in the succeeding verse (8*b*): ἐταπείνωσεν. This is a consideration which may seem to be of little importance. Its interest appears chiefly to be for those who wish to discern the literary form of the hymn. For them, it is consequently of significance to observe that, if verse 7*c* opens a new stanza, then both the first and second stanzas begin in a similar way:

    I: verse 6*a* ἐν μορφῇ Θεοῦ
    II: verse 7*c* ἐν ὁμοιώματι ἀνθρώπων

with identical prepositions, parallelism in the terms used (synonymous, μορφῇ : ὁμοιώματι, and antithetical, Θεοῦ : ἀνθρώπων) and two parallel participial constructions (ὑπάρχων, γενόμενος) which include an implied contrast. The two lines as separate units are antitheses:

(i) What He *was* by His fundamental constitution (ὑπάρχειν)
(ii) What He *became* by His choice to be incarnate (γενέσθαι)

This *Formanalyse* is confirmed in its correctness when we place verses 7*c* and 8*a* side by side:

    7*c*: ἐν ὁμοιώματι ἀνθρώπων γενόμενος
    8*a*: καὶ σχήματι εὑρεθεὶς ὡς ἄνθρωπος

These lines are linked by the parallelism of participial usage which includes two substantives which end in the syllables -μοτι and the couplet has an example of *homoeoteleuton*.

But this arrangement has an important bearing upon exegesis; and to this we now turn.

[1] *Op. cit., ad loc.*; Käsemann, 'Kritische Analyse', 75; Leivestad, *Christ the Conqueror* (1954), p. 113, n. 1; Michaelis, *Der Brief an die Philipper*, p. 38. Cerfaux, *Le Christ...*, p. 288 (E.T. p. 391).

[2] Dibelius, *ad loc.* This linking of *vv.* 7*c* and 8*a* was suggested by A. Deissmann, *St Paul* (1912), p. 169. It is accepted by Cerfaux, *op. cit.* pp. 382 f.

B. EXEGETICAL NOTES ON VERSES 7c–8

The main verb in verse 8b (ἐταπείνωσεν ἑαυτόν) is the natural starting-point; and mercifully it has a clear meaning in a section of the hymn which bristles with complicated constructions. Ταπεινοῦν means 'to humble, to humiliate'. Used with the reflexive pronoun ἑαυτόν, it means 'to humble oneself', the pronoun stressing that the action was free and voluntary (cf. Matt. xviii. 4 for a similar construction with the same verb). K. Barth lays stress on the importance of the reflexive, both in this verse and verse 7. 'It is thus no fate that overtakes him. Not even the will of the Father is mentioned as a ground of his performing this act of renunciation. He *wills* it so.'[1] Of His own unfettered choice He came into the world, a choice which included His pre-incarnate decision (*v.* 6) and His acceptance of the 'form of a servant'. By the same token He now is described as consenting to what P. Henry calls 'a double kenosis'[2] by following a path that will mean His humiliation.

The reader's attention is focused upon the verb ταπεινοῦν because it is the second main verb so far in the hymn. This fact links it with κενοῦν in verse 6. 'He emptied Himself...He humbled Himself.' The verb is flanked in the lines which precede and follow by participles which explain the attendant circumstances of humiliation. It is a verb which looks two ways. Our exegesis, therefore, may begin with the first line which is dependent upon ἐταπείνωσεν ἑαυτόν.

(i) *Humiliation and 'the likeness of men'*

The exact connotation of ὁμοίωμα is much controverted. Its usual meaning is 'likeness', 'form', 'appearance'. It is connected in LXX with μορφή, εἶδος, εἰκών, ἰδέα and σχῆμα, although there are no clear lines of distinction between the usage of the several words, as J. Behm says in his lexical study: 'Aber die hiermit bezeichneten Nuancen zwischen μορφή und Synonymen reichen bei dem wechselnden Gebrauch der Wörter nicht aus, um feste begriffliche Grenzen zwischen ihnen

---

[1] *The Epistle to the Philippians* (E.T. 1962), *ad loc.*
[2] 'Kénose', *DB Supp.* v (1950), 31.

aufzurichten.'[1] The term nearest in meaning to ὁμοίωμα in the group just quoted is εἰκών which J. Schneider regards as synonymous with it. There is a slight difference, however. Εἰκών represents the original, while ὁμοίωμα emphasizes a similarity which may imply a congruence, or admit a difference, between the original and the copy.[2] Schneider goes on to say that the basic meaning of ὁμοίωμα as 'image, likeness' can be applied in two ways. Sometimes it is used to mean 'the equal likeness', i.e. *Gleichbild*, of an original; at other times it means a resemblance of the original. In stating these two usages he puts his finger on the real exegetical difficulty in some New Testament texts. The fact of the matter is that ὁμοίωμα in its linguistic usage is ambiguous. The sharp alternatives are: its meaning as 'identity' or 'equivalence' and its meaning as 'similarity' or 'resemblance'. We may take an illustration from everyday English. A music teacher may show his pupil how a certain piece of music is to be played, and then encourage the student by saying, 'Now, play that as I have done'. He means, 'Play the composition in the *same way*, with the same accuracy, expression and emphasis, as I have shown you'. The student's attempt is to be a *Gleichbild* of the teacher's.

But the word 'like' can also mean 'in a similar way to'. This is a very common expression when we wish to compare one action or thing with another. 'He ran like lightning.' 'The aeroplane appeared in the sky like a silver bird.' There is no question here of literal identity, but rather of external resemblances which are observed by the eye.

These two different meanings of ὁμοίωμα are found in the New Testament. In the first sense, Romans vi. 5 may be quoted.[3]

[1] J. Behm, *TWNT*, IV, 752, *s.v.* μορφή.

[2] J. Schneider, *TWNT*, V, 191, *s.v.* Cf. R. C. Trench, *Synonyms of the New Testament* (1901), p. 34; M.–M., *Vocabulary of the New Testament, s.v.* ὁμοίωμα: 'As distinguished from εἰκών, which implies an archetype, the "likeness" or "form" in ὁμοίωμα may be accidental, as one egg is like another.'

[3] See full discussion in Schneider, *loc. cit.* 191–5; G. R. Beasley-Murray, 'Baptism in the Epistles of Paul', *Christian Baptism*, ed. A. Gilmore (1959), pp. 133 f.: 'The key term ὁμοίωμα means not simply "copy", but "likeness" or "form", in the sense that it expresses the being or essence of what is represented.' Similarly, G. Bornkamm, 'Taufe und neues Leben bei Paulus', *Das Ende des Gesetzes, Gesamm. Aufs.* I (1952), 42; R. Schnackenburg, *Baptism in the Thought of St Paul* (E.T. 1964), pp. 49–53.

'If we have been united in the likeness of his death', which seems to mean, 'in the same death that he died' on the cross. Also, Romans v. 14: 'in the likeness of Adam's transgression' may bear this sense, if Paul is teaching that in mankind's primal disobedience all are directly involved as though they themselves had transgressed the divine law. And, for a clear case of ὁμοίωμα = 'in the same manner as', Ignatius, ad Trall. IX, 2 may be cited.[1]

The second connotation which stresses the fact of resemblance between two objects is expressed in Apocalypse ix. 7: 'in appearance the locusts were like horses' (τὰ ὁμοιώματα τῶν ἀκρίδων ὅμοια ἵπποις).

With these two possibilities of meaning in mind, we may approach the Christological text of Philippians ii. 7. Otto Michel has clearly seen the issue involved. '...the Christological problem (is) whether Christ became Man completely and in the fullest sense, or whether He merely presented the picture of a Man, which appeared like a man, whereas, in actual fact, He remained in the world as a divine being (ein Gottwesen).'[2] W. Bauer phrases the question in a similar way. Does Philippians ii. 7 mean that, in His incarnate existence, Christ is fully and perfectly man, that His likeness to men means His full participation in their humanity; or that He was only seen to resemble men, since He is, in reality, in the world as a divine being?[3]

If the first alternative is chosen, then the question is forced upon us, Is it in all respects that He came to share our humanity? This is the point at which scholars have debated the 'type' of human nature which the incarnate Lord assumed, whether it was unfallen or fallen. The orthodox answer is that it was unfallen nature. P. Henry says that it is our nature He took in all respects, sin excepted (II Cor. v. 21).[4] Lightfoot seeks to find

---

[1] Ignatius, ad Trall. IX, 2: 'when his Father raised him up, as in the same manner his Father shall raise up in Christ Jesus us who believe in him' (Lake's translation in Loeb).

[2] Michel, 'Zur Exegese von Phil. 2, 5-11', 89-90.

[3] W. Bauer, Wörterbuch (Arndt and Gingrich, Lexicon, 1957), ad loc.

[4] Henry, 'Kénose', 30. But there are exceptions, e.g. Barth, Church Dogmatics, I, 2 (E.T. 1956), 151; Barrett, The Epistle to the Romans (1959), ad Rom. viii. 3; H. Johnson, The Humanity of the Saviour (1962), for full discussion. Surprisingly, J. J. Müller, Philippians and Philemon. p. 82 is to be included here.

support for this view by commenting on the use of the plural word ἀνθρώπων that 'Christ, as the second Adam, represents not the individual man, but the human race'.[1] But Käsemann has no difficulty in maintaining the point that all speculation about the natures of Christ is foreign to the hymn as a whole, and to this verse in particular.[2]

If we start from the assumption that the hymn has nothing to say about the inner relations of the 'natures' of Christ, or about the question how He who was divine could assume our humanity, there are three possible explanations of this line:

(a) The birth of Jesus

The full identification of the Incarnate one with humanity may be seen if the meaning of 'being born' is given to the participle γενόμενος. The sense is then that He was born into the world in exactly the same way as that in which all men are born. This understanding, which is championed by Cerfaux, Joüon and F. W. Beare,[3] depends upon taking the participle in its strict etymological sense, as in John viii. 58. The thought is thus parallel with that in Galatians iv. 4: God sent forth his Son, born of a woman. Some writers carry this line of interpretation a stage farther and see in the line a reference to the virgi-

[1] J. B. Lightfoot, *St Paul's Epistle to the Philippians*, p. 112; A. Plummer, *Philippians*, p. 46.

[2] 'Kritische Analyse', 76: 'All these statements are not meant to give a definition of being (*eine Wesensdefinition*) in the sense of the Christology of the early Church, but rather to speak of events in a connected series: He emptied himself, took the form of a servant, appeared as a human-like being; the fact of His becoming a man could be established (but) it is not here a question of the identity of a person in successive phases, but rather of the continuity of a miraculous occurrence.' Cf. Bultmann, *Theology*, I, p. 191: 'Paul does not speculatively discuss the metaphysical essence of Christ, or his relation to God, or his "natures", but speaks of him as the one through whom God is working for the salvation of the world and man.'

[3] Cerfaux, *Le Christ*, p. 390: 'The word (γενόμενος) is equivalent to "born of a woman"...to be born in the same way as men are born.' P. Joüon, 'Notes philologiques sur quelques versets de l'épître aux Philippiens', *RSR*, xxviii (1938), 300, renders: 'né à l'instar des hommes'. F. W. Beare cites the lines of the *Te Deum* as illustrative: 'When thou tookest upon thee to deliver man, thou didst not abhor the Virgin's womb', *Epistle to the Philippians*, p. 83. Compare Moffatt's translation: 'born in human guise': Michaelis, *An die Philipper*, p. 38.

nal conception of Jesus (so D. Edwards in a full discussion in his treatise on *The Virgin Birth in History and Faith*).[1] But this seems not altogether convincing.

(b) J. Weiss's exposition

Johannes Weiss, in an important exposition of the Pauline texts,[2] interprets Philippians ii. 7 in the light of Romans viii. 3: God sent forth his Son in the likeness of sin-dominated flesh. Paul does not say 'God sent his Son in the flesh of sin', for this would seem to him like blasphemy. He therefore uses an expression which is deliberately vague, because he finds himself under the pressure of an antinomy. On the one hand, Christ dealt with sin on the Cross at close quarters, and struck it a death-blow. On the other hand, Christ has personally no experience of sin (II Cor. v. 21). So Paul evades the difficulty by the use of a mediating expression, which shrinks from saying that He took sin upon Him, yet brings Him into a close relationship with it. Weiss argues that this same ambiguity is present in Philippians ii. 7. Paul does not say, *expressis verbis*, that He became man by the assumption of our nature, because he dare not express the complete humanity of Christ in view of his doctrine of human nature as in the grip of the demonic power of sin. Yet Christ *did* appear on earth in what appeared to human eyes as an earthly form which enveloped His divine form. But, in reality, says Weiss, this appearance is only a 'disguise, appropriate to the role which he played here'; and therefore, 'in this, Paul grazes the later heresy of "Docetism"'.[3]

[1] D. Edwards, *The Virgin Birth in History and Faith* (1943), pp. 73 ff. But *contra* V. Taylor, *The Person of Christ in the New Testament Teaching*, p. 217, n. 1 resists this suggestion. Cf. H. E. W. Turner, 'Expository Problems: The Virgin Birth', *ExT*, LXVIII, 1 (1956), 12.

[2] *Earliest Christianity* (E.T. vol. II, 1959 reprint), pp. 488 ff., and his *Christ: the Beginnings of Dogma* (E.T. 1911), pp. 110 ff. has an even fuller discussion of the meaning of ὁμοίωμα in Paul.

[3] Weiss, *Earliest Christianity*, II, 490; *Christ*, p. 115: 'It is not difficult to recognize here the germs of the later "Docetism", according to which Christ was held to have had only a phantasmal body, or the Gnostic doctrine, that the heavenly Aeon Christ descended into the man Jesus, to leave him again before death, so that it was only the man Jesus who actually suffered. Paul himself would have vehemently resisted these inferences, for the humanity of Christ, the suffering and the death are to him experiences of the entire person …But it is not to be denied that the two passages above quoted [Rom. viii.

Such a radical assessment of Philippians ii. 7 has not passed unchallenged;[1] but unfortunately Weiss's critics have not faced the meaning of the verse *in the context of the hymn*. Thus, it is really no argument to say, as V. Taylor does[2] (and the authorities he quotes in support of his view), that Paul elsewhere states unequivocally the full humanity of Christ. This begs the question about the 'Paulinity' of Philippians ii. 7, for it seems clear that this is traditional teaching which Paul is citing. It also overlooks the fact that Philippians ii. 7c is a single line of a hymn, and should not be taken in isolation from the rest of the composition. It may be that the coming of Christ in the semblance of human nature is all that this actual line declares;[3] but that the thought is developed and expanded in the next line.

3; Phil. ii. 7] very readily suggest a docetic interpretation.' F. C. Porter, *The Mind of Christ in Paul*, p. 210 awakens the suspicion that the hymn's Christology is Docetic: 'The veil of unreality is cast over his earthly life by phrases that seem to suggest that he was not really human'; but to cite Rom. viii. 3 as Paul's clear statement of his belief in Jesus' 'frail humanity' seems to overlook the similarity between Phil. ii. 6, 7 and that text.

[1] On general grounds Schneider has given a conclusive reply to Weiss, *TWNT*, v, 196; cf. F.-J. Leenhardt, *The Epistle to the Romans* (E.T. 1960), *ad* Rom. viii. 3.

[2] Taylor, *The Person of Christ*, p. 40.

[3] Cf. Michael, *Philippians*: 'The word (ὁμοίωμα) suggests similarity and nothing more; it does not imply, as the word *morphe* would have done, the reality of Christ's humanity' (92). 'To affirm likeness is at once to assert similarity and to deny sameness' (Dickson, Baird Lect. 1883, quoted by G. C. Martin, *The Century Bible* (n.d.), p. 165). This comment is true as far as the proper sense of ὁμοίωμα in Rom. viii. 3 is concerned, as Käsemann has noticed ('Kritische Analyse', 75). We are faced with the ambiguity of usage in the Pauline literature. In Rom. viii. 3 the sense is not 'Gleichbild' but 'Korrelat' or 'Analogie'; but if we draw the meaning from the usage in Rom. v. 14 and vi. 5, the above sentence will have to be re-written by reversing the meanings. This implies that the meaning of ὁμοίωμα can only be found by having regard to the context.

It may therefore be the case, as Dibelius has argued, that the lines of *vv.* 7c and 8a are strictly parallel and synonymous; and, for him, are a further instance of the author's facility in using different rhetorical terms and expressions with no apparent change of meaning. The demarcation lines of nuance which Bengel, Lightfoot, Henry and Michael draw seem to assume too rigid a distinction between μορφή, σχῆμα, and ὁμοίωμα, although we prefer to detect a progression of thought in the two lines (against Dibelius). See below, p. 206.

(c) O. Michel's treatment

A third way of taking this enigmatic phrase is stated in the full exegesis of Michel.[1] He starts from the premise that the New Testament declares the doctrine of the full manhood of the Lord. Only on this basis is it possible to affirm a valid doctrine of atonement. 'If Jesus did not attain to full humanity, there can be no judgment on sinful humanity in the event (of the Cross).' This is stated in Hebrews v. 1–10. And it is in the same Epistle that the root ὁμοιο- is used (cf. Heb. ii. 17; iv. 15). This formula, therefore, denotes the full participation of Christ in our human experience.

But in Philippians ii. 7 the unusual 'paraphrastic style' (*Umschreibungsstil*) betokens a 'lingering uncertainty' as to the unqualified humanity of Christ because (unlike the plain prose of Hebrews and other Pauline statements) 'the author is conscious of portraying something transcendent in the face of which any earthly method of expression can only be employed with a special hesitancy'. Therefore, 'hesitancy, caution and reflection' are important for this style of Apocalyptic writing in which the Biblical seer is endeavouring to put into human terms a vision of the supra-historical reality of the divine presence. The clearest examples of this reluctance to say that A *equals* B in a manner of literal identity are Daniel vii. 13 (ὡς υἱὸς ἀνθρώπων, ὡς παλαιὸς ἡμερῶν, cf. x. 16) and in the visions of Ezekiel (i. 26: ὡς ὅρασις λίθου, ὁμοίωμα θρόνου, ὁμοίωμα — דמות — ὡς εἶδος ἀνθρώπου; viii. 2 ἰδοὺ ὁμοίωμα ἀνδρός). In all these instances (and Enoch xxxi. 2, Apoc. i. 13 are in the same tradition) the use of ὁμοίωμα indicates the form in which someone divine, an angel or God, appears upon earth. The Apocalyptic writer shrinks from identifying him too closely in his human language, and employs this artifice of the ὁμοίωμα-formula to preserve the element of the numinous and the other-worldly. It is this special style—Michel calls it the 'epiphany style'— which accounts for the terminology in the Christ-hymn. 'Phil. ii. 7 is expressing the thought that even the self-emptying and humiliation have not destroyed or violated the secret of the pre-existent One. He is truly Man, but He is not merely Man.' This is the true explanation of the strange literary style and usages in

[1] 'Zur Exegese von Phil. 2.5–11', 90 ff.

the hymn. 'If it employs a large number of paraphrastic formulas, it is not because there is either ambiguity or uncertainty, but because there is a real necessity for these terms, on exegetical grounds. The Son of man has become the Servant of God and has trodden the path of humiliation and obedience, but at the same time He remains the Son of man, carrying out the eternal purpose of God on earth (I Cor. ii. 8). He is the appearance of Yahweh on earth. ...'

In following this line of interpretation, Michel is able to do justice to two salient facts in the verse. The first is that one would *expect* a clear statement of the full humanity of the incarnate Subject of the hymn, if any significance is to be attached to the foregoing depiction of His choice not to seek equality with God and His decision to take the form of a servant. To say that He did all this only to make a histrionic appearance upon earth as a god in disguise smacks of bathos and unreality. As Bonnard comments, 'notre texte ne décrit pas une comédie'.[1]

The second fact is that the text is *not* straightforward. There is no plain announcement, *homo factus est*. The coming of the Lord of glory to earth is wrapped in mystery; and His advent upon the scene of time is no everyday occurrence. There is an unexplained element, not only in His appearance but in His life upon earth. Käsemann is surely right in finding in His obedience the *differentia* which marks Him out as more-than-human, as verse 8*c* will show.[2]

We may accept Michel's line of interpretation as a valuable contribution to our understanding of the words, with the proviso that lines 7*c* and 8*a* are not tautologous. We detect a progression of thought in the two lines. The first line of the couplet announces His birth as the Divine in human form, leaving unexplained the issue whether this is a full Incarnation or simply a theophany. It is the next line which clinches the matter and declares that all His external appearance showed that He was an empirical man among men.[3]

---

[1] *L'épître aux Philippiens*, p. 44.

[2] 'Kritische Analyse', 75; similarly, this fact is expressed by Michaelis, *op. cit.* 38 and Schneider, *loc. cit.* 197: 'Denn Christus unterschied sich in seinem Menschsein von allen anderen Menschen dadurch, daß er gehorsam war und blieb.'

[3] Cf. Schneider, *TWNT*, v, who concludes his discussion by affirming the reality of our Lord's humanity, at the same time adding 'aber Christus ist

(ii) Humiliation and 'the appearance of a man'

The meaning of σχῆμα is outward appearance or form;[1] and, when the term is used with the verb εὑρίσκεσθαι, it denotes the external appearance of the incarnate Son as He showed Himself to those who saw Him in 'the days of his flesh' (Heb. v. 7, which Käsemann quotes as a 'concrete description' of what is stated tersely in Phil. ii. 8).[2] By this line the thought of the hymn is taken a stage farther. It contains an unmistakable witness to His personal humanity in its declaration that, in the eyes of those who saw His incarnate life, He was 'as a man'. The line, therefore, serves two purposes. It states, without equivocation, the reality of His humanity. That He was truly Man and not only, as the preceding words, 'in the likeness of men' might suggest, that He became 'like' a man, is made plain by the phrasing here.[3] The second purpose is to carry forward the record of the incarnate one and to lead up to His humiliation on the Cross (so Dibelius).

Yet even these words have not escaped the scrutiny of the critics and have become a centre of further controversy. There are two matters which are to be discussed.

Some writers have misconstrued the force of ὡς in the phrase ὡς ἄνθρωπος. It can be used where the real characteristics of a person or a thing are described (as in II Thess. iii. 15a, b; Jas. ii. 9 where its use is almost pleonastic).[4] The meaning is 'He was found to be a man'. A good parallel is Galatians ii. 17: 'we were found to be sinners', εὑρέθημεν...ἁμαρτωλοί. It certainly does not mean that to those who saw Him He was more than a

eben auch als Mensch im tiefsten Grunde seines Seins ein Wesen anderer Art gewesen' (197).

[1] Bauer–Arndt–Gingrich, Lexicon, ad loc. (804 f.) furnish a good illustration from Josephus of a king who exchanged his kingly robes for sackcloth and takes on a σχῆμα ταπεινόν. This Lexicon's translation of σχῆμα as 'outward appearance' (Erscheinungsweise) is approved by Käsemann, loc. cit. 75, comparing I Cor. vii. 31.

[2] E. Käsemann, Das wandernde Gottesvolk, p. 64.

[3] It is at this point that the verdict of Michel may be fully endorsed ('Zur Exegese von Phil. 2, 5–11', 90): 'Die ganze Christologie des Neuen Testamentes hängt an dem entscheidenden Ereignis, daß Jesus nicht nur menschenähnlich oder menschengleich war, sondern selbst ein Mensch war.'

[4] Bauer–Arndt–Gingrich, Lexicon, s.v. III c.

man (as Vincent and A. T. Robertson seem to imply).[1] The thought is simple. His σχῆμα was such that those who saw Him gained the impression that He was a Man; for it was by His σχῆμα (σχήματι = *dat. instrumentalis*) that this impression was registered. The use of the verb εὑρίσκεσθαι is appropriate to this meaning, for whereas εἶναι expresses the quality of a person or thing in itself, εὑρίσκεσθαι refers to the quality of a person or thing as it is discovered or recognized by others.[2]

Lohmeyer pointed out how un-Greek is the expression εὑρεθεὶς ὡς,[3] which he makes the starting-point for an elaborate theory that the underlying Semitic original of these words is to be discovered in the Aramaic of Daniel vii. 13: כבר-אנש meaning 'as a son of man'. This title he takes to mean 'a man carrying the appearance of a divinity', as in Enoch xlvi. 1 ff. and the Ezra Apocalypse (II Esdras xiii); cf. Apocalypse i. 13, xiv. 14.[4] On this reading, what is in view is not Christ's humanity but His transcendental state as the heavenly Man who came to earth to accomplish a redemptive mission for mankind. The grounds for Lohmeyer's theory are:

(*a*) He considers the meaning of σχῆμα which, he says, 'does not represent merely the physical, but also the spiritual or religious aspect'.[5] It is erroneous, then, to take 'as a man' to mean the 'natural aspects of His being'.[6] It conveys rather the idea of 'judgment and appreciation'[7] upon His moral character, His mental and spiritual state. It is a concept quite different from all that is implied in ὁμοίωμα which, as a tribute to His physical qualities, belongs to the beginning of His life. Not so with the second line. This relates to His earthly course; and depicts an office or status.

(*b*) Therefore this line (8*a*) is completely separate from what has gone before. It begins a new strophe, and 'can only serve to

---

[1] M. R. Vincent, *ICC*, p. 60; Robertson, *Paul's Joy in Christ*, revised ed., p. 73.
[2] Plummer, *Commentary*, p. 46, comparing Phil. iii. 9; I Cor. iv. 2; II Cor. v. 3, xi. 12. [3] *Kyrios Jesus*, pp. 8, 38 f.
[4] But cf. T. W. Manson, 'The Son of Man, etc.', in *Studies in the Gospels and Epistles* (1962), pp. 130 ff.
[5] Lohmeyer, *An die Philipper*, pp. 94–5: 'nicht den Gedanken einer naturhaften, sondern den einer sittlichen oder religiösen Bestimmtheit'.
[6] 'die naturhafte Bestimmtheit menschlichen Daseins'.
[7] 'aber enthält zugleich ein Urteil und eine Wertung'.

explain the thought of humiliation'.[1] But it is not as a man *simpliciter* that He is humiliated in death. It is in His office as Redeemer, i.e. as Son of man.

(c) The linguistic argument which depends upon the equivalence of ὡς ἄνθρωπος and כבר-אנש is appealed to. Lohmeyer never explains why the hypothetical *Vorlage* of this Danielic text fails to read ὡς υἱὸς ἀνθρώπου as in LXX instead of ὡς ἄνθρωπος.[2] And this disparity between the LXX of Daniel vii. 13 and Philippians ii. 8 is perhaps the most serious weakness of his novel theory. Most scholars are content to dismiss it, usually in an opprobrious aside (Käsemann, Michaelis).

Irrespective of the merits or demerits of Lohmeyer's linguistic argument, it is clear that his reference to the Son of man Christology in the psalm has commanded some widespread support. We have noticed the way in which some scholars have sought a background of the thought of the hymn in the myth of the *Urmensch*. Many more scholars have seen an identification of the Servant of Isaiah's prophecies and the Danielic Son of man figure in the lines of the two strophes.[3] That there is a cryptic allusion to 'the Son of man' in the hymnic line of verse 8a is believed by a number of writers.[4] There are two points which

[1] 'So ist also diese Zeile von der vorangegangenen deutlich geschieden; sie kann nur den Gedanken der Erniedrigung erläutern wollen.'

[2] But he does comment that Paul would write *kᵉbarnasha* as ὁ ἄνθρωπος (*Kyrios Jesus*, p. 40).

[3] For example, Michel, 'Zur Exegese von Phil. 2, 5–11', 80 ff.; O. Cullmann, *Christology*, pp. 174 ff.; Hunter, *Paul and his Predecessors²*, pp. 43 f., 86 f.; H. J. Schoeps, *Paul: The Theology of the Apostle in the light of Jewish Religious History* (E.T. 1961), p. 155, as well as Lohmeyer himself, *Kyrios Jesus*, p. 42.

[4] In addition to some of the above names: Rawlinson, *The New Testament Doctrine of the Christ*, p. 125; Barrett, 'New Testament Eschatology, ii', *SJT*, VI (1953), 235; E. M. Sidebottom, *The Christ of the Fourth Gospel* (1961), pp. 91–2; C. H. Dodd, *The Interpretation of the Fourth Gospel* (1953), p. 243, in reference to Paul's use of ὁ ἄνθρωπος as a Graecizing of the Semitic *barnasha*; and similarly, on the doctrine of I Cor. xv, R. Reitzenstein, *Die hellenistischen Mysterienreligionen³* (1956 reprint), p. 349; Richardson, *An Introduction to the Theology of the New Testament* (1958), p. 138 who refers to Jackson and Lake, *The Beginnings of Christianity*, I (1920), p. 380; E. Stauffer, *New Testament Theology*, pp. 108 ff.; T. Arvedson, *Das Mysterium Christi* (1937), 121 who includes 'Kyrios' as a translation of the Semitic 'Son of man'; and both are taken over from the primitive pre-Pauline community; J. Héring, *Le Royaume de Dieu et sa venue*, p. 170; E. Larsson, *Christus als Vorbild*, pp. 247 ff.

are held to support this belief. The main conviction is that Paul (or the *auctor* of the hymn) uses ἄνθρωπος as the equivalent of the full title ὁ υἱὸς (τοῦ) ἀνθρώπου which appears in the Gospels, in Acts vii and the Apocalypse. Both titles go back to the Aramaic *barnasha* in Daniel vii. 13. Paul never uses ὁ υἱὸς τοῦ ἀνθρώπου because it is barbarous Greek, but the idea of Son of man (in his character as revealing the hidden majesty of God, treading the *via dolorosa* and displaying his eschatological glory at the end of the Age) lives on in the Pauline letters under 'a new Christological theme-word' (E. Stauffer)[1] which gives linguistic expression to the same thing under a variety of terms (such as ἄνθρωπος, ἄνθρωπος ἐξ οὐρανοῦ, δεύτερος ἄνθρωπος, ἔσχατος Αδαμ, κεφαλή, εἰκών). This terminology is rooted in the contrast between the first Adam and Christ; and, as far as the Philippians-hymn is concerned, the lines 8*a* and *b* are characteristically related, for they bind together the two fundamental concepts of the hymn: the Son of man who is the last Adam and who enters upon His incarnate existence by assuming the nature of the sons of Adam; and the one who, as the Servant of the Lord who is destined to suffer, offers the exact opposite of Adam's primal failure—a complete obedience (line of verse 8*c*). Thus O. Cullmann explains the interrelation of the lines. 'A complete Christology in condensed form' is made up, he says, of this blend of the Son of man Christology and the Servant of God picture.[2] The acceptance of the office and mission of the atoning Servant is the means by which He shows Himself to be the true 'Son of man'. 'He who by nature was the only Godman, who deserved the designation by bearing the image of God, became man in fallen flesh through obedience, in which he proved himself precisely the Heavenly Man, and by which he accomplished his atoning work.'[3]

This involves, on an exegetical level, treating ὡς in the phrase 'as a man' as the equivalent of 'in the capacity of'.[4] The line now reads: 'And being made known by His appearance in

[1] *Op. cit.*, 'unter einem neuen christologischen Themawort' (p. 111 in his *Theologie des neuen Testaments*[4] (1948), p. 91). Cf. T. W. Manson, *The Teaching of Jesus*[2] (1935), pp. 233 f.

[2] Cullmann, *Christology*, pp. 179 ff., also W. Manson, *Jesus the Messiah* (1943), pp. 110 ff.   [3] O. Cullmann, *Christology*, p. 178.

[4] Cf. M.-E. Boismard, *St John's Prologue* (E.T. 1957), p. 52.

the status of the Man', i.e. the second Man (I Cor. xv. 47), of whom Adam was a τύπος (Rom. v. 14), and 'the new man' (Col. iii. 10).[1]

(iii) *Humiliation and 'obedient unto death'*

(a) Many commentators on the Pauline text have found the master-key of interpretation in the descriptions of the Suffering Servant of Isaiah.[2] We have already noted the way in which the phrase μορφὴν δούλου has been regarded as a translation of the verses in Isaiah lii. 13: 'my *servant* shall prosper' and 14: 'his appearance was so marred...and his *form* beyond that of the sons of men'. The verbal similarities between the Greek translation of Aquila and the text of Philippians ii have led some scholars (notably Cerfaux and Michel)[3] to posit a common dependence of both translations upon an older Greek translation of the Isaiah text than the LXX.

Both scholars find endorsement of this view in the structure of the lines of verses 7c and 8a. Michel observes the paradox of the Servant figure in the fourth Servant song. He is both unlike (lii. 14, liii. 3) and like the men to whom he comes and who look upon his form. From this fact Michel draws the inference that 'the Servant of God lives a life which separates him from men, but which does not take him out of humanity'. He is truly human, but stands apart from the rest of mankind. This 'apartness' of the Servant is 'an expression of his suffering, of his being cast out (*sein Herausgeworfensein*) from the normal existence of mankind. In this instance, we have a particular form of humanity before us, while it remains humanity itself.'[4] This strange paradox of One who is human and yet more-than-

---

[1] So Kittel, *TWNT*, ii, 394–5.

[2] The most elaborate treatment of the suggested parallels is that by L. Krinetzki, 'Der Einfluß von Jes. 52. 13–53. 12 par auf Phil. 2. 6–11', *ThQ*, cxxxix, 2 (1959), 157–93, 291–336. More recently, the same ground has been covered by A. Feuillet, 'L'hymne christologique de l'épître aux Philippiens (ii. 6–11)', *RB*, lxxii, 3 (1965), 352 ff.

[3] Cerfaux, *Le Christ*, pp. 390 f.; Michel, 'Zur Exegese von Phil. 2, 5–11', 92. Stanley, *Christ's Resurrection in Pauline Soteriology*, pp. 97 f. follows, somewhat slavishly, Cerfaux in this, as in many other matters. Cf. 'his conclusions may be accepted without further comment', 98). Also to be included in this group is Henry, 'Kénose', 46.

[4] Michel, 'Zur Exegese von Phil. 2, 5–11', 92.

human in His humiliation is the key to an understanding of the Subject of the Philippians-hymn. He becomes incarnate by accepting the form of a Servant (ii. 7: μορφὴν δούλου—the same word which Aquila's version of Isaiah lii. 14 uses to mark out the 'apartness' of the Servant). Yet He is genuinely one with the sons of men, whose griefs and sins He bears (liii. 4 f.). The lines of verses 7c and 8a, Michel concludes, are connected with a particular understanding of Isaiah lii. 14. In this case, however, His likeness to men and His resemblance to them is only another way of saying that His humanity is of a peculiar kind.

The subtlety and delicacy of Michel's argument have not been widely appreciated among those who look to the 'Ebed Yahweh portrait for a background to these lines. Verse 8b and c, however, has been seized upon as giving more apparent and cogent proof. Ἐταπείνωσεν ἑαυτόν, it is alleged, clearly echoes the LXX of Isaiah liii. 8: ἐν τῇ ταπεινώσει as the obedience of the 'Ebed (liii. 8, 12) εἰς θάνατον is pictured in the corresponding phrase γενόμενος ὑπήκοος μέχρι θανάτου in the hymn.[1] The outstanding difference lies in the insertion of the reflexive pronoun in Philippians ii. 8. It is the free act of Christ which leads Him to humiliation (cf. Isa. liii. 7).

The verbal agreements of the two passages may be granted. But there are, contra this identification, two objections to be launched.

In the first place, it is strange that, if the author of the hymn had wished to point to the Servant of Isaiah as the prototype of the Church's Redeemer, he should have omitted just those features in His humiliation which give to His sufferings their

---

[1] Cerfaux, Le Christ, pp. 390 f. and Henry, op. cit. 46 trace the words ὡς ἄνθρωπος to Isa. liii. 3: τὸ εἶδος (Aquila: μορφή) αὐτοῦ ἄτιμον ἐκλεῖπον παρὰ πάντας ἀνθρώπους· ἄνθρωπος ἐν πληγῇ ὤν, and the latter finds the obedience of Christ mirrored in the submissive lamb of Isa. liii. 7. This is very questionable in view of the difference between the voluntary nature of Christ's self-offering and the way in which the sacrificial lamb is brought to the shambles (Isa. liii. 7).

A further linguistic connection is made by L. C. Allen, 'Isaiah liii. 11 and its echoes', Vox Evangelica (1962), p. 27, who wants to render Isa. liii. 3 according to the second root of the Hebrew ידע: 'humbled by sickness' (ידוע חלי); and Isa. liii. 11: 'by his submission shall my righteous servant justify many' (בדעתו...עבדי). The submission of the Servant is an act of obedience.

eternal value, viz. His sin-bearing, vicarious work.[1] While the obedience of Christ is mentioned in the hymn, no hint is given as to how this obedience provides a rationale of His redemptive work (as in Romans v); and no clear statement is made of the interest which sinful men may have in His redemption. There is no allusion to the personal benefits which the Servant's work makes available (cf. Isa. liii. 4 f., 11 f.). In Christian terminology, there is no hint of *propter nos et propter nostram salutem.* Advocates of the '*Ebed Yahweh* background explain this omission by saying that the application of Christ's work to men is implied, if not explicitly stated, in the hymn. But it is singular that, if the author wanted to show that Christ was the fulfilment of the Servant, he should have left as implicit only what stands out most clearly in the fourth song—the Servant's sin-atoning ministry.[2] And there is no explicit mention of obedience in Isaiah liii.[3]

A second objection fastens on the way in which the '*Ebed Yahweh* view tends to be identified with the idea that Christ's humility provides a pattern of behaviour for Christians to imitate. The link between the two views is I Peter ii. 21–5. In this passage it is evident that the writer is using Christ's fulfilment of Isaiah liii as an incentive that his readers should follow His example and walk in His steps. He was the model of submissiveness under provocation. Let Christians who are provoked take Him as their example.

[1] In the few places in the New Testament where Isaiah's suffering Servant is used as a prefiguration of Christ, the atoning work of the Servant is prominent (e.g. Rom. iv. 25, v. 19), even in those contexts where such an allusion is not strictly required—for example, I Pet. ii. 21–5. As Bultmann has noted, in this passage there is little logical connection between the exhortation to slaves (ii. 18 ff.) to be submissive and the doctrine of the vicarious sufferings of Christ (ii. 24), 'Bekenntnis- und Liedfragmente im ersten Petrusbrief', *Coniectanea Neotestamentica*, xi (1947), p. 13.

[2] This omission is parallel with the use of the Servant theology in the speeches in Acts which employ the Servant terminology but contain no hint of a doctrine of vicarious sacrifice (except possibly in Acts viii. 32 f.). M. D. Hooker, *Jesus and the Servant*, p. 114 writes: 'It seems that the significance of Isa. 53 lay, for the author of Acts at least, not in the connection between suffering and the sin of others, but in the picture of humiliation.'

[3] Except in Symmachus' rendering (according to Eusebius) of נַעֲנֶה in Isa. liii. 7 by ὑπήκουσεν: Jeremias, *The Servant of God* (E.T. 1957), p. 97, n. 446.

The phrase ταπεινοῦν ἑαυτόν in Philippians ii. 8, according to some commentators, sets the same pattern before the Philippian Church. Paul is anxious to impress upon the Philippians the need for humility in their church's life (ii. 3: 'Do nothing from selfishness or conceit, but in humility count others better than yourselves'); and, at the same time, to call them to an obedient submission to his own Apostolic authority for their corporate good. So we find that the example of the obedient Christ is applied to the Philippians' situation directly following the citation of the hymn; and the word 'wherefore' (ὥστε) in verse 12 is the connecting-link between the example (ὑπήκοος) and the application (ὑπηκούσατε).[1] 'Il a obéi, donc (καθώς) obéissez', comments Bonnard.[2] We may compare the similar link in Hebrews v. 8 and 9 (ὑπακοήν — ὑπακούουσιν). The way in which the Philippian Christians are to obey is in submission to Paul's Apostolic directives, with an obedience which is referred to in such texts as II Corinthians ii. 9, vii. 15, x. 6; II Thessalonians iii. 4; Philemon 21.[3]

To many commentators the relevance of Christ's example to the situation at Philippi is too obvious to require further proof. To a community of Christ's people, harassed by intense strife, where pride had raised its ugly head, Paul would show, in the picture of an obedient and humiliated Lord, how sadly it was failing to appreciate His lowliness of mind and contradicting His spirit of obedience to the divine will. There could be no finer enforcement of his appeal for the conduct which befitted those who were 'in Christ' (ii. 5)[4] than this reminder of their

[1] This is the interpretation offered by Bonnard, *Philippiens*, p. 49; and Wohlenberg in his revision of Ewald's commentary (1923), p. 131, n. 1, on the ground that the expectation of the Parousia in verse 11 is the background to the call to holy living. For the construction with ὥστε in this setting, see I Cor. iv. 4, 5, xi. 33, xv. 58; Phil. iii. 20–iv. 1; I Pet. iv. 19.

[2] *Op. cit.* 49.

[3] Cf. Barth, *The Epistle to the Philippians* (E.T.), p. 69. He takes the exhortation back to i. 27 where Paul encourages the Church to be worthy of the Gospel and to stand fast in unity and loyalty. Similarly, Ewald, *ad loc.* and Müller, *Philippians and Philemon*, p. 90, n. 1.

[4] On this view 'in Christ' (v. 5) takes on a paradigmatic meaning, as Lohmeyer has expressed it. He regards the entire phrase as a 'kind of formula of citation', with the words ὃ καὶ ἐν Χριστῷ 'Ιησοῦ introducing an authoritative quotation. It paves the way for the hymn in which the

Lord who was both humble and obedient.[1] It is no exaggeration for Käsemann, then, to say that 'the ethical interpretation possesses here its stoutest bulwark',[2] when it gives 'decisive importance to the interpretation of the words ἐταπείνωσεν and γενόμενος ὑπήκοος'.

But we have already seen how fragile this 'ethical example' view of the hymn really is.[3] It is of the utmost importance to isolate the meaning of the terms in the hymn from the use which is made of them by Paul in the verses which precede and follow. The text of the hymn must be taken on its own, irrespective of the application which is made in the neighbouring verses. Once this is done, it becomes increasingly difficult to follow the 'ethical interpretation'. The hymn has little to say about the ethical intention of Jesus as though the author were holding up His virtues as a model to be copied. A clear illustration of reading back into the hymn ideas which are in the surrounding verses or found elsewhere in Paul is seen in the exegesis of Christ's obedience.

example of Christ is made authoritative for the Philippian community (*Kyrios Jesus*, p. 13).

By many scholars, 'in Christ' is taken as tantamount to 'in the Church': R. Bultmann, *Theology*, I, 311; *Existence and Faith* (1961), p. 142; J. Knox, *Jesus Lord and Christ* (1958 ed.), p. 181; E. Schweizer, *Church Order in the New Testament* (E.T. 1961), p. 94.

[1] So Müller, *Philippians and Philemon*, p. 77; Heinzelmann, *Die kleineren Briefe des Apostels Paulus*, p. 95 who renders *v*. 5: 'Seid eins in demütiger Liebe, wie Christus sie lebte', and goes on to expound the passage of *vv*. 6–11 on the assumption that Christ 'ist das Vorbild aller wahrhaft demütigen, in Liebe sich unter den Anderen herabbeugenden Willenshaltung'. Similarly, A. Schlatter, *Der Brief an die Philipper* (1928), p. 76: 'The Church must go the way of Jesus in that pure, selfless love, which can deny its own greatness and honour'; A. Plummer, *Commentary*, p. 40: 'The establishment of harmonious thought and action in a community requires from each individual the repression of all self-assertion and the renunciation of much that might be claimed. The whole life of Christ on earth is a unique pattern of such humility.' Bo Reicke ('Unité chrétienne et Diaconie', 210) has repeated this interpretation of the Apostle's purpose: 'Pourquoi l'apôtre rappelle-t-il aux lecteurs ce renoncement du Christ? Son intérêt est tout à fait pratique: il veut combattre l'ambition et la soif de dominer qui inspirent bien des chrétiens ...le Christ est le modèle de chaque membre de l'Église.'

[2] Käsemann, 'Kritische Analyse', 77: 'Der ethische Deutungsversuch besitzt hier ja sein stärkstes Bollwerk.'

[3] See above, ch. III and appendix A to ch. IV (pp. 84 ff.).

Michaelis makes this the all-controlling factor in His incarnation. The hymn turns upon 'the obedience of Christ to the Father's will' ('den Gehorsam Christi gegenüber dem Willen des Vaters').[1] Now this may very well be true; but it is only an inference from the text and from other cognate Biblical passages (notably Heb. x. 7 f.). As Barth has forcefully expressed it, the hymn 'is not concerned as to *whom* Christ obeyed in his self-humiliation as a man... (it) is interested rather in the fact *that* he obeys, in the attitude of submission and dependence he adopts'.[2] The line of verse 8c, therefore, says nothing about the inner relationships between the Father and the Son in the Godhead.[3] His obedience is simply noted as a fact. And no theory of redemption is suspended upon it (as it is in Rom. v. 19).[4] Further, Bornkamm has argued that the obedience is not an isolated act, but belongs to the whole course of His life, reaching its climax in death.[5]

Käsemann finds the main emphasis of this part of the hymn in the note of Christ's free act. 'The One who was equal with God became a slave and became obedient... To the question of the why of His abasement, the first strophe answers merely: of His own free will.' With this double insistence (in verses 7a: ἑαυτὸν ἐκένωσεν and 8b: ἐταπείνωσεν ἑαυτόν) on the free consent of Christ[6]—a feature which is absent in the '*Ebed Yahweh* descriptions—goes an emphasis upon what He *did*, not

[1] Michaelis, *Philippians*, p. 39; cf. Plummer, *Commentary*, p. 47 who boldly inserts 'obedient *to God*' on the ground that 'to God' is implied in *v.* 9. This is unwarrantable.

[2] Barth, *The Epistle to the Philippians*, p. 65 ('nicht...*wem*...sondern... für das Faktum, *daß* er gehorcht', in the original p. 63).

[3] For the nearest parallels to this heavenly dialogue, cf. *Barn.* xiv, 6 ff., *Asc. Isa.* x. 7 ff. and Naassene hymn in Hippolytus, *Elench.* v, 10 (cited by Käsemann, *Gottesvolk*, p. 64).

[4] His obedience 'was merely a valley lying across the way which had to be crossed en route to the heights of glory' (R. M. Hawkins, *The Recovery of the Historical Paul*, p. 252).

[5] G. Bornkamm, *Das Ende des Gesetzes*, p. 88: 'Die ὑπακοή Christi ist für Paulus nicht eine einzelne Tat, sondern das Kennzeichen seines Weges und Werkes im ganzen (Phil. 2. 8)'; Bonnard, *Philippiens*, p. 44.

[6] Käsemann, 'Kritische Analyse', 79. Cf. Ewald, *op. cit.* 120 who quotes the following references which illustrate the emphatic ἑαυτόν (-ούς) in Paul: I Cor. xi. 31, xiv. 4; II Cor. iii. 1, v. 12, viii. 5; Eph. v. 25, 28 and especially I Cor. xiii. 5.

It is doubtful whether there is any special significance in the change of

upon what He *was*.[1] The force of the lines which depict His humiliation and obedience is to set out the events by which the drama of salvation is carried forward.[2] The humiliation is but one event, one phase, in the way of the Redeemer as He travels from his high glory to the nadir of abasement, and thence to the place of universal lordship. But there is a special meaning in the limit of His obedience 'unto death'. This is His enslavement by the evil powers.

(*b*) For the majority of writers whose treatment of the lines we have examined above, the solemn words 'unto death' signify the utmost limit of the Son's obedience. As there is no greater love than that which is shown in the sacrifice of a man's life for his friends (John xv. 13), so there is no more exemplary obedience than the acceptance of the Father's will in the receiving of the cup of suffering and death. This 'will to die' (in Bernard's classic phrase)[3] in utter submission to God's redeeming purpose marks Him out as the true God-become-Man; for, as Lohmeyer says in a brilliant insight,[4] only a divine being can accept death as *obedience*; for ordinary men it is a necessity, to which they are appointed by their humanity (Heb. ix. 27).

Lohmeyer has drawn attention, however, to another aspect of Christ's obedience 'unto death';[5] and in this suggestion, as in others which he has made, he has been followed by later scholars. He has pointed out how in Jewish theology death is shown as a monarch, or even as a kingdom itself. So it may be, he infers, that our Lord's obedience unto death is like an entrance into this realm, a kind of *descensus ad inferos*.[6]

---

order (of ἑαυτόν) in *vv.* 7*a* and 8*b*, as Plummer believes. The variation is probably due to the desire to secure rhythmical lines, and to produce chiasmus.

[1] Käsemann, *loc. cit.* 72.

[2] G. Friedrich finds six different statements of the way of Christ from the glory of God to death, in *vv.* 7–8: He emptied Himself: took the servant's form; became like men: was found in appearance as a man: humbled himself: became obedient (*op. cit.* 109).

[3] *Non mors sed voluntas placuit sponte morientis* (*Ep.* cxc).

[4] Lohmeyer, *Kyrios Jesus*, p. 41; *Philipper*, p. 96.

[5] Lohmeyer, *Philipper*, p. 96; *Kyrios Jesus*, p. 43.

[6] For the *descensus*-doctrine, a little-known work of J. A. MacCulloch, *The Harrowing of Hell* (1930), discusses all the relevant texts: cf. W. Bieder, *Die*

Death itself, then, in this context becomes almost personified as a demonic power which enslaves men.[1] Christ's obedience means the utmost limit of His submission to the demonic forces which hold men in bondage. Käsemann has championed this understanding of the Incarnation and the death of Christ which, he says, belong together. 'They both have to do with an entrance into the control of the Powers', a conclusion which is confirmed by Hebrews ii. 15.[2] This latter text illustrates the teaching of human servitude to the Satanic powers which tyrannized over mortals and kept them in bondage through fear of death.[3] Jesus identified Himself to the full with this human fate, but with one obvious difference. He placed Himself under the yoke of submission to the elemental spirits of His own free will. When He was exalted by God, He broke the power of these forces of necessity and fate; and made it possible for those who base their lives on His victory to escape too. This, says Käsemann, is how the early Christian understood the soteriological drama of the *Christus victor*, who went to the utter limit of humiliation in His full identification with humanity.[4]

The data for this line of interpretation may be set down:

(i) The strongest point in its favour is the fact that verse 10 suggests that those agencies which now confess His lordship and victory are those to which He was subjected in His humiliation. They include τὰ καταχθόνια.[5] Ignatius, *ad Trall.* IX, 1

Vorstellung von der Höllenfahrt Jesu Christ (1949). For the New Testament evidence, see E. G. Selwyn, *The First Epistle of St Peter* (1947), pp. 319–22; C. E. B. Cranfield, *ExT*, LXIX (1958), 369–72; B. Reicke, *The Disobedient Spirits and Christian Baptism* (1946), pp. 231 ff.; H. Riesenfeld, 'La descente dans la morte', *Aux sources de la tradition chrét.* (1950), pp. 207 ff.

[1] See Käsemann, *Gottesvolk*, p. 100 for references.

[2] Käsemann, 'Kritische Analyse', 81.

[3] In addition to Heb. ii. 15 see II Tim. i. 10; Rom. viii. 38, 39; Acts ii. 27, 31; I Cor. xv. 55, 56 and Apoc. i. 18 (on which cf. MacCulloch, *op. cit.* p. 49). For death as the agent of Satan, cf. Dibelius, *Die Geisterwelt im Glauben des Paulus*, pp. 41–3.

[4] The background, according to Käsemann, *Gottesvolk*, pp. 98–105, is Gnostic, but is adapted to Christian usage. MacCulloch offers an alternative to this by concluding (286): 'we need go no further than Jewish-Christian circles to find the origin of the doctrine of the Descent. It required no formative influences from Pagan sources.'

[5] On καταχθόνια cf. W. Bousset, 'Zur Hadesfahrt Christi', *ZNTW*, XIX (1919/20), 50–66.

makes use of the same idea;[1] and both texts seem to depend upon the myth of the 'Journey to Hades'.[2] In the version of this myth which appears in the *Ascension of Isaiah*,[3] the powers of the underworld show their defeat by their worship of Christ.[4] And this is exactly the inference to be drawn from verse 10 of the hymn. The evil forces—the rulers of this age (I Cor. ii. 8)— which conspired to bring about the death of the Lord of glory are themselves dispossessed of authority and compelled to acknowledge the sovereignty of the exalted Christ.

(ii) The metrical structure of the hymn is set (according to Lohmeyer[5]) in triadic sections and phrases. The three 'states' through which Christ passed are 'divine–human–infernal', corresponding to the three stanzas of the first section. In each strophe 'this membership of each kingdom is pictured'; and at the triumphant conclusion of the hymn we see the three realms to which He has been subjected lying at the feet of the exalted One (Lohmeyer).

(iii) The hymn uses as its scaffolding the framework of the Gnostic redemption myth according to which the Redeemer is enslaved by the malevolent powers in the created world.[6] Yet in his enslavement he escapes from the realm of matter, and breaches the wall which separates the creation from God. Through his descent, death and return to heaven the Redeemer opens up the way for his followers. It is this ancient myth which lies in the background of the hymn, as of many references in the New Testament to Christ's death and resurrection.

Criticism of this approach as a whole may be concentrated upon the three points which are enumerated above.

(i) It may be questioned whether the reference to τὰ καταχθόνια implies that these infernal powers are hostile to Christ.[7] At all events, there is no hint of a mythical combat; and no

---

[1] Ignatius, *ad Trall.* IX, 1: 'Jesus Christ. . .was truly crucified and died in the sight of those in heaven and on earth and under the earth (ὑποχθονίων)'.

[2] Cf. Dibelius, *Die Geisterwelt*, pp. 203 ff. on the ancient 'Hadesfahrtmythus'.

[3] On the provenance of *Ascension of Isaiah*, cf. R. H. Charles, *The Ascension of Isaiah* (1900); and A. Harnack, *Geschichte der altchr. Litter.* II 1 (1897), pp. 573 ff.

[4] *Asc. Is.* xi. 23 ff.   [5] *Philipper*, p. 96; *Kyrios Jesus*, p. 43.

[6] Käsemann, *Gottesvolk*, pp. 98–105.

[7] Leivestad, *Christ the Conqueror*, p. 113.

clear indication that they are angelic beings at all. The expression in verse 10 may be a poetic pleonasm to signify the whole cosmos. All the world takes part in the worship of the enthroned Lord—this may be the message of the last part of the hymn, without exactly specifying three separate dominions.

The likeness of the *Ascension of Isaiah* myth (chs. vi–xi) to the theme of Philippians ii is certainly striking, as Dibelius has shown.[1] The basic scheme of descent and return is the same in both versions, but in details there is wide disparity. Perhaps the most outstanding difference is the motif of deception which runs through the *Ascension of Isaiah* drama. There, the *kenosis* of Christ is a stratagem which aims at concealing the identity of the incarnate one from the rulers of this world. This disguise-motif may be present in I Corinthians ii. 6–8; but it would be hard to detect it in Philippians ii where the Exaltation does not appear as the result of a victory gained through a ruse, but as the consequence of His self-abasement and obedience to the will of God His Father.

(ii) Lohmeyer's suggestion that verse 8 contains a mention of Christ's descent to Hades because of the requirements of metrical structure looks suspiciously like foisting a theory on the evidence. In order to give his view some semblance of plausibility he has to omit the words θανάτου δὲ σταυροῦ in verse 8*d*. In his view, this line breaks the metrical symmetry of the hymn, and is found now in the text because it is a Pauline gloss, added to the original hymn by the Apostle. If one is convinced that the entire hymn is built up on the principle of threes, then obviously this is a consideration which will weigh heavily. But we have already seen that other formal structures of the hymn are possible. It may be, however, that there are other reasons why this line should be deleted and regarded as an interpretative gloss.

Lohmeyer adds that his belief concerning the origin of this line is confirmed by the fact that the manner of the death— death upon a Roman cross—cannot take away from the death or add anything to its humiliation.[2] On his understanding of the teaching of this stanza, the chief element in Christ's death is His

[1] *An die Philipper*[3], p. 81.
[2] Lohmeyer, *Philipper*, p. 96: 'die Art dieses Todes ist vor dieser Wertung gleichgültig und kann ihm nichts wegnehmen oder seiner Niedrigkeit etwas hinzufügen'.

submission to the claims which death makes upon Him. The fact of death is all-important; the way in which He died is irrelevant to the hymn's theology.

With Dibelius, Michaelis, Stauffer and Cerfaux,[1] this line may be defended as authentically Pauline. But it is evident that this contention is just the one made by Lohmeyer and Käsemann;[2] for they maintain that the phrase was inserted by the Apostle's hand as he revised an existing liturgical hymn for inclusion in his Epistle to Philippi. The attitude which is taken up in regard to this line depends upon one's view of the hymn *in toto*—whether it is a Pauline composition or not. But we feel that Lohmeyer has overlooked the relevance of the line to the Philippian church for whom it would have special meaning. The Philippians lived in a Roman city where revulsion against the form of capital punishment mentioned in the line would be very strong.[3] For the Philippians at least, the addition of θανάτου δὲ σταυροῦ would emphasize the abject degradation of Christ's lowly obedience, and drive home the lesson that His identification with men reached the lowest rung of the ladder. Moreover, for a Jew, this attitude of disgust was shared, if for a different

[1] Dibelius, *An die Philipper*[3], p. 81; Michaelis, *op. cit.* 39; Stauffer, *New Testament Theology*, p. 284; Cerfaux, *Le Christ*, pp. 376, 382 and in 'L'hymne au Christ', *Recueil Lucien Cerfaux*, II (1954), 429 he defends the Pauline authenticity: 'Ce climax de l'hymne est sa signature paulinienne.'

[2] Käsemann, *loc. cit.* 82.

[3] This fact in the interpretation of *v.* 8 is brought out vigorously by Bornhäuser, *Jesus Imperator Mundi*, p. 23. Lohmeyer, it is true, seeks to place a paraenetic meaning on the phrase. By inserting it, Paul wished to remind the Philippians of their vocation as martyrs—in Lohmeyer's view, the *Leitmotiv* of the whole Letter—which would be no shame for them, for Christ's death on the cross was still more shameful. But he does not bring out the social and cultural relevance of the phrase in a letter addressed to Philippi, 'a city of Macedonia, the first of the district, a *Roman* colony' (Acts xvi. 12).
E. Esking, *Glaube und Geschichte in der theologischen Exegese Ernst Lohmeyers* (1951), p. 162, n. 2 shows how Lohmeyer's omission of the phrase θανάτου δὲ σταυροῦ is theologically motivated. The type of death is irrelevant (*Kyrios Jesus*, pp. 44f.) in his existential interpretation. It is the Lord's death *sub specie Dei* which gives it worth.
Cicero's expression of the Roman horror of the cross—*supplicium crudelissimum taeterrimumque* (*In Verrem*, v, 64: cf. v, 66: 'How shall I describe crucifixion? No adequate word can be found to represent so execrable an enormity'; *Pro Rabirio*, v, 10) is quoted as illustration. Cf. P. Winter, *On the Trial of Jesus* (1961), 'The Penalty of Crucifixion', pp. 62–6.

reason.[1] For him, death by crucifixion came under the rubric of Deuteronomy xxi. 23; for it meant that the victim was 'outside the pale of Israel; that he was *ḥérem*',[2] i.e. under a ban of excommunication from God's covenant. That this is a typically Pauline understanding of the death of the cross is seen from Galatians iii. 13 and from his references to the 'scandal' of the cross (I Cor. i–ii; Gal. v. 11, vi. 11 ff.).[3] The line of verse 8*d* may, with a degree of certainty, be regarded as Pauline, both because of its suitability in the Letter to the Philippians and because of its agreement with attested Apostolic doctrine.[4] The line may be treated as an insertion into the hymn, which (*pace* Lohmeyer here) means an extra humiliation in that it widens the scope of the descent of Christ who stooped to the tremendous limit of a death which placed Him under the wrath of God.

But—as we come back to a critique of Lohmeyer—there is no suggestion that in this uttermost humiliation a journey to the underworld is included; and no degree of cogency which he professed to find in a supposed triadic structure of the hymn can compensate for an absence of positive reference to such a thought.

(iii) As to the argument based on the use of the framework of Gnostic redemption mythology, enough has been said in earlier

---

[1] For the Jewish attitude to the cross, see lines 7 and 8 of the *pesher* on Nahum in the Qumran texts (published by J. M. Allegro, *JBL*, LXXV (1956), 89–95; cf. *JJS*, VII (1956), 71–2 on the terms תלה and תלה חי): 'This passage refers to the Lion of wrath who wreaked vengeance on the seekers after smooth things, and who used to hang men alive, as was never done before in Israel (אשר יתלה אנשים חיים אשר לא יעשה בישראל מלפנים), for he that is hanged alive on a tree...' *sc.* is accursed (Deut. xxi. 23) (J. T. Milik's translation, *Ten Years of Discovery in the Wilderness of Judea* (E.T. 1959), p. 73). See J. Klausner, *Jesus of Nazareth* (E.T. 1927), pp. 349 f. and E. Percy, *Die Botschaft Jesu* (1953), p. 172 on the disgrace of carrying the cross. [2] Davies, *Paul and Rabbinic Judaism* (²1955), p. 284.

[3] E. Schweizer, *Lordship and Discipleship* (E.T. 1960) (not in the original), p. 53: '...Paul has grasped the decisive point [in his doctrine of justification by grace]. In this connexion the particular manner of Jesus' death has also become important to him. Crucifixion is a manner of death which is under God's curse. The dishonour, the humiliation of Jesus has here become complete; vicariously and atoning for the Church Jesus has become a curse (Gal. 3. 13).'

[4] G. Strecker, 'Redaktion und Tradition im Christushymnus Phil. 2', *ZNTW*, LV (1964), 71 calls attention to the Pauline diction in the whole of *v.* 8.

parts of our study to show that, while there are external features which are common to the Gnostic and Christian dramas, there is much which distinguishes them.[1] What is common in this part of the hymn is the idea that death is a tyrant which exercises a baneful influence over men. The point of contact is most clearly to be seen in those writings which emanate from a Christian Gnostic source (e.g. *Odes of Solomon, Acts of Philip*).[2] There, death is brought into association with the devil. He is regarded as supreme in the kingdom of death. Inasmuch as Christ died, He placed himself under the power of Satan (cf. Luke xxii. 53), but voluntarily (John xiv. 30, 31); and in so doing and at length receiving His vindication from God, He broke that power. This, we submit, is the extent of the hymn's dependence upon extraneous demonology.

(*c*) A third line of investigation begins with the recognition that the coupling of humility and obedience is a feature which is prominent in Rabbinic thought. O. Michel[3] remarks that it is not accidental that in our Christ-hymn humiliation and obedience are brought together in such close inner unity, for it is precisely these two virtues which are spoken of in the same breath by the Jewish pietists.[4] Humility is an outstanding charac-

---

[1] G. Bornkamm finds the obedience of Christ to be the decisive *differentia*: 'Von höchster Bedeutung ist in unserm Text aber nun erst die Aussage über den *Gehorsam* Christi bis in den Tod.' He continues: 'there is no place in the act (of the Gnostic Redeemer who comes down into the fallen world of men and returns to his heavenly sphere with his redeemed souls) for obedience in humiliation and bodily suffering—death upon the cross. But for our hymn it is just at this point that the Christ-event finds fulfilment. Indeed, it is the obedience of Jesus which gives coherence to the whole. His giving up, in His pre-existence, of His equality with God and His descent into the human state of slavery take on meaning—as also does His exaltation to be Lord which follows—only because they are based on His obedience unto death' ('Zum Verständnis des Christus-hymnus Phil 2. 6–11', *Gesammelte Aufsätze*, II, 182).

[2] *Odes of Solomon*, xxxiii. 1 f., cf. xxix. 4, xv. 9; *Acts of Philip*, chs. cxv and cxii.

[3] O. Michel, 'Zur Exegese von Phil. 2, 5–11', p. 86. Similarly, E. Schweizer, *Erniedrigung und Erhöhung*, pp. 35 ff. and *NTS*, II (1955) as in n. 4 on p. 224. Davies, *Paul and Rabbinic Judaism*[2], pp. 262 ff.

[4] Obedience, humiliation and privation are closely associated. Hillel's words are classic: 'My humiliation is my exaltation, my exaltation is my humiliation' (S.-B., *Kommentar*, I, 774). Further examples in S.-B. I, 192 ff., 249 f., 921. For the interrelation of humility and exaltation in the New

teristic of life under the Torah, according to the witness of the Rabbinic literature. It is more than an isolated virtue; it is the quality of life which marks out the 'righteous people' (חסדים). But this teaching grew up in a world of realism.[1] The pietists who placed such emphasis upon undeviating devotion to the Law and its way of life knew full well that this pursuit would not be easy in a naughty world of sinners and indifferent men. Therefore, through experience and trial, there grew up the doctrine that the righteous man must inevitably suffer in a world like this.[2] But his suffering, humiliation and shame which came to him in pursuance of his vocation as the true servant of God would be followed by his exaltation and ultimate vindication. The whole of Jewish martyrology[3] is based on the twin facts of humiliation for the cause of God and the Torah, and exaltation by God. E. Schweizer gives a summary of this teaching:[4] 'Judaism frequently speaks of the righteous one who humbles himself or who voluntarily accepts humiliation by suffering and death in obedience to God. Suffering in particular is very valuable as atonement for one's own sins or vicarious atonement for other people's.' As a reward the righteous one is exalted by God, secretly already on earth, but especially in the world to come, where he finds his seat reserved for him in heaven, the

Testament cf. Matt. xvii. 4, xxiii. 12; Lk. xiv. 11, xviii. 14; II Cor. xi. 7; Phil. iv. 21; I Pet. v. 6; Jas. iv. 10. Cf. G. Bornkamm, *Jesus of Nazareth* (E.T. 1961), p. 202. Other references: Ecclus. iii. 19–23; I Clem. xxx, 2; Ignat. *ad Ephes.* v, 3; and especially *Wisdom*, ii. 12 ff., v. 1 ff., xviii. 20 ff.

[1] For the promise of a life of privation in devotion to the Torah, cf. *'Aboth* vi. 4: 'thou shalt live a life of trouble the while thou toilest in the Law' (Danby's translation).

[2] Cf. Enoch cviii. 7 (cited by Michel, *loc. cit.* 88). Michel comments: 'Humiliation and renunciation, humiliation and suffering go strictly together.'

[3] On Jewish martyrology see Schweizer, *Erniedrigung und Erhöhung*; E. Lohmeyer, *Die Idee des Martyriums im Judentum und Urchristentum* (1928) (known only from Esking's exposition, *op. cit.* pp. 223 ff.); Stauffer, *New Testament Theology*, Appendix I, pp. 331 ff. (texts on martyrdom); E. Lohse, *Märtyrer und Gottesknecht* (1955), pp. 66 ff.; T. W. Manson, 'Martyrs and Martyrdom' (i), *BJRL*, xxxix, 2 (1957).

[4] *Op. cit.* 42–3 (E.T. 30); cf. the same author's summary in 'Discipleship and Belief in Jesus as Lord from Jesus to the Hellenistic Church', *NTS*, II, 2 (1955), 88. E. Schweizer's discussion is sympathetically considered by M. Black, 'The Son of Man Problem in Recent Research and Debate', *BJRL* xlv, 2, 1963, 305 ff.

throne of glory, and there acts as a judge and executioner. This exaltation can also be pictured physically as an assumption from the earth, as an ascension to heaven.'

This outline which picks out the main elements in the Jewish martyr-theology has many points of contact with the drift of the hymn. There is confirmation of this in the Gospels where Jesus speaks of Himself as the Son of man humiliated on earth, rejected by men, exalted by God out of all suffering and judging men on His throne of glory. If we add to this scheme the idea of Israel's pious sufferers as the servants of God, who suffer vicariously for Israel, it is not difficult to see how this Christology grew up. Jesus is looked upon as the representative of His nation, fulfilling all that Israel was meant to be: and like the Son of man He is an 'inclusive personality', embodying in His person a great number of people. Like the servants of God in the nation's history, He treads the pathway of humiliation and rejection, unto death. All innocent suffering was regarded as atoning, often vicariously for all Israel;[1] and this explains why no explicit mention is made of His death as an atonement for sin.[2] On this view, the Christology is rudimentary and still awaits further development. The way in which the development will be made is seen in the extra line 'even the death of the cross', added by Paul. The text of the hymn says no more than that the obedience of Christ was perfect, but it is distinguished from that of other righteous men in Israel because He came from His pre-existent glory and claimed authority as the Son of man— Schweizer finds illustration of His uniqueness in His calling others to be His disciples, which none of His predecessors had done[3]—and taught that in His mission Israel's destiny came to realization. The addition made by the Apostle is important in the light of the way in which the Jewish martyrs faced the prospect of death. A. Büchler has drawn attention to an interesting feature of Jewish martyrology.[4] The Rabbis who faced

---

[1] Schweizer, *op. cit.* (E.T.), pp. 25 f.; E. Lohse, *op. cit.* pp. 29 ff.

[2] The obedience of Christ is μέχρι θανάτου. Phil. ii. 8 uses an expression familiar in a 'martyrdom' context—III Macc. vii. 16; cf. Phil. ii. 30; Apoc. ii. 10, xii. 11; Acts xxii. 4; I Clem. IV, 9.

[3] Schweizer, *op. cit.* (E.T.), p. 41.

[4] A. Büchler, *Studies in Sin and Atonement in the Rabbinic Literature of the First Century* (1928), pp. 189 ff. (quoted from Davies, *Paul and Rabbinic Judaism*[2], p. 284).

death were concerned not so much with the fact of death as with the peculiar form their deaths would take. For example, R. Ishmael in conversation with R. Simeon b. Gamaliel weeps, not because he is to be slain, but because he is to die by the sword 'in the same way as murderers, and as the desecrators of the Sabbath'. Now, as W. D. Davies has pointed out,[1] this is how we are to regard the 'death of the cross' in the eyes of a Rabbi. Yet what was to Paul the Rabbi a fearful σκάνδαλον becomes to him as a Christian the core of his teaching on the obedience of Christ. He who knew no sin was made 'sin' on our behalf (II Cor. v. 18 ff.); and He became a curse for us because His obedience was not simply unto death, but unto the accursed death of the cross (Gal. iii. 13). Paul thus directs the drift of the hymn's soteriological teaching—in its original form, somewhat vague and amorphous—into channels which are known to us from the Pauline literature.

As far as the original text of the hymn is concerned, the emphasis falls (in this view of the background of verse 8) on what Christ has done in fulfilment of His vocation. This vocation is drawn from the imagery of righteous sufferers in Israel who gave their lives for their faith and thus rendered some expiation to God.

While the correspondences in idea and application between Jewish martyr-theology and the teaching of the hymn are of interest, there are some outstanding differences. This view also assumes that the obedience is rendered to God; that the hymn's Subject stands in the Old Testament tradition as the eschatological Fulfiller of prophecy; that His death is related to sin. None of these things is said explicitly in the text. And so this understanding lacks the evidence to make it the definitive view.

C. SUMMING-UP

Our concern in this chapter has been with the humiliation and obedience of Christ. Directly related to this is the statement that He was born in human likeness and appeared on earth as a man. Amid the welter of diverse suggestions as to the meaning of these lines, the main features stand out. The hymn relates the Incarnation of the pre-existent One; it tells how He 'came down' and

---

[1] Davies, *op. cit.* p. 284.

took a human form, to all outward appearances showing that He was man. Yet inasmuch as He 'came down', as did none other, and remained, in His earthly form, still a divine (if simultaneously an incarnate) being,[1] the poet cannot call Him a man *simpliciter* as he might describe himself or his fellow-men. This accounts for the cumbersome language[2] and the adopting of the periphrastic style. This is the language of a divine epiphany—the manifestation of God in human form.

The earthly life of the 'manifested God' is summed up in one term: His obedience. It is not said to whom He was obedient. Indeed it seems to be unimportant, for the hymn shows little interest in biographical details.[3] There is no attempt at a full character study. The fact of His obedience is simply reported. Yet, because of who He is who is obedient, a more than ordinary significance attaches to this fact. If obedience is by definition a human characteristic, *this* obedience may underline further the reality of His identification with us men. He who 'came down' from God showed, as God, the very trait which marks humanity from the rest of creation—a sense of responsibility and the achievement of the true purpose of life.

Moreover, this obedience was carried to the farthest limit; for death is the end of all things which are mortal. He put Himself in an emphatic voluntary fashion under the control of death, man's last enemy. He yielded to its claim, although that claim was unlawful since He was divine and therefore not subject to death's régime.[4] At the climax of His earthly career He came

[1] This is perhaps the element of truth in Lohmeyer's theory of Anthropos (ὡς ἄνθρωπος)—'the one who carries this title is man, and at the same time, he is another. In his appearance his divine state is hidden', *Kyrios Jesus*, p. 40.

[2] G. Friedrich, *Der Brief an die Philipper*: 'Es heißt dann in dem Lied nicht einfach: Christus wurde Mensch, sondern es wird schwerfälliger, aber korrekter gesagt: er erschien in der Gleichgestalt des Menschen' (110).

[3] Lohmeyer, *Kyrios Jesus*, p. 37: 'Particulars of the historical life of Jesus are irrelevant in this presentation: what is of consequence is the stark factuality of his human existence.' It is therefore quite erroneous to try to relate His humiliation to some concrete aspect of His earthly life, e.g. His baptism (as Ewald does, *Philipper*, p. 125, n. 2).

[4] Lohmeyer writes finely: 'Es hätte in seiner Macht gelegen...dem Tode auszuweichen' (*Kyrios Jesus*, p. 41). Therefore His death is His own act and is given the character of a humble deed. Moreover, His death, because it is

under the sway of that which spells the very meaninglessness of all human existence. Not simply that He died, as all men must do. He became obedient to death—of His own free choice and with a specific purpose in view. For although He yielded to death, He did not remain under its tyranny. At the end of this line (of verse 8 c: γενόμενος ὑπήκοος μέχρι θανάτου), the close of the first half of the drama is reached, and the hymn reaches what the Greeks call its turning-point (περιπέτεια). The solemn ending μέχρι θανάτου seems to spell finality and doom for Him and the race to which He came. Life's meaninglessness is apparently and irrevocably confirmed as death engulfs Him, forgetful of the illegitimacy of its claim and that its 'victory' is possible only because He has consented to submit to its power. The new stanza will open with a new note, as the spoiler is itself despoiled, and the tyrant is overthrown; and, with this reversal of fortune and with the vindication of Christ, the sovereign love of God will be proved, His invincible care for men established and the purposefulness of life made evident.

But, at the end of the first section of the hymn, we trace the career of Christ to its nadir. From the glory of His Father's presence He has entered upon a historical existence. He has identified Himself with men in all the traits of humanity, not shrinking from the final identification in death. This is the lowest point in the dramatic parabola[1] as 'these three stanzas lead, in one great sweep, from the highest height to the deepest depth, from the light of God to the darkness of death' (Lohmeyer).[2]

the heavenly Man who dies and who dies of his own accord, is not the naturally-determined end of his life; it wears a 'religious-mythical' character —as all the acts of God in human history must do (op. cit. 43).

[1] This figure of speech is taken from E. Brunner, The Mediator (E.T. 1934), pp. 561–3.

[2] Lohmeyer, Philipper, p. 96. Suzanne de Dietrich, L'épître aux Philippiens (n.d.), p. 49 comments on the ultimacy of His obedience: 'Il descend dans ce gouffre dernier de la mort d'où seule la toute-puissance de Dieu pourra le retirer.'

CHAPTER IX

HIS EXALTATION

διὸ καὶ ὁ θεὸς αὐτὸν ὑπερύψωσεν
καὶ ἐχαρίσατο αὐτῷ
τὸ ὄνομα τὸ ὑπὲρ πᾶν ὄνομα (verse 9)

INTRODUCTION

Even to the reader of the English version of the text it is noticeable that, with the sentence of verse 9, a decisive turning-point
in the story of the hymn has been reached.[1] This is reflected in a
distinct change in the language and thought. At this juncture
the rôle of chief Actor in the drama of Incarnation and redemption changes. Attention has, up to this point, been focused upon
the self-humbling and obedience of the God-become-Man, with
the reflexive pronouns in verses 7 and 8 contributing to the
emphasis. The name of God is, so to speak, incidental to and
implicit in the drama, up to this stage.

But with verse 9 a shift of emphasis is apparent. Now it is God
the Father who, as it were, takes the initiative and becomes the
principal Actor in the new sequences of the second section of the
hymn.

This new beginning is even more obvious in the Greek[2] where
the language, which up to verse 9 has been terse and economical
with participial constructions (five in number) instead of main
verbs, becomes ornate and full of echoes of Old Testament
Semitic constructions and allusions. In place of the pronouns
there are proper nouns ('God' who is mentioned as the Subject
of a sentence for the first time in the hymn; 'Jesus'; 'Jesus
Christ'; 'God the Father'); and main verbs ('has highly exalted';
'has given') are followed by subordinate clauses with the para-
tactical copulative 'and' twice, rather than participles.

Both content and style confirm, therefore, Käsemann's

---

[1] See above, ch. II.
[2] E. Lohmeyer, *Philipper*, p. 96; W. Michaelis, *Der Brief an die Philipper*,
p. 41.

remark[1]—and he speaks for the commentators generally, since Lohmeyer first drew attention to these facts—that, at verse 9, there is 'a sharply marked change of subject. At this point we have to do with a new stage in the Redeemer's way. J. Jervell[2] has taken this contrast to the length of affirming that the hymn holds together—and none too successfully—two divergent Christologies. He argues that verses 6–8 are a fragment of Gnostic theology, based on the pre-existent 'Heavenly Man's' descent into the world; whereas in verses 9–11 we have a typically early Christian Christology, based on the Resurrection and Exaltation of Christ to be Lord and Son of God, whose sufferings are the gateway to His glory. 'In the Hellenistic Church, the two presentations are combined in order to give greater prominence to the cosmic importance of Christ.' Jervell makes much of the apparent disparity between the ideas in the two sections of the hymn, but overlooks the main thing which they have in common and the points of connection which show how well they are related. However much the two parts are different in style and syntax, they are complementary in one important respect. This is the controlling factor of *obedience and its vindication*. The humiliation of the incarnate One, who is the 'divine Hero' of the first part, is followed by the Exaltation at the hands of God. And it is this close connection which binds the two halves together.[3] On this understanding (which is supported by Michaelis and Käsemann), the link is found in the person of Christ Himself. He is the central theme of the first stanzas as His state and acts are related. He is equally at the centre of the second part, with the difference that He is there the recipient and the object rather than the subject of all that is said and done. But 'all the interest remains focused on Christ', as Michaelis says.[4] The two parts are two great chapters in His existence. 'As the humiliation signifies the obedience of Christ as self-humiliation, so the Exaltation is shown as Exaltation by God as He recompenses this

[1] 'Kritische Analyse', 82, drawing upon Lohmeyer, *Kyrios Jesus*, pp. 46 f.

[2] See Appendix to this chapter, pp. 247 f.

[3] Cf. Aristotle's directive on the unity of the plot: 'The unity of a plot does not consist, as some suppose, in its having one man as its subject. An infinity of things befall that one man, some of which it is impossible to reduce to unity; and in like manner there are many actions of one man which cannot be made to form one action', *Poetics*, 1451 a 16 ff.

[4] *Philipper*, p. 41.

obedience.'[1] The obedience of Christ is crowned by this act of Exaltation in which the Father raised Him from the dead, and elevated Him to the place of honour. The transition from humiliation to exaltation is denoted by the conjunction διό which prepares for what follows by introducing the result of His obedient submission unto death. The καί marks the element of reciprocity (Blass–Debrunner);[2] and the use of διό καί makes it clear that the best translation is 'that is why' (as at Luke i. 35; Rom. iv. 22).[3] He became obedient to the utmost limit of death; this is why God has lifted Him out of death and honoured Him. This sequence confirms Michaelis' view that Christ's obedience is the all-controlling theme of the hymn.

A. THE DIVINE INTERPOSITION

(i) *The debate over 'reward'*

Michaelis' interpretation has the advantage of a *prima facie* attractiveness. It certainly has more to commend it than some other views. It leaves open the ground on which Christ received His glory, although his use of the word 'recompense' may suggest that he has the thought in mind that Christ was rewarded for His obedience by the signal honour which God conferred upon Him. Many commentators take this view, especially those who write from a Roman Catholic standpoint. Thus, D. M. Stanley insists that 'the conception of Christ's exaltation as a personal reward for his obedience in undergoing death is characteristic of the theology of the whole passage. This is the one place in the whole *corpus Paulinum* where Christ's glorification appears in the context of his merit.'[4] This line of reasoning has been opposed

---

[1] Michaelis, *op. cit.* p. 40.

[2] Funk–Blass–Debrunner, *A Greek Grammar of the New Testament* (E.T. 1961), §§ 442, 12; 451, 5. The καί implies that God on His side responds in raising Jesus. The αὐτόν is emphatic by position, as is natural in a statement of reciprocity. He emptied *Himself*, and God exalted *Him*. So Plummer, *Commentary, ad loc.*; Lightfoot, *ad loc.*

[3] Cf. C. K. Barrett, *ad* Rom. iv. 22, *A Commentary on the Epistle to the Romans* (1957), p. 98.

[4] Stanley, *Christ's Resurrection in Pauline Soteriology*, p. 99, cf. p. 268: 'In the sequel [of the hymn], Christ's exaltation appears as the reward of this meritorious action.' Cf. F. Prat, *The Theology of St Paul²* (E.T. 1933), I, p. 312, n. 1 (*c*).
On the non-Roman side: R. S. Franks, *The Doctrine of the Trinity* (1953),

since the time of the Reformation. 'The idea of Christ's receiving his exaltation as a reward was repugnant to the Reformed theologians' (Vincent).[1] But their opposing view of this verse tended to do violence to the strict meaning of the words διὸ καί. Calvin translated these words by *quo facto*, 'which done', adding that the conjunction 'démonstre plustôt yci une conséquence de la chose, que non pas la cause et raison'.[2] It is extremely doubtful whether this rendering of διὸ καί by 'consequently' can be sustained. But equally there is no place for the notion of merit. The key is found in the precise meaning of the term 'reward'. R. Bultmann[3] has clarified the issue by remarking that, in the teaching of Jesus in the Gospels, He promises reward to those who are obedient without thought of reward. And in the context of the hymn, this is exactly the sense. It is not so much the thought that because He rendered this obedience He was glorified as that, having accomplished the mission He came into the world to fulfil, God interposed and reversed the seeming finality of death in raising Him to the place of dignity. The obedience of Christ did not force the hand of God, as a doctrine of merit implies.[4] The action of God is but the other side of that obedience, and a vindication of all that the obedience involved.

(ii) *Barth's view*

Reacting from all notions of merit and reward, Barth has gone to the opposite extreme.[5] For him, the διό of verse 9 does not divide the hymn into two separate parts. It simply marks another aspect of what has gone before. It marks the connection between two aspects of the same reality. The humiliated one is the exalted one, and as such is Lord over all. For His glory was apparent on earth in His humiliated state, and is merely dis-

p. 29: 'The keyword here is "wherefore" (διό) in verse 9, which introduces the principle of merit: it was by His obedience in dying that Christ merited Lordship.'

[1] *Philippians and Philemon*, ad loc.

[2] Calvin quoted by Bonnard, *Philippiens*, p. 45, n. 3.

[3] *Jesus and the Word* (E.T. 1934), pp. 78f. (1962 ed. pp. 62f.) and cf. G. Bornkamm, *Jesus of Nazareth* (E.T. 1960), pp. 137–43.

[4] Cf. Rom. iv. 4: 'Now to one who works, his wages are not reckoned as a gift (κατὰ χάριν) but as his due'; Rom. xi. 6; Eph. ii. 8.

[5] Barth, *The Epistle to the Philippians*, pp. 66 ff.

played at the Resurrection. When Barth comments thus on διό: 'It does not say that he who was humbled and humiliated was afterwards exalted, was indeed...rewarded for his self-denial and obedience', he has prejudiced our understanding of the verse by the use of the word 'rewarded' in a pejorative sense. If we substitute for this a less objectionable expression (to represent the Greek ἐχαρίσατο of verse 9b), it becomes apparent that the διὸ καί does mean exactly what Barth denies, viz., that God granted to Christ a vindication of His self-chosen humiliation in the conferring (χαρίζεσθαι) of the name which He did not previously have. This marks a new departure, and a new phase in Christ's existence which cannot (pace Barth) be read back into His incarnate life, which Barth interprets in terms of the divine incognito. What is important in Barth's complex exegesis is his insistence that it is the same Christ throughout every stage of the drama, although (according to the above criticism) he fails to do justice to the shift of emphasis and the new situation created by the vindication of Christ by God, which is marked by διὸ καί.

(iii) *Lohmeyer's interpretation*

Even more difficult of comprehension is Lohmeyer's exegesis, according to which the events portrayed in the Pauline verses exemplify the law *per aspera ad astra*.[1] When this law is expressed in Jewish terminology, it means that it is a universal rule that humiliation will issue in exaltation. It 'cannot be' otherwise in a universe where God is and rules. And it is this law—what Lohmeyer terms 'das göttliche Gesetz der Koinzidenz von

---

[1] *Philipper*, p. 97; *Kyrios Jesus*, p. 74: 'Die Einheit des Gedichtes ist sachlich das göttliche Gesetz: Per aspera ad astra; oder jüdisch gesprochen: durch menschliche Niedrigkeit zur göttlichen Hoheit.' Lohmeyer finds the antecedent of this principle in the Old Testament. It is related to the experience of the Jews as the elect of God who suffer in the earth. 'To be chosen by God means to suffer upon earth. This concept is first mentioned in Judaism by Deutero-Isaiah in the Suffering Servant Songs.' The law finds its highest illustration in the One in whom the election of Israel is fulfilled. He shows in His Incarnation how it is needful to accept humiliation in order finally to be exalted. 'If this paradox is the expression of the divine norm and a revelation of the divine being, then He who is ordained to be Lord must also bear and experience it (*sc*. suffering). In other words, in order to show Himself divine, it is necessary for Him to pass through time', *Philipper*, p. 93.

Niedrigkeit und Erhöhung'—which states that in our world the righteous servant of God will inevitably be called to a vocation of suffering, which will at length lead to his exaltation; this is indicated by the reversal of Christ's fortunes. It is true that what may be called a principle of the close association of humiliation and exaltation is found to be stated and exemplified in the scripture (Matt. xviii. 4, xxiii. 2; Luke xiv. 11, xviii. 14; II Cor. xi. 7; Phil. iv. 12; cf. I Clem. xiii),[1] and that the story of the hymn follows the pattern. But to take this line of reasoning to the extent which Lohmeyer does and to say that Christ is not explicitly named in verse 9 because it is a principle, and not a person, which is the main theme of the poem is surely a case of ὕστερον πρότερον. The hymn is not written to prove the validity of a principle. It depicts the humility and glory of a person who thereby illustrates the rule, but who is greater than it. It may be asked what has led Lohmeyer to take this unusual line of approach. E. Esking, in his study of Lohmeyer's concepts of *Faith and History*,[2] has supplied the answer by showing how the latter, with his philosophical presuppositions, is determined to eliminate the historical relations of the God-man and to set the contents of the hymn free from historical connections. In Lohmeyer's estimate it is not the 'worthiness' of Christ that is honoured, but this law which is being exemplified. His concern is with an ethical-philosophical law which can only be illustrated, never proved. And the events of Christ's humiliation and exaltation are just such an exemplifying.[3]

To start from an *a priori* philosophical conviction like this is hardly the best method of exegetical approach; and most subsequent writers have found fault with Lohmeyer's basic assumptions. It 'leads to confusion', remarks Bonnard,[4] as may well be expected when a speculative philosophical theory is superimposed upon a biblical text.

On the credit side, however, Lohmeyer has cleared up one

---

[1] Dibelius, *Die Formgeschichte des Evangeliums*[3] (1959), pp. 243 f. (E.T. of 2nd ed. 242 f.) says that I Clem. xiii contains a catena of Jesus' sayings.

[2] *Glaube und Geschichte*, p. 162.

[3] Lohmeyer says this in so many words: 'In this martyrdom (of Christ's) the law becomes apparent, according to which humiliation and exaltation are inseparably bound together', *Philipper*, p. 98.

[4] *Philippiens*, p. 45, n. 3.

vital matter.[1] He has shown that the Exaltation has to do with the cosmic lordship of Christ, who is installed as Lord of the universe and not simply as cultic Lord of the Church; and that the whole of the second part of the hymn is to be placed in a soteriological setting. Christ is Lord over all the world, and it is through Him that God works out His saving purposes in the world. This is the meaning of His being 'highly honoured' and accorded the 'name which is above every name'. Both phrases have been the focus of controversy; and to them we may turn.

B. THE SUPREME NAME

The vindication of Christ is expressed by the bestowal of 'the name' (reading τὸ ὄνομα with אABC; the definite article is omitted by DEFGKLP) 'above all names'. The precise meaning of this statement has been variously evaluated.

(i) The name—a personal title

The older commentators sought to trace the actual content of the name given to the glorified Christ. It can only be a curiosity of New Testament interpretation that the title 'Jesus' has been proposed (by Ellicott, Alford, Eadie and Robertson)[2] for, as P. Henry says,[3] Jesus had borne *this* name from His circumcision (Luke ii. 21) and what is envisaged in this hymn is the bestowal of a *new* name. Vincent and Meyer think of the composite name, 'Jesus Christ'; but there is no evidence for this; and the same verdict must be passed on the suggestion of υἱός (by Theodoret, Augustine and Pelagius).[4] A number of Church Fathers[5] opt for Θεός, but this suggestion faces the objection that the early documents of the New Testament do not adopt the second century practice of calling Jesus 'God' explicitly and in open declaration.[6]

---

[1] Lohmeyer, *Philipper*, p. 97 and *Kyrios Jesus, passim*.

[2] Cited by Michael, *Philippians*, p. 94 and Vincent, *Philippians and Philemon, ad loc.*

[3] 'Kénose', 35. Cf. Matt. i. 21, 25. But that the name of Jesus is the supreme name is maintained by W. L. Knox, *HTR*, XLI (1948), 238; Vincent, *op. cit. ad loc.*

[4] Cited by Henry, 'Kénose', 106, 126–7.

[5] E.g. Novatian, Gregory of Nazianzus, Cyril of Alexandria.

[6] Cf. Weiss, *Christ: The Beginnings of Dogma*, pp. 54 f. for this transition.

(ii) *The name—the office of lordship*

The last-named view prepares for the commonest understanding of the significance of the name.[1] In this view, more regard is paid to the fact that *God* bestows the superlative name upon Jesus than to the actual content of the name itself. Indeed, it must be confessed that we do not know what the name was, for the text is silent. The important thing is that it is God who gives to the exalted Jesus the all-excelling name. This, then, can be none other than the name of God Himself; and the name of God κατ' ἐξοχήν which, in the Old Testament, distinguishes Him from all rivals and idol powers is 'Lord' (Yahweh). This links with verse 11 which proclaims that 'Jesus Christ is Lord'.

This view gains further support from the train of thought in the entire hymn. God gave Him at the close of His earthly life and mission the name which might have been His in His pre-incarnate existence. This involves taking 'name' in the sense of office and power. God gave this to Christ because He chose to receive it not by exploiting His own privilege and claiming it for Himself, but because of His self-abnegation which was prepared to await the Father's pleasure and to receive it in His own way. The contrast between these alternatives is very forcefully expressed by the verbs οὐχ ἁρπαγμὸν ἡγήσατο and ἐχαρίσατο αὐτῷ.[2] He declined the opportunity to advance Himself by the assertion of His own right and to clutch at the power which might have been His in the exercise of His own lordship; now after a career of self-humbling and obedience there comes to Him in the Father's good pleasure (χάρις) the very thing He might have grasped, the 'name which is above every name' and the exercise of a universal dominion. The presuppositions of this view are:

(*a*) that ὄνομα carries the sense of the Old Testament שֵׁם which is 'not...a definite appellation, but (denotes) office, rank, dignity';[3]

(*b*) that this 'office, rank, dignity' which the glorified Christ receives are all expressive of the exercise of lordship. They may

---

[1] But W. Heitmüller, *Im Namen Jesu* (1903), pp. 65 ff. raises some important objections to this identification.

[2] Lohmeyer, *Kyrios Jesus*, p. 51 comments on the strophic parallelisms.

[3] J. B. Lightfoot, *St Paul's Epistle to the Philippians*, ad loc.

be predicated of Him because He is the Lord, the heavenly Kyrios. The root meaning of Κύριος is rulership based on competent and authoritative power, the ability to dispose of what one possesses.[1] It is essentially a functional term. God is sovereign possessor of all things because He is creator and sustainer; and He is called Lord because He has the right to use His possessions as He pleases. The same thought lies behind this name bestowed upon Christ. God assigns to Him the right to possess and to use all that God commits into His hand; He gives Him authority in heaven and upon earth (Matt. xxviii. 18);

(c) that Κύριος recalls the LXX translation of the covenant title Yahweh, and proclaims that Jesus Christ is installed in the place which properly belongs to God and exercises sovereign authority which God most rightly possesses.[2] The proof of this fact is supplied in the final lines of the hymn with their conscious reminiscence of the Old Testament (citing Isa. xlv. 23; cf. Isa. xlii. 8) and the open proclamation they contain of the lordship (κυριότης) of Jesus Christ.

This interpretation is linked with, and indeed is based upon, a corresponding understanding of ἁρπαγμὸν ἡγεῖσθαι as *res rapienda*. The train of argument is that Christ, in His pre-existence, declined to grasp what might have been His possession, viz. equality with God. At the close of His mission He returns to His Father's presence and is given the exact counterpart of what proved the substance of His choice. He is exalted to the rank of dignity of God as God's equal, exercising the very authority which God alone may properly exercise.

---

[1] *TWNT*, III, 1043 (= E.T. 9): *Kyrios* is he who can dispose of things or persons...; G. Harder, *Paulus und das Gebet*, pp. 190–2; L. Cerfaux, 'Kyrios', *DB Suppl.* Fasc. xxxiv, col. 202: 'Le substantif (τὸ) κῦρος apparaît depuis Eschyle avec la signification d'autorité souveraine, puissance de faire ou de ne faire, droit de décider...le κύριος celui qui a droit de disposer.'

[2] *TWNT*, III, 1094 (= E.T. 110): 'In ihm handelt Gott so, wie es das AT vom Κύριος aussagt' (In Him God acts in such a way as is said in the O.T. of the *Kyrios*).

J. Weiss, *Christ: The Beginnings of Dogma*, p. 52 remarks *à propos* of *vv.* 9–11: 'These names ['Lord', 'God' in Isa. xlii. 8, xlv. 22] which God jealously guards as his own prerogative, he has now surrendered to Christ...The granting of the name signifies according to ancient use, endowment with the power which the name denotes....Christ...definitely takes the place of the almighty God.'

(iii) *The name—God revealed to men*

A third possibility of interpretation is offered by Käsemann[1] and others who begin with the twin presupposition that (*a*) 'name' denotes the worth and the manifested character of an individual; it is the revelation of the inmost being of the one who carries it; and (*b*) Christ, in His pre-incarnate state, was God's equal as the Image which existed 'in God'. Therefore, it would be pointless to speak of an increase in the power of the Kyrios which the 'one equal with God' did not have before. If Christ were God's equal in His original status, then the exaltation can confer nothing greater upon Him. As Jervell has observed,[2] if verse 6 represents a maximum (Christ's being in the form of God and on an equality with God), then the 'step-up', the increase of power and fulness in the second section, is a senseless description; for how can a maximum be augmented?

Käsemann seeks an easement of this dilemma by giving a distinctive meaning to 'the name'.[3] 'The "more" (in the verb, "God did more than highly exalt him") is connected with the name. Christ is no longer the hidden Godhead (*das verborgene Gottwesen*). He is now revealed, and openly rules in the fullest sense. As far as the universe is affected by the proclamation of the new name, it no longer has to do with the unknown God, with what it itself calls Fate (*Schicksal*).'

On this way of taking the sense of τὸ ὄνομα, the conferring of the name is the designation of Christ as the Lord of the universe, holding the place *vis-à-vis* the world which God had up to that time held. Men, however, had not acknowledged this and had turned aside to false gods, a feature which is explained partly by the fact of their being sinners and partly by the fact that God was hidden and His character ambiguous (both elements are

---

[1] Käsemann, 'Kritische Analyse', 83, followed by Bornkamm, Jervell and Friedrich.

[2] *Imago Dei*, p. 212: Verses 9–11 represent 'eine Steigerung...Hier wird von einem Zuwachs an Machtfülle gesprochen. Doch ist dies wohl eigentlich sinnlos, denn V. 6 ὅς ἐν μορφῇ Θεοῦ ὑπάρχων bekundet ein Maximum.'

[3] *Loc. cit.* 85; but cf. Jervell, *op. cit.* p. 212, n. 153. For the Gnostic background of the hidden name of God cf. *The Gospel of Philip* 12 (102, 5–17) on which R. McL. Wilson, *The Gospel of Philip*, pp. 75 f. has written; and Quispel, in *The Jung Codex*, pp. 68 ff.

found in the New Testament—Romans i–ii for the first; Acts xvii. 22 ff. for the second). But now the old age of uncertainty and preparation is over. The times of ignorance are past; and God the invisible is plainly revealed in Christ, the Image of God in whom men may encounter Him. Indeed it is in Christ that they *must* encounter Him, for He is the God-appointed Judge and Lord. This is the import which Käsemann attaches to the lordship of Christ. 'Kyrios is God in His relation to the world. Only through Him does God deal with the world until the Parousia. He is *Deus revelatus*, the criterion and Judge of all history.'

C. THE EXALTATION

The verb ὑπερυψοῦν,[1] translated in the older English versions 'highly exalted', is generally taken as covering both the Resurrection (which is tacitly assumed), and the ascension. There is a parallel instance of this use of one term to cover the whole of Christ's triumph in I Peter iii. 18 ff. where 'made alive in the spirit' expresses the entire scope of His post-Resurrection ministry.[2] In both cases the act of Resurrection is included, but passed over in favour of a full emphasis upon the victory of Christ and His installation in the seat of power and might.

(i) *The verb ὑπερυψοῦν: its comparative force*

The exact sense of the verb needs a more careful definition, however. The issue in the exegesis of it is how the prefix ὑπερ- is to be taken. If ὑπερ- is given its full force and treated as a strict comparative, then the meaning will be that Christ is exalted to a place which He had not reached previously. This is clearly stated by Héring who comments that God has exalted His Son, giving Him 'une dignité supérieure à celle dont il avait joui dans

---

[1] The verb ὑπερυψοῦν is a New Testament *hapax*. The simplex form ὑψοῦν is regularly used for the ascension of Christ: John iii. 14, viii. 28, xii. 32, 34; Acts ii. 33, v. 31; *Odes of Sol.* xli. 12: 'He who was humbled and exalted by His own righteousness, the Son of the most High who appeared in the perfection of His Father.' For the nuance of the verbs, cf. J. G. Davies, *He ascended into Heaven* (1958), pp. 28 f.

[2] Cf. E. Schweizer, *Spirit of God* (1961), p. 102, following R. Bultmann, *Con. Neotest.* XI, 1–14. Cf. *ExT*, LXIX, 12 (1958), 369.

sa pré-existence'.[1] O. Cullmann has espoused this interpretation and set it at the heart of his exposition of Philippians ii. 6 ff.[2]

(ii) *The verb* ὑπερυψοῦν: *its superlative force*

According to a number of commentators no significance is to be attached to the prefix for two reasons. In the first place, the use of this particular verb is held to be derived from the LXX of Isaiah lii. 13: 'Behold my servant (ὁ παῖς μου: Aquila reads: ὁ δοῦλός μου) shall understand, and shall be exalted (ὑψωθήσεται) and extolled most highly.' Yahweh has set Him on high and committed an inheritance into His hand. This is the sense of 'He has highly exalted him'.

In the second place, it is said that the use of verbs with prefix in ὑπερ- is a characteristic Pauline usage.[3] The force of the

[1] *Le Royaume de Dieu*, p. 163 and the same writer's article 'Kyrios Anthropos' in *RHPR*, xvi (1936), 196–209: 'ὑπερυψοῦν et ἔδωκεν ὄνομα indiquent clairement l'investiture avec une dignité nouvelle et supplémentaire' (208).

[2] *Christology*, pp. 180 f. This interpretation is widely shared, e.g. by the following: Dibelius, *An die Philipper*[3], 79: 'Die Erhöhung gibt Christus mehr als er besessen; sonst würde es sich ja nur um Wiederherstellung, nicht um ὑπερυψοῦν handeln.' Ewald, *Philipper*, pp. 126 f. Lohmeyer, *Philipper*, p. 97 is apparently to be included here when he appends this comment: 'The name above every name' cannot be anything but the name of Lord as in the Old Testament, and with His receiving this is connected an elevation to the right hand of God also. This is a new marvel; for it means not only a new worthiness—the highest that it is possible to imagine— but also a new being. The form and existence of the Kyrios are bound up with this one "name".' Michaelis, *Zur Engelchristologie im Urchristentum* (1942), p. 44. Bonnard, *Philippiens*, p. 46: 'Le Christ reçoit une condition ou autorité plus grande encore que celle qu'il possédait avant son abaissement.' E. Stauffer, *New Testament Theology*, pp. 117 f. C. A. Anderson Scott, *Christianity according to St Paul* (1927), p. 272: 'That God when "He highly exalted him" gave Him the name and authority of Kyrios, the Lord, appears to indicate that Christ was after His resurrection admitted to higher glory than He had before.' Leivestad, *Christ the Conqueror*, p. 112: 'τὸ εἶναι ἴσα Θεῷ does not designate the original state of Christ, but a still higher rank, identical with that position to which he was finally exalted by God because of his humble self-abasement.' Hunter, *Paul and his Predecessors*, p. 50. H. A. A. Kennedy, *Commentary on Philippians*, p. 483. E. Andrews, *The Meaning of Christ for Paul*, p. 159: 'The latter [*sc.* His being equal with God] is a place of glory and honour surpassing that possessed in the pre-existence state.'

[3] Paul uses twenty word-formations with ὑπέρ. Cf. Caird, *The Apostolic Age*, p. 114. Limiting ourselves to the most striking examples, we may instance:

preposition is not to describe a different stage in Christ's existence in a comparative sense, but to contrast His Exaltation with the claim of other high powers, and thereby to proclaim His uniqueness and absoluteness (Michaelis).[1] 'God exalted him to the highest station' (Beare)[2] is a translation which forcefully expresses this thought, without any suggestion that He is elevated beyond His previous position.[3,4] The LXX version of Psalm xcvii (xcvi). 9: σὺ εἶ Κύριος ὁ ὕψιστος...σφόδρα ὑπερυψώθης ὑπὲρ πάντας τοὺς θεούς provides a close parallel of this superlative use of the preposition as the prefix of ὑπερ-

II Thess. i. 3: ὑπεραυξάνω; II Cor. iii. 10, ix. 14; Eph. i. 19, ii. 7, iii. 19: ὑπερβάλλω; II Cor. x. 14: ὑπερεκτείνω; Rom. viii. 26: ὑπερεντυγχάνω; Rom. viii. 37: ὑπερνικάω; Rom. v. 20; II Cor. vii. 4: ὑπερπερισσεύω. There are some expressive adverbs too: I Thess. iii. 10, v. 13 and Eph. iii. 20 (*c.* ὑπέρ)—a *hapax legomenon*: ὑπερεκπερισσοῦ.

[1] *Zur Engelchristologie*, p. 41.

[2] *Philippians*, p. 85: 'The thought is not that God exalts him to a higher rank than he held before, as *being in the form* of God. No such comparison between the pre-existent state of Christ and his exalted state is envisaged.'

[3] So G. Friedrich, *Philipper*, 'Jesus then is not only returned to the original form of being. He has not simply received the divine state which He formerly had, but is exalted beyond measure (*über alle Maßen*), so that He is now the Highest', 110.

G. Bornkamm, *loc. cit.*, 183 writes: 'One thing is certain, that this verse speaks not merely of a return of Christ to his pre-existent equality with God, but it gives him a new place.' This is the meaning of the composite form of the verb, which is pleonastic usage common in Hellenistic Greek and makes otiose Cullmann's rendering: 'er hat *mehr* getan, als ihn erhöht'. The *mehr* is not an accession of the fulness of power which He, as the equal with God, did not possess previously, but rather it is the manifestation of the worthiness of One who up to this time was hidden and the open and rightfully complete subjugation of the entire world. The installation of Christ as Lord in this cosmic sense explains why the verb is reinforced. Christ is promoted to the highest place and with the fullest power. E. Schweizer, *Erniedrigung*, p. 66, n. 286 accepts this: he renders '...hat Gott ihn überaus erhöht' and comments, 'Auch hier ist diese Erhöhung die Einsetzung in eine neue Würde'.

[4] Ὑψοῦν is 'used invariably in the LXX as a translation of *nasa* and *rum*, wherever in the Psalter the "elevation" or enthronement of either the king, the Anointed One, or Yahweh himself is under consideration'. So writes C. S. Mann, art. 'The New Testament and the Lord's Ascension', *CQR*, CLVIII (1957), 457. This is an important observation which leads us to think of the Exaltation of Christ in terms of His enthronement. There is, in this context, no comparison with His previous state. (Mann might have added the verb נבה, for which ὑπερυψοῦν is an LXX equivalent; cf. Euler, *op. cit.* 44.)

ὑψοῦν.[1] It is not the thought that Yahweh is on a step higher than other deities, but that He is unique and in a class apart because He is the incomparable One (Isa. xl. 18, xliv. 7; Jer. x. 6), and immeasurably greater than all idols. Käsemann's line of exegesis[2] accounts for the use of the strong verb with its reinforcing prefix and the significance of the phrase 'the name which is above every name', for, on his view, Christ is the World-Ruler who is manifestly enthroned above all the rulers and spirit-powers of the universe (as in Eph. i. 20, 21 where God elevates Him above all angelic Rulers, Authorities, Powers and Lords, above every name that is to be named not only in this age but in the age to come; and Heb. i. 4). He has received the name which is above all names, as Bengel observed, and not merely above all human names (*non modo super omne nomen humanum*). Käsemann takes this in a way which Bengel probably never dreamed about: Christ the *Cosmocrat* has the name above all the mythical powers.[3]

The conferring of the name is described in a way which betrays the imagery of an ancient ceremonial which may be detected elsewhere in the New Testament.[4] This is known to us from Egyptian enthronement ceremonies which set the enthronement of the divine king in three parts: exaltation, pre-

---

[1] Ὑπερυψοῦν is the LXX translation of the *niph'al* of עלה in this text from the Psalter. For a parallel usage of ὑπερυψοῦν in the superlative sense, I Clem. xiv, 5 may be cited: 'I saw the ungodly lifted high (ὑπερυψούμενον) ...as the cedars of Lebanon.'
Harder, *Paulus und das Gebet*, p. 58 finds an interesting parallel to the usage of ὑπερυψοῦν in Dan. iii. 65: εὐλογεῖτε πάντα τὰ πνεύματα, τὸν Κύριον ὑμνεῖτε καὶ ὑπερυψοῦτε αὐτὸν εἰς τοὺς αἰῶνας. This idea of cultic praise is, he says, the background of the Pauline text. 'The praising of the name in Greek-speaking Judaism is connected with ὑπερυψοῦν.'
[2] 'Kritische Analyse', 83 f.
[3] For the phrase 'above every name that is named', used of cosmic powers (apparently), cf. *The Gospel of Philip* 103 (124, 9–12), but the text is confused (R. McL. Wilson, *The Gospel of Philip*, p. 165).
[4] E. Schweizer, *Erniedrigung*, p. 65 (E.T. 65 f.) citing Jeremias *ad* I Tim. iii. 16 (*NTD*6 (1953), 22–3). The triple-action of this *Thronbesteigung* ceremony in Phil. ii. 9–11 is made up of (*a*) Elevation, *v.* 9*a*; (*b*) Proclamation of the Name, *v.* 9*b*; (*c*) Homage to the Enthroned one by gesture and confession, *vv.* 10 f. The same features of a ritual in three successive distichs are found in Heb. i. 5–14; Matt. xxviii. 18–20; cf. Jeremias, *Jesus' Promise to the Nations* (E.T. 1958), pp. 38–9. Full details of this enthronement rite are given by O. Michel, *Hebräerbrief*11 (*MeyerKomm.* 1960), p. 54.

sentation (before the gods) and enthronement (as the power of the office is seized). It is this cosmic setting which is prominent in the verse of the hymn in Philippians ii. 9. The name bestowed upon the victorious Christ is 'Lord' which derives from Isaiah xlv. 23, but this Old Testament citation is introduced incidentally to declare that Christ has now taken over the Rulership of the world. There is no cultic significance in the title (as Bousset thought),[1] but only a cosmic one as Christ is proclaimed as Lord, not of the Church, but of the whole universe. The final verses of the hymn confirm to Käsemann the correctness of this view as they unfold the universal homage which He receives as the 'criterion and Judge of all history', and the arbiter of all destiny.

[1] To summarize in a sentence or two Bousset's thesis, we may say that for him the origin of the title of *Kyrios* is to be sought in the Hellenistic communities, probably at Antioch, and in particular in their cultic veneration of Jesus which was modelled on that of the contemporary Hellenistic cults for which *Lord* was a current designation for the saviour-god. The *kyrioi* (I Cor. viii. 6) of these religions took their title from the cultus which grew up around them; and Bousset finds a parallel movement in the case of the use of the title of *Kyrios* as applied to Jesus. It is essentially a *cultic* term. See Bousset's *Kyrios Christos*[3] (1935), ch. III (75–104).

Lohmeyer took issue with this thesis on the ground that the confession in the Christ-psalm of Phil. ii (which he dated early) embraces the whole universe and is the expression of Christ's lordship over the cosmos and not the Church. The *Kyrios*-title speaks of Christ as World-ruler and not primarily as cultic deity, *Philipper*, pp. 97 f. and especially n. 6; *Kyrios Jesus*, pp. 60 f.: 'Es ist die entscheidende Wichtigkeit dieser Stelle [he is commenting on *vv.* 9–11], daß hier nicht von "einer gottesdienstlichen Verehrung", sondern von einer kosmischen Anbetung gesprochen ist.'

There has been a reaction to this (although Käsemann accepts Lohmeyer's view here, 'Kritische Analyse', 85). Jervell has challenged the methodological assumption and pointedly asks how the belief in the cosmic lordship of Christ could have grown up in a tradition which derives from 'a fragment of Eucharistic liturgy' which by its nature must be cultic: *Imago Dei*, p. 207, n. 135. And Cullmann, *Christ and Time* (E.T. 1951), pp. 186 f. has brought together the Church and the cosmos and placed both under the lordship of Christ. Both stand under the lordship of Christ, the Church consciously so and the world unwittingly. Therein lies the missionary task of the Church, to tell the world of an actual fact of which it is unaware. But there is no hiatus between the two concepts which are distinguishable but not separate, like two concentric circles.

D. SUMMING-UP

If we omit the exposition of Barth which is paradoxical and individualistic,[1] the interpretations fall into two main groups. There is no quarrel with the general understanding of the verse as depicting the reversal of Christ's fortune and His elevation from the depth of humiliation to the glory of His Father's acknowledgment in Resurrection and exaltation. The ground of this acknowledgment is a matter of some dispute, i.e. was it as a reward for His complete obedience, or was it an act of grace, 'the inversion, so to speak, of the self-emptying and of all the self-renunciation that followed upon it' (J. H. Michael)?[2] The latter seems more in keeping with the spirit of the passage and with the text itself. The term 'reward' by itself would need some closer definition.

The extent of His vindication and what it meant for Him is again an issue of debate. For one group of scholars the verse completes the thought of the earlier portion of the hymn. That which the pre-existent one refused to seize upon as His prize, namely equality with God, He is given in the good pleasure of God. Ἁρπαγμὸν ἡγήσατο and ἐχαρίσατο are correlatives.[3] This verse completes the circle of thought; and is a most illustrious example of the principle that humiliation leads to triumph. This principle is 'gloriously fulfilled in his own case' (Meyer). This suggestion chimes in with the Apostle's use of the passage in his Epistle. He is saying to the Philippians: As the obedient, self-effacing Lord was vindicated, so your lowliness of spirit, patterned on His, will not fail to produce the desired result in your church life. It is when the application is made like this that its incongruity is most obviously seen; and we shall revert to this point.

On the other hand, the controlling idea may be much simpler (or, as some think, only apparently so). God interposed when the obedience of Christ had run its course, and raised Him to the highest place. The stress falls upon the greatness of divine power which lifted Him from the thraldom of death; and this accounts for the emphatic verb: 'He *hyper*-exalted Him.'

---

[1] Schweizer, *Erniedrigung*, p. 66, n. 285, dismisses it in a sentence.

[2] J. H. Michael, *Philippians*, p. 93.

[3] So Stauffer, *New Testament Theology*, p. 284, n. 371.

HIS EXALTATION (VERSE 9)

As to the content of the name which is bestowed, there is now general agreement that this is to be understood in terms of *Kyrios*.[1] Admittedly, the precise content is not given and identification is not explicitly made, but it harmonizes with the drift of the passage that God gives to His obedient Son His own pre-eminent title;[2] and this is endorsed by verse 11. This name of Kyrios may well prove the most helpful starting-point from which to seek a path through the impasse of the two rival views of verse 9a. The repetition of the definite article in verse 9c prepares us for a declaration of the very name of God Himself. All that the Old Testament predicates of Yahweh—that He is exalted far above all demonic powers and idols and is worthy to receive the homage of the whole creation and that His name is all-excelling (the Rabbis spoke of 'Yahweh' as *šem hamᵉphôraš*)[3]

[1] E.g. Kennedy, *Philippians*, p. 438; Michael, *Philippians*, p. 94; Lohmeyer, *Kyrios Jesus*; Michaelis, *Zur Engelchristologie*, p. 42; Henry, col. 35; Käsemann, 'Kritische Analyse', 84; H. Bietenhard, *TWNT*, v, 272, ll. 9–11; Bornkamm, *loc. cit.* 183; Barth, *The Epistle to the Philippians*, 67; Beare, *Philippians*, p. 85; Bonnard, *Philippiens*, p. 46; F. C. Synge, *Philippians and Colossians* (1951), p. 32; C. A. A. Scott, *Christianity according to St Paul*, p. 272; K. Grayston, *Galatians and Philippians*, p. 94; P. Benoit, *Les épîtres*, p. 28, n. (*b*): 'Ce nom, c'est-à-dire ce titre, est celui de κύριος.' Cullmann, *Christology*, p. 217; *Idem*, art. 'The Kingship of Christ', etc. in *The Early Church* (E.T. 1956), pp. 105 f.; Stauffer, *New Testament Theology*, p. 118: *Idem*, *TWNT*, III, 105. J. Schmitt, *Jésus ressuscité*, p. 205; O. C. Quick, *Doctrines of the Creed*, p. 82; E. F. Scott, *Philippians*, p. 51; F. Tillmann, *Die Gefangenschaftsbriefe des heiligen Paulus*, p. 146: 'der über alle Namen ist, den Gott als Lohn und Gnadengeschenk Jesus verliehen hat. Es ist der Name Gottes selbst; der Name: Der Herr'; C. T. Craig, *The Beginning of Christianity* (1953), pp. 209 f. But Cerfaux, *Christ in the Theology of St Paul*, pp. 510 ff. has raised some objection to this identification.

[2] 'Gott ihm seinen eigenen Namen abtritt' (G. Friedrich, *Philipper, ad loc.*): 'Es ist Gottes eigener "Name", den er in seiner Erhöhung empfangen hat' (Bornkamm, *op. cit.* 183).

[3] For the meaning of 'the expressive name' (*šem hamᵉphôraš*) in Rabbinic thought, cf. Bousset–Gressmann, *op. cit.* 309 f. It was used to express all that the covenant name of Yahweh represented. Cf. C. Taylor, *Sayings of the Jewish Fathers²* (1897), pp. 66, 165–7. And on the importance of the Name in Jewish theology, cf. Lohmeyer, *Kyrios Jesus*, pp. 50 ff.; E. M. Sidebottom, *The Christ of the Fourth Gospel*, pp. 38 f. It may be significant that Jewish thought and expectation looked for the revelation of the *šem hamᵉphôraš* at the end of the present Age (*hā-'ôlām hazeh*); and viewed it as the eschatological sign that the new Age (*hā-'ôlām habā'*) had arrived (so G. Klein, *Der älteste christliche Katechismus* (1909), p. 44 quoting *Pes. Rabbati*: מכני שאינם סוד ש"; and cited by Harder, *op. cit.* 191). The name of God which is accorded to

—is applied to the exalted Christ at the behest of God Himself. The motion implied in ὑπερυψοῦν is such as to lead on naturally to the *sessio ad dextram Dei*;[1] and, as Foerster has shown in his study in *TWNT s.v.* κύριος, exaltation which is pictorially expressed by this metaphor connotes co-regency, i.e. the receiving and enjoyment of a dignity equal with God.[2] The name of Kyrios involves divine equality, for it authorizes Jesus to act in the capacity of God *vis-à-vis* the world, to receive the rightful obeisance of all created powers and to share the throne of the universe. If this is the important statement of this verse, there is no need (as Foerster says) to decide whether the *hyper* in the verb looks back to the beginning of the hymn or only means 'beyond all measure'. It betokens a status as Lord of all that can only be His at the completion of His redemptive mission by which God and the world are reconciled and that can only be His because the Father is pleased to commit it to Him. Equality with God which might have been His if He had snatched it (the *res rapienda* view of *harpagmos*) is hypothetical in more senses than one. It is a hypothetical interpretation of the biblical text. It is hypothetical also in the sense that equality with God could never have been seized in this way and wrested from the control of God. It is a status which can only be conferred as a gift; an office that can only be exercised in God's good will; a dignity which comes only as the recipient first treads the road of lowly

Christ in His glory is the index that the new Age has begun and that He is the Lord of the new Era—an interpretation which, if valid, has light to shed on *v*. 10.

[1] On the doctrine of *sessio*, see J. Daniélou, 'La session à la droite du Père', *The Gospels Reconsidered* (1961), pp. 68 ff. A. Seeberg, *Der Katechismus der Urchristenheit*, pp. 78 f. has an important consideration of this matter, maintaining that the *sessio* includes the subjugation of the spirits to the enthroned Christ and citing in evidence Eph. i. 20, iv. 8; Col. ii. 10, 11–13; I Cor. xv. 25; Polycarp, *ad Phil.* II, 1.

Käsemann ('Kritische Analyse', 85) draws out the significance of this in his remark that Christ is Lord of the new Aeon in the place He has received; and it is not by chance that elsewhere His lordship as *Weltherr* is acknowledged by the use of the Stoic τὰ πάντα formula (as in the texts above quoted and I Cor. viii. 6).

[2] W. Foerster, *TWNT*, III, 1088 (= E.T. 100): 'Sitting at the right hand of God connotes reigning with Him, i.e. divine status, as does the mere sitting in the presence of God.' Cf. G. B. Caird, 'To share the throne of God is to share the attributes of deity', *The Apostolic Age*, p. 46.

submission and self-denying obedience to God and his mission. It is the by-product, so to speak, of humility and service, something unsought-after which the disinterested Lord received not as a reward for what He had done or a prize for services rendered, but as the logical outcome of what obedience to God means in God's world and as the noblest illustration of God's power 'to exalt the humble and meek'.

APPENDIX

THE INTERPRETATION OF J. JERVELL

This note describes the unusual theory put forward by J. Jervell[1] in support of a partitioning of the Christ-hymn in Phil. ii. 6–11.

His discussion has the merit of addressing itself seriously to the issue: How are we to understand the relation of the exaltation of Christ to His pre-existence? (p. 212). A number of answers may be given, Jervell replies.

(i) The commonest view is that the exaltation represents a 'step up' in the place of Christ. Verses 9–11 speak of an increase of power. But this is quite pointless because in verse 6: ὃς ἐν μορφῇ Θεοῦ ὑπάρχων represents a maximum, for this phrase is a confession of Christ's deity which, by definition, cannot be increased. This assumes that Christ had divine equality in His pre-existence.

(ii) Verses 9–11 declare that the Heavenly Man has returned to His native place in a kind of 'as you were in the beginning' (restitutio in integrum). Christ the Urmensch appears again in the form of God which He had and laid aside. This is the view of Reitzenstein, Mysterienreligionen, pp. 357 ff. who adduces parallels to show the equivalence of μορφή and ὄνομα in Hellenistic religion. But Jervell exposes the weakness of this theory. The contrast is not between μορφή and ὄνομα but between the pre-existent μορφή of the Urmensch and His being hailed as Κύριος.

(iii) Verses 9–11 show the subordination of Christ in an emphatic manner. He is exalted to be Lord but He is so 'to the glory of God the Father' (v. 11). Jervell concludes from this fact: 'It seems that here a differently orientated Christology is being expressed, viz. one in which the human Christ is exalted to be Lord and Son of God, as in Rom. i. 3; Acts ii. 22 ff.; Luke xxiv. 19, etc.' Yet, if this is so, it is in open contradiction to the first part of the hymn which portrays Him as 'already God's Son in His pre-existence; in fact, more than the Son of God, He is Himself God' (p. 213). The difficult question is

---

[1] Imago Dei, pp. 212 f.

that of the identity of the Person. 'If we are really dealing here with a radical Kenosis, i.e. if "Form" equals "the inner being", "I", the true self, then where is the connection between the pre-existent and the earthly? But if "Form" equals the outward form, then the Incarnation of Christ is in danger and His Exaltation is merely an outward show; for He is only being given what He already has. His human form is merely a deceit; it is a mere covering for His divinity.'

From this analysis Jervell is driven to conclude that two diverse Christologies are set cheek by jowl in the hymn. In the first part, it is the Heavenly-Man-Christology of Him who came down from his pre-existent condition. There is no word of an ascension into heaven; but the accent falls simply upon His humility and *condescension*. In the second half, the teaching is that of the primitive Church that Jesus was promoted to lordship and sonship through His Resurrection and ascension (Acts ii. 36, v. 31; Rom. i. 3 f.).

Jervell's exposition is important because it faces the issues which others tend to skate over. It may be queried whether such a drastic conclusion as his is the only possible one. He sets out from the assumption that the pre-existent Christ was fully equal with God and no further enrichment of His state is therefore conceivable; but many scholars see the equality as an office which could only be His after His glorification and thus have no qualms about speaking of His 'new phase' of existence. Then, it may be doubted whether the second section of the hymn (*vv.* 9–11) does indeed teach a subordination of Christ to God as Jervell states ('Die Unterordnung Christi unter den Vater ist also in V. 9–11 deutlich hervorgehoben') on the basis of the phrase: εἰς δόξαν Θεοῦ πατρός. This may simply state that Christ is no rival of God, no 'second God', although in fact co-equal with God and partner of His throne. Moreover, it declares that the elevation of Christ to divine status is due to the Father's good pleasure (ἐχαρίσατο αὐτῷ, *v.* 9).

CHAPTER X

THE UNIVERSAL HOMAGE

ἵνα ἐν τῷ ὀνόματι Ἰησοῦ
πᾶν γόνυ κάμψῃ
ἐπουρανίων καὶ ἐπιγείων καὶ καταχθονίων
καὶ πᾶσα γλῶσσα ἐξομολογήσηται. (verses 10–11a)

The two final strophes (according to Lohmeyer's analysis) are
devoted to the praise of the name which ranks above all other
names. The English versions translate the introductory ἵνα by
'that', which disguises the two possible ways in which it may be
taken, whether as consequence ('so that in the name of Jesus
every knee should bow') or as purpose ('in order that in the
name of Jesus every knee might bow'). But the two ideas are
often confused in the thought and language of both Old and
New Testaments; and tend to run together.[1] That which God
has purposed in the exaltation of Christ follows, as His name
becomes the object of worship and praise. Three things may be
discussed in relation to this universal homage which is rendered
to His name.

A. THE OBJECT AND OCCASION OF THE HOMAGE

(i) Lord of the Church

Some older writers thought that this verse meant that the worship was directed to the Father in the name of Jesus (as in John
xvi. 23–4),[2] but the parallel words of verse 11b which describes
explicitly the act of reverence as paid directly to the Son and 'to

[1] F. M. Abel, *Grammaire du grec biblique* (1927), § 64, 4: 284; Funk-
Blass-Debrunner, *A Greek Grammar of the New Testament* (E.T. 1961), § 391.
[2] De Wette, Hofmann and Wohlenberg, as quoted by Henry, *Suppl. DB*,
col. 36. Michael, *Philippians*, p. 96, comments: 'Is the worship paid directly
to His Name, or to the Father *in* his Name? Each view has its advocates. It is
highly probable that the words speak of the direct ascription of worship to
the Son.' Lightfoot takes the same view, *op. cit.* 114, as does Henry, 'Kénose'.
Cf. Moule, *Philippians*, p. 69. Beare, *Philippians*, pp. 86f. and Heitmüller, *Im
Namen Jesu*, p. 67, take the other view, citing Eph. iii. 14.

the glory of God the Father', and the construction of this clause in 10*a* and *b* where the use of ἐν τῷ ὀνόματι implies that direct adoration is meant (as in I Kings viii. 44 and several places in the Psalter[1] as well as the common phrase, 'to invoke the name of the Lord'[2]) describe the exalted Christ as the recipient. In the phrase ἐν τῷ ὀνόματι Ἰησοῦ the genitive is not explicative but possessive. It is not 'the name Jesus', but 'the name which belongs to Jesus' that is meant.[3] And, as was noticed earlier, the name which God has conferred upon Him in His exaltation is most likely that of Lord. J. H. Michael is therefore justified when he explains that the 'Name of Jesus' stands for 'Jesus as bearing the new Name of Lord conferred on him by the Father'.[4]

If this is a sound conclusion, it helps to point to a correct understanding of the occasion which is referred to in the line: ἵνα ἐν τῷ ὀνόματι Ἰησοῦ πᾶν γόνυ κάμψῃ. There are two possibilities of interpretation. On the one side, the introductory phrase may mean that all creatures bow the knee and confess the lordship of Christ as they call upon His name.[5] The construction then is that of ἐν with the instrumental dative which is used to express the thought of the attendant circumstances of an action. The proclaiming of the name of Jesus is the accompanying circumstance of the submission. A parallel text would be Acts ii. 38.

A second view places the emphasis, not on the submission by itself, but on the proclaiming of the name which evokes the sub-

---

[1] Cf. Pss. lxiii. 5: ἐν τῷ ὀνόματί σου ἀρῶ τὰς χεῖράς μου; xliv. 10: ἐν τῷ ὀνόματί σου ἐξομολογησόμεθα; cv. 3: ἐπαινεῖσθε ἐν τῷ ὀνόματι τῷ ἁγίῳ αὐτοῦ.

[2] For the expression ἐπικαλεῖσθαι ἐν ὀνόματι Κυρίου representing the Hebrew קרא בשם יהוה see I Kings xviii. 24, 25, 26; II Kings v. 11; Ps. xx. 8, cxvi. 17; II Chron. xxviii. 15 as well as the well-known reference in Gen. iv. 26. These references imply the practice of the cult of Deity, and the expression comes over into the New Testament in such places as Acts ii. 21; Rom. x. 12 ff.; I Cor. i. 2.

[3] So Plummer, *Philippians*, p. 48.   [4] Michael, *Philippians*, p. 96.

[5] The knowledge of a name is a primitive idea. It implies, for example, the ability to render honour to the one who possesses the name, as in Judges xiii. 17. Ἐν τῷ ὀνόματι is a formula of invocation and worship in the LXX and in Col. iii. 17; Eph. v. 20. For uses in exorcism, cf. Mk. ix. 38, xvi. 17; Lk. ix. 49, and in healing the sick, Acts iii. 6, Jas. v. 14. Cf. Heitmüller, *op. cit.* 19 ff. for LXX usages.

mission of the creatures.[1] This is the view of many recent scholars who accept the translation offered by Bauer–Arndt–Gingrich: 'that when the name of Jesus is proclaimed (or mentioned) every knee should bow'.[2] The phrase ἐν τῷ ὀνόματι is not a formula of invocation here, as though the cosmic powers were invoking that name which Jesus has. Rather, its meaning is that when the name is uttered in the heavenly court they prostrate themselves in subjection and acknowledgment that this is the name over all. The importance of this distinctive meaning will be apparent as we proceed, for it marks a new departure in the interpretation of the closing stanzas of the hymn. On the first view, the calling of all creatures upon the name of Jesus is understood as a reverent submission to His lordship and authority; and a cultic confession of His God-given right to rule. This is in line with the earlier parts of the hymn. God has elevated Him to the place of honour and given Him His own name of Lord: now it is the natural thing that His rank and dignity should be acclaimed by the bending of the knee and the confessing of His name, although some commentators prefer to see in the homage which is rendered a worship of God which is offered in Jesus' name, i.e. on the ground of the lordship which God has given to Jesus (so G. Delling).[3] With this alternative assessment is bound up the wider issue of whether the early Church actually invoked Jesus in prayer and praise as distinct from addressing God in His name.[4] Most writers see in this Philippians-hymn a

[1] Thus the proclaiming of the name of Jesus is not the accompanying circumstance, but rather the efficient cause, of the submission: so Ewald, *Der Brief des Pl. an die Philipper*[3], p. 129, n. 2: 'The accent falls not on the act of submission but on the ἐν τῷ ὀνόματι Ἰησοῦ. The novelty is not the worship in general, but the worship in Jesus' name.'

[2] Bauer–Arndt–Gingrich, *Lexicon*, pp. 576 and 403; cf. C. F. D. Moule, *An Idiom-Book of New Testament Greek*[1], p. 78 (but cf. his second edition); and T. W. Manson, *The Beginning of the Gospel* (1950), p. 111; 'at the mention of the name Jesus'.

[3] On Philippians ii. 10, Delling, *Worship in the New Testament*, E.T. p. 106 says: 'Obviously (*sic*) it is not concerned with a worshipping of Jesus but of God which is offered "in the Name of Jesus", i.e. on the ground of the Lordship which God has given to Jesus (*v.* 11).' Barth similarly writes: 'The purpose of God's grace in giving Jesus the name "Lord" is, that…God may be worshipped by every creature' (*The Epistle to the Philippians*, p. 68).

[4] For example, P. Henry appends this note to the verse: 'Il [*sc.* St Paul] applique donc consciemment à Jésus un hommage qu'il sait réservé à

251

clear case of the evidence which leads to a positive answer to the question; for it shows that the glorified Jesus is the object of worship in the same way as the Jews invoked their covenant God.[1]

(ii) *Lord of the world*

The second way of understanding the text begins with Lohmeyer's decisive rejection of this cultic interpretation.[2] He writes: 'The scene here is that of an enthronement by means of which "the Lord of the world", having won a "victory", is proclaimed and acclaimed by the entire universe. . . .' There is no place for the Church as a confessing Church. It is 'cosmic acclamation of His lordship, and not religious worship, which is meant. Lordship signifies that He is, above all, Lord of the world, and not Lord of the Church.' These sentences are but one further instance of the way in which Lohmeyer's treatment of Philippians ii has proved a turning-point in our understanding of the whole hymn both in its structure and significance.[3] Continental scholars have taken these insights of Lohmeyer and developed them in considerable detail; but in each case they

Yahweh' ('Kénose', 36). The text is clear attestation of the divinity of Christ, he goes on to say.

[1] For a full treatment of the subject of the veneration of Christ in early Christianity, cf. Max Meinertz, *Theologie des Neuen Testamentes* (1950), I, 179–81; II, 75; Andrews, *The Meaning of Christ for Paul*, pp. 126–9.

[2] *Philipper*, p. 97; cf. *Kyrios Jesus*, p. 60: 'Es ist kosmische, nicht ekklesiastische oder "kultische" Betrachtung, und Herr sein bedeutet darum zunächst Herr der Welt, nicht aber Herr einer Gemeinde sein.'

[3] The influence is registered upon such writers as Käsemann, 'Kritische Analyse', 85; Bornkamm, 'Zum Verständnis des Christus-Hymnus', 183 in a most emphatic statement; Friedrich, *Philipper*, p. 111; Beare, *Philippians*, p. 86; Schweizer, *Erniedrigung*, pp. 63 f.; Dibelius, *Philipper*[3], p. 79; Michaelis, *Philipper*, pp. 42–3.

O. Michel expresses this newer interpretation in a concise way ('Zur Exegese von Phil. 2, 5–11', 95): 'This enthronement of the humiliated is not confined to the Church, but displays His temporarily interrupted authority over the world. . .The hymn praises the Redeemer's act of salvation and treats of the subjection of the powers by His Exaltation to be Lord. The Old Testament text (in Isa. xlv. 18–25) speaks of human beings who were directly wooed and won by God; in the New Testament paraphrase it is the saving act of the Redeemer who receives the rulership of the world and the acclamation of the powers. Subjection and Acclamation belong very closely together. . . (note 2: The confession here belongs within the cosmic setting to the act of the enthronement itself).'

start from this basic assumption that it is a piece of cosmic drama which is unfolded in the closing part of the hymn. We are not to think in terms of the Church's liturgical practice in her worship of Christ as the Lord of the community; we are to envisage, rather, the court of heaven (as in the imagery of Apocalypse v. 1–14, a chapter which Lohmeyer regards as identical in its symbolical meaning with Philippians ii. 9 ff.)[1] with the entourage of heavenly beings which greet the exalted Lord and offer to Him their homage. It is immaterial whether the text means that Jesus is the name above all or that Jesus has this name which is above all names, although Lohmeyer inclines to the second alternative. Both His being and His possession—what He is and what He has—add up to the same thing. He is Lord; and it is His lordly name which is announced in solemn fashion, and which evokes the submission of the spirit-powers in the presence of God.

In this scene the hymn takes us into the world of the eternal and the 'mythical'.[2] Lohmeyer finds it, therefore, in order to speak of the 'timelessness of eternity' (both here and in his interpretation of the Apocalypse's descriptions of the other world)[3] as he thinks of the poet caught up in the Spirit (the same Spirit which inspired the Old Testament scriptures; and this explains why use is made of Isaiah xlv. 23 without any introductory formula such as 'it is written', as in Romans xiv. 11) and attempting to portray with his words a scene which is 'out of this world'. His language then belongs to the eternal present of divine revelation as the humiliated and now exalted Lord takes His place in the heavenly realm and is greeted with divine honours. The entire universe salutes this triumph and confesses His dominion. Yet it is striking that it is the name 'Jesus' which is used. 'Into this timelessness steps, with singular importance, the name of a historical figure: it is the name of

[1] On Apoc. v. 1–14 Lohmeyer comments: 'The scene recalls in the most vivid way the enthronement of a new Ruler' (*HzNT: Die Offenbarung des Johannes* (1953 ed.), p. 51).

[2] Taking 'myth' to describe 'the use of imagery to express the other-worldly in terms of this world and the divine in terms of human life, the other side in terms of this side' (Bultmann, in *Kerygma and Myth*, 1 (E.T. 1953), 10).

[3] Lohmeyer, *Philipper*, p. 97; *Kyrios Jesus*, pp. 57 ff. and in his commentary on the Apocalypse *ut supra, passim*. But see the criticism by Cullmann, *Christ and Time*, p. 79.

Jesus.' It may seem incongruous that the earthly name is employed; but this has been done 'in order—so it seems—to remain in the realm of the historical', and to show that the revelation of God is made within the context of the humiliated and exalted Jesus. It is He who imparts meaning and value to the worship of God.

Lohmeyer leaves his discussion at that point. It is taken up by Käsemann who finds in the reference to the name of 'Jesus' *simpliciter* a characteristic which distinguishes myth from the Christian use which is made of myth in this hymn.[1] The human name of Jesus does not betray any interest in the historical Jesus as such; rather it focuses interest upon His obedience and its complementary vindication by God. The name holds together the two parts of the hymn, thereby telling us that 'the obedient One determines the universe and its history in this way (namely, He has passed through history as obedient at all points, even to the extremity of death; and is now installed as World-ruler)— and He alone as the obedient One. And what is meant in this case by obedience is plain from the interpretation of verses 7–8, viz., that humiliation is accepted as the possibility of freedom to serve. This is never proclaimed in the myth, which was, and always is, interested in apotheosis.[2] Here is its boundary, and here it is shown that the early Christian message is simply using the framework of the myth', breaking free from it at this crucial point by declaring that it is not concerned with a cult hero who is at length deified, but with the exaltation of *this One*— whose name is Jesus—who lived a life of self-denying abasement and obedience.[3] The name is the index of the distinctive Christian content which is added to the framework of the myth.

This complex discussion from the pen of Käsemann has taken

[1] 'Kritische Analyse', 89 f. Cf. J. M. Robinson, *A New Quest of the Historical Jesus* (1959), pp. 51 ff. The older criticism which fastened upon the name of Jesus as showing that it was the 'Jesus of history' who had been exalted is challenged by Robinson, *op. cit.* 88: 'A myth does not become historical simply by appropriating the name of a historical personage.'

[2] For apotheosis in this context cf. S. Lösch, *Deitas Jesu und antike Apotheose* (1933), sections I–II (1–67).

[3] '"Jesus" is the earthly name of Him who sacrificed His life on the cross. The Exaltation has not effaced the time of the humiliation; rather, the exalted one remains the crucified', comments G. Friedrich, *ad loc.*

us into a consideration of the meaning of the homage in its present relevance. We have now to return to see how it has been viewed by the older interpreters.

B. THE SCOPE AND SIGNIFICANCE OF THE HOMAGE

The universal scope of the adoration and confession is indicated by the use of the descriptive words: '*every* knee...*every* tongue'. There are two matters on which the expositors' attention has been concentrated. These are the use of the Old Testament citation; and the meaning of the triadic phrase: ἐπουρανίων καὶ ἐπιγείων καὶ καταχθονίων.

(i) *The use of Isaiah xlv. 23*

The LXX of Isaiah xlv. 23 runs: ὅτι ἐμοὶ κάμψει πᾶν γόνυ | καὶ ὀμεῖται πᾶσα γλῶσσα τὸν Θεόν with a variant reading of ἐξομολογήσεται in place of ὀμεῖται (read by א*B) in AQSᶜ. The setting of this passage in Isaiah xlv is of interest. Yahweh foretells the universal worship which one day will be offered to Him. 'I am God, and apart from me there is no other. I am the righteous One, and the saviour, and there is no other. Turn back to me and you will be saved, you who come from the ends of the earth. I am God and there is no other. By my own name I have sworn: from my mouth come words of righteousness and what I say cannot be turned aside, because every knee shall bend before me and every tongue shall confess to God' (Isa. xlv. 21 ff.). In this context the uniqueness of Israel's God is proclaimed and His universal triumph is hailed. The use which Philippians ii. 10 f. makes of the two parts of the *parallelismus membrorum* in the Isaiah text confirms to Lohmeyer[1]—and most commentators, with the exception of Harder,[2] follow him here—

---

[1] *Kyrios Jesus*, p. 57; the maximum value is placed upon the Old Testament allusions in the Philippians verses by Cerfaux, *Christ in the Theology of St Paul*, pp. 393 ff.; and Henry, 'Kénose', 47.

[2] *Paulus und das Gebet*, p. 59: he finds the *Vorbild* of Phil. ii. 10 f. not in Isa. xlv directly (as Lohmeyer believed), but in the Jewish '*Alenu* prayer which utilizes the Isaiah text. The relevant parts of the prayer run as follows:

כִּי לְךָ תִּכְרַע כָּל־בֶּרֶךְ
תִּשָּׁבַע כָּל־לָשׁוֹן
וְלִכְבוֹד שִׁמְךָ [הַגָּדוֹל] יְקָר יִתֵּנוּ

255

that the *auctor* of the hymn is drawing upon this prophecy and applying it to Christ. What God had announced as a future promise is now, for this hymn, a reality.[1] And in this realization the mould is broken as a larger fulfilment is actualized. The prophet had expected a turning to Yahweh of all the nations upon earth. The hymn extends the scope to include all sentient beings throughout the entire cosmos.[2] The exact scope of this acknowledgment is a matter of some dispute, but it is suggestive of a high doctrine of the place of the exalted Lord that this Old Testament prediction is taken over and re-applied to Him.[3] We may contrast here Romans xiv. 11 in which the same Old Testament verse is used in reference to God the Father and with the introductory formula: γέγραπται. The influence of Isaiah in the Philippians-psalm is unconscious and is not shown as an acknowledged quotation (as P. Henry notes).[4] The reason for this fact may lie in the peculiar capacity of the hymn-writer of Philippians ii. 6 ff. as one who felt himself standing in a pneumatic as distinct from a didactic succession,[5] composing

The main point which Harder emphasizes in support of his theory is that the *'Alenu* prayer contains also the phrase לכבוד which would account for the Pauline εἰς δόξαν Θεοῦ. In some Greek-speaking synagogue, he maintains, the Hebrew תשבע was rendered by ἐξομολογήσεται as in Phil. ii. 11 against the LXX's ὀμεῖται. This linguistic parallel is part of the evidence he marshals in defence of the thesis that 'der Philipperbriefhymnus ist auf jüdischem Gebetsgut aufgebaut' (59).

The dating of the *'Alenu* prayer is uncertain. The first half of the 3rd c. A.D. is the usual date, but its substance may be much earlier. 'That it expresses the conception of the Kingdom of God at the beginning of our era there is no question' (Moore, *Judaism*, 1 (1927), p. 434; cf. I. Elbogen, *Jüdischer Gottesdienst*, p. 143; Kohler, *Jewish Encycl.* 1, 336 ff.).

[1] 'That which has been decreed by God from eternity is now fulfilled in the eschatological present', O. Michel, 'Zur Exegese von Phil. 2, 5–11', 94 f.

[2] Bonnard, *L'épître aux Philippiens*, p. 46: 'It is not a matter of lordship over all the Gentiles, but over all living beings in the universe.'

[3] Henry, 'Kénose', 47: 'Le Christ, selon S. Paul, est digne des honneurs mêmes que l'A.T. réserve à Yahweh'; Bonnard, *op. cit.* 46: 'il est important de noter que l'élévation du Christ est décrite ici par un des textes les plus monothéistes de l'Ancien Testament. Jésus-Christ est élevé à la dignité même du Dieu de l'Ancien Testament.'

[4] The author of Phil. ii. 10 f. may be quoting Isa. xlv. 23 from the Targum. This would account for his use of the verb ἐξομολογεῖσθαι as also in Rom. xiv. 11. Cf. E. E. Ellis, *Paul's Use of the Old Testament* (1957), p. 144.

[5] This distinction between 'didaktischer und pneumatischer Rede' is made by Lohmeyer, *Kyrios Jesus*, p. 57. It is objected to by Delling, *Der Gottesdienst*,

under the direct afflatus of the Spirit. It does, however, bear an important testimony to his conception of the meaning of Christ's present place in the Father's presence. He is there as the sharer of the unique lordship of Yahweh and the rightful recipient of such worship and praise as God alone may command.

(ii) *The threefold division of the universe*

The phrase, 'of things in heaven, and things in earth, and things under the earth' is represented in the Greek by three adjectives with connecting particles. The A.V. and R.V. take the adjectives to refer to implied neuter nouns; hence 'things', a translation for which Lightfoot argues.[1] On his view, it is the whole created universe which joins in worship; and he thinks that the amplified phrase is a general expression for the whole universe of nature and men. He cites in support Psalm cxlviii in which Nature sings the praise of her Creator, and Romans viii. 22 where Paul speaks of 'all creation' as awaiting the redemption of Christ and as possessed of certain emotional qualities (verse 19: creation 'waits'; verse 22: 'is groaning in travail'). Although not many scholars share Lightfoot's interpretation, there is perhaps more to be said for it than this negative verdict—which is well-nigh universal[2]—would indicate. It may be questioned whether we are to interpret the phrase *au pied de la*

p. 96, n. 6 on the ground that the teacher is as much conscious of the inspiration of the Spirit as the 'pneumatic' (*der Geisterfüllte*) as I Cor. ii. 13 shows. But in the case of Paul he was both teacher and 'spiritual man' who knew the direct awareness of the Spirit's activity in such phenomena as speaking with tongues (I Cor. xiv. 6, 18, 19) and rapture (II Cor. xii. 1 f.). It is the latter type of experience (as in Apoc. i. 10, iv. 1) which has produced the Christ-hymn of our study.

For the latest suggestion concerning the respective rôles of charismatic prophet and teacher, 'Scripture-student', in the early Church, see A. N. Wilder, 'Form-history and the oldest Tradition', *Neotestamentica et Patristica: Festschrift Cullmann*, ed. W. C. van Unnik (1962), p. 7.

[1] Lightfoot, *Philippians*, p. 115, followed by Moule, *Philippians*, pp. 69 f.

[2] Some of the criticism is ill-founded. For instance, when Müller, *Philippians and Philemon*, p. 88, objects that the bowing of the knee and the confession of the tongue by the subjects of the triadic phrase must refer to personal beings because it is only in poetical parts of the scripture that we find inanimate nature personified, does he not overlook the fact that Phil. ii is exactly a poem in its structure and a 'myth' in its intention? See p. 253.

lettre; and imagine that the writer had in mind formal distinctions of denizens in three separate compartments of the universe. It may be that the phrase is a rhetorical pleonasm, expressed with the amplitude of poetic licence, for the whole universe. It is as though the writer were saying that the range of Christ's victory and sovereignty is all-embracing and complete and that there is no limit to it, without stopping to justify a poetic exaggeration.[1]

There are two other views which insist upon a literal reading of these words and seek to give a concrete application to the terms. By taking the epithets to be masculine in gender, the majority of exegetes see here a threefold division of the universe. On the one hand, the division is between angels in heaven, men upon earth and either the departed dead in Sheol[2] or demons under the earth.[3] This is the opinion of many older scholars. On the other hand, investigations which have utilized documents which relate to non-Christian beliefs have traced these terms to spirit-forces which the ancients thought to control the inhabitants in heaven, on earth and in the underworld. Scholars such as Seeberg and Dibelius[4] called attention to this strange litera-

---

[1] See Leivestad, *Christ the Conqueror*, pp. 113 f. for the same conclusion from a different angle; and F. X. Durrwell, *The Resurrection* (E.T. 1960), p. 114, citing J. Huby, *Les épîtres de la Captivité*[3] (1935), p. 314, n. 4, Paul 'meant by this triple designation to affirm the submission to Christ of all beings, animate and inanimate, in short, of the whole universe'.

[2] Thus Müller, *op. cit.* 88 and Alford, *ad loc.* This division goes back to Clement of Alexandria and Theodoret who writes: ἐπουρανίους καλεῖ τὰς ἀοράτους δυνάμεις, ἐπιγείους δὲ τοὺς ἔτι ζῶντας ἀνθρώπους καὶ καταχθονίους τοὺς τεθνεῶτας (quoted by Kennedy, *Phil. ad loc.*).

[3] So Chrysostom; Michaelis, *op. cit.* 42: 'men, angels, demons', and apparently Lohmeyer, *Kyrios Jesus*, p. 59, on the ground that three realms of existence are embraced: heaven, earth and hell, but he refuses to speculate further as to the inhabitants of these domains. The important thing is that it is the worship of the entire cosmos which is included. Cf. Ewald's confession that 'we know too little of the Apostle's ideas to be able to venture upon a decision' (*Philipper, ad loc.*).

[4] A. Seeberg, *Die Didache des Judentums und der Urchristenheit*, p. 81; and Dibelius, *Die Geisterwelt*, esp. pp. 11, 231 and *An die Philipper*[3], p. 79, which starts from two suppositions. First, Dibelius interprets the 'name above every name' (*v.* 9) as meaning the all-powerful name, i.e. the name which is more powerful than that of the spirits and is supreme in this spirit-world. Then, the term ἐπιγείων does not merely signify 'men upon the earth'. It refers to the spirits which motivate human activity. According to Eph. ii. 2

ture which describes how these mighty spirits were spoken of as in command of heaven, earth and the *tiers monde*; and E. Peterson's full-scale treatise[1] on this subject has convinced many interpreters that this is the background to the New Testament references, and to Philippians ii. 10–11 in particular.[2] On this latter view the text sets out, not the human adoration of Jesus, but the acknowledgment on the part of the mighty angelic powers which were thought to rule over the realms of the cosmos —astral, terrestrial and chthonic—that the exalted Christ is World-ruler. There is no cultic significance in this, but the open admission that these powers are now subservient to the One who is installed in the place of cosmic authority. The data for the view are:

(*a*) The division of the universe into three realms under the control of the mighty spirits is known in ancient cosmology, as Peterson has shown. There is evidence that the same views were shared by Jews who came under Greek influence, as part of the general development of angelology in later Judaism in the Greek period.[3] The closest linguistic parallels to this reference to the ἐπουράνιοι, the ἐπίγειοι and καταχθόνιοι are in two texts

the chief spirit whose locale is above the earth works in the sons of disobedience. See also I Cor. x. 20 f.; I Tim. iv. 1 f., as well as references to demonic activity in the Gospels and Acts. On this latter point, cf. J. M. Robinson, *The Problem of History in Mark* (1957), pp. 28 ff.

[1] E. Peterson, *HEIS THEOS* (1926), esp. pp. 159, 259 n. 2, 262 f., 326 f. for the threefold division of the cosmos in Hellenistic thought.

[2] So Dibelius, *ut supra*; Käsemann, 'Kritische Analyse', 86; Heitmüller, *Im Namen Jesu*, pp. 67, 322 ff. Schweizer, *Erniedrigung*, p. 66, n. 288; J. Michl, *Theol. Quart.* IV (1946), 450. F. W. Beare, *op. cit.* 86, 75; H. Traub, *TWNT*, V, 541–2: 'Hiermit ist keine verallgemeinernde Ortsangabe gemacht, sondern mit allen drei Gliedern ist an herrschende Geistermächte gedacht'; G. B. Caird, *Principalities and Powers*, ix, n. 10 who remarks that ἐπουρανίων in Phil. ii. 11 refers to heavenly beings in the same sense as Eph. iii. 10.

[3] See Cullmann, *Christ and Time*, p. 193 for references to Daniel, Ecclesiasticus and Enoch as well as the Talmud and Midrash. The Jews interpreted Psalm cx, which originally related to the conquest of Israel's enemies, as referring to the invisible powers which stood behind the nations. This prepared the way for the same process as we find in Phil. ii. 10 in its treatment of Isa. xlv which originally spoke of the worship of the Gentiles but is now applied to spirit-powers. For the teaching of angelic powers in control of the nations in later Judaism, cf. Caird, *Principalities and Powers*, ch. I.

which speak of demonic activity. These are in the great Paris magical papyrus;[1] and in the Ignatian letters.[2]

(b) O. Cullmann[3] has made the significant observation that, whenever in the New Testament and in early Christian literature the full lordship of Christ is asserted, His victory over the angel-powers is included. The confessions of faith in the early Church 'emphasize with characteristic regularity the subjection of the invisible powers under Him'; and Philippians ii. 6–11 is a notable illustration of this feature.

[1] P.Par. 574: 3041 ff. (3rd cent. A.D.) cited by Deissmann, *Light from the Ancient East*[4] (E.T. 1927), p. 261: 'And say thou whatsoever thou art, in heaven, or of the air, or on earth, or under the earth or below the ground' (ll. 35, 36 in C. K. Barrett's ed. *The New Testament Background: Selected Documents* (1956), p. 32). At line 32 the adjuration is directed to 'every daemonic spirit'. This is then elaborated to include: ἐπουράνιον ἢ ἀέριον εἴτε ἐπίγειον εἴτε ὑπόγειον ἢ καταχθόνιον. Cf. P.Lond. 46: 167 (4th cent. A.D.): ἵνα μοι ἦν ὑπήκοος πᾶς δαίμων οὐράνιος καὶ αἰθέριος καὶ ἐπίγειος καὶ ὑπόγειος. Dibelius cites an interesting text which also speaks of the submission of the demons (P.Oxy. XI, 1380, 164: οἱ...δαίμονες ὑπήκοοί σοι [γί]νο[ν]ται); and the way in which the demons were thought to have control of the various parts of the cosmos is clearly brought out in the texts quoted by Harder, *Paulus und das Gebet*, p. 58, n. 2: Apuleius, *Met.* XI, 5 f.: *te superi colunt, observant inferi, tibi respondent sidera*; P.Par. 2798: φύλαξόν με ἀπὸ παντὸς δαίμονος ἀερίου καὶ ἐπιγείου καὶ ὑπογείου; Livy I, xxxii, 10: *diique omnes caelestes, vosque terrestres, vosque inferni, audite*; Orphic fragment: τρία γένη, οὐράνιον καὶ ἐπίγειον καὶ τὸ μεταξὺ τούτων.

[2] Ignatius, *ad Trall.* IX, 1: 'Jesus Christ...was truly crucified and died in the sight of those in heaven and on earth and under the earth (βλεπόντων τῶν ἐπουρανίων καὶ ἐπιγείων καὶ ὑποχθονίων). For two different assessments of this text's witness to the historical Christ, see H. Schlier, *Religionsgeschichtliche Untersuchungen zu den Ignatiusbriefen* (1929), pp. 14 f., 67 ff., and Virginia Corwen, *St Ignatius and Christianity in Antioch*, pp. 94, 180, 184 f. Ignatius seems to be saying that the reality of Christ's death was attested by three sets of foes: the first class are the principalities and powers which crucified Him and were overthrown by that death (I Cor. ii. 8; Col. ii. 15); the second group are the enemies of the Lord on a human plane who brought about His death; while the third was '"the strong man" whom Christ has now bound, so that He might "spoil his goods", and release from Hades the awaiting spirits of the righteous who were "Christians before the time"' (J. Lawson, *A Theological and Historical Introduction to the Apostolic Fathers* (1961), p. 127). But the text is taken to represent 'the characteristic gnostic concept of the work of salvation as the work of cosmic liberation' by Bultmann, 'Bekenntnis- und Liedfragmente im 1. Pet.', 7–8; and Schlier, *Religionsgeschichtliche Untersuchungen*, pp. 14 ff.

[3] *The Earliest Christian Confessions*, E.T. 59–62; *Christ and Time*, p. 154, quoting Rom. viii. 38 f.; I Pet. iii. 22; I Tim. iii. 16; Polyc. II, 1. Add Heb. i. 6.

In adopting this line of approach, Cullmann has developed some suggestions which had earlier been made by Seeberg and Heitmüller.[1] These scholars sought to find the origin of the confession 'Jesus Christ is Lord' partly in the use of this formula in exorcism. When the name of Christ is mentioned, all the hostile demonic powers submit and fall down before Christ (as in Mark iii. 11, v. 6; cf. Mark ix. 38; Matt. vii. 22; Luke ix. 49, x. 17). In the second century, Justin's *Dialogue with Trypho* is a witness to the use of the name in casting out evil spirits and Justin adds that this expulsion is made possible because Christ is the 'Lord of the powers' (Κύριος τῶν δυνάμεων) and every demon is subject to Him (πᾶν δαιμόνιον ἐξορκιζόμενον νικᾶται καὶ ὑποτάσσεται).[2] In a similar context, Irenaeus uses not only the words ἐπουράνια, ἐπίγεια, καταχθόνια to denote the scope of Christ's lordship, but quotes Philippians ii. 10 in reference to the subjugation of the powers as they pay homage to Christ by bowing the knee and confessing with the mouth that He is Lord.[3]

From these attestations the inference is drawn that by the confession of His exalted position (contained in the formula, 'Jesus Christ is Lord' in verse 11) we are to understand that He is acknowledged as Lord of all angelic forces, especially malevolent demons. They are compelled to admit that He is the victor; and they show their submission by their prostration before Him.[4]

Käsemann[5] argues that the complete lordship of the risen Christ and the universal homage which is paid to Him by these angelic beings must imply that these powers which had been hostile to Him have been overcome. He finds confirmation of this teaching in Colossians i. 20 where Christ is hailed as the Reconciler of all things, both in heaven and on earth; and in Colossians ii. 15 which speaks of a disarming of the principalities

[1] Seeberg, *Die Didache*, p. 81; Heitmüller, *Im Namen Jesu*, pp. 65 ff.; 236 ff. Jervell, *Imago Dei*, pp. 207 f. seeks to connect the Name of Jesus with baptismal practice.
[2] Justin, *Dial.* LXXXV; cf. *ibid.* XXX, CXI, CXXI.
[3] Irenaeus, *adv. Haer.* I, 10. 1.
[4] This is clearly pictured in *Asc. Isa.* xi. 23 ff.; I Enoch xlviii. 5; and some scholars (e.g. Lohmeyer, *Kyrios Jesus*, p. 60 n.; Bultmann, *ZNTW*, xxiv (1925), 121 ff.) find it in I Tim. iii. 16; Ignatius, *Eph.* xix; *Odes Sol.* xvii. 6, xli. 6; and the Mandaean literature.
[5] Käsemann, 'Kritische Analyse', 87 ff.

and powers and their conquest by Christ upon the Cross. Thus he concludes:[1] 'The pacification of the universe is accomplished by the overthrow of those powers which up to that time claimed and played the rôle of the arbiters of Fate (*Schicksalsträger*). The coming-to-power (*Herrschaftsantritt*) of the Redeemer unites the universe by disarming them.[2] He is at once the Reconciler and Conqueror of the world. And this is not only to be "read between the lines", as Lohmeyer says; but it is explicitly stated when the worship and acclamation of the cosmic powers appear as an integral part of the enthronement of Christ. Only thus does the title and cry, "Kyrios Jesus Christ" take on all its depth and fulness.'

The inference that Käsemann has drawn from the texts in Colossians to the effect that Christ's dominion implies His conquest of the angelic powers is not necessarily to be used in interpreting Philippians ii. 10, 11. The hymn says nothing about a mythical combat and nothing about the victory He achieved over His enemies. The accent falls upon the universal domain of the risen Lord, and proclaims that there is no sphere which is outside His control.[3] It is a moot point whether we are to enquire who are referred to by each of the three terms and whether we are to think exclusively of angelic beings. But granting that spirit-powers are in view in this phrase, it is probably correct that these are hostile forces and that the confession they make is one wrung from them as a sign of their defeat and surrender to Christ as *Pantocrator*.

(*c*) Perhaps the strongest piece of evidence for the view that the hymn has the submission of spirit-powers in view in this

---

[1] Käsemann, *loc. cit.* 88, with reference to *Kyrios Jesus*, p. 67.

[2] Literally, 'by de-demonizing them' (*indem er sie entdämonisiert*). Friedrich follows Käsemann here with the same imagery: 'Since Christ is proclaimed as Lord of the world, all the powers are divested of power (*entmachtet*)', *Philipper*, p. 111.

[3] As in the parallel verse, Apoc. v. 13: 'And I heard every creature in heaven and on earth and under the earth and in the sea, and all therein, saying, "To him who sits upon the throne and to the Lamb be blessing and honour and glory and might for ever and ever!"', the homage is universal; but it would be wrong to import the notion of a victory after conflict into this scene, or to think of dwellers in separate compartments of the universe. In both texts it is a pictorial way of saying that the dominion is all-embracing. 'Heaven, earth, and the underworld embrace the total cosmos' (Leivestad, *Christ the Conqueror*, p. 114).

closing section is the setting of the verses as an enthronement drama.[1] The key-term is that translated 'confess' (ἐξομολο-γεῖσθαι). The older authorities took this verb to mean 'to proclaim with thanksgiving'.[2] The simple meaning is 'to declare openly or to confess publicly'; but there is a secondary sense derived from the LXX which puts the verb in a cultic context with the first meaning given above. It is easy then to see how this usage could lead commentators to think of the Church's witness to the lordship of Christ as expressed in the confession that is made. It is a natural assumption from this premise that the sense is something like this; All creation, the heavenly host, the Church upon earth and the deceased in Sheol, join to offer the thanksgiving of worship to the exalted Lord Christ, whether as a present fact or (more probably) as an eschatological hope when His redemption will have been completed. And the confession that is made is the personal witness of faith on the part of those who join in the chorus of acknowledgment.

Modern study has moved away from this understanding of the end of the hymn with a noticeable decisiveness. The real meaning of ἐξομολογεῖσθαι is not 'proclaim with thanksgiving' (as Lightfoot thought), but 'admit, acknowledge' in a neutral sense.[3] A word like 'own' or 'recognize' is a translation which many recent scholars favour.[4] The interpretation is in harmony

---

[1] Lohmeyer, *Philipper*, p. 97, n. 4: Peterson, *HEIS THEOS*, pp. 133 f.; J. R. Geiselmann, *Jesus der Christus*, p. 141 who distinguishes three acts of enthronement: proclamation of a new worthy name, act of worship (προσκύνησις) and acclamation. It is the merit of Peterson's study that he has described the way in which acclamation-formulas (such as *v.* 11: 'Jesus Christ is Lord') figured in ancient religious and political ceremonies (*HEIS THEOS*, p. 171, 3); but Lohmeyer, *Kyrios Jesus*, p. 60, n. 1 finds fault with his use of the term 'confession'.

[2] Lightfoot, *Philippians*, p. 115. 'All that ἐξομολογεῖσθαι of necessity means is "openly declare"; but LXX usage gives the verb the notion of praise or thanksgiving, and that idea is very appropriate here' (Plummer, *op. cit.* 49). M.–M., *Vocabulary*, p. 224 say: 'In the LXX the idea of "give thanks", "praise" is prominent.'

[3] This meaning is in line with the following construction of ὅτι and a noun clause; and not with the verb followed by a dative (as in Rom. xiv. 11 where the sense is 'praise': so Bauer–Arndt–Gingrich, *Lexicon, ad loc.*).

[4] For the newer meaning to be attached to ἐξομολογεῖσθαι cf. Michel, *TWNT*, v, 213: he translates as 'anerkennen', followed by Käsemann, Friedrich; Beare renders 'acclaim'; Norden, *Agnostos Theos*, pp. 277 ff.; J. Weiss, *Heinrici Festschrift* (1914), pp. 120 ff. N. P. Williams, *ExT*, LI (1940),

with this rendering of the verb.[1] It is not so much that creation confesses with personal response the lordship of Christ as that the angelic powers own His right because it is their duty so to do. It is not a confession of faith that they make in the modern sense of the term, but the open and irrevocable admission that this is the rightful Lord of the universe because God has installed Him in the seat of uncontested authority. It is their response to the divine epiphany which declares the sovereignty of the lordly Christ; and it is a response that they dutifully, if unwillingly, make.

This reading of the text fits in with the presupposition that they are alien powers which show their capitulation to Christ the conqueror by the admission they make. As Michel puts it, 'subjection and acclamation belong very closely together'.[2] The cosmic powers recognize their limitation and subjection as they own the pre-eminent rank of the Lord; and the confession on their lips, along with their attitude of lowly prostration on their knees,[3] is in keeping with this acknowledgment.

182–6, 215–20, in criticism of Norden, and especially E. Peterson, *HEIS THEOS*, p. 317.

Michel, in his article (*TWNT*, v, *s.v.*) regards the confession of Phil. ii. 10–11 as one made by the Church on earth in anticipation of the praise which will be offered by the Church at the end of the age (*loc. cit.* 214); but his essay 'Zur Exegese von Phil. 2, 5–11', 95, stresses the acclamation as part of the enthronement ceremony. While, however, it is not a confession of the Church, it is (he writes, *loc. cit.* 95, n. 2) 'a voluntary subjection of oneself to the new lordship, on the ground of a personal conviction, not merely of lip-service [*ein Wortbekenntnis*] in a limited sphere. The "confession" here belongs within a cosmic setting to the act of enthronement itself.' In this way, he is able to combine the setting of the formula 'Jesus Christ is Lord' in an enthronement ceremony and its place as a *Christian* declaration of faith in Christ.

[1] So Käsemann, 'Kritische Analyse', 87 who clearly indicates the significance: 'ἐξομολογεῖσθαι means the acclamation which from the oldest time has had a confirmed place at the enthronement. It is not confession in the narrow, modern sense, based on personal experience, not even a confession of faith [*ein Glaubensbekenntnis*], but an act of divine right, something which is a duty and which is binding in the presence of a divine epiphany. In this (act) there is not only a confession [*nicht nur bekannt*], but at the same time an open and irrevocable acknowledgment [*öffentlich und unverbrüchlich anerkannt*].' Similarly Lohmeyer, who remarks that the 'confession' is not an ἔκθεσις πίστεως in any ecclesiastical or 'cultic' sense (*Kyrios Jesus*, p. 60).

[2] 'Zur Exegese von Phil. 2, 5–11', 95.

[3] The bending of the knee is an expression of the greatest reverence and submission. It is a posture which is often found in the oriental world where

genuflection marks the humble approach of a worshipper who feels his need so keenly that he cannot stand erect before God. In contrast, the Hellenistic worshipper holds a free and upright posture (so Lohmeyer, *Kyrios Jesus*, p. 59). But it is doubtful if Lohmeyer's distinction should be accepted. Judaism knew both postures (Strack–Billerbeck, *op. cit.* II, 260 f.). The usual position was that of standing (S.–B. IV, 227 f., 230 *b*) as in the Old Testament, e.g. Jer. xviii. 20 and I Kings xviii. 15, xvii. 1, etc. But in cases of special need and extremity the suppliant falls upon his knees (e.g. Ezra ix. 5, 15; III Macc. ii. 1—prayer in time of distress). But there are other references which show how kneeling was thought of as the proper attitude to God: Ps. xcv. 6; Dan. vi. 10; I Esdras ix. 47; cf. Eusebius, *H.E.* v, v, 1: 'kneeled on the ground as is our familiar custom in prayer'. In the Gospels, men are described as standing for prayer: Luke xviii. 11, 13 (the publican as well as the Pharisee); and Jesus assumes that His disciples will stand (cf. Matt. vi. 5).

The contrast seems to be not between oriental and Greek habits and attitudes, but between the saying of prayers as a religious duty and the prostrating of the suppliant, in an acute sense of need and urgent pleading, before God. Thus Jesus who expects His followers to stand and pray (Mark xi. 25) and who Himself normally stood (John xi. 41, xvii. 1: except in Luke's Gospel where Jesus kneels in prayer) bows down in lowly submission and distress in the Gethsemane prayer (Mark xiv. 35; Matt. xxvi. 39; Luke xxii. 41). This distinction is strikingly confirmed by what André Parrot says in his essay on 'Gestures of Prayer in the Mesopotamian World' (*Maqqēl Shâqêdh: La Branche d'Amandier. Hommage à Wilhelm Vischer*, ed. J. Cadier (1960), pp. 177–80) that out of thousands of representations of men at prayer only four or five iconographs show the suppliants kneeling. The vast majority depict the worshipper standing or seated.

As an aid to the exegesis of Phil. ii. 10 we may conclude that kneeling in prayer is a mark of extreme abasement and submission (as in Eph. iii. 14) and denotes that the universal homage marks the subjection of those who so kneel to the lordship of Christ.

It could be suggested that kneeling for prayer is a mark of Gentile Christianity if one could safely build on the assumptions that Luke (or the *auctor ad Theophilum*) who shows a preference for this posture in the third Gospel and the Acts (see Luke xxii. 41 ff.; Acts vii. 60, ix. 40, xx. 36, xxi. 5) represents Gentile Christian practice in this matter; and that I Cor. xiv. 25; Ephesians iii. 14 also indicate the prayer habit of a Gentile believer. It may then be permissible to say that the allusion in the Christ-hymn to the bowing of the knee reflects its origin in a Hellenistic Christian community in which this custom was practised. But this is speculative. Cf. Delling, *Der Gottesdienst*, pp. 106 f.

Later Church practice is mentioned by C. F. D. Moule, *Worship*, p. 66: 'Perhaps bowing, kneeling, and prostration were in those days signs of special humility, intensity or anxiety.' We may add to his ref. to Origen, Tertullian, *de Orat.* XXIII; *Apol.* XXX; and for kneeling only on fast days, *de Corona*, III.

C. THE TIME OF THE HOMAGE

One remaining aspect of the verse falls to be noticed. It is the exegesis of the verb ἐξομολογεῖσθαι and its 'chronological' import. The issue is complicated by the textual uncertainty of this word. Most of the MSS read ἐξομολογήσεται (future indicative), while some authorities (including the MSS אB and 𝔓 46) have the aorist subjunctive ἐξομολογήσηται. The balance of witnesses is evenly divided, and most commentators confess to an uncertainty of the true reading on textual grounds alone. The future is perhaps the *lectio difficilior* inasmuch as a change to aorist subjunctive could easily be explained as an assimilation to the tense and mood of κάμψη.[1]

Happily, there is no need to form a hard-and-fast opinion about the choice of reading. That ε and η were interchanged in the post-classical period is attested in the papyri; and a similar lack of distinctness exists about the meanings of the two tenses in Hellenistic Greek, as Abel has shown.[2]

Both readings may therefore carry the meanings of two tenses, and we are still left with the choice: Does the universal homage belong to the future, at the time of the *Parousia*; or is it regarded as already taking place and contemporaneous with the age of the Church?

(i) *His present reign*

Over this issue there is a cleavage of opinion. Most scholars hold that the lordship of Christ which the acclamation declares is a present fact consequent upon His ascension and return to His Father's presence. 'The cosmic homage is the effect of the exaltation of Christ, which means his heavenly enthronement';[3] and this has taken place at His ascension and receiving of the supreme name. The universal acclaim that He is Lord is the creation's response to His return to the divine scene and His entry upon the lordship which is now committed to Him. From

---

[1] But, on the other hand, the reverse procedure may have been adopted to bring the tense of Phil. ii. 11 into line with the future in Isa. xlv. 23.

[2] *Grammaire du grec biblique*, §§ 59, 270 f. For the suggestion that the aorist here may have an inchoative sense (cf. Funk–Blass–Debrunner, § 331) cf. J. Héring, *ad* II Cor. x. 6 (*Commentaire du N.T.* VIII (1958), p. 79, n. 2.

[3] Leivestad, *Christ the Conqueror*, p. 114; Cullmann, *The Earliest Christian Confessions*, pp. 59–62.

a cultic standpoint, then, which views His glory *sub specie aeternitatis*, His dominion is already acknowledged and His triumph over all His foes complete.[1] On the other hand, if there is no cultic significance in this acclamation, the subjugation of the powers is a thing of the past and followed directly upon His installation as *Cosmocrator*.[2] He has now achieved His triumph and entered upon His reign over His vanquished foes.

(ii) *His future rule*

This view has to meet the objection that the present experience of the Church in its conflicts and trials does not confirm the impression that all things are now subject unto Christ. C. D. Morrison writes, therefore:[3] 'The period of Christ's lordship was far from one of the powers' subjection or defeat, but rather the period of conflict with them.' It is undeniable that this motif of conflict and tension runs through the Pauline writings; and later Christian literature (e.g. Irenaeus' *adv. Haer.* i, 10) placed the subjection of the evil powers in an eschatological future as something still to happen.[4] The tension is one which belongs to Christian thought in many phases; and Cullmann's *schema* of the interrelation between present actuality and future realiza-

[1] Delling, *Der Gottesdienst*, p. 101 (not in E.T.): 'In any case this adoration is not limited to the future, but occurs also now in the present (since Jesus is already at this time Lord)'; and H. Schlier, *Principalities and Powers in the New Testament* (E.T. 1961), pp. 47–8.

[2] Peterson, *HEIS THEOS*, pp. 259 n. 2, 262 f., 226 f. introduces the parallels which speak of the victory of the sun-god over the astronomical elements and his lordship over the threefold divisions of the universe; and Käsemann ('Kritische Analyse', 88) finds the relevance of this idea in the victory of Christ over the spirits which were thought to be the controllers of man's Fate. Christ as the Conqueror of all has taken over from these powers, declared the régime of Necessity to be at an end and brought all the powers throughout the universe under His sovereign sway. His enthronement is the signal that their reign is over and their power to influence men as 'arbiters of human destiny' (*Schicksalsträger*) is taken away. It is the decisive moment in 'the change of Lordship' (*Herrschaftswechsel*). Similarly, Bornkamm interprets the triumph of Christ as 'an emancipation (of humanity) from the tyranny of the world-powers' (*loc. cit.* 187).

[3] *The Powers That Be* (1960), pp. 116–19 (esp. 119); cf. E. Schweizer, *NTS*, ii, 2 (Nov. 1955), 95, 96.

[4] Cf. Cullmann, *The Earliest Christian Confessions*, pp. 61 f.

tion is perhaps the best-known method of accounting for both strains in Christian thinking.[1]

Applied to the present problem of exegesis, this principle means that 'the Christians of the first generation believe in the eschatological triumph of Christ, because they believe in the triumph already won by Him. They believe in the future Kingdom of God because they believe in the present reign of Christ.'[2] Both the actuality of His present lordship and the continuance of the hostile powers against the Church as they disengage themselves temporarily from the bonds that attach them to their master Christ are taught in the New Testament. They are subject to Christ, but not yet annihilated. Christ reigns (I Cor. xv. 25), having taken His place in the heavenly court (Apoc. iii. 21; Heb. i. 8–14; Rom. viii. 34; Col. iii. 1; Eph. i. 21 f.; Heb. x. 13, i. 3–6, viii. 1; Acts ii. 34, v. 31, vii. 55; I Pet. iii. 22; I Clem. XXXVI, 5; Polycarp, *Phil.* II, 1; Barn. XII, 10), with the angelic host already submissive to Him (I Pet. iii. 22; I Tim. iii. 16). Yet, in a paradox, there is still opposition and conflict; and He waits for the day of His open victory (I Cor. xv. 25 b; Rom. xvi. 20: cf. Heb. ii. 8, x. 13) and the Church is still engaged in conflict and lives under the shadow of the persecutor (Eph. vi. 10 f.; Phil. i. 28 f.; I Thess. ii. 18, iii. 5; II Tim. ii. 8 ff.; Apoc. ii–iii; xii; xvii).

(iii) *Can the paradox be resolved?*

Must this paradox lie unresolved? Are the twin facts of Christ's present lordship and the Church's oppression by the very powers which acknowledge His authority to be set side by side, like parallel lines which never meet?

The fact that the enthronement scene is pictured (as in Apoc. v. 1–14) in a hymn may put us on the track of an answer to these questions. Within the structure and setting of this Christological hymn we are caught up in the drama of redemption and lifted into the presence of God's heavenly court. His voice is heard in

---

[1] Cullmann, *ibid.* and for his discussion of what he calls 'the relation of tension between the middle and the end' (*Spannungsverhältnis zwischen Mitte und Ende*) of the Church's history, see *Christus und die Zeit* (1946), p. 136 (E.T. *Christ and Time*, p. 154); and 'The Kingship of Christ, etc.', *The Early Church*, pp. 105 ff. Cf. Barrett, *From First Adam to Last*, pp. 89 f.

[2] Cullmann, *The Earliest Christian Confessions*, p. 62.

the bestowal of the Name which is above all names. The humiliated and exalted Christ is proclaimed and acclaimed as Lord of all the spiritual forces throughout the universe. All these powers fall down and submit to His God-endowed right. As in a vision of the final restoration of all things (the *apokatasta-sis* of New Testament thought[1]), His sovereign sway is complete and no dissentient voice is heard. The scene is the presence of God for whom there is no past, present or future. Already now in His sight the world's salvation and reconciliation is a *fait accompli*;[2] but the Church sees it only in prospect and vision. The Church knows it only as an article of faith and hope.[3] For the Church which is still on earth, it is a time of conflict and sore trial, cruel persecution and endurance of the tyranny of many enemies. But in the hymn the Church is caught up from earth to heaven, from the scene of conflict and duress into the presence of the all-conquering Lord, from the harsh realities of what is to the glorious prospect and promise of what will be, because it is so

[1] As in Eph. i. 10; Rom. xi. 32; I Cor. xv. 27–8; Col. i. 20. For the word, cf. Acts iii. 21.

[2] 'Il est incontestable que la Seigneurie du Christ est présentée [in the hymn] comme un fait accompli, et non comme un but à atteindre', remarks Bonnard, *op. cit.* 46. Michaelis comments: 'Verses 10, 11 are not to be understood as eschatological statements. As the hostile powers are included, it cannot be at the Last Day that they at length worship, since (in Col. ii. 15) already with the Exaltation of Christ God has pronounced judgment on these powers' (*An die Philipper*, p. 42).

[3] Cullmann speaks of an anticipation of the end when the Church gathers at the Supper meal. 'Here happens even now what really will take place only at the end' (*Christ and Time*, p. 155). The Eucharist thus anticipates the end. The presence of Christ in answer to the call *Maranā thâ*: 'our Lord, come', at the Table is a foretaste of His presence at the end of the Age. In the Supper celebrations there is 'concretized' (*konkretisiert*) the entire situation of redemptive history in the present, as what lies *sub specie temporis* in the future is brought into the present *sub specie Dei*. The Supper is an anticipation of the Kingdom of God and the express lordship of Christ.

It is along this line that Lohmeyer might have argued, had he developed his treatment in *Kyrios Jesus*, pp. 65–7. Mention may be made of the recent discussion of the reign of Christ by C. F. D. Moule, *The Birth of the New Testament* (1962), ch. VI. His statement (102) 'At moments of Christian worship, time and space are obliterated and the worshipping Church on earth is one in eternity with the Church in the heavenly places' (citing Heb. xii. 22 ff.), confirms the line of interpretation adopted above. The connection between Heb. xii. 18 ff. and Phil. ii. 10 f. is brought out by W. Hahn, *Gottesdienst und Opfer Christi* (1951), pp. 113 f.

already in God's sight. The Christ-hymn enables the Church to see beyond the present in which the Head of the Church reigns invisibly and powerfully—but known only to faith—to that full proof of His reign in the heavenly sphere in which all the powers are veritably subject to Him and His dominion is manifestly confessed.

CHAPTER XI

THE CHRISTOLOGICAL CONFESSION

ὅτι Κύριος Ἰησοῦς Χριστός
εἰς δόξαν Θεοῦ πατρός (verse 11 *b, c*)

INTRODUCTION

The Christ-hymn reaches its climax in the utterance of the whole cosmos: 'Jesus Christ is Lord.' The accent falls on the last word which is placed first in the Greek phrase, and thereby given special force.[1] The term Κύριος is, as P. Henry says, the culminating point of the entire passage.[2] Here particularly, the revelation of the name as Kyrios completes the sense of the second half of the hymn.

At the new sentence of verse 9 a decisive turn in Christ's fortunes has been registered. God has exalted Him and bestowed upon Him the supreme name. But the reader is left in suspense as to what this name is and what it signifies. The lines which follow build up the suspense by reporting that the name which Jesus has been given is one which evokes a cosmic submission and a universal acclaim. Finally, in the formula which all creation takes upon its lips, this name is at length made manifest; it is the name of Kyrios. With artistic skill and by careful design, the author of the hymn has held back the most important term in the composition; and introduces it in a heavily-accented line as the finale and climax of the entire psalm.[3]

[1] The word 'Lord' is 'emphatic by position' (Plummer, *Philippians*, p. 49).

[2] Henry, 'Kénose', col. 37. Bonnard, *L'épître aux Philippiens*, p. 47, takes the opposite view in his suggestion that the accent falls on the words '*Iēsous Christos*'. 'It is to Jesus Christ, and not to any of the other spiritual authorities which are in the universe that the sovereign authority now belongs.' But the two interpretations amount to much the same thing. Jesus Christ is the Lord of the universe; and the Lord of the world is none other than He.

[3] This holding back of the name of 'Lord' reminds us of a stylistic trait found in Hebrews in which the author keeps back the personal name of Jesus 'generally as the climax of an impressive phrase or phrases' (Moffatt, *ICC* (1924), p. lxiii). The instances are Heb. ii. 9, iii. 1, iv. 14, vi. 20, vii. 22, xii. 2, xiii. 20. Cf. V. Taylor, *The Names of Jesus* (1954), p. 7.

271

The line, 'Jesus Christ is Lord', serves a number of purposes. It reveals the identity of the name, adumbrated in the earlier verses. It states the theme of the cosmic homage, for the lordship of Christ is both the reason why all the powers bow down and submit, and the actual content of their acclamation as they cry: Jesus Christ is Kyrios. Moreover, this confession of the title Lord gives meaning to the redemptive event[1] which began with the *katabasis* of the pre-existent One from His glory into a life of servitude, humiliation and death, and is completed by a corresponding *anabasis*, as He is taken up by divine power, installed in the seat of authority and given the very name of God Himself, the name of Kyrios. To interpret further the saving significance of the name, we may say that it was for the receiving of this name that He 'came down' and accepted His humiliation; and now, with His receiving of the name, His mission is completed and His goal reached. The line, thus interpreted in the light of the whole hymn, is the symmetrical and logical completion of the career of Christ, and the final step in His journey back to the celestial region from which He emerged. It is also the last act in the drama of salvation and the assurance that what God purposed to do has now in fact been accomplished. Jesus Christ is Lord because God has made Him so, thus achieving His redeeming purposes.[2]

A. 'TO THE GLORY OF GOD THE FATHER'

If this conclusion is accepted, it seems hard to justify the presence of the extra line: εἰς δόξαν Θεοῦ πατρός. Many commentators are embarrassed by this 'tail-piece'; and a variety of explanations which seek to account for its significance has been forthcoming.

There is little to be said in the favour of those suggestions which would make the phrase part of the confession, whether in the sense that creation's confession includes the phrase (as Vincent takes it[3]), or taking the phrase to mean 'in the glory of

---

[1] 'Hier wird die Heilsbedeutung des Christusgeschehens offenbar' (Friedrich, *Philipper* (*NTD*), p. 111).

[2] Michaelis, *Der Brief an die Philipper*, p. 43, comments: The adoration is directed to the praise of 'God the Father...whose redemptive purpose Christ has fulfilled'.

[3] *ICC*, p. 63; and Peterson, *HEIS THEOS*, p. 133 who reads the confession as 'Jesus Christus Herr sei zur Ehre Gottes'.

God the Father', as a number of scholars do. Thus Meinertz interprets the sentence in the light of John i. 18 (the Logos is 'in the bosom of the Father').[1] By His exaltation He returns to that pre-existent state; and is proclaimed as Lord in His Father's glory. Similarly, Prat renders boldly the last lines:[2] 'que toute langue confesse que le Seigneur Jésus-Christ est entré dans la gloire de Dieu le Père'. This is inadmissible because it has mistaken the significance of the title Κύριος by placing it as an adjective; and given a wrong sense to the prepositional phase εἰς δόξαν Θεοῦ πατρός.

It seems conclusive that the phrase should be separated from the text of the confession, brought into the ἵνα-clause of the preceding lines, and regarded as a liturgical conclusion of the entire hymn. All praise, honour and power finally belong to God the Father. The ultimate note of the hymn is thus not, as we earlier suspected, the lordship of Christ, but the glory of the Father.[3] This is a solution which harmonizes with its liturgical origin, for the last line forms a sort of doxology which rounds off the whole.[4] But there are some oustanding difficulties to be faced.

The authorship of the words has, as we have seen, been a matter of debate. J. Jeremias[5] (followed by E. Schweizer and G. Friedrich)[6] proposes that this phrase is a Pauline addition to the original version of the hymn on the ground that it is separated from the verb ἐξομολογήσηται to which it belongs; and in any case, εἰς (τὴν) δόξαν is 'an expression which Paul loves. The Apostle's thought does not rest, it should be noted, until it comes to rest in

[1] Meinertz, *Theol. d. NT*, II, 67; similarly O. Casel, *The Mystery of Christian Worship*, etc. (E.T. 1962), p. 147, renders the text: 'Jesus Christ is Lord in glory (*doxa*) = in the being of God'; and Durrwell, *The Resurrection*, p. 114: 'Jesus Christ is Lord in the glory of God the Father.'

[2] *La Théologie de saint Paul*, I (1938), p. 373, following the Vulgate.

[3] So Dibelius writes: 'The entire solemn description [following the proclamation of the Κύριος name] finds its goal in the rhetorical clause which refers to the Father, *v.* 11' (*An die Philipper*[3], ad loc.).

[4] It is doxology which proceeds from the contents of the psalm, and is not to be referred to an eschatological future, as E. Peterson believed (*Zeit. f. Syst. Theol.* VII (1928–9), 698: quoted by Dibelius and Henry). The origin of the doxology is most probably to be traced to the liturgical use of the hymn.

[5] Art. cit. *Studia Paulina*, pp. 153 ff.

[6] Schweizer, *Erniedrigung*, p. 52, n. 224 (not in E.T.); *Idem*, 'Anmerkungen zur Theologie des Mk', *Neotestamentica et Patristica*, 43; Friedrich, *Philipper*, p. 111.

the glory of God.'[1] Both these arguments for the later addition of the phrase from the hand of Paul have already been touched upon.[2] Jeremias has a stronger argument when he remarks that this line breaks the metrical symmetry of the piece.[3] He believes that 'the whole hymn is built up in couplets';[4] and on this arrangement the line is 'odd man out', with no corresponding partner to form a couplet.

Opinion is divided over the origin of the line; but if it is a Pauline gloss it is possible to suggest why it was added. There must be some powerful motive behind its insertion inasmuch as (on Jeremias' analysis) it destroys the precise order of the whole composition. Käsemann submits tentatively that the thought is brought in 'to give expression to a "subordinationist" Christology, as in I Corinthians xv. 28'.[5] On this suggestion, Paul adds the phrase in order to safeguard the unity of the Godhead—for him as a Jew, a precious inheritance with which he never parted, for all his concern to assert the universality of the Gospel and the divinity of Christ.[6] The acclamation that Jesus Christ is Lord may well have suggested—as we shall observe later—that the exalted Christ is a 'second God', having taken His place on His Father's throne as His consort and partner. But this to the Apostle is an intolerable thought if it violates the Biblical monotheism, or if it suggests that Christ is there as God's rival who has set up His throne in opposition to that of His Father.

The final line which declares that He is Lord to the glory of

---

[1] Jeremias, *loc. cit.* 154, n. 2; in this observation he is anticipated by J. Schmitt who writes concerning the phrase εἰς δόξαν Θεοῦ that it 'semble bien trahir la main de l'Apôtre terminant son exposé selon sa manière habituelle, par une doxologie à "Dieu le Père"' (*Jésus ressuscité*, p. 97).

[2] See above, p. 34, n. 1.

[3] So Friedrich, *Philipper*, p. 111: 'das Gefüge des Liedes stören'.

[4] Jeremias, *loc. cit.* 153; so Schweizer, *Erniedrigung*[2], p. 93, n. 373: 'scheinen rhythmisch überzuschießen'; and R. Bultmann who, independently of Jeremias, wrote in 1949 in reference to εἰς δόξαν Θεοῦ πατρός: 'It is an extra third line of the Christ-hymn whose construction I regard differently from Lohmeyer. Whereas he claims throughout that there are verses of three lines, I believe that there are two-line verses all the way through, up to the final verses', 'Bekenntnis- und Liedfragmente im 1. Petrusbrief', *Con. Neotest.* XI (1949), 6, n. 10.

[5] 'Kritische Analyse', 89.

[6] Andrews, *The Meaning of Christ for Paul*, pp. 131 f.: 'Paul an uncompromising monotheist' is his chapter heading.

the Father underlines that all these suggestions are false. He lives and reigns in heaven (I Cor. xv. 25), not as a δεύτερος Θεός (as in the second century title[1]), but as a sharer in the glory of that full equality with God which is the Father's gift to His obedient Son. 'No competition between the Members of the Godhead has resulted, since Christ is no insurgent, but the obedient One' (Friedrich).[2] The homage which is paid to Christ in His glory in no way detracts from the worship of God the Father, for, as this line stresses, the homage is rendered to the glory of the Father.[3]

This explanation would account for the hypothetical Pauline insertion. It springs from his concern to preserve the inviolability of the one God, the Father;[4] for, it is maintained,[5] Jesus (in Paul's theology) is not hailed as God, but as His Christ. There is a subordinationist strain which runs through his statements about the relations of the Godhead.[6] And the addition of the doxology is an indication that Paul would not allow to pass unchallenged any suspicion of a duality within the Godhead.

[1] E.g. in Justin Martyr, *I Apol.* xiii, 3; cf. II Clem. i, 1: 'we must think of Jesus Christ as of God': Ignatius, *Rom.* iii, 3 and *proem.*: vi, 3; *Smyr.* i, 1: x, 1; *Trall.* vii, 1.

[2] *Philipper*, p. 111; cf. Bonnard, *Philippiens*, p. 46: 'Jésus-Christ est élevé à la dignité même du Dieu de l'Ancien Testament...mais il ne lui ravit pas cette dignité.'

[3] Most commentators on the Pauline text make this point: Bonnard, *op. cit.* 47, citing Calvin: 'Le Père est glorifié au Fils'; Heinzelmann, *Philipper*, p. 96, comparing John v. 23, xii. 44 f.; Henry, 'Kénose', 37 quoting John xvii. 1–5; Müller, *The Epistles to the Philippians and Philemon*, p. 89; Beare, *Philippians*, p. 87, who has apposite quotations from the Old Testament to show that there is there no conflict between the kingly rule of Yahweh and that of the Messianic king (esp. Ezek. xxxiv). Cf. S. Mowinckel, *He That Cometh* (E.T. 1956), pp. 172 ff. There is a parallel expression in *The Odes and Psalms of Solomon* (1909), p. 103, 'and it became to me for the praise of the Most High, and of God my Father' (Rendel Harris). The reference is x. 5.

[4] The characteristic New Testament idiom is that God is the Father and the title 'Lord' is almost completely confined to Jesus: so Lohmeyer, *Probleme paulinischer Theologie* (1954), pp. 9–29; and *ZNTW* xxvi (1927), 169 ff. Cf. I Cor. viii. 6; Rom. i. 7; II Cor. i. 2, 3.

[5] By, e.g., W. Morgan, *The Religion and Theology of Paul* (1917), p. 54; P. Feine, *Theologie d. N.T.*² (1911), p. 257; cf. V. Taylor's discussion of these passages, *The Person of Christ*, pp. 57 ff.

[6] As in I Cor. iii. 23, xi. 3, xv. 28; Gal. iv. 4; Rom. viii. 3, 32.

Comment on this line of reasoning must await our study of the significance of the lordship of Christ. But it may be argued that Paul's addition (or the presence of the line in the hymn, if it belonged to the *Urschrift*) is directed, not so much against a doctrine of two Gods as against the idea that there is any rivalry within the Godhead. The line is there as a bulwark against the wrong notion that the exalted Lord is Kyrios in His own right.[1] The drift of the entire hymn has run counter to this notion. He chose not to use His state as One in the form of God to aspire to His own end. He forfeited His equality with God, whether in the sense of letting go what He had or refusing to grasp at that which was within His reach. He chose, instead of a selfish act, an act of humiliation in obedience to some power outside Himself. And now there is given to Him as His Father's gracious gift the very thing He might have aspired to and called His own: the lordship over the entire cosmos.[2] This is the motif which runs through the hymn from beginning to end. The pre-existent One subordinated His own desire and refused to claim His lordship in opposition to God. The humiliated One was obedient, to the final stage of His life. The exalted Lord has His glory and exercises His authority, not in any selfish manner or as a rebel against God, but to the Father's lasting honour until He hands over the authority to the God from whom He derives it (I Cor. xv. 27–8). Seen in this light, the last line may be no afterthought, added by another hand, although it undoubtedly expresses Pauline theology. It simply reiterates the *Leitmotiv* of the whole hymn, and stresses the sovereignty of God the Father and the obedience of His co-equal Son. But if the hymn is a series of couplets, the doxology was added in the spirit of the entire piece.

If the deduction we have drawn, in the above paragraph, about the Father–Son relationship is valid, very little may be

---

[1] Lohmeyer, *Philipper*, 93, obscures this when he writes: 'und wird Kyrios wieder durch die eigene Tat'. The lordship is secured by God's gift, not 'His own deed', surely!

[2] Bo Reicke has recently expounded this aspect of the hymn with great insight ('Unité chrétienne et Diaconie', p. 210: 'La toute-puissance du Christ dans ce monde ne se base pas sur une aspiration de puissance, mais sur la diaconie'; 211: 'c'est seulement par son renoncement à toute domination que Jésus a acquis cette majesté'.

added by way of explanation of the title πατήρ in verse 11 *c*.[1] Lohmeyer[2] was perhaps the first to raise the question: of whom is God the Father, in this passage? Is He the Father of believers? Against this, we may note that Christians have not been mentioned in the foregoing hymn. Is He the Father of Christ? If so, he remarks, there may be an implicit allusion to the primitive Christian title 'Son of God'; but it must be admitted that there is no clear reference to this. He is finally reduced to the explanation that God is surnamed as 'the Father of the world', although he grants that this is an uncommon expression.

E. Käsemann poses the same queries as to the meaning of the enigmatic phrase εἰς δόξαν Θεοῦ πατρός.[3] Like the other scholars of whom we have spoken, he would prefer to regard the phrase as a Pauline addition, but chooses to retain it as original in the hymn on the Form-analytical ground that the line is required at the conclusion of the third major strophe (following Lohmeyer's analysis). He sums up: 'so we are left with the conclusion that, at this point, a Christian idiom is employed which is able to refer to God as the Father in the absolute sense, and yet, at the same time, to mean by the term the Father of Christ and Christians. In that case, here, and here only, do we see the Church being brought into the scope of the eschatological event which is portrayed, and do we understand it as a redemptive event.'

It is the last phrase of Käsemann's commentary on the words which puts us on the scent of the most likely view. The hymn is concerned with the interrelation of two worlds, the divine and the human.[4] It tells the story of One who came down 'from above' and lived 'below' in this earthly order. At length, He returned to His place 'above', and received the submission of the whole cosmos. In spatial and kinetic terminology, the circle

[1] It is interesting (but probably the fact is non-significant) to observe the use of κάμπτειν and description of God as πατήρ in Eph. iii. 14. See C. Masson, *Épître aux Colossiens* (1950), p. 95, n. 4.

[2] *Philipper*, p. 98; *Kyrios Jesus*, pp. 61 f. His explanation as 'Father of the world' is confirmed, he says, if the line belongs to the confession. But this is improbable; and faces Käsemann's objection that the demonic powers would not call God 'Father' ('Kritische Analyse', 89).

[3] *Loc. cit.* 89.

[4] This contrast of two orders of existence is found elsewhere in the New Testament: Romans i. 3–4; I Tim. iii. 16; Apoc. v. See E. Schweizer, *Spirit of God*, pp. 57 f. and *Idem*, *Erniedrigung und Erhöhung*, p. 104.

of His mission is complete; and heaven and earth are united by this act. The entire creation—heaven, earth and the underworld—pay their homage and bend the knee in token of this world-wide reconciliation, for He is Lord of all the powers. And the reconciliation means that the universe is restored to its rightful Lord who in turn, by His redemptive act, has reinstated the Fatherly rule of God over all His universe.[1] Lordship and Fatherhood are bound together, for His lordship is the cosmic sign that the victory is won; and 'the word "Father" betokens that now God and the world are "reconciled" and united'.[2] God is the Father of the universe which is now brought back to cosmic harmony because He is the Father of His Son through whom the reconciliation is effected; and the imperious call to those who sing this hymn is to confess the lordship of Christ by their obedience, even as He came to His lordship along the path of a humble obedience.

B. THE LORDSHIP OF CHRIST

The preceding section has used the term 'Christ's lordship' with some frequency. It is necessary to examine this concept more closely at the close of the exegesis, since it is the dominating theme of the hymn as a whole. What are we to understand by the acclamation that Jesus Christ is Lord? This question narrows the field of enquiry to the meaning of the lordship of Christ in this context. 'To make clear the religious import of the use of the name "Lord" by the early Christians, one would have to cite the whole of the New Testament', as J. Weiss observes;[3] but our present task is considerably less ambitious, with one text only before us.

[1] The work of Jesus as high-priest who returns to the heavenly sanctuary is seen by Lohmeyer to be the same thought in a different idiom. 'By this return He completes the work of unifying God and the world' (*Kyrios Jesus*, p. 81). But Héring is critical of this line of reasoning, *Le Royaume de Dieu*, p. 178.

[2] Lohmeyer, *Philipper*, p. 98: 'Darum kann in dem Worte "Vater" davon gesprochen werden, daß jetzt Gott und Welt "versöhnt" und eines sind.' The word 'versöhnt' may be an allusion, in Lohmeyer's mind, to the 'Sohn Gottes' through whom the reconciliation is achieved—a play on the word which cannot be reproduced in English.

[3] *Christ: the Beginnings of Dogma*, E.T. p. 46.

Ernst Lohmeyer acutely saw that one of the reasons why Philippians ii. 6 ff., in his view, could not be easily fitted into the type of Christology represented in Acts was that Christ in the passage is proclaimed as Lord of the world, not Lord of the Church. Yet he holds that the Christology of this Christ-psalm goes back to the oldest form of Christianity. This is the issue between him and W. Bousset, which he sees as sharply dividing them.[1] In the closing scene of the enthronement of Christ, the world as a whole submits, and not simply the Church. Indeed, there is no mention of a confessing Church. Furthermore, it is not religious worship which is offered to the regnant Christ, but cosmic acclamation of Him as Lord. It is not the song of the redeemed, but the cry of the subjugated, that is contained in the words 'Jesus Christ is Lord'. And the formula runs 'Lord', not 'our Lord'; the latter title belongs to the Church for it expresses a personal relationship between the believers and the Head of the cult, the former title is that which relates the world to its new Ruler.[2] The personal element comes out in the use of 'Christ' (which does not mean Messiah, as in the Acts-Christology), but from the order of the words in the text it is clear that Christ is a proper name.[3] The sense of the whole is: Jesus Christ—as He is known to Christians—is the Lord of the universe. Nothing could be further from a cultic setting, for the scene is on a world scale, and it is the cosmic powers

[1] Lohmeyer, *Philipper*, p. 97, n. 6 and his introductory remarks in *Kyrios Jesus*, pp. 1 f.; Käsemann, 'Kritische Analyse', 84 f.; A. B. Macdonald, *Christian Worship in the Primitive Church*, p. 126; J. R. Geiselmann, *Jesus der Christus*, p. 145. See p. 53, n. 4 for Bousset's title; and G. Vos, 'The Kyrios-Christos Controversy', *Princeton Theological Review*, XII (1914), 636 ff.; xv (1917), 21–89.

[2] Geiselmann, *Jesus der Christus*, p. 133: 'Es ist auch nicht wahrscheinlich, daß Paulus den Erhöhten als Kyrios des gesamten Kosmos preist. Für Paulus ist Jesus "unser" Herr, der im Kult der Kirche verehrte Kyrios. Die absolute Formel: Kyrios Jesus Christos (Phil. 2, 11) begegnet uns noch einmal Kol. 2, 6. Und dort sagt uns Paulus, daß er diese Formel der Paradosis verdanke.'

In this line of argument, Geiselmann is asserting the pre-Pauline character of the hymn and the conclusion that confession of Christ as 'the Lord' is traditional Christian belief, which Paul takes over and personalizes by adding the possessive pronoun 'our' ('my Lord' is found only once, in Phil. iii. 8: Cerfaux, 'Kyrios', *DB Suppl. loc. cit.* col. 222).

[3] Lohmeyer, *Philipper*, p. 98: *Kyrios Jesus*, pp. 60–1.

which humble themselves in acknowledgment of a new world-Ruler.

In a way which Lohmeyer does not exactly explain, the origin of this faith in the cosmic Christ is traced to the Eucharist;[1] and therein, as J. Jervell has noticed, lies the weakness of his theory.[2] It is not easy to see what the Christians' cultic meal has to do with the universal admission, owing to Christ's *force majeure*, of the cosmic powers. But as to the setting of this psalm in its transcendental aspect of Christ's heavenly enthronement and lordship over more-than-human powers, Lohmeyer seems to have proved his point.

If his conclusion about the Kyrios-title in this passage be accepted, it is less simple to follow him in his further conviction that, as this is a pre-Pauline fragment, it belongs to the oldest Christianity and emanates from the Jerusalem Church.[3] The impression one gains of this community is that it was a species of Jewish heterodoxy, a conventicle within the parent, Judaic fold rather than a community fired with the knowledge of the cosmic Lord who is sovereign over all the earth and whose kingly sway is exercised over all creatures. Nor is it convincing to find in the hymn a development of the Petrine kerygma which says that He is Lord of all (Acts x. 36), as Geiselmann would have us believe.[4] The 'Lord of all' must surely be governed by the first part of the verse: 'the word sent unto the sons of Israel'. A more germane parallel would be *Barnabas* v, 5: 'He is Lord of all the cosmos'; or I Peter iii. 22: 'Who is at God's right hand, having gone into

---

[1] Lohmeyer, *Kyrios Jesus*, pp. 65–7. Cf. Cerfaux, 'L'hymne au Christ-Serviteur de Dieu', *Miscellanea Historica* (1946), p. 130; Harder, *Paulus und das Gebet*, pp. 57 ff.; N. A. Dahl, 'Anamnesis', *ST*, 1 (1947), 85, n. 1, who all follow Lohmeyer in his conclusion. More recently, Lucetta Mowry, *The Dead Sea Scrolls and the Early Church* (1962), p. 245 has placed Phil. ii. 6 ff. in the setting of the Lord's Supper: 'The hymn in Philippians 2: 6–11 to the glorified Servant is...appropriate for a eucharistic service of worship.'

[2] Jervell, *Imago Dei*, p. 207, n. 135.

[3] Lohmeyer, *Kyrios Jesus*, p. 66: 'ein Stück ältester eucharistischer Liturgie...seine palästinensische Herkunft'; *Philipper*, p. 98: 'in diesem zusatzlosen "Herr" altes ererbtes Gut vorliegt'.

[4] Geiselmann, *Jesus der Christus*, p. 145: 'In the veneration of the Lord as Lord of the whole world this hymn which Paul had received as a tradition develops liturgically the kerygma of Peter which preaches that Jesus Christ is Lord of all (Acts x. 36).'

heaven, angels, authorities and powers under His control'; or I Timothy iii. 16; or Apocalypse xix. 16.

Because of the similarities between the scenario of the hymn and Hellenistic parallels in the stories of the gods who came down and thereafter were apotheosized—and especially in the final part of the drama where the imagery of the enthronement of Christ is drawn from an ancient ritual of the coronation of a deity (with the acts of proclaiming a new name, the abasement of his foes and the acclamation of his worthiness and greatness) —later scholars have seen the lordship of Christ against a more developed background. According to them, His lordship means His control of the spirit-powers and His acceptance of the office which they formerly held. In the Hellenistic world spirit-forces were thought to be the arbiters of human life and, by the movements of the stars, to regulate man's destiny.[1] Men were held in bondage to these superstitions which to Hellenistic man were not a triviality on the fringe of his life, but a real force to be reckoned with and an issue of serious and practical importance.[2] For this situation of men in the iron grip of Necessity and Fate the proclamation of Jesus Christ as Kyrios had, for the Church and the world in which it lived in the first century, a prime significance. For it announced that the régime of the hostile forces which controlled human life is now at an end, and henceforth God is known, not as a mysterious and capricious Fate,[3] but as the Father of Jesus Christ into whose hands the destinies of life are committed. The lordship of Christ is the announcement of His cosmocracy from the throne of the universe, which is the throne of God. He is God revealed, God in His relations

---

[1] W. Bousset has written a full description of this type of *Aberglaube: Kyrios Christos*[3], pp. 185 ff. The key sentence is this: 'Dependent upon that world (above our world, the stellar region where the stars are gods and where all is order, harmony, beauty and goodness) is the whole world of human life and destiny, for it is those heavenly powers which determine the lives of men.' Cf. G. Murray, *Five Stages of Greek Religion* (1935 ed.), pp. 138 ff.

[2] Bousset, *op. cit.* 186: The stars 'are no mere powers, dead and cold; they are gods, to whom men pray as they lift up their hands—this is a right thing to do, however illogical'.

[3] In the sense that men's destinies were thought to be fixed at birth by the stars and were settled; but they could be altered by such phenomena—quite accidental—as comets and unusual movements of the heavenly bodies. See Tarn–Griffith, *Hellenistic Civilisation* (3rd ed. 1952), pp. 347, 351.

with the world.[1] The exalted Lord is the promise that a new chapter in the world's history has begun and a new beginning for men's hopes made possible. His enthronement declares a freedom from the tyranny of Fate and all the malevolent powers which enslaved ancient man; and a freedom for God, for the *Cosmocrator* is none other than the obedient One. This is the meaning of the confession for the Church, as Käsemann sees it.[2] He writes: 'For by the proclaiming of the obedient One as the Lord of the universe (*Kosmokrator*), the bounds are drawn which separate the old and new world, and the Christian community is thereby called afresh into that sphere in which it has to live, to work and to suffer, the sphere of being "in Christ", of humility and obedience and the liberty of the redeemed. In that sense the hymn is a confession. Confession in the early Christian community serves to mark the boundaries between the old and the new age, boundaries which in daily life are threatened with obliteration constantly.' What this confession proclaims is that 'the world belongs to the obedient One; and that He is Lord of the world in order that we may become obedient. We do not become obedient by means of an example (*ein Vorbild*); but through the word which witnesses that we belong to Him.'[3]

From this excerpt of Käsemann at the conclusion of his 'kritische Analyse' we can gain some understanding of his view of Christ's lordship and its relevance to the Church. It is set in a framework which has little connection with the Church's worship; rather the primary application of the lordship is to the cosmic spirit-powers which admit their subservience to the enthroned Christ. They utter the cry: He is Lord. The Church overhears this and identifies herself with it, thereby committing herself to His sovereign rule. She thus confesses that she too belongs to the *Regnum Christi*, and that her life and witness in the world are to be marked by the same devotion to God, the same humiliation and obedience, as brought her Lord to His throne. And, amid all the tangled problems and vicissitudes of life, she knows that human life and the world's future are in the hands of Him whom God has appointed as His vice-gerent until the end of time.

[1] Käsemann's phrase, 'Kritische Analyse', 85.
[2] *Loc. cit.* 94 f. [3] *Loc. cit.* 95.

C. SUMMING-UP

The way in which the hymn borrows the ascription of worship which, in the first instance, was written in reference to the cultic worship of Yahweh,[1] and the use it makes of the imagery of an ancient enthronement ritual in which a heavenly being is proclaimed as 'Lord of the spirits',[2] both express the unique status which the Christians accorded to the ascended Jesus. In the citation of the Old Testament text the inference is clearly intended that the Lord Jesus is the Object of devotion and honour alongside the covenant God, Yahweh. And in the bestowal of a new name and the cosmic homage which this act evokes there is the implication that 'Kyrios is not merely a general designation of high rank, but a name which has almost become the proper name of God. Christ is thus exalted not into a general circle of divine beings alone, he definitely takes the place of the almighty God.'[3]

Yet, in both lines of thought which are interwoven in the hymn so that we should not be faced with the choice of either-or, the notion of a rivalry within the Godhead is scouted, and there is no thought that Christ is a usurper, nor any suggestion of a crude binitarianism. For the worship of the exalted Lord is 'to the glory of the Father'. The Biblical monotheism is safeguarded;[4] and the purpose of the Father-God is seen to be honoured in the high place accorded to His Son.

[1] Confirmation of this is found in Rom. xiv. 11 on which Paul comments, 'So each of us shall give account of himself to *God*' (*v.* 12, including in the citation the phrase λέγει Κύριος).

[2] This title is taken from I Enoch xlviii. 5: 'All who dwell on earth shall fall down and worship before him, and will praise and bless and celebrate with song the Lord of spirits' (*Enoch*, ed. R. H. Charles (1925), p. 66). In the preceding verses 2 and 3, there is a reference to the naming of the Son of man.

[3] Weiss, *Christ: the Beginnings of Dogma*, p. 52.

[4] Bonnard, *Philippiens*, p. 47; 'le monothéisme biblique est sauvegardé'; Heinzelmann, *Philipper*, p. 96: 'Kommt Gott dabei [*sc.* that Christ is Lord, and is to be worshipped] nicht zu kurz? Gibt es jetzt nicht zwei Götter? Nein, der Monotheismus bleibt fest.'

PHILIPPIANS II. 5–11 IN ITS FIRST CENTURY SETTING

A. THE 'SITZ IM LEBEN' OF THE HYMN

In this closing section of our study our task is to enquire into the meaning of the passage in the setting of the community which first used it or heard it. When the scope of the enquiry is framed in this way, it is clear that certain presuppositions are being made. These presuppositions may be summed up in a sentence: Philippians ii. 6–11 is an independent, hymnic composition in praise of the cosmic dominion of the Kyrios, Jesus Christ. We have now to address ourselves to enquiring into the hymn's setting in the New Testament period, its *Sitz im Leben der alten Kirche*. But there are two separate issues involved here. There is the meaning of the passage in the context of Paul's letter; and there is the meaning of the Christ-hymn on its own, i.e. before its incorporation into the hortatory context of the Apostolic Epistle. It is conceivable that the two meanings may in no way coincide.[1] One can imagine that Paul would utilize the hymn for his own purposes, without necessarily implying that the original sense of the hymn is to be understood in the use he makes of it. The recognition of this fact is really the decisive factor in the newer interpretation of the passage.

(i) *The 'ethical Interpretation'*

On the older view, the verses were regarded as an integral part of the letter; and Paul glides easily from his exhortation to the Philippians to be selfless and humble-minded into a recital of the humility of Christ. The humbled Christ is set forth as an example of the Christian's humility; the obedient Son is described as an incentive to the Christians' obedience to God as represented by

---

[1] This possibility is endorsed by what G. R. Beasley-Murray has recently written *à propos* of this passage: it is 'necessary to distinguish between the intention of the hymn and the meaning it would have had for the apostle', *Peake's Commentary on the Bible* (²1962), p. 986 (sect. 861 *d*).

Paul's apostolic authority (*v.* 12); Christ's vindication in honour is a spur to ethical endeavour, and an illustration of the divine law that 'he that humbleth himself shall be exalted'.

But, as we have already noticed, there are some serious objections to this so-called 'ethical interpretation'. The syntax of verse 5, τοῦτο φρονεῖτε ἐν ὑμῖν ὃ καὶ ἐν Χριστῷ 'Ιησοῦ, presents an insuperable difficulty once it is recognized that Paul did *not* say: 'Let this mind be in you which was also in Christ Jesus' (A.V.), but rather: 'Act as befits those who are in Christ Jesus.' The Lord's name is used as a pendant to what follows, and not as the introduction of a portrait of His character and actions which are meant to be imitated. Then, there is the fact that Paul never uses the earthly life of Jesus as an *exemplum ad imitandum,* as though he were suggesting that all that a Christian has to do is to follow in the Master's footsteps (contrast I Peter ii. 21).[1] The controlling motive of Pauline ethics is not imitation, but death and resurrection. It involves a death to sin in baptism and a sharing of His risen life in the Spirit. Finally, it becomes very difficult on the view we are criticizing to give any satisfactory sense to the second half of the hymn. If Paul were simply inculcating an acceptance of humility on the ground that Christ was humble, why does he go on to speak of Christ's triumph and honour? An American scholar, R. M. Hawkins,[2] has placed a

---

[1] 'The thought that Christ has given an example (*Vorbild*) for His own which they are, on their part, to emulate, appears only on the fringe of the NT', E. Lohse, 'Nachfolge', *RGG*[3], col. 1288. Lohse's discussion of the Pauline teaching in I Cor. xi. 1; I Thess. i. 6 concludes that 'this does not think of Christ as an example (*Vorbild*) through imitation of whom one becomes similar or equal to Him; but it means that a Christian's relationship to Christ as his Lord is confirmed by his obedience. The Churches are not directed to a prominent moral example but are called to live in a way that is proper in the sphere of Christ's lordship, to be obedient, as He Himself was obedient.'

[2] *The Recovery of the Historical Paul* (1943), pp. 252 f. The effect (of the hymn as a whole) must have been 'to make each proud self-glorifying Christian think, "I will be like Christ; I will ever be conscious of my true dignity; I will stoop to a temporary subjection of myself to my fellow in the hope that God will see the merit of my self-abnegation, and exalt me far above this fellow to whom I temporarily submit myself". It could but accentuate the divisions and the rivalries, although it suggested the method of humility as the goal to the realization of the superiority each one thought himself to possess. Such an assumption of humility as a means to self-exaltation is utterly contemptible.' Hawkins cuts the knot of this problem by

finger on this difficulty by showing that verses 9–11 have no relevance to Paul's ethical admonition. Indeed, the record of the Exaltation of Christ could be a barrier to the exhortation because it could lead to false motives and the acceptance of unworthy ends. The Philippians may have reasoned that it would be good to suffer the inconvenience of a mock humility in the confidence that God would eventually exalt them—as He did Christ—to a place of superiority.

(ii) *An alternative proposal*

Once the hymn's significance in its original form is detached from the use Paul makes of it, we are relieved of these irritating difficulties of interpretation. But the question presses: why, then, did Paul recount the story of Christ as an adjunct to his ethical stimulation of the Philippian Church? If it is not his business to set before them an example of the humble and obedient Lord, to what purpose is he led to pass from the call of ii. 1–4 to verses 5–11? The clue to the answer is found in two parts of the hymn: in the words of verse 5 b: ὃ καὶ ἐν Χριστῷ 'Ιησοῦ, and the confession of verse 11: Κύριος 'Ιησοῦς Χριστός.

(a) *Verse 5b*

The problems of the exegesis of verse 5 b have been mentioned in some detail. It is permissible to read the cryptic words as implying that Paul is summoning the Philippians to act in such a way as befits their standing in Christ Jesus, i.e. as members of His Church.[1] He is reminding them of what they should be as

regarding ii. 5–11 as a post-Pauline interpolation into the text of Philippians. This is a desperate expedient, for which there is no justification—whether textual or other—and is unnecessary once it is recognized that ii. 6–11 is an independent hymn which is being quoted *in toto*. Cf. Jervell, *op. cit.* 209: 'Paul is quoting—as is evident—as the hymn cuts short his presentation. As a matter of fact, only verses 6–8 are necessary to illustrate the exhortation in verses 2–3; but because Paul had a hymn in front of him he continues with verses 9–11. These verses, in this context, serve no purpose.'

[1] Cf. K. Grayston, *Commentary*, p. 91: '"Think this way among yourselves, which also you think in Christ Jesus, i.e. as members of His Church." In other words, this attitude of mind (described in verses 1–4) they are to have in their personal relations, because it is the only attitude proper to those who are "in Christ".'

those who are 'in Him'.[1] This characteristic Pauline phrase is the bridge along which his thought travels to a recital of the events of salvation by which they came to be Christians. He is saying in effect: This is how you came to be incorporated into Christ—for the hymn tells you of His 'way' from glory to ignominy and shame; and thence to glory again—and you are 'in Him'; and, as such, you are called to live a life which has His redeeming acts as its foundation.[2] On this view, the hymn is only loosely dependent upon the ethical admonition, yet it is important in that it supplies the objective facts of redemption on which an ethical appeal may be made. The Apostolic summons is not: Follow Jesus by doing as He did—an impossible feat in any case, for who can be a 'second Christ' who quits His

---

[1] Cf. R. Bultmann, *Theology*, I, 311: '"In Christ", far from being a formula for mystic union, is primarily an *ecclesiological* formula' (italics in the original); *Idem, Existence and Faith* (1961), p. 142; E. Schweizer, *Church Order in the New Testament*, p. 94. Suzanne de Dietrich, *L'épître aux Philippiens* (n.d.), p. 48 writes: 'Toute l'éthique paulinienne n'est autre chose qu'une vie "en Christ", c'est-à-dire une vie qui a en Jésus-Christ son principe et sa fin.' And that motif is realized as the believer appropriates and works out in experience all that the crucified and risen Christ has done for him, as she explains forcefully (*op. cit.* 12–14, citing Col. iii. 1–4; cf. 50). Her title for the Philippians verses is: 'Soyez entre vous comme il faut être en Christ' (*op. cit.* 43).

For the variety of meanings to be attached to the Pauline ἐν Χριστῷ see A. Schweitzer, *The Mysticism of the Apostle Paul* (E.T.[2] 1953), pp. 122 ff.; W. Schmauch, *In Christus* (1935), pp. 68–102; F. Büchsel, '"In Christus" bei Paulus', *ZNTW*, XLII (1949), 141–58; F. Neugebauer, 'Das paulinische ἐν Χριστῷ', *NTS*, IV (1957–8), 124–38; J. A. Allan, 'The "in Christ" Formula in Ephesians', *NTS*, V (1958–9), 54–62; M. Bouttier, *En Christ* (1962).

[2] Käsemann, 'Kritische Analyse', p. 91; 'The technical formula "in Christ" refers beyond doubt, whatever else we can say about it, to the event of salvation. It is soteriological in character, as, according to Paul, the state of being in Christ is arrived at only through the sacrament. Paul therefore regards this hymn as setting forth the event of salvation...(which) is inseparable from, and forms the foundation of, the status of being a Christian' ('Das Heilsgeschehen ist unteilbar und begründet insgesamt oder gar nicht den Christenstand'). Without the aid of this insight there is no solution to the difficulty which F. C. Porter, *The Mind of Christ in Paul*, p. 210, raises: 'They (*sc.* the verses in Philippians) require a Christ whom men cannot regard as an example, because he is not really man. The Christ of the hymn was divine before he was human, and is now divine with a still higher title and authority.' The second part of Porter's statement is doubtless true but it is a *petitio principii* to start from the assumption that the heavenly Christ is set forth as an example.

heavenly glory and dies in shame and is taken up into the throne of the universe? The appeal and injunction to the Philippians in their pride and selfishness are rather: Become in your conduct and church relationships the type of persons who, by that *kenosis*, death and exaltation of the Lord of glory, have a place in His body, the Church.

(b) Verse 11 b

The declaration of the lordship of Christ in verse 11 echoes the same thought. In the context of the hymn the words are in the style of an acclamation-formula, by which the spirit-powers admit that their homage is due to the enthroned Kyrios. The Church—as Lohmeyer's insight revealed—is not present in the heavenly enthronement scene. But 'Jesus Christ is Lord' *is* a Christian confession (Rom. x. 9; I Cor. xii. 3; II Cor. iv. 5, cf. Col. ii. 6; I Peter iii. 15; Acts x. 36); and in any case it is the confessing Church which sings the hymn, thereby identifying herself with the confession made by the subdued cosmic forces in the celestial world, although the lordship of Christ means far more to her than to them. In so doing, she is caught up to share the Redeemer's final victory in the Jubilee of the reconciled universe.[1] This victory is *de jure* a present reality, for He is exalted and is the object of all creation's worship, with angelic powers bowing down before Him. But *de facto* the triumph is a future expectation, for the end is not yet, and the principalities and powers are very real in the influence they exert against the *ecclesia pressa et militans* on earth. But when the hymn is sung, and His lordly power owned and confessed, the Church shows that, even now and here on earth, there is a present Reign of Christ; and that she is called to live (and to suffer) under that lordship of Him who is the Head of the Church. The application of this teaching would not be lost on the first readers of the quoted

[1] Here again our conclusion owes much to Käsemann's summing-up: 'With this hymn, the Christian Church on earth makes her simultaneous response to the adoration of the Powers which is taking place before the throne of God. She is thus caught up into the eschatological event, and is a witness on earth of the enthronement of Him who was obedient. It is not necessary that she should be proclaiming what has happened to herself. While she is proclaiming Christ as the Ruler of the cosmos, the new era is made visible in the Church. It is apparent that the obedient One is setting forth those who are obedient', 'Kritische Analyse', pp. 94–5.

hymn in the Philippian Letter. As they were *cives* of the Empire, called to live worthily of Rome and all that the Empire stood for, so they are bound to a higher loyalty and to a heavenly Lord (Phil. i. 27, iii. 20 f.).

(iii) *A suggested baptismal context*

A more precise *Sitz im Leben* has been suggested in recent studies; and as this is but the logical conclusion to the line of interpretation adopted above, it may now be examined. The confession of Christ as Kyrios (in the hymn's context) betokens His victory over the spirit-rulers and spells an end to their régime. The convert who confesses this lordship may well have seen in it a means of passing from the domain of tyrannical forces and fears into the liberty and joy of Christ (Rom. viii. 15, 21, 38 f.; Gal. iv. 1 ff., v. 1 ff.; Col. i. 12 f., ii. 8–15, 20; Acts x. 38; Apoc. i. 18).

It is a well-known fact that this confession of Jesus as Lord was made in baptism.[1] Likewise, the use which the hymn makes of the concept of 'the name' of Jesus (*vv.* 9, 10) suggests a baptismal motif as we recall that early Christian initiation was administered in the name of the Lord Jesus (Acts ii. 38, viii. 16, x. 48, xix. 5; I Cor. i. 12 f., vi. 11; Jas. ii. 7; cf. Matt. xxviii. 19 f.). The unusual expressions μορφή Θεοῦ/δούλου may have some connection with the baptismal theology, as J. Jervell argues.[2] The believer was united with Christ in the sacramental experience wherein he put off the 'old nature' and put on Christ, 'the new man' in whose image he was renewed and reborn.[3] By submitting to this act of baptism 'into Christ' he is called to live out the life of Christ as he becomes conformed to that image. Thus Christ 'takes shape' (μορφοῦσθαι)[4] in him from the moment of baptism onwards; and this implies, on its negative side, a death to sin and a conformity to His death in the watery grave of baptism (Rom. vi. 4 ff. in the light of Phil. iii. 10: συμμορφιζόμενος τῷ θανάτῳ αὐτοῦ) and an increasing identification with His 'form' by the Spirit in this life, a process to be

---

[1] Cf. J. Crehan, *Early Christian Baptism and the Creed* (1950).

[2] *Imago Dei*, p. 208.

[3] Rom. vi. 3 ff., xiii. 14; I Cor. x. 2 (by inference); Gal. iii. 27; Eph. iv. 20–4; Col. iii. 9 ff.; Tit. iii. 5.

[4] Gal. iv. 19; cf. Eph. iv. 20; Rom. xiii. 14; Gal. ii. 20; Col. i. 27, 28; ii. 6.

completed in the resurrection of the body when Christians will take on the full shape of the glorified body of the risen Lord.[1]

It is true that this line of interpretation requires a good deal of subtle and intricate cross-fertilization of thought on the part of the readers; but if baptism meant to the early Church all that modern scholarship holds that it did mean,[2] then the citation of this hymn (with these undertones and allusions making their powerful appeal) will have suggested the following to the Philippian Christians. Paul is admonishing them to adopt the highest ways of life by recalling to them their standing in Christ. He was the divine Image who became incarnate in human likeness (ἐν ὁμοιώματι ἀνθρώπων γενόμενος). The Philippians are reminded that they are destined to share that pre-existent likeness, and even now are to be transformed into that image, which is Christ's.[3] The place where this metamorphosis began for them was their baptism as they renounced the old nature of Adam's likeness and received the new nature of Christ's image imprinted upon them. They confessed their allegiance to the new Man as Lord of all, as they invoked His name and passed into His Kingdom. All that is involved in being 'in Christ' (as by nature they were 'in Adam') is concentrated in the baptismal rite, with its implications of an imprinting of a new image and of a change of lordship. And this new life in His likeness is to be worked out in moral endeavour and practical living; for, as Jervell puts it, baptism is the place in the experience of the early Christians where soteriology and ethics meet.[4] In accepting the challenge of life in Christ they will 'become what they are', they will work out in actual fact all that is potentially declared in baptism, viz. that they are no longer members of the old

[1] II Cor. iii. 18; Rom. viii. 29; Phil. iii. 21; I Cor. xv. 49.

[2] We think especially of the results produced by the so-called 'exegesis in depth' of the Church of Scotland's *Interim Reports of the Special Commission on Baptism* (1955 ff.); cf. W. F. Flemington, *The New Testament Doctrine of Baptism* (1948).

[3] This statement presupposes the equation of μορφή and εἰκών (Jervell, *Imago Dei*, pp. 204 f.). Thus, the references to Christ as the Image of God are relevant: II Cor. iv. 4-6; Col. i. 15, iii. 9 ff.; Eph. iv. 24.

[4] Jervell, *op. cit.* 208: 'The hymn must not be interpreted either in a purely ethical or in a purely soteriological way, but a starting-point should be found where soteriology and ethics come together, that is, in the sacrament.'

Adam and in his image, but are members of the new Adam and re-fashioned in His likeness.[1]

The hymn is a solemn reminder[2] to them that they have received in baptism the divine image and that they belong to this new Age in which the exalted Christ is the world-Ruler. All authority is committed to Him, and He exercises it in His Church visibly, even as He exercises world-dominion in the heavenly world. The Church, by the citation of this Christ-hymn, is summoned to live in that world as those who belong to the coming era, and to actualize in their relationships *hic et nunc* the quality of life which is the life of the Age to come in which the enthroned Christ is sovereign.[3]

(iv) *The soteriological significance*

The hymn may, however, be treated on its own, as having an independent existence; and our closing section will be concerned to elucidate its significance as a self-contained unit, as a specimen of early Christian hymnody. In the classification of early Christian hymnic fragments which was attempted above, Christological hymns formed a major group. Philippians ii. 5–11 is distinguished by the fact that it is perhaps the most illustrious

---

[1] Cf. C. H. Dodd, *The Epistle to the Romans* (*MNTC*, 1932), p. 93: 'The maxim all through is: *Werde das was Du bist* ('Become what you are'). The Christian is a member of Christ: he must see to it that in the empirical life of moral endeavour he becomes more and more that which a member of Christ should be.'

[2] The word 'reminder' carries the dynamic sense which N. A. Dahl gives to ἀνάμνησις in Paul. It is more than a mental reflection, but implies a reliving of the events which are called to mind.

[3] The hymn stands in direct contrast with the Jewish apocalyptic hope and with those parts of the New Testament which are influenced by it. On the apocalyptic view, the salvation of the world is a future event which God will bring about at the last day. This Age = the *hā-'ôlām hazeh* will give place to the Messianic Age or the Age to come = the *hā-'ôlām ha-bā'* (cf. Davies, *Paul and Rabbinic Judaism*[2], pp. 285 ff.; *Torah in the Messianic Age and/or the Age to Come* (1952)). The Christ-hymn proclaims a present salvation for the world in Christ now as, by His Exaltation, He has bound together heaven and earth, and already raised up His people to sit with Him in the heavenly places. The world's salvation is thus a *fait accompli*, and holds out, as Käsemann has acutely noticed, 'Kritische Analyse', 92, no eschatological hope in the futuristic sense of that term. It is, we may submit, the most compelling evidence in the New Testament for the teaching of a realized Eschatology.

example of New Testament Christ-hymns. It stands out as an ode sung to Christ in praise of Him and His achievement. But its significance for Christology should be carefully defined. The stress falls more on what He has accomplished than upon who He was. It is the record of His acts, more than of His character and traits of personality, that occupies the centre of interest. The descriptions of His person in verses 6 ff. serve mainly to prepare for the record of His obedience which in turn is a pendant to His present status as exalted Lord of the universe. It is the lordship of Christ which gives us the right clue to an appreciation of the hymn as a whole; and it is His high destiny as 'Cosmocrator' or world-Ruler which marks the *ultima Thule* of the hymn's recital. In other words, the passage is an aretalogy in honour of Christ the Lord, which recounts His deeds and His ultimate triumph; and directs our thought to His present office and rank, as it proclaims Him worthy of all homage and worship.

If this observation is soundly based, it supplies us with a guiding line of interpretation. These verses, cast in lyrical and liturgical form, portray a soteriological drama. They are not a piece of Christological speculation which answers our question who Christ was, but the record of a series of events of saving significance which declare what He did and how He became worthy of cosmic power. The drama of verses 6 ff. tells how it came about that Christ has received a cosmocracy and why He is now installed as the heavenly Kyrios, with all creation under His control. As befits a drama, the language is picturesque and set in the form of a story. It should, therefore, be interpreted as such, and not as a piece of dogmatic theology,[1] and certainly not as though the terms used were borrowed from classical philosophy.[2] Moreover, the hymn is not concerned with the inner

---

[1] The attempt to make the hymn's Christology conform to the Athanasian Creed—as those who arraigned A. S. Geyser on a charge of heresy have recently tried to do—is surely misconceived. The gravamen of the charge against Professor Geyser of Pretoria University was that he taught that God 'gave him (*sc.* Christ) a higher status after his resurrection than before; and that this teaching detracted from the true and eternal godhead of Christ, as defined in the Athanasian Creed' (Report, 'Heresy in South Africa', *The Hibbert Journal*, LXI (1962), 12 f.).

[2] Especially the terms μορφή, σχῆμα, and ὁμοίωμα. Cf. T. O. Wedel's exposition (*ad* Eph. ii. 4–5, *IB*, x (1953), 642): 'The New Testament. . . (is) never wearied of repeating—as a creed does in more stylized mold—the

relationships of the Godhead, but is arranged so as to tell the events of the Redeemer's way in a connected series.[1] The 'plot' is told in spatial terms and by the use of a kinetic imagery—thus we read of a divine being, who is not identified with God, but is on a par with Him. He is faced with a choice, which He makes. The consequence of this momentous decision is an epiphany, as He who was 'above' came 'down'. His appearance is marked by self-humbling and obedience to the farthest point, to death. The imagery of movement is continued in the thought that God lifted Him up and bestowed upon Him a kingly name and office, before which angelic powers and the entire cosmos bend down in submission. The epiphany is thus completed; and the incarnate One resumes a place in the celestial sphere. In so doing He has joined together heaven and earth; and brought under His authority those cosmic powers which up to that point had had control in the realms of creation. In this sense they are 'reconciled' and brought into unity and harmony with the divine will. For the hymn, this is the soteriology which is important; and it is Christ's present Rule that is of supreme moment.

The author's main interest lies in seeking an answer to the pressing issue of human destiny and purpose in life. He seems to draw into his picture of the pre-existent, humiliated and victorious Lord many strands of Christological speculation and theory. He is dependent upon a variety of categories as he sets

essence of the gospel. Always this is in the form of drama. Christian faith is based upon a story, an epic. It is verb-theology, not a series of abstract propositions. Something has happened....' The last statement is strikingly illustrated by the hymn. The important words are not the nouns, but the verbs ('thought it not', 'emptied Himself', 'becoming obedient', God 'exalted' and 'bestowed', 'every knee should bow', 'every tongue confess').

[1] Käsemann, 'Kritische Analyse', p. 71: 'Not a relationship, but an event, a "drama", is here portrayed, in which various phases follow one another...Christology is here set forth to view in the framework of soteriology'; 76: 'All these statements are not intended to give a definition of essence in the sense of the Christology of the early Church, but rather to speak of events in a connected series...It is not a matter of the identity of a person in different phases, but of the continuity of a miraculous happening'; 80: 'The underlying myth embraces the idea of "God becoming man" in successive phases, in the continuity of the drama of salvation, which is connected together by miracle, and because of that presents contrasts. At the same time, it would be wrong to derive a *kenosis* teaching from our hymn; for the humiliation is merely one phase in the way of the Redeemer, and as such it cannot be isolated and should not be so.'

forth the meaning of the incarnation, the *kenosis* and the glorification of Christ. It is not surprising that scholars have been able to detect a bewildering array of categories, so that the verses of this short tribute appear like a Christological miscellany with many contributions: a Son of Man dogmatic; oriental or Greek mythology (Lucifer? the Titans? Herakles?); the first–second Adam speculation of Jewish thought; Hellenistic Jewish concepts of Wisdom; the Servant of Yahweh concept, a 'Paidology'; an Emperor motif; a divine Hero, θεῖος ἀνήρ, Christology; an enthronement ritual of an oriental monarch; an Iranian or Gnostic redemption myth; all these categories have been suggested, with varying degrees of plausibility.

The hymn, however, refuses to yield its deep secrets; and it is possible that many factors have influenced the poet's thinking. But, whatever the background to this story of Christ may be, the twin concepts of humiliation and exaltation which figure so prominently in Jesus' teaching[1] and which are exemplified in His earthly and post-resurrection life[2] must have been in the forefront of his mind as he composed this tribute to the Church's Lord.

B. THE QUESTIONS OF AUTHORSHIP AND PROVENANCE

The author is debtor to many traditions, and in particular, to both a Hebraic and Hellenistic thought-world. The former inheritance is shown in his use of the Old Testament, both by allusion and by explicit citation, certain Semitic expressions in his writing and his doctrine of 'the name'. The latter is apparent in his cosmology of two worlds, below and above, his possible reference to the Greek gods and heroes who 'came down' and his statement about the mighty angels which control the regions of the universe. Clearly, the author of Philippians ii. 6–11 stands at the junction of two cultures and two religious traditions. His background is Jewish, but it is Greek ideas which stand at the forefront of his mind; and he is concerned, as a Christian, to relate the Gospel to the larger world of Hellenism.[3]

---

[1] Matt. xviii. 4, xxiii. 12; Lk. xiv. 11, xviii. 14.

[2] Cf. Mark viii. 31–ix. 1.

[3] While, therefore, there is evidence that the earliest followers of Jesus worshipped Him as their Lord, and accorded Him such divine honours as

This hymn, we may suggest, has cultic significance in that it hails the Church's Lord; but it is equally a missionary manifesto of some Christian or Christian group whose outlook reaches

belonged properly to their covenant God (F. C. Burkitt, *Christian Beginnings*, pp. 51 f. against Bousset's denial that the believers at Jerusalem used the title 'Lord' for Jesus; and G. Dix, *Jew and Greek: A Study in the Primitive Church* (1953), p. 79 for the view that Jesus was the object of a liturgical cultus from the beginning), certain features of Phil. ii. 6 ff. point to a later origin of the hymn it embodies. These are such Hellenistic elements as the threefold division of the cosmos, the concept of two orders of existence and the emphasis on the freely willed choices of Jesus. More importantly, there is a singular absence of those features which are found in the Jerusalem kerygma; for this see C. H. Dodd, *The Apostolic Preaching and its Developments*[2] pp. 17 ff.; R. B. Rackham, *The Acts of the Apostles*[14] (1951), p. lxx; A. M. Hunter, *The Unity of the New Testament* (1946). The following items in this early statement of the gospel of Christ are missing from Phil. ii:

(i) The origin of Jesus from the house of David (Acts ii. 25 ff., xiii. 16–40; cf. Rom. i. 3; II Tim. ii. 8);

(ii) His fulfilment of Messianic prophecy (Acts ii. 16, iii. 18, 24, x. 43; Rom. i. 2; I Cor. xv. 3–4);

(iii) His being 'sent by the Father' to the Jewish nation (Acts x. 36; cf. xiii. 23, 32);

(iv) His ministry, teaching and preaching (Acts. ii. 22, iii. 22, x. 37 f.);

(v) His death by crucifixion, according to the 'settled' purpose of God (Acts ii. 23, iii. 13 f., v. 30, x. 39; cf. xiii. 27 ff.);

(vi) His Resurrection in accord with the scriptures (Acts ii. 24, 32, iii. 13, iv. 11, v. 31, x. 40. He is now exalted 'as Messianic head of the new Israel' (Dodd, *op. cit.* p. 22), Acts ii. 33;

(vii) The promise that He will come again (Acts iii. 21: so Dodd, *op. cit.* p. 23; but this is criticized by J. A. T. Robinson, 'The Most Primitive Christology of all?', *JTS*, VII (1956), 177 ff.; *Jesus and His Coming* (1957), pp. 144 ff. In any event, Acts iii 21 looks ahead to a future appearance of Christ, whether as Judge (in the sense of Acts x. 42) or as full Messiah (but cf. E. Schweizer, *Lordship and Discipleship*, p. 57, n. 3).

Even in those places where Phil. ii. 6 ff. contains language which is similar to that of the early speeches, it is a moot point whether in fact the two documents mean the same thing. For example, the term παῖς Θεοῦ is an ambiguous title, with a different flavour in the two sources. In the Acts record, Jesus is *God's* Servant; but this is not explicit in Phil. ii. 7. Again, Acts ii. 36 declares that by the Resurrection Jesus is made Lord and Christ, but this may mean no more than 'Head of the Messianic community' rather than 'Lord of all creation', as in Phil. ii. 9–11. To say, moreover, as J. A. T. Robinson does (*Jesus and His Coming*, p. 147) that the 'fore-appointment' (προχειρίζεσθαι) 'for you' (*sc.* the Jews) in Acts iii. 20 is the equivalent of Christ's pre-existence in Phil. ii. 6 is precarious. There is a much richer understanding of Christ's person and office implied in the Philippians reference.

forth to the world beyond the confines of Jewish Christianity and sees that the cosmic Christ, the universal Lord, is the one true answer to the religious quests of the Graeco-Roman world. This thesis may be supported in two ways. First, the hymn may be contrasted with a product of early Christianity which is sensitive to its Jewish inheritance and which has addressed its message to a community in which emphases of Jewish faith are especially pronounced. The section in I Corinthians xv. 3 ff. fits this description. Then, by sketching the religious and cultic situation in the world of the Empire in the first century, we may be able to see the relevance of the hymn as a presentation of Christ which is directed to this scene.

(i) *Two 'traditional' passages compared: I Corinthians xv. 3–5 and Philippians ii. 5–11*

It is an instructive exercise to compare the Philippians hymn with the *pericope* I Corinthians xv. 3 ff.:[1]

> For I delivered to you as of first importance what I also received:
> that Christ died for our sins in accordance with the scriptures,
> that he was buried,
> that he was raised on the third day in accordance with the scriptures,
> and that he appeared to Cephas, then to the twelve.

This passage is universally acknowledged as traditional material which Paul has taken over,[2] and which he quotes to introduce his discussion of problems connected with the Resurrection hope at Corinth. Its character as a fragment of pre-Pauline *paradosis* is shown by the marks it carries of being a credal formulation. The following are the most noteworthy points:

(*a*) The introductory verbs παραλαμβάνειν and παραδιδόναι

---

[1] For recent discussions of this passage, cf. E. Lichtenstein, 'Die älteste christliche Glaubensformel', *Zeit. für Kirchengeschichte*, lxiii (1950), 1–74; B. Gerhardsson, *Memory and Manuscript* (1961), pp. 299 ff. The older studies of A. Seeberg, *Der Katechismus der Urchristenheit* (1903), pp. 45–58; and E. Norden, *Agnostos Theos* (1913), pp. 269 ff. had already detected the confessional character of the words.

[2] J. Jeremias, *The Eucharistic Words of Jesus* (E.T. 1955), pp. 129 ff.; R. H. Mounce, *The Essential Nature of New Testament Preaching*, pp. 90 ff.; A. M. Hunter, *Paul and his Predecessors*[2] (1961), pp. 15 ff., 117 f.

are the equivalents of two rabbinical technical terms used for the receiving and transmission of a tradition, קבל מן and מסר ל.[1]

(b) The fourfold repetition of ὅτι seems to indicate the presence of material which the Apostle is citing.

(c) There are a number of un-Pauline traits in the language which is used: the phrase κατὰ τὰς γραφάς is found nowhere else in Paul who usually says καθὼς γέγραπται; the plural word for 'sins' is not typical of Paul's writing and in those places where it is found in his authentic literature, it can be fairly obviously shown that he is dependent upon general Christian usage. His own preference is for the word in the singular, with the sense of 'Sin' (as a personified power); certain turns of phrase such as ὤφθη (only here and in the hymnic I Tim. iii. 16), ἐγήγερται (only in this chapter and in the credal II Tim. ii. 8) and οἱ δώδεκα, are untypical of Paul.

(d) Jeremias has taken the investigation a stage farther by submitting that there are signs that this section is a translation of a Semitic original. The name of Jesus is avoided; the passive voice of the verb ἐγήγερται is used as a periphrasis for the divine name; the word ὤφθη (instead of ἐφάνη) is explained by the fact that the putative Hebrew original נראה would have the double meaning 'He was seen' and 'He appeared'; the placing of the subject of the last clause in the dative (Κηφᾷ = Aramaic כיפא) after a passive verb, instead of the expected ὑπό with the genitive; the double reference to the Old Testament scriptures.[2] All this, according to Jeremias, suggests that I Corinthians xv. 3 b–5 arose in a Jewish-Christian *milieu*. And this is confirmed by verse 11 which states that what Paul is reproducing was identical with the common proclamation of the Apostles at Jerusalem.

There are two distinct conclusions which have been drawn. The first is that I Corinthians xv. 3 ff. embodies 'a piece of primitive Christian tradition—παράδοσις...as if Paul were reciting a connected fragment of catechism' (J. Weiss).[3] The style and form of the Greek text reinforce this verdict which is generally shared. But recent scholarship has taken the *Sitz im Leben* of this catechetical matter back to the Jerusalem Church,

[1] Dibelius, *From Tradition to Gospel*, p. 21 citing *'Aboth* i. 1: Moses received the oral law from God on Sinai, and committed it to Joshua.
[2] For the meaning of this 'Schriftprinzip' cf. Lichtenstein, *loc. cit.* 9–25.
[3] *Der erste Korintherbrief* (*MeyerKomm.* 1925), p. 347.

and interpreted E. Meyer's remark, that we have here the oldest document of the Christian Church in existence, in a literal way.[1] Against Heitmüller's[2] and Dibelius'[3] view that I Corinthians xv. 3 ff. is a summary of belief held in Hellenistic Christianity and was mediated to Paul through the Hellenistic Church, it is now contended that the *paradosis* emanated from the primitive Palestinian Church.[4] It represents, says B. Gerhardsson, 'a logos fixed by the college of Apostles in Jerusalem'.[5] A. M. Hunter, who in 1940 opined that the text came from the Church at Damascus as 'a creed perhaps taught him (Paul) by Ananias before his baptism',[6] now in his revision of *Paul and his Predecessors* prefers, in view of the linguistic data, to think that the tradition stemmed from the mother Church at Jerusalem;[7] and Gerhardsson has set this conclusion on a theological basis, viz. Paul's respect for Jerusalem as the eschatological city of God from which the word of the Lord would proceed in the last days.[8]

If this assumption concerning the provenance of the Corinthian catechesis may be accepted, then that text and Philippians ii. 6–11 are comparable. Both antedate Pauline Christianity and go back to the early days of the Christian mission; and both belong to the confessional life of the Church. But they are very different in content. I Corinthians xv. 3–5 is a *credo* which is meaningful in a community where the Jewish inheritance of the Christian faith is strong; where forgiveness of sins is a burning issue, and the heartfelt cry of the believer is (as the Reformation age phrased it): 'Wie kriege ich einen gnädigen Gott?' Moreover, it is a Christian community in which the portrait of Jesus is painted on an Old Testament canvas, and in which the argument from Messianic prophecy is accepted as cogent.

In Philippians ii. 6 ff. the message is coming to grips with the world of Hellenism; and the crucial issues under debate are the purposelessness of existence and the conquest of those agencies which tyrannized over Hellenistic man. The live question is not

---

[1] E. Meyer, *Ursprung u. Anfänge des Christentums*, III (1923), p. 210.
[2] *ZNTW*, XIII (1912), 320–37 (quoted by Hunter, *op. cit.* p. 17).
[3] *From Tradition to Gospel*, p. 18.
[4] Seeberg, *Der Katechismus*, p. 268 had expressed the view that the catechetical formula (*Glaubensformel*) went back to the period 'shortly after the death of Christ'.
[5] *Memory and Manuscript*, p. 297.   [6] *Paul and his Predecessors*[2], p. 16.
[7] A. M. Hunter, *op. cit.* pp. 117 f.   [8] B. Gerhardsson, *op. cit.* pp. 274 ff.

seen as the resolution of the problem of man's guilt before the holy God of the Old Testament, but the assurance that God in Christ is in control of the universe and that life has meaning.

It is to E. Schweizer that the credit must go for discerning the different *milieux* from which the two parts of scripture are drawn.[1] We may set the features side by side in order more clearly to see the contrast. The main presupposition which underlies this analysis is an insight which J. R. Geiselmann has stated.[2] This is to the effect that it is as important to notice what the Philippians-hymn *does not* say as to build upon what it *does* say. If we apply this rule, we can set down the following:

I CORINTHIANS XV. 3 FF.	PHILIPPIANS II. 6 FF.
The humanity of Jesus is the starting-point of the Christology. The career of Christ is set in a linear, eschatological framework; it is composed of a historically determined progression: 'died, buried, raised, appeared'.	It is the pre-existent 'Form of God' who stands at the head of this Christology. The movement is in terms of a descent from the world above to the world below. His coming is *into*, with a true humanity only equivocally expressed, rather than arising *from*, humanity. He 'appears' rather than 'is born' or 'is sent' by the Father.
Christ's mission is 'according to the scriptures'. A Jewish background is assumed, with a doctrine of two covenants, two Ages. The Messiah fulfils the prophecy and inaugurates the Messianic era in His earthly life.	The *schema* is set in a Hellenistic frame of two worlds, the heavenly and the earthly; and the Incarnation is the bridge between two orders of existence, the divine and the human; and no feature marks out the earthly existence but its obedience.
Christ died 'for our sins' and in fulfilment of all that was written of Him. It was a sin-atoning death, on a cross; and for the sake of His people.	The death of the Lord is the end of His earthly career and the last stage of His obedient way from heaven to earth. No atoning significance is attached to

[1] E. Schweizer, *Erniedrigung*, pp. 112 ff.; *Lordship*, pp. 114 ff. See his later contribution, 'Two New Testament Creeds compared. 1 Corinthians 15: 3–5 and 1 Timothy 3: 16', *Current Issues in New Testament Interpretation*, ed. W. Klassen and G. F. Snyder (1962), pp. 166–77.

[2] *Jesus der Christus*, p. 146.

I CORINTHIANS XV. 3 FF.	PHILIPPIANS II. 6 FF.
	it; and the Church is not prominent. What He does is done for the whole of the race.
The saving work of Christ is completed at the Resurrection. This is God's affirmation. It is needed as part of the apologetic against Jewish detractors who argued that Jesus was a blasphemer who died under the ban of God, and was therefore a Messianic pretender. The Resurrection reverses this verdict and is God's attestation of His Messiahship (as in the Acts-kerygma).	The Resurrection is passed over in favour of the Exaltation which is all-important. It is this which signifies that He is the exalted One on the throne to whom all the cosmic powers are subject.
The appearance of the living Christ is to His disciples who needed to be assured of His personal presence; who needed the message of pardon on the ground of His death for their sins; who faced a world of sceptical fellow-Jews who shared their need: How can a man be right with God?	The ascended Lord appears to angels; and receives the homage of the astral powers which own His lordship as Lord of all (*Pantocrator*). This fact brings comfort to the Church of the Hellenistic world in which men live in fear of hostile stars and wrestle with the meaninglessness of life which is ruled by Fate and Necessity. The Church sings the hymn; and in so doing, she confesses (with the powers above) that He is Lord of the universe and human destiny is in His hands. Life has a purpose; and freedom from fear is possible

We have stated the contrasts in bold relief; and have not stopped to indicate some of the points of similarity which the two representations of the Christian message have in common. Jesus Christ for both wings of the Church is the same person, but is interpreted in a different light according to the varying needs of the situation. It is the same basic conviction—that God was in Christ reconciling the world unto Himself—which runs through the whole New Testament, but as the Church moves away from her Jerusalem birthplace and her Palestinian home, she confronts new situations and inherits new problems in the communication of her 'word of salvation'. With Hellenistic man as the potential convert and church-member, she must transpose the message of Christ into an idiom which he will appreciate, and present him with an understanding of the significance of Christ which will meet his need. We may presume that the emergence of a new missionary situation, which fell across the path of the Church's progress when some men of Cyprus and Cyrene, members of the school of the martyred Stephen, began their work, prompted the development of this Christology and cognate soteriology. These men came to Antioch (Acts xi. 19 ff.), and addressed themselves to the evangelization of the Greeks with a message of Jesus as Kyrios.[1] The mission to the Hellenistic world opened at this juncture. It met with initial success, and drew into its orbit the contribution of Saul of Tarsus. But it is possible that the foundations of the wider appeal had already been laid by the thought, preaching and influence of Stephen. There is some affinity between the record we have of his theology and that of the Philippians-psalm, especially if (as W. Manson's study allows us[2]) we bring in the emphases of the letter to the Hebrews. In Stephen we have a candidate for the authorship of the hymn. He was a Hellenistic Jewish Christian, of wide sympathies and with depth of penetration into the mystery of Christ.[3] He saw beyond the bounds of a Jewish-Christian mission, to a universal Church, and this con-

---

[1] The significance of the statement 'Jesus Christ is Lord' in this missionary context is well assessed by H. Riesenfeld, 'The Mythological Background of New Testament Christology', *The Background of the New Testament and its Eschatology* in honour of C. H. Dodd (1956), p. 94: 'The sentence "Jesus Christ is Lord"...was fitted to transcend all frontiers and thus made the world mission possible.'

[2] W. Manson, *The Epistle to the Hebrews* (1951).

[3] M. Simon, *St Stephen and the Hellenists in the Primitive Church* (1958), cf. A. F. J. Klijn, 'Stephen's Speech—Acts vii. 2–53', *NTS*, IV (1957), 25–31, and earlier, 'Stephen's Vision in Acts vii. 55–6' by H. P. Owen, *NTS*, I (1954), 224–6. Cullmann writes: 'Apart from Paul, Stephen was perhaps the most significant man in the early Church. According to the little we know of his theological views, he grasped what was new in Jesus' thought better than almost anyone else' (*Christology*, p. 183).

viction was his because he 'saw that the Messiah was on the throne of the Universe'.[1] He was 'the crucified Son of Man to whom the throne of the world and the Lordship of the Age to come belonged' (Manson).[2] Some links of terminology between Stephen's speech in Acts vii and the text of the Christ-hymn;[3] his practice of prayer to *Maran*-Jesus as the exalted Son of man in the glory of God and the heavenly Kyrios;[4] his grasp of the universality of the Christian faith which embraces humanity at large;[5] his background in Jewish Hellenism and the inheritance into which his followers entered at Antioch[6] about which G. Dix writes: 'it was a bastion of Hellenism in the Syriac lands...the inevitable meeting point of the two worlds';[7] and the lexical, stylistic and theological affinities between Stephen's *plaidoyer* for the truth and finality of the Christian gospel and the Christology of Hebrews[8]—all these features are worthy of consideration when we seek to anchor the Christ-hymn in the historical stream of the early Church.

[1] Manson, *The Epistle to the Hebrews*, p. 31.   [2] *Op. cit.* 32.
[3] See appendix to Part III, pp. 312 f.
[4] Acts vii. 59 records the prayer: 'Lord Jesus, receive my spirit.' The fact that Stephen is described as taking the title 'Lord' upon his lips may or may not be significant; but it is impressive that this sentence contains an invocation of Jesus as the Christians' *Maran* in a similar way to that in which the confessing Church would take the hymnic acclamation 'Kyrios Jesus Christ' in Phil. ii. 11, and thereby give expression to her faith. In both instances, it is the exalted Jesus who is invoked as heavenly Kyrios; and who is directly addressed in prayer.
[5] See W. Manson, *ut supra.*
[6] 'The Hellenistic message undoubtedly represents one step towards Christian emancipation. It is at least very likely that the Antioch community, where a peculiar type of Christianity, Greek in language and spirit, was elaborated...was actually founded by some disciples of Stephen', writes M. Simon, *St Stephen*, p. 112.
[7] *Jew and Greek*, p. 33; cf. II Macc. iv. 9 for an illustration.
[8] The points of contact between Phil. ii and the Christology of Hebrews are numerous: the exordium of Heb. i. 1–4 moves in the same thought-world as the Philippians hymn, with the notes of heavenly glory and pre-existence, a *katabasis* into this world, and a return to the celestial world. Then, the obedience of the incarnate Christ (in Phil. ii. 7 f. and Heb. v. 5 ff.) is common teaching. The emphasis in Hebrews falls on the Exaltation of Christ more than on His Resurrection which, in fact, is mentioned only once in the Epistle (xiii. 20). Both Christologies employ the imagery of an enthronement ritual as the exalted Lord is worshipped by the angelic host. And both seem to lay under tribute the teaching of a divine Hero who comes

At all events, the relevance of the confession, 'Jesus Christ is Lord' in the early decades of the Church's life must have been apparent. We turn now to consider the world of Graeco-Roman culture and religion into which the Church came, and to note something of the relevance of its proclamation and cultus.

(ii) The first century background and challenge

Many factors contributed to make the Hellenistic age one of instability and fear.[1] There were the political confusions which followed in the wake of Alexander's world-shaking influence and its demise. The wars and the disturbances of the balance of power brought an unsettlement to the lives of ordinary men. As was inevitable following the political upheavals and conflicts, social misery and economic ruin appeared on the scene; and these features contributed further to the sense of futility which

from the world above and blazes a trail as ἀρχηγός and πρόδρομος, thus making it possible for men to follow to the heavenly world without fear. Both Christological teachings operate with categories of the two worlds.

It would be an interesting side-light on the enigmatic οὐχ ἁρπαγμὸν ἡγήσατο, in Phil. ii. 6, if we could interpret the preposition ἀντί in Heb. xii. 2 to mean: Jesus, the pioneer and perfecter of our faith, who *instead of* the joy that was set before Him endured the cross, despising the shame, etc. (cf. Heb. xi. 25, 26 for the thought of a choice and its consequences)—as Michel, *Hebräerb.* pp. 293 f. and Schweizer, *Lordship*, p. 73, n. 1 consider possible.

For the discussions of the interrelation of Phil. ii and Heb. initiated in this way by Lohmeyer, *Kyrios Jesus*, pp. 70 ff., cf. Käsemann, *Das wandernde Gottesvolk*, esp. pp. 61 ff., whose treatment of the text and thesis that Christ is the pioneer, who through His Incarnation and victorious and expiatory death has opened up a way for His people into the homeland, have influenced subsequent discussion; Leivestad, *Christ the Conqueror*, pp. 178 ff.; Michel's commentary *ut supra* who questions some of Käsemann's Gnostic analogies; and, for the Christology in particular, G. Bornkamm, *Gesamm. Aufsät.* II, 'Das Bekenntnis im Heb.', 188 ff., esp. 197 ff.

Manson, *The Epistle to the Hebrews*, p. 97 finds that both Hebrews and Phil. ii are based on a Wisdom Christology fashioned to meet the needs of a world mission.

[1] For this section we are indebted to: A.-J. Festugière, *Personal Religion among the Greeks* (1960 ed.), pp. 40 ff.; W. W. Tarn and G. T. Griffith, *Hellenistic Civilisation*[3] (1952), chs. IX and X; F. C. Grant, *Roman Hellenism and the New Testament* (1962); G. Murray, *Five Stages of Greek Religion* (1935 ed.), ch. IV: 'The Failure of Nerve'; P. Wendland, *Die hellenistisch-römische Kultur*[2] (1912), pp. 106 ff.; A. D. Nock, *Conversion* (1933) (later edit. 1961).

fell across the spirit of Hellenistic man. On the intellectual level, probably the most significant influence was that which came with a new view of the cosmos provided by Greek science. The new geocentric astronomy, although adumbrated by Heraclides (c. 360 B.C.) and earlier by Eudoxus (c. 408–355 B.C.), was formulated by Hipparchus (c. 190–126 B.C.), and immediately and enthusiastically brought into relation with everyday life through the astrologers who were interested in locating the realms of the gods or the forces governing human life in the sphere of the fixed stars. On this view, the planets did much to alter the scheme of human life, and the region below the moon was a source of constant daemonic interference. The geocentric cosmology taught that the earth floated freely in space, surrounded by seven or eight concentric spheres which rotated about it, always in perfect harmony and obedient to eternal laws. As far as religion was affected by this newer scientific theory, it meant that a drastic re-thinking of the Homeric theology was required. No place could be found for the pantheon on Mount Olympus and the realm of the gods could not be located in any mundane sphere. There was no place for them except the outer regions of starry space—unless they were to be identified with the stars. And this identification came about, chiefly through the advent of oriental astrology which 'with its accompanying astral religion and dominant fatalism, lay like a nightmare upon the soul'[1]—or, to change the metaphor, 'fell upon the Hellenistic mind as a new disease falls upon some remote island people' (Gilbert Murray).[2] The effect of this was that, with the new scientific world-view which placed emphasis upon transcendence, universal law and cosmic order, religion entered upon a phase of pessimism and despair. The scientists had given an important place to the stars and planets in the systems. The astrologers made capital of this by teaching that everything in this world is governed by astral powers which determine the lot of humanity. Moreover, these powers are indifferent to the individual man; and the doctrine of Destiny which had earlier been applied to public affairs was now transferred to private life. Men were made to feel that all things were

[1] P. Wendland, 'Hellenistic Ideas of Salvation in the light of ancient Anthropology', *AJT*, XVII (1913), 345–51 (345).

[2] *Five Stages of Greek Religion*, p. 144.

ruled by an evil Necessity (ἀνάγκη) and Destiny (εἱμαρμένη)[1] which from birth—and the particular constellation or conjunction of the stars or planets under which a person was born was of decisive importance—determined 'the entire course of our lives, and which nothing can enable us to escape'.[2]

But escape was promised along certain paths: mysticism, occultism and ascetic practices. By seeking fellowship with a mighty god who is able to raise his protégés above the hopeless round of Necessity and above the regions controlled by the powerful astral deities;[3] by the cults of Serapis, Isis and Asclepius who are hailed in the aretalogies of contemporary writers as mightier than εἱμαρμένη and who offer victory over Destiny (τύχη) to their devotees;[4] and by renunciation, asceticism and magic—in these ways the yearning of Hellenistic man for 'salvation' and a sense of harmony with the remote eternal world of the divine was expressed. Men confessed that life was one of uncertainty and fear; and sought to escape from the mesh of inevitability. The universe seemed cold and unfriendly;

[1] For this see, in addition to the above, Festugière, *L'idéal religieux des Grecs* (1932), pp. 66 ff., 101 ff.; D. Amand, *Fatalisme et liberté dans l'antiquité grecque* (1945); W. C. Greene, *Moira: Fate, Good and Evil in Greek Thought* (1944); G. H. C. Macgregor and A. C. Purdy, *Jew and Greek: Tutors unto Christ* (1936), pp. 231 ff., 291 ff.

[2] Festugière, *Personal Religion*, p. 41.

[3] Wendland, 'Hellenistic Ideas of Salvation', p. 347. He cites the following prayers:

(i)   To Serapis: 'Preserve me from the might of the stars, Hold me back from the cruel compulsion of fate, Allot me a happy destiny, bless my life, O Lord, with all goodness; for I am thy slave and thy protégé' (Dietrich, *Abraxas*, p. 178).

(ii)   In the Mithras Liturgy (ed. by Dietrich, 1910): a prayer to be freed from the bitter and inexorable compulsion of fate.

(iii)   Hermetic prayer of thanks: 'No threatening shall obtain power over me. No spirit, no demon, no ghost, nor any other evil apparition from the underworld shall oppose me, because of thy name which I bear in my heart' (Dietrich, *Abraxas*, p. 195).

[4] Isis is greater than εἱμαρμένη and has power to deliver man (Festugière, *HTR*, XLII (1949), 209 ff., 223, 233 f.). Lucius, in Apuleius, *Met.*, is beset by Fate, the blind goddess; but 'the day of deliverance dawns for thee' (XI, v, 4), through the merciful Isis (XI, xv, 1-4: 'by the providence of the mighty Isis he doth triumph joyfully over his Fortune') whose aretalogy is: 'I am victorious over Destiny. Destiny (τύχη) obeyeth me' (Aretalogy to Isis Cymaea which contains the words, cited by Festugière, *L'idéal religieux*, p. 101: ἐγὼ τὸ ἱμαρμένον νικῶ).

indeed the stars which religious thought had earlier deified were positively malevolent and hostile;[1] and life lacked any sense of purpose or significant meaning. The heart's cry of this man was:

> I, a stranger and afraid
> In a world I never made;[2]

or, as Belloc's lines put it:[3]

> Strong God, which made the topmost stars
> To circulate and keep their course;
> Remember me, whom all the bars
> Of sense and dreadful fate enforce.

To such a person the Christian gospel came as one of deliverance and hope. The three basic needs of the Hellenistic age which Wendland has described[4] were met in the message of the early missionaries. In the first place, men craved a freedom from the power or tyranny of evil spirits. Then, as they groaned under the weight of astral religion, which made them the sport and plunder of the star-gods, they cried out for some mighty god who would be able to control a relentless and pitiless fate and to deliver them from bondage to the archons and from the rule of εἱμαρμένη and ἀνάγκη. Thirdly, the soul of man, conscious of its divine origin, strove for redemption from its foreign and unrelated companion, the body. It sought deliverance from all that is sinful, finite and mortal.

C. THE ESSENTIAL TEACHING OF THE HYMN

It is with the second of the above features that the Christ-hymn in Philippians ii is directly concerned. The relevance of this will be even clearer if we compare the hymn in Ignatius, ad Ephes. xix which makes explicit what is implied in the Philippians-

---

[1] Therefore, the endeavour was, in Tarn–Griffith's expression, to 'short-circuit the stars' (op. cit. 351), i.e. to reverse the destiny they decreed, and to break their spell.
Tarn–Griffith, op. cit. 345 f., speak of the doctrine of *heimarmene* as 'one of the most terrible doctrines which ever oppressed humanity'.

[2] A. E. Housman. See ch. VII above, note 4 on p. 180.

[3] Quoted by F. C. Grant, *Roman Hellenism and the New Testament*, p. 48.

[4] 'Hellenistic Ideas', p. 348; cf. for a similar list, Tarn–Griffith, op. cit. 351 ff.; Macgregor–Purdy, *Jew and Greek*, pp. 235 ff.

psalm. The 'Song of the Star' is, as we have seen, a dramatic account of the Incarnation of Christ. His epiphany as an astral Power[1] means the pulling down of the old kingdom (παλαιὰ βασιλεία διεφθείρετο), as all magic and superstition is dissolved, and every bond of evil is taken away, along with ignorance. The Incarnation marks the overthrow of the reign of those malign astral powers which rule men by holding them in the chains of Fate. Man's last enemy, death, has to yield as God's age-old plan of eternal life comes to pass. In this hymn—this description is justified because the planets gathered as a chorus round the epiphany star, as the choir gathered round the altar in pagan ceremonial[2]—it is not said how the victory of Christ is won, but a clue is offered in the line: πῶς οὖν ἐφανερώθη τοῖς αἰῶσιν; Probably we should translate this (with Bultmann):[3] 'How then was He manifested to the Aeons?' The hymn speaks of Christ's appearing to the angelic powers which were thought of as inhabiting the stars and planets. But His light far surpasses theirs, and is acknowledged as a *nova*. They admit to His supremacy and hail Him in a song of praise and acclamation as the Lord of all.

This scene, cast in dramatic form, is parallel with the climax and finale of Philippians ii. 6–11. The mighty spirits of all creation bow down and exclaim 'Jesus Christ is Lord'. The scenery is different, but the meaning is the same. It is the open confession that Christ is *Pantocrator* and sovereign over all rivals. The astral deities prostrate themselves in admission that their régime is ended.

This is the triumphant declaration which the hymn sounds

[1] This star is evidently not the nativity star of Matt. ii. 2 ff. (cf. W. K. L. Clarke, 'The rout of the Magi', *Divine Humanity* (1936), pp. 41 ff.). It is regarded by Schlier, *Rel. Unter. zu den Ignatiusbriefen*, p. 28, as a symbol of the ascending Redeemer on his way back into the celestial spheres; but this view involves some transposition of the text and is criticized by H.-W. Bartsch, *Gnostisches Gut und Gemeindetradition bei Ignatius von Antiochien* (1940), pp. 154–9; and V. Corwen, *St Ignatius and Christianity in Antioch*, pp. 176 ff.

[2] Cf. Ignatius, *ad Rom.* II, 2.

[3] *Theology*, I, 177, II, 154 after Schlier, *Rel. Unter. zu den Ignatiusbriefen*, pp. 28 ff.; but there is objection to this from V. Corwen, *St Ignatius and Christianity in Antioch*, who translates 'the ages' (178) in the time sense. But the use of τοῖς αἰῶσιν in *Eph.* VIII, 1 is against her here. The reference in the latter is to 'the Church well-known to the spiritual powers'; and probably in canonical Ephes. iii. 9.

forth. It proclaims that the humiliated and obedient Christ is Lord of all spirit-powers. Life, therefore, is under His rule and derives its purpose from the meaning which His incarnate existence gives to it. Above all, it assures us that the character of the God whose will controls the universe and human destiny is to be spelled out in terms of Jesus Christ. He is no arbitrary power, no capricious force, no pitiless, indifferent Fate. His nature is Love, and His concern for the world is most clearly expressed in the enthronement of Christ who came to His glory by a life of humble submission to His will and a complete obedience unto death. The universe over which God reigns is one in which true nobility and lordship can come only in this way, for He who is now the Lord of all creation first humbled Himself and accepted the rôle of a slave. His title to lordship—and this is the theme of His teaching as of His life upon earth[1]—can be interpreted only in terms of self-denying service for others.

The relevance of the hymn has not been exhausted with the passing of the first-century world and its ethos. While we no longer share the primitive cosmological theories and are no longer terrified by astral gods and demons, we face some of the deep issues which Hellenistic man encountered. For him—and for many of *our* contemporaries—there is little meaning in some aspects of the Christian message. The argument from prophecy is of small consequence; the understanding of estrangement from God in terms of guilt makes little appeal; but the questions that lie aback the fears and uncertainties of the ancient world still persist in a modern scientific age. Are we at the mercy of blind cosmic forces, impersonal and inevitable? Has life a meaning outside of this world? Is the universe friendly? And if there is a God behind and above the phenomena, does He live and rule in love and concern for His creatures?

The Christ-hymn which has been the theme of this academic exercise has something to teach in reply to these questionings in the mind and soul of modern man. And it is an answer spelled out in terms of the humiliation and Exaltation of Jesus Christ.

---

[1] The teaching of the ἦλθον-logia (especially Mark x. 45; cf. Mark ii. 17; Matt. v. 17; Luke xii. 49, xix. 10; John ix. 39; x. 10; xii. 27) is germane here (cf. Lk. xxii. 24–7; John xiii. 1 ff.).

APPENDIX A

ACTS VII AND PHILIPPIANS II

The following note investigates the links of thought and terminology which join Stephen's speech and its sequel in Acts vii and the Christological passage in Phil. ii.

(*a*) Acts vii. 55 f. 'He gazed into heaven and saw the glory of God, and Jesus standing at the right hand of God; and he said, "Behold, I see the heavens opened, and the Son of man standing at the right hand of God.'

This statement speaks of the glorified Son of man, a declaration which is even more pronounced if the καί of verse 55 be regarded as epexegetical: 'He saw the glory of God, *even* Jesus at the right hand of God.' The vision of Stephen recalls those confessional formulas which describe the pre-existent glory of Christ as the divine image: Col. i. 15; Heb. i. 3; II Cor. iv. 6; cf. Jas. ii. 1 and I Cor. ii. 8; and Phil. ii. 6 is to be added if the term ἐν μορφῇ Θεοῦ carries the sense of 'being in the glory of God' (cf. John xvii. 5, 24).

Moreover, the heavenly Christ is entitled ὁ υἱὸς τοῦ ἀνθρώπου—a title which is found only here outside the Gospels in the New Testament (Apoc. i. 13, xiv. 14 are doubtful). May it be that Stephen's statement brings together exactly those two strands of Christological teaching that are present in Phil. ii. 6 ff.—Christ as the Heavenly Man who radiates the divine image, because He is 'in the form of God'? The idea of the glory (δόξα) of God is found also in Acts vii. 2. Certainly, even if the details are not to be pressed, the conception of the risen Christ in exalted glory, is the picture we have in both Stephen's speech and the Philippians psalm (ii. 6, 9–11).

(*b*) Stephen's remarks concerning the idolatry of the Jews and their worship of the heavenly bodies may reflect some appreciation of the angels as the guardians of the nations (Acts vii. 42 f.) or even of the angelic powers which control the destinies of men upon earth. This notion goes back to Deut. iv. 19 (LXX), is amplified in the book of Daniel and receives a classic formulation in Jubilees xv. 31 f. where the idea is expressed that every nation has its special star-angel which leads it into idolatry: 'over all (nations) He hath placed spirits in authority to lead them astray from Him'. Israel alone is excepted, but in Pauline thought (of which there are anticipations in the report of Stephen's polemic) the giving of the Law and the ministry of angels are both related to the baneful influence of the 'elemental spirits' which hold men in bondage. P. Benoit[1] makes the

---

[1] 'Paulinisme et Johannisme', *NTS*, IX (1962–3), 193–207.

comment: 'Behind the Law of Moses the promulgation of which Jewish tradition attributed to the ministry of angels (Gal. iii. 19; Acts vii. 38, 53; Heb. ii. 2)...Paul sees the celestial powers which tyrannized over the ancient world (Gal. iv. 3, 9; Col. ii. 8).'[1]

There may be a link-up with the thought of the hymn that these astral powers which claimed the homage and fear of men are themselves claimed as suppliants before the *Pantocrator* (Phil. ii. 10 f.).

(c) The title 'The righteous one' (Acts vii. 52) may have some affinity with the concept of the servant in later Judaism. E. Schweizer in his *Erniedrigung* has shown the widespread influence of the notion of the suffering and righteous one in Judaism, whence it came over into Christianity. This figure, which has many historical applications in Judaism, is known as 'the servant of God'. He is distinguished by his obedience to God and his vocation of suffering unto death—the twin concepts which lie at the back of the description of the incarnate existence in the hymn. May it be that Stephen is conscious of this line of teaching in his designation of Jesus as the righteous One whom the fathers opposed and persecuted—a thought which comes over into the hymn as 'He humbled himself and took the rôle of a servant, and became obedient unto death'?

For the relation of this passage in Phil. ii to 'the Greek-speaking community which had gathered around Stephen and his circle', see now D. Georgi, 'Der vorpaulinische Hymnus Phil. 2, 6–11'.[2]

APPENDIX B

SOME RECENT STUDIES

The foregoing treatment of Philippians ii. 5–11 as a *carmen Christi* was completed as a piece of academic research in January 1963. The purpose of this appendix is to pass under review some of the discussions on the passage which have appeared in the last three years, and to relate them to the author's 'history of interpretation'. What is offered is a miniature *Forschungsbericht* covering the years 1963–66, but the author makes no claim to having mentioned all the available material. Three areas are delimited.

A. FORM-ANALYSIS

The debate over the literary form of the verses continues. J. Jeremias[3] offered a short defence of his earlier views in the light of the criticisms of G. Bornkamm (noted above, p. 190). He reiterated, with linguistic

---

[1] *Loc. cit.* 203.   [2] In *Zeit und Geschichte* (1964), p. 292.

[3] 'Zu Phil. ii. 7: ἑαυτὸν ἐκένωσεν', *Novum Testamentum*, VI, 2/3 (1963), 182–8.

evidence to support his case, the view that ἑαυτὸν ἐκένωσεν is a legitimate translation-equivalent of Isaiah liii. 12 (M.T.: הערה למות נפשׁו); and proceeded to justify this interpretation of the kenosis as a reference to the Cross by observing the place of the phrase in the hymn's structure. In particular, he drew attention to the use of chiasmus: ἑαυτὸν ἐκένωσεν : ἐταπείνωσεν ἑαυτόν (*vv.* 7, 8) —a feature which is found more than once in the first part of the hymn (in strophes I/II), along with the presence of antithetic parallelism. The third strophe (*vv.* 9–11) with its strongly accentuated διὸ καί marks the reversal of Christ's fortunes (περιπέτεια) and so stands apart from the earlier verses which are closely knit and speak of one theme: the sacrifice of Christ's death.

G. Strecker[1] has made two points which are relevant to formcritical considerations. He wishes to remove the whole of verse 8 as a Pauline gloss on the ground of its strongly Pauline language (71, n. 34); and he argues that Jeremias' description of 'the three states of Christ's existence' in the hymn must be challenged in view of the way in which the pre-existence is dismissed in a single participial line (*v.* 6*a*): ἐν μορφῇ Θεοῦ ὑπάρχων. He concludes: 'Die Präexistenz des Christus ist danach nur der Hintergrund, von dem die Inkarnation sich abhebt; nicht die drei Seinsweisen sind Inhalt des Liedes, sondern die Erniedrigung des Präexistenten und seine Erhöhung zum Kyrios' (p. 70). From these conclusions he builds up the hymn in two stanzas, each containing three sets of couplets. Verse 8 is omitted from the pre-Pauline *Vorlage*.

Against this view may be maintained that (i) it overlooks the possibility of chiasmus and antitheses in what is (on Strecker's showing) a lyrical composition, which require the presence of verse 8; and more significantly (ii), if ἑαυτὸν ἐκένωσεν is the main verb with not only λαβών but also γενόμενος and εὑρεθείς dependent upon it, the last two participles read most unnaturally. It is far more reasonable to treat them syntactically as looking forward to a main verb. And this requires a verb in the following line, i.e. in verse 8.

A. Feuillet[2] takes over Strecker's literary theory *in toto*, and uses it to explain a difficulty to which reference was earlier made, viz. the lack of coherence and chronological sequence in the hymn's tracing the course of the Lord's incarnate life (see above, p. 186). On Feuillet's understanding, the reference to the Cross in verse 7 (here following Jeremias) needed some explanation, as it would fall

---

[1] 'Redaktion und Tradition im Christus-hymnus Phil 2', *ZNTW*, LV (1964), 63–78.
[2] 'L'hymne christologique de l'épître aux Philippiens (ii. 6–11)', *RB*, LXXII, 3, 4 (1965–6), 352–80, 481–507.

strangely on Greek ears. 'C'est pourquoi l'Apôtre a jugé bon d'ajouter un éclaircissement' (494).

On this reading of the situation behind the Pauline insertion of verse 8, the extra couplet simply duplicates by way of amplification the message of the Cross in verse 7. It was added (so Feuillet avers) to clarify the (implicit) reference to Christ's sacrifice in the earlier verse. To be sure, it does emphasize just those features which are found in the '*Ebed Yahweh* picture—humiliation and suffering unto death; and captures the spirit of the suffering Servant. But the circumlocutory manner in which the couplet is written is a point against its being a later insertion unless it is thought that Paul wishes to 'improve' the hymn before him by adding an extra couplet in conscious imitation of the existing piece. It seems far more likely that his hand may be traced in only the last three words of the verse.

B. AUTHORSHIP

In this area of discussion too there is no *opinio communis*. The non-Pauline authorship is taken as 'assured' by R. H. Fuller,[1] whose views of the hymn's *Sitz im Leben* will be noticed later. Other commentators speak with less conviction. Whether Paul utilized and adapted an already existing text or composed a lyrical passage *ad hoc* is a question which Bo Reicke[2] prefers to leave *au suspens*. E. Larsson[3] refuses to regard authorship as a matter of decisive significance, adding that 'if Paul has taken over this "hymn" from tradition, he has interpreted it from the standpoint of his own theology'. Larsson does not deal with the question of 'redaction', i.e. the possibility that the hymn's original form and meaning may have been modified when it was taken over from tradition by the Apostle.

The legitimacy of the argument against Paul's authorship on the ground of word-usage has been queried by R. M. Grant[4] at various places in his discussion of New Testament integrity (64 f., 175, 194, 201). For those who deny the Pauline authorship of Phil. ii. 6–11, it is probably the style and liturgical content of the piece which is the decisive index. And the chief issue remains whether the Christology of the passage can be satisfactorily fitted into the Pauline period or betrays marks which stamp it as a pre-Pauline formulation. This brings us directly to the major question of the hymn's setting in early Christianity.

[1] *The Foundations of New Testament Christology* (1965), p. 204.
[2] 'Unité chrétienne et Diaconie', 209.
[3] *Christus als Vorbild*, p. 231.
[4] *A Historical Introduction to the New Testament* (1963).

C. INTERPRETATION

Chapter IV, Appendix A, referred to E. Larsson's arguments in support of the 'ethical interpretation' of the *crux* in verse 5: τοῦτο φρονεῖτε ἐν ὑμῖν ὃ καὶ ἐν Χριστῷ Ἰησοῦ. A. Feuillet[1] is persuaded by Larsson's exegesis and accepts the implied understanding of ἦν in the second part of the verse. With deeper penetration, however, G. Strecker[2] has raised the question whether these two rival views (the 'ethical-paradigmatic' interpretation which sees the hymn as setting out Christ's example to be followed, and Käsemann's ecclesiological view of ἐν Χριστῷ and the subsequent soteriological drama of verses 6–11) are mutually exclusive. He finds fault with each when the other is excluded from the total picture, and discovers (in the spirit of the post-Bultmannian school) a method of combining the two ideas. This is his suggestion that the admonition included not only the thought of the Church's being constituted through the Cross but also the reflection on the ethical norms of the Lord's conduct (*Verhalten*) which had been set forth in the event of the Cross. More speculatively he bases on his view that verse 8 is a Pauline gloss the superstructure that by this 'redactional reference to the obedience of the Crucified' there is introduced the ethical accentuation which derives from the Pauline theology of the Cross (77, 78). But we have already seen that this elimination of verse 8 is questionable.

The most interesting area of debate is that of the hymn's *Sitz im Leben der alten Kirche*.

With the pre-Pauline origin taken as an accepted starting-point among those who have addressed themselves to the task of locating the passage in the stream of early Christianity, it is still possible to maintain that the Christology belongs to the very earliest stratum of the New Testament. A. Feuillet[3] does this in the latest contribution to the debate. He rests his case on the double ground of (i) the doctrine of the Cross, which at Phil. ii. 8 and in the early kerygmatic preaching in Acts is proclaimed as a fact, but with no expiatory value yet accorded to it; and (ii) the designation of Christians as a people who call on the name of the Lord. Here again, he says, the thought of verse 10 matches this description and belongs to an 'archaic' theology of the Name whose presence is found in Acts. In short, the hymn is primitive because it is practically interested only in the two 'stages' of Christ's life—'les abaissements couronnés par la mort sur la Croix et l'exaltation glorieuse qui en est la contrepartie' (500). His pre-existence is contained in a participial phrase,

---

[1] 'L'hymne christologique', 504, n. 145.
[2] 'Redaktion und Tradition', 66 f. [3] *Loc. cit.* 487.

which shows that no decisive importance was attached to it in the early Jerusalem community to which the original hymn may be attributed.

There are a number of serious objections to this reconstruction, apart from the logical difficulty of basing an argument on verse 8 which Feuillet has deleted from the original text as a later Pauline addition. Probably he wished to read the full meaning of the Cross into verse 7 which is interpreted as an overt allusion to Isaiah liii. 12, although he grants that no atonement for sins is mentioned in the hymn (357). This omission, we observed, is striking and casts some doubt on the strict identification of the Philippians hymn text with Isaiah lii–liii, which Feuillet accepts (380). Of more importance is the cosmic setting of the Christological drama, particularly verses 10, 11 in which the universal acclamation of the lordship of Christ is made by spiritual powers, not men and not the Church. There is thus no link with 'those who invoke the name' in the early Jewish-Christian community. Nor are we persuaded that the compression of the thought of pre-existence into a participial line need imply a passing over of this 'stage'. A pre-temporal existence ἐν μορφῇ Θεοῦ seems required to give meaningful force to the decision of verse 6b which in turn leads on to the declaration of verse 7. Such a pre-existent state clearly implies, as R. H. Fuller[1] remarks, a more developed Christology than may be credited to the earliest Palestinian Church. Fuller goes on[2] to make the important point that 'the exaltation Christology of the second strophe was probably quite foreign to Aramaic Christology'.

'Rather its *Sitz im Leben* must be sought in Hellenistic *Jewish* Christianity.' This sentence summarizes the position of Fuller[3] which is enlarged in his statement: 'We would propose that Phil. 2. 6–11 is the product of Hellenistic Jewish missionaries working in a mainly Hellenistic gentile environment. They were sensitive to its outlook and needs, and used materials provided by the sophia and anthropos myth already current in Hellenistic Judaism, by the Hellenistic world view, and by the earlier Hellenistic Jewish kerygma. There is no need to look further afield for the origin of this hymn' (206).

With this description of the type of Christianity in which the hymn was born, our final chapter is largely in agreement. There we proposed that the original author of the hymn stood 'at the junction of two cultures and two religious traditions. His background is Jewish, but it is Greek ideas which stand at the forefront of his mind; and he

---

[1] *The Foundations of New Testament Christology*, p. 235, n. 4.
[2] *Op. cit.* 205. [3] *Ibid.*

is concerned, as a Christian, to relate the Gospel to the larger world of Hellenism' (297).

Professor Fuller, however, is disposed to place the passage at a later stage in Christological development than that of early Hellenistic Jewish Christianity on the ground that a 'three stage' Christology is envisaged (as an advance on the 'two stages' of Rom. i. 3 f.); the notion of a freely willed choice which has replaced the idea of the Son's being 'sent' by the Father; and the completeness of His enthronization which admits of no concession to the Church's continuing struggle against unsubdued demonic powers. But (as Strecker observed) the pre-existence is only cursorily touched upon, and while necessary, we would contend, to give full meaning to the Incarnation, it is not as developed as in Col. i. 15 ff. and the prologue to the Fourth Gospel where the pre-existent One's activity as Creator and Sharer of the divine throne is explicitly mentioned. It looks as if Phil. ii. 6 depicts the very earliest beginnings of that Christian cosmic Christology which came to full maturity in the later literature. The emphasis in the sentence ἑαυτὸν ἐκένωσεν may be explained as a Christian motif added in order to stress the voluntariness of Christ's acceptance of humanity. It may then have a polemical purpose and serve to mark out the Incarnation from rival notions (e.g. Wisdom's coming to men). Moreover, that no clear evolutionary line in Christological development is possible is shown by the return of the 'sending' motif in the Fourth Gospel which confronts (as Fuller shows) the situation in the Gentile mission. His last argument which concerns the finality of the exalted One's complete victory and enthronement over all cosmic forces is of some import. Our discussion of verses 10, 11 sought to show that the paradox of a complete subjugation and hint of 'not yet' may be resolved by having regard to the liturgical origin of the passage. It is in worship that the Church which celebrates by this ode to Christ, His redemption and glory, reaches forward to claim the fulness of that redemption and to share here and now that glory.

The reference to the missionary purpose of this psalm made by Fuller[1] chimes in with our tentative supposition that it was the school of Stephen (see above, pp. 304 f.) which gave notable impetus to the Hellenistic Jewish mission. Dieter Georgi[2] has also suggested this proposal. He argues that the hymn utilizes the framework of the sophia-myth but re-interprets it in the light of the early Hellenistic Jewish claim that placed Jesus on a par with Yahweh as Lord of the world. This claim would be treated as blasphemous by Jews; and

---

[1] *Op. cit.* 206.
[2] 'Der vorpaulinische Hymnus Phil. 2, 6–11', 263–93.

there is a further polemic overtone in the contrast between Wisdom (which Hellenistic Judaism equated with the eternal Law of God) and Jesus. The Christian version of the sophia-story (portrayed in the Hellenistic *Wisdom of Solomon*) energetically teaches that the embodiment of divine Wisdom has appeared in space and time in the figure of Jesus—and in a historical event which is recent and factual. The pattern of His mission is one of humiliation–exaltation, based on the presentation of the wise, righteous man in the Wisdom literature. Yet the thought of pre-existence is not absent, as E. Schweizer[1] has recently emphasized. It is a moot point, however, which we raised earlier, whether the descriptions of Wisdom in the texts referred to (e.g. Wisd. xviii and Ecclus. xxiv), which set forth her universal command, are of the same order of grandeur and cosmic sweep as the exalted terms of Phil. ii. 10, 11. But, as we suggested, the parallels between Wisdom embodied in the righteous and obedient man of later Judaism and the incarnate and vindicated Christ are remarkable, and the former may well have served as starting-points for the development of this type of Christological speculation in response to the opportunities created by the Hellenistic Jewish mission.[2]

[1] *Erniedrigung*[2] (1962), pp. 102 f.   [2] So Georgi, *loc. cit.* 292 f.

SELECT BIBLIOGRAPHY

A. DICTIONARIES, ENCYCLOPAEDIAS AND SOURCE-BOOKS

The Apocrypha and Pseudepigrapha of the Old Testament (ed. R. H. Charles, 2 vols.). Oxford, 1913.

Die Religion in Geschichte und Gegenwart (3rd ed. by K. Galling, 1956–65). Tübingen.

Theologisches Wörterbuch zum Neuen Testament (ed. G. Kittel and G. Friedrich). Stuttgart, 1933– .

The Vocabulary of the Greek Testament (ed. J. H. Moulton and G. Milligan). London, 1914–29.

Kommentar zum Neuen Testament aus Talmud und Midrasch (ed. H. L. Strack and P. Billerbeck), i–iv. Munich, 1956.

A Greek–English Lexicon (ed. H. G. Liddell–R. Scott–H. S. Jones). Oxford, 1940.

A Greek–English Lexicon of the New Testament and other early Christian Literature (ed. W. F. Arndt and F. W. Gingrich as an adaptation of W. Bauer's *Griechisch-Deutsches Wörterbuch zu den Schriften des Neuen Testaments und der übrigen urchristlichen Literatur*, Berlin, 1952). Cambridge and Chicago, 1957.

A Greek Grammar of the New Testament, etc. (ed. R. W. Funk as a translation of F. Blass–A. Debrunner, *Grammatik des neutestamentlichen Griechisch*, Göttingen, 1959). Cambridge and Chicago, 1961.

B. BOOKS AND ARTICLES REFERRED TO IN THE TEXT

Abel, F.-M. *Grammaire du Grec biblique* (Paris, 1927).

Adam, A. *Die Psalmen des Thomas und das Perlenlied als Zeugnisse vorchristlicher Gnosis* (Berlin, 1959).

Allen, L. C. 'Isaiah liii. 11 and its Echoes', *Vox Evangelica* (ed. R. P. Martin) (London, 1962).

Amand, D. *Fatalisme et liberté dans l'antiquité grecque* (Louvain, 1945).

Andrews, E. *The Meaning of Christ for Paul* (New York/Nashville, 1949).

Arvedson, T. *Das Mysterium Christi. Eine Studie zu Mt 11, 25–30* (ASNU, 7) (Uppsala, 1937).

—— 'Phil. 2, 6 und Mt. 10, 39', *ST* v, i–ii (1951), 49–51.

Audet, J.-P. *La Didachè: Instructions des Apôtres* (Paris, 1958).

Badham, F. P. 'Phil. II. 6 'Αρπαγμός', *ExT*, xix (1908), 331.

Baillie, D. M. *God Was in Christ* (London, 1948).

Baird, W. R. Jnr. 'Current Trends in New Testament Study', *Journal of Religion*, Chicago, xxxix, 3 (1959).

Barclay, W. 'Great themes of the New Testament—I. Philippians ii. 1–11', *ExT*, lxx, 1 and 2 (1958), 4–7; 40–4.

Barnikol, E. *Der marcionistische Ursprung des Mythos-Satzes Phil. 2. 6–7* (Kiel, 1932).

Barr, J. *The Semantics of Biblical Language* (Oxford, 1961).

—— 'The position of Hebrew Language in Theological Education', *The International Review of Missions*, l, 200 (1961), 435–44.

Barrett, C. K. 'New Testament Eschatology: II', *SJT*, vi, 3 (Sept. 1953), 225–43.

—— *The New Testament Background: Selected Documents* (London, 1956).

—— *The Epistle to the Romans* (Black's N.T. Commentaries) (London, 1959).

—— 'The Background of Mark 10: 45', *New Testament Essays: Studies in memory of T. W. Manson*, ed. A. J. B. Higgins (Manchester, 1959).

—— *From First Adam to Last* (London, 1962).

Barth, K. *Erklärung des Philipperbriefes* (Zurich, 1928 = 1947). (E.T. *The Epistle to the Philippians*, London, 1962.)

—— *Church Dogmatics*, 1/2 (E.T. Edinburgh, 1956).

—— *Church Dogmatics*, iv/1 (E.T. Edinburgh, 1956).

Barth, M. 'The Old Testament in Hebrews', *Current Issues in New Testament Interpretation. Essays in honor of O. A. Piper*, ed. W. Klassen and G. F. Synder (London, 1962).

Bartsch, H.-W. *Gnostisches Gut und Gemeindetradition bei Ignatius von Antiochien* (Göttingen, 1940).

Bartsch, H.-W. (ed.). *Kerygma and Myth*, 1 (E.T. London, 1953).

Baur, F. *Paulus, der Apostel J.-C.* (Stuttgart, 1845).

Beardslee, W. A. *Human Achievement and Divine Vocation in the Message of Paul* (SBT, 31) (London, 1961).

Beare, F. W. *A Commentary on the Epistle to the Philippians* (Black's N.T. Commentaries) (London, 1959).

—— 'New Testament Christianity and the Hellenistic World', *The Communication of the Gospel in New Testament Times* (SPCK Theological Collections) (London, 1961).

—— *St Paul and his Letters* (London, 1962).

Beasley-Murray, G. R. 'Baptism in the Epistles of Paul', *Christian Baptism* (ed. A. Gilmore) (London, 1959).

—— 'Philippians', *Peake's Commentary on the Bible*[2] (ed. M. Black and H. H. Rowley) (London, 1962).

Beet, J. A. *A Commentary on St Paul's Epistles to the Ephesians*, etc. (London, 1890).

Behm, J. 'μορφή', *TWNT*, IV, 750–60.

Benoit, P. *Les épîtres de S. Paul: Aux Philippiens*, etc. (Bible de Jérusalem) (Paris, 1959).

Bevan, E. *Hellenism and Christianity* (London, 1921).

Bieder, W. *Die Vorstellung von der Höllenfahrt Jesu Christi. Beitrag zur Entstehungsgeschichte der Vorstellung vom sog. Descensus ad inferos.* (Abh. TANT, 19) (Zürich, 1949).

Bietenhard, H. 'ὄνομα', *TWNT*, V, 242–81.

Binder, A. W. *Biblical Chant* (New York, 1959).

Bindley, T. H. *The Oecumenical Documents of the Faith* (revised by F. W. Green) (London, 1950).

Black, M. 'The Pauline Doctrine of the Second Adam', *SJT*, VII, 2 (1954), 170–9.

Blackman, E. C. *Marcion and his Influence* (London, 1948).

Boer, W. P. de. *The Imitation of Paul* (Kampen, 1962).

Boismard, M.-E. *St John's Prologue* (E.T. London, 1957).

—— *Quatre Hymnes baptismales dans la première épître de Pierre* (Lectio divina, 30) (Paris, 1961).

Bonnard, P. *L'épître de S. Paul aux Philippiens* (CNT, x) (Paris, 1950).

Bonsirven, J. *L'évangile de Paul* (Paris, 1948).

Boobyer, G. H. *St Mark and the Transfiguration Story* (Edinburgh, 1942).

Bornhäuser, K. *Jesus Imperator Mundi (Phil. 3, 17–21 und 2, 5–11)* (Gütersloh, 1938).

Bornkamm, G. 'Christus und die Welt in der urchristlichen Botschaft', *Das Ende des Gesetzes: Paulusstudien. Gesammelte Aufsätze: Band I.* (Beitr. zur evang. Theol. 16) (Munich, 1952, ³1961).

—— 'Zum Verständnis des Christus-Hymnus, Phil. 2. 6–11', *Studien zu Antike und Urchristentum. Gesammelte Aufsätze: Band II* (Beitr. zur evang. Theol. 28) (Munich, 1959).

—— 'Das Bekenntnis im Hebräerbrief', *Studien zu Antike und Urchristentum. Gesammelte Aufsätze: Band II* (Beitr. zur evang. Theol. 28) (Munich, 1959).

—— *Jesus of Nazareth* (E.T. London, 1961).

Bousset, W. 'Zur Hadesfahrt Christi', *ZNTW*, XIX (1919/20), 50–66.

—— *Die Religion des Judentums im späthellenistischen Zeitalter³* (revised by H. Gressmann) (Tübingen, 1926).

—— *Kyrios Christos: Geschichte des Christusglaubens von den Anfängen des Christentums bis Irenaeus* (FRLANT, 4) (Gottingen, ²1921, ³1926).

Bouttier, M. *En Christ. Étude d'exégèse et de théologie pauliniennes* (Paris, 1962).

Bouyer, L. "Ἁρπαγμός', *RSR*, xxxix (1951-2) in honour of J. Lebreton, 281-8.

Brockington, L. H. 'The Septuagintal Background to the New Testament use of δόξα', *Studies in the Gospels: Essays in memory of R. H. Lightfoot* (ed. D. E. Nineham) (Oxford, 1955).

Bruce, A. B. *The Humiliation of Christ* (Edinburgh, 1876, = 1955 reprint).

Bruce, F. F. 'The Epistle to the Philippians: An extended paraphrase', *The Evangelical Quarterly*, xxxv, 1 (1963), 45-51.

Brunner, E. *The Mediator* (E.T. London, 1934).

—— *The Christian Doctrine of Creation and Redemption, Dogmatics*, II (E.T. London, 1952).

Büchler, A. *Studies in Sin and Atonement in the Rabbinical Literature of the First Century* (Jews' College Publications, no. 11) (London, 1928).

Büchsel, F. *Theologie des Neuen Testaments*[2] (Gütersloh, 1937).

Bultmann, R. 'Die Bedeutung der neuerschlossenen mandäischen und manichäischen Quellen', *ZNTW*, xxiv (1925), 100-46.

—— *Jesus and the Word* (E.T. London, 1934 = 1962).

—— 'Bekenntnis- und Liedfragmente im ersten Petrusbrief', *Coniectanea Neotestamentica*, xi (Lund, 1947), 1-14.

—— *Theology of the New Testament* (London, E.T. I, 1952; E.T. II, 1955).

—— 'Ignatius und Paulus', *Studia Paulina: in honorem J. de Zwaan*, ed. J. N. Sevenster and W. C. van Unnik (Haarlem, 1953). (E.T. in *Existence and Faith*, ed. S. M. Ogden, London, 1961.)

—— 'Mythos und Mythologie im NT', *RGG*[3], iv (1960), 1278-82.

Burkitt, F. C. *Christian Beginnings* (London, 1924).

Burney, C. F. *The Aramaic Origin of the Fourth Gospel* (Oxford, 1926).

Bywater, I. (ed.). *Aristotle's Poetics* (Oxford, 1909).

Cabrol, F. and Leclerq, H. *Monumenta ecclesiae liturgica: Reliquiae liturgicae vetustissimae.* (Part I, Paris, 1900).

Cadier, J. (ed.). *Maqqél Shâqédh: La Branche d'Amandier: Hommage à Wilhelm Vischer* (Montpellier, 1960).

Caird, G. B. *The Apostolic Age* (London, 1955).

—— *Principalities and Powers* (Oxford, 1956).

Carpenter, L. L. *Primitive Christian Application of the Doctrine of the Servant* (Durham, N. Carolina, 1929).

Casel, O. *The Mystery of Christian Worship* (E.T. London, 1962).

Cerfaux, L. 'L'hymne au Christ—Serviteur de Dieu', in *Miscellanea historica Alberti de Meyer* (reprinted in *Recueil Lucien Cerfaux*, II: *Études d'Exégèse et d'Histoire Religieuse* (Bibl. Ephem. Theol. Lovan. VI–VII), Gembloux, 1954).

—— 'Kyrios', *DB Suppl.* Fasc. XXIV, Paris, 1950.

Cerfaux, L. *Le Christ dans la théologie de S. Paul*[2] (Lectio divina, 6) (Paris, 1954). (E.T. *Christ in the Theology of St Paul*, London, 1959.)

Champion, L. G. *Benedictions and Doxologies in the Epistles of Paul* (Diss. Heidelberg) (published privately, 1934).

Charles, R. H. *See* Morfill, W. R.

—— (ed.). *The Ascension of Isaiah* (London, 1900).

Cholmondeley, F. G. 'Harpagmos', *ExT*, VII (1895-6), 47 f.

Clarke, W. K. L. *New Testament Problems* (London, 1929).

—— *The Divine Humanity* (London, 1936).

Clemen, C. *Primitive Christianity and its non-Jewish Sources* (E.T. Edinburgh, 1912).

Colpe, C. *Die religionsgeschichtliche Schule. Vorstellung und Kritik ihres Bildes vom gnostischen Erlösermythos* (FRLANT, 78) (Göttingen, 1961).

Conzelmann, H. *Die kleineren Briefe des Apostels Paulus: Der Brief an die Kolosser*,[9] (NTD, 8) (Göttingen, 1962).

Cooper, L. *Aristotle on the Art of Poetry* (Oxford, 1913).

Corwen, V. *St Ignatius and Christianity in Antioch* (New Haven, U.S.A., 1960).

Craig, C. T. *The Beginning of Christianity* (New York/Nashville, 1953).

Cranfield, C. E. B. 'The Interpretation of 1 Peter iii. 19 and iv. 6', *ExT*, LXIX (1958), 369-72.

Creed, J. M. 'The Heavenly Man', *JTS*, XXVI (1925), 113-35.

—— 'Recent Tendencies in English Theology', *Mysterium Christi* (ed. G. K. A. Bell and A. Deissmann, London, 1930).

Crehan, J. *Early Christian Baptism and the Creed* (London, 1950).

Cullmann, O. *The Earliest Christian Confessions* (E.T. London, 1949).

—— *Christus und die Zeit* (Zürich, 1946). (E.T. *Christ and Time*, London, 1949, [2]1962.)

—— 'Paradosis et Kyrios', *RHPR*, XXX (1950), 16-30.

—— 'The Tradition', in *The Early Church* (E.T. London, 1956).

—— 'The Kingship of Christ', in *The Early Church* (E.T. London, 1956).

—— *Peter: Disciple, Apostle, Martyr* (E.T. London, 1953, [2]1962).

—— *Early Christian Worship* (SBT, 10) (E.T. London, 1953).

—— *Die Christologie des Neuen Testaments* (Tübingen, 1957). (E.T. *The Christology of the New Testament*, London, 1959.)

—— 'The Reply of Professor Cullmann to Roman Catholic critics', in *SJT*, XV, 1 (1962), 36-43.

Dahl, N. A. 'Christ, Creation and the Church', *The Background of the New Testament and its Eschatology* (ed. W. D. Davies and D. Daube) (Cambridge, 1956).

—— 'Anamnesis: Mémoire et Commémoration dans le christianisme primitif', *ST*, 1, i (1947), 69–95.

Daniélou, J. 'La session à la droite du Père', *The Gospels Reconsidered—Studia Evangelica* (ed. K. Aland *et al.*) (Berlin, 1959).

Daube, D. *The New Testament and Rabbinic Judaism* (Jordan Lectures, 1952) (London, 1956).

Davies, J. G. *He Ascended into Heaven* (London, 1958).

Davies, W. D. *Paul and Rabbinic Judaism. Some Rabbinic Elements in Pauline Theology* (London, 1948, ²1955).

—— *Torah in the Messianic Age and/or the Age to Come* (JBL Monograph series, 7) (Philadelphia, 1952).

Dawe, D. G. 'A Fresh Look at the Kenotic Christologies', *SJT*, xv, 4 (1962), 337–49.

Deissmann, G. A. *Paulus: Eine kultur- und religionsgeschichtliche Skizze²* (Tübingen, 1925). (E.T. *St Paul*, London, 1925).

—— *Light from the Ancient East* (E.T. ⁴London, 1927).

Delling, G. *Der Gottesdienst im Neuen Testament* (Göttingen, 1952). (E.T. *Worship in the New Testament*, London, 1962.)

Dibelius, M. *Die Formgeschichte des Evangeliums³* (ed. G. Bornkamm) (Tübingen, 1959). (E.T. *From Tradition to Gospel*, London, 1934.)

—— *Die Geisterwelt im Glauben des Paulus* (Göttingen, 1909).

—— *An die Thessalonicher: an die Philipper* (HzNT) (²1923, ³1937).

—— 'Der himmlische Kultus nach dem Hebräerbrief', *ThBl*, xxi (1942), 1–11.

Dietrich, A. *Abraxas. Studien zur Religionsgeschichte des spätern Altertums* (Leipzig, 1891).

Dietrich, S. de. *L'épître aux Philippiens* (Lyons, n.d.).

Dillistone, F. W. *Jesus Christ and his Cross* (London, 1953).

Dix, G. *Jew and Greek. A Study in the Primitive Church* (London, 1953).

Dodd, C. H. *The Epistle to the Romans* (MNTC) (London, 1932).

—— *The Bible and the Greeks* (London, 1935).

—— *The Apostolic Preaching and its Developments* (London, 1936, ²1944).

—— Review of *TWNT*, *JTS*, xxxix (1938), 287–93.

—— *According to the Scriptures* (London, 1952).

—— *The Interpretation of the Fourth Gospel* (Cambridge, 1953).

Dölger, F. J. *Sol Salutis. Gebet und Gesang im christlichen Altertum²* (Liturgiegeschichtliche Forschungen, 4/5) (Munich, 1925).

Dugmore, C. W. *The Influence of the Synagogue upon the Divine Office* (Oxford, 1944).

—— 'Lord's Day and Easter', *Neotestamentica et Patristica in honorem O. Cullmann* (ed. W. C. van Unnik) (Leiden, 1962).

Duhm, A. *Gottesdienst im ältesten Christentum* (Tübingen, 1928).

Dumaine, H. 'Dimanche', *Dict. d'arch. chrét. et de lit.* IV (Paris, 1920).

Duncan, G. S. *Jesus Son of Man* (London, 1948).

Dupont, J. 'Jésus-Christ dans son abaissement et son exaltation d'après Phil. ii. 6–11', *RSR*, XXXVII (1950).

Durrwell, F. X. *The Resurrection* (E.T. London, 1960).

Edwards, D. *The Virgin Birth in History and Faith* (London, 1943).

Ehrhardt, A. A. T. 'Jesus Christ and Alexander the Great', *JTS*, XVLI (1945), 45–51 (= *EvT*, I–II (1948–9), 101–10).

Elbogen, I. *Der jüdische Gottesdienst in seiner geschichtlichen Entwicklung*[4] (Hildesheim, 1931 = 1962).

Ellis, E. E. *Paul's Use of the Old Testament* (Edinburgh, 1957).

Eltester, F.-W. *Eikon im Neuen Testament* (ZNTW Bh. 23) (Berlin, 1958).

Engnell, I. '"Knowledge" and "Life" in the Creation story', *Wisdom in Israel and in the Ancient Near East* (ed. M. Noth and D. Winton Thomas) (Leiden, 1960).

Ernesti, H. F. 'Phil. II. 6–11 aus einer Anspielung auf Gen. II.–III. erläutert', *TSK*, XXI (1848), 858–924; XXIV (1851), 596–630.

Esking, E. *Glaube und Geschichte in der theologischen Exegese Ernst Lohmeyers* (ASNU, 18) (Lund/Copenhagen, 1951).

Euler, K. *Die Verkündigung von leidenden Gottesknecht aus Jes 53 in der griechischen Bibel* (Beitr. z. Wiss. vom A. u. NT, IV, 14) (Stuttgart, 1934).

Ewald, P. *Der Brief des Paulus an die Philipper* (Zahn's Kommentar zum NT, XI: revised G. Wohlenberg) (Leipzig, 1923).

Feine, P. *Theologie des Neuen Testaments*[2] (Leipzig, 1911; [8]Berlin, 1951).

Festugière, A.-J. *L'idéal religieux des Grecs et l'Évangile* (Étude bib.) (Paris, 1932).

—— *La révélation d'Hermès Trismégiste*, I–II (Étude bib.) (Paris, 1944–49).

—— 'À propos des Arétalogies d'Isis', *HTR*, XLII (1949), 209 ff.

—— *Personal Religion among the Greeks* (Berkeley, Los Angeles, Cal., 1960 ed.).

Feuillet, A. 'L'homme-Dieu considéré dans sa condition terrestre (Phil. II. 5 seq. et parall.)', *RB*, LI (1942), 58–79 (= *Vivre et Penser*, 2nd ser.).

Filson, F. V. *Jesus Christ the Risen Lord* (New York/Nashville, 1956).

Flanagan, N. 'A note on Philippians iii. 20, 21', *CBQ*, XVIII (1956), 8–9.

Flemington, W. F. *The New Testament Doctrine of Baptism* (London, 1948).

Flew, R. N. *Jesus and His Church* (London, 1938, 1943).

Foerster, W. 'ἁρπαγμός', *TWNT*, I, 472–4.

—— 'κύριος', *TWNT*, III, 1038–94.

Forsyth, P. T. *The Person and Place of Jesus Christ* (London, 1909).

Franks, R. S. *The Doctrine of the Trinity* (London, 1953).

Fridrichsen, A. 'Quatre conjectures sur le texte du NT', *RHPR*, III (1923).

Friedrich, G. *Die kleineren Briefe des Apostels Paulus: Der Brief an die Philipper*[9] (NTD, 8) (Göttingen, 1962).

Frisque, J. *Oscar Cullmann. Une théologie de l'histoire du salut* (Tournai, Belgium, 1960).

Fuller, R. H. *The Mission and Achievement of Jesus* (SBT, 12) (London, 1954).

Funk, R. W. *See* Blass–Debrunner under A.

Furness, J. M. 'The authorship of Phil. 2. 6–11', *ExT*, LXX, 8 (1959), 240–3.

Gander, G. 'L'hymne de la Passion. Exégèse de Philippiens i. 27–ii. 18' (unpublished Diss. Geneva, 1939).

Geiselmann, J. R. *Jesus der Christus. Die Urform des apostolischen Kerygmas als Norm unserer Verkündigung und Theologie von Jesus Christus* (Stuttgart, 1951).

Gerhardsson, B. *Memory and Manuscript. Oral Tradition and Written Transmission in Rabbinic Judaism and early Christianity* (ASNU, 22) (Lund, 1961).

Gewiess, J. 'Zum altkirchl. Verständnis der Kenosisstelle (Phil. II. 5–11', *ThQ*, CXX (1948), 463–87.

Gifford, E. H. *The Incarnation. A Study of Philippians ii. 5–11* (London, 1897 (= The Expositor, 1896), 1911 (ed. H. Wace)).

Goguel, M. *Introduction au nouveau Testament*, Tome IV (Paris, 1925).

—— *The Birth of Christianity* (E.T. London, 1953).

Goodenough, E. R. *By Light, Light. The Mystic Gospel of Hellenistic Judaism* (New Haven, Conn., 1935).

Gore, C. *The Incarnation of the Son of God* (Bampton Lectures) (London, 1891).

Grant, F. C. *An Introduction to New Testament Thought* (New York/Nashville, 1950).

—— *Roman Hellenism and the New Testament* (Edinburgh, 1962).

Grant, R. M. (ed.). *Gnosticism: An Anthology* (London, 1961).

Grayston, K. *The Epistles of Paul to the Galatians and Philippians* (Epworth Preacher's Commentary) (London, 1957).

Greene, W. C. *Moira: Fate, Good and Evil in Greek Thought* (Cambridge, Mass., 1944).

Grenfell, B. P. and Hunt, A. S. *The Oxyrhynchus Papyri.* Part XV (London, 1922).

Griffiths, D. R. 'ἁρπαγμός and ἑαυτὸν ἐκένωσεν', *ExT*, LXIX (1958), 237–9.

327

Guignebert, C. 'Quelques Remarques d'exégèse sur Phil. 2. 6–11', *RHPR*, III (1923), 522–32.

Hahn, A. and G. L. *Bibliothek der Symbole und Glaubensregeln der alten Kirche* (Hildesheim, 1897 = 1962).

Hahn, W. *Gottesdienst und Opfer Christi* (Göttingen, 1951).

Hall, F. J. *The Kenotic Theory* (New York, 1898).

Hamman, A. *La Prière. I: Le Nouveau Testament* (Bibliothèque de Théologie) (Tournai, 1959).

Hanson, S. *The Unity of the Church in the New Testament. Colossians and Ephesians*. (ASNU, 14) (Uppsala, 1946).

Harder, G. *Paulus und das Gebet* (Neutest. Forschungen, I, 10) (Gütersloh, 1936).

Harris, J. R. *The Odes and Psalms of Solomon* (Cambridge, 1909).

Hartmann, S. S. *Gayōmart: Étude sur le syncrétisme dans l'ancien Iran* (Uppsala, 1953).

Haupt, E. *Die Gefangenschaftsbriefe* (MeyerKommentar, 8–9) (Göttingen, 1902).

Hawkins, R. M. *The Recovery of the Historical Paul* (New York/Nashville, 1943).

Heinzelmann, G. *Die kleineren Briefe des Apostels Paulus: Der Brief an die Philipper*[8] (NTD, 8) (Göttingen, 1955).

Heitmüller, W. *In Namen Jesu. Eine sprach- und religionsgeschichtliche Untersuchung zum NT speziell zur altchrist. Taufe* (FRLANT, 1/2) (Göttingen, 1903).

Hendriksen, W. *New Testament Commentary: Exposition of Philippians* (Grand Rapids, 1962).

Henry, P. 'Kénose', Supplément au *Dictionnaire de la Bible*: Fasc. XXIV, 7–161 (Paris, 1950).

Héring, J. 'Kyrios Anthropos', *RHPR*, XVI (1936), 196–209.

—— *Le Royaume de Dieu et sa venue* (Bibliothèque théologique) (Paris/Neuchâtel, 1937, 1959).

—— *Die biblischen Grundlagen des christlichen Humanismus* (Zürich, 1946).

—— *La seconde épître de Paul aux Corinthiens* (CNT, VIII) (Paris/Neuchâtel, 1958).

Holtzmann, H. J. *Lehrbuch der NT Theologie* (revised by A. Jülicher and W. Bauer), II (1911).

Holtzmann, O. *Das neue Testament nach dem Stuttgarter griechischen Text*, II (Leipzig, 1926).

Hooke, S. H. *Alpha and Omega* (London, 1961).

Hooker, M. D. *Jesus and the Servant. The Influence of the Servant Concept of Deutero-Isaiah in the New Testament* (London, 1959).

Howard, W. F. *Christianity according to St John* (London, 1943).

Humbert, P. 'Trois notes sur Genèse I' *Interpretationes ad vetus Testamentum pertinentes Sigmundo Mowinckel* (Oslo, 1955).

Hunter, A. M. *Paul and his Predecessors* (London, 1940, ²1961).
—— *The Unity of the New Testament* (London, 1946).
—— *Interpreting Paul's Gospel* (London, 1954).
—— *Introducing New Testament Theology* (London, 1957).
—— *Galatians to Colossians* (Layman's Commentary) (London, 1960).
Jacob, E. *Theology of the Old Testament* (E.T. London, 1958).
Jaeger, W. 'Eine stilgeschichtliche Studie zum Philipperbrief', *Hermes*, L (1915), 537–53.
Jammers, E. 'Christliche Liturgie', *RGG³*, IV (1960), 407 f.
Jeremias, J. 'Zwischen Karfreitag und Ostern', *ZNTW*, XLII (1949), 194–201.
—— 'Zur Gedankenführung in den paulinischen Briefen', *Studia Paulina in honorem J. de Zwaan* (ed. J. W. Sevenster and W. C. van Unnik) (Haarlem, 1953).
—— *Die Briefe an Timotheus und Titus* (NTD, 9) (Göttingen, 1953).
—— *The Eucharistic Words of Jesus* (E.T. Oxford, 1955, London, ²1966).
—— 'παῖς', *TWNT*, V, 653–713. (E.T. *The Servant of God* (SBT, 20), London, 1958.)
—— *Jesus' Promise to the Nations* (SBT, 24) (London, 1958).
Jervell, J. *Imago Dei: Gen. i. 26 f. im Spätjudentum, in der Gnosis und in den paulinischen Briefen* (FRLANT, 76) (Göttingen, 1960).
Johnson, H. *The Humanity of the Saviour* (London, 1962).
Jonas, H. *Gnosis und spätantiker Geist*, I (FRLANT, 63) (Göttingen, 1954).
—— *The Gnostic Religion* (Boston, U.S.A., 1958).
Jones, G. V. *Christology and Myth in the New Testament* (London, 1956).
Jones, M. *The Epistle to the Philippians* (WC) (London, 1918).
Joüon, P. 'Notes philologiques sur quelques versets, etc.', *RSR*, XXVIII (1938), 299–310.
Käsemann, E. *Das wandernde Gottesvolk. Eine Untersuchung zum Hebräerbrief* (FRLANT, 37) (Göttingen, 1961).
—— 'Kritische Analyse von Phil. 2. 5–11', in *Exegetische Versuche und Besinnung: erster Band* (Göttingen, 1960).
Kattenbusch, F. "Ἁρπαγμόν? Ἄπραγμον! Phil. 2, 6. Ein Beitrag zur paulinischen Christologie', *TSK*, CIV (1932), 373–420.
Keet, C. C. *A Liturgical Study of the Psalter* (London, 1928).
Kelly, J. N. D. *Early Christian Creeds* (London, 1950).
Kennedy, E. C. *Martial and Pliny* (Oxford, 1952).
Kennedy, H. A. A. *The Epistle to the Philippians* (The Expositor's Greek Testament, ed. W. R. Nicoll) (London, 1903).
—— *St Paul and the Mystery Religions* (London, 1913).
—— *St Paul's Conceptions of Last Things* (London, 1904).

Kidd, B. J. *A History of the Church to A.D. 461*. 2 vols. (Oxford, 1922).

Kittel, G. 'δόξα', *TWNT*, II, 236–56.

Kittel, H. *Die Herrlichkeit Gottes. Studien zu Geschichte und Wesen eines neutestl. Begriffes* (Göttingen, 1935).

Klausner, J. *Jesus of Nazareth* (E.T. London, 1927).

Klein, G. *Der älteste christliche Katechismus* (Berlin, 1909).

Kleinknecht, H. and Kittel, G. 'εἰκών', *TWNT*, II, 387–96.

Kleist, J. A. (ed.). *Ancient Christian Writers*, vol. VI (London, 1957 ed.).

Knox, J. *Jesus Lord and Christ* (a trilogy comprising *The Man Christ Jesus*; *Christ the Lord*; and *On the Meaning of Christ*) (New York, 1958).

Knox, W. L. 'The "Divine-Hero" Christology in the New Testament', *HTR*, XLI, 4 (1948), 229–49.

Kögel, J. *Christus der Herr* (Beitr. z. Ford. christl. Theologie, XI) (Göttingen, 1908).

Kraeling, C. H. *Anthropos and Son of Man. A study in the religious Syncretism of the Hellenistic Orient* (New York, 1927).

Kraemer, C. J. 'Pliny and the Early Christian Church service', *JCP*, XXIX (1934), 293–300.

Kroll, J. *Die christliche Hymnodik bis zu Klemens von Alexandreia* (Verzeichnis der Vorlesungen an der Akademie zu Braunsberg, Sommer-Semester) (Königsberg, 1921).

Kümmel, W. G. 'Jesus und der jüdische Traditionsgedanke', *ZNTW*, XXXIII (1934), 105–30.

Lampe, G. W. H. (ed.). *A Patristic Greek Lexicon*, Fasc. 1 (Oxford, 1961).

Larsson, E. *Christus als Vorbild. Eine Untersuchung zu den paulinischen Tauf- und Eikontexten* (Acta Sem. Neotest. Upsal. XXIII) (Uppsala, 1962).

Lawlor, H. and Oulton, J. E. L. *Eusebius*, 2 vols. Translation and Commentary (London, 1927).

Lawson, J. *A Theological and Historical Introduction to the Apostolic Fathers* (New York, 1961).

Lawton, J. S. *Conflict in Christology* (London, 1947).

Leenhardt, F.-J. *The Epistle to the Romans* (E.T. London, 1960).

Leivestad, R. *Christ the Conqueror* (London, 1954).

Lenski, R. C. H. *The Interpretation of St Paul's Epistles...to the Philippians* (Columbus, Ohio, 1937).

Lichtenstein, E. 'Die älteste christliche Glaubensformel', *Zeitsch. f. Kirchengesch.* LXIII (1950), 4–74.

Lieberman, S. *Hellenism in Jewish Palestine. Studies in the Literary Transmission, Beliefs, and Manners of Palestine in the I Century B.C.– IV C.E.* (New York, 1950).

Lietzmann, H. 'Die liturgischen Angaben des Plinius', *Geschichtliche Studien Albert Hauck zum 70. Geburtstag* (Leipzig, 1916).

—— 'Symbolstudien, VII–XII', *ZNTW*, xxii (1923), 257–79.

—— *Messe und Herrenmahl* (Bonn, 1926). (E.T. *Mass and the Lord's Supper*, date of preface 1953, Oxford.)

—— *An die Korinther I–II*[4] (HzNT, revised by W. G. Kümmel) (Tübingen, 1949).

—— *The Founding of the Church Universal*[2] (E.T. London, 1950).

Lightfoot, J. B. *Ignatius. The Apostolic Fathers*, ii (London, 1889).

—— *St Paul's Epistle to the Philippians* (London, 1868, [4]1896).

—— *St Paul's Epistles to the Colossians and to Philemon* (London, 1904).

Lohmeyer, E. *Kyrios Jesus: Eine Untersuchung zu Phil. 2, 5–11* (Sitzungsberichte der Heidelberger Akademie der Wissensch., Phil.-hist. Kl., Jahr. 1927–28, 4. Abh.) (Heidelberg, 1928, [2]1961).

—— *Christuskult und Kaiserkult* (Tübingen, 1919).

—— *Die Idee des Martyriums im Judentum und Urchristentum* (Zeit. f. Syst. Theol. 5) (1928).

—— *Der Brief an die Philipper*[8] (MeyerKommentar) (Göttingen, 1930; 9th ed. revised by W. Schmauch, 1953).

Die Briefe an die Kolosser und an Philemon[9] (MeyerKommentar) (Göttingen, 1953).

—— *Die Offenbarung des Johannes*[2] (HzNT) (Tübingen, 1953).

—— *Gottesknecht und Davidsohn* (Symbolae Biblicae Upsalienses, 5) (Lund, 1945; [2]Göttingen, 1953).

—— *Probleme paulinischer Theologie* (Darmstadt, 1954).

Lohse, E. *Märtyrer und Gottesknecht* (FRLANT, 46) (Göttingen, 1955).

—— 'Imago Dei bei Paulus', *Libertas Christiana: Festschrift F. Delekat* (Munich, 1957).

—— 'Nachfolge', *RGG*[3], iv (1960), 1286–8.

Loofs, F. 'Kenosis', Hastings' *Encyclopaedia of Religion and Ethics*, vii (1914), 680–7.

—— 'Das altkirchliche Zeugnis gegen die herrschende Auffassung der Kenosisstelle (Phil. 2. 5 bis 11)', *TSK*, c (1927/28), 1–102.

Lösch, S. *Deitas Jesu und antike Apotheose* (1933).

Lueken, W. 'Der Brief an die Philipper', *Die Schriften des Neuen Testaments*[2] (Göttingen, 1917).

MacCulloch, J. A. *The Harrowing of Hell* (Edinburgh, 1930).

MacDonald, A. B. *Christian Worship in the Primitive Church* (Edinburgh, 1934).

Macgregor, G. H. C. 'Principalities and Powers', *NTS*, i (1954), 17–28.

Macgregor, G. H. C. and Purdy, A. C. *Jew and Greek: Tutors unto Christ* (London, 1936).

Machen, J. G. *The Origin of Paul's Religion* (1925 (= Grand Rapids, 1947)).

Mackintosh, H. R. *The Doctrine of the Person of Jesus Christ* (Edinburgh, 1913).

Mann, C. S. 'The New Testament and the Lord's Ascension', *CQR*, CLVIII (1957).

Manson, T. W. *The Teaching of Jesus*² (Cambridge, 1935).

—— *The Church's Ministry* (London, 1948).

—— *Ministry and Priesthood: Christ's and Ours* (London, 1953).

—— 'Martyrs and Martyrdom (i)', *BJBL*, XXXIX, 2 (1957).

—— 'The Son of Man, etc.', *Studies in the Gospels and Epistles* (Manchester, 1962).

Manson, W. *Jesus the Messiah* (London, 1943).

—— *The Epistle to the Hebrews* (London, 1951).

Martin, G. C. (ed.). *Ephesians, Colossians, Philemon and Philippians* (The Century Bible) (Edinburgh, 1902).

Martin, R. P. *An Early Christian Confession: Philippians ii. 5–11 in recent Interpretation* (London, 1960).

—— *Worship in the Early Church* (London, 1964).

Marty, J. 'Étude des textes cultuels de prière contenus dans le NT', *RHPR*, III, 4/5 (1929), 234 ff.; (1930), 366 ff.

Mascall, E. L. *Christ, the Christian and the Church* (London, 1946).

Masson, Ch. *L'épître de S. Paul aux Colossiens* (CNT, x) (Paris, 1950).

Maurenbrecher, M. *Von Nazareth nach Golgotha* (1909).

Maurer, W. *Bekenntnis und Sakrament*, I (Berlin, 1939).

McArthur, A. A. *The Evolution of the Christian Year* (London, 1953).

McCasland, S. V. '"The Image of God" according to Paul', *JBL*, LXIX (1950), 85–100.

M'Neile, A. H. 'Adam', *Hastings' Dictionary of the Bible* (one-volume ed.) (Edinburgh, 1909).

Meinertz, M. *Theologie des Neuen Testamentes*, vols. I, II (Bonn, 1950).

Metzger, B. M. 'A reconsideration of certain arguments against the Pauline authorship of the Pastoral Epistles', *ExT*, LXX, 3 (1958), 91–4.

Meyer, E. *Ursprung und Anfänge des Christentums* (3 vols.), III (Stuttgart/Berlin, 1923).

Meyer, H. A. W. *The Epistle to the Philippians: Commentary on the New Testament* (E.T. London, 1897).

Michael, J. H. *The Epistle of Paul to the Philippians* (MNTC) (London, 1928).

Michaelis, W. *Der Brief des Paulus an die Philipper* (Theologischer Handkommentar) (Leipzig, 1935).

—— *Zur Engelchristologie im Urchristentum* (Zürich, 1942).

—— 'μιμέομαι', etc., *TWNT*, IV, 661–78.

Michel, O. 'Zur Exegese von Phil. 2, 5–11', *Theologie als Glaubenswagnis, Festschrift Karl Heim* (Hamburg, 1954).

—— *Der Brief an die Römer*[10] (Meyer) (Göttingen, 1955).

—— *Der Brief an die Hebräer*[9] (Meyer) (Göttingen, 1955).

—— 'ὁμολογέω', *TWNT*, v, 199–220.

Michl, J. 'Die "Versöhnung" (Kol. i. 20)', *ThQ*, IV (1948), 451 ff.

Milik, J. T. *Ten Years of Discovery in the Wilderness of Judaea* (SBT, 26) (E.T. London, 1959).

Moffatt, J. *An Introduction to the Literature of the New Testament*[3] (Edinburgh, 1918).

—— *Love in the New Testament* (London, 1931).

Mohler, S. L. 'The Bithynian Christians Again', *JCP*, xxx (1935), 167–9.

Moore, G. F. *Judaism in the First Centuries of the Christian Era* (3 vols.) (Oxford, 1927–30).

Morfill, W. R. and Charles, R. H. *The Book of the Secrets of Enoch* (Oxford, 1896).

Morgan, W. *The Religion and Theology of Paul* (Edinburgh, 1917).

—— *The Nature and Right of Religion* (Edinburgh, 1926).

Morrison, C. D. *The Powers that be* (SBT, 29) (London, 1960).

Moule, C. F. D. *An Idiom-Book of New Testament Greek* (Cambridge, 1953).

—— *The Epistles to the Colossians and Philemon* (CGT revised) (Cambridge, 1957).

—— *Worship in the New Testament* (London, 1961).

—— *The Birth of the New Testament* (London, 1962).

Moule, H. C. G. *The Epistle to the Philippians* (CB) (Cambridge, 1899).

Moulton, J. H. *Grammar of New Testament Greek*, I (Edinburgh, 1908).

Moulton, J. H. and Milligan, G. *Vocabulary of the Greek New Testament* (London, 1914–30).

Mounce, R. H. *The Essential Nature of New Testament Preaching* (Grand Rapids, 1960).

Mowinckel, S. *He that Cometh* (E.T. Oxford, 1956).

Mowry, L. *The Dead Sea Scrolls and the Christian Church* (Chicago, 1962).

Müller, J. J. *The Epistles of Paul to the Philippians and to Philemon* (New London Commentaries) (London, 1955).

Munck, J. 'La vocation de l'Apôtre Paul', *ST*, I (1947), 131–45.

—— 'The New Testament and Gnosticism', *ST*, xv (1961), 181–95. (= *Current Issues in New Testament Interpretation: Essays in honor of O. Piper*, ed. Snyder, G. F. and Klassen, W. (London, 1962), 224–38.)

Murray, A. V. *Personal Experience and the Historic Faith* (London, 1939).

Murray, G. *Five Stages of Greek Religion*[2] (London, 1935).

Nauck, W. *Die Tradition und der Charakter des ersten Johannesbriefes* (Wissenschaftliche Untersuchungen zum NT, 3) (Tübingen, 1957).

Nielen, J. M. *Gebet und Gottesdienst im Neuen Testament* (Freiburg, 1937).

Nilsson, M. P. *Greek Popular Religion* (E.T. New York, 1947).

—— *Greek Piety* (E.T. Oxford, 1948).

Nineham, D. E. 'Eye-witness testimony and Gospel tradition', *JTS*, XI, 2 (1960).

Nock, A. D. 'Early Gentile Christianity', *Essays on the Trinity and the Incarnation* (ed. A. E. J. Rawlinson) (London, 1928).

—— *Conversion* (Oxford, 1933 (later ed. 1961)).

—— *St Paul* (London, 1938).

Nock, A. D. and Festugière, A.-J. *Corpus Hermeticum*, I–II (Collection des Universités de France) (Paris, 1945).

Norden, E. *Agnostos Theos: Untersuchungen zur Formgeschichte religiöser Rede* (Leipzig/Berlin, 1913; Stuttgart, 1956 (= ⁴1923)).

—— *Die antike Kunstprosa*, I (Leipzig, 1913).

Odeberg, H. *The Fourth Gospel interpreted in its relation to Contemporaneous Religious Currents in Palestine and in the Hellenistic-Oriental World.* (Uppsala/Stockholm, 1929).

Oepke, A. 'κενόω', *TWNT*, III, 661 f.

Oesterley, W. O. E. *The Jewish Background of the Christian Liturgy* (Oxford, 1925).

Pedersen, J. *Israel, Its Life and Culture*, vols. I–II, III–IV (London/Copenhagen, 1926).

—— 'The Fall of Man', *Interpretationes ad vetus Testamentum pertinentes Sigmundo Mowinckel* (Oslo, 1955).

Percy, E. *Untersuchungen über den Ursprung der johanneischen Theologie* (Lund, 1939).

—— *Die Probleme der Kolosser- und Epheserbriefe* (Lund, 1946).

—— *Die Botschaft Jesu. Eine traditionskritische und exegetische Untersuchung* (Lund, 1953).

Peterson, E. *HEIS THEOS. Epigraphie, formgeschichtliche und religionsgeschichtliche Untersuchungen* (FRLANT, 24) (Göttingen, 1926).

—— 'La libération d'Adam de l'ἀνάγκη', *RB*, LV (1948), 199–214.

—— *Frühkirche, Judentum und Gnosis. Studien und Untersuchungen* (Freiburg/Rome/Vienna, 1959).

Plummer, A. *A Commentary on St Paul's Epistle to the Philippians* (London, 1919).

Porter, F. C. *The Mind of Christ in Paul* (New York, 1931).

Porter, H. B. *The Day of Light* (London, 1960).

Prat, F. *The Theology of St Paul* (E.T. 2 vols., London, 1933).

Purdy, A. C. *See* Macgregor, G. H. C.

Quasten, J. *Musik und Gesang in den Kulten der heidnischen Antike und christlichen Frühzeit* (Liturgiegeschichtliche Quellen und For-schungen, 25) (Münster, 1930).

Quick, O. C. *Doctrines of the Creed* (London, 1938).

Quispel, G. 'The Jung Codex and its Significance', *The Jung Codex* (E.T. ed. Cross, F. L., London, 1955).

Rackham, R. B. *The Acts of the Apostles*[14] (WC) (London, 1951).

Rall, H. F. *According to Paul* (New York, 1944).

Ramsey, A. M. *The Glory of God and the Transfiguration of Christ* (London, 1949).

Ratcliff, E. C. 'Christian Worship and Liturgy', *The Study of Theology* (ed. Kirk, K. E.) (London, 1939).

Raven, C. E. *Apollinarianism* (Cambridge, 1923).

Rawlinson, A. E. J. *The New Testament Doctrine of the Christ* (London, 1926).

Reicke, B. *The Disobedient Spirits and Christian Baptism* (ASNU, 13) (Copenhagen/Lund, 1946).

—— *Glaube und Leben der Urgemeinde: Bermerkungen zu Apg. 1–7* (Abh. T. ANT, 32) (Zürich, 1957).

—— 'Unité chrétienne et Diaconie', *Neotestamentica et Patristica in honorem O. Cullmann* (ed. van Unnik, W. C.) (Leiden, 1962).

Reitzenstein, R. *Poimandres. Studien zur griechisch-ägyptischen und frühchristlichen Literatur* (Leipzig, 1904).

—— *Das iranische Erlösungsmysterium* (Bonn, 1921).

—— *Die hellenistischen Mysterienreligionen nach ihren Grundgedanken und Wirkungen* (Leipzig/Berlin, 1927; Stuttgart, 1956).

Rengstorf, K. H. 'δοῦλος', *TWNT*, II, 264–83.

Richardson, A. *An Introduction to the Theology of the New Testament* (London, 1958).

Rickaby, J. *The Epistles of the Captivity* (London, 1911).

Ridderbos, H. N. *Paul and Jesus* (E.T. Philadelphia, 1958).

Riesenfeld, H. 'La descente dans la morte', *Aux sources de la tradition chrétienne. Mélanges M. Goguel* (Neuchâtel, 1950).

—— 'The Mythological Background of the New Testament Christology', *The Background of the New Testament and its Eschatology*, ed. Davies, W. D. and Daube, D. (Cambridge, 1956).

—— 'Sabbat et Jour du Seigneur', *New Testament Essays in memory of T. W. Manson*, ed. Higgins, A. J. B. (Manchester, 1959).

Robertson, A. T. *A Grammar of the Greek New Testament in the light of Historical Research* (London/New York, 1914).

—— *Paul's Joy in Christ* (Nashville, 1917; later ed. n.d.).

Robinson, H. W. *The Cross of the Servant* (London, 1926; reprinted in *The Cross in the Old Testament*, London, 1957).

Robinson, J. A. T. *The Body. A Study in Pauline Theology* (SBT, 5) (London, 1952).
—— *Jesus and his Coming* (London, 1957).
—— *Twelve New Testament Studies* (SBT, 34) (London, 1962).
Robinson, J. M. 'A Formal Analysis of Col. i. 15–20', *JBL*, LXXVI (1957), 270 ff.
—— *The Problem of History in Mark* (SBT, 21) (London, 1957).
—— *A New Quest of the Historical Jesus* (SBT, 25) (London, 1959).
Rossowsky, S. *The Cantillation of the Bible* (New York, 1957).
Sabatier, A. *The Apostle Paul. A Sketch of the development of his doctrine* (London, 1903).
Sass, G. 'Zur Bedeutung von δοῦλος bei Paulus', *ZNTW*, XL (1941), 24–32.
Schlatter, A. *Die Theologie des Neuen Testaments*, vol. 2: *Die Lehre der Apostel* (Stuttgart, 1910).
—— 'Der Brief an die Philipper', *Erläuterungen z. NT* (Stuttgart, 1928).
Schlier, H. *Religionsgeschichtliche Untersuchungen zu den Ignatiusbriefen* (ZNTW, Bh. 8) (Giessen, 1929).
—— *Die Verkündigung im Gottesdienst der Kirche* (Köln, 1953).
Schmauch, W. *In Christus. Eine Untersuchung zur Sprache und Theologie des Paulus* (Neutestamentliche Forschungen, 9) (Gütersloh, 1935).
Schmidt, K. L. '"Homo Imago Dei" im alten und neuen Testament', *Eranos-Jahrbuch*, XV: *Der Mensch* (Zürich, 1948).
Schmithals, W. *Die Gnosis in Korinth. Eine Untersuchung zu den Korintherbriefen* (FRLANT, 66) (Göttingen, 1956).
Schmitt, J. *Jésus ressuscité dans la prédication apostolique. Essai de théologie biblique* (Paris, 1949).
Schnackenburg, R. *La Théologie du Nouveau Testament* (Studia Neotestamentica: Subsidia, I) (Bruges, 1961).
—— *Baptism in the Thought of St Paul* (E.T. London, 1964).
Schneider, J. *Doxa. Eine bedeutungsgeschichtliche Studie* (NT Forschungen, 3) (Gütersloh, 1932).
—— 'ὁμοίωμα', *TWNT*, v, 191–7.
Schoedel, W. R. 'The Rediscovery of Gnosis', *Interpretation*, XVI, 4 (1962) (Richmond, Virg., 1962), 387–401.
Schoeps, H. J. *Paul. The Theology of the Apostle in the light of Jewish Religious History* (E.T. London, 1961).
Schumacher, H. *Christus in seiner Präexistenz und Kenose nach Phil. 2, 5–8*. Part I: *Exegetisch-kritische Untersuchung* (Rome, 1914); Part II: *Historische Untersuchung* (Rome, 1921).
Schürer, E. *History of the Jewish People in the Time of Jesus Christ*. 5 vols (E.T. Edinburgh, 1885).

Schweitzer, A. *The Mysticism of the Apostle Paul*[2] (E.T. London, 1953).

Schweizer, E. *Erniedrigung und Erhöhung bei Jesu und seinen Nachfolgern* (Ab. T. ANT, 28) (Zürich, 1955; [2]1962). (E.T. with adaptation *Lordship and Discipleship* (SBT, 28), London, 1960.)

—— 'Discipleship and Belief in Jesus as Lord from Jesus to the Hellenistic Church', *NTS* II, 2 (1955), 87–99.

—— *Church Order in the New Testament* (SBT, 32) (London, 1961).

—— *Spirit of God* (E.T. = *TWNT*, VI, 394–449) (London, 1961).

—— 'Anmerkungen zur Theologie des Markus', *Neotestamentica et Patristica in honorem O. Cullmann* (ed. van Unnik, W. C.) (Leiden, 1962).

—— 'Two New Testament Creeds compared', *Current Issues in New Testament Interpretation. Essays in honor of O. Piper* (ed. Klassen, W. and Snyder, F. G.) (London, 1962).

Scott, C. A. A. *The Fellowship of the Spirit* (London, 1921).

—— *Christianity according to St Paul* (Cambridge, 1932).

—— *Footnotes to St Paul* (Cambridge, 1935).

Scott, E. F. *The Epistles to the Colossians, to Philemon and to the Ephesians* (MNTC) (London, 1930).

—— *The Epistle to the Philippians* (IB) (New York/Nashville, 1955).

Scott, W. (ed.). *Hermetica. The ancient Greek and Latin Writings which contain Religious or Philosophical Teachings ascribed to Hermes Trismegistus*, I–IV (London, 1924–36).

Seeberg, A. *Der Katechismus der Urchristenheit* (Leipzig, 1903).

—— *Die Didache des Judentums und die Urchristenheit* (Leipzig, 1908).

Sellers, R. V. *Two Ancient Christologies* (London, 1954).

Selwyn, E. G. *The First Epistle of St Peter* (London, 1947).

Sidebottom, E. M. *The Christ of the Fourth Gospel* (London, 1961).

Simon, M. *Hercule et le christianisme* (Paris, 1955).

—— *St Stephen and the Hellenists in the Primitive Church* (London, 1958).

Smedes, L. B. *The Incarnation: Trends in Modern Anglican Thought* (Diss. Amsterdam) (Kampen, n.d.: about 1953).

Somerville, D. *St Paul's Conception of Christ or the Doctrine of the Second Adam* (Edinburgh, 1897).

Srawley, J. H. *The Early History of the Liturgy*[2] (Cambridge, 1947).

Stählin, G. 'ἴσος', etc., *TWNT*, III, 343–56.

Stanley, D. M. 'The Theme of the Servant of Yahweh in Primitive Christian Soteriology and its Transposition by St Paul', *CBQ*, XVI (1954), 385–425.

—— 'Carmenque Christo quasi Deo dicere', *CBQ*, XX (1958), 173–91.

—— *Christ's Resurrection in Pauline Soteriology* (Analecta Biblica, 13) (Rome, 1961).

Stauffer, E. *New Testament Theology* (E.T. London, 1955).

Stauffer, E. 'θεός' (in NT), *TWNT*, III, 103–22.

Stevenson, J. *The New Eusebius* (London, 1957).

Stewart, J. S. *A Man in Christ* (London, 1935).

Stewart, R. A. *Rabbinic Theology* (Edinburgh, 1961).

Synge, F. C. *Philippians and Colossians* (Torch Bible Commentary) (London, 1951).

Tarn, W. W. and Griffith, G. T. *Hellenistic Civilisation*[3] (London, 1952).

Taylor, C. *Sayings of the Jewish Fathers* (Cambridge, 1897).

Taylor, V. 'The Origin of the Markan Passion sayings', *NTS*, I (1954), 159–67.

—— *The Names of Jesus* (London, 1954).

—— *The Atonement in New Testament Teaching*[3] (London, 1958).

—— *The Person of Christ in New Testament Teaching* (London, 1958).

Thornton, L. S. *The Common Life in the Body of Christ*[3] (London, 1950).

—— *The Dominion of Christ. The Form of the Servant*, II (London, 1952).

Tillmann, F. *Die Gefangenschaftsbriefe des heiligen Paulus*[4], ed. M. Meinertz and F. Tillmann: *Der Philipperbrief* (Bonn, 1931).

Tinsley, E. J. *The Imitation of God in Christ* (London, 1960).

Toynbee, A. *A Study of History*, vol. VI (London, 1939).

Traub, H. '(ἐπ)ουράνιος', etc., *TWNT*, V, 538–43.

Trench, R. C. *Synonyms of the New Testament* (London, 1901).

Turner, H. E. W. 'Expository Problems: The Virgin Birth', *ExT*, LXVIII, 1 (1956).

Unnik, W. C. van (ed.). *Neotestamentica et Patristica. Festschrift Oscar Cullmann* (Leiden, 1962).

—— *Tarsus or Jerusalem* (E.T. 1962, London).

Vincent, M. R. *The Epistles of Paul to the Philippians and to Philemon* (ICC) (Edinburgh, 1897).

Vos, G. 'The Kyrios-Christos controversy', *Princeton Theological Review*, XII (1914), 636 ff.; XV (1917), 21–89.

Wainwright, A. W. *The Trinity in the New Testament* (London, 1962).

Warren, W. 'On ἑαυτὸν ἐκένωσεν', *JTS*, XII (1911), 461–3.

Weber, F. *Jüdische Theologie auf Grund des Talmuds und verwandter Schriften* (Leipzig, 1897).

Weiss, J. *Beiträge zur paulinischen Rhetorik* (Göttingen, 1897).

—— *Christus: Die Anfänge des Dogmas* (Religionsgeschichtl. Volksbücher) (Tübingen, 1909). (E.T. *Christ: The Beginnings of Dogma*, London, 1911.)

—— *Neutestamentliche Studien Georg Heinrici zu seinem 70. Geburtstag* (Leipzig, 1914).

—— *Der erste Korintherbrief* (MeyerKommentar) (Göttingen, 1925).

338

—— *Earliest Christianity.* 2 vols. (New York, 1959) (also published as *The History of Primitive Christianity*, London/New York, 1937). (E.T. *Das Urchristentum*, Göttingen, 1917.)

Wendland, P. *Die hellenistisch-römische Kultur*[2] (HzNT) (Tübingen, 1912).

—— 'Hellenistic ideas of salvation in the light of Anthropology', *AJT*, XVII (1913), 345–51.

Werner, M. *The Formation of Christian Dogma* (E.T. London, 1957).

Westerman, C. 'Liturgie', *RGG*[3], IV (1960), 1204 f.

Williams, A. L. *The Dialogue with Trypho* (London, 1930).

Williams, N. P. 'Great texts reconsidered: Matt. xi. 25–27 = Luke x. 21, 22', *ExT*, LI (1940), 215–20.

Wilson, R. McL. *The Gnostic Problem* (London, 1959).

—— *The Gospel of Philip: Translated from the Coptic text, with an Introduction and Commentary* (London, 1962).

Windisch, H. Review of Lohmeyer's *Kyrios Jesus* in *TLZ*, XI (1929), 246 ff.

—— *Paulus und Christus. Ein biblisch-religionsgeschichtlicher Vergleich.* (Unter. z. NT, 24) (Leipzig, 1934).

Wolff, H. W. *Jesaja 53 im Urchristentum*[3] (Berlin, 1953).

ADDITIONAL BIBLIOGRAPHY

Benoit, P. 'Paulinisme et Johannisme', *NTS*, IX (1962–3), 193–207.

Black, M. 'The Son of Man Problem in Recent Research and Debate', *BJRL*, XLV (1963), 305–18.

Bruce, F. F. *An Expanded Paraphrase of the Epistles of Paul* (Exeter, 1965).

Feuillet, A. 'L'hymne christologique de l'épître aux Philippiens (ii. 6–11)', *RB*, LXXII, 3, 4 (1965–6), 352–80, 481–507.

Fuller, R. H. *The Foundations of New Testament Christology* (London, 1965).

Georgi, D. 'Der vorpaulinische Hymnus Phil. 2, 6–11' in *Zeit und Geschichte*, Dankesgabe an Rudolf Bultmann zum 80. Geburtstag, ed. E. Dinkler (Tübingen, 1964).

Grant, R. M. *A Historical Introduction to the New Testament* (London, 1963).

Jeremias, J. 'Zu Phil. ii. 7: ἑαυτὸν ἐκένωσεν', *Novum Testamentum*, VI, 2–3 (1963), 182–8.

Krinetzki, L. 'Der Einfluss von Jes. 52. 13 – 53. 12 par auf Phil. 2. 6–11', *ThQ*, CXXXIX (1959), 157–93, 291–336.

Scroggs, R. *The Last Adam* (Oxford, 1966).

Strecker, G. 'Redaktion und Tradition im Christus-Hymnus Phil 2', *ZNTW*, LV (1964), 63–78.

SUPPLEMENTARY BIBLIOGRAPHY

Arnold, C. E. *The Colossian Syncretism. The Interface between Christianity and Folk Belief at Colossae* (Wissenschaftliche Untersuchungen zum NT, 2.77) (Tübingen, 1995; Grand Rapids, 1996).

Bailey, J. L., and Vander Broek, L. D. *Literary Forms in the New Testament* (Louisville, Ky., 1992).

Bandstra, A. J. ' "Adam" and "the Servant" in Phil. 2:5 ff.', *Calvin Theological Journal*, i (1966), 213-16.

Basevi, C., and Chapa, J. 'Philippians 2.6-11: The Rhetorical Function of the Pauline "Hymn" ', *Rhetoric and the New Testament*, ed. S. E. Porter and T. H. Olbricht (*JSNT* Supplement Series 90) (Sheffield, 1993).

Bloomquist, L. G. *The Function of Suffering in Philippians* (*JSNT* Supplement Series 78) (Sheffield, 1993).

Bockmuehl, M. ' "The Form of God" (Phil. 2:6): Variations on a Theme of Jewish Mysticism', *JTS*, xlviii n. s. (1997), 1-23.

Brucker, R. *'Christushymnen' oder 'epideiktische Passagen'?* (FRLANT 176) (Göttingen, 1997).

Cabaniss, A. *Pattern in Early Christian Worship* (Macon, Ga., 1989).

Caird, G. B. *Paul's Letters from Prison* (New Clarendon Bible) (Oxford, 1976).

Collange, J.-F. *L'épître de Saint Paul aux Philippiens* (CNT) (Paris/Neuchâtel, 1973) (E.T. *The Epistle of Saint Paul to the Philippians* [London, 1979]).

———. *De Jésus à Paul. L'éthique du Nouveau Testament* (Geneva, 1980).

Contri, A. 'Il "Magnificat" alla luce dell'inno christologico di Filippesi 2, 6-11', *Marianum*, x.1 (1978), 164-68.

Dahl, N. A. 'Euodia and Syntyche and Paul's Letter to the Philippians', *The Social World of the First Christians: Essays in Honor of Wayne A. Meeks*, ed. L. M. White and O. L. Yarborough (Minneapolis, 1995), 3-15.

Davis, C. J. *The Name and Way of the Lord. Old Testament Themes, New Testament Christology* (*JSNT* Supplement Series 129) (Sheffield, 1996).

Deichgräber, R. *Gotteshymnus und Christushymnus in der frühen Christenheit* (Studien zur Umwelt des NT, 5) (Göttingen, 1967).

Dinkler, E. 'Das Kreuz als Siegeszeichen', *ZfTK*, lxii (1965), 1-20 (= *Signum Crucis* [Göttingen, 1967]).

Dunn, J. D. G. *Christology in the Making* (London/Philadelphia, 1980; second ed.; Grand Rapids, 1996).

Eckman, B. 'A Quantitative Metrical Analysis of the Philippians Hymn', *NTS*, xxvi (1980), 258-66.

Fee, G. D. 'Philippians 2:5-11: Hymn or Exalted Pauline Prose?', *BBR*, ii (1992), 29-46.

———. *Paul's Letter to the Philippians* (NICNT) (Grand Rapids, 1995).

Fowl, S. E. *The Story of Christ in the Ethics of Paul. An Analysis of the Function of the Hymnic Material in the Pauline Corpus* (*JSNT* Supplement Series 36) (Sheffield, 1990).

Gamber, K. 'Der Christus-Hymnus im Philipperbrief in liturgiegeschichtlicher Sicht', *Biblica*, li (1970), 369-76.

Gloer, W. H. 'Homologies and Hymns in the New Testament: Form, Content and Criteria for Identification', *PRS*, xi (1984), 115-32.

Gundry, R. H. 'Style and Substance in 'The Myth of God Incarnate' according to Philippians 2:6-11', *Crossing the Boundaries. Essays in Biblical Interpretation in Honour of Michael D. Goulder*, ed. S. E. Porter, P. Joyce and D. E. Orton (Biblical Interpretation Series 8) (Leiden, 1994).

Hammerich, L. L. *Phil. 2,6 and P. A. Florenskij* (Det Kongelige Danske Videnskabernes Selskab, Historisk-filosofiske Meddelelser, xlvii, 5) (Copenhagen, 1976).

Hawthorne, G. F. *Philippians* (WBC 42) (Waco, Tex., 1983).

————. 'The Imitation of Christ: Discipleship in Philippians', *Patterns of Discipleship in the New Testament*, ed. R. N. Longenecker (Grand Rapids, 1996).

Hays, R. B. *The Moral Vision of the New Testament* (New York, 1996).

Hengel, M. *The Son of God* (E.T. London, 1976).

————. 'Hymn and Christology', *Studia Biblica* 1978 III. Papers on Paul and Other New Testament Authors, ed. E. A. Livingstone (*JSNT* Supplement Series 3) (Sheffield, 1980 = *Between Jesus and Paul: Studeis in the Earliest History of Christianity* [London/Philadelphia 1983]). German version: 'Hymnus und Christologie', *Wort in der Zeit. Festgabe für Karl Heinrich Rengstorf zum 75 Geburtstag*, ed. W. Haubeck and M. Bachmann (Leiden, 1980).

————. ' "Sit at My Right Hand!" The Enthronement of Christ at the Right Hand of God and Psalm 110:1', *Studies in Early Christology* (Edinburgh, 1995).

————. 'The Song about Christ in Earliest Worship', *Studies in Early Christology* (Edinburgh, 1995).

Hofius, O. *Der Christushymnus Philipper 2, 6-11* (Wissenschaftliche Untersuchungen zum NT, 17) (Tübingen, 1976).

Hooker, M. D. 'Philippians 2,6-11', *Jesus und Paulus. Festschrift für W. G. Kümmel*, ed. E. E. Ellis and E. Grässer (Göttingen, 1975). (= *From Adam to Christ* [Cambridge, 1990]).

Hoover, R. W. 'The *Harpagmos* Enigma: A Philological Solution', *HTR*, lxiv (1971), 95-119.

Howard, G. 'Phil. 2:6-11 and the Human Christ', *CBQ*, xl (1978), 368-87.

Hurtado, L. W. 'Jesus as Lordly Example in Phil. 2:5-11', *From Jesus to Paul. Studies in Honour of Francis Wright Beare*, ed. J. C. Hurd and G. P. Richardson (Waterloo, 1983).

————. *One God, One Lord* (Philadelphia, 1988).

Jeremias, J. 'Zur Gedankenführung in den paulinischen Briefen', *Studia Paulina in Honorem J. de Zwaan*, ed. J. N. Sevenster and W. C. van Unnik (Haarlem, 1953).

Jewett, R. 'Conflicting Movements in the Early Church as Reflected in Philippians', *Novum Testamentum*, xii (1970), 362-90.

Karris, R. J. *A Symphony of New Testament Hymns* (Collegeville, Minn., 1996).

Käsemann, E. 'A Critical Analysis of Philippians 2:5-11', *God and Christ. Existence and Province (Journal for Theology and Church*, 5) (E.T. New York, 1968).

Kennel, W. *Frühchristliche Hymnen? Gattungskritische Studien zur Frage nach den Liedern der frühen Christenheit* (Wissenschaftliche Monographien zum Alten und Neuen Testament, 71) (Göttingen, 1995).

Kim, S. *The Origin of Paul's Gospel* (Wissenschaftliche Untersuchungen zum NT, 2.4) (Tübingen, 1981; Grand Rapids, 1982).

Lattke, M. *Hymnus. Materialen zu einer Geschichte der antiken Hymnologie* (Freiburg/Göttingen, 1991).

Losie, L. A. 'A Note on the Interpretation of Phil. 2,5', *ExT,* xc (1978), 52-54.

Manns, F. 'Philippians 2, 6-11: A Judeo-Christian Hymn', *Theology Digest,* xxvi/i (1978), 4-10.

Marcheselli, C. C. 'La celebrazione di Gesù Cristo Signore in Fil 2, 6-11. Riflessioni letterario-storico-esegetiche sull' inno cristologico', *Ephemerides Carmeliticae,* xxix (1978), 2-42.

Martin, R. P. 'Some Reflections on New Testament Hymns', *Christ the Lord. Studies Presented to Donald Guthrie,* ed. H. H. Rowdon (Leicester, 1972).

————. *Philippians* (New Century Bible) (London, 1976; Grand Rapids, 1980).

————. 'New Testament Hymns: Background and Development', *ExT,* xciv (1983), 132-36.

————. *Reconciliation. A Study of Paul's Theology* (revised ed.; Grand Rapids, 1989; reprint Eugene, Oreg., Pasadena, Calif., 1997).

————. 'Hymns, Hymn Fragments, Songs, Spiritual Songs', *Dictionary of Paul and His Letters,* ed. G. F. Hawthorne, R. P. Martin and D. G. Reid (Downers Grove, Ill., 1993).

Martin, R. P., and Dodd, B. J., eds. *Where Christology Began: Essays on Philippians 2* (Louisville, Ky., 1998).

Melick, R. R. *Philippians, Colossians, Philemon* (Nashville, 1991).

Mengel, B. *Studien zum Philipperbrief* (Wissenschaftliche Untersuchungen zum NT, 2.8) (Tübingen, 1982).

Minear, P. S. 'Singing and Suffering in Philippi', *The Conversation Continues. Studies in Paul and John in Honor of J. Louis Martyn,* ed. R. T. Fortna and B. R. Gaventa (Nashville, 1990).

Moule, C. F. D. 'Further Reflexions on Philippians 2:5-11', *Apostolic History and the Gospel. Biblical and Historical Essays Presented to F. F. Bruce on His 60th Birthday,* ed. W. W. Gasque and R. P. Martin (Exeter/Grand Rapids, 1970).

SUPPLEMENTARY BIBLIOGRAPHY

———. 'The Manhood of Jesus in the NT', *Christ, Faith and History*, ed. S. W. Sykes and J. P. Clayton (Cambridge, 1972).

Mountain, C. M. 'The New Testament Christ-Hymn', *The Hymn*, xliv.1 (1993), 20-28.

———. 'The New Testament Epiphany-Hymn', *The Hymn*, xlv.2 (1994), 9-17.

Murphy-O'Connor, J. 'Christological Anthropology in Phil. II.6-11', *RB*, lxxxiii (1976), 25-50.

Nagata, T. 'Philippians 2:5-11. A Case Study in the Contextual Shaping of Early Christology'. Unpublished Ph.D. dissertation, Princeton Theological Seminary (1981).

O'Brien, P. T. *The Epistle to the Philippians* (New International Greek Testament Commentary) (Grand Rapids, 1991).

———. 'The Gospel and Godly Models in Philippians', *Worship, Theology and Ministry in the Early Church*, FS R. P. Martin, ed. M. J. Wilkins and T. Paige (*JSNT* Supplement Series 87) (Sheffield, 1992).

O'Neill, J. C. 'Hoover on *Harpagmos* Reviewed, with a Modest Proposal concerning Philippians 2:6', *HTR*, lxxxi (1988), 445-49.

Pannenberg, W. *Jesus—God and Man* (E.T. London, 1968).

Perkins, P. 'Philippians: Theology for the Heavenly *Politeuma*', *Pauline Theology* 1, ed. J. M. Bassler (Minneapolis, 1991).

Peterlin, D. *Paul's Letter to the Philippians in the Light of Disunity in the Church* (Novum Testamentum Supplement Series 79) (Leiden, 1995).

Pretorius, E. A. C. 'A Key to the Literature on Philippians', *Neotestamentica*, xxiii (1989), 125-53.

Rowland, C. C. *The Open Heaven. A Study of Apocalyptic in Judaism and Early Christianity* (London, 1982).

Sanders, J. T. *New Testament Christological Hymns. Their Historical and Religious Background* (Society for New Testament Studies Monographs, 15) (Cambridge, 1971).

Schenk, W. *Die Philipperbrief des Paulus* (Stuttgart, 1984).

Schweizer, E. 'Paul's Christology and Gnosticism', *Paul and Paulinism. Essays in Honour of C. K. Barrett*, ed. M. D. Hooker and S. G. Wilson (London, 1982).

Seeley, D. 'The Background of the Philippians Hymn (2:6-11)', *Journal of Higher Criticism*, i (1994), 49-72.

Segal, A. F. *Two Powers in Heaven. Early Rabbinic Reports about Christianity and Gnosticism* (Leiden, 1977).

Silva, M. *Philippians* (Wycliffe Exegetical Commentary) (Chicago, 1988).

Steenburg, D. 'The Case against the Synonymity of *Morphê* and *Eikôn*', *JSNT*, xxxiv (1988), 77-86.

Stenger, W. 'Two Christological Hymns (Phil. 2:6-11; 1 Tim. 3:16)', *Introduction to New Testament Exegesis* (Grand Rapids, 1993).

Strimple, R. B. 'Philippians 2:5-11 in Recent Studies: Some Exegetical

Conclusions', *Westminster Theological Journal,* xli (1979), 247-68.

Talbert, C. H. 'The Problem of Pre-existence in Phil. 2:6-11', *JBL,* lxxxvi (1967), 141-53.

Thekkekara, M. 'A Neglected Idiom in an Overstudied Passage (Phil 2:6-8)', *Louvain Studies,* xvii (1992), 306-14.

Wanamaker, C. A. 'Philippians 2. 6-11: Son of God or Adamic Christology?', *NTS,* xxxiii (1987), 179-93.

Way, D. V. *The Lordship of Christ. Ernst Käsemann's Interpretation of Paul's Theology* (Oxford, 1991).

Weder, H. *Das Kreuz Jesu bei Paulus* (FRLANT, 125) (Göttingen, 1981).

Wengst, K. *Christologische Formeln und Lieder des Urchristentums* (Studien zum NT, 7) (Gütersloh, 1972).

Wick, P. *Der Philipperbrief* (Beiträge zur Wissenschaft vom Alten und Neuen Testament, 135) (Stuttgart/Berlin/Köln, 1994).

Witherington, B. W., III. *Friendship and Finances in Philippi* (Valley Forge, Penn., 1994).

——. *Jesus the Sage. The Pilgrimage of Wisdom* (Minneapolis, 1994).

——. *Paul's Narrative Thought World* (Louisville, Ky., 1994).

Wong, T. Y.-C. 'The Problem of Pre-existence in Philippians 2, 6-11', *Ephemerides Theologicae Lovanienses,* lxii (1986), 267-82.

Wrege, H.-T. 'Jesusgeschichte und Jüngergeschick nach Joh 12, 20-23 und Heb 5, 7-10', *Der Ruf Jesu und die Antwort der Gemeinde. Festschrift für J. Jeremias,* ed. E. Lohse (Göttingen, 1970).

Wright, N. T. 'ἁρπαγμός and the Meaning of Philippians 2:5-11', *JTS,* xxxvii n.s. (1986), 321-52 (revised version: *The Climax of the Covenant. Christ and the Law in Pauline Theology* [Edinburgh, 1992], 56-98).

Wu, J. L. 'Liturgical Elements', *Dictionary of Paul and His Letters,* ed. G. F. Hawthorne, R. P. Martin and D. G. Reid (Downers Grove, Ill., 1993).

INDEX OF AUTHORS

INDEX OF SUBJECTS

INDEX OF PASSAGES QUOTED

356

OTHER ANCIENT AUTHORS AND WRITINGS

INDEX OF PASSAGES

Eusebius
   Historia Ecclesiastica
   III, xxxiii, 1–3   7
   v, ii, 2   62, 146
   v, v, 1   265
   v, xxviii, 5   9
   VII, xxx, 10   2
   VIII, xii, 2   140

Faustus of Reji, I, 1   5

Gospel of Philip
   12   238
   103   242

Heliodorus VII, xx, 2   144

Hippolytus
   Elench. v, 10   216

Horace
   Carmen saeculare, 8   8
   Odes, IV, xii, 9–10   8

Ignatius
   Epistula ad Ephesios
   IV   2, 10
   IV, 1–2   10
   V, 3   224
   VIII, 1   310
   XVII, 2   22
   XIX   2, 11, 40, 160 261, 309
   XIX, 2, 3   11
   XX, 1   117, 119
   Epistula ad Magnesios
   V, 2   104
   IX, 1   2
   Epistula ad Romanos
   proem.   275
   II, 2   310
   VI, 3   73
   IX, 5   275
   Epistula ad Smyrnaeos
   I   2
   I, 1–2   22
   I, 1   275
   X, 1   275
   Epistula ad Trallianos
   VII, 1   275
   IX   2, 22
   IX, 1   218, 219, 260
   IX, 2   201

Irenaeus
   adversus Haereses I, x, 1   267

Isidore
   Epistulae IV, 22   144

Justin Martyr
   Apologia
   I, xiii, 3   275
   I, lxv   2
   I, lxvi   2
   I, lxvii   2
   I, lxvii, 3 2
   Dialogus cum Tryphone Judaeo
   XXX   261
   LXIII   4
   LXXXV   261
   CXI   261
   CXXI   261

Livy
   Annales I, xxxii, 10   260

Mandaean literature   261

Nag Hammadi
   Apoc. of John
   11. 18–21   xxvii
   Gospel of the Egyptians
   58. 23–59.4 xxvii
   Hypostasis of the Archons
   86. 28–87.3 xxvii
   94. 20–28   xxvii
   94. 36–95.7 xxvii
   Origin of the World
   103. 6–21   xxvii

Odes of Solomon
   x. 5   275
   xv. 9   223
   xvii. 6   261
   xix   39
   xxix. 4   223
   xxxi   39
   xxxiii   39
   xxxiii. 1 f. 223
   xli. 6   261
   xli. 12   239

Origen
   contra Celsum VII, 67   9

INDEX OF
GREEK, LATIN AND SEMITIC WORDS

SUPPLEMENTARY
INDEX OF AUTHORS (1997)

SUPPLEMENTARY SCRIPTURE INDEX (1997)